The Legal System of England and Wales

The Legal System of England and Wales is an ideal choice for all students looking for a modern, contemporary and innovative textbook on this core area of the law, as its clear explanations, carefully developed learning tools and focus on modern case law help bring the subject to life.

This fully updated new edition includes significantly revised coverage of statutory interpretation; a clarified and consolidated chapter on legal professionals; more on new pathways to qualification in the legal profession, and on diversity and well-being; and a new chapter on legal skills. *The Legal System of England and Wales* will also help students translate knowledge successfully to an assessment situation (whether examination, tutorial preparation or coursework) through the acquisition and development of key skills, such as problem-solving and application, critical reasoning and evaluation and research and referencing. The accompanying digital learning resources have also been updated, including additional video and audio content.

The Routledge Spotlights series brings a modern, contemporary approach to the core law curriculum, which will help students to:

- Move beyond an understanding of the law.
- Refine and develop the key skills of problem-solving, evaluation and critical reasoning, which are essential to assessment success.
- Discover sources and suggestions for taking your study further.

By focusing on recent case law and real-world examples, Routledge Spotlights will help you shed light on the law, understand how it operates in practice and gain a unique appreciation of the contemporary context of the subject.

Support material for this text can be found here: https://www.englishandwelshlegalsystem.co.uk

Ryan Murphy is Professor of Legal Education and Pro-Vice Chancellor and Executive Dean of the Faculty of Humanities and Social Sciences at Swansea University.

Frances Burton is former Senior Lecturer in Law at Buckingham University, former Chancery Barrister who has, for many years, taught a wide range of subjects, including both much of the knowledge and the skills which are the subject of this book, and both on academic and vocational courses at a variety of British and international institutions. As a retired judge, she has also had many years' experience of the operation of the rule of law in the UK from the judicial perspective as well as from those of the practitioner and the academic.

SPOTLIGHTS

SHEDDING LIGHT ON THE LAW

Routledge Spotlights Series

A new textbook series designed to help you translate your knowledge of the law to assessment success.

AVAILABLE NOW:

EU Law, Gerard Conway

Equity & Trusts 2nd edition, Scott Atkins

Tort Law, Timon Hughes-Davies and Nathan Tamblyn

Contract Law 2nd edition, Tracey Cooper and Ewan Kirk

Public Law 3rd edition, Michael Doherty and Noel McGuirk

Tort Law 2nd edition, Timon Hughes-Davies, Nathan Tamblyn and Matthew Channon

The Legal System of England and Wales 2nd edition, Ryan Murphy and Frances Burton

SPOTLIGHTS
SHEDDING LIGHT ON THE LAW

The Legal System of England and Wales

SECOND EDITION

RYAN MURPHY AND FRANCES BURTON

Routledge
Taylor & Francis Group
LONDON AND NEW YORK

Designed cover image: Shutterstock

Second edition published 2026
by Routledge
4 Park Square, Milton Park, Abingdon, Oxon, OX14 4RN

and by Routledge
605 Third Avenue, New York, NY 10158

Routledge is an imprint of the Taylor & Francis Group, an informa business

First edition published by Routledge 2020

British Library Cataloguing-in-Publication Data
A catalogue record for this book is available from the British Library

Library of Congress Cataloging-in-Publication Data
Names: Murphy, Ryan (Law teacher) author | Burton, Frances (Frances R.), 1941– author
Title: The legal system of England and Wales / Ryan Murphy and Frances Burton.
Description: Second edition. | Abingdon, Oxon [UK] ; New York, NY : Routledge, 2026. | Series: Spotlights series | Includes bibliographical references and index.
Identifiers: LCCN 2026005732 | ISBN 9781032641812 hardback | ISBN 9781032641805 paperback | ISBN 9781032641829 ebook
Subjects: LCSH: Law—England | Law—Wales
Classification: LCC KD660 .M87 2026
LC record available at https://lccn.loc.gov/2026005732

ISBN: 978-1-032-64181-2 (hbk)
ISBN: 978-1-032-64180-5 (pbk)
ISBN: 978-1-032-64182-9 (ebk)

DOI: 10.4324/9781032641829

Typeset in Joanna
by Apex CoVantage, LLC

CONTENTS

Guide to the Spotlights Series xix
Preface xxi
Table of cases xxiii
Table of legislation xxix

1 INTRODUCTION TO 'LAW' AND THE 'LEGAL SYSTEM' 1

2 SOURCES OF LAW 27

3 INSTITUTIONS OF THE LEGAL SYSTEM 47

4 LAW-MAKING IN ENGLAND AND WALES I – PRIMARY LEGISLATION 63

5 LAW-MAKING IN ENGLAND AND WALES II – DELEGATED (SECONDARY) LEGISLATION 109

6 STATUTORY INTERPRETATION 151

7 THE JUDICIARY 191

8 THE COURT STRUCTURE 225

9 PRECEDENT 247

10 CIVIL JUSTICE 273

11 CRIMINAL JUSTICE 299

12 THE JURY 323

13 ADMINISTRATIVE JUSTICE AND THE TRIBUNAL SYSTEM 353

14 DISPUTE RESOLUTION (DR) 373

15 LEGAL PROFESSIONALS 417

16 SKILLS FOR LEGAL STUDY 449

Index 479

DETAILED CONTENTS

Guide to the Spotlights Series xix
Preface xxi
Table of cases xxiii
Table of legislation xxix

1 INTRODUCTION TO 'LAW' AND THE 'LEGAL SYSTEM' 1
Introduction 1
What is law? 2
The function(s) of the law 4
Preserving public order 5
Reflecting and influencing values of a society 7
Regulating the powers of institutions of the state 8
Protecting individual freedoms 10
Regulating relationships 10
Resolving disputes 11
Law and legal theory 11
Legal systems and their classification 14
Common law systems 16
Civil law 16
Religious systems 17
The legal systems of the United Kingdom 18
Scotland 19
Northern Ireland 19
England and Wales 19
The European Union 21
Themes and contexts within this book 21
Legal skills 22
A blueprint for the book 23
Companion website 24

2 SOURCES OF LAW 27
Introduction 27
The nature of sources of law 28
Legislation 29
Primary legislation 29
Secondary (or delegated) legislation 29
Legislation of the Senedd Cymru 30
Common law 31
Custom and practice 32
Equity 34
Books of authority 36

International law 38
Categorising the law of England and Wales 39
Common law and statute 39
Common law and equity 40
Constitutional or ordinary law 40
Criminal law and civil law 40
Public law and private law 41
Procedural or substantive law 41
Summary 41
Hierarchy of norms and sources 42
Conclusion 44
Companion website 45

3 INSTITUTIONS OF THE LEGAL SYSTEM 47
Introduction 47
Institutions of law-making 48
The legislature 48
House of Commons 49
House of Lords 50
Crown in Parliament 52
The executive 52
Monarch 52
The UK government 53
Executive agencies, non-departmental public bodies 54
The Civil Service 55
The judiciary 55
Separation of powers 55
Separation of powers within the legal system of England and Wales 57
The website 60

4 LAW-MAKING IN ENGLAND AND WALES I – PRIMARY LEGISLATION 63
Introduction 63
Parliamentary sovereignty 64
Primary legislation – classification 65
'Nature of the bill' classification 66
Public bills 66
Private bills 66
Hybrid bills 67
'Origin of the bill' classification 68
Government bills 68
Private members' bills 70
Influences on law-making 72
Manifesto pledges 72

Royal Commission reports 75
Public inquiries 76
Law Commission reports 81
International law obligations 83
Pressure groups 83
Public pressure 84
Legislative process 86
Pre-legislative process 86
Consultation: Green and White Papers 86
Speech from the Throne – the King's Speech 87
Drafting 87
Passage through Parliament – the legislative process 88
Statement of compatibility 89
House of Commons – first reading 89
House of Commons – public reading 90
House of Commons – second reading 91
House of Commons – programme motion and order 91
House of Commons – committee stage 92
House of Commons – report stage 94
House of Commons – third reading 94
House of Lords – procedure 94
Royal Assent 95
Coming into force and commencement 96
Post-legislative review 98
'Special procedures' 98
Conflict and the Parliament Acts 99
Preservation 102
Transfer of powers to the European Union 103
The legislative landscape: flat or contoured? 104
Conclusion 106
The website 107

5 LAW-MAKING IN ENGLAND AND WALES II – DELEGATED (SECONDARY) LEGISLATION 109
Introduction 109
Nature and scope of secondary legislation 110
Need for secondary legislation 114
Detail vs principle and the need for expertise 115
Updating of rules 115
Expansion of the state 115
Speed of response and emergencies 116
To implement EU law 117
The dangers of secondary legislation 118
Types of secondary legislation 119
Orders in Council 119

Statutory instruments 120
Commencement orders 121
Orders in Council 122
Regulations 123
Remedial orders 124
Devolution 126
Regulatory reform orders and control of public bodies 126
Byelaws 129
Rules, codes of conduct and codes of practice (tertiary legislation) 131
Passage of statutory instruments 132
Negative resolution procedure 133
Affirmative resolution procedure 134
Other methods of making statutory instruments 135
Scrutiny of delegated legislation 136
Committees of Parliament 137
Joint Committee on Statutory Instruments (JCSI) 137
Delegated Legislation Committees (DLCs) 138
House of Lords Secondary Legislation Scrutiny Committee (SLSC) 139
Departmental Select Committees (DSCs) 141
Judicial scrutiny of delegated legislation 142
Conclusion 148
The website 149

6 STATUTORY INTERPRETATION 151
Introduction 151
The importance of statutory interpretation 152
For the legal system 152
For students (of law and otherwise) 153
The need for statutory interpretation 155
The multiple or uncertain meanings of words 155
Poor drafting 156
The difficulties of turning policy into 'law' 157
New situations 159
Approaches to parliamentary drafting 160
The 'natural' as opposed to the 'legal' meaning of words 161
Conclusions on the need for statutory interpretation 163
The dangers of statutory interpretation 163
Tools, rules and principles of statutory interpretation 166
The orthodox 'rules' of statutory interpretation – a rejection 166
Literal rule 167
Golden rule 168
Mischief rule 169
Concluding remarks on the rules 169
The aims, principles and presumptions of statutory interpretation in the modern context 170

The aim and purpose of statutory interpretation 170
Overarching considerations 172
Statutes are always speaking 172
The place of mischief 173
The Interpretation Act 1978 173
The Human Rights Act 1998 and European influence 174
Presumptions 174
Against a change in the common law 175
Against ousting the jurisdiction of the court 175
Against a violation of international law 175
Against a violation of fundamental rights of individuals (the presumption of legality) 176
That legislation applies prospectively 176
Exclusion of the Crown 177
Rules of language 177
Ejusdem generis ('of the same kind') 178
Expressio unius est exclusio alterius ('express mention of one thing, excludes another') 178
Expressum facit cessare tacitum ('statement ends implication') 179
Interpretative aids – internal 179
Other sections within the Act, including schedules 179
Long and short title 180
Headings, marginal or side notes 180
Introductory sections 181
Interpretative aids – external 181
Dictionaries 182
Law Commission reports and other pre-legislative reports 182
Consultation papers 183
Statutes in *pari materia* 183
The use of Hansard as an aid to interpretation – the rule in *Pepper v Hart* 184
Explanatory notes 186
Conclusion 187
The website 188

7 THE JUDICIARY 191
Introduction 191
Nature of judging and role of the judiciary 191
Judicial office-holders 196
Appointment of judges 200
Context 200
Justices of the Supreme Court 202
Judicial Appointments Commission 202
Pay and training 206
Pay 206
Training 206

Complaints, discipline and removal from judicial office 207
Complaints 208
Public perception and behaviour of the judiciary 209
Retirement 213
Judicial independence and neutrality 213
Judicial neutrality 215
Judicial immunity 217
Diversity in the judiciary 218
The problem 218
The solution 221
The website 222

8 THE COURT STRUCTURE **225**
Introduction 225
The framework of senior and inferior courts 226
The inferior courts 228
The senior courts 229
Magistrates' Courts – civil and criminal jurisdiction 230
Criminal jurisdiction 230
Civil cases 231
The County Court – civil jurisdiction only 231
Appellate jurisdiction of the County Court 233
The High Court – civil jurisdiction 233
The tracks system and case management 235
The Court of Appeal – civil jurisdiction 236
The Supreme Court 237
The Judicial Committee of the Privy Council 237
The criminal court system 238
The Magistrates' criminal jurisdiction 238
The Crown Court 240
Appellate jurisdiction of the Crown Court 240
Court of Appeal – criminal jurisdiction 241
Supreme Court 241
The Judicial Committee of the Privy Council 242
The Criminal Cases Review Commission (CCRC) 242
The influence of European courts 243
A critical approach to the court structure 244
Conclusion 245
The website 245

9 PRECEDENT **247**
Introduction 247
The rationale and practical considerations for precedent 248
The rationale 248
Practical considerations 250

The reporting of cases 250
Discerning the 'value' of judgments 253
Establishing the binding element 253
The elements of a case 253
The material facts 253
Ratio decidendi 254
Obiter dicta 255
Concluding thoughts on *ratio* and *obiter* 256
The precedential hierarchy 257
The Supreme Court 257
The senior courts 261
Court of Appeal (civil division) 261
Court of Appeal (criminal division) 262
High Court (appellate and first instance jurisdiction) 262
The Crown Court 262
The inferior courts 263
The European courts 263
Court of Justice of the European Union (CJEU) 263
Decisions of the European Court of Human Rights 264
Mechanisms for avoiding or correcting precedent 266
Distinguishing 266
Reversing 267
Overruling 267
Per incuriam 268
Persuasive or non-binding precedent 268
Ratio of a court lower in the hierarchy 269
Dissenting judgments in previous cases 269
Minority judgments in previous cases 269
Decisions of courts outside of England and Wales 269
Academic thinking and law reform 270
Final thought 270
Conclusion 271
The website 271

10 CIVIL JUSTICE 273
Introduction 273
Terminology and a little history 274
Civil justice pre–Lord Woolf 275
Civil justice post–Lord Woolf 277
The Jackson Report 277
The Briggs Report 277
From dispute to trial 278
Paying for legal services 279
Civil Procedure Rules (CPR) 281
Overriding Objective (part 1) 282

Pre-action steps 282
Issue and the tracks 286
Starting proceedings (Part 7) 286
Courts' power of case management (Parts 1 and 3) 287
Issuing 287
Responding to particulars (Part 9) 287
Offers to settle (Part 36 Offers) 288
Allocations 288
Small claims track (Part 27) 289
Fast track (Part 28) 289
Multi-track (Part 29) 290
The civil trial process 290
Remedies 292
Interim relief 292
Damages 293
Equitable remedy 293
Costs (Parts 43–47) 293
Enforcement (Parts 70–74) 294
Appeals 295
But will there be a trial at all? 295
The website 296

11 CRIMINAL JUSTICE 299
Introduction 299
The criminal justice system in summary and some terminology 300
Detecting crime and keeping order: police organisation and investigation powers and safeguards for the citizen 302
The police role in getting the accused to court 304
The police station, detention, questioning and associated powers 307
Detention, treatment and questioning 308
Taking samples 309
Search of premises 310
Charging the accused 311
The criminal court process 312
The summary trial process 312
Either-way offences before the Magistrates and/or the Crown Court 313
Allocation procedure 314
Indictable offences 315
Trial on indictment in the Crown Court 316
The Crown Court trial process 317
The order of speeches and evidence 317
The prosecution case 317
The defence case 318
Closing speeches 319

Summing up 319
Verdict 319
Sentencing 320
Appeals 320
The website 321

12 THE JURY 323
Introduction 323
The importance of the jury 324
Origins 324
The rationale for jury trial 325
The function and forms of jury trial 327
Function of a jury 328
Criminal trials 328
Bench trials in criminal matters 330
Civil 333
Coroners' courts 335
Jury selection 336
Summoning 336
Eligibility 337
Ineligibility 337
Disqualification 338
Grounds for excusal or deferral 340
From summons to serving 341
Challenges 341
Challenging the array 342
Challenge for cause 342
Standby (and jury vetting) 343
Underpinning principles 344
Majority decisions 344
'Jury equity' 345
Confidentiality of deliberation 346
Juror behaviour 348
Proposed reforms to the jury system – the Leveson Review 350
The website 351

13 ADMINISTRATIVE JUSTICE AND THE TRIBUNAL SYSTEM 353
Introduction 353
Administrative law and justice 354
Courts and tribunals 356
Distinction between courts and tribunals 358
The administrative court 359
Supervisory jurisdiction over other courts, tribunals and authorities 359
Judicial review 359
The tribunals service – reformed framework of the tribunals 361

The First Tier and Upper Tribunal 363
First-tier Tribunal 363
The General Regulatory Chamber (GRC) 363
The Social Entitlement Chamber (SEC) 363
Health, Education and Social Care Chamber 364
Immigration and Asylum Chamber 364
Property Chamber 364
Tax Chamber 364
War Pensions and Armed Forces Compensation Chamber 364
The Upper Tribunal 364
Administrative Appeals Chamber 364
Tax and Chancery Chamber 365
Lands Chamber 365
Immigration and Asylum Chamber 365
How cases are heard in tribunals 365
Employment tribunals and other 'different' tribunals 366
Ombudsmen 366
Inquiries 367
Concluding thoughts on administrative justice 370
The website 370

14 DISPUTE RESOLUTION (DR) 373
Introduction 373
Principles of dispute resolution (DR) 374
Types of DR 376
Mutually exclusive or hybrid forms of DR? 376
Rationale for dispute resolution (DR) 379
Party control of the process 379
Costs 381
Appropriate forum for discussion 381
Arbitration 382
Arbitration Act 1996 (as amended by the Arbitration Act 2025) 383
Rationale of the Arbitration Act 1996 384
General provisions of the Arbitration Act 1996 387
Party choice 388
Powers of court 389
Powers and duties of arbitrators and the arbitral tribunal 392
Common examples of arbitration 393
Commercial arbitration 393
Faith-based arbitration 394
Family law arbitrations 398
Role of ABTA 398
Advantages and disadvantages of arbitration 399
Mediation 400
Principles of mediation 400

Examples of mediation in the legal system of England and Wales 402
Mediation in family cases 402
Court-based schemes 402
Other forms of dispute resolution 404
Encouraging the use of dispute resolution 404
Compulsion 405
Encouragement from within the formal legal system 411
Small claims track 411
The Commercial Court 412
Government encouragement 412
Summary of use of DR *within* the formal legal system 414
Conclusion 414
The website 415

15 LEGAL PROFESSIONALS 417
Introduction 417
A historical perspective on the legal professions (11th–20th century) 418
The modern development of the legal professions 419
The 1970s and the Benson Report 419
1980s to the mid-1990s: the push for liberalisation 420
The 2000s and the Clementi Review 421
The regulation of the professions and legal services 422
Contemporary legal professionals 422
The Legal Services Act 2007 423
The regulatory framework 424
The Legal Services Board 424
The independent professional regulators 425
Reserved legal activity and authorised persons 426
The unregulated legal profession 428
The work of the professions 430
The work of solicitors 430
The work of barristers 431
Education and training for legal professionals 433
Solicitors – the current route to qualification 436
Degree-level study 437
The Solicitors Qualifying Examination (SQE) 437
Qualifying Work Experience (QWE) 438
The test of character and suitability 438
Concluding comments on the route to qualification 438
Barristers – the current route to qualification 439
Academic stage – degree-level study and legal knowledge 439
Vocational stage 439
Pupillage 440
Qualification 440
Complaints 441

Complaints and discipline against solicitors 441
Complaints against barristers 442
The Legal Ombudsman 443
The future of the legal profession 444
Conclusion 446
The website 447

16 SKILLS FOR LEGAL STUDY 449
Introduction 449
Establishing good study environments and study habits 449
Study environment(s) 449
Study habits 450
Schedule and routine 450
Note-taking 451
Finding support 452
Understanding learning resources 453
Preparing for assessments and making the most of feedback 453
The skill and importance of critical thinking 453
Academic study skills 458
Keeping your knowledge up to date 458
Deploying legal terminology 460
Researching 461
Referencing, academic integrity and ethics 462
Academic integrity and ethics 462
Generative artificial intelligence for legal study 463
Generative artificial for practice 465
Reading 467
Reading with purpose 467
Reading for context 467
Reading for specific knowledge 467
Reading for analysis 468
Reading strategically 469
Reading different sources 470
Conclusion on reading 470
Writing 470
The mechanics of writing 470
Essays 471
Problem/hypothetical questions 474
The broader skills developed by legal study 477
The website 477

Index 479

GUIDE TO THE SPOTLIGHTS SERIES

The Routledge Spotlights series is an exciting new textbook series that has been carefully developed to help give you a head start in your assessments. We've listened to lecturers and examiners to identify what it takes to succeed as a law student, and we've used that to develop a brand-new series of textbooks that combines detailed coverage of the law together with carefully selected features designed to help you translate that knowledge into assessment success.

AS YOU READ
sections at the start of each chapter introduce you to the key questions and concepts that will be covered within the chapter to help you to focus your reading.

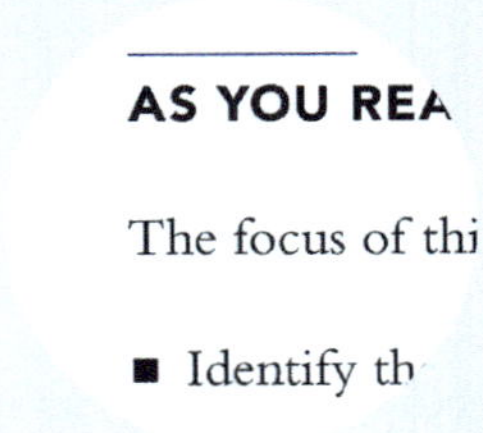

KEY LEARNING POINTS
throughout each chapter highlight important principles and definitions to aid understanding and consolidate your learning.

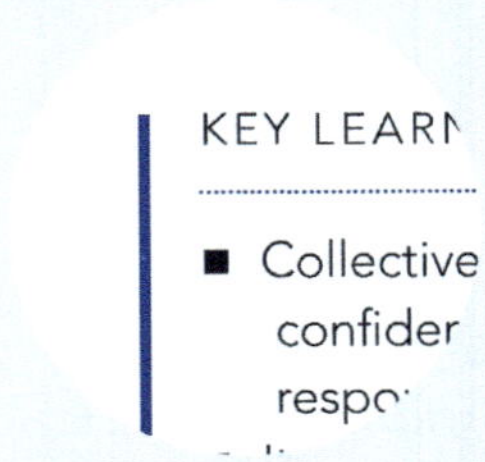

EXPLAINING THE LAW
brings the subject to life through the use of practical examples to provide valuable context to your learning.

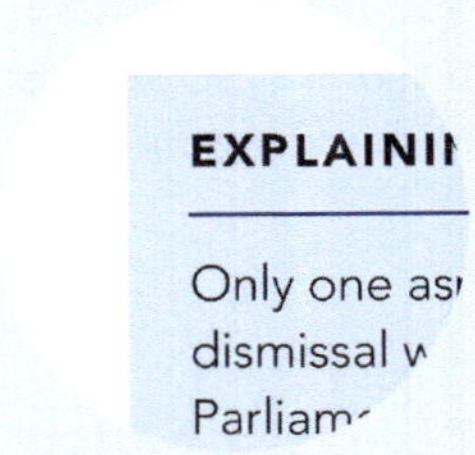

ANALYSING THE LAW
invites you to consider your own response to legal dilemmas and debates. Critical thinking is key to assessment success and with this feature, our authors invite you to critique the law or evaluate conflicting arguments in a debate.

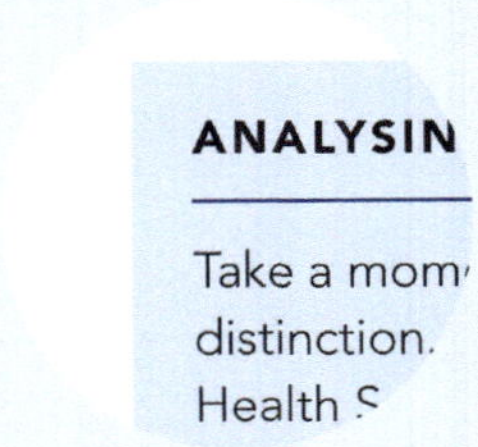

APPLYING THE LAW

Problem questions will form a large part of your assessment and **Applying the law** allows you to develop your problem-solving skills by showing how the law can be applied to a given situation. Learn how to interpret the law and apply it to any problem question.

MAKING CONNECTIONS

will help you impress examiners, showing you how a topic fits into the bigger picture, not just of the wider subject but also across the legal curriculum.

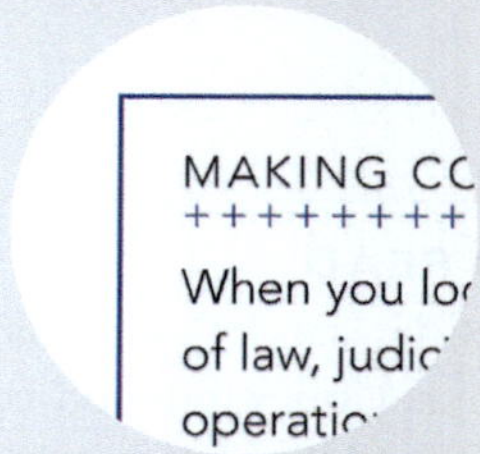

POINTS TO REVIEW

bring together all of the principles and themes for the chapter, helping to reinforce your learning.

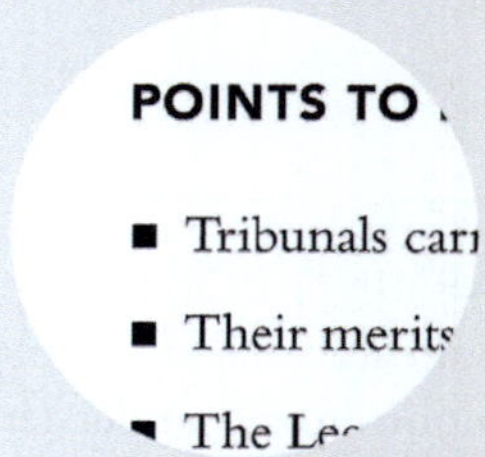

TAKING IT FURTHER

Reading widely impresses examiners! **Taking it further** provides annotated lists of journal articles, book chapters and useful websites for further reading which have been carefully selected to help you to demonstrate an enhanced understanding of the topic.

PREFACE

This text was first published more than 6 years ago, and the world has changed considerably in the intervening period. The UK has since left the transition period following its exit from the European Union. We have come through the other side of a global pandemic involving unprecedented risk and restriction of freedoms and witnessed a succession of Prime Ministers of short tenure that speak to the febrility of the political arena. Political uncertainty, conflict and the rise of AI have also shaped the global context in which English and Welsh law operates.

Each of these events has left an indelible mark on our understanding of the law and of the legal system. Despite these changes, and the many more considered throughout the updated version of this text, the fundamental aim of *The Legal System of England and Wales* remains constant. We hope that the text still provides a contemporary, accessible and rigorous treatment to the core curriculum of the legal system of England and Wales. We hope it offers clear explanations without oversimplification.

As well as a general update of all aspects of the text, there have been some transformational changes. The chapter on statutory interpretation has been re-written to move away from a mechanical application of the 'rules' to one that gives a deeper and more nuanced analysis of the process of judicial decision-making in this area. The chapter on the professions has been tightened and updated to reflect the new pathways to practice and a greater focus on the regulatory environment. The chapter on the European Union has been removed from the text (but still available on the companion website) to make way for a more detailed and overt consideration of legal skills. We think that these developments enhance the text and make it even more useful to those seeking to understand the legal system.

Texts of this length do not get written without the encouragement and belief of very many people, and the authors would like to acknowledge the support of these individuals. Our warmest thanks go to our respective families and colleagues who tolerate the trials of the writing process, including late nights and cries from behind closed doors of 'But why won't this text format properly?'

Ryan would like to thank his eldest son, Peter (age 12), for his supportive comments and bright mind; his youngest son, Simon (age 9), for his curiosity for life and for always making them smile; and his wife, Sarah-Jane, for her boundless patience for the immoveable place that this book now holds in the family. Since the last edition, the Murphy household has grown to include a new pet, Bill. Bill is a cockapoo, and whilst a steadfast and loyal companion, he has shown no interest in the second edition whatsoever.

Frances would like to thank her daughter Janey (janeyburton.com) for prioritising reading, all the way through, the first manuscript during the hectic pre-submission weeks, when there was a lot of it to fit together after the extended years of work and development.

We would also like to thank our colleagues and students for providing inspiration and advice on the style and content of what, we hope, is a fresh and modern examination of the legal system of England and Wales. In particular, we are grateful to Michael Jarrett, who provided us with an early draft of what became the chapter on civil justice in the first edition of the textbook.

We are very grateful to those at Taylor & Francis who have maintained unwavering faith in a project that has taken much longer than intended to deliver in its second edition. Patience and support have been maintained, from the original commissioning editor, Fiona Briden, through to our most recent interaction with Chloe James, Emily Kindleysides, Sanika Shah and others. We are enormously grateful for their part in bringing this book to the world.

Ryan Murphy (Swansea University) and Frances Burton (University of Buckingham) April 2026

TABLE OF CASES

A (Wardship: Fact Finding: Domestic Violence) [2015] EWHC 1598 (Fam) ... 210
Adler v George [1964] 2 QB 7 (QB) ... 169
Agricultural, Horticultural and Forestry Industry Training Board v Aylesbury Mushrooms Ltd [1972] 1 WLR 190 (QBD) ... 144
AG v BBC [1980] 3 All ER 161 (HL) ... 358
AG v Cooper [2010] EWCA Civ 464, [2011] QB 976 ... 218
AI v MT (Alternative Dispute Resolution) [2013] EWHC 100 (Fam), [2013] 2 FLR 371 ... 395–396, 400
Alassini v Telecom Italia [2010] ECR I-2213 ... 408
Al Khatib v Masry [2004] EWCA Civ 1353, [2005] 1 FLR 381 ... 401
Al Rawi v The Security Service [2011] UKSC 34, [2012] 1 AC 531 ... 196
Amministrazione delle Finanze dello Stato v Simmenthal Case 106/77 [1978] ECR 629 ... 104
Anderton v Ryan [1985] AC 560 (HL) ... 259
Assange v The Swedish Prosecution Authority [2012] UKSC 22 ... 175
Associate Provincial Picture House v Wednesbury Corporation [1947] 1 KB 223 (HL) ... 360
Attorney General v Davey [2013] EWHC 2317 (Admin), [2014] 1 Cr App R 1 ... 349
Attorney General v Fraill [2011] EWHC 1629 (Admin), [2011] 2 Cr App R 21 ... 349
Austin v Mayor and Burgesses of the London Borough of Southwark [2010] UKSC 28, [2011] 1 AC 355 ... 259
AWG v Morrison [2006] EWCA Civ 6, [2006] 1 WLR 1163 ... 216
Ayinde v London Borough of Haringey [2025] EWHC 1040 (Admin) ... 466

Belhaj v DPP [2018] UKSC 33 ... 176
Belvedere Court Management v Frogmore Development [1997] QB 858 (CA) ... 157, 164
BH (AP) v The Lord Advocate [2012] UKSC 24, [2013] 1 AC 413 ... 105
Black-Clawson v Papierwerke [1975] AC 591 (HL) ... 175, 180
Boddington v British Transport Police [1999] 2 AC 143 (HL) ... 129
Bombay v Municipal Corporation [1947] AC 58 (PC) ... 177
Bremer Vulcan v South India Shipping [1980] 2 WLR 905 (CA); [1981] AC 909 (HL) ... 383, 387, 388
British Railways Board v Pickin [1974] AC 765 (HL) ... 127, 143
Burchell v Bullard [2005] EWCA Civ 358, [2005] BLR 330 ... 407
Burmah Oil Ltd v Lord Advocate [1965] AC 75 (HL) ... 146
Bushel's Case (1670) 124 ER 1006 ... 345

Cab Housing Ltd v The Secretary of State for Levelling Up [2022] EWHC 208 (Admin), [2022] PTSR 1027 ... 178
Carlill v Carbolic Smoke Ball [1893] 1 QB 256 (CA) ... 31
Carltona v Commissioners of Works [1943] 2 All ER 560 (CA) ... 144
Cassell v Broome [1972] AC 1027 (HL) ... 249
Central London Property Trust Ltd v High Trees House [1947] KB 130 (KB) ... 199, 255
Channel Tunnel Group v Balfour Beatty Construction [1993] AC 334 (HL) ... 389, 394
Cheney v Conn [1968] 1 WLR 242 (Ch) ... 65
Cherry & Others v Advocate General [2019] CSIH 49, [2019] SLT 1097 ... 20
Cherry v Advocate General for Scotland [2019] UKSC 41, [2019] 3 WLR 589 ... 21, 205
Churchill v Merthyr Tydfil CBC [2023] EWCA Civ 1416 ... 410
Circle Freight International Ltd v Medeast Gulf Exports Ltd [1988] 2 Lloyd's Rep 427 (CA) ... 392
Commissioners for Her Majesty's Revenue and Customs v London Clubs Management [2020] UKSC 49 ... 184
Cookson v Knowles [1979] AC 556 (HL) ... 268
Cooper Brookes (Wollongong) Property Ltd v Federal Commissioner for Taxation [1981] HCA 26 ... 166
Costa v ENEL, Case 6/64 [1964] ECR 585 ... 15, 104
Cotham School v Bristol City Council [2025] EWHC 1382 (Ch) ... 34
Council of Civil Service Unions v Minister for the Civil Service [1985] AC 374 (HL) ... 120, 144, 361
Cowl v Plymouth City Council [2001] EWCA Civ 1935, [2002] 1 WLR 803 ... 405
Crinion v IG Markets Ltd [2013] EWCA Civ 587, [2014] 2 All ER (Comm) 55 ... 211
Cukurova v Sonera [2014] UKPC 15, [2015] 2 All ER 1061 ... 383

Dallah v Pakistan [2010] UKSC 46 ... 391
Dallas v United Kingdom (2016) 63 EHRR 13 ... 349
Dammermann v Lanyon Bowdler LLP [2017] EWCA Civ 269 ... 294
Davis v Johnson [1978] 1 All ER 841 (CA); [1979] AC 264 (HL) ... 184, 185, 199, 262
Denetower Ltd v Toop [1991] 1 WLR 945 ... 157
Digital Rights Ireland, Joined Cases C-293/12 C-594/12 [2014] ECR I-845 ... 94
Dimes v Grand Junction Canal Proprietors (1852) 10 ER 301 ... 217
Director of Public Prosecutions of the Virgin Islands v William Penn [2008] UKPC 29 ... 342
Director of Public Prosecutions v Bull [1995] QB 88 (QB) ... 182, 183
Donoghue v Stevenson [1932] AC 562 (HL) ... 199, 254
DPP v Vivier [1991] 4 All ER 18 (QBD) ... 178
Dunnett v Railtrack Plc [2002] EWCA Civ 303, [2002] 1 WLR 2434 ... 406
Duport Steels Ltd v Sirs [1980] 1 WLR 142 (HL) ... 164

Earl de la Warr v Miles (1881) 17 ChD 535 (CA) ... 33
Earl of Oxford's Case (1615) 1 Ch Rep 1 ... 35

F and Thompson (FC) v Secretary of State for the Home Department [2010] UKSC 17, [2011] 1 AC 331 ... 124
Fisher v Bell [1961] 1 QB 394 (QB) ... 161–163
Fitch v Rawling (1795) 2 H BL 393 ... 33

Gallie v Lee [1969] 2 Ch 17 (CA) ... 261
Geddes v Secretary of State for the Home Department [2024] EWHC 66 ... 178, 179
General Medical Council v BBC [1998] 3 All ER 426 (CA) ... 358
Georgi Ivanov Elchinov, Case C-173/09 [2010] ECR I-8889 ... 263
Gow v Grant [2012] UKSC 29, [2013] SC (UKSC) 1 ... 225
Graham v Dodds [1983] 1 WLR 808 (HL) ... 268
Great Peace Shipping v Tsavliris Salvage [2002] EWCA Civ 1407, [2002] 4 All ER 689 ... 261
Grey v Pearson [1857] 6 HL Cas 61 ... 168

Hall v Simons [2003] 3 All ER 673 (HL) ... 443
Halsey v Milton Keynes General NHS Trust [2004] EWCA Civ 576; [2004] 1 WLR 3002 ... 337, 401, 407, 408, 412
Harber v HMRC [2023] UKFTT 1007 (TC) ... 466
Harding v Wealands [2006] UKHL 32; [2007] 2 AC 1 (HL) ... 186
Hassam v Rabot [2024] UKSC 11 ... 175
Hayes v Chief Constable of Merseyside [2011] EWCA Civ 911; [2012] 1 WLR 517 ... 307
Hedley Byrne v Heller [1964] AC 465 (HL) ... 254
Heydon's Case [1584] Co Rep 7a ... 169
Hickman v Blake [2006] EWHC 12 (QB), [2006] 3 Costs LR 452 ... 408
Hinz v Berry [1970] 2 QB 40 (CA) ... 253
Hirst v United Kingdom (No 2) [2005] ECHR 681 ... 89, 165
Hyman v Hyman [1929] AC 601 (HL) ... 396

Industrial Cleaning Equipment v Intelligent Cleaning Equipment & Another [2023] EWCA Civ 1451 ... 264
Ipswich Board of Finance v Clark [1973] Ch 323 (Ch) ... 198
IRC v Hinchy (1960) AC 748 (HL) ... 168
Ivey v Genting Casinos [2017] UKSC 67 ... 256

Jivraj v Hashwani [2010] EWCA Civ 712, [2011] 1 All ER 50 ... 396
Jivraj v Hashwani [2011] UKSC 40, [2011] 1 WLR 1872 ... 396
Jones v DPP [1962] AC 635 (HL) ... 168
Jones v Kernott [2011] UKSC 53, [2012] 1 AC 776 ... 225
Jti Polska v Jakubowski [2023] UKSC 19 ... 261

Kadi and Al Barakaat International Foundation v Council and Commission [2008] ECR I-6351 ... 15
Knauer v Ministry of Justice [2016] UKSC 9, [2016] AC 908 ... 259, 268
Kobler v Austria [2003] ECR I-10239 ... 218
Kuruma v R [1955] AC 197 (PC) ... 306

L, M and P v Devon County Council [2021] EWCA Civ 358 ... 255
The Law Debenture Trust Corporation v Ukraine [2023] UKSC 11 ... 37
Lindner v Rawlins [2015] EWCA Civ 61 ... 357
Lipton v BA Cityflyer [2024] UKSC 24 ... 264
Lloyd v Wright [1983] QB 1065 (CA) ... 380
London Street Tramways v London County Council [1898] AC 375 (HL) ... 257

Madzimbamuto v Lardner-Burke [1969] 1 AC 645 (HL) ... 64
Magor and St Mellons Rural District Council v Newport Corporation [1950] 2 All ER 1226; [1952] AC 189 ... 165
Malone v United Kingdom (1984) 7 EHRR 14 ... 9
Manchester City Council v Pinnock [2010] UKSC 45, [2011] 2 AC 104 ... 265
Mancini v DPP [1942] AC 1 (HL) ... 318

Mandla v Lee [1983] 1 All ER 1062; [1983] QB 1 (CA) ... 154, 182
Marbury v Madison (1803) 5 US 137 ... 40, 143
Marks & Spencer Plc v Commissioners of Customs & Excise [2003] EWCA Civ 1448, [2004] 1 CMLR 8 ... 37
Marks v Minister of Justice [2022] NIQB 57 (QBD) ... 184
Mattison v Hart [1854] 14 CB 357 ... 168
Mazur v Charles Russell Speechlys LLP [2025] EWHC 2341 (KB) ... 427
McKenzie v McKenzie [1970] 3 All ER 1034 ... 429
Mercer v Denne [1905] 2 Ch 538 (CA) ... 33
Miller v Jackson [1977] QB 966 (CA) ... 254
Miller v Prime Minister [2019] EWHC 2381 (QB), [2019] 9 WLUK 81 ... 20
M'Naghten's case (1843) 10 Cl & Finn 200 ... 318
Mohamed v Secretary of State for Foreign and Commonwealth Affairs [2008] EWHC 2048 (Admin), [2009] 1 WLR 2579 ... 38
Morelle v Wakeling [1955] 2 QB 379 (CA) ... 268
M v Home Office [1994] 1 AC 377 (HL) ... 8

Nazir v Begum [2024] EWHC 378 (KB) ... 182
Newhaven Port and Properties v East Sussex County Council [2015] UKSC 7, [2015] 2 WLR 601 ... 33
News Corp UK Ltd v Commissioners for HMRC [2023] UKSC 7 ... 173
Northern Counties Securities Ltd v Jackson & Steeple Ltd [1974] 1 WLR 1133 (Ch) ... 66

O'Hara v Chief Constable of the Ulster Constabulary [1997] AC 286 (HL) ... 306
OVM Petrom v Glencore [2015] EWHC 666 (Comm) ... 37
Oxford County Council v Oxford City Council [2006] UKHL 25, [2006] 2 AC 674 ... 33

Paramount Airways Limited (No 2), Re [1993] Ch 223 (CA) ... 156
Parr v Keystone Healthcare [2019] EWCA Civ 1246, [2019] 4 WLR 99 ... 251–252, 294
Pepper (Inspector of Taxes) v Hart [1993] AC 593 (HL) ... 91, 184–186
Peter Farrar v Leongreen Limited [2017] EWCA Civ 2211, [2018] 1 P&CR 17 ... 249
PGF II v OMFS [2013] EWCA Civ 1288, [2014] 1 WLR 1386 ... 409
Pham v Secretary of State for the Home Department [2015] UKSC 19, [2015] 1 WLR 1591 ... 37
Phillips v The Secretary of State for Foreign, Commonwealth and Development Affairs [2024] EWHC 32 (Admin) ... 183, 186
Pioneer Shipping v BTP Tioxide (The Nema) [1982] AC 724 (HL) ... 390
Pius v Fearnley [2013] EWHC 2216 (Ch) ... 218
Porter v Magill [2001] UKHL 67, [2002] 2 AC 357 ... 144, 338, 342
Practice Direction (Citation of Authorities) [2012] 1 WLR 780 ... 251
Practice Direction Judgments: Form and Citation [2001] 1 WLR 194 ... 252
Practice Direction Judicial Precedent [1966] 1 WLR 1234 ... 259, 268
Practice Note (Mode of Address: Lord Justice Butler-Sloss) [1994] 1 FLR 866 ... 220
Practice Statement [1994] 1 WLR 14 (QB) ... 412
Prescott v Birmingham Corp [1954] Ch 210 (CA) ... 144

QX v Secretary of State for the Home Department [2024] UKSC 26 ... 268

R v Abdroikov [2007] UKHL 37, [2007] 1 WLR 3538 ... 337–338
R (on the application of Accident Exchange Ltd) v Broom [2017] EWHC 1530 (Admin) ... 287
Radmacher v Granatino [2010] UKSC 42, [2011] 1 AC 534 ... 199, 219
R v Allen (1872) LR1 CCR 367 ... 155
R v Antoine [2001] 1 AC 340 (HL) ... 328
R (on the application of Ball) v Hinckley and Bosworth Council [2024] EWCA Civ 433 ... 179
R v Barry [1992] 95 Crim App R 384 (CA) ... 309
R v Barton [2020] EWCA Crim 575 ... 256–257
R (Black) v Secretary of State for Justice [2017] UKSC 81 ... 177
R v Brandford [2016] EWCA Crim 1794, [2017] 4 WLR 17 ... 345
R (BskyB) v Chelmsford Crown Court [2012] EWHC 1295 (Admin) ... 212
R (Countryside Alliance and others) v Attorney General [2007] UKHL 52, [2008] 1 AC 719 ... 101
R v Davis [2008] UKHL 36, [2008] 3 WLR 125 ... 37
R v Derek William Bentley (Deceased) [1998] 1 Cr App 21 (CA); [2001] 1 Cr App R 21 (CA) ... 242, 262
Reed Executive Plc v Reed Business Information Ltd (No 2) [2004] EWCA Civ 887, [2004] 1 WLR 3026 ... 407
Reilly (No 2) v Secretary of State for Work and Pensions [2016] EWCA Civ 413 ... 176
R (on the application of FDA) v Minister for the Cabinet Office [2024] EWHC 1729 (Admin) ... 176, 181

R v Galbraith [1981] 1 WLR 1039 (CA) ... 318
R v Hare [1934] 1 KB 354 (CA Crim) ... 180
R v Horncastle [2009] UKSC 14 ... 265
R (HS2 Alliance) v Secretary of State for Transport [2014] UKSC 3, [2014] 1 WLR 3253 ... 43, 106
Richardson v Chief Constable of Essex [2011] EWHC 773 (QB), [2011] 2 Cr App R 1 ... 307
Ridehalgh v Horsfield [1994] Ch 205 (CA) ... 294
R (Jackson) v Attorney General [2005] UKHL 56, [2006] 1 AC 262 ... 64, 101, 214
R v James [2006] EWCA Crim 14, [2006] QB 588 ... 270
R v J, S, M [2010] EWCA Crim 1755, [2011] 1 Cr App R 5 ... 331, 332
R v Judge of the City of London Court [1892] 1 QB 273 (CA) ... 167
R (Liverpool City Council) v Local Commissioner for Local Government [2001] 1 All ER 462 (CA) ... 367
R v Mason [1981] QB 881 (CA) ... 343
R v McKenna (William James) [1960] 1 QB 411 (CA) ... 325
R v Medical Appeal Tribunal *ex parte* Gilmore [1957] 1 QB 574 (CA) ... 361
R v Miller [1993] 97 Cr App R 99 (CA) ... 309
R (on the application of Miller) v The Prime Minister; Cherry and Others v Advocate General for Scotland [2019] UKSC 41, [2019] 3 WLR 589 ... 9, 21, 199, 205, 353, 360
R (Miller) v Secretary of State for Exiting the European Union [2016] EWHC 2768 (Admin), [2017] 1 All ER 158 ... 205
R (Milton) v Crown Prosecution Service [2007] EWHC 532 (Admin) ... 183
R v Mizra; R v Connor and Rollock [2004] UKHL 2, [2004] 1 AC 1118 ... 347
R v Montila [2004] UKHL 50 ... 180
R v National Insurance Commissioner, *Ex parte* Hudson [1972] AC 944 (HL) ... 259
R (Nicklinson) v Ministry of Justice [2014] UKSC 38, [2014] 3 WLR 200 ... 72
R (on the application of O) v Secretary of State for the Home Department [2022] UKSC 3, [2022] 2 WLR 343 ... 170, 181, 185
R (Oceana) v Upper Tribunal [2023] EWHC 791 (Admin) ... 175
Rolf v de Guerin [2011] EWCA Civ 78, [2011] CP Rep 24 ... 408
Rothermere v Times Newspapers Ltd [1973] 1 WLR 448 (CA) ... 334
Royal Bank of Canada v Ministry of Defence [2003] EWHC 1841 (Ch) ... 413
Royal College of Nursing v DHSS [1981] AC 800 (HL) ... 159, 163
R (P, G and W) v Secretary of State for the Home Department and Another [2019] UKSC 3, [2019] 2 WLR 509 ... 369
R v Pintori [2007] EWCA Crim 1700; [2007] Crim LR 997 ... 343
R v Ponting [2015] Crim LR 318 (CA) ... 346
R v Prichard (1836) 7 C&P 303 ... 328
R (on the application of Privacy International) v Investigatory Powers Tribunal and Others [2019] UKSC 22, [2019] 2 WLR 1219 ... 37
R (on the Application of Quintavalle) v Secretary of State for Health [2003] UKHL 13, [2003] 2 AC 687 (HL) ... 172, 180
R (Prolife) v British Broadcasting Corporation [2003] UKHL 23, [2004] 1 AC 185 ... 214
R (Reilly No 2) v Secretary of State for Work and Pensions [2014] EWHC 2182 (Admin) ... 144, 146
R (Reilly) v Secretary of State for Work and Pensions [2012] EWHC 2292 (Admin), (2012) 156(32) SJLB 31 ... 145
R (Reilly) v Secretary of State for Work and Pensions [2013] UKSC 68, [2014] AC 453 ... 116, 144
R v R (Marital Exemption) [1992] 1 AC 599 (HL) ... 267
R v Secretary of State for the Environment, *ex parte* Hammersmith and Fulham London Borough Council and Others [1991] 1 AC 521 (HL) ... 143
R v Secretary of State for the Home Department *ex parte* Fire Brigades Union [1995] 2 AC 513 (HL) ... 121–122, 357
R v Secretary of State for the Home Department *ex parte* Simms [2002] 2 AC 115 (HL) ... 176
R v Sheffield Crown Court *Ex parte* Brownlow [1980] QB 530 (CA) ... 344
R v Shivpuri [1987] AC 1 (HL) ... 259
R v Simpson [2003] EWCA Crim 1499, [2004] QB 118 ... 262
R v Somerset County Council, *ex parte* Fewings [1995] 1 WLR 1037 (CA) ... 144
R (T) v Chief Constable of Greater Manchester Police [2014] UKSC 35; [2014] 3 WLR 96; [2015] AC 49 ... 369
R v Thompson [2010] EWCA Crim 1623, [2011] 1 WLR 200 ... 349
R v Twomey [2013] ECHR 577 ... 327
R v Twomey, Blake, Hibberd and Cameron [2011] EWCA Crim 8, [2011] 1 WLR 1681 ... 332
R v Wang (Cheong) [2005] UKHL 9, [2005] 1 WLR 661 ... 345
R v Watson [1988] QB 690 (CA) ... 320
R (West) v Parole Board [2005] UKHL 1, [2005] 1 WLR 350 ... 260
R (Whiston) v Secretary of State for Justice [2014] UKSC 39, [2015] AC 176 ... 260

R v Young [1995] QB 324 (CA) ... 348
R (Youngsam) v The Parole Board [2017] EWHC 729 (Admin); [2017] 1 WLR 2848 ... 255, 260
R (on the application of UNISON) v Lord Chancellor [2017] UKSC 51, [2017] 3 WLR 409 ... 58, 360

sE Asian Fire Bricks Sdn Bvd v Non-Metallic Mineral Products Manufacturing Employees Union [1981] AC 363 (PC) ... 361
Serafin v Malkiewicz [2020] UKSC 23 ... 212
Seventh Earl of Malmesbury v Strutt [2008] EWHC 424 (QB), [2008] 5 Costs LR 736 ... 381, 409, 410
Sirros v Moore [1975] QB 118 (CA) ... 217
Smith v Hughes [1960] 1 WLR 830 (QB) ... 169
Solicitor General v Stoddart [2017] EWHC 1361 (QB) ... 349
Sumukan v Commonwealth Secretariat [2006] EWHC 1148 (Comm), [2006] 1 All ER (Comm) 621 ... 391–392
Sussex Peerage Case (1844) 11 C & Fin 85 ... 167

Tanfern Ltd v Gregor Cameron-Macdonald [2000] 2 All ER 801 (CA) ... 233
Thoburn v Sunderland City Council [2002] EWHC 195 (Admin), [2003] QB 151 ... 40, 43, 44, 105, 106
Thomas v News Group Newspapers [2001] EWCA Civ 1233, CA ... 158
Total Metal Manufacturing v Tungsten [1955] 1 WLR 761 ... 255
TuneIn v Warner Music UK Ltd [2021] EWCA Civ 441 ... 264

Vauxhall Estates v Liverpool Corp [1932] 1 KB 733 (KB) ... 104
Walker v Innospec Ltd [2017] UKSC 47 ... 176
Ward v James (No2) [1966] 1 QB (CA) ... 333
Westminster City Council v Asylum Support Service [2002] UKHL 38 ... 186
Whiteley v Chappell [1868] LR QB 147 ... 167
Williams v Fawcett [1986] QB 604 (CA) ... 261
Woolmington v DPP [1935] AC 462 (HL) ... 318
Wyld v Silver [1963] 1 QB 169 (CA) ... 33

Yeo MP v Times Newspaper Ltd [2014] EWHC 2853 (QB), [2015] 1 WLR 971 ... 334
Young v Bristol Aeroplane Co Ltd [1944] KB 718, [1944] 2 All ER 293 (CA) ... 261

TABLE OF LEGISLATION

Abortion Act 1967 ... 72, 84, 160, 163
s 1 ... 159–160
Access to Justice Act 1999 ... 231, 280, 381, 412
s 4(4)(c) ... 381
s 54 ... 236
Act of Settlement 1701 ... 200
Art. 7 ... 200
Acts of Parliament (Commencement) Act 1793 ... 97
Acts of Union 1707 ... 19, 96
Administration of Estates Act 1925 ... 168
Administration of Justice (Miscellaneous Provisions) Act 1933 ... 333
s 6 ... 333
Administration of Justice Act 1969
ss 12–15 ... 236
Administration of Justice Act 1985 ... 420, 425
Airports Act 1986
s 63 ... 130
American Constitution First Amendment 1791 ... 5
Arbitration Act 1996 ... 383–387, 388, 389, 392, 393, 394
s 1 ... 386, 387, 389, 394
s 1(a) ... 387
s 1(b) ... 380, 387
s 1(c) ... 387, 389
s 2(1)–(3) ... 385
s 3 ... 386, 388
s 5 ... 385, 386
s 7 ... 385, 386
s 8 ... 385, 386
ss 9–11 ... 385
s 9(1), (4) ... 389
s 11 ... 386
s 12 ... 389
s 13 ... 386
s 14, 15 ... 386, 388
s 16 ... 386, 388
s 18 ... 386, 389
s 19 ... 386
s 20 ... 388
ss 20–21 ... 386
s 23 ... 388
s 23(1) ... 388
s 23(4) ... 388
s 24 ... 386
s24(1)(a–c) ... 340, 389
s 24(1)(d) ... 390
s 25 ... 386
s 26 ... 386
s 28 ... 386
s 29 ... 386, 392, 393
s 30 ... 386, 392, 393
s 32 ... 386
s 33 ... 386, 388, 392, 393
s 34 ... 386, 388, 392, 393
ss 35–37 ... 386
s 38 ... 392
s 40 ... 386
s 41 ... 386
s 41 (3) ... 393
ss 42–45 ... 386
s 46 ... 386, 392
s 48 ... 386
s 48(4) ... 393
s 48(5) ... 393
s 49 ... 386
s 51 ... 386
s 56 ... 386
s 59 ... 386
s 60 ... 386
s 61 ... 386, 393
s 64 ... 386
ss 66–68 ... 385, 386, 390, 391
s 69 ... 386, 390, 391
s 69(3) ... 390
s 71 ... 386
s 72 ... 386
s 80 ... 386
s 81 ... 386
s 82 ... 386
s 166 ... 389
Sch. 1 ... 388
Practice Direction, PAC 3.1(3) ... 375
Arbitration Act 2025 ... 82, 383–387, 391
Armed Forces Act 2006
s 219A ... .339
s 220 ... 339
s 221A ... 339
s 222 ... 339
Sch. 2A, paras. 2–5 ... 339
Automated Vehicles Act 2024 ... 82

Bereavement Benefits (Remedial) Order 2023, SI 2023/134 ... 125
Berne Convention for the Protection of Literary and Artistic Works 1886 ... 39, 83

Bill of Rights 1689 ... 43, 105
Art. 9 ... 43
Broads Authority Act 2009
s 11 ... 132

Cardiff Bay Barrage Act 1993 ... 67
Channel Tunnel Rail Link Act 1996 ... 67
Child Maintenance and Other Payments Act 2008 ... 364
Children Act 1989 ... 10, 234, 396
s 2 ... 396
Children Act 2004 ... 78
s 11 ... 308
Children and Families Act 2014 ... 402
Child Support Acts 1991–1995 ... 364
City of London Corporation (Open Spaces) Act 2018 ... 67
Civil Contingencies Act 2004 ... 116
ss 1, 20 ... 116
Civil Liability Act 2018 ... 175
Civil Partnership Act 2004 ... 10, 234
Civil Procedure Rules (CPR) 1998, SI 1998/3132 ... 232, 235, 236, 280–284, 288, 291, 292, 295, 313, 314, 373, 376, 377, 381, 404, 409, 414
Pt. 1 ... 282, 287, 404, 406
r. 1.1 ... 235–236
r. 1.4 ... 405
r. 1.4(2)(e) ... 405, 409
Pt. 3 ... 287
r. 3.1(2)(m) ... 409
Pt. 9 ... 287, 290
Pt. 12 ... 288
Pt. 14 ... 287
Pt. 15 ... 287
Pt. 16 ... 286
Pt. 22 ... 286
Pt. 23 ... 292
Pt. 25 ... 292
Pt. 26 ... 289
r. 26.4 ... 405
r. 26.4(2) (2A) ... 405
Pt. 27 ... 289
Pt. 28 ... 289–290
Pt. 29 ... 290
Pt. 31 ... 291
Pt. 32 ... 291, 292
Pt. 36 ... 288
Pt. 41 ... 293
Pts. 43–47 ... 293–294
Pt. 52 ... 236, 295
Pts. 70–74 ... 294–295
Pt. 72 ... 295
Pt. 79 ... 295
Pt. 83 ... 295
Pt. 89 ... 295
Commonhold and Leasehold Reform Act 2002 (CLARA 2002) ... 364
Common Law Procedure Act 1854 ... 333
s 1 ... 333
Commons Act 1876
s 29 ... 33
Commons Registration Act 1965
s 22(1)(b) ... 33
Commons Registration Act 2006 ... 33
Companies Act 2006 ... 10
Constitutional Reform Act 2005 ... 93, 196, 197, 202, 203, 205, 236, 245, 282
s 2(1) ... 196
s 3 ... 214
s 3(1) ... 205
s 3(6) ... 205
s 5(1) ... 197
s 5(a) ... 197
s 7 (1) ... 197
s 7(2)(b) ... 206
s 17 ... 214
s 23 ... 51, 58, 229
s 26(3)(a), (b) ... 202
s 26(5) ... 202
s 27(1) ... 202
s 27(2) ... 202
s 27(5) ... 202
s 27(8) ... 197
s 61 ... 202
s 63 ... 204
s 64(1) ... 221
s 64(2) ... 221
ss 66–94B ... 203
s 108 ... 208
s 137 ... 213
s 137A ... 222
Sch. 8 ... 202
Sch. 12 ... 202
Consumer Rights Act 2015 ... 4, 10, 102, 279
Contempt of Court Act 1981 ... 358
s 1 ... 215
s 8 ... 347, 348
Contracts (Applicable Law) Act 1990 ... 10
Copyright Act 1911 ... 83
Copyright Designs and Patents Act 1988 ... 159, 160
Coronavirus Act 2020 ... 94, 116, 117, 118
Coroners Act 1988 ... 335, 359
s 11(5) ... 335

Coroners and Justice Act 2009 ... 320
s 7(2) ... 335
s 10(2) ... 335
s 37 ... 206
Sch. 6, paras 5A–5D ... 339
Countryside Act 1968
s 41 ... 130
County Court Act 1981
s 66(3) ... 333
County Court Act 1984 ... 232
County Court Rules ... 282
Courts Act 1971 ... 229, 244, 245
Courts Act 2003
s 63(1) ... 220
Courts and Legal Services Act 1990 ... 111, 201, 231, 421
s 1 ... 111
s 1(1A) ... 111
s 1(9) ... 111
s 1(a)–(b) ... 112
s 10 ... 112
s 27 ... 421
s 62 ... 443
s 120 ... 111
Crime and Courts Act 2013 ... 303
s 17 ... 232
Sch. 9 ... 232
Crime and Disorder Act 1998
s 51 ... 313, 315
ss 51B, 51C ... 239
Criminal Appeal Act 1968 ... 240
s 33 ... 241
Criminal Appeal Act 1995 ... 242
s 2 ... 240
Criminal Attempts Act 1981 ... 82
Criminal Damage Act 1971
s 1(3) ... 6
Criminal Justice Act 1967 ... 344
Criminal Justice Act 1982
s 37(2) ... 132
Criminal Justice Act 1988 ... 122
ss 35, 36 ... 7
ss 108–117 ... 122
Criminal Justice Act 2003 ... 238, 239, 313, 316, 340
s 43 ... 121, 329, 330–331
s 44 ... 329, 330, 331
s 44(2)–(4) ... 331
s 44(5) ... 331
s 142 ... 320
s 170 ... 239
ss 177, 226A, 226B, 227, 228 ... 339
s 321 ... 337
Criminal Justice and Courts Act 2015 ... 6, 231, 347
ss 46–50 ... 312
s 68 ... 337
s 117 ... 310
Criminal Justice and Public Order Act 1994 ... 319
Criminal Law Act 1977 ... 329
Criminal Procedure (Insanity) Act 1964
s 4A(2) ... 328
Criminal Procedure (Right of Reply) Act 1964
s 1 ... 319
Criminal Procedure (Scotland) Act 1995
s 210A ... 339
Criminal Procedure and Investigations Act 1996
s 6, 7A, 8 ... 317
Criminal Procedure Rules (CrimPR) 2015 ... 313, 316
PD. 3A ... 316
PD. IV.42.1, 2 ... 341
PD. IV.42.4 ... 341
Criminal Procedure Rules 2025 ... 313
Pt. 9 ... 313

Dangerous Dogs Act 1991 ... 85
Data Retention and Investigatory Powers Act 2014 ... 83, 94
Defamation Act 2013 ... 334
s 11 ... 334, 335
Defence of the Realm Act 1914 ... 85
Deregulation and Contracting Out Act 1994 ... 126
Digital Economy Act 2017 ... 82
Directive 93/104/EC Concerning Certain Aspects of the Organization of Working Time ... 117
Directive 2008/52/EC On Certain Aspects of Mediation in Civil and Commercial Matters ... 406
Art. 3(a) ... 406
Disability Discrimination Act 1995 ... 84
Dissolution and Calling of Parliament Act 2022 ... 49
Divorce Reform Act 1969 ... 268
Domestic Abuse Act 2021 ... 103

Easter Act 1928 ... 97, 98, 121
s 2(2) ... 98
Economic Crime and Corporate Transparency Act 2023 ... 424
s(1)(3)(a)–(e) ... 424
Education Act 2002 ... 123, 124
ss 19–40 ... 123
ss 76–96 ... 123
s 119 ... 123
s 120 ... 124
ss 157–74 ... 123

Education Act 2011 ... 10
Education (School Teachers' Appraisal) (England) Regulations 2012, SI 2012/115 ... 115, 123
Employment Rights Act 1996 ... 10, 366
Employment Tribunals Act 1996 ... 358, 366
Environment Protection Act 1980 ... 179
Equality Act 2010 ... 306, 366
s 4 ... 154
s 136 ... 274
Equal Pay Act 1970 ... 268
Estate Agents Act 1979 ... 363
European Communities Act 1972 ... 43, 103, 105, 117
s 2(2)(a) ... 117
Sch. 2 ... 117
European Convention on the Protection of Human Rights and Fundamental Freedoms ... 10, 38, 45, 72, 74, 80, 89, 121, 124, 146, 161, 166, 174, 176, 195, 243, 264, 327, 332, 408
Art. 5 ... 307
Art. 6 ... 314, 332, 347, 391, 407, 408
Art. 7 ... 97
Art. 8 ... 9, 124, 125, 396
Art. 9 ... 5, 10
European Parliamentary Elections Act 1999 ... 101
European Union Act 2011 ... 93, 103
s 2(2) ... 29
s 4(1)(a)–(m) ... 103
Sch. 1 ... 29
European Union (Withdrawal) Act 2018 ... 118, 128, 136, 263, 264
s 6(1) ... 264
s 6(4)(a) ... 264
s 8(1) ... 117
Sch. 7 ... 136

Family Law Act 1986 ... 82
Family Law Act 1996 ... 402
Family Law (Scotland) Act 2007 ... 225
Family Procedure Rules (FPR) 2010 ... 234, 341, 402
Fatal Accidents Act 1976 ... 406
Finance Act 1976 ... 184, 185
Finance Act 2012 ... 132
Sch. 29 ... 132
Finance Act 2025 ... 93
Financial Services Act 2012 ... 132
Financial Services and Markets Act 2000 ... 10, 102, 132
ss 137A–141A ... 132
First Statute of Westminster 1275 ... 32
Fiscal Compact Treaty ... 103
Fixed Terms Parliament Act 2011 ... 49, 87, 93
Food Act 1984
s 60 ... 130
Forced Marriage Act 2007 ... 4
Forced Marriage Act 2017 ... 4
Fraud Act 2006 ... 82

Gender Recognition Act 2004 ... 234
Government of Ireland Act 1914 ... 101
Government of Wales Act 1998 ... 30, 48
Government of Wales Act 2006 ... 18, 30
s 112 ... 30
Sch. 7 ... 30
Greater London Authority Act 1999
s 385 ... 132
Growth and Infrastructure Act 2013 ... 34
s 15(1) ... 34
s 15C ... 34
s 16 ... 34
Sch. 1A ... 34

Harbours, Docks and Piers Clauses Act 1847
s 18 ... 130
Health Act 2006 ... 177
High Speed Rail (London–West Midlands) Act 2017 ... 67
High Speed Rail (West Midlands–Crewe) Act 2021 ... 67
Homicide Act 1957
s 2 ... 318
House Of Lords Act 1999 ... 51
House of Lords Reform Act 2014 ... 51
Human Fertilisation and Embryology Act 1990 ... 172, 180
s 3(1) ... 172
s 3(2) ... 172
s 3(3) ... 172
Human Rights Act 1998 ... 10, 43, 45, 73, 74, 89, 93, 105, 124, 161, 174, 195, 265, 329
s 2 ... 265
s 2(1) ... 265
s 3 ... 174, 265–266
s 4 ... 80, 124, 125, 195
s 10 ... 124
s 19 ... 89
Humber Bridge Act 2013 ... 67
Hunting Act 2004 ... 99, 100, 101, 102

Illegal Migration Act 2023 ... 89
Inclosure Act 1857
s 12 ... 33
Income Tax Act 1952 ... 168
s 25 ... 168
Industrial Training Act 1964 ... 144
s 1(4) ... 144

Inquiries Act 2005 ... 76, 77, 368
s 1 ... 59, 368
s 1(1)(a)–(b) ... 368
s 10 ... 59, 77, 193, 368
Insolvency Act 1986
s 238 ... 156
Intellectual Property (Unjustified Threats) Act 2017 ... 82
International Copyright Act 1886 ... 83
Interpretation Act 1978 ... 173, 174
s 4 ... 97, 98
s 6 ... 173
s 8 ... 173

Jobseekers Act 1995 ... 116
s 17 ... 145
s 17A ... 116
Jobseekers (Back to Work Schemes) Act 2013 ... 145
Jobseekers Allowance (Employment, Skills and Enterprise Scheme) Regulations 2011, SI 2011/917 ... 116, 144–145
Judicature Act 1873
s 25(11) ... 35
s 87 ... 419
Judicature Acts 1873–5 ... 40, 229, 241, 245, 419
Judicial Appointments Order 2008, SI 2008/2995
Sch. 1 ... 201
Judicial Discipline (Prescribed Procedures) Regulations (2014) SI 2014/1919 ... 208
Judicial Pensions and Retirement Act 1993
s 3(1) ... 213
s 26(1) ... 213
Sch. 5 ... 213
Judicial Review and Courts Act 2022 ... 147
s 1 ... 147
s 2 ... 147
Juries Act 1974 ... 336, 337, 342, 347
s 1 ... 337
s 2(1)–(3) ... 336
s 6(1) ... 336
s 8(1), 9(1), 9(A), 9AA ... 340
s 12(4) ... 342
s 12(6) ... 342
s 17 ... 344
s 17(3), (4) ... 345
s 20 ... 336
s 20(5)(d) ... 338
ss 20A–20D ... 347, 349
ss 20A–20G ... 339
ss 20E–20G ... 347
Sch. 1 ... 338
Justice and Security Act 2013 ... 176

Land Drainage Act 1991
s 66 ... 132
Landlord and Tenant Act 1985 ... 10
Landlord and Tenant Act 1987 ... 157, 164
s 6 ... 157
s 12 ... 157
Landlord and Tenant Act 1988 ... 82
Land Registration Act 2002 ... 10, 182, 364
Law Commission Act 2009 ... 81
s 1 ... 82
Law Commissions Act 1965 ... 81
s 1 ... 81
s 3(1) ... 81
s 3A ... 82
Leasehold Enfranchisement Act 1967 ... 365
Leasehold Reform, Housing and Urban Development Act 1993 ... 364
Legal Aid, Sentencing and Punishment of Offenders Act (LASPO) 2012 ... 29, 278, 281
Legal Services Act 2007 ... 422–425, 427, 430, 441, 443
s 1 ... 423
s 2 ... 424
s 3 ... 425
s 4 ... 425
s 12 ... 426
s 14 ... 428
s 17 ... 428
s 18 ... 426
s 19 ... 426
Sch. 2 ... 424, 427
Sch. 4 ... 425
Legal Services Authority Act 1987 ... 381
Legislative and Regulatory Reform Act 2006 ... 126
s 1, 2 ... 126
Life Peerages Act 1958 ... 51
Limitation Act 1980
s 11 ... 287
Limited Liability Partnerships Act 2000 ... 431
Local Government Act 1972
s 235 ... 129
s 235(3) ... 129
Local Government Byelaws (Wales) Act 2012 ... 129

Magistrates' Courts Act 1980 ... 231
s 17A ... 313
s 18A ... 238
s 19 ... 239
ss 19–23 ... 313
s 20 ... 239
Magna Carta 1215 ... 43, 324, 325, 327
Art. 39 ... 324

Marriage Act 1949 ... 10
Marriage (Same Sex Couples) Act 2013 ... 75, 234
Matrimonial Causes Act 1973 ... 234, 268
Mental Capacity Act 2005 ... 339
Mental Health Act 1983 ... 339
s 7 ... 339
s 17A ... 339
Military Lands Act 1892
s 14 ... 130
Monken Hadley Common Act 2022 ... 67
Municipal Corporations Act 1835 ... 73

National Insurance Act 1946 ... 116
Nationality, Immigration and Asylum Act 2002
s 104 ... 179
National Security Act 2023 ... 305
Neonatal Care (Leave and Pay) Act 2023
s 1 ... 121
Neonatal Care (Leave and Pay) Act 2023 (Commencement No 1) Regulations 2023, SI 2023/904 ... 121
New York Convention on the Recognition and Enforcement of Foreign Arbitral Awards 1959 ... 39
Northern Ireland (Temporary Provisions) Act 1972 ... 123
s 1(3) ... 123
Northern Ireland Act 1998 ... 184
ss 84–86 ... 123

Offences Against the Person Act 1861
s 57 ... 155
Official Secrets Act 1911 ... 344, 346
Official Secrets Act 1920 ... 317, 344, 346

Paraffin (Maximum Retail Prices) (Revocation) Order 1979, SI 1979/797 ... 134
Parliament Act 1911 ... 29, 49, 51, 88, 99, 100, 101, 102, 107
s 1(1) ... 99
Parliament Act 1949 ... 29, 49, 51, 88, 99, 101, 102, 107
Parliamentary Constituencies Order of 1969 ... 135
Parliamentary Standards Act 2009 ... 49, 364
Partnership Act 1890 ... 431
Patents Court (Financial Limits) (No 2) Order 2011, SI 2011/1402 ... 111
Pension Service Pensions and Judicial Offices Act 2022 ... 213
Police and Criminal Evidence Act (PACE) 1984 ... 6, 78, 132, 304–305, 306, 307
Code A ... 306
Code A–I ... 305
Code C ... 307, 308, 309
Code C, Annex B ... 307
Code C 16.5 ... 312
Code D ... 309
Code E, F ... 307, 309
s 1(6), 2 ... 306
s 17 ... 310
s 24 ... 305
s 24(5) ... 305
s 29 ... 307
s 37, 37A ... 311
s 37B ... 311
s 38 ... 312
s 56 ... 307
s 58 ... 307
s 61 ... 310
s 61A ... 310
s 63S ... 310
s 64A ... 309
s 66 ... 132
s 76(2)(a), (b) ... 309
Police Reform Act 2002 ... 304
Police Reform and Social Responsibility Act 2011 ... 304
Powers of Criminal Courts (Sentencing) Act 2000 ... 313
Promissory Oaths Act 1868
s 6A ... 214
Prosecution of Offenders Act 1985
s3(2) ... 238
s 10 ... 311
Protection from Harassment Act 1997 (PFHA) ... 158
Protection of Freedoms Act 2012
s 113 ... 331
Public Bodies Act 2011 ... 127, 128, 362
s 7 ... 128
s 8 ... 128, 139
Public Health Act 1875
s 164 ... 130
Public Health Act 1936
s 231 ... 130
Public Health (Control of Disease) Act 1984 ... 116, 136
s 45R ... 136
Public Health Acts Amendment Act 1907
s 82 ... 130
Public Libraries and Museums Act 1964
s 19 ... 130
Public Order Act 1986 ... 6
ss 1–4, 4A, 5 ... 6

Race Relations Act 1976 ... 154, 268
Railways Act 2005
s 46 ... 132
Regulation of Investigatory Powers Act 2000 ... 132

Regulatory Reform Act 2001 ... 126
Representation of the People Act 1983 ... 89
Representation of the People Act 1985 ... 89
Restriction of Offensive Weapons Act 1959 ... 161
s 1 ... 161
Restriction of Offensive Weapons Act 1961 ... 163
Road Traffic Act 1988 ... 178
Road Traffic Acts ... 238, 279, 301, 329
Royal Assent Act 1967 ... 96
s 1 ... 96
Rules of the Supreme Court ... 282

Safety of Rwanda (Immigration and Asylum) Act 2024 ... 176
Sale of Goods Act 1979 ... 4, 10
School Teachers' Pay and Conditions Order 2014, SI 2014/2045 ... 124
Scotland Act 1998 ... 43, 105
Senior Courts Act 1981 ... 200, 219, 229
s 2 ... 197
s 2(1)(b) ... 236
s 2(3) ... 220
s 11 ... 213
s 11(3) ... 200
s 28A ... 359
s 29(3) ... 232, 359
s 69(1) ... 333
Serious Organised Crime and Police Act 2005 ... 305
Sex Disqualification (Removal) Act 1919 ... 419
Sexual Offences Act 1959
s 1 ... 182
Sexual Offences (Amendment) Act 2000 ... 101
Sexual Offences Act 2003 ... 124, 125
s 1 ... 183
s 82 ... 124
Sexual Offences Act 2003 (Remedial) Order 2012, SI 2012/1883 ... 124, 125
Social Security Contributions and Benefits (Northern Ireland) Act 1992
s 9A ... 125
Solicitors Act 1974 ... 442
s 11(1) ... 236
s 43 ... 442
Special Immigration Appeals Act 1997 ... 366
Statute of Labourers 1351 ... 228, 230
Statutory Instruments Act 1946 ... 120, 122
s 1(1) ... 120
s 5(1) ... 134
Street Offences Act 1959
s 1(1) ... 169
Supreme Court Act 1981, *see* Senior Courts Act 1981
Supreme Court of Judicature Act 1873 ... 36

Terrorism Act 2000 ... 133, 184
Theft Act 1968 ... 238, 329
Town Police Clauses Act 1847
s 68 ... 130
Trade Union and Labour Relations (Consolidation) Act 1992 ... 132
s 199 ... 132
s 207 ... 132
Transport Act 1962 ... 129
Treasure Act 1996 ... 335
Tribunals, Courts and Enforcement Act 2007 ... 201, 226, 354, 361, 362
s 51 ... 201
Tribunals of Inquiry (Evidence) Act 1921 ... 76

UNCITRAL Model Law on International Commercial Arbitration (United Nations) 1985 ... 383, 384
Union with Ireland Act 1800 ... 18
Union with Scotland Act 1707 ... 18
Union with Wales Act 1536–1543 ... 18
United Nations Convention against Torture 1984 ... 39
United Nations Convention on the Rights of the Child 1989 ... 39

Value Added Tax Act 1994 ... 173
Vienna Convention on the Law of Treaties 1969 ... 10, 39
Voyeurism (Offences) Act 2019 ... 72

War Crimes Act 1991 ... 101
War Damages Act 1965 ... 146
Weights and Measures Act 1985 ... 105
Welsh Church Act 1914 ... 101
Working Time Regulations 1998, SI 1998/183 ... 117

Youth Justice and Criminal Evidence Act 1999 ... 318

1

CHAPTER 1 INTRODUCTION TO 'LAW' AND THE 'LEGAL SYSTEM'

INTRODUCTION

There are few, if any, who will make it through to adulthood without having come across the terms 'law' and 'legal system'. The concepts not only dominate and regulate, often without our conscious recognition, our day-to-day interactions with each other and the state but also are part of our shared cultural conscience. Aspects of law and the legal system are never far from the public eye, with countless hours of popular culture and endless pages of the press devoted to portraying (sometimes highly inaccurately) law, justice and legal systems in action.

Even though the 'law' is an accepted part of our daily lives, there are few who will be asking the key questions: what is 'law', and what is meant by the 'legal system'? Fewer still will peer behind the curtain to question the nature, purpose and *effectiveness* of the law and the legal system within which it operates. This chapter is not as ambitious as to seek to provide definitive answers to questions of the purpose or nature of law or to provide a conclusive answer as to the necessary or sufficient features of the 'legal system', but rather, it is to get the reader to *start* to think about these things. Indeed, the rest of this textbook is dedicated to exploring aspects of the legal system of England and Wales.

This chapter has a number of interrelated aims. First, it considers the concepts of 'law' and 'legal system' and how they relate to legal theory. Secondly, the chapter considers how these concepts translate into the legal system of England and Wales. Finally, the chapter identifies some of the central themes that will be explored throughout the rest of the textbook and outlines how to make the most of the pedagogical features of the text.

AS YOU READ

This chapter and the next will probably be amongst the most challenging to read for someone new to the study of law; however, perseverance is a key legal skill. As you read, try to think about how the concepts under discussion can relate to real-life experiences of the legal system that you know best.[1] Of all the chapters, it is to this one that you should return frequently. It seeks to give you the framework necessary for understanding the rest of the textbook.

By the end of this chapter, the reader should have an **emerging understanding** of the difference between 'law' and 'legal system'. You should be able to consider critically *the functions*

1 If you have experience of other legal systems, then turn this to your advantage by considering how what you learn about the legal system of England and Wales compares with what you know about your own system.

DOI: 10.4324/9781032641829-1

and purpose of law and legal rules and how these contrast with the functions and purpose of other forms of 'rule'.

You will also be able to **differentiate between** different legal systems and what this may mean for the law that emerges and how the law is administered in that jurisdiction. You will thus be able to **describe** how the different jurisdictions within the UK interact.

WHAT IS LAW?

Subsequent chapters of this text will explore the different *sources* of particular laws and will look at the process for creating specific categories of law. This section seeks to explore – in an accessible and straightforward way – the concept of 'law' in its broadest sense, unrelated to *particular* laws. In this way, 'What is law?' is a question that has troubled the minds of lawyers, academics, politicians, judges and the public for centuries, and it is not proposed that this textbook will be able to articulate a wholly satisfactory answer in one short chapter. The question of 'What is law?' provokes such interest because all concentrations of human population throughout history develop a system of laws, although the nature, form and sophistication of those laws can vary quite significantly.[2]

At its most basic level, we could explain the law *as a collection of rules that seek to govern behaviours, relationships and disputes*. This definition of 'law' is attractive for its simplicity and, all else excluded, is neat and reasonably accurate. It is also an incomplete definition, ignoring as it does other 'rules' that may exist. The fact that law does not operate in a vacuum is a key theme that we return to throughout the text. Law is, of course, not the only form of rule by which we live and by which our behaviour is regulated. There is a multitude of 'rules' that vary in both effect and formality, and 'laws' are just one of these sorts of rules. To take some examples:

- Families may develop 'rules' for how time is spent and on the activities that are allowed or are prohibited. For example, on the time permitted to use mobile phones or social media.
- Clubs and societies may have rules that seek to regulate the governance of the club's activities. For example, on how the committee members are appointed, elected or removed.[3]
- Universities will have 'rules' as to assessment processes or on how feedback on work is produced and delivered. For example, there may be rules on how examinations and other assessments are conducted and coursework submitted.

2 David Howarth, 'On the Question "What Is Law?"' (2000) 6 Res Publica 259.

3 For example, the Society of Legal Scholars is an academic membership society and has, as you might expect of a group of academic lawyers, its own set of rules – <https://www.legalscholars.ac.uk/wp-content/uploads/2021/12/REVISED-SLS-RULES-2021.pdf>.

- A school will have rules as to the behaviour of its pupils. For example, there may be set sanctions linked to specific actions, or there may be guiding principles or values to which it is expected that students will adhere.
- Games and sports will have 'rules' as to conduct that govern the way in which the game or sport is played. For example, in chess there are rules as to the permissible movements of each playing piece.
- Within social groups of friends or within wider society, there may be certain, albeit soft, social rules that seek to govern how we act in certain situations. For example, there are so-called unspoken rules of social conduct and the concept of personal space.
- As between companies, or within particular sectors of the economy, there are soft rules which govern conduct and behaviours. They operate on a 'shared understanding' of the rules for which there may be no formal, legal consequence for breach.[4]
- There are also certain moral codes by which people seek to live their lives. For example, there are those who will not consume meat or animal products.
- There are also religious observances and rules that dictate the behaviour of individuals who are part of particular religious communities. For example, many faiths have rules about the preparation and consumption of certain foods and rituals and rules about prayer and worship.
- Workplaces will set rules for the conduct of their employees. For example, particular codes of dress or rules governing the use of social media during work hours.

It is also important to note that these categories of rules are not *static*, *exhaustive* or *mutually exclusive*. Over time – and according to particular political, social, economic and cultural considerations – rules can become more or less formal, and formerly 'informal' rules can become law. A rather stark example of this was the changing nature of the aforementioned 'personal space' during the Covid-19 pandemic. What had always been a soft social norm of respecting the 'personal space' of others became increasingly formalised into strict government guidance as a way of attempting to control the spread of the coronavirus.[5]

In this way, it must be true that *legal* rules have additional or distinguishing characteristics that differentiate them from these other types of rules. The inherent fluidity to this categorisation can make identifying those characteristics very difficult. Again, at the risk of oversimplifying matters, laws could be said to be rules that the state and society agree should be deemed as such and for which there are state-endorsed consequences for breach. Laws are, as a result, a more *formal* form of rule. In this way, law is elevated above other forms of rule due to its endorsement by the state – through legislation or case law – as an expression of the values and beliefs of a society with state-sanctioned consequences for breach. The following section turns attention towards the *function* or *purpose* of such law.

4 Although a breach of these conventions or 'soft law' may lead to 'hard law' being enacted. For example, the failure of the press to self-regulate effectively came to light during the 'phone hacking' scandal in the UK, and the subsequent Leveson Inquiry led to calls (at the time of writing, still resisted) for *legislatively* backed standards of conduct.

5 For example: <https://assets.publishing.service.gov.uk/government/uploads/system/uploads/attachment_data/file/883116/Staying_at_home_and_away_from_others__social_distancing_pdf>.

THE FUNCTION(S) OF THE LAW

Another way to consider the concept of law is to think about the *purpose of law* and the *function* that it plays in society, and then the question moves from 'What is law?' to 'Why do we need law?' This helps us understand the importance of law to society but can also help us assess whether particular laws have met their aims and ambitions. This latter point is particularly important as having a *critical* understanding of the law will help in understanding calls for reform.

ANALYSING THE LAW – APPROACHING LEGAL STUDY

An ability to **assess** the law critically is one of the crucial academic and practical legal skills that form the basis of much of the academic study of law and, indeed, its practice. When engaging with a piece of legislation for the first time, it is worth taking a step back and trying to understand not only **how** the law applies but also **what** the law was seeking to achieve.

This 'purpose' can be at a very abstract level, for example, whether the law was intended to **shape** and **change** behaviour within a community[6] or whether it was aimed at **reflecting** existing expectations of behaviour within a society[7]or whether it was intended to consolidate fragmented laws into a single piece of legislation (a process termed 'consolidation').[8]

At a more focussed level, the 'purpose' of the law may be understood as the very concrete outcomes that the legislation was seeking to achieve – for example, a decrease in the level of knife-related crime amongst young people may be the purpose of a piece of legislation that increased the 'stop and search' powers of the police, such as is the case under the various codes of PACE.

Understanding **purpose** (at all levels) is important for a number of reasons. In this context, by understanding the purpose of law, it is possible for the observer to comment critically on the impact (potential or actual) of law on society. As will be examined in Chapters 4 and 5 – on primary and secondary legislation, respectively – the context to the passing of a particular law can have a profound impact on its effectiveness. Equally, how courts approach the interpretation of the law will also have a sizeable impact on its application, as is discussed in Chapter 6.

6 For example, the Forced Marriage Acts 2007 and 2017.

7 For example, the theory of Sir Frederick Maine, set out in his seminal work *Ancient Law* (first published Murray 1861, reprinted 1906), in which he identified the socio-legal trend of earliest societies where the custom was first established, and then the regulating law followed only later.

8 For example, the consolidation of earlier commercial statutes into the Sale of Goods Act 1979, and later into the Consumer Rights Act 2015.

The website that accompanies this textbook contains more detailed examples of specific legislation, with exercises for exploring their role, function and effectiveness.

What follows is a concise consideration of the main functions of law. These help shape not only the *substantive* law but also how and why a particular *form* of law has been adopted. It is also worth noting that these are only a snapshot of the multiple purposes that law may be trying to achieve at any given point and that they should not be viewed as mutually exclusive or exhaustive (i.e. a law may be seeking to achieve more than one purpose at a time).

PRESERVING PUBLIC ORDER

It is first important to attempt to define the term 'public order' before considering the function of law in 'preserving' that public order. The difficulty is that the concept of public order is rather broad and heavily contested. It is a phrase often found in the mouths of politicians, to be used as a mechanism of social control and to counter activism against government policy.

Moving away from the political, this concept can mean different things to different disciplines, and the term can even have specific jurisdictional meanings within different legal systems.[9] For the purposes of this section, a broad understanding of *public order* is adopted and, in this sense, is understood to be the balance between competing freedoms – most notably the freedoms of association[10] and assembly[11] on the one hand and the rights of broader society to go about its business uninterrupted on the other. A thread that runs through *some* of the notions of public order is a need to protect public security and the proper functioning of the state.

The law performs an important function of 'preserving public order' by restricting or regulating certain freedoms. In England and Wales, the law performs this function in a number of ways, but, most notably, through the criminal law. Certain behaviour that threatens public order can, therefore, lead to criminal sanctions, such as imprisonment.

9 For example, within the European Union, the term 'public order' is an amalgamation of the concepts of 'public policy' and 'public security'.

10 That is, the fundamental workers' right to join workers' associations and/or other organisations, including political organisations, provided they are peaceful and do not threaten public order or breach other legislation or rules protecting public order, termed in some legislation 'the Queen's Peace' or, since 2022, 'the King's Peace'.

11 That is, the right in, for example, Article 9 of the European Convention on Fundamental Freedoms, and the First Amendment to the American Constitution (added 1791), to allow political, religious or other meetings of any kind for which people may lawfully wish to meet to discuss or indulge in other activities (which would cover everything from a sewing circle, through going to church, to a political meeting).

EXPLAINING THE LAW – PUBLIC ORDER OFFENCES

The Public Order Act 1986 sought to codify, clarify and modernise the common law[12] offences against public order and to place them under the authority of an Act of Parliament. The main offences that seek to preserve public order are:

- Riot[13]
- Violent disorder[14]
- Affray[15]
- Fear or provocation of violence[16]
- Intentional harassment, alarm or distress[17]
- Harassment, alarm or distress[18]

It is of interest to note that public order offences under the Act are often commissioned at the same time as other offences such as assault,[19] arson[20] or criminal damage.[21]

There is also a concern that a failure to deal with threats to public order (which are often accompanied by violence to persons or property) can allow them to spread across the country, causing a complete breakdown of the functioning of the state. By way of example, in 2011 public order was threatened by mass rioting across the UK following the shooting of Mark Duggan during an attempted arrest in London.[22] The riots quickly spread across the UK, with more than 3,000 arrests for public order and other offences related to significant damage to property and looting.

In the trials that followed, and as an indication of the seriousness with which a threat to public order is treated, the courts were seen to treat those involved with the riots harshly. Adam Ahmadzai was a ringleader of a set of rioters who was initially sentenced to four years' imprisonment following a guilty plea to charges of violent disorder, robbery, criminal damage and burglary. The Crown Prosecution Service thought that

12 The 'common law' is that body of law which is made by judges and is explored, in detail, in Chapter 2, 'Sources of Law'.
13 Public Order Act 1986 s1.
14 Public Order Act 1986 s2.
15 Public Order Act 1986 s3.
16 Public Order Act 1986 s4.
17 Public Order Act 1986 s4A.
18 Public Order Act 1986 s5.
19 For example, common assault (the basic offence under the common law, committed by assault [threat] and battery [physical action on the person of the victim]) or the more detailed offences under the Offences Against the Person Act 1861 or more recent more specialised statutes, such as Criminal Justice Acts or Police Acts, etc.
20 Criminal Damage Act 1971 s1(3).
21 See Criminal Damage Act 1971 s(1).
22 <https://www.bbc.co.uk/news/uk-england-london-14842416>.

this sentence was 'unduly lenient'[23] and referred the matter to the Court of Appeal, which quashed the original sentence and replaced it with a sentence of seven years.

More recently, in 2024, civil disorder broke out following the stabbing and murder of young girls attending a dance class in Stockport. The riots began as rumours of the identity of the suspect fuelled anti-immigrant and Islamophobic feeling across the country. More than 1,000 people were charged with disorder-related offences, with some high-profile cases of sentencing being reported. Primary amongst these was the case of Lucy Connolly, who was sentenced following messages posted on social media. She was sentenced to 31 months' imprisonment.[24] A further high-profile case related to the Stockport Riots was that of Peter Lynch, who was convicted of violent disorder following incidents outside a hotel housing migrants. He was sentenced to two years and eight months but subsequently committed suicide in prison. Some of these charge and sentencing decisions sparked global debates about freedom of speech and how that is to be balanced against the need to maintain public order. They go to show the difficult balance of interests that are sometimes at play in a legal order, but also of the very fundamental importance and gravity with which the maintenance of public order is treated.

REFLECTING AND INFLUENCING VALUES OF A SOCIETY

This function of law is fairly broad and encompasses much of the function of law in a developed society. The way in which law regularly achieves this function is to capture, regulate and enforce expected standards of behaviour (often through the criminal law). In many situations, there is a shared, societal understanding of what we expect of our fellow citizens. Some of these standards are deemed important enough to be enshrined in law so that they have the endorsement of the state and also the ability to be enforced or, for non-compliance, to be punished. To take an obvious example, the law reflects an accepted societal position that citizens should not be able to kill another citizen. Thus, the legal system of England and Wales, with all the usual caveats and conditions[25] about the risks of oversimplification, recognises murder as a criminal offence. With the uncertain *deterrent* effect of laws or strict sentencing governing such important questions,[26] the law of murder is less about encouraging citizens *not* to kill one another unlawfully but more about recognising the fact that we accept such behaviour as morally[27] wrong and wish to issue sanctions against those who violate that

23 This is a technical area of criminal law governed by ss35 and 36 of the Criminal Justice Act 1988 but, for our purposes, it is possible for the Crown Prosecution Service to refer cases to the Court of Appeal where the sentence appears not to be sufficient.

24 The sentencing remarks of the judge can be found here. <https://www.judiciary.uk/wp-content/uploads/2024/10/R-v-Lucy-Connolly.pdf>.

25 Such as self-defence, etc.

26 Andrew Ashworth, 'The Common Sense and Complications of General Deterrent Sentencing' (2019) 7 Crim LR 564.

27 Whether we derive that moral judgment from some internal mechanism or by reference to religious beliefs.

standard. Those laws that 'reflect' societal norms are normally relatively uncontroversial, other than in the detail or at the fringes of their application.[28] As a result, it could be argued that one of the functions of law is to *reflect* and create consequence for non-compliance with already-accepted standards of behaviour.[29]

There are also laws that seek actively to *influence* or *change* the accepted standards of behaviour within a society. These rules are often based on a changed understanding of the world and can be fuelled by technological or medical advances. The law's purpose here is to introduce, through state action, new accepted standards of behaviour for the benefits of its citizens.

TAKING THINGS FURTHER – LAW AS AN AGENT FOR CHANGE

The website that accompanies this text charts a seemingly small development in the law that has played a part in changing societal attitudes and which exemplifies this function of law and relates to the increased regulation on the use of safety equipment in cars.

This function of law can be controversial, and it is often that there is not a shared acceptance that regulation of activity or behaviour is necessary. Such action that is intended to *lead* society rather than reflect it is often for the protection of the health, safety and well-being of the population. It is for this reason that the creation of such laws in the legal system of England and Wales is normally reserved to Parliament, rather than to judges through the common law, as it is Parliament that is directly answerable to the people.[30]

REGULATING THE POWERS OF INSTITUTIONS OF THE STATE

Within the legal system, it is true to say that all are subject to the law.[31] This applies as much to the government of the day[32] (and their agents) or public authorities as it does to individual citizens. It is here that the law performs a *constitutional* function in delineating and controlling the powers of the state. This coin has two sides – the law *grants* powers to the state and *controls* and sets the limits of those powers.

In English and Welsh law, each and every action of a public body or the government that conflicts with specific rights requires a legal basis that enables that action. This is sometimes known as the principle of legality.[33] There are various legal sources for the lawful use of state powers, and the function of the law in this instance is to create lawful authority for the

28 To put this differently, most in society would agree that murder ought to be prohibited, but there will be less agreement as to what should fall inside the scope of the definition of *murder*.

29 This is at the heart of Maine's theory that in primitive societies, the law followed accepted social standards and culture.

30 This split between the powers and functions of the state is considered in greater detail in Chapter 3, 'Institutions of the Legal System'.

31 This is a core element of the rule of law, which is one of the founding principles of the British constitution. See the influence of the theory of John Locke, that freedom is everyone being subject to the law laid down by a legislature that applies to everyone.

32 *M v Home Office* [1994] 1 AC 377 (HL).

33 Jason Varuhas, 'The Principle of Legality' (2020) 79 CLJ 578.

exercise of public powers. The law adds a *legitimacy* to and *accountability* for the actions of those with public powers. For example, in the case of *Malone*[34] the European Court of Human Rights held that the UK violated an individual's right to a private life (Article 8 of the European Convention on Human Rights) by requiring the interception of his telephone conversations without a specific statutory authority.

The parallel function of law is to ensure that those exercising public powers do so within the limits of their lawful authority. If there is no lawful basis for the exercise of public power, then the action can be challenged before the courts. Such exercise of power beyond legal authority is known as *ultra vires* and can render actions or decisions unlawful and void. The challenge before the court is called 'judicial review' and is discussed further in Chapter 13, on administrative law.

EXPLAINING THE LAW – PROROGATION OF PARLIAMENT

A fairly recent example of the control of government power will help demonstrate this important function of the law in controlling the powers of the institutions of the state. In the autumn of 2019, Boris Johnson, leader of the Conservative government and Prime Minister, prorogued Parliament[35] for five weeks, leaving the legislature with little time to scrutinise the government in the run-up to the date on which the UK was due to leave the European Union ('Brexit Day' or 'Exit Day'). The issue of sufficient parliamentary control over the UK's rescinding its membership of the EU was (and still is) deeply contentious. A number of parties alleged that this was unlawful and so brought the issue before the courts.

Following a complicated, but expedited, journey through the courts, the matter ended up before the Supreme Court in the *Miller* case,[36] which was faced with the politically charged question of whether the Prime Minister had acted unlawfully in advising the Queen to prorogue Parliament for such a long time at such a constitutionally significant moment. The Supreme Court ruled that the power to prorogue Parliament had *limitations*, chiefly that it could not be used where it 'has the effect of frustrating or preventing, without reasonable justification, the ability of Parliament to carry out its constitutional functions as a legislature and as the body responsible for the supervision of the executive'.[37] As the Prime Minister had not put forward a 'reasonable justification' for the length of the prorogation, he had acted beyond the limits of his power to request prorogation. This led the Supreme Court to the inevitable conclusion that the advice to the Queen was unlawful and void, and so was the prorogation.

34 *Malone v United Kingdom* (1984) 7 EHRR 14.

35 Ending the particular parliamentary session in readiness for a new Speech from the Throne (this is a ceremonial proceeding at the State Opening of Parliament that lays out the laws that the government will bring forward in the parliamentary session and is commonly referred to as the King's or Queen's Speech).

36 *R (on the application of Miller) v The Prime Minister* [2019] UKSC 41, [2019] 3 WLR 589.

37 ibid [50].

PROTECTING INDIVIDUAL FREEDOMS

The previous subsection explored the principle of legality insofar as it considered the role that law has to play in governing state exercise of power. If we turn our attention to the *individual*, then law plays an equally important role in protecting individual rights and freedoms.

Unlike in the case of the exercise of power by public authorities, which requires specific lawful authority, English and Welsh law has embraced the principle that individuals are entitled to conduct their business free from interference *unless* the law dictates otherwise.[38] In this way, the law, when not regulating the behaviour of individuals, performs the function of protecting individual freedoms and liberties. This can happen through the common law or through Acts of Parliament. As just one example, the Human Rights Act 1998[39] protects, amongst other things, the freedom of expression.[40] This means that individuals have the right to hold opinions and to give and receive information without interference from any public authority. If a public body wishes to interfere with that right, then it must comply with certain legal standards, and it cannot do so in an arbitrary or disproportionate way.

REGULATING RELATIONSHIPS

In order to live life in an ordered and structured manner, there needs to be some degree of certainty about the relationships we form. The law assists in this by providing a framework for governing relationships. This happens in multiple aspects of our personal and professional lives and covers a wide range of relationships.

From the perspective of an individual, the law (as periodically amended) provides a framework for regulating marriages,[41] civil partnerships,[42] tenancies,[43] land ownership,[44] parenthood[45] and education.[46] It governs the goods we buy,[47] the services we receive[48] and the work that we undertake.[49] The law also functions to regulate the relationships within[50] and between[51] businesses and how international commerce is governed.[52] At a more abstract level, the law can also govern the relationship between states.[53]

38 A basic principle of English constitutional law articulated by AV Dicey, *Introduction to the Study of the Law of the Constitution* (Macmillan 1885).

39 An Act of Parliament that incorporates the European Convention on Human Rights into English and Welsh law.

40 Article 9 ECHR.

41 Marriage Act 1949.

42 Civil Partnership Act 2004.

43 Landlord and Tenant Act 1985.

44 Land Registration Act 2002.

45 Children Act 1989.

46 Education Act 2011.

47 Consumer Rights Act 2015.

48 Financial Services and Markets Act 2000.

49 Employment Rights Act 1996.

50 Companies Act 2006.

51 Sale of Goods Act 1979.

52 Contracts (Applicable Law) Act 1990.

53 Vienna Convention on the Law of Treaties 1969.

RESOLVING DISPUTES

The law also functions as a method for people to resolve disputes in a potentially dispassionate and objective way. The law provides the institutions,[54] the procedures[55] and the personnel[56] that facilitate the resolution of disputes. Chapter 8 ('The Court Structure'), Chapter 7 ('The Judiciary'), Chapter 15 ('The Legal Professionals') and Chapter 14 ('Dispute Resolution') will give a more detailed examination of the framework for resolving disputes, of which court proceedings provide only one way, and several forms of non-court dispute resolution (N-CDR) also offer others of differing degrees of formality.

TAKING THINGS FURTHER – WHEN FUNCTIONS COLLIDE

It is clear that the functions outlined can sometimes coincide and overlap. Equally, it is possible that some of the functions operate in tension and risk colliding. The website that accompanies this textbook explores situations where the functions of law may come into conflict and poses some questions as to how that conflict might be managed or resolved.

LAW AND LEGAL THEORY

As well as an understanding of what law may be and why we may need it in a functional sense, there is a whole branch of legal study dedicated to the theoretical underpinnings of the *nature* of law – this branch of study is termed 'jurisprudence'.[57]

> MAKING CONNECTIONS – LAW AS A 'DISCIPLINE'
>
> The growth of the discipline and profession of law risks reducing the law to a 'subject' to be 'studied'.[58] Great care should be taken in treating law as an isolated academic discipline. Without the need of being overly philosophical, law is a construct of humankind. It does not exist without humans or society. For this reason, it should not be detached from the human experience. Law does not exist in a vacuum but is a product of economics, philosophy, culture, politics, sociology and a whole lot more. By understanding how these disciplines interact with and exert influence on law, a much richer understanding of law can be achieved. Also, recognising how these disciplines bleed into each other will help understand some of the peculiarities of the law and the legal system.

54 For example, the courts and tribunals.

55 For example, the rules of evidence and court procedures.

56 Through members of the legal profession, judges and court officials.

57 The word 'jurisprudence' comes from *juris prudentia*, Medieval Latin, the study of the philosophy of law.

58 Indeed, the authors both make a living from researching and teaching the discipline of law at universities!

Not only does jurisprudence seek to explain the nature of law; it also seeks to explain the *legitimate basis* of the law and its purpose. Essentially, jurisprudence allows us to make sense of the law and to question whether, amongst other things, a particular law is *valid* as a law. In this way, jurisprudence seeks to locate and explain the authority of the law by reference to underlying philosophies or principles and to consider the limits of that authority and legitimacy. It is important to have an awareness of the major legal philosophies as they can often help explain the approach of legal systems to particular issues at particular points in time. Each approach to legal theory has its adherents and detractors, and none perfectly describes or prescribes the operation of the legal system. In many ways, the different jurisprudential approaches could be seen as lenses through which we can examine the law and its qualities. The major schools of legal theory are outlined in Table 1.1, but the list is

Table 1.1 Major schools of legal theory

Theory	*Description*	*Theorists/influence*
Natural law theory/natural rights	A belief that there is a higher form of law that transcends the law of man and that is independent of, and superior to, the law of any state. It is based on an understanding of the law of 'nature' that is common to all societies. Law, according to this theory, is rational and capable of being reasoned. The proponents of this theory suggest that law is just and fair – that is, there is a link between natural law and morality. Although now largely fallen out of favour, the principles of natural law (e.g. inalienable rights) still find some support in the principles and law of international human rights.	Aristotle St Thomas Aquinas Hobbes Locke Fuller Dworkin (partially!)
Legal positivism	Fundamentally different to 'natural law'. A positivist would suggest that law is only 'law' when it is recognised as such by a human-made authority.	A. Austin Bentham Hart Kelsen Raz

Theory	*Description*	*Theorists/influence*
	Under this theory, the content of law is not questioned on the basis of a moral judgement. Law's validity derives from sovereignty and authority. There is a focus on the procedures by which a law is passed rather than on its moral quality.	
Legal realism	Legal realism focusses less on high-level principles and more on how the law operates and is determined in practice – that is, evidence of real-world impact. Law is resolved through conflict rather than consensus. According to this theory, the judiciary and the courts are the central protagonist in determining the remit of law because disagreements about the law tend to be settled by courts.	Wendell Holmes Llewelyn
Critical legal studies	Critical legal studies (CLS) shares some features of legal realism in that it does not focus on law as an abstract concept but as one that is grounded in real-world experience. Critical legal studies notes the failings and biases of the law and the legal system. A common feature of CLS is the idea that the institutions of the legal system uphold and reinforce existing political structures.	Marx Pyle Ungar

(Continued)

Table 1.1 *(Continued)*

Theory	*Description*	*Theorists/influence*
	According to critical legal studies, law is often used as a way of asserting majoritarian rule over minority groups and giving a gloss of legitimacy to state action.	

not intended to be exhaustive, with an almost-endless supply of other constantly evolving jurisprudential theories.[59]

To those new to the study of law, jurisprudence can feel detached and difficult. The theories can be conceptually challenging as the developments and 'sub-theories' clash and overlap. For the purposes of understanding a textbook on the legal system of England and Wales, it is worth remembering that 'there's nothing so practical as good theory'.[60] To put this differently, legal theory can be used to explain *why* certain choices are made within a legal system and also to advocate for how they might be done differently or 'better'. Bearing in mind that individuals may *want*, *need* or *expect* different things from the legal system and the law may help understand the compromises that are often reached in the formulation and execution of the law.

TAKING THINGS FURTHER – JURISPRUDENCE IN ACTION

The companion website to this text has some exercises based on fictitious legal scenarios. You can use these to test and expand your understanding of the different theories presented previously. There are explanations of how different legal theories would resolve the questions posed, and there is an introduction to Fuller's hypothetical 'Speluncean Explorers' case study – a fictional scenario intended to explore how different schools of legal theorists would treat the moral and legal case of cannibalism.[61]

LEGAL SYSTEMS AND THEIR CLASSIFICATION

Attention now turns from notions of law to the concept of the 'legal system', as this is a necessary precursor to discussing the 'English and Welsh' legal system. In much the same way as a definition of 'law' is difficult to settle upon, the term 'legal system' is equally flexible and can mean different things in different contexts to different people. This textbook adopts a particularly broad understanding of the concept of 'legal system' as being the collection of

59 For example, Marxist theories of law, feminist jurisprudence or law and economics.

60 Kurt Lewin, 'Problems of Research in Social Psychology' in Dorwin Cartwright (ed), *Field Theory in Social Science: Selected Theoretical Papers* (Harper & Row 1951) 169.

61 Lon Fuller, 'The Case of Speluncean Explorers' (1949) 62 Harv L Rev 616.

sovereign processes and institutions that govern the creation, enforcement and interpretation of the law and the legal rules of a particular body or state. The legal system is the way in which the *process* of law is managed, moderated and controlled. Whilst legal systems are most readily associated with countries or states – indeed, this is a textbook about the legal system of England and Wales – it is also true that legal systems can be created as between groups of countries. In this way, legal systems can also overlap and interact.

MAKING CONNECTIONS – THE EUROPEAN UNION

+++++++++++++++++++++++++++++++++++++

The European Union is a good example of an international organisation that has a developed and sophisticated legal system that sits both outside and as part of the legal heritage of its 27[62] member states. This legal system – which has processes for the creation and enforcement of laws by independent institutions – was created through the pooling of the sovereignty of its members.

In the seminal *Costa*[63] case, the Court of Justice of the European Union articulated its own understanding of the legal system of the EU in terms of its key features and the source of its legitimacy. The Court held that:

> The . . . [T]reaty has created its own legal system which, on the entry into force of the treaty, became an integral part of the legal systems of the member states and which their courts are bound to apply.
>
> By creating a community of unlimited duration, having its own institutions, its own personality, its own legal capacity and capacity of representation on the international plane and, more particularly, real powers stemming from a limitation of sovereignty or a transfer of powers from the states to the community, the member states have limited their sovereign rights and have thus created a body of law which binds both their nationals and themselves.[64]

Within the context of the EU at least, a legal system was characterised by certain key features – sovereignty, unlimited duration, institutions and real power. This formulation is repeated in subsequent cases emanating from the European Union and represents a core part of its identity as an emerging legal system that values its autonomy and self-determination. In this way, the Court of Justice of the European Union was able to assert its own authority and reject simply accepting the rules of another law-making entity – in this instance, the UN Security Council – in the *Kadi*[65] case.

Many of the features identified by the CJEU in *Costa* are common across different legal systems, including the presence of institutions, independence and sovereignty.

62 Formerly 28 members before the UK departed.

63 Casse 6/64 *Costa v ENEL* [1964] ECR 585.

64 ibid at para 3.

65 Case C-402/05 *Kadi and Al Barakaat International Foundation v Council and Commission* [2008] ECR I-6351.

Legal systems can vary significantly from jurisdiction to jurisdiction. Each is a unique product of its history, its social development, its economic and theological environment. In this way, it can be difficult to categorise the different types of legal system reliably, and these sorts of labels are only partially useful. Labels can be helpful in that they seek to draw together similar treatment of law, institutions and processes. In this early chapter, which is attempting to introduce fundamental concepts, the intention is to outline some of the common legal systems and their features but not subject them to a detailed consideration.

COMMON LAW SYSTEMS

Common law systems tend to be those that place particular importance on the decisions of courts. Case law forms an important *source* of law, and judges are particularly powerful actors within the legal system. This does not mean that judge-made law is the *only* source of law in a common law legal system. It should be noted that common law systems also have legislation that usually takes priority when it conflicts with judge-made law. The legal system of England and Wales is a common law system, but there are many others around the world – including the United States of America, Singapore, Israel, Canada and Australia. In this way, the former colonies of the British Empire and the British Colonies often absorbed English and Welsh common law principles into their legal systems. Common law systems are typical where there is not a highly codified body of statutory law and the common law then 'fills the gaps' between particular Acts of Parliament, or in areas of law that lend themselves to judge-led resolution (such as contract law and the law of tort).

Another central feature of the common law is the system of precedent – discussed further in Chapter 9 – meaning that courts are, subject to considerations of hierarchy and certain rules of principle, *bound* by the decisions of other courts. It is this concept of *stare decisis*[66] that gives the common law certainty and allows for its refinement in an incremental way.

CIVIL LAW

In contrast with the common law, a system adhering to the civilian law tradition is more likely to be based on 'codes' that seek to codify and bring areas of law together into a single set of written rules. Those jurisdictions adopting a civilian tradition often adopt a written constitution and accompanying written criminal and civil codes which set out the principles of their legislation. These codes are more flexibly drafted than the statutes of common law jurisdictions since codes are deliberately more widely framed than a common law jurisdiction statute (which tends to include within it all the required detail to achieve the purpose of the statute). Civil law approaches expect the more flexible codes of their jurisdictions to cover more widely expressed situations from which civil law judges will abstract a sufficiently widely framed meaning to meet the purpose of the code's law, including perhaps in situations not even envisaged when the code was originally drafted.

66 That is to 'stand by things decided' in Latin.

The civil law system is the prevalent one of continental Europe and much of Africa. The reason for this tells a lot about the history of empire(s) in Europe and Africa with clear influences of Roman law and, later, the Napoleonic Codes, which spread throughout the European countries conquered by Napoleon through their colonies during his time as Emperor of the French.

RELIGIOUS SYSTEMS

A third type of system can be seen by those states that base their legal structures around a religious text or belief system. This text is the fundamental source of law and the source of the legitimacy of other forms of law, such as decided cases or legislation. The most common form of religious state in modern times is that of Islam, with countries such as Saudi Arabia and Iran basing their legal system around the tenets of the Islamic faith. Sources of law tend to focus on the core religious texts as well as the writings of prominent religious scholars or prophets. There are also states which base *aspects* of their law on religious rules, and other aspects are more akin to common or civilian law traditions. A further example would be the Vatican City State, which relies on a form of Canon law based on the Catholic teachings of Christianity.

This sort of legal system should not be confused with the use of dispute resolution systems based on religion. The former governs the law-making and framework of the entire legal system, while the latter is just an accommodation of the legal system to allow people to use religious principles to settle their disputes. These forms of religious dispute resolution, such as Beth Din[67] or the Muslim Arbitration Council,[68] are discussed in greater detail in Chapter 14 on dispute resolution.

ANALYSING THE LAW – THE COMPARATIVE AND PLURALISTIC APPROACH

The preceding is just a brief sketch of the main forms of legal system that are present in different states. In reality, there are many that 'borrow' from the different traditions and so are described as 'pluralistic' or 'hybrid' legal systems. The most obvious, for the sake of this text, is Scotland, as this system borrows from both the common and civilian law tradition. As with much in law, categories are only ever the *starting* point of analysis, and there is much overlapping and cross-fertilisation of legal systems. In this way, legal systems should not be viewed as 'dead' or 'settled', and there will commonly be development and evolution of systems over time, such as the mutual influence of the EU and English legal systems on each other during the latter's membership of the former.

There is a whole branch of legal study dedicated to comparative law, and you should bear in mind other systems as you progress through this textbook.[69] Comparative law is

67 Used by those of the Jewish faith.

68 Used by those of the Islamic faith.

69 Peter de Cruz, *Comparative Law in a Changing World* (4th edn, Routledge 2018).

often more than just *describing* different legal systems but involves an analysis of their similarities and differences. By comparing the approaches of law to common problems or to structures, we can often learn more about our own system. Understanding similarities can be important, and English and Welsh courts often look to the solutions adopted in other common law jurisdictions when considering whether to change or develop the common law.

THE LEGAL SYSTEMS OF THE UNITED KINGDOM

One of the core characteristics of a legal system is that it has a defined geographical/jurisdictional scope. This allows us to understand the limitations of a legal system and how it interacts with other systems. This text concerns itself with the legal system of England and Wales, but it would be remiss (as similar texts do) to overlook the fact that the United Kingdom has a system of systems that coexist and share certain common traditions and institutions. There are a number of jurisdictions and 'countries' that exist within the broader banner of 'UK' or 'British' or 'English' (or, indeed, 'Welsh') law. They also interact and collide at times, and this can impact on the understanding of the individual systems.

The terminology applied to describe the law as applied within the United Kingdom is often deployed loosely with little thought for, or link to, the precise *legal or common-sense meaning* of the words used. It is, therefore, important to deal with some basic terminology first before considering the detail of the system that is the subject of this book. It is here that we start to see some of the differences between the term 'law' and the term 'legal system'.

The United Kingdom is shorthand for the United Kingdom of Great Britain and Northern Ireland. Great Britain is comprised of England, Wales and Scotland, and this is then 'united' with Northern Ireland to form the UK. Of itself, and for historical reasons,[70] the UK does not have a single legal system but rather is a collection of legal systems with certain shared institutions (such as the Supreme Court[71] and the Westminster Parliament). For our purposes, there are **five** different forms of 'law' that are relevant – the law of the UK (that applies across *all* of the constituent jurisdictions), Scots law, English and Welsh law, Welsh law[72] and Irish law. There are also international laws that will be discussed where relevant throughout the remainder of the text.

70 The UK was formed out of a series of Acts of Union with Scotland (1707), Ireland (1800) and Wales (1536–1543).

71 Which is the highest civil court for all civil cases in the UK and the highest criminal court for England and Wales and Northern Ireland.

72 Legislation passed under the devolved authority of the Government of Wales Act 2006.

There are then **three** distinct legal systems in operation within the UK: that of *England and Wales*,[73] *Scotland* and *Northern Ireland*.

TAKING THINGS FURTHER – THE COMMONWEALTH, BRITISH OVERSEAS TERRITORIES AND CROWN DEPENDENCIES

The website that accompanies this text provides an opportunity to explore how the various legal systems of the UK interact with the nations of the Commonwealth, the British Overseas Territories and the Crown dependencies. Although many of these nations and territories have their own fully developed legal systems, it is useful to understand the broader picture and to consider the process and challenges of sharing institutions whilst seeking to develop a sense of independent identity.

SCOTLAND[74]

The legal system of Scotland is a hybrid system, calling as it does on both civil and common law traditions. Following the Acts of Union 1707, which created the UK Parliament, Scotland retained its own legal system. This means that it has its own courts and legal principles, notably in terms of property and criminal law. Historically, Scotland has always been influenced by France, with which it always had close relations from the Middle Ages. Scottish monarchs regularly found French spouses more often than English ones, and inevitably, this led to French influence in the upbringing of underage monarchs who succeeded fathers to the throne.

NORTHERN IRELAND[75]

The legal system of Northern Ireland is more closely aligned to the English and Welsh system than to Scots law, and many of the principles that underpin the common law find their origins in English and Welsh law. Nonetheless, Northern Ireland has its own legal system and capacity for law-making, as well as a court system to administer the law.

ENGLAND AND WALES

When we discuss the 'English legal system' or 'English law', we are in fact talking about the law and legal system of England and Wales. The *single* legal system that operates throughout England and Wales is often forgotten due to the frequent shortening of the term to 'English law'. There are no 'separate' courts for Wales, although this has been debated as a future potential development. Even though certain powers to make law have been devolved to the Senedd

73 There is an ongoing and lively debate as to whether Wales should become a distinct jurisdiction – National Assembly for Wales, *Inquiry into the Establishment of a Separate Welsh Jurisdiction* (2012) <https://www.gov.wales/sites/default/files/consultations/2018-01/131217finalsummaryen.pdf>.

74 For more information on the Scottish legal system, see Bryan Clark and Gerard Keegan, *Scottish Legal System Essentials* (3rd edn, Edinburgh UP 2012).

75 For a more detailed consideration of the legal system of Northern Ireland, see Brice Dickson, *Law in Northern Ireland* (Hart-Bloomsbury Professional 2018).

Cymru and Welsh Government, the *system* of law, including the courts and professions, is fused together. The textbook will touch upon devolution and its ongoing influence on the law of England *and* Wales.

TAKING THINGS FURTHER – DEVOLUTION IN WALES

The website that accompanies this text contains resources on the process of devolution in Wales. Having two legislative bodies – the Senedd and the UK Parliament – operating within a single legal system can be confusing and difficult to navigate. It is, however, important that you understand the place of Welsh law in the legal system of England and Wales. A solicitor who qualified in England and has only practised in England may nonetheless be confronted by a matter of Welsh law even when appearing in a court in England. The same is true of the reverse situation. The website explores a brief history of the process of devolution before considering the notion of 'territorial extent', which means the legal system in which a particular law is recognised and can be applied by the courts. The website contrasts this with the concept of territorial application, which means the territorial area in which a law takes effect, or the geographical boundary for application.

The remainder of this textbook is concerned with the combined legal system and jurisdiction of England and Wales – how law is made, its institutions and the people who work within it.

The case concerning the attempted prorogation of Parliament (discussed previously) gives some indication of why knowing about the different jurisdictions and how they interact is important.

ANALYSING THE LAW – THE CASE OF PROROGATION (AGAIN!)

As discussed previously, this case concerned the UK government using its prerogative powers to prorogue the UK Parliament. This action was governed by UK constitutional law.

The prorogation led to actions challenging the legality of the government's action being taken in two[76] of the jurisdictions of the UK: notably by Joanna Cheery in the Scottish Inner House[77] and the High Court of England and Wales by activist Gina Miller.[78] The Scottish court found that the action was unlawful. The English court found that the action was lawful. Although a rare occurrence, the cases demonstrate that

76 Further cases, which did not progress, were also heard in the courts of Northern Ireland.

77 Actions were taken by a cross-party group of 75 MPs and lords. *Cherry & Others v Advocate General* [2019] CSIH 49, [2019] SLT 1097.

78 *Miller v Prime Minister* [2019] EWHC 2381 (QB), [2019] 9 WLUK 81.

there are inherent risks of operating multiple legal systems within a close political union. In this case, the matter was resolved by the Supreme Court, which acts as the highest court of the UK (i.e. for England and Wales *and* Scotland) for all civil matters.[79] It ruled that the prorogation was, indeed, unlawful. By having a single Supreme Court to resolve differences in judgments, the UK is able to avoid divergence amongst its constituent legal systems on important matters such as constitutional law.

The interactions of the systems can be complex and confusing. However, having an understanding not only of the systems but also of the circumstances that brought us to this situation is useful. Knowing that the UK is a political union that was achieved through particular milestones and prevailing economic, political and social conditions will help one understand some of its 'quirks' and institutional structures.

THE EUROPEAN UNION

The United Kingdom was, until January 2020, a member of the European Union. The EU has an independent legal system and also provided an important source of law for the legal system of England and Wales. During the more than 40 years of membership, the legal systems had intertwined and cross-fertilised each other to a significant degree that continues to prove challenging to untangle.

In various chapters, this textbook will touch upon those challenges as they apply to particular aspects of the law and will consider the future impact of EU law on the legal system of England and Wales. As you read, try to think about how those challenges could be reduced or eliminated.

THEMES AND CONTEXTS WITHIN THIS BOOK

The legal system is just that – a *system* of interacting norms, institutions and people. It is easy to forget that, as a system, the reader should be wary of looking at any individual part of the 'system' in isolation. Not only will this give a skewed outlook, but it will also risk overlooking ways in which the 'system' as a whole can be improved. Even if studying substantive areas of law – such as contract, tort or public law – it should never be forgotten that those areas are underpinned, constrained and enabled by the *system* discussed in this textbook. In this way, the legal system is both the frame of the umbrella that unites as a whole the various, disparate

79 *Miller & Cherry v Advocate General for Scotland & The Prime Minister* [2019] UKSC 41, [2019] 3 WLR 589.

areas of law *and* the safety net intended to correct any undesirable effects arising from the development of the law.

Legal study is made much easier when connections are made between different parts of the system. In this way, a study of a 'legal system' is much more than just about 'how' things are done or by whom and should certainly not be seen as something to be treated as 'introductory'. The legal system is the machine that makes the law work. One way of making those connections is to identify themes that unite the different parts of the system. The following two themes will emerge as you read this text and should be considered as you read the individual chapters.

- *Theory and practice.* The book will introduce you to the processes and structures of the legal system of England and Wales as *intended* to apply. It will quickly become apparent that how the system operates in *practice* can be different, sometimes very different. Assessing why the 'law in the books' may be different to the 'law in action' is a very important legal skill and one which this text hopes to help you develop.
- *Distribution of power.* The formulation, execution and operation of law is intrinsically linked to where 'power' lies (e.g. as between Parliament and the government or the government and the judiciary or the government and the people). This textbook considers the impact of 'power' (legal, political, social, economic) on the operation of the law and on the way in which the legal system operates.

LEGAL SKILLS

A study of the 'legal system' should always be accompanied with an appreciation of the legal skills necessary to understand its operation. Much has been written about the notion of 'legal skills', and there are many excellent texts that are dedicated to the topic. However, there is no universal definition as to what the term means, and different authors and educators sometimes use it to mean different things. This textbook adopts an open approach to the term and treats it as including:

- General transferable skills (such as communication and analysis)
- Legal study skills (such as legal research and case analysis)
- Practical legal skills (such as advocacy or drafting)

This textbook has been designed in such a way as to *embed* the acquisition, development and mastery of certain key legal skills, behaviours and competences. The authors have sought to *integrate* these skills into the design of the text and the activities and questions we encourage you to answer as you read and on the website. The text also has a chapter that seeks to bring to life those legal and academic skills that you will need to succeed in the study of law.

Interspersed in the text are diagrams intended to simplify or give a visual representation of the various processes, and there are comment 'boxes' throughout that provide opportunities to:

- Explore a given aspect of the legal system in greater detail
- Analyse the law by considering the implications of a given feature or development or by considering proposals for law reform
- Apply the law by considering how a particular legal rule operates in practice
- Make connections between different chapters of the textbook or to different areas of substantive law in order to gain a better understanding of the contextual detail of the law
- Take things further by directing the reader to additional resources or thinking points or by making reference to further material available on the companion website

This integrated approach works well in the written form for certain skills – such as legal research or written communication – but perhaps less well for others such as advocacy. Whereas there is much to be gained from the textbook itself, the companion website contains a significant range of further activities and examples that seek to develop your skills further. This balanced approach to providing both information and skills is one of the defining features of this textbook and its website. The accompanying website contains the following:

- *Long podcasts.* To form a series of 'mini-lectures' on the major chapters of the text. This will draw upon the key components and bring them to life with further examples and explanations as well as advice on how to get the most out of legal study.
- *Short podcasts.* These will cover recent developments and examples that seek to keep the readers' knowledge and understanding up to date and to provide additional information on the development of the law and the legal system.
- *Legal exercises.* In the form of questions and activities designed to encourage the application of the law or its critical analysis.
- *Multiple-choice questions.* In order to highlight areas of strength and weakness in understanding of specific topics and to provide feedback on performance.
- *Study advice.* This takes the form of general advice on the study of law and specific, worked examples of student work with strengths and weaknesses identified.

A BLUEPRINT FOR THE BOOK

The rest of this text will explore particular dimensions of the legal system of England and Wales. The book is split into four main sections, as outlined in Figure 1.1.

While the individual chapters are designed to give an isolated examination of the detail of each topic, the reader should be mindful of how that topic fits into the broader *system*. This will give a better overview of the legal system as a whole and also enrich understanding of the individual topics.

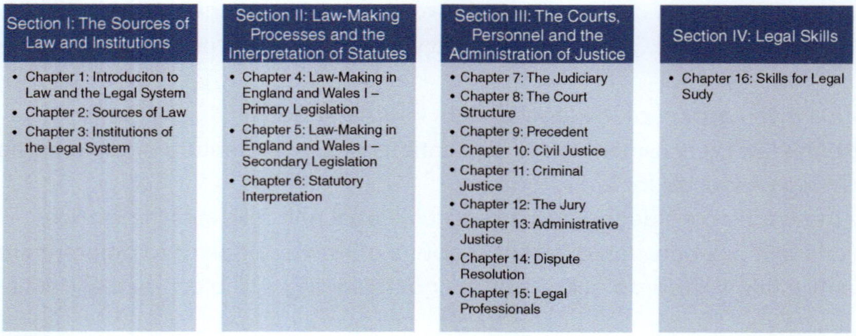

Figure 1.1 Structure of the book.

COMPANION WEBSITE

The website that accompanies this textbook contains many useful resources that you can use to consolidate and further your knowledge of the law, to hone your skills of critical analysis and to test your knowledge.

2

CHAPTER 2
SOURCES OF LAW

INTRODUCTION

In determining the law of a legal system, it is normal to turn to its formal, written constitution in the first instance. This will give an indication of the institutional actors capable of passing binding law under prescribed conditions. The legal system of England and Wales is different, lacking as it does a formal, written (so-called) codified constitution. This, when coupled with its common law (judge-made law) heritage, means that determining and categorising the sources of English and Welsh law can be more difficult than for other legal systems. Yet being able to determine and classify sources is important as it not only gives a legal system its distinct character but also enables somebody unfamiliar with a particular area of law to identify its general principles and detailed rules.

This chapter will explore the major sources of English and Welsh law and attempt to put forward ways of categorising and ordering those sources. It will also introduce you to the concept of there being a hierarchy of norms,[1] with some sources of law taking priority over others within the legal system. Subsequent chapters will explore some of these sources in much greater detail, for example, when talking about case law, primary legislation and delegated legislation. This chapter will make cross-references to other chapters so that you can see how these sources operate both independently and alongside each other. Even though greater treatment will be given in those individual chapters, it is important not to lose sight of the bigger picture of sources provided here.

AS YOU READ

This chapter focusses on **describing the major sources of law**, and so you should focus your reading on those key definitions. Being able to **distinguish and categorise** sources of law is another skill to be developed during your reading of this chapter.

By the end of this chapter, you should have a broader understanding of how different sources of law **interact, and be able critically to discuss** any overlaps that exist. In considering the different sources of law, it is important to be able to **rank the sources in terms of priority** so as to demonstrate **critical understanding of the hierarchy of norms** in the legal system of England and Wales.

1 Another way of saying 'legal rules'.

DOI: 10.4324/9781032641829-2

THE NATURE OF SOURCES OF LAW

Almost all legal systems around the world are based on a formal, written constitution. The constitution will establish the legal system and explain how the relationship between its constituent parts is to be governed. The United Kingdom is one of a small number of states that lack a fully codified, written constitution.[2] This is an important part of a system's legal culture as it allows for a more flexible system of government and a wider variety of sources to be used as law. It also adds to the evolutionary character of the law and the system that administers it.

As you will undoubtedly come to learn if you formally study law in depth, just because the legal system of England and Wales lacks a formal, codified constitutional document does not mean that it lacks constitutional rules or an order of priority amongst its sources.

The following sections will outline the major sources of law (see Figure 2.1) in the English and Welsh legal system before turning to questions of how we can classify the relationship between them or the hierarchy that may (or may not) exist between those sources.

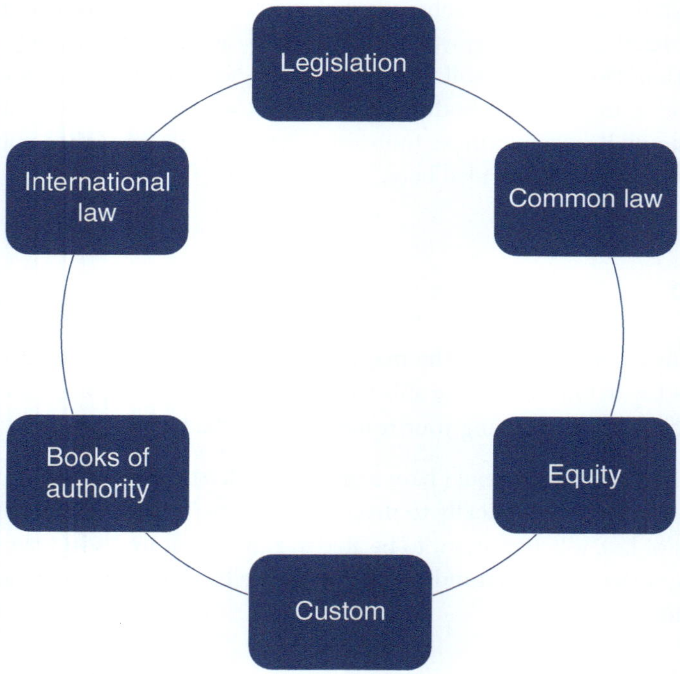

Figure 2.1 Major sources of law.

2 Israel and New Zealand also lack a codified constitution.

LEGISLATION

The term 'legislation' is taken to mean the statutory law of England and Wales, including Acts of Parliament (primary legislation) and delegated legislation (secondary legislation) – mostly statutory instruments, usually fleshing out a piece of primary legislation, that is, providing for the detailed implementation of the statute which authorises that further detail to be legislated for by a Minister of the government.[3] This subsection will briefly outline these two sources of law, leaving their detailed discussion to their dedicated chapters later in this work (Chapters 4 and 5).

PRIMARY LEGISLATION

Primary legislation consists of Acts of the United Kingdom Parliament which, for our purposes, have application in England and Wales. Parliament, in this sense, is taken to be the House of Commons, House of Lords and the Monarch acting in combination. Prior to becoming an Act of Parliament, the draft piece of legislation is referred to as a 'bill'. Such legislation is normally made with the involvement of each part of Parliament, but there are circumstances[4] where either additional requirements are necessary to enact the legislation[5] or the consent of the Lords is not needed.[6] There are different ways in which Acts of Parliament can be classified and categorised (e.g. as a government bill or a private members' bill), but the process for their passage remains broadly the same. The full law-making process is explored in great depth in the chapter dedicated to primary legislation (Chapter 4).

SECONDARY (OR DELEGATED) LEGISLATION

Secondary (or delegated) legislation consists of those measures that are made, normally by government Ministers, with the authority of Parliament.[7] The vast majority of pieces of secondary legislation take the form of statutory instruments, but there are also other forms of secondary legislation, such as Orders in Council and byelaws. Secondary legislation is discussed in greater detail in a subsequent chapter of this textbook (Chapter 5). For present purposes, it is worth noting that the majority of secondary legislation derives its authority from an Act of Parliament; they are subject to that authority, and any powers exercised under secondary legislation must be compatible with that specific Act of Parliament.

3 Examples are found in many modern statutes as this has become a preferred way of legislating now, when the principles of the legislation are dealt with in the main statute and the detailed implementation then included in an associated statutory instrument (S.I.); for example, the Legal Aid, Sentencing and Punishment of Offenders Act 2012, commonly referred to as 'LASPO' required a good deal of additional implementation work to be done because of its radical cuts to legal aid, and much of this is in the Legal Aid, Sentencing and Punishment of Offenders Act 2012 (Consequential, Transitional and Saving Provisions) Regulations 2013.

4 Discussed in Chapter 4.

5 For example, the referendum requirements of the European Union Act 2011 s2(2) and Schedule 1.

6 Due to the provisions of the Parliament Acts 1911 and 1949.

7 Discussed in Chapter 5.

Secondary legislation is, therefore, largely dependent on primary legislation for its continued existence and can be challenged before the courts if it falls short of any requirement in its 'parent' act.

LEGISLATION OF THE SENEDD CYMRU

During the last 30 years, the United Kingdom has been through a period of structural and constitutional change known as devolution whereby powers have flowed out to certain geographical regions and nations. The devolved nations are Scotland, Northern Ireland and Wales. For a textbook on the 'English legal system', which is more properly known as the unified legal system of England and Wales, a brief consideration of post-devolution Wales is necessary. This will allow you to differentiate devolved competences from the unified legal system of England and Wales that is subject to the bulk of discussion in this text.

As part of the process of devolution, there is now a Senedd Cymru[8] and a Welsh government. In certain areas, the Senedd is able to pass both primary and secondary legislation, and these form part of the law as it applies to Wales. In contrast with the unlimited legislative competence of the UK Parliament, the Senedd has to act within the limits of the powers conferred upon it by the devolution settlement.[9] Since 2011, the Senedd (and formerly the National Assembly for Wales) has had the power to pass Acts of Senedd Cymru. These 'acts' are to be regarded as primary legislation for Wales and should not be confused with Acts of Parliament, as the former have a much more limited scope of application (both substantively and geographically) and derive their authority from an Act of the United Kingdom Parliament.[10]

The Senedd can only pass primary legislation in defined areas. These areas of devolved power include policy areas such as agriculture, culture, economic development, education, transport, housing, etc.[11] This principle of constrained legislative competence means that a draft measure can be referred directly to the Supreme Court if there is doubt as to whether the Senedd has acted within its competence.[12] This is the only time that the Supreme Court hears cases as a court of first instance rather than an appellate court, demonstrating the constitutional significance of properly defining devolved and reserved areas.

TAKING THINGS FURTHER

Chapters 4 and 5 consider the principles underpinning, and processes for the creation of, primary and secondary legislation. The website that accompanies this text also contains examples of each form of legislation, with annotations on how they are structured and

8 Or Welsh Parliament, formerly known before 2020 as the National Assembly for Wales.

9 Started by the Government of Wales Act 1998.

10 Government of Wales Act 2006.

11 ibid. Schedule 7 lays down the 'subjects' for which the Senedd can legislate.

12 ibid s112.

research exercises designed to help you to familiarise yourself with each type of source. It is always beneficial to take the abstract descriptions and analysis of particular sources given in texts such as this and to explore what those principles and sources look like in particular, concrete measures.

If you are studying any substantive legal subjects, you could explore the legislation (primary, secondary and devolved) that influences that area of law.

This will help you contextualise the substantive legal rules within the broader legal system. Equally, it is beneficial to look at legislation on areas that you have not previously studied or that you may never study. This will allow you to focus on the features and style of the legislation without becoming overly distracted by the content. Once you are familiar with the way in which primary and secondary legislation is structured and the sometimes esoteric language that is used, you will find legal study more straightforward.

COMMON LAW

The second major source of law in England and Wales comes in the form of cases decided by courts. This is often referred to as the 'common law', although, as mentioned later, the term 'common law' can have many different meanings, and it is important to use the term correctly in its proper context. It can refer to the case law itself and to the classification of the legal system.

The use of case law defines the legal system of England and Wales to the extent that it is referred to as a 'common law system' and is contrasted with other systems, such as those following a civil law tradition, that rely less heavily upon the use of judges in developing the law. Under the common law, there are stricter rules about the binding nature of judicial decisions and a stronger hierarchy of courts.

If you continue with further legal study, then it is inevitable that you will notice that certain areas of the law are dominated by the common law, with very little legislative activity. For example, the law of contract is primarily a common law subject with many of the major principles – such as offer and acceptance[13] – having been developed by the courts. Equally, the law of murder in criminal law is a common law offence.[14]

The common law developed organically out of local custom and practice in the different regions of England, and from the 11th century onwards, a more consistent application of

13 *Carlill v Carbolic Smoke Ball* [1893] 1 QB 256 (CA).

14 Although sentencing on conviction is statutory.

principle was developed from these decided cases.[15] This led to a body of law that, by the 13th century, was slowly becoming 'common' across the English territory (as it was then). It is this general applicability of common law principles across the whole of the legal system of England and Wales that differentiates the common law from continuing local customs (discussed next).

In order to develop legal certainty and consistency further, the doctrine of *stare decisis* was adopted, whereby courts followed previous decisions by other courts when factual situations were suitably similar, and those facts raised the same legal issue. This adds certainty to the system as individuals can refer to decided cases to predict how their dispute will be settled. This principle still survives today and makes up the basis of the rules of binding precedent. It also explains the need to record cases in the law reports for subsequent reference by lawyers, judges and the public. The precise and technical rules of precedent are discussed in detail in Chapter 9 of this work.

Through case law, judges have a mechanism of developing law. In this way, judges not only interpret and apply the law but also are active participants in its creation. This can be through the refinement of existing case law (allowing for an organic development of the law) or through the development of new principles. Judges can also develop understanding of the law through their interpretation of legislation. As the number of pieces of legislation, as well as their length, has grown over time, the judiciary now spend a greater proportion of time interpreting statutes than was once the case.

CUSTOM AND PRACTICE

The concept of 'custom and practice' as a source of law is one that receives little attention from modern writers, but it is a source that remains important in certain (albeit limited) circumstances. It should be remembered that it was a filtering and refinement of local custom and practice that led to the development of the principles of the common law, and therefore, custom has historically contributed a great deal to the development of the legal system. In modern times, custom remains relevant where there is long-standing practice (normally the conferral of a right) that is restricted to a specific area or locality. This contrasts with the common law, which is not restricted to a specific area and applies generally.

Not all customs will be recognised as a source of law, and there are certain requirements for such recognition by the courts. Most importantly, the right claimed must have existed since 'time immemorial'. This is a legal concept that was defined by the first Statute of Westminster 1275 and is deemed to relate to the first year of the reign of Richard I in 1189, the date 'whereof the memory of man runneth not to the contrary' or the limit of legal memory. If it is

15 For more on the history of the common law, see Harry Potter, *Law, Liberty and the Constitution: A Brief History of the Common Law* (Boydall Press 2015).

possible to demonstrate that a particular right has not been generally exercised until relatively modern times, then a claim based on custom is likely to fail.

This is evident in the case of *Newhaven Port*,[16] in which the Supreme Court noted that 'bathing [in the sea for pleasure] could rarely be a right obtained by custom and usage'[17] because such an activity was first recorded in the 18th century and so had not been relied upon since time immemorial. As a result of this requirement, most customs relate to rights associated to specific local professions (such as rights of fishermen[18] or agricultural rights[19]) or local traditions (such as the holding of country fairs on parcels of land[20] or rights of recreation).[21] In addition, the custom must exist as a *right* rather than because it has been granted with the permission of another person (such as a landowner granting permission in the form of a licence for a person to fish on their land[22]). This system of local law will remain important to maintaining the character of certain localities and has been recognised in certain statutory frameworks.

Most famously, in recent times, the ongoing importance of local customary law is underlined in the law (statutory and common) surrounding 'village greens'. The concept of a village green is different in popular literature and in law. The former conjures pictures of green space located in the centre of idyllic English villages, often with a pond and a maypole. In the words of Lord Hoffman, '[n]o doubt there were, and perhaps are, village greens like that, but the law took a more prosaic view of the matter'.[23] One of the ways in which a person can demonstrate that a parcel of land is a village green is if it is a space 'on which the inhabitants of any locality have a customary right to indulge in lawful sports and pastimes'.[24] Under the Commons Registration Act 2006, such land could traditionally be registered as a village green with important consequences for development, as it is a criminal offence to prevent access to a common space such as a village green.[25] Thus, if a person could demonstrate that a customary right existed over a piece of land, then that person could have it registered and therefore frustrate (or at least reduce) development of the land. Registration of a village green was recently used as an attempt to protect West Beach in Newhaven. Although the *Newhaven*[26] case was decided on another definition of 'village green', the use of a customary right to secure registration is still a

16 *Newhaven Port and Properties v East Sussex County Council* [2015] UKSC 7, [2015] 2 WLR 601.

17 ibid [35].

18 *Mercer v Denne* [1905] 2 Ch 538 (CA).

19 *Earl de la Warr v Miles* (1881) 17 ChD 535 (CA).

20 *Wyld v Silver* [1963] 1 QB 169 (CA).

21 *Fitch v Rawling* (1795) 2 H BL 393.

22 *Earl de la Warr v Miles* (1881) 17 ChD 535 (CA).

23 *Oxford County Council v Oxford City Council* [2006] UKHL 25, [2006] 2 AC 674 [4] (Lord Hoffmann).

24 Commons Registration Act 1965 s22(1)(b). The other two possibilities being 'land which has been allotted by or under any Act for the exercise or recreation of the inhabitants of any locality or . . . on which the inhabitants of any locality have indulged in such sports and pastimes as of right for not less than 20 years'.

25 Inclosure Act 1857 s12 and Commons Act 1876 s29.

26 *Newhaven Port and Properties v East Sussex County Council* [2015] UKSC 7, [2015] 2 WLR 601.

possibility (one recognised by the Supreme Court),[27] and so custom as a source of law is likely to have some continuing importance that should not be too readily ignored.

The government has attempted to curtail this type of defensive registering as a means of blocking planned developments by tightening the requirements of registration via the Growth and Infrastructure Act 2013. This will reduce the use of custom as a source of law as it will no longer be possible to register a village green in reaction to planning proposals.[28]

Equally, the use of 'village green' status to protect customary or other rights is also narrowed by other competing sources of law and, in particular, statutory requirements. As was demonstrated recently in *Cotham School*,[29] a village green cannot be registered where it would go against the land's statutory purpose. Here, a school playing field had been registered as a village green, but the entry on the register was subsequently deleted as its use for customary rights was not compatible with its statutory use for education purposes. This demonstrates not only the careful balance but also the hierarchy between different sources of law.

EQUITY

As the common law developed, its rules became much more rigid and procedural. Equally, the range of remedies available under the common law was limited. Litigants had to bring their claim using one of a prescribed set of 'writs' which laid out the nature of the action that was being brought. As new circumstances arose, new writs were not always conceived. As a result, those bringing an action either had to make their circumstances artificially satisfy one of the existing writs or risk having their claim struck out. In achieving the balance between legal certainty and flexibility, the common law appeared to have favoured certainty. This led to potentially unjust decisions being made under the common law.

Where the common law failed to provide an adequate solution due to its inflexibility, individuals began to petition the King directly. The weight of these cases gradually increased, and the King passed them to his Lord Chancellor to decide as 'Keeper of the King's Conscience'. Free from the constraints of the strict rules of the common law, the Lord Chancellor was able to decide cases according to broader notions of fairness or *equity*. Given that the Lord Chancellor was normally a member of the clergy, the judgments given in equity were seen to have a moral, rather than a strictly legal, weighting.

27 ibid [134].

28 The Growth and Infrastructure Act 2013 s16 amends the Commons Act 2006 by inserting a new section (s15C), which reads as follows: 'The right under section 15(1) to apply to register land in England as a town or village green ceases to apply if an event specified in the first column of the Table set out in Schedule 1A has occurred in relation to the land ("a trigger event").' Schedule 1A triggering events include applications for planning permission, a development plan that identifies the land as a potential site for development.

29 *Cotham School v Bristol City Council* [2025] EWHC 1382 (Ch).

This practice eventually developed into one in the 15th century that was facilitated by a parallel route within the court system, where cases were heard by the Court of Chancery, although it was a while before this specific court was so designated: Sir Thomas More, as Lord Chancellor, sat in what is now called the 'Old Hall' in Lincolns Inn, which dates from the late 15th century.

Due to the uncertain nature of the decisions taken in equity, principles or 'equitable maxims' developed to guide the decision-making process of the Court of Chancery. These maxims were intended to be high-level guiding principles. They included, but were not limited to, the following:

- **Equity acts in personam.** This means that equity is concerned with persons, and jurisdiction need not be exerted over property since a decision acted on the conscience of the individual before the court, who could then be required to carry out that decision, which might then affect property.
- **He who comes to equity must come with clean hands.** Those who seek an equitable remedy must not have acted unconscionably in the matter concerned.
- **Between equal equities, the first in order of time shall prevail.** Where there are two equal equitable claims, then the one that arose first will prevail.

The resolution of disputes by recourse to equity also had a distinct set of remedies attached that differed from common law damages. These equitable remedies include estoppel, specific performance and injunctive relief. These remedies were always discretionary and remain so to this day, which contrasts starkly with common law remedies which are awarded as of right.

This development of equity from an informal system into a quasi-distinct justice system continued, and the rules became more concrete and inflexible over time as a way of dealing with the criticism that the notion of 'fairness' was subjective and an inability to predict outcomes in a given case was damaging to legal certainty. Moreover, the situation of two sets of courts exercising seemingly equal jurisdiction was bound to lead to confusion and conflict. This conflict came to a head in 1615 in the *Earl of Oxford's case*,[30] where the case progressed first through the common law courts and a decision was made that a transfer of land was void under a specific statute. A further action, involving one different party, but covering essentially the same issue, was brought in the equitable Court of Chancery. The Lord Chancellor granted an injunction to prevent enforcement of the common law judgment. As a result, the common law (in the ordinary courts) and the law of equity (in the Court of Chancery) came into conflict, and it was only after the intervention of the King that the conflict was resolved. James I made a declaration that equity takes priority over the common law when they are in conflict. This prioritisation of equity was brought into statutory effect by the Judicature Act 1873 (s25(11)).

With the uncertainty and delay of the Court of Chancery and the more rigid application of the equitable maxims, there were calls for a unified court system that brought together equity

30 *Earl of Oxford's Case* (1615) 1 Ch Rep 1.

and the common law. This was achieved by the Supreme Court of Judicature Act 1873, which established the High Court and brought the law of equity into the same system as that of the common law. Although still housed within a separate division (the Chancery Division) to that where common law claims were heard (the King's Bench), the two sets of law were within one unified system with greater clarity about the division of jurisdiction. The law itself was not fused, but rather, the claims on equity and/or common law could be heard within a single structure, the High Court. It is in this form that equity acts as a source of law. It is part of a unified legal system but retains a distinct set of rules and principles (based on the equitable maxims) that can be applied to a case, particularly where a common law solution or remedy would seem to be unfair, inappropriate or likely to lead to injustice.

MAKING CONNECTIONS – THE LAW OF EQUITY

For those studying for a degree in law, you will undoubtedly come across equitable principles and equitable remedies in other areas of study. There are entire areas of substantive law – such as the law of trusts – that are governed by equitable principles. In addition, there are many other areas of law – such as contract, intellectual property and family law – where the law of equity plays an important part, specifically in relation to remedies.

BOOKS OF AUTHORITY

Given the lack of consistent record-keeping in terms of judicial decisions prior to the 17th century, books of authority are treated as representing authoritative and accurate reflections of the common law as it stood at that time. These were texts written by contemporary jurists of the period and are taken to reflect the judicial decisions and practice of that era. There are numerous authors who have been held to hold such authority, including, but not limited to:

- Glanvill's *Treatise on the Laws and Customs of the Realm of England* (1189).
- Bracton's *On the Laws and Customs of England* (1250).
- Coke's *Institutes of the Lawes of England* (1628–1644).
- Blackstone's *Commentaries on the Laws of England* (1765). The work consists of four volumes relating to broad areas of law: the rights of persons, the rights of things, of private wrongs, of public wrongs.

These books of authority can still be relied upon as authoritative sources of the law and are still used in court today, either where the common law has not significantly changed or where a reading of these texts may cast a new light on the issue at hand. As recently as March 2023, the Supreme Court relied upon Blackstone's *Commentaries* when considering a contested debt between Russia and Ukraine in the context of the ongoing conflict.[31] In 2019, the Supreme Court relied upon passages of Blackstone's *Commentaries on the Laws of England* in deciding a matter related to the security services,[32] and references to the commentaries on 'public wrongs' have proved useful when discussing criminal law, particularly basic and fundamental principles of criminal justice.[33] These cases powerfully demonstrate the ongoing relevance and pertinence of books of authority to significant legal questions of the 21st century.

EXPLAINING THE LAW – THE INFLUENCE OF ACADEMIC WRITINGS

A distinction ought to be drawn between these 'books of authority' and modern academic writing. Both can be cited in court cases, but only the former is regarded as being an authoritative statement of the law. Nonetheless, the writings of expert academics in law journals have certainly influenced judges in coming to conclusions on the law. For example, Lord Justice Auld in *Marks & Spencer*[34] used the analysis provided by Dr Sara Drake (an academic specialising in EU remedial law)[35] to frame his decision on a significant tax matter.[36]

Judges also often point to academic criticism of the law when advocating a change in the law. This is notable in the recent judgment of the High Court in *OMV Petrom*,[37] where the extensive criticism of the position of the Court of Appeal by Professor Trietel in the *Law Quarterly Review* was cited.[38]

This raises two important points. First, we must distinguish between *authoritative* statements of the law which form an independent source of law for the legal system and the writing of academics that may only influence court decisions. Second, and despite their non-binding nature, modern writers can help *shape* the law through their writing.

31 *The Law Debenture Trust Corporation v Ukraine* [2023] UKSC 11 [204].

32 *R (on the application of Privacy International) v Investigatory Powers Tribunal and Others* [2019] UKSC 22, [2019] 2 WLR 1219 [32] and a more substantive treatment in *Pham v Secretary of State for the Home Department* [2015] UKSC 19, [2015] 1 WLR 1591 [97] and [106]. This reference is by no means unusual, and you will find reference to Blackstone (and other writers) peppered through the law reports at all levels.

33 *R v Davis* [2008] UKHL 36, [2008] 3 WLR 125 [5].

34 *Marks & Spencer Plc v Commissioners of Customs & Excise* [2003] EWCA Civ 1448, [2004] 1 CMLR 8.

35 Sara Drake, '*Vouchers v VAT*: Issues of Direct Effect and National Time Limits Raised by the *Marks and Spencer* Case' (2003) 28(3) EL Rev 418.

36 *Marks & Spencer Plc v Commissioners of Customs & Excise* [2003] EWCA Civ 1448, [2004] 1 CMLR 8, [29] (Auld LJ).

37 *OVM Petrom v Glencore* [2015] EWHC 666 (Comm).

38 Guenter Trietel, 'Damages for Breach of Warranty of Quality' (1997) 113 LQR 188.

INTERNATIONAL LAW

The contribution of international law to the legal system is important, but it acts as a less direct source than other forms of law discussed in this chapter. There are two particularly noteworthy forms of international law that are sources of law for the legal system of England and Wales.

First, and more controversially, there exists a body of law called *jus cogens*, which are peremptory norms of international law from which it is impossible to derogate. This means that the rights and obligations classified as *jus cogens* cannot be displaced by agreements between different countries or by the independent actions of a particular country. There is no generally accepted list of *jus cogens*, but they include things like the prohibition against state torture.

These principles may influence the way in which judges decide cases under the common law, but their precise status as a 'source' of law is less certain. As noted in *Mohamed v Secretary of State for Foreign and Commonwealth Affairs*,'[39] [w]hile customary international law is a source of the common law, the precise manner in which it is received into English law is a question determined by English and Welsh law'.[40] In this way, it is clear the *jus cogens* are at the least an *influence* on English and Welsh law and at the most are an independent source of law. If you study public international law, then you will be likely to explore the academic debates that surround such examples of the *jus cogens*.[41]

Second, there are international treaties signed by the UK with other sovereign states or with international organisations, such as the United Nations or the World Trade Organisation. The nature of these treaties is to bind, at the international level, those states (known, normally, as 'contracting parties') to certain commitments. There are two primary ways in which international treaties can become part of domestic, national law. The method of incorporation will depend on whether the country/state in question is a monist state or a dualist state. *Monist states* are those where international law becomes part of domestic law when a particular treaty is signed by the government. The legal system of England and Wales does not follow this model and, to preserve the sovereignty of Parliament, follows the dualist model.

Under the dualist model, any agreement made by the government at the international level must be *incorporated* into domestic law by legislation. More specifically for the legal system, this will require an Act of Parliament to be passed in the normal way through the Houses of Parliament. Thus, although the UK was an original signatory of the European Convention on Human Rights in the early 1950s, the substantive rights contained within it did not become part of the law of England and Wales until Parliament passed the Human Rights Act in 1998. Until that point, the only rights that people had were those available as a matter of *international*

39 *Mohamed v Secretary of State for Foreign and Commonwealth Affairs* [2008] EWHC 2048 (Admin), [2009] 1 WLR 2579.

40 ibid [184].

41 For a flavour of that debate, see Matthew Saul, 'Identifying Jus Cogens Norms: The Interaction of Scholars and International Judges' (2015) 5 AJIL 26 or Ulf Linderfalk, 'What Is So Special About Jus Cogens? – On the Difference Between the Ordinary and the Peremptory International Law' (2012) 14 IntCLRev 3.

law, and this precluded those who had been the victim of a violation of human rights – as defined in the Convention – from launching an action in the courts of England and Wales. In this way, international treaties act as a source of law for the English and Welsh legal system when they have been incorporated but potentially can be a source of *rights in international law* for British citizens when they are signed and ratified by the UK government.

The use of international law treaties is widespread and can cover a surprising array of subject matter from cross-border commercial matters, such as intellectual property[42] or recognition of arbitration agreements[43] from other countries, to public law matters, such as principles relating to the rights of children[44] and agreements against the use of torture.[45] The use of international treaties is so widespread that there are even treaties governing the use, interpretation and effect of other international treaties! The Vienna Convention on the Law of Treaties, also known as the 'Treaty of Treaties', has 85 articles governing a common way of understanding, interpreting, terminating and suspending the operation of treaties.

CATEGORISING THE LAW OF ENGLAND AND WALES

Having briefly dealt with the individual sources of law, it is important to spend some time exploring the different ways in which law can be categorised. This is helpful for further understanding the varying roles that these sources play in the legal system. This is distinct from earlier discussions of 'common law' as a way of describing a whole *system*. Here we are talking about common law as a source of law. It is also worth noting that when people refer to the 'common law', they may be referring to one of many different definitions/understandings of the common law. By understanding the following subsections, you will be able to contextualise the different usages of the phrase 'common law' as a source of law and avoid understandable misunderstandings. The following is not intended to be an exhaustive consideration of the way in which law can be classified, not least because there are limitless ways in which we could try to sort and label law. The purpose is rather to give an indication of terminology and to introduce you to the idea that sources of law can be categorised differently for different purposes.

COMMON LAW AND STATUTE

Another way of categorising law is to make a distinction between common law and statutory law. Here, *common law* is normally being used to describe all case law. This is a broad conception of case law and can include the principles of equity (found within case law) and even cases

42 Berne Convention for the Protection of Literary and Artistic Works (1886).

43 Convention on the Recognition and Enforcement of Foreign Arbitral Awards (1959), also known as the New York Convention.

44 United Nations Convention on the Rights of the Child (1989).

45 United Nations Convention against Torture (1984).

that do not have precedential value. Statute is used, in this instance, to cover both primary and secondary legislation.

COMMON LAW AND EQUITY

Another typical distinction is between equity and common law. These are both forms of case law, and the difference is one of historical fact (discussed previously). People making this distinction are normally interested in comparing the rigidity of the rules of the old common law system and the broader equitable principles that were applied first by the Lord Chancellor directly and later by the Court of Chancery. Understanding the distinction is still important because equitable remedies are not available as of right, as is the case under the common law, and are discretionary. This means that although the Judicature Acts sought to *fuse* the institutional organisation of equity and the common law, they remain distinct sources of law, albeit, as has been said, 'now flowing along the same channel'. In this way, being cognisant of the different context within which the phrase 'common law' is used can impact on our ability to understand a given case or the analysis of a particular case.

CONSTITUTIONAL OR ORDINARY LAW

The classification of law as 'constitutional' or 'ordinary' law is important in countries that have formal, codified constitutions. This is because constitutional law is a superior form of law that has special rules and procedures that govern its creation, and it normally takes priority over conflicting 'ordinary' law. For example, in the United States, the Supreme Court can strike down Acts of Congress (primary legislation) that are incompatible with the US Constitution.[46]

Traditionally, such a distinction has been unnecessary in the legal system of England and Wales as, with the lack of a formal written constitution, there was no higher source of law than Acts of Parliament. While this position is still broadly true, judicial developments in the early 21st century have suggested that there is a subset of constitutional law statutes that have a certain priority when they clash with 'ordinary' statutes. What makes this all the more striking is that there is no difference in the procedure for making so-called constitutional statutes.[47] This development is taken up later in the section on the hierarchy of norms, and also in the substantive chapter on primary legislation.

CRIMINAL LAW AND CIVIL LAW

A further division in the classification of law comes in the form of the differences between civil and criminal law. When we talk of *civil law* in this way, we mean the branch of law that governs the relationship between individuals (particularly where that relationship breaks down), as opposed to criminal law, which seeks to redress wrongs done by individuals against the state. The civil law therefore encompasses private law disputes (such as breach of contract, negligence and matrimonial disagreements, etc.), whereas the criminal law deals with offences of varying seriousness (such as murder, theft, speeding, etc.).

46 *Marbury v Madison* (1803) 5 US 137.

47 *Thoburn v Sunderland City Council* [2002] EWHC 195 (Admin), [2003] QB 151.

Civil and criminal law are both subject to their own sets of procedures and have their own language for describing similar aspects of cases. There are more important differences, such as the standard of proof required to be successful in a given case with the 'balance of probabilities' being used in civil cases and 'beyond all reasonable doubt' forming the criminal standard. Due to the significant differences in process, there are dedicated chapters on the civil (Chapter 10) and criminal justice (Chapter 11) systems later in this work.

PUBLIC LAW AND PRIVATE LAW

In some ways, this categorisation is a broader version of the distinction between criminal law and civil law. Public law concerns the relationship between the individual and the state, and also between the different institutions of the state. In this way, criminal law is a form of public law as it concerns the way in which the state redresses offences against it. Other branches of public law include constitutional law (which is concerned with the creation of government and the regulation of the powers of the state and the rights of individuals against the state) and administrative law (which is concerned with the activities of government agencies, such as those administering social security or other welfare payments). The cornerstone of public law is the concept of 'judicial review', whereby individuals can challenge the actions of the government (or its agents) before a court.

Private law, on the other hand, governs the relationship between individuals and is often used synonymously with the term 'civil law'.

PROCEDURAL OR SUBSTANTIVE LAW

This method of categorisation relies less on the type of source under discussion but rather more on its purpose. Substantive law lays down the principles of a given area of law, for example, the required elements of a criminal offence. Substantive law establishes the rights and obligations of an individual in a given situation. Procedural law will set out the rules and principles by which that substantive law is *administered* (e.g. the steps needed to bring a valid claim in the High Court for a breach of contract or various rules of evidence).

SUMMARY

As we have seen previously, there are numerous ways in which we can classify law or attempt to distinguish between different types of sources of law. This is a useful skill for a person wishing to study the English and Welsh law in greater detail as it will allow for a concept with several possible meanings to be understood in its proper context. The rest of this text will assume that the reader has mastered these distinctions. As the text progresses to more detailed, and analytical, discussion, it would be easy to discard the messages in this chapter. This temptation should be avoided, as a proper grounding in basic terminology and the fundamental sources of the legal system of England and Wales is crucial to understanding the more technical aspects of the system and the principles by which it operates.

TAKING THINGS FURTHER – TESTING YOUR UNDERSTANDING

The website that accompanies this textbook has exercises by which you can test your knowledge and understanding of these classifications and to enable you to be sure that you understand the correct use of key terminology in this chapter. Although it takes time to become familiar with the unique language of law and of legal sources, the greater the immersion that you have into it, the faster your understanding will develop.

HIERARCHY OF NORMS AND SOURCES

The presentation of the sources of law should not be studied in isolation. It is, of course, essential to understand and to be able to describe the basic sources of law of the English and Welsh legal system that were laid out previously. The first part of the chapter dealt with this aspect of the law. It is also important to be able to categorise, compare and distinguish between the various sources of law and legal systems. The second part of the chapter dealt with this aspect.

It is of equal importance to consider the normative framework within which these sources operate. This turns the legal sources into a series of interacting (and sometimes conflicting!) norms, some of which have priority over others. It is this aspect of the law that is dealt within this final section. Given the lack of a fixed constitutional document, it can be very difficult to ascertain and understand the order of priority amongst this multitude of sources. What makes this task even more difficult is that the position of particular sources may move over time or, at the least, our understanding of how these sources interact can change and develop as the legal system continues to develop and evolve. Also, there is disagreement (amongst academics and the institutions) about the ordering of these sources, and this adds to the richness of the discourse.

MAKING CONNECTIONS – CONSTITUTIONAL LAW

++++++++++++++++++++++++++++++++++++

Further chapters of this textbook continue to explore certain constitutional principles. The rule of law, parliamentary sovereignty and the separation of powers are not sources of law themselves, but these principles (and their interpretation) do impact on how the sources of law are understood and can give a different gloss to a particular piece of law, or even to a whole category of sources. These constitutional principles underpin the way in which the framework of the law is to be understood. These concepts are returned to in later chapters, but if you are also studying constitutional law, then you will delve even deeper into these concepts.

A textbook on the legal system of England and Wales written at the turn of the 20th century would have reflected a much different hierarchy of norms than is presented here. We currently stand at the start of a new era in the development of the relationship between sources with the courts seemingly keen (albeit, so far, in mainly non-binding statements) to drive forward a new understanding of how the sources interact. What follows is a brief conceptualisation of the hierarchy between the different sources of law.

Even though the English and Welsh legal system lacks a formal written constitution, it still has forms of constitutional law that take priority over other, non-constitutional sources. This constitutional law is formed through the adherence to certain principles and a core of so-called constitutional statutes that take priority over ordinary law. This was first established in the *Thoburn*[48] case. These statutes are partly entrenched and, unlike other statutes, can only be repealed through the express actions and words of Parliament. There is no definitive list of such constitutional statutes, but the following have been held to be included in the definition:

- European Communities Act 1972 (now repealed)
- Human Rights Act 1998
- Bill of Rights 1689
- Magna Carta 1215
- Scotland Act 1998

It is these principles and constitutional statutes that sit at the apex of the hierarchy of norms and take priority over other conflicting pieces of 'ordinary law', unless that ordinary law expressly repeals the constitutional statute.

To complicate things further, the Supreme Court, in its *HS2*[49] judgment, suggested that not all these constitutional statutes are equal and that there may even be an order of priority between them. This is a developing area of UK constitutional law, and the effect of the judgment is not quite certain, as resolution of this hierarchy between constitutional statutes was not necessary to decide the case at hand. The suggestion – but it was only a suggestion – in this case was that the principle of parliamentary privilege over its own internal affairs[50] would take priority over the primacy of European Union law that bound the UK during its membership.[51] The implication is that ordering these sources and determining priorities is a matter for the courts to decide in cases where a conflict arises.[52]

Most recently, the Supreme Court, some 20 years after the decision in *Thoburn*,[53] has cast doubt over the ongoing relevance of the priority of so-called 'constitutional statutes'. In *Allister*,[54] the court refused to engage with an analysis of whether the Northern Ireland Protocol was

48 *Thoburn v Sunderland City Council* [2002] EWHC 195 (Admin), [2003] QB 151, also known as the '*Metric Martyrs* case'. An important case on the relationship between EU law and an Act of Parliament.

49 *R (HS2 Alliance) v Secretary of State for Transport* [2014] UKSC 3, [2014] 1 WLR 3253.

50 Derived from Article 9 Bill of Rights 1689.

51 European Communities Act 1972.

52 *R (HS2 Alliance) v Secretary of State for Transport* [2014] UKSC 3, [2014] 1 WLR 3253, [207].

53 And interestingly, the present case was also about the UK's relationship with the European Union in the form of the Northern Ireland Protocol, which was intended to govern trade.

54 *Re Allister* [2023] UKSC 5.

in conflict with the earlier (undoubtedly constitutional) Acts of Union. It termed the debate about constitutional statutes 'academic'[55] and seemed to be adopting a much more orthodox view of parliamentary sovereignty. The Court managed to resolve the dispute without having to consider whether the Protocol conflicted with a prior constitutional statute. This could be seen as the Court distancing itself from the line of reasoning in *Thoburn* and *HS2*, but it did not go so far as to make a definitive statement on the principles. This leaves the hierarchy of norms in an uncertain state but does show the ability of the common law to develop and evolve over time, both refining and dispensing with principles.

Following next, and subject to the constraints and doubts of the constitutional law just discussed, come 'ordinary' statutes. By 'ordinary' we mean Acts of Parliament that are not constitutional in the *Thoburn* sense.[56] This would cover the vast majority of Acts of Parliament. These, due to the principle of parliamentary sovereignty, take priority over all the other sources. This is a principle of long-standing[57] and one that is discussed further in the chapter on law-making.

Sitting below statutory law is the common law, in the sense of the totality of case law. Acts of Parliament can displace the common law, and where the two come into conflict, the former takes priority over the latter. Even within the broad definition of case law, the principles of equity take priority over the rules of the common law.[58]

Similarly, there is a hierarchy between the judgments of different courts. The binding rules of precedent (discussed in a later chapter) make certain judgments more authoritative than others. This is an important point not always remembered by those who are studying the law for the first time. Thus, not only does a Supreme Court judgment take priority over judgments from any other court in the legal system of England and Wales; it is also more authoritative in its statements of the law.

The position of secondary legislation is fairly subordinate. It takes its authority from a parent Act (an Act of Parliament) and can be annulled through judicial review by courts where it is held to have been passed *ultra vires*.

CONCLUSION

This chapter was intended to give an introduction to the major sources of law within the legal system. Reading this chapter will have provided an overview that will be invaluable for the

55 ibid at [66].

56 For debate on the meaning of this term, see Farrah Ahmed and Adam Perry, 'The Quasi-Entrenchment of Constitutional Statutes' (2014) 73 CLJ 514.

57 Michael Gordon, 'The Conceptual Foundations of Parliamentary Sovereignty: Reconsidering Jennings and Wade' [2009] PL 519.

58 Alastair Hudson, *Equity and Trusts* (9th edn, Routledge 2016) 14.

more detailed and analytical chapters on specific sources or aspects of the legal system that follow. More importantly, the chapter deconstructed some of the different ways in which legal terminology can be used to describe different facets of a single concept (most importantly, the 'common law'). Being aware of this rich and multifaceted use of language will improve your understanding not only of the legal system but also of any substantive legal subjects that you may study.

The chapter should also prompt you to think about how sources of law interact and how the system seeks to resolve conflict between sources when they arise. The centrality of the courts to resolving this conflict underlines the judiciary's importance in the common law system. Also, the evolutionary nature of the legal system of England and Wales should be apparent from the analysis in this chapter. The common law developed out of custom over a period of hundreds of years and was partly fused with the principles of equity after the two had existed in tandem for many years. This staged progress has also allowed for the absorption of international law principles into English and Welsh law. The incorporation of the ECHR (through the Human Rights Act 1998) and the UK's membership of the European Union have caused the most significant shift of the last 100 years in how legal sources are used and understood. This change to our understanding of how legal sources interact is something that is ongoing and will continue to trouble the courts in the future. This only goes to further demonstrate the fluid and dynamic nature of the legal system.

TAKING THINGS FURTHER

The website that accompanies this textbook contains many useful resources that you can use to consolidate and further your knowledge of the law, to hone your skills of critical analysis and to test your knowledge. This includes a set of multiple-choice questions (MCQs) that can be used to test your knowledge and understanding of the material.

COMPANION WEBSITE

The website that accompanies this textbook contains many useful resources that you can use to consolidate and further your knowledge of the law, to hone your skills of critical analysis and to test your knowledge.

3

CHAPTER 3
INSTITUTIONS OF THE LEGAL SYSTEM

INTRODUCTION

There is a myriad of institutions involved in the operation of the legal system of England and Wales. The powers that these institutions exercise and how they interact with each other have a profound impact on the nature of the legal system as well as the character, form and legitimacy of the law that they create and administer.

This chapter explores the institutional landscape for the legal system in England and Wales. It is one of a series of chapters that seeks to provide an overview of the institutions and law-making processes of the legal system. It concludes with a brief account of an important constitutional principle – separation of powers – that affects the distribution of power within the legal system, a central theme of this textbook.

AS YOU READ

The chapter provides a framework for understanding the major **institutions of the legal system**, but there will be a focus on those institutions that have a role in the **law-making process** or in the **administration of justice**. By the end of this chapter, you should be able to **identify the core institutions of the legal system** and critically consider their role, powers and functions.

In considering the institutions, you should **think critically about the nature of 'power' and influence** and be able to **evaluate the relationship between these institutions**. This involves understanding their *function* and their constitutional legitimacy. Any student of law will struggle to understand the legal system by just learning the institutions, in a standalone manner, without understanding the relationship with other chapters of this textbook. The ability to draw out themes that cross different areas of study is one that is particularly valuable to a student of law. As you read the distinct sections, attempt to **synthesise the information so as to consider the nature of power and its distribution across the different institutions of law-making**.

DOI: 10.4324/9781032641829-3

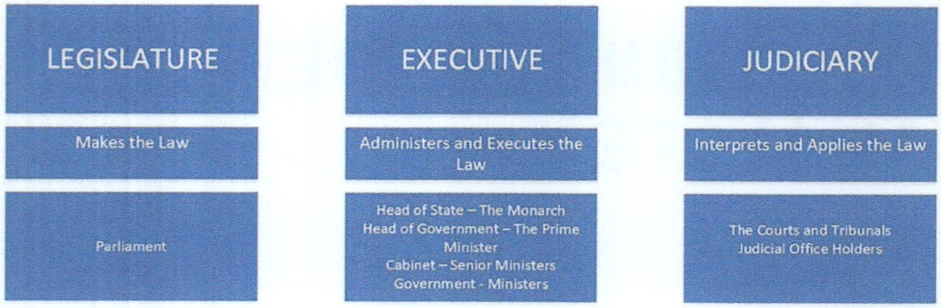

Figure 3.1 The branches of the state.

INSTITUTIONS OF LAW-MAKING

The following sections will seek to distinguish between those institutions that make the law and those that are responsible for the administration of justice. As with all aspects of the legal system, these labels are only partly effective in describing the roles, which is in part due to the fluid nature of the powers of such institutions within the legal system of England and Wales.

At its most basic, we can separate the institutions of the state into three parts – the *executive* branch, the *legislative* branch and the *judicial* branch. Figure 3.1 considers the major functions of each branch, and the subsections that follow consider the role in the legal system played by the major actors of each branch.

THE LEGISLATURE

Within the English and Welsh legal system, the UK Parliament is the legislature.[1] This means that the primary law-making body is Parliament. The UK's Parliament has two functions:

- To pass laws
- To hold the executive to account

It is the *legislative*, or law-making function, with which this textbook is concerned. The precise details of *how* law is made can be found in Chapters 4 and 5, but the remainder of this section is concerned with the structure of Parliament. The purpose of this section is to give the reader the necessary context for them to be able to understand the terminology used in later chapters. Although there are two chambers[2] within the UK Parliament, there are actually three constituent elements: the House of Commons, the House of Lords and the King in Parliament.

1 Although Wales also has a devolved Senedd Cymru with 96 members, created by the Government of Wales Act 1998, which has limited powers in respect of Wales, including legislation and taxes. The number of members of the Senedd recently increased from 60.

2 So-called bicameral system.

In order for bills to become Acts of Parliament, they need to pass successfully through all three[3] constituent parts.

HOUSE OF COMMONS

The lower house comprises 650 Members of Parliament (MPs), who are directly elected to represent constituencies across England, Wales, Scotland and Northern Ireland. Elections take place every five years, unless Parliament is dissolved earlier by order of the King on the advice of the Prime Minister.[4] Elections are held according to universal suffrage and by a system known as 'first past the post', which means that the candidate with the most votes within an area becomes the MP for that constituency. Members of Parliament draw a salary that is set by the Independent Parliamentary Standards Authority.[5]

Within the UK electoral system, there are two main parties[6] with a number of other, smaller parties,[7] who tend to gain a lesser number of seats at General Elections than the two main parties. On rare occasion, sometimes one of these smaller parties is needed to form a coalition with one of the two largest, which would otherwise not be able to form a government without such assistance: for example, in the coalition government of Conservatives and Liberal Democrats in 2010, when the previous Labour government was defeated in the General Election. There are also several MPs who sit as 'independents' (i.e. those without an affiliation to a particular party).[8] In some senses, the House of Commons is regarded as the 'superior' chamber due to the fact that its members are elected by the people, and this gives them, and the laws they pass, democratic legitimacy.

The House of Commons also has many committees that help it hold the government to account and assure the efficient passage of legislation – some of these committees are considered in greater detail in Chapters 4 and 5.

Within the 650 elected Members of Parliament, there are also several officials who perform important functions within the House of Commons. Chief amongst these is the Speaker, who is elected from amongst the MPs and who chairs sessions of the House of Commons, maintains order and can suspend a particular sitting. The Speaker is supported by a number of Deputy Speakers and a Clerk, who is neither a member of the House nor a civil servant and is responsible for advising the Speaker (and MPs) about parliamentary process. The Leader of the House of Commons is responsible for organising government business within the House.

3 Under certain circumstances, discussed in Chapter 4, bills can become Acts of Parliament without the approval of the House of Lords under the provisions of the Parliament Acts 1911 and 1949.

4 The Dissolution and Calling of Parliament Act 2022 repealed the Fixed-Term Parliament Act 2011, which had curtailed the monarch's prerogative power to dissolve Parliament at the request of the government.

5 A statutory body established by the Parliamentary Standards Act 2009.

6 Labour and Conservative.

7 For example, the Liberal Democrats, Scottish Nationalist Party, Democratic Unionist Party, The Independent Group for Change, Plaid Cymru, Green Party and Sinn Fein.

8 Either through choice or, as happened to 21 former Conservative MPs in autumn 2019, because they defied their former leader's instructions and had party support withdrawn.

TAKING THINGS FURTHER – THE OFFICERS OF PARLIAMENT

The website that accompanies this textbook has further information on the principal officers of Parliament. On the website, there is a podcast that seeks to explore the impact of these officers on the legal system and, in particular, on the law-making processes within the legal system. These officers are not normally considered in a text on the legal system, but the view taken here is that the personality and approach of the officers generally (and the Speaker particularly) can have a significant impact on the way in which Parliament goes about its law-making task. For example, John Bercow stepped down as Speaker on 31 October 2019, and his ten-year term demonstrates the significant impact that a Speaker can have on the legal system, given it coincided with the UK's exit from the European Union.

HOUSE OF LORDS

The upper house consists at the time of writing of 826[9] largely appointed[10] peers. The peers are divided into Lords Spiritual and Lords Temporal. The Lords Spiritual are the 26 bishops of the Church of England, and the Lords Temporal are a mixture of hereditary peers[11] and so-called life peers[12] who are appointed by the Monarch on the advice of the Prime Minister.

The House of Lords is an integral part of the legislative process – a proposal for a piece of law may technically start its life in either the Commons or the Lords – but certain conventions and procedures have sought to restrict the activities of the Lords to reflect the fact that its members are not elected but rather appointed or in their position as a consequence of birth. These conventions and processes seek to allow the democratically elected House of Commons to take precedence whilst still valuing the expertise that the Lords can bring as a 'revising' chamber.

For example, the Lords can no longer *veto* bills but rather, as a result of the Parliament Acts 1911 and 1949, can only force a delay for the length of a parliamentary session. Equally, the Lords are unable to prevent the passage of a 'money bill'.[13] The impact of these restrictions for law-making is considered in greater detail in Chapter 4.

Even with the softening of the power of the House of Lords, there remains a live controversy about the place of the House of Lords in the modern legal system, particularly in relation to the position of the bishops and hereditary peers.

---

9 From a report in September 2025 <https://researchbriefings.files.parliament.uk/documents/CBP-10219/CBP-10219.pdf>.

10 There are still 92 hereditary peers who sit as a matter of birth right and who are elected from a pool of around 750 eligible peers.

11 Those whose titles and peerage can be inherited.

12 Those whose titles and peerage cannot be passed on by inheritance.

13 A bill that relates to government spending or taxation.

ANALYSING THE LAW – REFORM OF THE HOUSE OF LORDS

The proper composition and role of the House of Lords have been the subject of fierce debate for decades.[14] There have been significant reforms to date, with the Parliament Acts of 1911 and 1949 severely restricting the Lords' legislative role and the Life Peerages Act 1958, which both introduced the concept of appointed 'life peers' and also allowed women to sit for the first time in the House. The House of Lords Act 1999 was a significant change, with the size of the chamber reducing by half through the drastic reduction to 92 hereditary peers.[15] Since that significant reform, things have somewhat stalled. There have been further reforms, including the removal of the House of Lords judicial function to the newly established Supreme Court in 2009,[16] and less radical reform, such as the introduction of additional ways for members of the Lords to leave the House (through resignation, retirement and exclusion).[17]

There have been further efforts for more significant reform under the coalition government of 2010 between the Liberal Democrats and the Conservatives, with a proposed bill[18] to transform the House into an elected chamber. These plans were abandoned when it became clear that back-bench Conservatives would not support the bill. The Burns Report,[19] published in 2017, recommended a further reduction in the size of the House and a restriction of terms to 15 years, but this also appears to have been lost in the political and constitutional tumult of Brexit and post-Covid financial recovery.

The Labour government's 2024 manifesto[20] included a promise to immediately modernise the House of Lords through the introduction of a mandatory retirement age of 80 and to abolish the remaining hereditary peers. At the time of writing, the House of Lords (Hereditary Peers) Bill 2024–2026 was making its way through the parliamentary process and had been returned to the House of Commons for debate of the amendments proposed by the Lords. If this Bill does pass and become law, it would certainly be the biggest constitutional reform to the Lords for nearly 30 years.[21]

14 For a flavor, see Mark Ryan, 'A Referendum on the Reform of the House of Lords?' (2015) 66(3) NILQ 223; Lord Bingham, 'The House of Lords: Its Future' [2010] PL 261; Stephen Tierney, 'A New Wave of Constitutional Reform for the UK?' (2009) 15(3) EPL 289.

15 When one retires or otherwise vacates their space there is provision for a by-election amongst the remaining eligible peers to become one of the 92.

16 By virtue of the Constitutional Reform Act 2005 s23.

17 By virtue of the House of Lords Reform Act 2014.

18 House of Lords Reform Bill 2012.

19 *Report of the Lord Speaker's Committee on the Size of the House* (published on 31 October 2017) <www.parliament.uk/documents/lords-committees/size-of-house/size-of-house-report.pdf>.

20 <https://labour.org.uk/wp-content/uploads/2024/06/Labour-Party-manifesto-2024.pdf>.

21 You can monitor the progress of the Bill here: <https://bills.parliament.uk/bills/3755/stages>.

What is evident from the brief consideration of reform is that the issue of House of Lords reform is an ongoing debate and that some changes to the legal system happen in an evolutionary, rather than revolutionary, way. There are occasional 'jumps' (such as the change precipitated in 1911, 1999 and 2009) towards reforms, but there are often small 'steps' (such as the change in 2014).

Maintaining an up-to-date understanding of the evolution of the legal system is crucial to success in legal study and will allow for a form of 'horizon scanning' that ensures that future plans for reform (and their likelihood for success) can be identified.

Much like for the House of Commons, there are also several officers within the Lords who have the role of ensuring the efficient operation of the chamber. Some are mirrors of officers in the Commons – including the Lord Speaker and Leader of the House of Lords – but there are also others that are particular to the Lords. The most notable of these is Black Rod,[22] who is the King's representative in Parliament and is responsible for maintaining order in the Lords and who also takes part in the ceremonial aspects of the State Opening of Parliament.

CROWN IN PARLIAMENT

As well as playing an important symbolic and substantive role in the administration of justice and the exercise of executive power, the Monarch also plays an important part in the life of Parliament. He is responsible for the State Opening and the dissolution of Parliament that leads to a General Election.

The Monarch's technical role in law-making is considered in greater detail in Chapter 4, but for present purposes, it is enough to note that the King must give his Royal Assent to all primary legislation before it can become a valid Act of Parliament.

THE EXECUTIVE

Executive power within the legal system of England and Wales is exercised by a number of different individuals and public bodies. Some of the more prominent institutions of the executive are considered in the following sections, as this provides useful information and context for the detailed discussion that follows.

MONARCH

The Monarch is the original source of executive power in the legal system. As a result, King Charles III is the symbolic Head of State. There are still some powers that are recognised as being personal to the Monarch. Examples include the appointment of the Prime Minister

22 Named after the ebony staff that this officer carries on ceremonial occasions. Black Rod is not a peer but is usually knighted if not already of that rank and is now appointed after a search for an appropriate holder, although the post used to rotate amongst the armed forces. The post-holder at the time of writing is Lieutenant-General Edward Davis (having been appointed in July 2025).

and, on advice, the appointment of the other Ministers that form His Majesty's Government. The majority of prerogative powers of the Monarch are now exercised either on the advice of the Prime Minister or directly by Ministers on behalf of the Monarch. Even where the Monarch *appears* to have wide-ranging discretion, there are certain conventions that dictate how that discretion is exercised. The selection of the Prime Minister is a good example of how the legal system tolerates an unelected Monarch that would otherwise offend against democracy.

EXPLAINING THE LAW – CHOOSING THE PRIME MINISTER

The office of the Prime Minister, Keir Starmer at the time of writing, is one of the four Great Offices of State,[23] and the person occupying that position is a very visible and important part of the legal system as the head of the government. Prime Ministers are chosen by the Monarch according to the Monarch's prerogative powers. Given the importance of the role, it might be surprising that an unelected Monarch is able to select the head of the UK government. However, certain *conventions* have arisen that allow for a legitimate Prime Minister to be selected.

First, the Monarch will always select a Prime Minister who sits in the House of Commons (i.e. an MP). This ensures that there is a democratic link to the people and that the democratically elected house has the best opportunity to hold the Prime Minister to account.

Second, the Monarch will always select a Prime Minister who can command the confidence of the House of Commons. Although an incumbent Prime Minister will have the first opportunity to demonstrate this, most normally the person with the best chance of securing the confidence of the Commons will be the leader of the party who secures the most seats at a General Election. This means that the government will normally be formed by whoever 'wins' an election, and so their mandate comes from the electorate and the government has democratic legitimacy.

THE UK GOVERNMENT

This is the most obviously recognisable part of the executive within the legal system of England and Wales. The UK government is led by a Prime Minister and a Cabinet of their most senior Ministers.[24] By convention, all government Ministers also sit in Parliament (in either the Lords or the Commons), so that they are answerable and accountable to Parliament for their actions and must subscribe to a specific code of conduct policed by the Prime Minister.[25]

23 Alongside the Home Secretary, Foreign Secretary and Chancellor of the Exchequer.

24 Including, amongst others, the Chancellor of the Exchequer, the Foreign Secretary, the Home Secretary, the Lord Chancellor and Justice Secretary and the Defence Secretary.

25 Cabinet Office *Ministerial Code* (November 2024) <www.gov.uk/government/publications/ministerial-code>.

As discussed previously, the Prime Minister and his Ministers will usually be drawn from the political party which won the most seats at a General Election.[26] They may govern by majority (when they have more than half of the available seats in the House of Commons), by minority (when they have more seats in the House of Commons than any other political party but still fewer than half of the seats) or in coalition with another party.

The government organises its work within departments that are aligned to particular policy areas.[27] It is these government departments that turn the aspirations of the Cabinet into policy and proposals for law. For the purposes of this textbook, the Ministry of Justice (MoJ) is amongst the most important of the government departments. The MoJ is responsible for the effective operation of the legal system, including, but not limited to:

- The operation of the courts and tribunals[28]
- The funding of Legal Aid[29]
- Prisons
- Probation

The government has a particularly prominent role in law-making within the legal system of England and Wales. As the government is responsible for the way in which time is given to particular proposals in Parliament, it also has a great deal of influence over the way in which matters become law. Individual Ministers may have the power to pass delegated legislation.

EXECUTIVE AGENCIES, NON-DEPARTMENTAL PUBLIC BODIES

Supporting the work of the governmental departments are executive agencies and non-departmental public bodies. Executive agencies are more closely interwoven with the work of the department with which they are affiliated. These bodies are assigned their own budgets and managed separately but retain a particularly close relationship with their associated department and Minister. Within the Ministry of Justice, for example, the Legal Aid Agency, His Majesty's Courts and Tribunals Service and His Majesty's Prison Service are all executive agencies.

These executive agencies are to be contrasted with non-departmental public bodies. These bodies are further detached from the department that sponsors them and have a greater degree of autonomy. These public bodies are free from ministerial interference, and the bodies are accountable to Parliament for their activity, including budgets. Nonetheless, they retain an important place in the legal system and can have significant influence over how the system is administered. Amongst the multitude of such public bodies, some of those most relevant to a textbook on the legal system include the Judicial Appointments Commission, the Law Commission, the Legal Services Board and the Sentencing Council.

26 Occasionally, elections do not provide a majority government, and so parties may form coalition government amongst themselves; this happened between the Conservatives and the Liberal Democrats following the 2010 election.

27 There are (at the time of writing) 24 ministerial departments, 20 non-ministerial departments and more than 417 agencies and other public bodies <www.gov.uk/government/organisations>.

28 A task it performs through the executive agency: His Majesty's Court and Tribunals Service (HMCTS).

29 Through the executive agency: the Legal Aid Agency.

As the textbook progresses, the importance of the role of some of these bodies will become clearer.

THE CIVIL SERVICE

Given that governments will change every five years or so,[30] it would be inefficient if the entire machinery of the executive also had to change when a new government was elected. The Civil Service is a permanent workforce of politically neutral employees of the Crown. Civil servants are there to implement the policies of the elected government. The work of civil servants is spread amongst the government departments, each of which has a senior civil servant, known as a Permanent Secretary.

THE JUDICIARY

The judicial function is undertaken by the judiciary (judges and the magistracy) and within the courts and tribunals of England and Wales. The courts are assisted in their task by court officials and the legal professions. In this way, the judicial branch of the state contributes the following to the legal system of England and Wales:

- Application of principles of law that can be used to resolve disputes[31]
- Processes by which disputes are to be settled, including application of rules of evidence and procedural rules[32]
- Organisation of court buildings that can be used to hear and determine disputes[33]
- Personnel, including judges, who, by virtue of qualification and experience, are deemed appropriate for appointment to adjudicate on disputes, and jurors who hear the most serious criminal cases[34]

Much of the remainder of this textbook is concerned with considering in some detail these judicial functions and how they contribute to the operation of the legal system of England and Wales.

SEPARATION OF POWERS

The preceding section of this chapter has accounted for the individual role of specific institutions and bodies within the legal system, with a focus on those responsible for law-making and the administration of justice. There is a risk that these institutions are viewed as wholly independent and separate, each providing their own piece of the puzzle that is the legal system. This approach may help develop *knowledge* but will do little to aid your *understanding* of the system. The truth of the matter is that the legal system is infinitely more complex, with

30 And in recent times, much more frequently!

31 See Chapter 6 ('Statutory Interpretation') and Chapter 9 ('Precedent').

32 See Chapters 10, 11 and 13 on civil, criminal and administrative justice, respectively.

33 See Chapter 8 ('The Court Structure') and Chapter 14 ('Dispute Resolution').

34 See Chapter 7 ('The Judiciary') and Chapter 12 ('The Jury').

the institutions interacting and colliding as they go about their functions and exercise their powers.

To manage conflict and to understand properly the interactions, one must turn to fundamental constitutional principles. Of most immediate relevance is the separation of powers, as it is this principle that seeks to manage and regulate the distribution of state powers.

> MAKING CONNECTIONS – THE INSTITUTIONS AND PUBLIC LAW
>
> The doctrine of separation of powers touches upon one of the core substantive subjects covered in most studies of law – public law, which is sometimes also characterised as 'constitutional law'. The discussion of separation of powers here is relatively brief and is intended to aid your understanding of the mechanics of the legal system, rather than an in-depth exploration of the theoretical structures of the state.[35]
>
> Any extended study of the law and legal system will involve considering the constitutional principles that govern the distribution and control of powers between the different organs of the state. Some of those principles are discussed here and in other chapters, but it may be that you return to them to consider them in greater detail at a later point in your studies, or you may analyse them from a more theoretical standpoint. In addition to the separation of powers (discussed here), the **rule of law** and **parliamentary sovereignty**[36] define the character of the British constitution and, thereby, the legal system.

Under the (sometimes) flexible doctrine of separation of powers, the power of the state is dispersed over many institutions and actors. This splitting, or separation, of powers is achieved in order to ensure that power is used legitimately, that it is not concentrated in too few institutions and that there are adequate checks and balances in place to prevent abuse. In recent history,[37] the institutions of the state have been categorised using the labels described earlier in this chapter – *legislature*, *executive* and *judiciary*. The separation of powers goes further than merely *describing* those institutions but takes the analysis one step further by considering how those institutions interact and how they provide checks and balances to one another.

Whilst the categories or labels in Figure 3.1 earlier are important, they only tell part of the story and are descriptive in nature. What is perhaps more important is the way in which the separation operates in practice. For this reason, there are also different *models* of how separation of powers can operate within a legal or political system. Some of these models are based

35 For such an examination, see Michael Doherty, *Public Law* (3rd edn, Routledge 2022).

36 Discussed in Chapter 4.

37 John Baker, *An Introduction to English Legal History* (5th edn, OUP 2019).

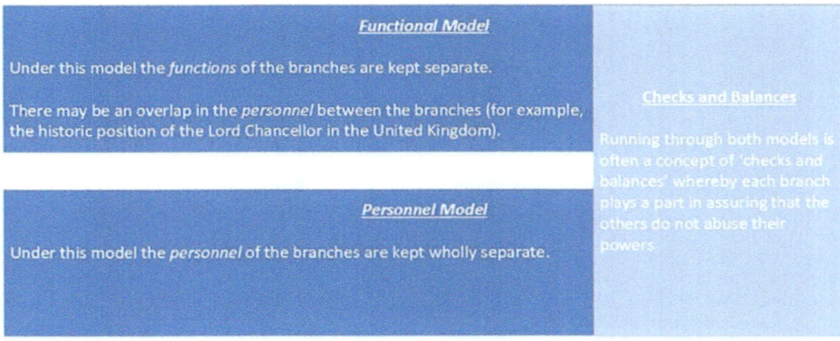

Figure 3.2 The models of separation of powers.

on the principle of non-interference in the work of the other branches, whilst others focus on each branch providing a 'check' on the other branches. Figure 3.2 shows the two major models.

As one example, the Constitution of the United States of America takes a particularly strict and formal approach to separation of powers in the American legal system, with the functions of the legislature (Congress – Article I), the executive (President[38] – Article II) and the judiciary (the Supreme Court and inferior courts – Article III) clearly codified and defined and assigned to particular personnel. As we shall see shortly, and by contrast, the legal system of England and Wales takes a more mixed and dynamic approach.

SEPARATION OF POWERS WITHIN THE LEGAL SYSTEM OF ENGLAND AND WALES

The legal system of England and Wales exhibits the features of both models and adopts a mixed approach to the question of separation of powers. Rather than adopting a very fixed and rigid approach, the legal system accommodates or tolerates overlaps of functions or personnel between the branches but prevents abuse of power through the utilisation of 'checks and balances'. Figure 3.3 demonstrates how some of the remaining (and historic) overlaps operate and how the 'checks and balances' seek to militate against abuse.

The checks and balances, or so the argument goes, allow the legal system to operate efficiently and flexibly, but in such a way that does not lead to concentrations or abuses of power. It also means that, whilst the system is working, overlaps between functions or personnel are not deemed to be problematic.

The more flexible and evolutionary approach to separation of powers means that the institutional structure of the legal system is able to adapt and change over time. This is not to say that there are not watershed and more substantial changes that shift the balance of the legal system towards more or less formal forms of separation of powers. For example, the

38 And administration.

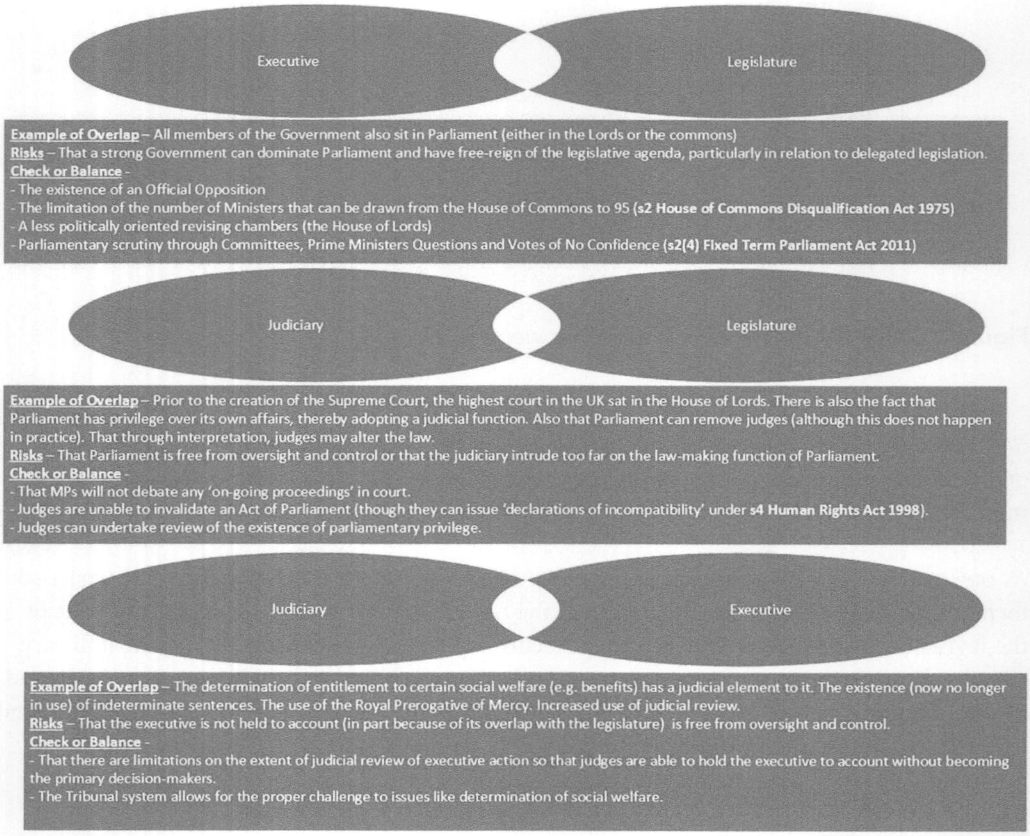

Figure 3.3 Managing the overlaps between the branches of state.

Judicial Committee of the House of Lords operated for many years from within Parliament despite it being the highest court of England and Wales and despite the fact that its judges were also members of the House of Lords. The constitutional objection to the situating of judicial function within Parliament was addressed by the creation of the Supreme Court in 2009, which further separated the personnel and structures of the judiciary and the legislature.[39] There is an argument that the move to a wholly separate building with a new name has emboldened the court to take a more interventionist approach to protecting separation of powers (as in the *Miller* and *Unison*[40] judgments).

Even with rules outlining the relationship between the constituent parts of the legal system and proper checks and balances, the evolutionary and sometimes informal nature of the legal system can often lead to 'gaps' in the system of accountability, which is at the heart of the doctrine of separation of powers. A good example of tensions that can emerge from an informal separation of powers can be seen through the increasing use of judges as Chairs of public inquiries.

39 Constitutional Reform Act 2005 s23.

40 *R (Unison) v Lord Chancellor* [2017] UKSC 51, [2017] 3 WLR 409.

ANALYSING THE LAW – JUDGES AS LEADERS OF INQUIRY

Public inquiries can be used in several circumstances[41] but are often used following on from major scandals or public disasters. Such inquiries[42] can make recommendations for changes to the law.[43] The government can propose[44] *judges* to lead such inquiries. The benefits of judges leading inquiries are apparent:

- They often have expertise in the subject matter of the inquiry.
- They have authority and credibility with the public, and so the outcomes of the inquiry are more likely to be viewed as being 'acceptable'.
- They have experience of dealing with complex and emotive factual situations.
- They are used to questioning witnesses.

They have an ability to foresee some of the practical consequences of any recommendations of changes to the law.

When acting as Chairs of such inquiries, the judges are not acting in their normal judicial capacity in the sense of overseeing a trial in a typically adversarial process. However, the increasing trend of appointing judges to lead inquiries also brings particular challenges that demonstrate the problems of blurring the distinction between personnel and functions of the executive and the judiciary:

- The *political* and very public nature of some inquiries can cause a blurring in the mind of the public of the judicial function (which is concerned with questions of law and not questions of politics). This can be seen in the high levels of scrutiny faced by Lord Justice Leveson during his leadership of the inquiry into press standards.
- Linked to the preceding point, there is a risk that inquiries bring to light tensions between members of the government and the judiciary. Again, the Leveson Inquiry provides useful evidence of this with the then Education Secretary Michael Gove being openly critical of the direction of the inquiry with an equally robust response from Lord Justice Leveson.[45] Although judges are not acting in a judicial capacity when leading inquiries, it would be naïve to assume that those witnessing these public tensions can draw that distinction, and these outbursts on both sides risk the reputation of the independence of the judiciary.

The fact that the formal recommendations may be adopted and become law brings the judge closer to becoming a law-maker.[46]

41 Inquiries Act 2005 s1.
42 These inquiries form part of the administrative justice system, discussed in greater detail in Chapter 13.
43 As happened with the reform of police screening checks following the Bichard Inquiry into the Soham murders.
44 On consultation with other senior members of the judiciary as specified in s10 Inquiries Act 2005.
45 Who made the rather pointed comment to the Education Secretary: 'I don't need to be told about the importance of free speech, I really don't.' The transcript may be found at the National Archives, <www.discovery.nationalarchives.gov.uk/>.
46 This statement is made with the full recognition that any recommendations would still need to be formally adopted into law.

In closing, it is worth noting that the constitutional principle of separation of powers has a demonstrable impact on the shape and powers of the institutions of the legal system of England and Wales. This, in turn, affects the *operation* of the legal system and the *outputs* of the law-making process. For this reason, as you continue to read this textbook, reflect on how the institutional *shape* and the relationship between the different institutions impact on the effectiveness of the legal system as a whole.

THE WEBSITE

The website that accompanies this textbook contains many useful resources that you can use to consolidate and further your knowledge of the law, to hone your skills of critical analysis and to test your knowledge. This includes a set of multiple-choice questions (MCQs) that can be used to test your knowledge and understanding of the material.

4

4

CHAPTER 4
LAW-MAKING IN ENGLAND AND WALES I – PRIMARY LEGISLATION

INTRODUCTION

Under an orthodox examination of the hierarchy of norms, primary legislation sits at the apex of a complex pyramid of legal sources (as discussed in Chapter 2). Original sovereignty lies with Parliament, and Acts of Parliament have paramount importance within the legal system. Such Acts of Parliament are collectively referred to as 'legislation', or 'statutes'. An understanding of how such primary legislation is made (i.e. how the original sovereignty is *executed*) is, therefore, fundamental to any study of the legal system and, indeed, the study of substantive legal subjects.

This chapter explores the nature of primary legislation (i.e. Acts of Parliament or statutes) and of how such legislation is passed. The text that follows will examine the different types of Acts of Parliament, the detailed process by which a policy idea becomes a law and the roles of the various institutions in the law-making process.

The very fabric of the legal system of England and Wales is an interwoven blend of law and politics – a fact often forgotten by those lawyers who concentrate heavily on the common law. This multidisciplinary understanding of law is nowhere more apparent than in the law-making process. Acts of Parliament are not made in a legal vacuum, and politics (and economics) influence not only the process of law-making but also the outcomes of that process. The consequence of such a relationship, and what it means for the nature and character of law, is an important theme that runs through the analysis of this chapter. Students of law often struggle with marrying law and other disciplines, but noting the links between different disciplines can help you understand the material better.

AS YOU READ

Much of this chapter is concerned with the classification of Acts of Parliament and with giving detailed information on the process by which policy is 'concretised' into law. It is important that, as you read, **you do more than just memorise** this information. By the end of this chapter, you should be able to **identify different types of Acts of Parliament** and discuss what impact the origin of a bill may have on the application of the law.

In considering the legislative process, you should **think critically about the nature of the law-making process** and be able to **evaluate the relationship between legal and political**

DOI: 10.4324/9781032641829-4

considerations. A much-needed skill for any student of law is the ability to draw out themes that cross different areas of study. As you read the distinct sections, attempt to **synthesise the information so as to explore the theme of** *democratic input* into the legislative process.

PARLIAMENTARY SOVEREIGNTY

Central to an understanding of law-making within the legal system of England and Wales is the doctrine of parliamentary sovereignty. This is a principle that holds that Parliament is the supreme legislative body of the legal system and that no person or body can challenge the law that Parliament passes.[1]

> MAKING CONNECTIONS – PUBLIC LAW
>
> As well as being an important feature of the legal system of England and Wales, parliamentary sovereignty is also a fundamental *constitutional* principle for the United Kingdom. If you are studying, or will study, constitutional, EU or public law, then you will undoubtedly return to the principle of parliamentary sovereignty and consider it in more detail than space here allows.
>
> There are many debates about the continued importance of the doctrine and particularly whether it was weakened by the UK's membership of the European Union.[2] The website that accompanies this textbook contains a short podcast that further explores the relationship between the domestic and international legal orders, with a specific focus on parliamentary sovereignty.

In practical terms, and in relation to this chapter, the importance of parliamentary sovereignty lies in the fact that primary legislation (Acts of Parliament) has a special status. Acts of Parliament are a manifest expression of Parliament's sovereignty, and so all other forms of law – such as secondary law or case law (both discussed in subsequent chapters) – must not violate, and cannot overturn, primary legislation. This is a marked difference to other legal systems, such as that of the United States of America, where the American Supreme Court has the power to 'strike down' primary legislation that violates the Constitution. No such power has (yet) been expressly[3] recognised by the English and Welsh legal system. Understanding the

1 This principle has long been recognised in the case law – *Madzimbamuto v Lardner-Burke* [1969] 1 AC 645 (HL) 723 (Lord Reid); *R (Jackson) v Attorney General* [2005] UKHL 56, [2006] 1 AC 262 [102] (Lord Steyn).

2 For a flavour of the debate, see Nicholas Barber, 'The Afterlife of Parliamentary Sovereignty' (2011) 9(1) IJCL 144; Mark Elliott, 'Parliamentary Sovereignty Under Pressure' (2004) 2(3) IJCL 545.

3 Some *obiter* (non-binding) comments by the House of Lords in *Jackson* have suggested that under certain circumstances the courts may dispense with the doctrine of parliamentary sovereignty – *R (Jackson) v Attorney General* [2005] UKHL 56, [2006] 1 AC 262 [102] (Lord Steyn).

nature, function and process for passing primary law is therefore of paramount importance to understanding other parts of the system and is a lens through which the other chapters of the textbook could be viewed.

PRIMARY LEGISLATION – CLASSIFICATION

Flowing from the idea of parliamentary sovereignty is the principle that Parliament may legislate on any matter it wishes.[4] It achieves this legislative function through primary legislation. While going through the law-making process, pieces of intended primary legislation are initially referred to as 'bills', and once the legislative process is complete, they are then called 'Acts of Parliament'. These Acts of Parliament make up the statutory law of the legal system. Although primary legislation consists mainly of Acts of Parliament,[5] there are different ways in which we could categorise those acts. The following section (and Figure 4.1) seeks to expand upon and explain those categories.

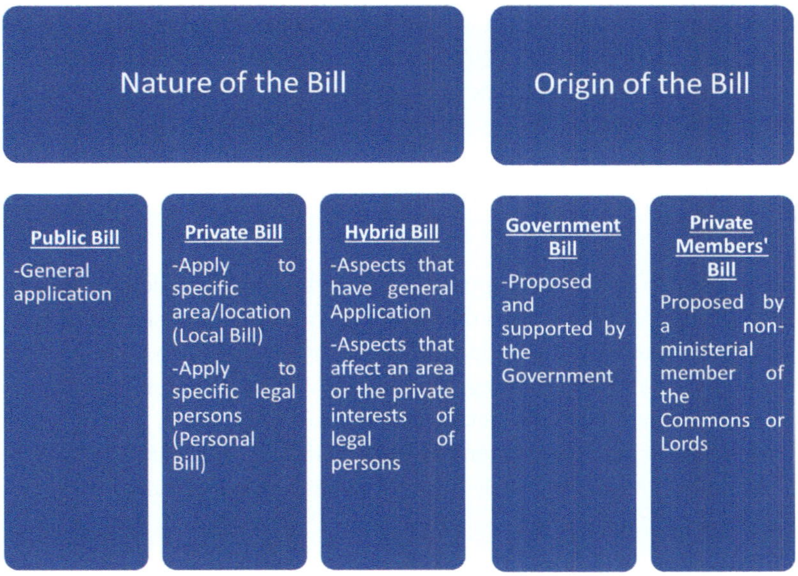

Figure 4.1 Classification of bills.

4 See, for example, the case of *Cheney v Conn* [1968] 1 WLR 242 (Ch) for authority that Parliament's law is the highest form of authority in the British constitutional legal order.

5 Technically, Orders in Council, made by the king, that have no statutory basis are also a form of primary legislation. Orders in Council (both those with and those without statutory basis) are discussed in the next chapter, on secondary legislation.

The categories 'nature of the bill' and 'origin of the bill' are not mutually exclusive, and a bill will be a combination of the two categories (for example, a government public bill or a hybrid private members' bill).

'NATURE OF THE BILL' CLASSIFICATION

Under this system of classification, there are public bills, private bills and hybrid bills, and they are differentiated by either their geographical scope of application or as to the effect that they have on the whole population or a specified group of natural or legal persons.[6]

PUBLIC BILLS

Public bills have general application in the UK or for one or more of the constituent countries.[7] Public bills are the most common type of bill. This has not always been the case; in the 17th and early 18th centuries, during the Industrial Revolution, in order to allow for the development of infrastructure, and later, as Parliament had a role in granting divorces, private bills greatly outnumbered public bills.

Between the 2010–2012 and 2017–2019[8] parliamentary sessions, there were some 311 public bills that became Acts of Parliament, usually introduced into the House of Commons by the government. In parliamentary sessions 2019–2021 and 2021–2022, there were a further 98 bills that gained Royal Assent and became Acts of Parliament. Most lately, in the parliamentary session of 2022–2023, a total of 67 bills gained Royal Assent, and in the session that has most recently ended (2023–2024), there were only 23 bills that received Royal Assent.[9] Parliament itself publishes interesting data on the progress of bills in a given parliamentary session.[10]

If passed through the legislative system, public bills become public general acts.

PRIVATE BILLS

These are bills that are not of general application but which apply to defined geographical regions or locations (local bills) or specific groupings of people (private bills). Due to their potentially oppressive nature on individual private interests, these private bills are subject to additional requirements in order to safeguard individual rights. The full legislative procedure for public bills is discussed in greater detail later, and this section only highlights some deviation from that normal process when passing private bills. The parliamentary process is much less flexible for private bills, partly in order to ensure legal certainty for those individuals affected.

6 A 'legal person' being a company or organisation that has legal personality – Northern Counties Securities Ltd v Jackson & Steeple Ltd [1974] 1 WLR 1133 (Ch).

7 England, Wales, Scotland and Northern Ireland.

8 The 2017–2019 parliamentary session was the longest since the Civil War and was brought to an end in October 2019 to allow for a new legislative agenda to be put forward in a Queen's Speech.

9 These numbers speak to the rate of Royal Assent but say nothing about the importance or scale of the law they contain.

10 <https://www.parliament.uk/business/publications/commons/sessional-returns/>

One additional hurdle for private bills is the requirement that those promoting the bill must publish in national newspapers the fact that the bill has been brought forward.[11] Those who oppose the bill can then, within restrictive time frames, petition Parliament to prevent the measure from proceeding. If members of either House then register their opposition to the bill in the second reading, it is referred to an 'Opposed Bill Committee'. An Opposed Bill Committee must determine, after listening to evidence in the manner of a court, whether the *need* for a bill has been established. If it has, then it proceeds to the next stage of the legislative process, but if the need has not been proved, then the bill will be lost.[12] An example of this can be found in the Highgate Cemetery Bill introduced in 2020–2021 and which passed through an Opposed Bill Committee and became an Act in 2022. No such 'necessity' test is required for public bills.

Private bills are now typically supported/proposed by public authorities (such as Local Councils) in order to extend or augment their existing public law powers. For example, the Hertfordshire County Council (Filming on Highways) Act 2014 empowers the named Council to restrict the use of the public highway or permit film-makers to place objects on the highway for the purpose of making a film. Similarly, the Humber Bridge Act 2013 allows the operators of the Humber Bridge to charge tolls for use of the bridge. Private bills can also be used to grant additional (or amended) powers to individual companies or associations, such as the Monken Hadley Common Act 2022 or the City of London Corporation (Open Spaces) Act 2018.

HYBRID BILLS

These bills have a mixed function in that they are of general application (like public bills) but affect specific people or organisations (like private bills) in a way that is different to other people generally affected by the bill. National infrastructure projects that have a specific impact on a local area would be likely to require a hybrid bill. For example, the High Speed 2 rail project to connect London and Birmingham required such a hybrid bill – the High Speed Rail (London – West Midlands) Act 2017, as did the High Speed Rail (West Midlands – Crewe) Act 2021. Other examples include the Cardiff Bay Barrage Act 1993 and the Channel Tunnel Rail Link Act 1996.

The procedure for the introduction of a hybrid bill is a modified version of that required for a public bill – the full procedure for public bills is discussed in a later section. For example, a hybrid bill does not require those supporting the bill (normally the government) to demonstrate that the bill is necessary – as is required for private bills – but it does give those interested an opportunity to have their views heard by a Select Committee before the bill is referred to the relevant Public Bill Committee. The Select Committee can suggest amendments aimed at compensating those affected by the bill.

Hybrid bills are used infrequently, with fewer than 30 being introduced since 1990, and only one has received Royal Assent since 2021. At the time of writing, the Holocaust Memorial

11 Richard Kelly, 'Private Bills in Parliament: House of Commons Background Paper' (Standard Note, SN/PC/06508, 2014) 3.
12 ibid 6–7.

Bill is awaiting consideration of amendments from the Lords as part of the 2024–2025 parliamentary session.[13]

APPLYING THE LAW – HYBRID BILLS

The passage of the (unsuccessful) House of Lords Reform Bill in 2012 further clarifies the restricted nature and narrow scope of hybrid bills. During the passage of the bill, Jacob Rees-Mogg (MP) raised the question as to whether it was a hybrid bill as it affected a certain category of bishops within the Church of England and their ability to sit in the reformed House of Lords. In rejecting that view, the Speaker of the House stated:

> [A] Hybrid Bill is a Public Bill that affects a particular private interest in a manner different from the private interest of other persons or bodies of the same category or class. The key phrase here is 'private interest'. The only interest of bishops affected by the Bill is that of being part of the legislature. That is a public interest, not a private one. Accordingly, no question of hybridity arises.[14]

Thus, only bills that affect private interests and not public offices will be considered as hybrid.

'ORIGIN OF THE BILL' CLASSIFICATION

Alternatively, it is possible to classify bills according to who proposes the bill. In this regard, there are two major forms of a bill, discussed next. They are government bills and private members' bills.

GOVERNMENT BILLS

These are, as the name suggests, proposed and supported by the government. Although not as numerous as private members' bills, they have a much greater chance of success. Government bills go through the full legislative procedure, discussed later in this chapter.

Table 4.1 examines the prevalence and success rates of government bills over the past 20 years, split at five yearly intervals.[15]

13 Having been introduced as long ago as the 2022–2023 session!

14 HC Deb 9 July 2012, vol 548, col 23.

15 The table to 1997–1998 is based on data from the Department of Information Services, 'Summary of Public Bills Introduced Since 1983–84' (Standard Note, SN/PC/02283, 2013) 2, and the table from then until 2016–2017 is based on data from House of Commons Library, 'Number of Public Bills Introduced and Gaining Royal Assent Since 1997' (Briefing Paper, 2017). Subsequent data is gathered directly from the session reports of the House of Commons.

Table 4.1 Success rate for government bills

Parliamentary sessions	*Number of government bills introduced*	*Number of government bills completing legislative process*
1983–1984 to 1987–1988	254	247
1988–1989 to 1992–1993	216	205
1993–1994 to 1997–1998	196	194
1998–1999 to 2002–2003	172	159
2003–2004 to 2007–2008	192	166
2008–2009 to 2012–2013	131	116
2013–2014 to 2016–2017	110	98
2017–2019 to 2019–2021[16]	104	95

Table 4.1 demonstrates two trends that should be borne in mind when considering government bills. Firstly, that the number of such bills has declined since the 1980s. This should not be seen as the government doing 'less', as the overall length of Acts of Parliament has grown dramatically in the last century. In 1950, for example, there were 720 pages of primary legislation spread over 50 general acts, whereas in 2007, there were 3,186 pages of primary legislation spread over only 31 public acts.[17] This has implications for the effectiveness of scrutiny, as the amount of parliamentary time to consider these matters has not dramatically increased. It also obviously has an impact on comprehension, since the complexity of modern legislation and the system of amendment of earlier acts affected by later legislative provisions mean that an entire, lengthy, statute often needs to be read as a whole, including the consequential amendments of other acts, before its ultimate effect can be understood.

Secondly, the vast majority of government legislation that is proposed as a bill will become law. It may, as is discussed later, be amended, but fundamentally, the legal system is structured in such a way that the government is able to pass the bills that it wishes to pass. This raises

16 It has not been possible to disaggregate progress of Government Bills from other types of Bills for later parliamentary sessions.

17 Based on the data from Richard Cracknell, 'Acts and Statutory Instruments: The Volume of UK Legislation 1950–2014' (Standard Note, SN/SG/2911, 2014) 4–7.

questions about the ability of Parliament to keep an adequate check on what the government is doing and to give full scrutiny to the laws that are put before it. This is partly a consequence of the tendency of the electoral system of the United Kingdom to return strong majority governments. The government is then able to use its majority to force measures through Parliament.

PRIVATE MEMBERS' BILLS

These are to be distinguished from private bills, discussed earlier. Private members' bills are those introduced by members of the House of Commons or Lords but are not supported by the government. They are likely to be public bills. Very many such bills get proposed every year – more in number than government bills. Table 4.2 indicates the number of private bills introduced since the 1980s and their rate of success.[18]

Table 4.2 The success of private members' bills

Parliamentary sessions	*Number of private members' bills introduced*	*Number of private members' bills completing legislative process*
1983–1984 to 1987–1988	531	83
1988–1989 to 1992–1993	615	69
1993–1994 to 1997–1998	550	82
1998–1999 to 2002–2003	487	35
2003–2004 to 2007–2008	470	15
2008–2009 to 2012–2013	560	28
2013–2014 to 2016–2017	520	29
2017–2019 to 2019–2021[19]	509	21

18 The table to 1997–1998 is based on data from the Department of Information Services, 'Summary of Public Bills Introduced Since 1983–84' (Standard Note, SN/PC/02283, 2013) 2, and the table from then until 2016–2017 is based on data from House of Commons Library, 'Number of Public Bills Introduced and Gaining Royal Assent Since 1997' (Briefing Paper, 2017). Subsequent data is gathered directly from the session reports of the House of Commons.

19 It has not been possible to disaggregate private members' bills from other types of bills for more recent parliamentary sessions.

If we compare Table 4.2 to Table 4.1 for government bills, then we can note two important differences. Firstly, two to three times the number of private members' bills are introduced in each time period when compared to the number of government bills. Secondly, the success rate for private members' bills is significantly less than that of government bills. It could be argued that this reduces the effectiveness and diversity of legislation and further illustrates the government's dominance of Parliament's agenda.

The very limited success of private members' bills is principally owing to the fact that the government controls the parliamentary timetable, and there is very limited opportunity for private members' bills to be allocated sufficient time to progress through the system. Under parliamentary procedure, for 13 Fridays, private members' bills are timetabled in preference to government bills, thus allowing guaranteed time for a wider range of legislation to be discussed.

Private members' bills can be introduced to the House of Commons in the following ways:

1. *By ballot.* In every parliamentary session, 20 names are drawn from all those MPs who have an interest in bringing forward a private members' bill.[20] Those members are given priority in presenting their bill and can have them allocated to the Fridays discussed earlier that are set aside for private members' bills, and therefore, they have much greater prospect of success.
2. *By virtue of the 'ten-minute' rule.* A member may, on specified days, attempt to gain permission to present a bill.[21] The member has ten minutes (hence the name) in which to make a speech recommending the bill to the House.
3. *By presentation.* Any MP can propose a bill to be considered and choose a day for second reading.[22] As the government controls the parliamentary timetable, these bills rarely progress through the legislative process.

Most private members' bills are proposed in the full knowledge that they are unlikely to become law. This is partly because the government often does not assign adequate time for a bill to proceed or because they can be quite easily defeated. The Voyeurism (Offences) Bill 2017–2019 was defeated on presentation at second reading by a single shout of 'object' when the bill was brought before Parliament and its title read.[23] The purpose of the Bill was to make 'up skirting' a particular criminal offence.

Due to the rarity of success, they are often proposed as a way of raising awareness on a particular issue and allowing for debate that may spark public interest and convince the government to take up a bill. The Assisted Dying Bill 2014–2015, presented by Lord Falconer, is an excellent example of a bill that is intended to provoke debate, particularly

20 Standing Order 14(9).

21 Standing Order 23.

22 Standing Order 57.

23 The Conservative MP Sir Christopher Chope, who objected, has stated that he did so on the basis of the procedure used and not the substantive merits of the Bill.

when considering the reference that was made to that Bill in the Supreme Court's judgment in *Nicklinson*.[24] In *Nicklinson*, the Supreme Court strongly suggested that Parliament consider again the issue of assisted suicide in order to ensure the UK's continued compliance with the European Convention on Human Rights.[25] Further bills on assisted dying have been introduced to subsequent sessions of Parliament, for example, the Assisted Dying Bill 2021–2022, sponsored by Baroness Meacher. Ten years after Lord Falconer's attempt, Kim Leadbeater has taken up the cause with the Terminally Ill Adults (End of Life) Bill in the 2024–2026 session.

Despite how rarely they are passed, some extremely important Acts of Parliament – including those deemed by the government to be too controversial to be promoted – began their lives as private members' bills. Perhaps the clearest example of this is the bill that became the Abortion Act 1967, which was introduced by David Steel, MP, and sought to allow for lawful abortions where they were carried out by registered medical practitioners.

Equally, the government may sometimes pick up legislation that has failed to make it through as a private members' bill and seek to include it in its own legislative programme, particularly where there is strong public support. The Voyeurism (Offences) Bill 2017–2019, mentioned earlier, is a good example of this, where Theresa May's government took the failed private members' bill and legislated on the issue by passing the Voyeurism (Offences) Act 2019.

INFLUENCES ON LAW-MAKING

To consider only the official stages of the legislative process can give a distorted understanding of the purpose of that legislation – a theme more closely examined in Chapter 6, on statutory interpretation. Bills do not appear from the ether, fully formed and devoid of historical and political context. In order to gain a better understanding of the formal law-making process, it is important to understand the institutions, events and principles that can lead to legislative proposals long before they are formalised into a draft bill to be presented to Parliament.

The list of influences (Figure 4.2), discussed next, should not be viewed as either exhaustive or as acting fully independently of the others in the list. It is often a combination of these factors working in tandem (and others) that eventually leads to a piece of legislation being brought forward.

MANIFESTO PLEDGES

Before a General Election, each political party will produce a manifesto.[26] The manifesto will detail the principles and policies that the party will seek to achieve or implement

24 *R (Nicklinson) v Ministry of Justice* [2014] UKSC 38, [2014] 3 WLR 200 [166].

25 ibid [300]–[301] (Lady Hale), who went even further and would have granted a declaration of incompatibility, which would have put additional pressure on Parliament to review the issue.

26 An unofficial collection of all party manifestos can be found at the following link: <www.politicsresources.net/area/uk/man.htm>.

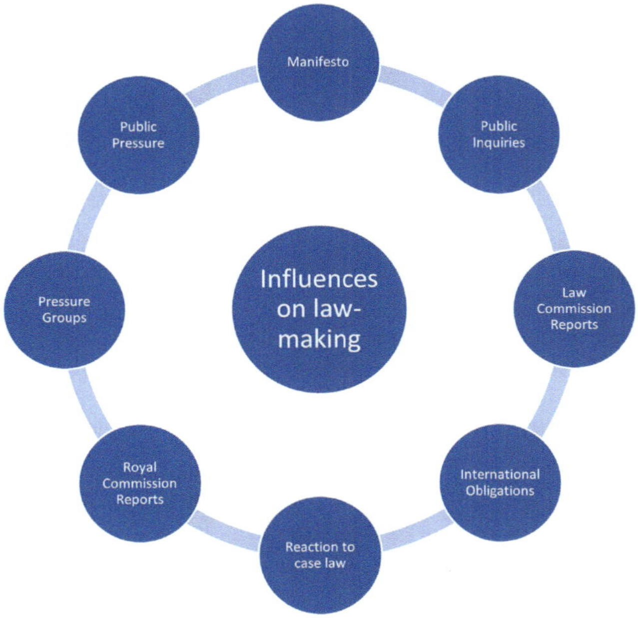

Figure 4.2 Influences on law-making.

should they be returned to government. Manifestos can be high-level political statements, such as Robert Peel's Tamworth Manifesto[27] of 1834, which sought to change the direction and philosophy of the Tory Party and which is seen as the starting point of the modern Conservative Party. From the principles of modern conservatism in the Tamworth Manifesto flowed support for particular pieces of legislation that would have previously been unpalatable to a Tory leader.[28] Peel spoke in terms of principle in his manifesto, but those principles could be seen to influence later law-making, such as support for the passage of the Municipal Corporations Act 1835.

Equally, manifestos can contain precise and specific promises to enact specific types of legislation. As a result, and from the late 19th and throughout the 20th centuries, the promises contained within a party manifesto began to form the core of the legislative programme that the government would adopt during their time in office. A clear example of this is the Human Rights Act 1998.

27 This was not a manifesto in the modern sense of the word. It was, as was the practice of that time, an address to Peel's own constituency but that was reproduced in the popular press. Nonetheless, it went further than previous examples and is one of the earliest illustrations of a party political statement of aims if returned to government.

28 See, for example, the Municipal Corporations Act 1835.

EXPLAINING THE LAW – 'BRINGING RIGHTS HOME'

When seeking election in 1997, the Labour Party placed a strong emphasis on civil liberties and human rights protection within their manifesto. The manifesto stated thus:

> Citizens should have statutory rights to enforce their human rights in the UK courts. We will by statute incorporate the European Convention on Human Rights into UK law to bring these rights home and allow our people access to them in their national courts.[29]

Shortly after Tony Blair came to power, his Labour government passed the Human Rights Act 1998 in order to make good on his manifesto promise to incorporate the European Convention on Human Rights (ECHR) into law of England and Wales.

A manifesto adds democratic legitimacy to the laws brought forward by the government as the proposals are seen to have the consent or approval of the populace. Obviously, the extent to which the voting public read or understand party manifestos is debatable, as is the implication that a person voting for a particular party agrees to every item in a manifesto. Recent research on the European level suggests that policy documents, such as a manifesto, do not have a significant impact on voter behaviour.[30] Nonetheless, a manifesto does provide a link between the wishes of the electorate and the legislation that is eventually passed through Parliament.

It is important to note that a manifesto is in no way legally binding and has only political force within the legal system. However, that political force should not be underestimated. In 2010, the UK returned a hung Parliament – the first since the 1970s – with no political party gaining an overall majority. This situation led to the forming of a coalition government between the Conservative Party and the Liberal Democrats. As neither party was returned with a majority, their ability and willingness to abide by their original (very different) manifestos were a constant source of political tension.

ANALYSING THE LAW – THE POLITICAL FORCE OF MANIFESTOS

Perhaps the most striking recent examples of the political force of manifestos come from the legislative programme of the coalition government. The Liberal Democrats' 2010 manifesto contained the following promise: 'We will scrap unfair university tuition fees so everyone has the chance to get a degree, regardless of their parents' income.'[31] As they did not gain an overall majority to form a government, they entered into a coalition with the Conservatives.

29 Labour Party Manifesto 1997. Can be accessed at <www.labour-party.org.uk/manifestos/1997/1997-labour-manifesto.shtml>.

30 James Adams, Lawrence Ezrow and Zeynep Somer-Topcu, 'Is Anybody Listening? Evidence that Voters Do Not Respond to European Parties' Policy Statements During Elections' (2011) 55(2) AJPS 370, 375.

31 Liberal Democrat Manifesto 2010, 33.

The coalition agreement anticipated changes arising out of Lord Browne's Review into the funding of Higher Education.[32] Eventually, the coalition announced a policy that ran counter to the Liberal Democrats' manifesto promise in that it *increased* the cap on tuition fees. This caused a great deal of controversy both within the party[33] and within the constituencies that had elected Liberal Democrat MPs. While 29 Liberal Democrat MPs either voted against the government's policy or abstained, 27 Liberal Democrat MPs voted for the plan.[34]

Governments legislating for important matters *not* contained within their manifesto can be equally controversial. Another example from the 2010 elections serves to illustrate the point. The coalition government introduced the Marriage (Same Sex Couples) Bill into Parliament in January 2013. The Bill, now Act, sought to extend the institution of marriage to people of the same sex. Such a piece of legislation was not anticipated by the Conservative's 2010 manifesto and provoked a great deal of debate within the Conservative Party (and within their supporters in the wider public). As the Bill progressed through the legislative procedure, more than 30 references were made, by MPs and Lords who opposed the Bill, to the fact that the Bill was not included in the manifesto and that the changes proposed to the institution of marriage were of such importance that a clear democratic mandate should be required.[35]

David Cameron's manifesto pledge to deliver an EU referendum following the 2015 General Election is another example of the political force of referendum commitments. Putting into action the decision to rescind its membership of the European Union remained a key priority of Theresa May's Conservative manifesto in 2017 and Boris Johnson's in 2019.

ROYAL COMMISSION REPORTS

Royal Commissions are set up by the government on an ad hoc basis, and their purpose is to review an area of law and, where appropriate, make recommendations for improvements and reform.[36] Such Commissions are normally constituted of those with a specific interest or specific expertise in the area under review. Although created by the government, they are non-

32 Lord Browne, 'Securing a Sustainable Future for Higher Education' (12 October 2010).

33 Given that all Liberal Democrat MPs had signed a pledge with National Union of Students to vote against tuition fee increases.

34 This included key members of the leadership, including Nick Clegg and Vince Cable.

35 On Second Reading in the Commons: HC Deb 5 February 2013, vol 558, cols 130, 157, 158, 165, 173, 174, 181, 182, 184, 188, 190, 200, 216, 227.

On Third Reading in the Commons: HC Deb 21 May 2013, vol 563, cols 1162 and 1169.

On Second Reading in the House of Lords: HL Deb 3 June 2013, vol 745, cols 945, 965, 984, 993, 1004, 1013, 1017, 1019, 1025, 1091, 1091, 1094, 1097, 1107.

HOL (745, 10) 3 June 2013 cols 945, 965, 984, 985, 993, 1004, 1013, 1017, 1019, 1025, 1091, 1094, 1097, 1107.

36 C.f. Some Royal Commissions, including, for example, those on the preservation of historical manuscripts, have taken on a quasi-permanent existence.

political and are to be independent of government control. The government may then adopt the recommendations of the Commission through the passage of Acts of Parliament.

The effectiveness[37] of a Royal Commission is in part determined by the political will to adopt its recommendations. This is sometimes hampered by the delay of up to four years between the establishment of the Commission and its report being published. Such a delay will mean that, often, a Royal Commission that is set up by one government could end up reporting to a different government if there has been a General Election in the intervening period. In light of the work of the Law Commission and the increased availability of public inquiries, the use of Royal Commissions has become less common than it once was. However, there are still occasional *calls* (even if these are not heeded) for Royal Commissions to be established. For example, Nick Clegg, during his time as Deputy Prime Minister, called for a Royal Commission to be established into the possibility of reforming Britain's drug laws.[38] The position of Royal Commissions seems, therefore, to be residual, as it falls in the space created between the work of inquiries (which often deal with scandals and reviews sparked by specific incidents) and matters related purely to law reform (even if they have a social dimension), which are within the purview of the Law Commission.

There have been no new Royal Commissions since the Blair government of the 1990s, which established the Royal Commission on the Reform of the House of Lords in 1999 and which reported in 2000.[39]

PUBLIC INQUIRIES

There are a range of different types of inquiry that may be established within the legal system of England and Wales.[40] However, it is statutory inquiries set up in response to scandals or catastrophic events that most frequently form an influence on future law-making. Such inquiries have seen an increase since the establishment of the Inquiries Act 2005, which created a statutory framework for the establishment of such inquiries by Ministers.[41] Figure 4.3 gives an indication of the structure of the Inquiries Act 2005 and some indication of the powers under it. It is unlikely that you will need to know the detail of the Inquiries Act 2005, but the diagram is intended to give some indication of the layout of an Act of Parliament that contributes to the generation of ideas for reform.

Public inquiries can be an excellent conduit for law reform and act as an increasingly important influence on law-making. However, their purpose is not solely (or even, in some cases, primarily) to propose changes to the law. Inquiries are set up primarily as fact-finding exercises but can make recommendations for changes to the law.

37 If effectiveness is measured by recommendations becoming law.

38 <www.bbc.co.uk/news/uk-20722527>.

39 <https://www.gov.uk/government/publications/a-house-for-the-future-royal-commission-on-the-reform-of-the-house-of-lords>.

40 Land inquiries and other statutory schemes of inquiry.

41 Prior to this, and in accordance with the Tribunals of Inquiry (Evidence) Act 1921, major inquiries had been established via a resolution in both Houses of Parliament.

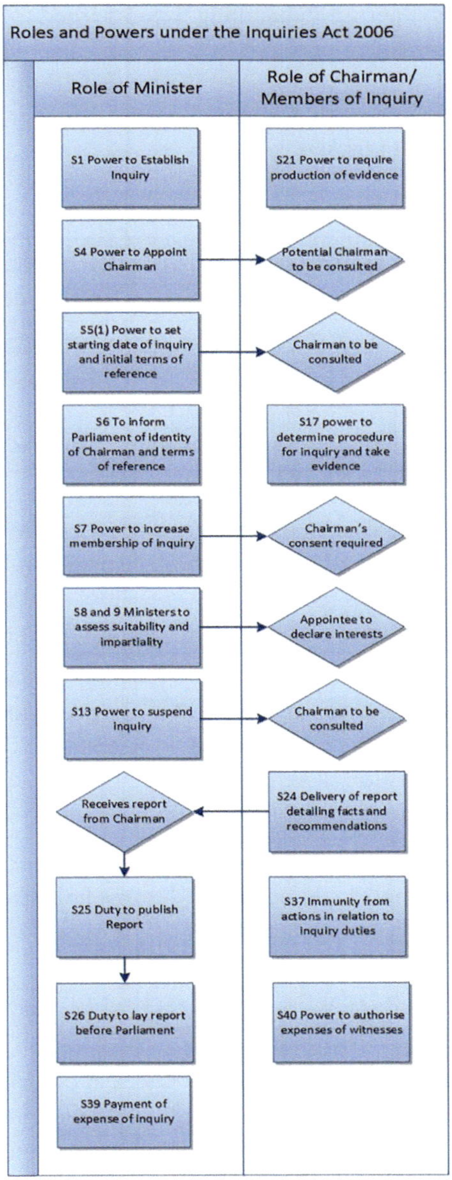

Figure 4.3 Structure of the Inquiries Act 2005.

In the years leading up to and following on from the Inquiries Act 2005, there has been an increased reliance on public inquiries, particularly those chaired by senior members of the judiciary,[42] as a method of reviewing the effectiveness of public bodies and as a response to public scandals. Judges are often appointed to lead inquiries because of their experience of

42 The power to appoint a judge can be found in Inquiries Act 2005 s10.

dealing with evidence, their expertise in handling witnesses and their ability to foresee the consequences of their recommendations.

Recent examples of public inquiries, their reason for establishment and the impact of their recommendations are detailed in Table 4.3.

Table 4.3 Recent public inquiries

Chairman[43]	*Event leading to establishment of inquiry*	*Recommendations and influences on changes in the law*
Michael Bichard	Questions over child protection following on from murder of two schoolgirls by Ian Huntley	Criminal Records Bureau checks for those working with children
Lord Laming	Questions over the failings of social services and other agencies after the death of Victoria Climbié	Changes to child protection processes in the Children Act 2004, including the establishment of a (now defunct) national database for agencies to share information
Lord Laming Dame Janet Smith	Questions over the effectiveness of checks on doctors following the conviction of serial killer Harold Shipman	Recommended changes to the supervision of doctors and their ability to access and administer certain drugs
Sir William Macpherson	Murder of black teenager Stephen Lawrence in a racially motivated attack	Changes to police practice in light of finding that the Metropolitan Police Service was institutionally racist
Robert Francis	High mortality rates at Stafford Hospital and concerns about patient care	Some 290 recommendations; some, such as the limitation on the use of 'gagging clauses' in employment law, have been implemented by changes in the law
Lord Scarman	The Brixton Riots	Radical changes to police procedure and a new code of police behaviour introduced in the form of the Police and Criminal Evidence Act 1984

43 The word 'chairman' is used as it is the language used in the legislation.

Lord Justice Leveson	The News International phone hacking scandal	Recommended additional regulation of the press; partly implemented under a new statutory framework
Sir Martin Moore-Bick	Events that led to a fire that killed a number of people within Grenfell Tower in London	Phase 1 recommendations including further training of fire services on combustible materials and the placing of particular duties on owners of high-rise buildings Phase 2 recommendations focussed on the important role of local authorities in preventing such disasters, with 58 recommendations
Sir Wyn Williams	The miscarriages of justice that led to the imprisonment of postmasters due to a failure of technology	First volume urging swift action around compensation; final recommendations not complete at the time of writing
Baroness Hallett	To examine the UK's response to the Covid-19 pandemic	First recommendations relating to the government's preparedness for a Covid-like national emergency, including the establishment of a whole-system civil service committee and regular pandemic response exercises to test readiness

The report of an inquiry may make recommendations that find their way into law. This is not to say that *all* inquiries will make recommendations for changes to primary law. Moreover, not all recommendations will be taken up by the government, particularly given that many will report to a subsequent government rather than the one that established it. Inquiries are often perceived to be 'a lightning conductor for the anger of the public',[44] and this can affect their effectiveness if they are set up (and report) in haste. One of the clearest examples of an emotive public inquiry leading to questionable use of law is the Bichard Inquiry into the Soham murders.

44 Lord Butler, 'Despite the Doubts over Leveson and the Mid-Staffs Report, Public Inquiries Still Play a Vital Role' *The Guardian* (London, 26 March 2013), www.theguardian.com/commentisfree/2013/mar/26/public-inquiries-vital-healing-holding-account.

ANALYSING THE LAW – THE BICHARD INQUIRY

The majority of recommendations proposed by public inquiries help improve the legal system and substantive law. However, sometimes they have unintended consequences, as illustrated by the Bichard Inquiry into the so-called Soham murders.

While working as a caretaker in a secondary school, Ian Huntley murdered Holly Wells and Jessica Chapman. A public inquiry was launched in 2004 to investigate the events that led to the death of the two girls and Huntley's ability to gain employment in a school despite having previous allegations of sexual conduct with underage girls.

The Bichard Inquiry that followed suggested changes to the system of criminal records checks in order to safeguard against those with certain criminal offences (or allegations of criminal offences) working with children. The recommendations of the inquiry led to the proliferation in the use of an enhanced Criminal Records Bureau check for those working with, or unsupervised around, children. It also led to police forces improving their record-keeping in order to furnish bodies with criminal records disclosures.

In the aftermath of the inquiry, and its report, the use of enhanced criminal records checks increased dramatically, and many offences (and warnings) of dubious relevance and those committed when the offender was very young were kept on file and disclosed to potential employers. This eventually led to the Supreme Court, in *R(T)*[45] in 2014, ruling that the lack of safeguards in the system and its disproportionate[46] impact breached T's human rights and so supported the Court of Appeal's declaration of incompatibility of the legislation with rights contained in the European Convention on Human Rights.[47] The declaration of incompatibility prompted the government[48] to scrap the CRB system and replace it with a less restrictive system of checks operated by the Disclosure and Barring Service.

In this instance, the inquiry raised the profile of a problem beyond that which was necessary and did little to help achieve a balanced and appropriate solution to the problem. Indeed, the clamour for justice and 'lessons to be learned' in light of the Soham murders contributed significantly to the overburdening of the CRB system and to the breaches of individuals' right to a private life under the European Convention on Human Rights.

45 *R(T) v Greater Manchester Police* [2014] UKSC 35, [2014] 3 WLR 96.

46 ibid [121] (Lord Reed).

47 A power under the Human Rights Act 1998 s4.

48 Perhaps hastily in not awaiting the judgment of the Supreme Court – a point recognised by the Supreme Court: ibid [3] (Lord Wilson).

LAW COMMISSION REPORTS[49]

The Law Commission is an independent body established by the Law Commissions Act 1965 'for the purpose of promoting the reform of the law'.[50] Unlike Royal Commissions, the Law Commission is a permanent body dedicated to law reform which, in limited circumstances, can investigate areas of its own motion and not just at the request of the government. Regardless of the source of the initiative for a review of an area of law, all proposed works need to be approved by the Lord Chancellor.[51] The Commissioners, of which there are four, and a Chairman are appointed by the Lord Chancellor but are independent of government control. Nonetheless, there is a strong working relationship between the Commission and the government.

The function of the Law Commission is to

> keep under review all the law with which they are respectively concerned with a view to its systematic development and reform, including in particular the codification of such law, the elimination of anomalies, the repeal of obsolete and unnecessary enactments, the reduction of the number of separate enactments and generally the simplification and modernisation of the law.[52]

The preceding extract demonstrates that one of the *statutory* functions of the Law Commission is to seek to be an influence for changes in the law.

The Law Commission has a rolling programme of projects, and most recently, the 13th programme of reform was launched in December 2017. The 13th programme is looking, amongst others, at the following issues:[53]

- Burial of the dead
- Automated vehicles
- Electronic signatures
- Modernising of trusts law
- Museum collections
- Residential leaseholds
- Smart contracts
- The immigration rules
- Surrogacy

49 <https://www.lawcom.gov.uk/.>

50 Law Commissions Act 1965 s1.

51 Government Ministers may refer matters to the Commission, but the Commission is under no obligation to take forward projects on this basis.

52 Law Commissions Act 1965 s3(1).

53 Details of all projects within the 13th programme can be found here: <https://webarchive.nationalarchives.gov.uk/ukgwa/20240605042804/https://lawcom.gov.uk/document/programmes-of-law-reform/>.

As can be seen from the preceding list, the work of the Commission is varied. In 2023, the Chair of the Law Commission announced a delay to agreeing and publishing the 14th programme of work. This means that the Commission, for the time being, will be focussing on existing projects from the 13th programme and other work referred to them by Ministers. At the time of writing, there had been no further update.

TAKING THINGS FURTHER – INVESTIGATING LAW REFORM

The programme of reform instigated by the Law Commission is constantly evolving, and projects are often at very different stages. Investigating the status of ongoing projects can be very useful as it provides you with insights into the perceived problems of the law as it currently stands and some indication of possible solutions identified by the Commission. It can also be interesting to reflect on those proposals that have not been taken forward into legislative change.

A great deal of information about the present and past work of the Commission can be found on their website – www.lawcom.gov.uk.

As a result, these areas are likely to influence law-making in the near future, not least because before undertaking a review, the Law Commission must seek from the government, through the Lord Chancellor, an undertaking 'that there is a serious intention to take forward law reform in this area'.[54] In an effort to improve the implementation of Law Commission proposals and to bring about greater transparency in government responses, the Law Commission Act 2009 also requires the Lord Chancellor to report to Parliament the status of Commission proposals.[55]

A number of important Acts of Parliament have followed Law Commission recommendations, including the Criminal Attempts Act 1981, the Family Law Act 1986, the Landlord and Tenant Act 1988 and the Fraud Act 2006, all of which made significant changes to the law in relation to areas of concern identified by the Commission. The most recent completed programme (the 12th) provided the basis for the Digital Economy Act 2017 and Intellectual Property (Unjustified Threats) Act 2017.[56] Equally, big changes were brought about to the system of dispute resolution by the Arbitration Act 2025, which came from a review by the Law Commission of the Arbitration Act 1996. The Automated Vehicles Act 2024 created a framework for the safe implementation of use of self-driving cars and demonstrates the legal system wrestling with new technological advancements.[57]

54 Law Commission, *Protocol Between the Lord Chancellor (on Behalf of the Government) and the Law Commission* (Law Comm No 321, 2010) para 6.

55 Law Commission Act 2009 s1 inserting a new section, s3A, into the Law Commission Act 1965.

56 Law Commission, *Annual Report 2018–19* (Law Comm No 274, 2019).

57 As noted in the Law Commission, *Annual Report 2024–5* (Law Comm No 418, 2025).

INTERNATIONAL LAW OBLIGATIONS

As a dualist state, the United Kingdom must incorporate its international law obligations (most frequently found in international treaties) into domestic law through either primary or secondary legislation. This is to be contrasted with monist states (such as France and Germany), where international obligations become law at the moment that the international treaty is ratified. The dualist nature of the UK means that international law obligations can have a strong influence on law-making within the legal system. There will continue to be an influence over law-making from the EU even though the UK has rescinded its membership.

Although a great deal of legislation that is inspired by the international legal order is of EU origin, this is not always the case. The Berne Convention of 1886 prompted changes to the intellectual property law of the UK, and its provisions were incorporated partly by the International Copyright Act 1886. International influences on the process of law-making in England and Wales are ongoing, and subsequent amendments of the Berne Convention have led to further changes to UK law via Acts of Parliament. For example, when the Convention was revised in 1908, some of these changes were realised by the Copyright Act 1911.

TAKING THINGS FURTHER – THE COMPANION WEBSITE

The website that accompanies this textbook further explores the influence that international courts can have on the legal system. There is a podcast examining the judgment of the Court of Justice of the European Union on the validity of the European Data Retention Directive. This Directive was ruled to violate fundamental rights, and as a consequence, the UK government hastily[58] passed the Data Retention and Investigatory Powers Act 2014 to deal with the vacuum created. The podcast describes these developments and also analyses the way in which the DRIP Act 2014 was passed.

PRESSURE GROUPS

Pressure groups can be an important, if sometimes controversial, influence on the law-making process. Pressure groups seek to campaign on set issues or to protect certain groups of people or specific interests. As such, they normally focus on a single policy or set of contexts on which they campaign for law reform.

Some examples of successful campaigns led by pressure groups are included in Table 4.4.

Caution should be exercised when attempting to measure the impact of pressure groups on law-making as it is often a combination of factors that eventually leads to changes in the law. It would be unusual for a government, when proposing a new public bill, to indicate that a

58 In the words of Lord Phillips of Sudbury: 'this measure has been rushed, helter-skelter, through both Houses. It is fair to say that the vast majority of Members in both Houses are deeply worried by all that but have none the less accepted the view of the Government as to the need for that expedition.' HL Deb 17 July 2014, vol 755, col 722.

Table 4.4 Successful pressure group campaigns

Organisation	*Nature of campaign*	*Outcome*
Stonewall	Lowering the age of consent for sexual intercourse between homosexual men so that it matched that for heterosexual sexual intercourse	Partial victory in 1994 with a reduction in the age of consent from 21 to 18
Disablement Income Group (and others)	Equal rights for those with disabilities in relation to access to employment and the provision of services	Enactment of the Disability Discrimination Act 1995, which prevented discrimination on the basis of disability and required employers and service providers to make reasonable adjustment to accommodate those with disabilities
Pro-Life Alliance	Sought repeal of the Abortion Act 1967	Failed to secure repeal of the Abortion Act but was an instrumental pressure in having the latest date reduced from 28 to 24 weeks

pressure group was responsible for the introduction of the legislation. It would not normally be sensible for the government to recognise external bodies as having determinative influence over law-making. Moreover, pressure groups often have persistent and permanent campaigns that stretch for many years, and thus, tracing their direct influence on government policy can be difficult. Nonetheless, their influence is important, can be controversial and should not be overlooked.[59]

PUBLIC PRESSURE

Although closely linked to the concept of pressure groups, there can be more generalised public pressure that leads to changes in the law. This tends to come about due to events that lead to media attention.

For example, following a number of high-profile cases where young children were mauled by dogs, there was a great clamour in the popular press for greater controls over what came

59 Riccardo de Caria, 'The Constitutional Right to Lobby on the Two Sides of the Atlantic: Between Freedom and Democracy' (2013) 2 CJICL 452, 455.

to be known as 'dangerous dogs'. The outcome of that media pressure was the passing of the Dangerous Dogs Act 1991. The Act categorises certain 'types' of dog and cross-breeds of those types as needing special control.

ANALYSING THE LAW – THE DANGEROUS DOGS ACT 1991

Much like public inquiries, considered earlier, a major problem of this type of pressure is that it can lead to hasty and ill-considered legislation. Again, the Dangerous Dogs Act 1991 is a prime example of the criticisms that can be levelled at public pressure gaining too much influence in the law-making process.

The Dangerous Dogs Act 1991 had an expedited journey through Parliament. It was not put out for public consultation. The Bill passed through all stages of the Commons within 24 hours, with the debates programmed to continue until 4:00 a.m. to ensure that it could be debated in the Lords and passed before the parliamentary session ended.

In practice, the Dangerous Dogs Act 1991 has been heavily criticised, and much of the criticism could have been resolved had the Bill been properly scrutinised and more carefully considered. For example, choosing to ban 'types' rather than 'breeds' has led to great confusion. The intention was to allow judgments to be made by courts based on physical characteristics of the dog. In hindsight, the quality and effectiveness of the Act is to be questioned. There are now more pit bulls in the UK than before the passage of the Act, and by concentrating so heavily on types, the Act is not sufficiently focussed on the behaviour of owners. It also required, at that time, a mandatory destruction order issued by a Magistrate, allowing the courts very little discretion in assessing the subjective danger that a particular dog creates.

One member of the House of Lords has deemed it 'the most outrageous law ever passed in Parliament. It is probably worse in some respects even than the suppressive tendencies of war-time legislation and the Defence of the Realm Act (regardless of national security)'.[60] Although this comment was couched in rather strong language, the dangers of hastily passed legislation should not be ignored.

Public policy issues also tend to re-occur over time, particularly if legislation is poorly drafted and struggles to address fundamental issues in a way that can develop over time. In the early 2020s, a new breed of dog, the XL bully type, was involved in several mauling incidents, including those where the victim died from their injuries. Following a period of public outrage, the breed was added to the list of dangerous dog breed types covered by the Act in 2023.[61]

60 HL Deb 20 January 1993, vol 541, col 933.

61 The Dangerous Dogs (Designated Types) (England and Wales) Order 2023 SI 2023/1164 s2.

In spite of the preceding, public pressure can lead to positive changes in the law and act as an important conduit for democratic input into the law-making process. There is now a formally recognised mechanism for such public influence through the government's e-petition website.[62] When a petition gains 10,000 signatures, the government department responsible for the policy area will give a response. Should the petition receive 100,000 signatures, then it is passed to the Backbench Business Committee, who consider whether to table the issue for debate in the House of Commons.

LEGISLATIVE PROCESS

The following section will explore the law-making process (Figure 4.4) from the pre-legislative process that leads to a particular piece of legislation, through the specific procedures through which primary legislation is required to pass and finally deal with scrutiny of an Act after it has been brought into force.

PRE-LEGISLATIVE PROCESS

This term is most commonly used to refer to the stages that a government bill will go through before being presented to Parliament. Not all bills, or even all government bills, will go through all the procedures discussed in the following sections. The order in which the stages happen (particularly in relation to drafting and the Speech from the Throne – known as the King's Speech) can also vary.

CONSULTATION: GREEN AND WHITE PAPERS

A government will sometimes put out ideas for legislation to public consultation. This takes place via Green and White Papers, named for the colour of paper on which they were traditionally printed. The former set out broad proposals on potential legislation and ask for

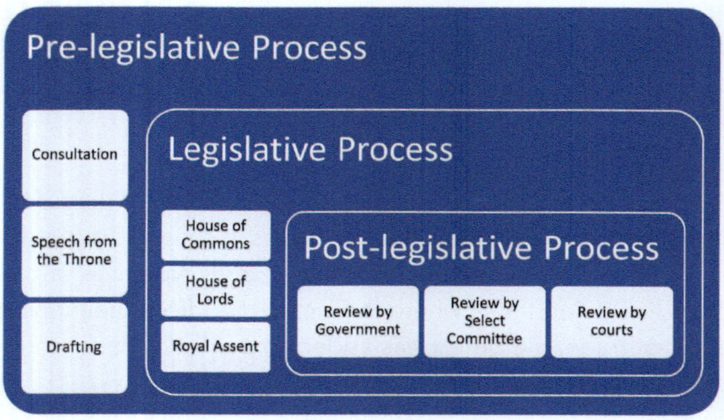

Figure 4.4 The legislative process.

62 <https://petition.parliament.uk/>.

comments and feedback. They are often discursive and explore the context which has led to the government considering legislation and lay down various options for resolving the issues.

The latter, on the other hand, give much firmer details of the direction that the government would like to take on a particular policy, but they are still consultation documents. As such, Green Papers are not definitive statements of policy but are rather invitations for final comment before the government decides to bring forward (or not bring forward) primary legislation.

SPEECH FROM THE THRONE – THE KING'S SPEECH

The State Opening of Parliament is an important ceremonial event within the legal system of England and Wales. It happens in the House of Lords and signifies the beginning of a new session of Parliament. Since the passing of the Fixed-Term Parliament Act 2011 and its coming into force in 2012, it was intended to become normal practice for the State Opening to happen in late spring/early summer as opposed to later in the autumn or early winter. However, as is often the case, the 'law in the books' does not represent practice on the ground. The coming to power of Boris Johnson led to a Queen's Speech being held in the autumn of 2019, and the Fixed-Term Parliament Act itself was repealed in 2022.

As part of the State Opening of Parliament, the Monarch gives a Speech from the Throne, more commonly known as the 'King's Speech'. This Speech explains the bills that the government intends to bring forward in that parliamentary session. The legislative programme is not designed by the King personally but is drawn up by a Cabinet Committee called the Legislation Committee. Given government control of the parliamentary timetable, these bills are likely to take up a significant period of parliamentary time in the session. The Speech is then debated in both the Commons and the Lords.

DRAFTING

Bills may be, and increasingly are, published in draft form as part of public consultation. Government bills are drafted by specialist lawyers within the Office of the Parliamentary Counsel. They must take the specific policy ideas of the various government departments and formalise them into the bill that will be introduced to Parliament. There has been much pressure in recent years to decrease the overly legalistic language used in Acts of Parliament, and it is the task of Parliamentary Counsel to ensure that acts are legally effective but also accessible to, and understandable by, the public.[63]

MAKING CONNECTIONS – STATUTORY INTERPRETATION

The difficulties caused by poor drafting are considered in Chapter 6, on statutory interpretation, but it is worth reinforcing the fact that the task facing those drafting public bills is formidable. They must find a form of words that is broad enough to cover every situation envisioned by the policymaker (including, where appropriate, future scenarios that may arise due to technological advances), but not so broad as to inadvertently extend the Act beyond its intended purpose.

63 <www.gov.uk/government/collections/good-law>. See also Peter Butt, *Modern Legal Drafting: A Guide to Using Clearer Language* (3rd edn, CUP 2013) Ch 6 and 7.

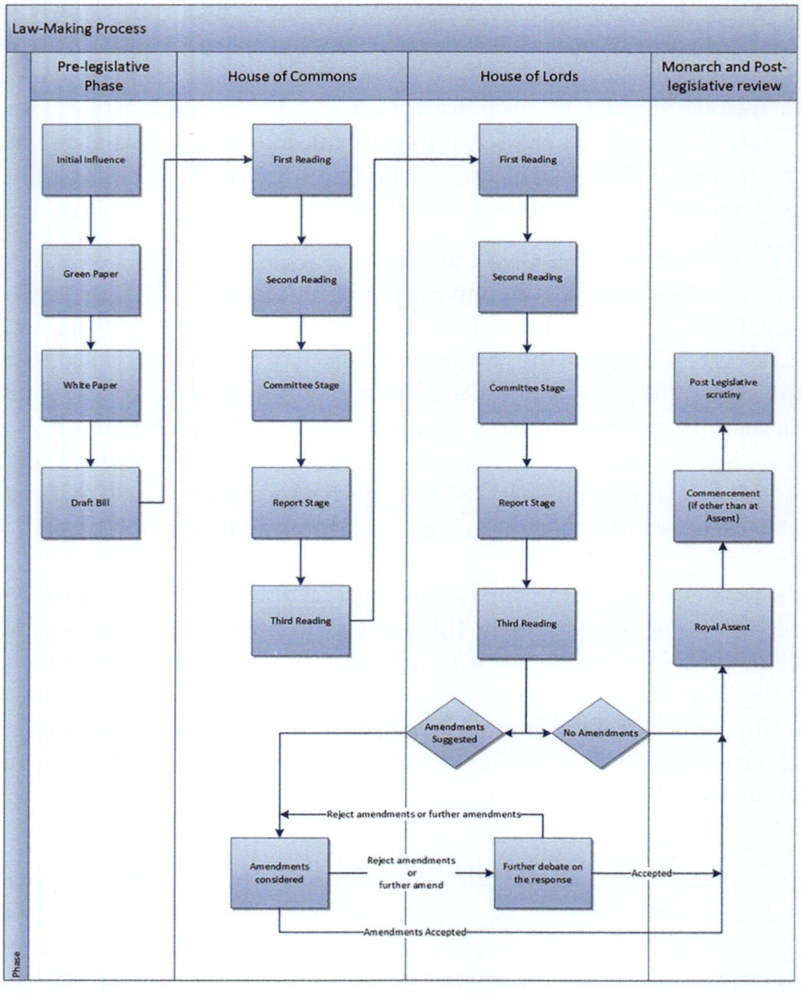

Figure 4.5 The law-making process – primary legislation.

PASSAGE THROUGH PARLIAMENT – THE LEGISLATIVE PROCESS

Most bills may begin their lives in either the Commons or Lords but must[64] receive support from both Houses before being sent on to the Monarch for Royal Assent. Money bills will begin their life in the Commons, and by convention, matters governing the judicial system or bills seeking to implement Law Commission recommendations will start their life in the Lords. Otherwise, bills may start their progress through Parliament in either House.

Figure 4.5 gives a visual representation of the major stages in the law-making process both in the Commons and in the Lords for a public bill. These are then explored more fully later, so

64 Subject to the limitations of the Parliament Acts 1911 and 1949, discussed later.

referring back to Figure 4.5 will help the reader track the process in a more fluid manner. The diagram assumes that a bill has started in the House of Commons.

STATEMENT OF COMPATIBILITY

Since the Human Rights Act 1998 came into force in 2000, all government bills are subject to a so-called statement of compatibility. Under s19 of the Human Rights Act 1998, the Minister responsible for a particular bill must, before the second reading,

> make a statement to the effect that in his view the provisions of the Bill are compatible with the Convention rights ('a statement of compatibility'); or
>
> make a statement to the effect that although he is unable to make a statement of compatibility the government nevertheless wishes the House to proceed with the Bill.

It was very rare for a bill not to receive a statement of compatibility. This is largely because a government Minister will not wish to state openly that an Act may be incompatible with the European Convention on Human Rights. One example of a bill that did not receive such a statement was the failed House of Lords Reform Bill introduced by the then Deputy Prime Minister Nick Clegg in 2012. The bill proposed large-scale changes to the composition of the House of Lords, including the introduction of elected members. The Deputy Prime Minister explained that he was unable to give a statement of compatibility because the proposed system of electing members of the Lords would exclude prisoners,[65] and this was in contravention of the *Hirst*[66] judgment of the European Court of Human Rights.[67]

More recently, in 2023, the then Home Secretary Suella Braverman did not make a statement of compatibility for the Illegal Migration Act 2023. The Act was a deeply controversial Act of Parliament that is intended to control the stem of migration to the UK, particularly by those migrants entering the UK illegally by small boats. The failure to be able to provide a statement of compatibility significantly raised the profile of the Bill and was a source of debate throughout its passage,[68] even involving an MP requesting a point of order before the Home Secretary had risen to introduce the Bill.[69]

HOUSE OF COMMONS – FIRST READING

The first reading stage is the formal introduction of the bill to the House. It is presented to the House by the Clerk, who reads out the short title of the bill. The bill will then be ordered to be printed, alongside the explanatory notes for a government bill, and a date will be set for second reading.

---

65 House of Lords Reform Bill 2012–2013 clause 6 citing the Representation of the People Acts 1983 and 1985.

66 *Hirst v United Kingdom (No 2)* [2005] ECHR 681.

67 <www.publications.parliament.uk/pa/bills/cbill/2012-2013/0052/en/13052en.htm> paras [248]–[249].

68 At pretty much every stage of its progress, the absence of a statement was noted and debated: HC Deb 27 March 2023, vol 730, col 769 at Committee Stage; HC Deb 26 April 2023, vol 731, col 784 at Report Stage; HL Deb 10 May 2023, vol 829, col 1800 at Second Reading; HL Deb 24 May 2023, vol 830, col 877 at Committee Stage; HL Deb 28 June 2023, vol 831, col 703 at Report Stage.

69 HC Deb 13 March 2023, vol 729, col 573.

HOUSE OF COMMONS – PUBLIC READING

Between the publication of a bill and its committee stage, it was once possible that the government or the House of Commons put the bill out for 'public reading'. This involved public consultation on the bill, the outcome of which is communicated to the relevant committee.

Pilot public readings were given to four bills in the 2010–2012 and 2012–2013 sessions:

- Small Charitable Donations Bill 2012–2013 (government pilot)
- Children and Families Bill 2012–2013 (House of Commons pilot)
- Protection of Freedoms Bill 2010–2012 (government pilot)
- Draft Care and Support Bill 2012 (government pilot)

ANALYSING THE LAW – PUBLIC READING STAGE PILOT

The results of the public reading stage pilots were mixed.

The Protection of Freedoms Bill received some 500 comments from 250 participants, but the collated responses were not made available to all Committee members in advance of the Committee commencing its scrutiny, thus hampering the utility of the comments.[70] In addition, the comments were not systematically referred to but were used to inform the approach taken by individual members of the Committee. It could be argued that such an approach risks ignoring comments that do not accord with a specific member of the Committee's view.

The Draft Care and Support Bill similarly received around 1,000 responses, and so public appetite for comment is strong in some areas. This is enhancing the public's engagement with the legislative process and should be encouraged. However, the Small Charitable Donations Bill received only 85 comments, many of which were from those who had already been involved with the Bill before this stage. In none of the preceding cases did the public reading comments lead directly to amendments being tabled.

As the Leader of the House of Commons noted in 2012, 'the pilot results indicate that approaches to consultation should be carefully tailored to the Bill'.[71] As a result of the mixed response to public readings, the government will not bring forward plans to extend the pilots to all public bills. The experimentation (even if it was not taken forward) demonstrates the flexibility and agility of the legal system to change.

70 Richard Kelly, 'Public Reading Stage of Bills' (Standard Note, SN/PC/06406, 2014) 7.

71 HC Deb 17 January 2013, vol 556, cols 44WS–45WS.

HOUSE OF COMMONS – SECOND READING

The second reading of a bill focusses on the principles underpinning the bill. For government bills, the Minister responsible for the proposal will give a statement to the House outlining the purpose of the bill.

> MAKING CONNECTIONS – THE WIDER USE OF THE MINISTERIAL STATEMENT
>
> The importance of the ministerial statement should not be understated. If the meaning of particular words in an Act of Parliament is unclear, then a court may rely on ministerial statements in interpreting those words. This is known as the rule in *Pepper v Hart*[72] and is discussed in greater detail in Chapter 6, on statutory interpretation.

The bill is then debated, and eventually, a vote on the Floor of the Chamber is held. Amendments that members (including the Minister responsible for the bill) will be likely to table in the committee stage can be considered and recommended for adoption at the committee stage, but the amendments themselves are not made during the second reading.[73] Those in support of the bill will be asked by the Speaker of the House to signify their approval for the bill to pass the second reading by calling 'aye', while those opposed to the bill will call 'no'. If there is a clear and definite majority for 'aye', then the bill is 'read a second time', and if there is a clear and definite majority for 'no', then the bill will fail to gain second reading. If there is any doubt, then a full division is declared, and members of the Commons will go through one of two lobbies[74] to signify whether they agree to the bill receiving its second reading.

It is rare for government bills to require a full division, and rarer still for such a bill to be defeated at second reading. Failure of a government bill to receive a second reading will normally be followed by the abandonment of the measure. This happened with the Shops Bill introduced by Margaret Thatcher in the 1980s, which sought to change the Sunday trading laws within the UK. Private members' bills more frequently fail to progress beyond second reading, particularly where they are, as a matter of principle, controversial, such as the Assisted Dying (No 2) Bill 2015.

HOUSE OF COMMONS – PROGRAMME MOTION AND ORDER

Immediately after the bill is read for a second time, a programme order will be passed, following a programme motion, and this will act as a timetable for the remainder of the bill's time in the Commons. It commits the bill to the relevant Public Bill Committee, sets a

72 *Pepper v Hart* [1993] AC 593 (HL).

73 For example, the Minister responsible for the Intellectual Property Bill 2014 made comments in the second reading about plans he had for making amendments to the bill at the committee stage. See HC Deb 20 January 2014, vol 574, col 40.

74 An MP can also register an abstaining vote by passing through both the aye and no lobby.

deadline for consideration by the Committee and makes arrangements for the third reading, which follows the committee stage. If a bill passes second reading, it is extremely unusual for a programme motion to be denied, not least because there is not normally a debate over the order.

As a programme order will set the amount of time that the bill will be debated, it is an important, if often overlooked,[75] part of the law-making process. For example, it was the prospect of failure to agree a programme order that finally forced the coalition government to withdraw the radical House of Lords Reform Bill in 2012.[76] The Bill would have paved the way for an elected House of Lords. It passed second reading with a strong 90+ majority, but the Labour Party withdrew its support due to the restricted time allowed for debate in the programme order.[77] With the prospect of defeat, through a combination of Conservative backbenchers and Labour Party MPs, the government withdrew the programme motion, thus suspending the progress of the Bill. The Bill was formally abandoned later in the year.[78]

The European Union (Withdrawal Agreement) Bill 2017–2019 also failed to secure a majority for its programme order and so fell at the dissolution of Parliament.

HOUSE OF COMMONS – COMMITTEE STAGE

It is at the committee stage that the most thorough scrutiny of the bill can take place. This happens on a clause-by-clause basis, enabling the detail of the bill to be fully explored. The committees that consider the bill can suggest amendments, and these can then be debated again by the whole of the Commons at the report stage. The following section explores the different committees that may be involved at the committee stage.

PUBLIC BILL COMMITTEE

The most common form of committee used is the Public Bill Committee.[79] These are ad hoc committees established specifically for considering a specific bill and are named after the bill (e.g. the Modern Slavery Bill 2014–2015 was committed to the Public Bill Committee on Modern Slavery).

The constitution of the Public Bill Committee will roughly reflect the composition of the House of Commons and will normally consist of a minimum of 16 members up to a maximum of around 50 MPs. Thus, the party of government who has the greatest number of seats in the House of Commons will also make up the majority of the Committee. The result of this is that many of the changes that are proposed in the Committee will be suggested by the government, and it is less likely that amendments that the government disapproves of will be approved by the Committee.

75 Few of the major textbooks on the English and Welsh legal system cover it at all.

76 HC Deb 3 September 2012, vol 549, cols 35–42.

77 Labour would have preferred unrestricted time to discuss the contents of the Bill.

78 HC Deb 3 September 2012, vol 549, col 35.

79 These, before 2006, were known as 'Standing Committees'.

Since the replacement of Standing Committees with Public Bill Committees in 2006, such committees can also take evidence from interested parties. This means that external organisations can contribute more directly to the passage of individual bills. For example, the Modern Slavery Bill heard evidence from the Director of Public Prosecutions, the Director of the National Crime Agency, barristers who specialise in human rights law and the head of the Bishops' Conference Office for Migration Policy.[80]

SELECT COMMITTEE

Certain bills can be committed to a Select Committee in place of a Public Bill Committee after second reading. The Select Committees are permanent bodies and are aligned to government departments. This practice has fallen into disuse, as Select Committees can now be involved earlier in the process before a bill is formally placed before Parliament. For example, the draft Consumer Rights Bill 2014–2015 was considered by the Business, Innovation and Skills Select Committee as part of pre-legislative scrutiny.[81] However, some bills involving the armed forces[82] are examined by a Select Committee as part of the full legislative process. The most recent Armed Forces Bill to be considered in this way is the Armed Forces Bill 2019–2021, 2021–2021, considered in Select Committee on 25 March 2021. It gained Royal Assent in December 2021. Occasionally, private bills do get referred to Select Committees, for example, the Malvern Hills Bill 2024–2026, which sought to create and confer powers on a trust to manage the Malvern Hills, is at the time of writing before a Select Committee.

COMMITTEE OF THE WHOLE HOUSE

It is also possible for the committee stage of the House of Commons, much as it does in the Lords, to be taken on the floor of the House. This is known as a Committee of the Whole House. This tends to be reserved for matters of great constitutional importance, such as the Constitutional Reform Act 2005.[83] Bills that seek to change the composition of Parliament will also be debated in this way. A recent example is the House of Lords (Hereditary Peers) Bill 2024–2026, which seeks to abolish the remaining hereditary peers in the House of Lords and was committed to a Committee of the Whole House whilst passing through the Commons.

Equally, those bills that are so uncontroversial that a Public Bill Committee would not be a beneficial use of parliamentary time can be considered by a Committee of the Whole House. Private members' bills often are heard in this way, as are private bills. All finance bills go to a Committee of the Whole House; see, for example, the Finance Act 2025.

In addition, if bills need to pass through Parliament very quickly, then it may be appropriate to have a Committee of the Whole House.[84] This was the case for the Data Retention and

80 <www.parliament.uk/business/news/2014/july/modern-slavery-bill-evidence-programme-announced>.

81 For example, <www.parliament.uk/business/committees/committees-a-z/commons-select/business-innovation-and-skills/inquiries/parliament-2010/gvt-draft-consumer-rights-bill> 20 August 2014.

82 Particularly the five yearly bill that allows Parliament to maintain a standing army and governs certain aspects of discipline of the armed forces.

83 And for example, the Human Rights Act 1998, the Fixed Terms Parliament Act 2011 and the European Union Act 2011.

84 For more examples, see Department of Information Services, 'Bills Whose Commons Committee Stage Has Been Taken in Committee of the Whole House' (Standard Note, SN/PC/05435, 2013) 2–5.

Investigatory Powers Act 2014, which was passed over a few days in response to a case from the European Court of Justice.[85] The Corona Virus Act 2020 was both constitutionally significant in the powers it granted to Ministers to limit freedom but also had to be passed with rapidity and so was committed to a Committee of the Whole House and passed the major stages of the Commons within 1 day.

On extremely rare occasions, it is possible for a bill to pass through a Committee of the Whole House before then being committed to a Public Bill Committee. This happened with the Human Fertilisation and Embryology Bill, which contained various controversial clauses (such as those on admixed embryos)[86] that required a full debate, as well as very technical clauses that would benefit from thorough scrutiny in a Public Bill Committee, where evidence can be gathered from experts.

HOUSE OF COMMONS – REPORT STAGE

After the Committee has concluded its work, the bill is returned to the Floor of the House, where there is further debate, and the bill may be amended again. If the committee stage has made amendments to the bill, then it is open for MPs at the report stage to suggest reversing these changes. The report stage is important as it is potentially the last opportunity for the Commons to make amendments to the bill.

HOUSE OF COMMONS – THIRD READING

Immediately following on from the report stage (often on the same day) is the third reading. In the Commons, amendments are not permitted at the third reading, but there is a final – normally short – debate on the merits of the bill. The debate is then followed by a vote on whether the bill should be permitted to proceed. Failure to secure a bill's third reading will normally mean that the bill will be lost.

HOUSE OF LORDS – PROCEDURE

If a bill begins in the Commons, then it follows an almost-identical procedure when it arrives in the House of Lords. The key differences in procedure are:

- The first reading of a bill in the House of Lords always passes without discussion.
- There is no programme motion, and the corresponding programme order, in the House of Lords, and so debates may last longer than in the Commons.
- By default, bills at the committee stage in the Lords are committed to the Whole House rather than in a Public Bill Committee. In the past, the House of Lords has occasionally committed to a Special Standing Committee[87] so that the House can receive specialist evidence from interested parties before the debate is re-committed to the Committee of the Whole House.[88]
- Unlike the position in the House of Commons, bills can be amended at the third reading stage in the Lords.

85 Joined Cases C-293/12 and C-594/12 *Digital Rights Ireland* [2014] ECR I-845.

86 Embryos of mixed human and animal DNA.

87 Now known as Special Public Bill Committee.

88 For example, the Inheritance and Trustees Powers Bill in 2013.

ANALYSING THE LAW – THE HOUSE OF LORDS

The lack of a programme motion and the convention of holding the Committee Stage on the Chamber Floor is not just a historical anomaly. These practices reconfirm the important constitutional function of the House of Lords as a revising chamber and a place where detailed debate can take place in a way that is not always possible in the Commons. Indeed, the important scrutiny function of the House of Lords is often highlighted when reform is discussed. While reform of the House of Lords is a constant discussion point, it is important not to forget the value of a revising chamber.

Additionally, there is a procedure, known as committing to 'Grand Committee', where the bill is taken out of the main chamber and discussed in a separate room. This is an option available only to bills in the Lords. This is ostensibly a time-saving measure but is technically still part of a Committee of the Whole House in that all members are able to attend should they wish, and for this reason, only a single bill per day can be considered in this way. The major difference between a bill in the grand chamber and those discussed in the main chamber is that amendments proposed in the Grand Committee must be adopted by unanimity.

AMENDMENTS

If no amendments are made by the second House that considers the bill, then it progresses to Royal Assent.

If amendments are made in the non-originating House, then they must be agreed by the House in which the bill originated. For example, a bill starting in the House of Commons that is subsequently amended in the Lords must be returned to the Commons for those (and other) amendments to be debated and agreed. If the amendments are accepted, the bill progresses to Royal Assent. If there continues to be disagreement between the two Houses, then the bill 'ping-pongs' back and forth until one of three situations occurs:

- The parliamentary session ends.
- There is 'double insistence' by which one House insists on disagreement with an amendment and the other House insists on its support for the amendment.[89] The last time this happened was for the European Parliamentary Elections Bil (1997–1998)
- The Houses come to an agreement.

The first two scenarios will normally result in the bill being lost, whilst the third option results in the bill being sent for Royal Assent.

ROYAL ASSENT

When a bill has completed its passage through the Houses of Parliament, it is sent for Royal Assent. Royal Assent is the (now largely symbolic) involvement of the sovereign within the

89 This is something of which the political parties are keenly aware and seek to avoid by strategically 'amending amendments'.

law-making process. The process of Royal Assent emphasises the historical importance of the Monarch as the source of law within the legal system of England and Wales. It is at the point of Royal Assent that a bill becomes an Act of Parliament.

Although it is with the giving of Royal Assent that a bill becomes an Act, the process has been little more than a ceremonial technicality for the past three centuries. By convention, the Monarch would only withhold the Royal Assent on the advice of the government,[90] and the last time that assent was refused was in 1708, when Queen Anne declined to give the Royal Assent to the Scottish Militia Bill.[91] It is to be remembered that even if it is a ceremonial technicality, a bill cannot come into force unless it has Royal Assent.

Traditionally, assent was given in person. The Monarch would take his or her place on the throne in the House of Lords and listen to the bills being read before assent was granted. This gave way, in the time of Henry VIII, to a new procedure of assent by commission by which members of the Privy Council gave assent personally on behalf of the Monarch. This was, in turn, largely replaced, by virtue of the Royal Assent Act 1967, by a procedure whereby the Monarch can give their assent in writing using letters patent.[92] This written form is now the way in which the vast majority of bills receive Royal Assent. Assent, under the written procedure, is said to have been granted when both Houses of Parliament have been informed by their respective presiding officers that assent has been received.

TAKING THINGS FURTHER – THE COMPANION WEBSITE

Acts of Parliament are structured in a fairly rigid manner. The website that accompanies this textbook contains a podcast with a fully annotated statute to allow you to see the various features of an Act of Parliament on a piece of legislation that is currently in force.

You can access Acts of Parliament at the following web address: www.legislation.gov.uk. You can also access bills currently before Parliament at Parliament's website: https://bills.parliament.uk/.

COMING INTO FORCE AND COMMENCEMENT

Before the end of the 18th century, an Act of Parliament would be deemed to come into force on the first day of the parliamentary session in which it was introduced. This would mean

90 There is even some doubt as to whether under convention the Monarch can *ever* withhold assent, regardless of the advice of her Ministers. See Nick Barber, 'Can Royal Assent Be Refused on the Advice of the Prime Minister?' (UK Constitutional Law Association, 25 September 2013) <http://ukconstitutionallaw.org/2013/09/25/nick-barber-can-royal-assent-be-refused-on-the-advice-of-the-prime-minster>, and this issue has arisen again in the Brexit context – Robert Craig, 'Could the Government Advise the Queen to Refuse Royal Assent to a Backbench Bill?' (UK Constitutional Law Association, 22 January 2019) <https://ukconstitutionallaw.org/2019/01/22/robert-craig-could-the-government-advise-the-queen-to-refuse-royal-assent-to-a-backbench-bill>.

91 A bill which sought to settle the Scottish army following on from the Acts of Union 1707.

92 Royal Assent Act 1967 s1.

that most legislation was introduced retrospectively and would be 'backdated' to the start of the session. This practice was increasingly seen as unfair[93] as it could mean laws having retrospective effect for nearly a year. As such, the Acts of Parliament (Commencement) Act 1793 changed the position so that the Clerk of the Parliaments[94] had to endorse an Act with the date that it received Royal Assent, and it was from this date that an Act would normally come into force.

This has the consequence that although a bill becomes an Act upon receiving Royal Assent, this does not mean that it necessarily comes into force immediately. The current position is to be found in the Interpretation Act 1978. Section 4 of the Act reads as follows:

> An Act or provision of an Act comes into force –
>
> a Where provision is made for it to come into force on a particular day, at the beginning of that day;
> b Where no provision is made for its coming into force, at the beginning of the day on which the Act receives Royal Assent.

There is therefore a continuum of commencement with acts that come into force at different times. Some acts come into force fully and immediately on receiving Royal Assent. Others come into force on a predetermined date. Others still will come into force on a date to be determined by some additional process, such as through the passage of an Order in Council or a vote in the Houses of Parliament. In the case of some statutes, for any enabling sections requiring preparations to be made before the bulk of the Act can come into force, only those enabling sections will come into force immediately, and the rest of the Act can be brought into force sequentially at a date, or dates, to be determined either at the time the Act is passed or later.

EXPLAINING THE LAW – THE IMPORTANCE OF COMMENCEMENT

An example of the importance of commencement can be demonstrated by reference to the Easter Act 1928. This Act was duly passed in the last century, but despite containing only two sections, it has not yet come into force almost 100 years later. Its intention was 'to regulate the date of Easter Day' to curtail the practice of having a floating date for Easter Sunday, which can currently fall on dates between late March and late April.[95]

93 It would now be regarded as a breach of the modern conception of the rule of law. See European Convention on Human Rights Article 7 and Tom Bingham, *Rule of Law* (Penguin 2011).

94 The Clerk is also responsible for the pronouncement of Royal Assent.

95 For example, in 2008, Easter fell on 23 March, whereas it will fall on 25 April in 2038.

Section 1 set the date for Easter as the first Sunday after the second Saturday in April. However, commencement was to happen via an Order in Council that was to be laid before the Houses of Parliament for approval. The requirements, including the 'regard' that is to be had to the view of any church, of commencement are found in Easter Act 1928 s2(2). Due to historic disagreement within established Christian churches as to the setting of a date for Easter, the necessary order has yet to be laid before Parliament.

Although you may question the importance of setting a date for Easter, it is an important example of the dangers of simply finding statutes on the internet and assuming that they are fully in force. You should always be aware as to whether the Act as a whole is in force.

Section 4 of the Interpretation Act 1978 also makes it clear that *individual provisions* of an Act can come into force at different times. The power to bring part of an Act into force is normally delegated to a Minister. This process is achieved through the passage of a commencement order, which is a form of secondary legislation (discussed further in the next chapter). This is an important, but sometimes confusing, feature of the legal system. The consequence is that those involved in the application of the Act in question – including the legal professions – must be aware which parts of an Act are in force at any one time, as well as if the act as a whole is in force at all.

POST-LEGISLATIVE REVIEW

Following on from the granting of Royal Assent, acts introduced by the government will be the subject to formal post-legislative scrutiny.[96] This involves the government department responsible for that area of policy preparing a command paper for the relevant Select Committee on how the Act has operated in practice and whether it has achieved its objectives.[97] The Select Committee can then, if it deems it necessary, undertake a fuller review of the operation of the Act in question.[98]

'SPECIAL PROCEDURES'

Later 19th- and early 20th-century discussion of the legislative process would encompass only the preceding (or even only elements of the preceding) procedure. Providing that the bill had made it through both the Commons and the Lords and had received Royal Assent, then that was all that was to be considered. If a bill failed to make it through the process, then it was lost at the end of the parliamentary session.

96 <www.gov.uk/government/publications/post-legislative-scrutiny-the-governments-approach>.

97 This is independent of any other statutory review that may be necessary.

98 Fuller details of the process can be found in the Cabinet Office's 'Guide to Making Legislation' (2025) 290–9.

More recently, there are numerous additional procedures that must be discussed when examining the law-making process of the legal system in its modern context. These special procedures and processes arise from the modern context under which Parliament legislates and are designed to deal with, amongst other things, the potential for conflict between the Houses, the transfer of powers to the European Union and the possibility of preserving a bill that fails to make it through both Houses in a single parliamentary session.

CONFLICT AND THE PARLIAMENT ACTS

The growth of democratic accountability and the increased importance of the lower chamber of Parliament led to questions being asked about the equality of arms between the House of Commons and the House of Lords. More particularly, the ability of the unelected House of Lords permanently to frustrate the will of the democratically elected House of Commons was controversial.

The tension over the powers of the upper chamber boiled over in the early 20th century when the House of Lords rejected the budget (in the form of a finance bill) of the Liberal government in 1909. In response, the Prime Minister of the day threatened to request that the King create sufficient new Liberal Peers to force legislation through the Lords and to prevent conflicts over future finance bills. The outcome of the political tussle was the Parliament Act 1911. The compromise that was reached in that Act was a reduction in the power of the Lords and made the Commons the de facto superior legislating chamber.

The major innovation of the Parliament Act 1911 was the removal of the Lords' power of absolute veto for most bills. After the Parliament Act 1911, the Lords could only delay a bill (other than a money bill)[99] for two whole parliamentary sessions. Under the Act, the rejected bill could then proceed to the Monarch for Royal Assent if it was rejected in the third session. This power of delay was reduced further by the Parliament Act 1949, so that a bill could only be delayed for around a year (over two sessions). Thus, a bill presented by the Commons in a second successive session can now progress straight to Royal Assent if rejected a second time by the Lords.

The 1949 Act has proved to be controversial in that it had to be passed using the powers of the 1911 Act! This was because the Lords had already rejected proposals to introduce the 1949 bill on two previous occasions. Thus, we are left with a slightly unusual situation in that a bill that was proposed to *amend* the 1911 Act had to *rely* on the 1911 Act in order to be passed.

Figure 4.6 illustrates the operation of the Parliament Act 1911 as amended in 1949 and how it was used to pass the Hunting Act 2004. The controversies associated with the Hunting Act are discussed later in this section.

The reduction of the powers of the House of Lords is obviously an important development in the democratisation of the system and in the process of reform of the upper chamber. Despite this, it is important to keep a sense of perspective about the use of the Acts. As well

99 Which can only be delayed for one month – Parliament Act 1911 s1(1).

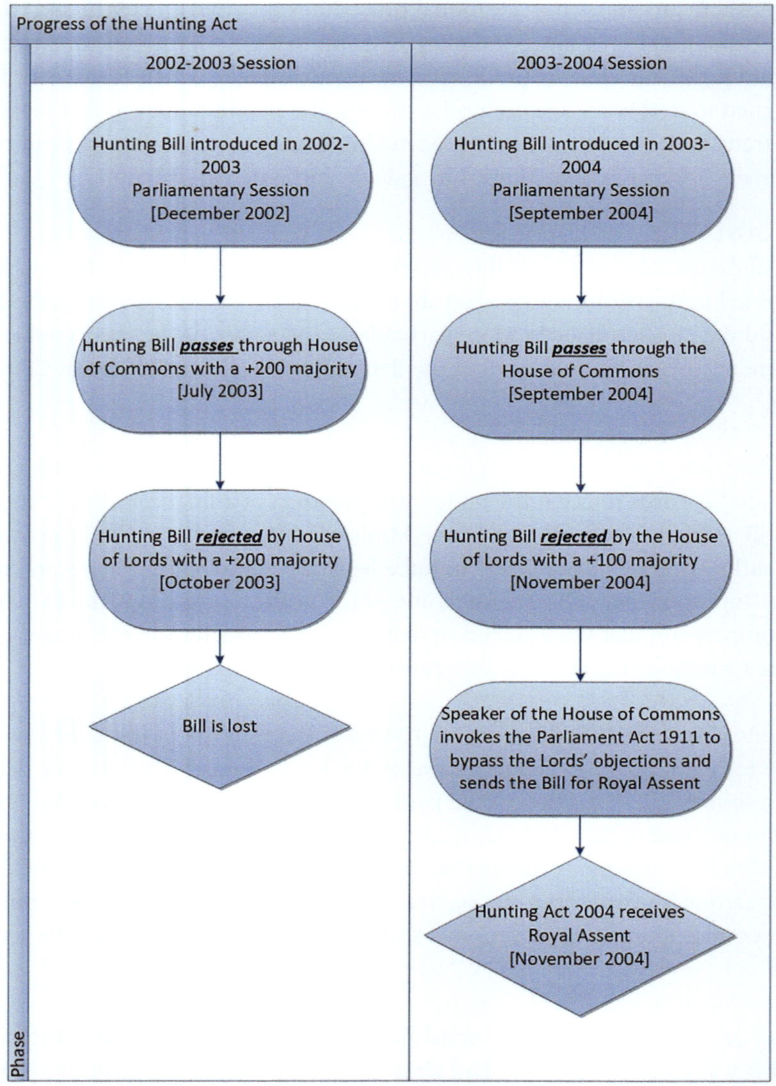

Figure 4.6 Progress of the Hunting Act 2004.

as reinforcing the supremacy of the elected Commons, the Parliament Act 1911 also acts as an important deterrent for the Lords. It encourages them to use their power of delay in a more discriminating fashion. By preserving some of the power of the Lords, essentially now a power to delay, it does not completely undermine the role of the upper chamber as a place for revising and scrutinising legislation.

The provisions of the Parliament Act itself are rarely called upon and have been used to force the passage of only seven bills:

- Welsh Church Act 1914
- Government of Ireland Act 1914
- Parliament Act 1949
- War Crimes Act 1991
- European Parliamentary Elections Act 1999
- Sexual Offences (Amendment) Act 2000
- Hunting Act 2004

It is of interest to note that only one of the Acts just listed – the War Crimes Act 1991 – was enacted by a Conservative government. This leads on to a further important, but indirect, function of the Parliament Acts, which was to redress, in part, the inbuilt Conservative dominance of the House of Lords. Also, the threat of the use of the powers under the Parliament Act can be a galvanising force in the passage of contentious bills – meaning that the Lords are always debating in its shadow.

ANALYSING THE LAW – THE PARLIAMENT ACTS 1911 AND 1949

With fewer than ten bills in more than a century requiring recourse to the powers of the Parliament Act 1911, its importance could be questioned. However, it is vital to view the Parliament Act 1911 as an early stepping stone in the broader process of Lords reform. Moreover, the debate that surrounded the enactment of the Parliament Act 1911 has contributed to other developments that have had a more immediate impact on the legislative process. For example, the development of the Salisbury Convention in the mid-1940s was strongly influenced by recent memory of the events that led to the 1911 Act. The constitutional convention[100] named for Lord Salisbury holds that any government bill that seeks to achieve a manifesto commitment will not be voted down[101] by the Lords. In many cases, this avoids the need to have recourse to the Parliament Act 1911.

The most recent use of the Parliament Act was by Tony Blair's Labour government to secure the passage of the Hunting Act 2004. This Act banned certain forms of hunting, including those of wild mammals by dogs. This was, and continues to be, a controversial piece of legislation.[102] In a bid to prevent the operation of the Act, numerous challenges have been brought concerning its legality.[103] For the purposes of a chapter on the law-making process of England and Wales, it is the *Jackson*[104] case that laid down important principles about the use of the Parliament Acts.

100 A *constitutional convention* is a non-legal rule that actors within the English and Welsh legal system consider themselves (for constitutional reasons) to be bound by. See Nicholas Barber, 'Laws and Constitutional Conventions' (2009) 125 LQR 294.

101 A bill may be *amended* provided that the amendment does not stop the bill from progressing (i.e. it cannot be a 'wrecking amendment').

102 <https://petition.parliament.uk/petitions/205852>.

103 *R (Countryside Alliance and others) v Attorney General* [2007] UKHL 52, [2008] 1 AC 719.

104 *R (Jackson) v Attorney General* [2005] UKHL 56, [2006] 1 AC 262.

EXPLAINING THE LAW AND MAKING CONNECTIONS – THE *JACKSON* CASE

The case was brought by members of the Countryside Alliance, including Jackson, who argued that the Parliament Act 1949 should not have been passed using the 1911 Act, as the former amended the latter. They argued that any legislation passed under the Parliament Act 1911 was not, in fact, primary legislation but delegated legislation. This, so the appellants argued, meant that the 1949 Act was invalid, and so the Hunting Act 2004, passed under the procedures of the 1949 Act, was also invalid.

The challenge failed, with Lord Bingham stating that the Parliament Act 1911 did 'effect an important constitutional change, but the change lay not in authorising a new form of sub-primary parliamentary legislation but in creating a new way of enacting primary legislation'.[105]

The case is important because it demonstrated that Parliament can itself alter the law-making process through a regular Act of Parliament.

PRESERVATION

Traditionally, a bill that does not attain Royal Assent by the end of the parliamentary session in which it was introduced would be lost. This adds certainty to the position and status of bills. Also, in the days before Parliament sat frequently, it would stop bills being maintained for a number of years. This position was changed by Tony Blair's government in 1998 when the Financial Services and Markets Bill 1998–1999 was carried over between sessions. The procedure of carry-over is particularly important where very long and technical bills[106] are introduced, which require extensive scrutiny at the committee stage. If 'carry-over' was not possible, then there is the risk that bills would be (even more frequently) rushed through the parliamentary process with insufficient checks or scrutiny.

The beginning of the 2004–2005 session of Parliament saw the formalisation of a procedure of 'carry-over' into a House of Commons Standing Order. The Consumer Rights Bill is an example of an important legislative measure that was carried over from the 2013–2014 period into the 2014–2015 session before becoming the Consumer Rights Act in 2015.[107] Similarly, the controversial HS2 Bill, which paved the way for the completion of a high-speed rail link between Birmingham and London, and which runs to some 413 pages, was subject to carry-over in the same session.[108] Moreover, it was already envisioned at that time that the HS2 Bill might be carried over to the 2015–2016 session,[109] and in fact, it did not receive the Royal Assent until 23 February 2017.

105 ibid [24] (Lord Bingham).

106 The Financial Services and Markets Act 2000 had some 433 sections and 22 schedules.

107 HC Deb 28 January 2014, vol 574, col 834.

108 HC Deb 29 April 2014, vol 579, cols 771–4.

109 ibid.

The power of carry-over can only be used for bills introduced in the Commons that have yet to be sent up to the Lords. This last restriction does arguably limit the effectiveness of the power of carry-over, but the very existence of the power indicates the willingness of the Commons to adapt its procedures better to suit the modern environment in which legislation is drafted. This is particularly important, as noted previously, in the case of bills that contain a significant amount of technical information. It also ensures that adequate time can be allocated to long and technical bills.

The Domestic Abuse Bill 2017–2019 was almost a casualty of the power struggle between Parliament and the government during the unlawful prorogation of September 2019. Despite strong cross-party support, the Bill was not, initially, subject to a carry-over motion and so seemed to have been lost. Following the Supreme Court's ruling that that prorogation that had caused the loss had been unlawful, the Bill was recovered and was subject to a carry-over motion before the (lawful) prorogation in October 2019.[110] This means that the Bill, now the Domestic Abuse Bill 2017–2019 to 2019–2020, resumed its passage through the law-making process, eventually becoming the Domestic Abuse Act 2021.

TRANSFER OF POWERS TO THE EUROPEAN UNION

The General Election of 2010 returned a coalition government between the Conservatives and the Liberal Democrats. Despite the parties holding almost diametrically opposed views on aspects of European integration, the coalition agreement proposed amending the European Communities Act 1972 so as to require a referendum if there was to be a further transfer of powers to the European Union. This aspect of the coalition agreement was achieved not through amendment of the European Communities Act 1972 but rather by the passage of new primary legislation in the form of the European Union Act 2011. Indeed, the EUA 2011 went further and set up numerous restrictions on how future developments of the EU were to be achieved through primary legislation, had we remained members.

The language of the EU Act 2011 was densely drafted, but the core of the Act's provisions was about specific 'trigger events' that would require a referendum before the UK ratifies an EU treaty.[111] For example, if the EU was granted new exclusive competence or existing competences had been extended, or if an EU institution was granted new powers to impose sanctions on the member states, then a referendum would be triggered.

The reality of the situation, however, is more complicated than the face of the Act suggests. During the UK's remaining membership of the EU, there was not the need for a referendum under the EUA 2011. This was despite the fact that there had been new treaties affecting the balance of powers within the EU during this time.[112] The preceding is simply an example of different processes as clearly there will be no further transfer of powers to the EU now that the UK has rescinded its membership.

110 Details of the Bill, and its legislative history, can be found at <https://services.parliament.uk/Bills/2017-19/domesticabuse.html>.

111 European Union Act 2011 s4(1)(a)–(m).

112 For example, the Fiscal Compact Treaty.

THE LEGISLATIVE LANDSCAPE: FLAT OR CONTOURED?

This chapter has very much focussed on how individual bills become Acts of Parliament. However, it is important to remember that Acts of Parliament do not operate in a vacuum and will often interact with and contradict each other. The legal system in operation in the UK has a long-established principle, that of 'implied repeal', that helps deal with the question of inconsistencies between Acts of Parliament in a pragmatic way.

Implied repeal has traditionally been understood, from cases such as *Vauxhall Estates*,[113] to mean that where you have inconsistencies between two acts, the most recent Act is seen to impliedly repeal the older act. As such, the orthodox view of the legal system in England and Wales has been of a flat legislative landscape, with all Acts of Parliament equally being subject to the doctrine of implied repeal.[114] The basis of implied repeal lies in the doctrine of parliamentary sovereignty.

The preceding means that acts could not become 'entrenched' and acts (no matter their importance) were all equal. However, modern developments have put increasing pressure on this concept, and we can now see that discovering which acts take priority in the case of conflict is now more complex.

> MAKING CONNECTIONS – PUBLIC LAW
>
> ++++++++++++++++++++++++++++
>
> The debate about the extent to which Acts of Parliament can be repealed impliedly by later Acts of Parliament will be explored in much greater depth in modules that you may study on public law, constitutional law or European Union law. However, a basic understanding of the position is necessary for an understanding of the operation of the English and Welsh legal system and of law-making.

Due to membership of the European Union and the case law of the Court of Justice of the European Union,[115] it was recognised that EU law would take priority over conflicting national law regardless of when that national law was passed.[116] This called into question the principle of implied repeal for the legal system of England and Wales as a later Act of Parliament had to always give way to a piece of prior EU law.

113 *Vauxhall Estates v Liverpool Corp* [1932] 1 KB 733 (KB).

114 See this interesting blog piece by Mark Elliot, 'Reflections on the HS2 Case: A Hierarchy of Domestic Constitutional Norms and the Qualified Primacy of EU Law' (UK Constitutional Law Association, 23 January 2014) <http://ukconstitutionallaw.org/2014/01/23/mark-elliot-reflections-on-the-hs2-case-a-hierarchy-of-domestic-constitutional-norms-and-the-qualified-primacy-of-eu-law>.

115 Case 6/64 *Costa v ENEL* [1964] ECR 585.

116 Case 106/77 *Amministrazione delle Finanze dello Stato v Simmenthal* [1978] ECR 629.

The English and Welsh courts were faced with the question of whether to apply the doctrine of implied repeal to matters concerning EU law in the *Thoburn*[117] case.

EXPLAINING THE LAW – *THOBURN*

The case concerned the Weights and Measures Act 1985, which gave equal legal authority to measurements of weight in both pounds and kilograms. A later amendment of the Act by secondary legislation in 1994, brought about to comply with EU law and made under the powers of the European Communities Act 1972, prohibited pounds being used as the *primary* indicator of weight in the UK. Thoburn was convicted for using scales that did not comply with the amended 1985 Act but that would have complied with it as originally enacted.

Thoburn argued that the Weights and Measures Act 1985 (as originally enacted) had impliedly repealed the powers under the European Communities Act 1972. As a result, the later amendment to the 1985 Act using the 1972 Act was invalid.

Lord Justice Laws, in the High Court, disagreed with this argument and made some important comments *obiter* about the nature of legislation and law-making in the legal system of England and Wales. He stated that '[w]e should recognise a hierarchy of Acts of Parliament: as it were "ordinary" statutes and "constitutional" statutes. The two categories must be distinguished on a principled basis'.[118] As a result of this, he stated that '[a] constitutional statute can only be repealed, or amended in a way which significantly affects its provisions touching fundamental rights or otherwise the relation between citizen and State, by unambiguous words on the face of the later statute'.[119]

The outcome of *Thoburn* was that some 'constitutional' statutes, such as the European Communities Act 1972, were immune from implied repeal and can only be repealed by express words in subsequent Acts of Parliament. This principle, that some Acts of Parliament may be immune from implied repeal, survives the UK ending its membership of the EU. This is clear from *Thoburn* itself, where Lord Justice Laws identified other statutes, including the Human Rights Act 1998, the Scotland Act 1998, the Bill of Rights 1689 and Magna Carta, as other acts of similar status.[120] This means that, albeit to a limited extent, the legal system now has a two-tiered system of primary legislation. Although these cases were decided in the context of EU law, the principles underpinning them have been extended in subsequent cases in other contexts.[121] The principle also applies even though the European Communities Act 1972 has now been expressly repealed.

117 *Thoburn v Sunderland City Council* [2002] EWHC 195 (Admin), [2003] QB 151.

118 ibid [62] (Laws LJ).

119 ibid [63] (Laws LJ).

120 ibid [62].

121 For a Scottish case on the effect of the Scotland Act 1998, see *BH (AP) v The Lord Advocate* [2012] UKSC 24, [2013] 1 AC 413 [30] (Lord Hope).

The *Thoburn* case is also an excellent example of external influences – in this case the EU – transforming our understanding of the domestic legal system. In the *HS2*[122] case, involving the planned high-speed rail link between London and Birmingham, the Supreme Court indicated, *obiter*,[123] that even amongst constitutional statutes, there may be an order of priority.[124] This suggests that the legal has a multidimensional legislative framework, with certain pieces of primary law taking priority over others. As was discussed in an earlier chapter, the position in *Thoburn* has been thrown into question by the recent Supreme Court judgment in *Allister*.[125]

It is important to remember this when assessing the impact of particular pieces of legislation that have a constitutional flavour. It is no longer sufficient to view each piece of legislation in isolation, and it is important not only to think of whether it is of a constitutional nature itself but also whether it will conflict with earlier acts or principles of a constitutional nature. This task of identifying 'constitutional' Acts of Parliament is complicated by the fact that they will, until labelled as such by a court, appear to be a regular Act of Parliament. So-called constitutional acts will follow the same procedure as any other Act of Parliament in their passage through the legislative process.

CONCLUSION

The law-making process, as it applies to primary legislation, is complex and highly politically charged. However, it is crucial for those wishing to understand the legal system of England and Wales to appreciate fully the importance of every step of the process that leads to primary legislation. Without understanding the *context* of how an Act of Parliament came into force, it can be difficult to understand how it was intended to apply and how it will be received by both the courts and the wider public.

Moreover, and beyond the mere mechanics of the law-making process, with its many steps and procedures, it is important to note some of the broader themes that arise out of the discussion in this chapter. First, the process tells us something about the involvement (or lack thereof) of citizens in that process. At present, the role of participatory democracy in the legal system is somewhat limited. Citizens elect their MPs (who are only part of the legislature), and thereafter, the role of the individual member of the public is largely over until the next General Election, some five years hence. The legal system has informal channels through which the individual may influence law-making, such as exerting pressure on the government to introduce specific policies. Increasingly, there are also more formal channels for recognising the role of the citizen *in the process* of law-making. These are genuine steps towards greater participation of citizens, including the launch of e-petitions and the (albeit failed) pilots of

122 *R (HS2) v The Secretary of State for Transport* [2014] UKSC 3, [2014] 1 WLR 324.

123 The concept of *obiter dictum* is discussed further in Chapter 9, but for the purposes of this chapter, it is to be understood as a non-legally binding part of a court judgment.

124 See *R (HS2) v The Secretary of State for Transport* [2014] UKSC 3, [2014] 1 WLR 324 at [79] and [203].

125 See *Allister* [2023] UKSC 5.

a public reading stage. The success of these developments led to mixed engagement with the opportunities.

Secondly, and due partly to the inbuilt propensity for dominance of Parliament by the government,[126] the effectiveness of the system of scrutiny of legislation is in question. The debates in the Houses of Commons and Lords and the work of the Public Bill Committees are intended to be the primary method of scrutiny within the legal system. Their work is undermined by the control of government of the parliamentary timetable, and the increase in length and complexity of statutes only exacerbates the problem. The problem of effective scrutiny has traditionally been made even worse by the tendency for General Elections to return strong majority governments able to pass legislation by sheer force of will. It has yet to be seen whether coalition governments will happen more frequently in the future and how this will impact on the law-making process. These two factors may act as a force for reducing government control, in particular in the Commons, in the future.

Thirdly, and although it may not always seem this way, the English and Welsh legal system is progressive and evolutionary. It is not a fixed system and is capable of organic changes that subtly, but importantly, and sometimes irreversibly, change the direction and nature of law-making. The most noteworthy of these in the last two centuries is probably the Parliament Acts 1911 and 1949, which allowed Parliament to legislate in a new way. More subtle changes, not normally discussed in English and Welsh legal system textbooks, include the change to accommodate carry-over of bills and the evolving system of standing orders that regulate Parliament but that allow for flexibility to be injected into the system. This organic development is a key feature of the whole legal system and will be returned to in subsequent chapters.

Fourthly, and finally, as much as this textbook encourages you to view your study of individual modules as interconnecting parts of a single system, it is equally important not to divorce law from its political, economic and social contexts. Law does not just appear fully formed and without figurative 'baggage'. An individual Act of Parliament is a product of its time, of the political climate and of the society from which it comes. It is important to remember this in any study of the legal system. Much law is the realisation of politics, and the more you understand about the *political process*, the more you will understand the *legal process*.

THE WEBSITE

The website that accompanies this textbook contains many useful resources that you can use to consolidate and further your knowledge of the law, to hone your skills of critical analysis and to test your knowledge. This includes a set of multiple-choice questions (MCQs) that can be used to test your knowledge and understanding of the material.

126 For a reconsideration of the issue of executive dominance of Parliament, see Grégoire Webber, 'Parliament and the Management of Conflict' [2014] PL 100, 102–4.

5

CHAPTER 5
LAW-MAKING IN ENGLAND AND WALES II – DELEGATED (SECONDARY) LEGISLATION

INTRODUCTION

If, as discussed in the previous chapter, primary law sets out the framework of the legal system, then secondary legislation is designed to flesh out the detailed rules and enables the decisions that operate under that framework to be taken. Alternatively called delegated or subordinate legislation, secondary legislation is largely the exercise of law-making powers under the *authority* and *control* of Parliament.

Such delegated legislation is an increasingly important part of a legal system that operates in the context of expansive government activity and of complex and technical regulatory environments. From tax to the control of public spaces, from the setting of constituency boundaries to the control of a global pandemic, secondary legislation affects all aspects of the legal (and political) system.

This chapter will explore the different forms of delegated legislation and how they are made. More importantly, the chapter will examine the extent of powers that can be exercised under and through secondary legislation and how that power is controlled by various actors within the legal system. A major theme of this chapter is how secondary legislation is scrutinised both within and outside of Parliament.

AS YOU READ

Think about the different forms of secondary legislation and the different purposes they may be trying to achieve. From the examples given, consider whether the different forms of secondary legislation *achieve* those purposes. Assess the **effectiveness** of the methods of scrutiny and how these methods interact with each other and how they might be improved.

Consider the different roles of Parliament, the executive and the judiciary in formulating and scrutinising secondary legislation.

DOI: 10.4324/9781032641829-5

NATURE AND SCOPE OF SECONDARY LEGISLATION

This textbook presents, for reasons of efficacy, primary legislation (i.e. Acts of Parliament) in a distinct chapter from secondary legislation. However, they should not be viewed as wholly separate instruments but rather as interacting and complementary forms of legislation. Typically, primary legislation sets down principles, and secondary legislation attempts to achieve the detailed implementation of those principles. Primary legislation is like the rigid skeleton of the English and Welsh legal system,[1] and secondary legislation fleshes out that skeleton.

TAKING THINGS FURTHER – SEEKING OUT SECONDARY LEGISLATION

This is a topic for which it is particularly useful for you to explore some concrete examples of secondary legislation. It is possible to browse much of the secondary legislation currently in force via a government website – www.legislation.gov.uk/browse. Visiting this website regularly can help keep you up to date with recent legislative developments.

A word of warning should be attached to the use of the aforementioned website. With more than 3,000 statutory instruments – a particular type of secondary legislation – published each year, it is easy to get lost or distracted by the volume of legislative output. You can search the database for more relevant pieces of secondary legislation, or use it to get a feel of the form, structure and style of such delegated legislation.

The companion website that accompanies this text contains a podcast where the author talks through the structure of a piece of secondary legislation, some comprehension activities to test your understanding of such legislation and even a hypothetical problem question that will allow you to apply your comprehension skills.

Given the central position of Parliament's sovereignty in the law of England and Wales, most secondary legislation comes into force under Parliament's authority.[2] Such secondary legislation is authorised by a piece of primary law – an Act of Parliament – known as the parent or enabling Act. This will dictate to whom powers are delegated, what the powers are to be used for and how the delegated legislation is to come into force. Being familiar with the proposition that a parent Act will contain all the information related to the passing of a

1 Which is not to say that those bones cannot be broken and recast if needed.

2 Certain prerogative powers of the Monarch can be exercised by Orders in Council, some of which are not required to be laid before Parliament.

piece of a secondary legislation will help you understand the symbiotic relationship between primary and delegated legislation. That relationship is explored in what follows in the context of the Courts and Legal Services Act 1990.

EXPLAINING THE LAW – THE COURTS AND LEGAL SERVICES ACT 1990: THE RELATIONSHIP BETWEEN PRIMARY AND SECONDARY LEGISLATION

The Courts and Legal Services Act 1990 makes provision for secondary legislation on a number of issues related to the day-to-day operation of the courts and the allocation of claims to the High Court or other courts. This is the parent act, and Section 1 empowers the Lord Chancellor[3] to allocate categories of cases to various courts by way of secondary legislation.

The Act also sets certain limits and conditions on exercise of the discretion of the Lord Chancellor. For example, any changes to the balance of shared jurisdiction between the High Court and County Court are subject to the approval of the Lord Chief Justice, who is the head of the judiciary in England and Wales.[4] For other changes, mainly to the sole jurisdiction of the High Court or County Court, the Lord Chancellor must consult with various members of the judiciary.[5] The Court and Legal Services Act 1990 also details that secondary legislation made by the Lord Chancellor in exercise of these powers is to be made but can be annulled by a resolution of either House of Parliament.[6]

In 2011, the Lord Chancellor exercised the powers under the Act and made a piece of secondary legislation called the Patents Court (Financial Limits) (No 2) Order 2011.[7] This Order set a limit of £500,000 for claims brought in what were the patents county courts.[8]

Certain consequences flow from the fact that the power for most secondary legislation comes from the authority of Parliament. First, the power to create the secondary legislation is vested only in the person (or persons) named in the parent Act. In the preceding example, this is the Lord Chancellor.

3 A government position bestowed by the King on the advice of the Prime Minister. Since changes brought about by the Constitutional Reform Act 2005, the Lord Chancellor usually now also holds the post of Secretary of State for Justice, but the positions are legally distinct.

4 Courts and Legal Services Act 1990, s1(1A).

5 ibid s1(9).

6 ibid s120.

7 The Patents Court (Financial Limits) (No 2) Order 2011, SI 2011/1402.

8 These are now a specialist list of the High Court called the Intellectual Property Enterprise Court.

Secondly, the content of secondary legislation is limited to the scope given to it by the parent Act. This can have a positive and negative dimension. The positive dimension is that the Act may give express powers to do X, Y and Z, and the person making the secondary legislation may not go beyond the powers so given. The negative dimension is that an Act may expressly prevent powers from being used in a specific way. In the preceding example, the Act gives the Lord Chancellor the positive power to confer jurisdiction over certain cases to the High Court and County Court and, in the negative dimension, prohibits him from conferring jurisdiction for judicial review on the County Court.[9]

Thirdly, and linked to the previous point, secondary legislation is challengeable if it is outside the powers given by the parent Act. For example, if the Lord Chancellor attempted to use the Act to change the jurisdiction of the *Crown Court*, it would be possible to challenge the legality of the secondary legislation as it would be going beyond the powers (to manage the jurisdiction of the County Court and the High Court).

A previous chapter of this textbook explained that Acts of Parliament, due to the sovereignty of Parliament, cannot be challenged in court. The same does not apply to secondary legislation, which can be challenged through the courts. This process is known as judicial review, and its effectiveness is discussed in the section on scrutiny of secondary legislation.

MAKING CONNECTIONS – JUDICIAL REVIEW

++++++++++++++++++++++++++++++++

If you study public law, then you will explore, in great detail, the principles of judicial review. The vast majority of judicial review claims revolve around alleged misuse of powers conferred by Acts of Parliament, including those involving secondary legislation. This aspect of public law is increasingly important given the growth of secondary legislation and the scant scrutiny that Parliament is able to give to such delegated legislation.

The number of pieces of secondary legislation passed every year has increased in the past five decades. This is compounded by the fact that the average *length* of each piece of delegated legislation has also grown dramatically in the same period. Figures 5.1 and 5.2[10] depict the growth in the number of statutory instruments (the main form of delegated legislation) in recent years and the number of pages contained within those statutory instruments.[11]

9 Courts and Legal Services Act 1990 s1(a)–(b) and s10, respectively.

10 See <www.legislation.gov.uk/uksi>.

11 This does not include other forms of SI, including those in Wales and Northern Ireland.

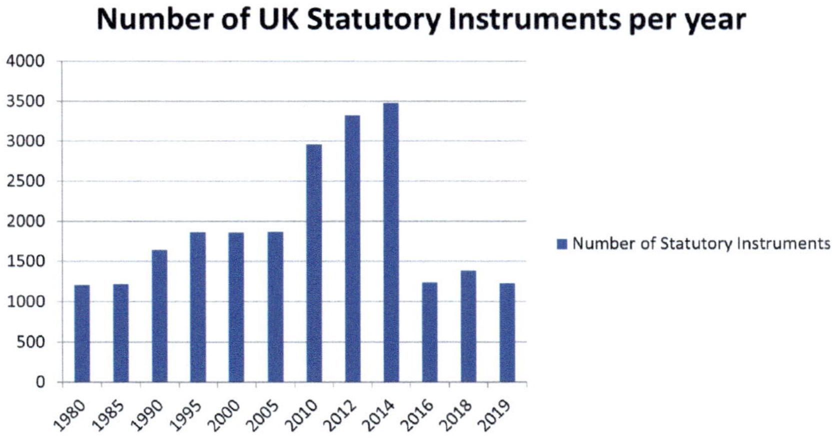

Figure 5.1 Number of statutory instruments, 1980–2019.[12]

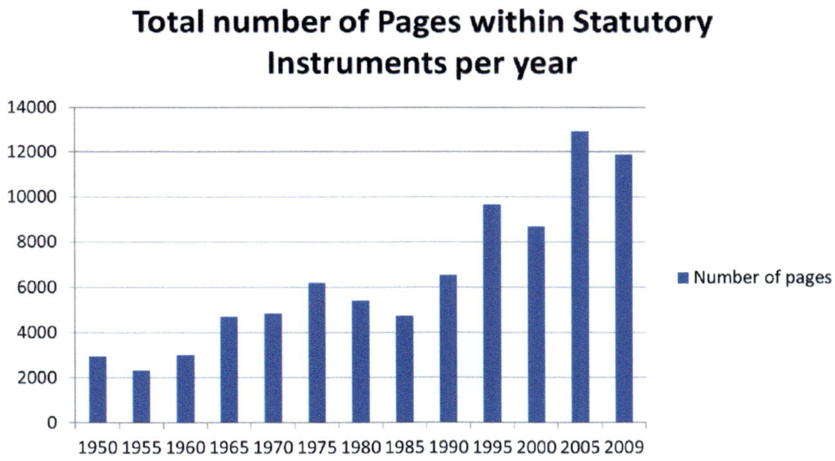

Figure 5.2 Number of pages of statutory instruments, 1950–2009.[13]

Figures 5.1 and 5.2 demonstrate that while the number of UK SIs has doubled in 20 years, the number of pages has increased sixfold. This growth, when coupled with the concurrent exponential growth in the average length of Acts of Parliament,[14] has put increased pressure on the parliamentary process and has arguably led to a reduction in the effectiveness of scrutiny (a theme developed later in this chapter).

12 Based on data in Richard Cracknell, 'Acts and Statutory Instruments: The Volume of UK Legislation 1850–2014' (Standard Note, SN/SG/2911, 2014).

13 These are the total number of pages passed in the years specified. Based on the data in the parliamentary note based on data in Richard Cracknell, 'Acts and Statutory Instruments: the Volume of UK Legislation 1850–2014' (Standard Note, SN/SG/2911, 2014). The last year for which data is available is 2009.

14 See previous chapter on primary legislation for detail on this point.

The charts also show a rapid contraction in the number of UK SIs laid between 2016 and 2019. This is partially a result of the Brexit negotiations, which have had a stultifying effect on the legislative programme of the last two or three parliamentary sessions. It remains to be seen whether there will be a post-Brexit uplift in the volume of secondary legislation, but one is expected given that the government will have significant powers to change existing legislation upon the UK leaving the EU. After initially seeing a rise post-2019, it can be seen that a 'new normal' of around 1,500 per year is settling in. This suggests that the peaks seen between 2010 and 2014 will not be returned to in the current circumstances.

Given the growth of secondary legislation, it would be easy to question whether it would be desirable to reduce the amount of such delegated legislation so that it can be properly scrutinised. However, and before making such a drastic judgement, it is important that we assess *why* delegated legislation is necessary. From this perspective we can see the relationship between competing interests of efficient and thorough scrutiny on the one hand and timely law-making on the other. The following section will explore the need for secondary legislation so that an informed judgement about its important but unusual place in legal system can be made.

NEED FOR SECONDARY LEGISLATION

Before discussing the procedure for passing delegated legislation, it is important to understand *why* such legislation is necessary (Figure 5.3) and why it is not always possible for Acts of Parliament to deal directly with the matters covered by secondary legislation. What follows is

Figure 5.3 The need for secondary legislation.

not intended to be exhaustive but to indicate why, as a matter of public policy, we may need at times to rely on delegated legislation.

DETAIL VS PRINCIPLE AND THE NEED FOR EXPERTISE

Secondary legislation complements primary legislation in that the latter deals with principles and the former with details.[15] It is often the case that Parliament has neither the time nor the expertise to deal with some of the technical detail required for certain policy areas.

The governance of education is a clear example of where Acts of Parliament leave much of the *detail* of regulation to secondary legislation, normally passed by the Secretary of State for Education. At the time of writing, there were 43 pieces of secondary legislation concerned with education in the year 2025 and 24 in the first three months of 2026, compared with 53 in 2018 and 36 in 2017.[16] Although importance should not be inferred from the volume of secondary legislation alone,[17] it can be an indication of areas that lend themselves to secondary legislation. In relation to education, secondary legislation also provides for a further, linked, purpose, and that is creating a national regulatory framework for certain professions. Thus, there is secondary legislation on the system of performance management that is applicable to teachers, as to include this level of detail in an Act of Parliament would be confusing and create a system that was difficult to change.[18]

UPDATING OF RULES

Sometimes it is difficult for Parliament to legislate for every situation and to foresee later developments that will change the context in which primary legislation is applied. Statutory instruments are useful, therefore, in providing flexibility in systems to allow for them to be updated. Similarly, where rules and procedures have a statutory basis but need to be altered annually, then it would not make sense to pass a new Act of Parliament to achieve this. This last point is caveated with the fact that we do have a new Finance Act every year, however, owing to the changes made in the annual budget delivered to Parliament by the Chancellor of the Exchequer when they plan the nation's annual expenditure each year. Updates to the tax codes that operate within the legal system are an example of the type of updating that is achieved primarily by secondary legislation. More directly, the civil and criminal procedure rules that govern the procedures for bringing actions in the criminal and civil courts are updated by secondary legislation.

EXPANSION OF THE STATE

Since the end of the Second World War in 1945, and partly in response to the Beveridge Report,[19] the ambit of what the government is responsible for providing and regulating has

15 This is, of course, just the theoretical position, and the reality might vary quite considerably!

16 <www.legislation.gov.uk/secondary?title=education>.

17 There were, for example, more than 1,200 pieces of secondary legislation governing trunk roads in 2013. <www.legislation.gov.uk/secondary?title=trunk%20road>.

18 The Education (School Teachers' Appraisal) (England) Regulations 2012, SI 2012/115.

19 William Beveridge, *Social Insurance and Allied Services* 1942.

significantly increased. This includes the establishment of the NHS, of various forms of social assistance[20] and the implementation of the National Insurance Scheme.[21] This broadening of the state required a whole series of institutions, processes and regulations to govern how the welfare system was to operate. It would not be practical for Parliament to manage and debate this level of detail. Even in more recent times, alterations and new schemes involving benefit payments have been achieved using secondary legislation. For example, the government's controversial scheme that, on threat of sanction, forced people into unpaid periods of work was achieved through secondary legislation[22] that was made on the basis of the Jobseeker's Act 1995.[23] Given the constantly evolving nature and the development of new schemes in areas such as social security, it would not be sensible for such matters to be subject to constant Acts of Parliament in order to change.

SPEED OF RESPONSE AND EMERGENCIES

At times, it is imperative that legislation be passed quickly. It may be that there is some emergency that requires a rapid response and to wait for Parliament to act through primary legislation would put in jeopardy some important public interest. Parliament spends a number of weeks of the year in 'recess'[24] and does not sit at these times. During these (sometimes very long) periods of recess, MPs normally carry out constituency work. Moreover, even when sitting, it may be proper for decisions to be taken more quickly than the parliamentary process allows.

The Civil Contingencies Act 2004 provides for such powers to pass emergency secondary legislation. It allows *senior* members of the government to pass secondary legislation at times of national emergency.[25] In this context, a national emergency is one that threatens human welfare, will cause serious damage to the environment or in situations of war or times when terrorism threatens the security of the UK.[26]

Equally, the UK's response to the Covid-19 pandemic was first controlled by emergency secondary legislation enacted by virtue of the Public Health (Control of Disease) Act 1984. The government then passed the Coronavirus Act 2020 in order to accrue to itself further powers (and powers with fewer restrictions) to pass secondary legislation to control the pandemic. Despite being 102 sections long (with 29 schedules), it passed through Parliament in four sitting days.

20 Including income support, council tax benefit, jobseekers allowance and the state pension.

21 National Insurance Act 1946.

22 Jobseekers Allowance (Employment, Skills and Enterprise Scheme) Regulations 2011, SI 2011/917. These regulations were successfully challenged in court in the case of *R (Reilly) v Secretary of State for Work and Pensions* [2013] UKSC 68, [2014] AC 453 for not providing the requisite details required by the parent act. This case is further discussed later.

23 Jobseekers Act 1995 s17A.

24 Precise dates can be found at <www.parliament.uk/about/faqs/house-of-commons-faqs/business-faq-page/recess-dates/recess>.

25 Civil Contingencies Act 2004 s20.

26 Civil Contingences Act 2004 s1.

TAKING THINGS FURTHER – LEGISLATING AT TIMES OF EMERGENCY

The website that accompanies this textbook demonstrates how ministerial power can be used to respond to an emergency and considers the benefits and challenges of this approach. There is a podcast that contains an analysis of the Coronavirus Act 2020 and the powers it provides the government.[27]

TO IMPLEMENT EU LAW

The European Union has played an integral part in the development of the law of England and Wales over the last 40 years. This is nowhere more evident than when it comes to a discussion of secondary legislation. European Union law, particularly those pieces passed in the form of directives, was often implemented not by primary legislation but by secondary legislation. The European Communities Act 1972 conferred upon Government Ministers powers to make secondary legislation

> for the purpose of implementing any EU obligation of the United Kingdom, or enabling any such obligation to be implemented, or of enabling any rights enjoyed or to be enjoyed by the United Kingdom under or by virtue of the Treaties to be exercised.[28]

In light of more specific enabling Acts discussed earlier and later, the ECA 1972 gave quite broad powers to Ministers to pass secondary legislation implementing EU law obligations. Although there were limitations on what Ministers could do with the powers under the ECA,[29] the powers affected a number of very important policy areas and gave Ministers a great deal of discretion in how to implement EU law. For example, the EU passed a directive[30] in the early 1990s requiring its member states to regulate maximum working hours and to ensure that there were adequate rest breaks and minimum periods of annual leave for workers. These rules were incorporated into the legal system of England and Wales via a piece of secondary legislation – the Working Time Regulations[31] – in 1998.

The UK left the European Union on 31 January 2020 and entered into a transition period that came to an end on 31 December 2020. During this time, the effect of the European Communities Act 1972 was maintained. At the end of the transition period, the powers of Ministers to make legislation under the ECA 1972 disappeared. This does not mean that the UK's (former) membership of the EU will cease to be of relevance to secondary legislation. Indeed, untangling the EU and English and Welsh legal systems will be partly achieved through

27 See also the following link for an interesting blog on the dangers of the coronavirus legislation: <https://ukconstitutionallaw.org/2020/06/09/jake-hinks-the-coronavirus-act-2020-an-example-of-excessive-executive-dominance/>.

28 European Communities Act 1972 s2(2)(a).

29 These limitations, including those on taxation and criminal matters, can be found in Schedule 2 of the Act.

30 Directive 93/104/EC concerning certain aspects of the organization of working time [1993] OJ L307/18.

31 The Working Time Regulations 1998, SI 1998/1833.

secondary legislation. The process of leaving the EU has brought a new suite of powers to government Ministers to pass secondary legislation deemed 'necessary' to address issues caused by Brexit during the transition period and beyond. Many of these powers are contained within the European Union (Withdrawal) Act 2018 and include so-called Henry VIII powers (discussed elsewhere in this chapter) to pass regulations that amend primary legislation. These powers can be found in s8(1) of the EU(W)A. The section allows Ministers to take measures to deal with 'deficiencies' in assimilated EU law and to remedy any 'failure of EU law to operate effectively'.

THE DANGERS OF SECONDARY LEGISLATION

Whilst the previous section makes for a compelling set of non-exhaustive reasons that the legal system benefits from the existence of secondary legislation, there are also considerable dangers or concerns with their overuse. This section will briefly outline those dangers, but it is important that you keep them in mind as you read the remainder of the chapter. The dangers can be summarised by:

- The concentration of power in the government
- The increasing scope of secondary legislation
- The increased scale of use of secondary legislation
- The lack of proper scrutiny

The most prominent risk is that secondary legislation is increasingly being made to pass very significant law-making powers into the hands of the executive. The previous section noted that secondary legislation is positively used for detail or updating of technical rules, but it can also be used to influence broad policy areas. This cuts across the role of Parliament as the legislature and makes it more challenging to hold the executive to account. This danger becomes most acute where secondary legislation contains so-called Henry VIII clauses. These are powers for Ministers to pass secondary legislation that *amends* primary legislation.

The concerns, about effective scrutiny and accountability, particularly with the use of Henry VIII clauses more generally, are brought into sharp focus when considering their use in the context of Brexit. This has two dimensions. One is the staggering breadth of areas that may be subject to change using the powers of the European Union (Withdrawal) Act 2018. This is due to the fact that membership of the EU covered a broad range of policy areas. Similar concerns could be raised around the Coronavirus Act 2020.

This links to a separate danger of lack of proper scrutiny of secondary legislation. The process that secondary legislation goes through is discussed later in the chapter, and the theme of proper scrutiny will be discussed at that time, but it is important to make a few points here. First, that the processes lead to variable levels of full scrutiny. Second, that the government typically has a majority in Parliament and so can more easily get secondary legislation (and the primary legislation needed to empower Ministers) through the system. Finally, the volume of secondary legislation is significant, and this itself means that the time available for scrutiny can be limited.

When these two dangers (wide-ranging powers and lack of proper scrutiny) converge, it becomes apparent that significant parts of English and Welsh law may be subject to change by Ministers with only partial scrutiny by Parliament. This raises significant concerns about accountability and democratic legitimacy.[32]

There is a final danger to be discussed in this section, and this relates to the lack of clarity that sometimes comes with significant amounts of secondary legislation. There is a risk that the executive 'over-implement' the policy objectives. This is demonstrated clearly by the legislative response to the coronavirus pandemic. In tackling the pandemic, the government brought forward primary legislation, secondary legislation and also issued 'guidance'.[33] Given the complexity and the pace of development, the lines between these different responses were often blurred. The police were accused of 'over'-implementing the guidance by treating it as if it were law. Equally, Boris Johnson misled Parliament in his obfuscation between the different forms of applicable rules relating to illegal gatherings at the heart of government.

The aforementioned dangers are only lightly sketched in order to contextualise the sections that follow and focus your attention on how these dangers may manifest themselves and jeopardise some of the necessity of secondary legislation in the legal system.

TYPES OF SECONDARY LEGISLATION

So far, this chapter has sought to discuss secondary legislation as a single concept. However, there are various different types of secondary legislation that serve different purposes and seek to address different needs.

ORDERS IN COUNCIL

Orders in Council are made directly on the authority of the King. They are formally passed by the Privy Council in the name of the Monarch. There are two recognised forms of Orders in Council, those with a statutory basis (discussed later as part of the section on statutory instruments) and those with no statutory basis.

Those that are passed without statutory authority – prerogative Orders in Council – have the force of primary legislation. Although, as previously mentioned, there is a formal role for the

32 See, for example, <https://ukconstitutionallaw.org/2020/06/09/jake-hinks-the-coronavirus-act-2020-an-example-of-excessive-executive-dominance/>.

33 Non-binding advice to citizens.

Privy Council, the measures are normally proposed by the government. Orders in Council made under the prerogative powers are often used in relation to those who are seen to have some sort of relationship with the Crown. In the *GCHQ*[34] case, for example, there were prerogative powers embodied through an Order in Council that allowed the Secretary of State for the Civil Service to alter the terms and conditions of employment of civil servants. Similarly, there are prerogative powers to pass Orders in Council in relation to appointments to certain public offices and to certain positions within the Church of England. In the modern context, the most important prerogative Orders in Council relate to international relations and the powers to enter into binding international treaties. Recent Orders in Council passed under prerogative powers have also included making changes to the Royal Charters that govern various universities.[35]

STATUTORY INSTRUMENTS

The majority of delegated legislation is achieved using so-called statutory instruments (SIs). These are passed under the authority of an Act of Parliament (the parent Act) and are numbered consecutively by the year in which they were made.

The use of such delegated legislation is governed by the Statutory Instruments Act 1946. This Act defines *statutory instruments* as the *expression* of the exercise of a power conferred on the King or a Minister by an Act of Parliament to 'make, confirm or approve orders, rules, regulations or other subordinate legislation'.[36] Thus, statutory instruments are the documented exercise of powers conferred by statute on the King or his Ministers.[37] The Statutory Instruments Act 1946 also makes provision for the numbering, printing and publication for sale of SIs. As discussed later in this chapter, the Statutory Instruments Act 1946 also plays an important part in laying down the procedure for Parliament to scrutinise and approve/reject statutory instruments.

TAKING THINGS FURTHER – USING LEGISLATION.GOV.UK

Examples of statutory instruments can be found on the government's legislation website.[38] This allows you to browse SIs by year or search for specific SIs on specific topics. Visiting the website frequently will give you an idea of the sorts of issues that can be governed by SIs. For example, if you search for the word 'education', then you will see that there are more than 2,500 SIs relating to education. It is unlikely that you will need to know the detailed substance of any of these Sis, but (quickly) reading some of them will give a clear insight into the way in which SIs are used and the way in which they are drafted.

34 *Council of Civil Service Unions v Minister for the Civil Service* [1985] AC 374 (HL).

35 In July 2014, the Charters of the University of Bath and Surrey were altered by Orders in Council.

36 Statutory Instruments Act 1946 s1(1).

37 Including Ministers of the devolved institutions of Scotland, Wales and Northern Ireland.

38 <www.legislation.gov.uk/uksi>.

Each SI opens with a statement that indicates *who* is making use of the delegated powers and under the authority of which Act the use of power is being made. All SIs also come with explanatory memoranda. The purpose of the explanatory memoranda is to:

- Set out the *objective(s)* of the SI.
- Explain the *context* of the SI (including its relationship with other pieces of delegated legislation).
- Set out the *territorial scope* of the SI and confirm, where necessary, its compliance with the European Convention on Human Rights.
- Include a statement on the *policy* behind the SI. This is particularly useful as it is easy to view legal provisions in a vacuum and thus overlook the political context within which they are adopted.
- Where public *consultation* has taken place, the explanatory memoranda will explore the themes of the responses and also any changes made to the SI in light of those changes.
- Set out any details of *impact assessments* (on business, charities and the public sector).

Just as 'secondary legislation' is a blanket term that covers a host of different measures, the term 'statutory instrument' can also be used to describe a number of different pieces of secondary legislation. The rest of this section explores the major forms of statutory instrument that exist within the legal system of England and Wales.

COMMENCEMENT ORDERS

Acts of Parliament frequently do not come into force on the day that they receive Royal Assent. Indeed, individual sections of acts may come into force at different times. The coming into force of a section, set of sections or whole Acts of Parliament is governed by a form of statutory instrument called 'commencement orders'. For example, Section 1 of the Neonatal Care (Leave and Pay) Act 2023 (which creates a new statutory right to leave) came into force in August 2023 as a result of a commencement order.[39]

The original Act will delegate powers to pass commencement orders, normally to Ministers. There are around 150 commencement orders passed in each year. Leaving the control of commencement to Ministers may mean that acts, despite being validly passed, will never come into force. The most famous of these, as discussed in the previous chapter, is the Easter Act 1928, which is still awaiting a commencement order but which has not otherwise been repealed. It is even possible that aspects of Acts of Parliament are repealed before they are commenced – for example, the possibility of a trial without jury in serious or complex fraud cases was found in Criminal Justice Act 2003 s43, but this was repealed before it was ever brought into force by a commencement order.[40]

There are times when leaving to a Minister the decision as to the commencement of an Act can risk abuse of powers. This is well-illustrated by the *ex parte Fire Brigades Union*[41] case.

39 The Neonatal Care (Leave and Pay) Act 2023 (Commencement No 1) Regulations 2023, SI 2023/904.

40 Chapter 12 deals with jury trials and s43 in greater detail.

41 *R v Secretary of State for the Home Department ex parte Fire Brigades Union* [1995] 2 AC 513 (HL).

EXPLAINING AND ANALYSING THE LAW – ABUSE (AND NON-USE) OF COMMENCEMENT ORDERS

In this case, the government maintained certain non-statutory powers to compensate the victims of crime To place the scheme on a more transparent foundation, Parliament passed the Criminal Justice Act 1988, which was designed, *inter alia*, to provide a new *statutory* scheme for compensation. The relevant sections[42] of the CJA were to be brought into force through a commencement order. The Secretary of State refused to bring forward a commencement order and continued to rely upon the old non-statutory powers to develop a new tariff of compensation.

The House of Lords, in *ex parte Fire Brigades Union*, was asked whether the Secretary of State's action was unlawful due to an abuse of power (i.e. the refusal to bring forward commencement). The issue was whether a Secretary of State had the ultimate and unfettered discretion to refuse ever to bring forward a commencement order or whether he just had the power to decide when commencement would happen. This is an important point and links to some of the issues discussed elsewhere in this chapter on the *scrutiny* of secondary legislation.

In deciding the case, the judiciary had to consider the *purpose* of secondary legislation and the role of Parliament and the executive in the execution of primary law. The House of Lords held that those with the discretion to introduce secondary legislation could not completely refuse to exercise that discretion as this would 'frustrate the will of Parliament expressed in a statute'.[43] Ministers needed to keep their minds open to the possibility of commencing an Act and should not introduce new schemes that were incompatible with the scheme foreseen by the statute.

This finding tells us two important things about the law-making process. First, the use of secondary law by government Ministers is about a *separation of functions* between Parliament and the executive. The powers of the latter are subservient to the powers of the former. Secondly, the courts are charged with the duty of ensuring that the powers conferred by Parliament are not abused. This form of judicial scrutiny is explored in greater detail later in this chapter.

ORDERS IN COUNCIL

Orders in Council that stem from the prerogative powers of the Crown are discussed earlier. In addition, there are also Orders in Council that come in the form of statutory instruments. This means that their use is governed by the Statutory Instruments Act 1946. They have, traditionally, been used in relation to important matters of state, such as those pertaining to the devolved institutions. For example, from the 1970s through to the turn of the century,

42 In particular, Criminal Justice Act 1988 ss 108–17.

43 *R v Secretary of State for the Home Department ex parte Fire Brigades Union* [1995] 2 AC 513 (HL), 552 (Lord Browne-Wilkinson).

a substantial amount of legislation passed for Northern Ireland was achieved via Orders in Council. These were used at times when the Parliament of Northern Ireland was suspended and overall control of the region was reverted to Westminster. An Order in Council will be made via statutory instrument (as opposed to the prerogative), where the powers granted to the Crown stem from an Act of Parliament. In relation to the situation in Northern Ireland, the power to pass Orders in Council in the form of statutory instruments came from the Northern Ireland (Temporary Provisions) Act 1972.[44]

REGULATIONS

Where an Act of Parliament leaves the detailed fleshing out of policy to statutory instruments, the powers will frequently be exercised via regulations. This is important where an Act of Parliament creates a framework for a particular policy area or profession but where it does not have the capacity (or expertise) to create the detail. The governance and regulation of compulsory education and the teaching profession provide an excellent example of when regulations in the form of statutory instruments will be used.

EXPLAINING THE LAW – USING REGULATIONS TO PROVIDE DETAIL: TEACHERS

The Education Act 2002 sets out certain requirements for schools. It is a fairly long Act, with some 217 sections and 22 schedules. It establishes certain bodies related to the provision of education (such as the School Teachers' Review Body)[45] and sets the outline of the national curriculum[46] and the requirements for the governance of maintained schools[47] and independent schools.[48] Despite the length of the Act, it is only a *framework* and represents a fraction of the legislation needed to establish and maintain the environment for compulsory education.

As such, the Act delegates powers for some of the detail of the system to be created, maintained and amended by the Secretary of State for Education. This is achieved largely through the passage of regulations in the form of statutory instruments. For example, the arrangements by which teachers' performance in the classroom is assessed were laid down by regulations.[49] It would have been a poor use of parliamentary time to debate and consider a system of performance management

44 Northern Ireland (Temporary Provisions) Act 1972 s1(3). These powers were largely repealed by the advent of devolution in 1998. However, the Queen did retain certain powers to make Orders in Council in the form of statutory instruments in the Northern Ireland Act 1998 ss84–6.

45 Education Act 2002 s119.

46 Education Act 2002 ss76–96.

47 Education Act 2002 ss19–40.

48 Education Act 2002 ss157–74.

49 For example, the Education (School Teachers' Appraisal) (England) Regulations 2012, 2012/115.

for a single profession. It is much better, provided there is adequate parliamentary oversight, for the Department of Education to use their expertise to create such a system of appraisal.

As a side note, and to pick up a major theme of the textbook as a whole, although this section is about a specific type of statutory instrument, it is important not to lose sight of the fact that, often, different types of statutory instrument interact. Indeed, many Acts of Parliament envisage different forms of delegated powers and different ways of exercising those powers. For example, and still within the Education Act 2002, implementation of the working conditions and pay of teachers as recommended by the School Teachers' Review Body is achieved via an Order in Council.[50] The result is that, particularly where the policy area is complex, different types of SIs are used to achieve different purposes, but they complement each other in the overall framework.

REMEDIAL ORDERS

Since the coming into force of the Human Rights Act 1998 in 2000, Ministers have acquired powers to make direct changes to primary legislation under limited circumstances.[51] If a court has declared a provision of UK law to be incompatible[52] with rights under the European Convention of Human Rights the powers of the Secretary of State are activated. An example of this happening was in relation to the Sexual Offences Act 2003 which was amended via a remedial order: the Sexual Offences Act 2003 (Remedial) Order 2012.[53]

EXPLAINING/ANALYSING/APPLYING THE LAW – REMEDIAL ORDERS UNDER THE HUMAN RIGHTS ACT 1998

The Sexual Offences Act 2003 contained provisions[54] for those convicted of certain sex offences to notify the police of their home address and of any plans to travel abroad. Where the sentence was in excess of 30 months, the offender was subject to the notification requirement for an indefinite period of time. In the case of *F and Thompson (FC)*,[55] it was held that the indefinite period of the requirement, with no opportunity for review, was incompatible with Article 8 of the European Convention on Human Rights. As such, the Supreme Court issued a declaration of incompatibility

50 Education Act 2002 s120. An example of such an order is the School Teachers' Pay and Conditions Order 2014, SI 2014/2045.

51 Human Rights Act 1998 s10.

52 Human Rights Act 1998 s4.

53 The Sexual Offences Act 2003 (Remedial) Order 2012, SI 2012/1883.

54 Sexual Offences Act 2003 s82.

55 *F and Thompson (FC) v Secretary of State for the Home Department* [2010] UKSC 17, [2011] 1 AC 331.

under Section 4 of the Human Rights Act 1998. This triggered the powers of the Home Secretary, who passed a statutory instrument – in the form of a remedial order – to remove the inconsistency in the Act.[56] This was achieved by directly amending the Sexual Offences Act 2003 so that it allowed the opportunity for review.

From the perspective of the legal system, these remedial orders are interesting as they are a (rare) example of the different institutions of law-making working together in order to reform the law. The courts identify a problem (the inconsistency with an ECHR right), the government proposes a solution (in the form of the order) and the legislature have the final say on whether to pass that solution into law (by affirming the remedial order). This has been described by some as a 'constitutional dialogue'[57] between the organs of state. This is a positive and welcome development, but it is not without its controversies – some of which you will explore further if you undertake further study of constitutional law. The major criticisms come in two forms. First, that the power to issue such a declaration gives the judiciary a significant amount of power. Although a government is not *legally* obliged to act upon such a declaration, there is a great deal of *political* force that will militate in favour of reform. Secondly, the constitutional 'dialogue' is not so much a dialogue as it is a series of events triggered with little *discussion* between the various branches of the state. Once the court has issued the declaration, then the matter is essentially one for the government, given that SIs are rarely rejected by Parliament.

The process for passing a remedial order is more involved than with passing a regular statutory instrument (as described in detail later). For this reason, the use of remedial orders is relatively rare – at the time of writing, there have been fewer than 30 such orders issued. The most recent at the time of writing is the Bereavement Benefits (Remedial) Order,[58] following the Supreme Court decision[59] on the incompatibility of the Social Security Contributions and Benefits (Northern Ireland) Act 1992 s9A with Article 8 of the ECHR.

The Minister responsible must explain to Parliament the context that has, in that Minister's view, led to a need for a remedial order. The *proposal* for a draft remedial order must be laid before Parliament for 60 days, during which the Joint Committee on Human Rights will also report on the necessity and appropriateness of the order. The Minister will also seek representations from interested parties during this time. After the 60 days have lapsed, the Ministers will communicate to Parliament the nature of representations made and lay the draft

56 See the Sexual Offences Act 2003 (Remedial) Order 2012, SI 2012/1883.

57 Tom Hickman, 'Constitutional Dialogue, Constitutional Theories and the Human Rights Act 1998' [2005] PL 306.

58 The Bereavement Benefits (Remedial) Order 2023, SI 2023/134.

59 *In the matter of an application by Siobhan McLaughlin for Judicial Review (Northern Ireland)* [2018] UKSC 48.

order for a further 60 days, after which the Minister will attempt to gain approval for a motion passing the order.

DEVOLUTION

To add a further level of complexity, in addition to UK statutory instruments, the devolved institutions are also able to make SIs. There are generally between 200 and 300 SIs issued by the Senedd Cymru every year.[60] That compares with around double the number issued by the Scottish Parliament, reflecting, in part, the greater devolved powers that Scotland has.[61] Similarly, Northern Ireland makes between 300 and 500 SIs each year. The Senedd Cymru, the Northern Irish Assembly and Scottish Parliament are responsible for the oversight and scrutiny of statutory instruments in relation to non-reserved matters.

REGULATORY REFORM ORDERS AND CONTROL OF PUBLIC BODIES

The Legislative and Regulatory Reform Act 2006, which built on powers conferred in earlier acts,[62] allows Ministers to amend Acts of Parliament in order to promote efficiency in regulation and to reduce burdens on business and the economy. The provisions of Enabling Acts that empower Ministers to amend primary law are also known as 'Henry VIII clauses', and the dangers of these have been laid out earlier.

EXPLAINING THE LAW – HENRY VIII CLAUSES

The Legislative and Regulatory Reform Act 2006 gives wide-ranging powers to Ministers to amend primary legislation, but this does not give them *carte blanche* to amend primary law without safeguards. For example, the Act only allows Ministers to remove or reduce *burdens* on any person. Section 1 gives a relatively wide definition to the term 'burden', including 'a financial cost; an administrative inconvenience; an obstacle to efficiency, productivity or profitability; or a sanction, criminal or otherwise, which affects the carrying on of any lawful activity'.[63]

A Minister wishing to use the powers under the Act must also satisfy certain tests found within Section 2. This has both positive and negative aspects. On the positive side, the use of a regulatory reform order **must**:

1. Not be capable of being achieved via non-legislative means
2. Be proportionate to the aim of the policy
3. Strike a balance between the public interest and the impact on any individual

60 <www.legislation.gov.uk/wsi>.

61 <www.legislation.gov.uk/ssi>.

62 The Regulatory Reform Act 2001 and the Deregulation and Contracting Out Act 1994.

63 Legislative and Regulatory Reform Act 2006 s1.

On the negative side, the use of a regulatory reform order **must not**:

1. Remove necessary protection
2. Prevent the exercise of a right by another person who may have a legitimate expectation to exercise that right
3. Amend an Act that is of 'constitutional significance'

These tests, and the limitations on the *substantive* reach of such orders,[64] have the potential to act as a safeguard on the quite extraordinary powers to amend primary legislation.

The reduction of burdens on the economy may, at first hearing, sound like a perfectly reasonable proposition and removing *unnecessary* regulatory burdens on individuals or businesses is something to be welcomed. However, the Act is, and its predecessors were, controversial as they allow the government to undo and change things done by Act of Parliament without Parliament always being able to scrutinise the change fully. It could be argued that if an Act of Parliament is defective, then it is for *Parliament* and not the *government* (in the form of a regulatory reform order) to remedy the problem. This is important as a matter of principle due to the legislative supremacy of Parliament and the constitutional rule that no other institution should be able to challenge or question the authority of Parliament.[65] As such, the *principle* behind regulatory reform orders and similar Henry VIII clauses has been criticised.[66]

The fear of regulatory reform orders is grounded on the precedent that it sets rather than the use to which the powers have been put. Regulatory reform orders have, thus far, been sparingly used (fewer than 100 since 2001), and there is little evidence that they have been abused. However, subsequent Acts of Parliament have been modelled on the LRRA. For example, the Public Bodies Act 2011 is another, more recent example of an enabling Act that contains significant powers given via Henry VIII clauses. The Act grants powers to Ministers to amend primary legislation to abolish, merge, amend and alter the powers of public bodies. Ostensibly about efficiency and disbanding needless 'quangos',[67] the original Bill contained insufficient safeguards. Amendments

64 They cannot be used, for example, to vary existing, or introduce new, taxes (s5) or create or vary more serious criminal offences (s6).

65 *British Railways Board v Pickin* [1974] AC 765 (HL) 'In earlier times many learned lawyers seem to have believed that an Act of Parliament could be disregarded in so far as it was contrary to the law of God or the law of nature or natural justice, but since the supremacy of Parliament was finally demonstrated by the Revolution of 1688 any such idea has become obsolete.' 782 (Lord Reid).

66 For the LRRA, see Tarunabh Khaitan, "'Constitution' as Statutory Term' (2013) 129 LQR 589, 597 and for Henry VIII clauses see Daniel Greenberg, 'Dangerous Trends in Modern Legislation' [2015] PL 96, 105.

67 Quangos (quasi-autonomous non-governmental organisations) were organisations to which the government had devolved public law powers.

brought about during the passing of the Act significantly curtailed the potential abuse by introducing safeguards on the use of powers under the Act. For example, a Minister cannot use the powers to remove or move powers of a judicial nature, to remove enforcement mechanisms for obligations on Ministers or to make changes to measures that act as scrutiny or oversight of actions of Ministers.[68] Similar to the LRRA 2006, the powers under the Public Bodies Act 2011 can only be used if the Minister is satisfied that changes are necessary for, *inter alia*, reasons of efficiency and economy.[69] Embodied in the Act is also a test of proportionality, meaning that use of the powers to abolish a public body must be appropriate and necessary for achieving the policy aim.[70] The inclusion of a proportionality test indicates that the use of any powers under the Act is subject to judicial review by the courts.

At the time of writing, the powers under the Public Bodies Act 2011 have been used on fewer than 50 occasions to abolish a wide variety of bodies, most recently the abolition of the Public Works Loan Commissioners.[71]

In summary, the 2006 and 2011 Acts are not dramatic in terms of their *material* scope, and there are safeguards and restrictive tests that must be satisfied in order to use the powers within. It is always possible, should the powers be abused, to launch a judicial review in the courts to challenge the legality of a piece of secondary legislation. However, it is the creeping erosion of the *role* of Parliament in the law-making process that is problematic. In a system where the government typically dominates the process, the increased use of Henry VIII clauses –which enable Ministers to change Acts of Parliament using delegated legislation – is concerning. This concern is exacerbated where Parliament's *scrutiny* of the use of such powers is weak. This is a point taken up later.

ANALYSING THE LAW – DISENTANGLING OUR MEMBERSHIP OF THE EUROPEAN UNION

The UK's decision to leave the European Union has brought into sharp focus the use of Henry VIII powers and the potential for abuse. The EU Withdrawal Act 2018 contains significant powers for the government to make amendments to the statute book as a result of the UK's departure from the EU. The government gains wide powers under s8 to pass secondary legislation to prevent or remedy any 'failure of retained EU law to operate effectively' or 'any other deficiency in retained EU law'. These powers have been criticised for their potential to be abused.

68 Public Bodies Act 2011 s7.

69 ibid s8. This has led to some speculation as to which bodies will be targeted by the use of the powers under the Act – see Stuart Bushell, 'In the Balance' (2012) 156 SJ 19, who argues to preserve the Legal Services Board, which was the quango responsible for regulating the legal services field. The body was nonetheless replaced by the Legal Services Commission, which was itself replaced by the Legal Aid Agency (LAA) on 1 April 2013.

70 Public Bodies Act 2011 s7.

71 <www.legislation.gov.uk/all?title=%22The%20Public%20Bodies%22%20abolition>.

BYELAWS

Byelaws are primarily used as a method of achieving decentralised law-making. That is to say that they are normally passed by those with a strong connection with a particular area in order to regulate that area. As a result of this, most byelaws are passed by local authorities. They are important for two reasons. They act as a form of subsidiarity[72] and bring decision-making closer to the individuals affected and are therefore more likely to engage the affected communities. Additionally, they allow for differentiation in that one rule or law may be appropriate as a solution in one area but not in another.

Like most other pieces of secondary legislation, byelaws are made under the authority of an Act of Parliament, and the powers granted must be exercised in a manner consistent and compatible with a way that is in accordance with the parent act. A great number of byelaws made by local authorities[73] are made under the Local Government Act 1972. This Act, via Section 235, enables councils to pass byelaws to ensure 'good rule and government and suppression of nuisances'. This may seem fairly wide-ranging, but Section 235 is a 'catch-all' provision that applies only where other Acts do not provide for powers to pass byelaws.[74] Local authorities, therefore, have more specific powers to make byelaws under various Acts of Parliament. Table 5.1 gives some indication of the sorts of byelaws that can be passed, by a variety of persons, under the authority of various Acts of Parliament. Table 5.1 is not an exhaustive list of such powers but is presented in order to demonstrate the breadth of powers that can be made available via byelaws. These include the regulation of public services, the control of places of national strategic importance and the behaviour of people in specific locations.

The importance of byelaws to those with delegated power lies in the fact that such people can only do things that they have expressly been given the powers to do. Thus, locating the precise nature of the power conferred, and the procedure to be followed, is crucially important to the validity of any byelaw passed. These byelaws made by local authorities in England used to have cumbersome 'confirmation' procedures involving central government.[75] Since 2016, the process for a great number of byelaws in England was streamlined, and they are now more easily passed, with only a light touch 'leave' being granted by the relevant department.[76] This precedes local publication and consultation with those affected. The growth of 'standard form' byelaws on things like the rules governing access to and use of public places raised the question as to whether the requirement of 'confirmation' by central government was still a sensible use of ministerial time and led to the 2016 reforms.

72 A principle that action should be taken at the lowest level unless there are compelling reasons for it to be taken at a higher level.

73 For example, organisations like Transport for London and airport operators have powers to pass byelaws. The British Railway Board had also been given powers to pass byelaws by the Transport Act 1962 – for discussion of these byelaws, see *Boddington v British Transport Police* [1999] 2 AC 143 (HL).

74 Local Government Act 1972 s235(3).

75 The system is different in Wales – see Local Government Byelaws (Wales) Act 2012. In Wales, byelaws can be made directly by 'legislating authorities', including Councils, but only after the formalities of the Act are satisfied.

76 The Byelaws (Alternative Procedure) (England) Regulations 2016, SI 2016/165.

Table 5.1 Examples of powers conferred through byelaws

Enabling act	***Purpose of byelaws passed under authority of its enabling act***
Town Police Clauses Act 1847, s68	Regulating, inter alia, the conduct of hackney carriage drivers (taxi drivers) and the number of people that they can carry; fixing the rate of fares; dealing with lost property in hackney carriages
Harbours, Docks and Piers Clauses Act 1847, s18	Regulating, inter alia, the use of a harbour, dock or pier; the powers of the harbour master; admission of vessels into the harbour; warehousing, etc.; regulating the use of fires or cranes or weighing machines
Public Health Act 1875, s164	Regulation of places of public recreation (such as public walks or pleasure grounds)
Military Lands Act 1892, s14	The use of land held for military purposes, including securing the public against danger
Public Health Acts Amendment Act 1907, s82	Regulating the use of the seashore, including the erection of temporary structures (for example, booths or tents); sales taking place on the seashore; control of riding and driving
Public Health Act 1936, s231	Regulating public bathing, including the times during which bathing is permitted; clothing to be worn by bathers
Public Libraries and Museums Act 1964, s19	Regulating the use of libraries and museums, including the conduct of users
Countryside Act 1968, s41	Ensuring the protection of country parks, picnic sites from damage; maintaining public order
Food Act 1984, s60	Regulating marketplaces, including buildings, stalls and pens; preventing obstructions; preventing spread of fires
Airports Act 1986, s63	Securing safety of aircraft; controlling operation of aircraft; prohibiting access to parts of the airport; restricting advertising

Enabling act	*Purpose of byelaws passed under authority of its enabling act*
Land Drainage Act 1991, s66	Securing efficient working of the drainage system
Greater London Authority Act 1999, s385	Ensuring proper management of Trafalgar Square and Parliament Square Garden by persons using those Squares
Railways Act 2005, s46	Regulating aspects of railway transport, including rules associated with ticketing; fare evasion; obstructions; conveyance of bicycles; prevention of nuisance; prohibition of smoking
Broads Authority Act 2009, s11	Registration of vessels; rules on exemptions from registration; timing of registration; setting of registration fees

Given the number of local authorities and, by extension, the potential number of byelaws that apply across the geographical area covered by the legal system, there is a risk that law becomes inconsistent and unclear. In a bid to allow for some level of consistency, there has been a move to the use of model byelaws which Councils (or others) can use as a framework for making byelaws.

Byelaws that create criminal offences are tried in a magistrates' court, and the punishment, determined by the specific byelaw, will be a fine typically at level 2, 3 or 4 on the standard scale.[77] As a result, the breach of a byelaw will not lead to a custodial sentence. Where the proposed changes to the process of confirmation apply, there is also the potential for fixed-term penalties to replace fines.

RULES, CODES OF CONDUCT AND CODES OF PRACTICE (TERTIARY LEGISLATION)

There is another category of legislation – normally referred to as 'tertiary' legislation – that covers extremely technical rules and procedures that govern a very narrow range of matters within a policy area. Although these powers stem from Acts of Parliament, their use receives little (or no) scrutiny from Parliament. It is typical, where tertiary legislation is appropriate, for the parent Act to make provision for the making of regulations that can themselves further delegate powers to make rules.

77 Currently, for England and Wales, between £500 and £2,500. Criminal Justice Act 1982, s37(2).

The following contains some examples of the use of such tertiary legislation in the English and Welsh legal system:

- The rules that govern the operation of the powers of the Church of England are governed by rules developed (under statutory authority) by the leaders of the established church.
- There are also rules governing the minutiae of the tax and finance system. The Finance Act 2012 extended the powers of Her Majesty's Revenue and Customs to make provision for technical rules relating to VAT via tertiary legislation.[78]
- The Financial Services and Markets Act 2000, as amended by the Financial Services Act 2012, confers powers on the Financial Conduct Authority to make rules for the conduct of those covered by the Act.[79]
- The Police and Criminal Evidence Act 1984 permits the Secretary of State to develop codes of practice that the police must adhere to when exercising their powers under the Act.[80] The powers covered by such a code of conduct include those governing police search powers, detention and questioning and seizure of property.
- ACAS has powers under the Trade Union and Labour Relations (Consolidation) Act 1992 to issue codes of practice relating to the relationship between employers and trade union officials.[81] These codes are not legally binding but can be taken into consideration in any legal proceedings.[82]
- The exercise of powers under the Regulation of Investigatory Powers Act 2000 is also subject to codes of practice developed as tertiary legislation.

PASSAGE OF STATUTORY INSTRUMENTS

The passage of secondary legislation does not follow a single procedure, such as that which applies to primary legislation, and there are several ways in which it can be made. The important point to note is that the Act which authorises the passage of a particular piece of secondary legislation will also normally dictate the procedure to be followed.

Unlike Acts of Parliament, secondary legislation is not drafted by the Office of the Parliamentary Counsel but by individual government departments. This has the potential to cause problems in the consistency and quality of legislation. This is an aspect of secondary legislation that is discussed later. Once drafted, a statutory instrument is then completed or 'made' when it receives the signature of the person authorised by the Act to make such instruments. The majority of statutory instruments are required to be laid before Parliament either in draft form or, in some cases, after they have been 'made' by the relevant Minister. The

78 Finance Act 2012 Schedule 29.

79 Financial Services and Markets Act 2000 ss137A–141A.

80 Police and Criminal Evidence Act 1984 s66.

81 Trade Union and Labour Relations (Consolidation) Act 1992 s199.

82 ibid s207.

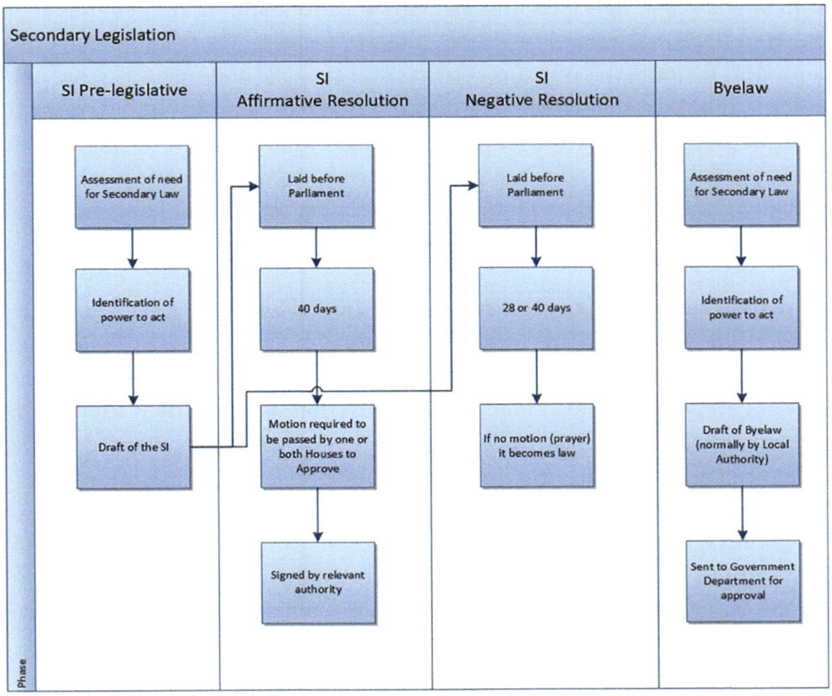

Figure 5.4 The process for adopting secondary legislation.

Act of Parliament that authorises the making of a particular piece of secondary legislation will also determine the method by which Parliament shall approve the instrument.

Once statutory instruments have completed the procedure laid down in the parent Act, they are numbered consecutively in the year in which they are approved. For example, the Proscribed Organisations (Name Changes) Order[83] was the 2,210th statutory instrument of 2014. It would therefore be labelled as SI 2014/2210.[84]

The rest of this section will explore the various procedures (Figure 5.4) that govern the passage of the major forms of statutory instrument. It should be noted that there are many more methods for making statutory instruments than are listed here, but the vast majority are made using the negative or affirmative resolution procedures listed in what follows.

NEGATIVE RESOLUTION PROCEDURE

This is a passive form of approval in that it does not require specific action on the part of Parliament in order for the statutory instrument to become law. Under the negative resolution

83 This Order added the 'Islamic State' as an alternative name for the terrorist group the 'Islamic State of Iraq and Syria' (ISIS) to the Terrorism Act 2000. This is an example of the 'updating' function of statutory instruments.

84 Full citation would be: The Proscribed Organisations (Name Changes) (No. 2) Order 2014, SI 2014/2210.

procedure, an SI will come into force unless there is a successful motion (in the form of a prayer directed to the King) passed in either House to annul it. There are 40 days in which to secure a motion to annul the measure. Having said this, the successful passage of a motion does not of itself annul the measure, and a measure that has been 'made' will remain effective until an Order in Council is passed to revoke it.[85] This further weakens the effectiveness of parliamentary scrutiny and could be said to undermine the legitimacy of secondary legislation. This is a theme discussed further on in relation to the problems caused by statutory instruments.

It is rare for statutory instruments to be prevented from coming into force via the negative resolution procedure. This is for two (interlinked) reasons. First, time to consider and debate such a motion in the Commons is extremely limited and in the hands of the government. This means that it is not guaranteed that a negative motion, particularly if supported by only a small number of backbench MPs, would be given any parliamentary time. Secondly, the government is likely to have a majority in the Commons, and so any motion would require the government's own backbenchers to vote against (or abstain) in any division on a negative motion. The last time a motion under the negative resolution procedure was successful was in the 1970s.[86] In this way, many of the problems caused by the dominance of government, discussed in the chapter on primary legislation, are also relevant when talking about secondary legislation.

In the interim report for the parliamentary session for 2022–2023, it was noted that around 67% of draft SIs were required to be considered using the negative resolution procedure.[87] This is a broadly consistent pattern over recent years.

AFFIRMATIVE RESOLUTION PROCEDURE

This is a more rigorous process and requires a motion to be passed in both Houses[88] authorising the SI within a specified number of days (normally 40). Thus, unlike the negative resolution procedure, scrutiny is active in that it requires action on the part of Parliament for the SI to become law. Given the stricter requirements, SIs which require an affirmative resolution tend to be on more important issues that should not come into force by default but that should be subject to active scrutiny by Parliament.

As with the negative resolution procedure, there is little opportunity for Parliament to amend the SI, and they must approve it or reject it in its entirety. Again, much like the negative resolution procedure, it is rare for an SI not to pass the necessary procedure to become law. The last time that an SI failed to receive approval under the affirmative resolution procedure was in the late 1960s and 1970s, when Parliament rejected the draft version of the

85 Statutory Instruments Act 1946 s5(1).

86 Paraffin (Maximum Retail Prices) (Revocation) Order 1979, SI 1979/797.

87 <https://committees.parliament.uk/publications/40146/documents/196168/default/> at [38].

88 Or, in the case of SIs related to financial matters, the House of Commons only.

Parliamentary Constituencies (England) Order in the Winter of 1969 and the Dock Labour Scheme in 1978.

ANALYSING THE LAW – A CLOSER LOOK AT PARLIAMENTARY SCRUTINY

What made that rejection of the draft Parliamentary Constituencies Order of 1969 even more extraordinary (and indeed a parliamentary first) was that the Home Secretary, who laid the Orders before Parliament, also argued that they should not be passed.[89] The failure to secure the passage of the Parliamentary Constituencies Order in 1969 is a reminder of the *political* context within which law operates. The orders in question concerned proposed changes to the development and make-up of electoral constituencies. The Labour Home Secretary in that instance – James Callaghan – laid the secondary legislation before Parliament based on the recommendations of the Boundary Commission. For a number of reasons, including the perceived bias against the Labour Party,[90] he then went on to recommend that Parliament not approve the orders.

This saga had followed on from a failed Labour bill to redraw the electoral map in the previous session[91] and is indicative of the politics that are involved with law-making. We should be careful not to make assumptions about the route that legislation will follow based solely on a bald reading of the Act in question. It would have been easy to assume in the preceding scenario that a piece of legislation proposed by the government would be supported by that government.

The split in the proportions of draft SIs considered by the House of Lords Secondary Legislation Scrutiny Committee in the latest completed session, 2022–2023, is available on the website.[92] It demonstrates that the vast majority of SIs are approved using the negative resolution procedure. Parliament plays only a passive role under that procedure. This is then compounded by the sheer number of SIs passed in a session. These two factors combined lead to serious questions being asked about the effectiveness of the scrutiny of law-making in the legal system.

OTHER METHODS OF MAKING STATUTORY INSTRUMENTS

Most statutory instruments will follow either the straightforward affirmative or the negative resolution procedures detailed earlier. However, the Act which dictates the powers to pass secondary legislation can also create new methods of scrutiny or, more typically, variations to

89 HC Deb 12 November 1969, vol 791, cols 428–32.

90 ibid cols 436, 451, 453.

91 That had been wrecked by the House of Lords.

92 For a more detailed report, see <https://committees.parliament.uk/publications/40146/documents/196168/default/>.

existing methods. This means that there are potentially an endless number of ways in which statutory instruments can be passed.

One example of an amended process relates to secondary legislation passed under the powers of the European Union (Withdrawal) Act 2018, which introduced a new 'sifting' process intended to help manage the volume of legislation that would need to be passed to deal with leaving the European Union.[93] The process involves an additional step of 'sifting' statutory instruments proposed to be passed using the negative procedure for matters related to leaving the European Union. If the committee(s) set up for this purpose feel it necessary for there to be greater scrutiny, they may recommend that the procedure be upgraded from the negative to the affirmative process. The relevant Minister is not obliged to follow this recommendation but must make a written statement if they disagree.

Equally, the response to emergency situations may mean that waiting the normal 28 or 40 days to turn a 'laid' instrument (a draft) into a 'made' instrument (a law) may not be practicable. This was the case during the global Covid-19 pandemic. More than 500 statutory instruments were passed between 2020 and 2022 using a process where the instrument is first 'made' (i.e. brought into law) before it is laid before Parliament for scrutiny. The vast majority of these were made under the emergency powers of the Public Health (Control of Disease) Act 1984.[94]

SCRUTINY OF DELEGATED LEGISLATION

A theme of both law-making chapters of this textbook is the extent to which legislation is properly scrutinised before it becomes law. Both primary and secondary legislations are subject to control and scrutiny from Parliament and others. This is particularly important for delegated legislation as, without the involvement of Parliament, there is a risk that the democratic link to the people is lost. This would undermine the *legitimacy* of legislation. The preceding analysis of the different methods for passing secondary legislation has highlighted how these processes are intended to provide sufficient room for scrutiny, whilst ensuring that legislation can efficiently be passed. The rest of this section will explore not only the way in which scrutiny happens but also the *effectiveness* of those scrutiny mechanisms.

It should be noted from the outset that statutory instruments – the major form of delegated legislation – find their basis in an Act of Parliament. Thus, Parliament has made an active choice to provide for such delegation, and the creation and control of those powers are in the hands of Parliament. Those granted powers under such an Act cannot go further than the Act permits. As such, a well-drafted parent Act can go a long way to reducing the risk of abuse.

93 European Union (Withdrawal) Act 2018 Schedule 7.

94 Public Health (Control of Disease) Act 1984 s45R.

COMMITTEES OF PARLIAMENT

As well as the formal process required for the passage of secondary legislation, there is also additional scrutiny by a system of committees in Parliament. These provide a more detailed process of scrutiny than is possible in the limited time available in the main chamber of the Commons or Lords. There are numerous committees that undertake different tasks in relation to scrutinising pieces of delegated legislation. The purpose of these committees is to provide a complete system of scrutiny that is based on the distinct separation of functions between the legislature and the executive. In this way, Parliament is able to act as a check on the powers of the government.

The remainder of this section will explore the major parliamentary committees that are involved in scrutinising the use of delegated legislation. These include:

- The Joint Committee on Statutory Instruments
- Delegated Legislation Committees
- House of Lords Secondary Legislation Committee (formerly the Committee on the Merits of Statutory Instruments)
- Departmental Select Committees

JOINT COMMITTEE ON STATUTORY INSTRUMENTS (JCSI)

The JCSI is a committee of both the Commons and the Lords, and its primary function is to draw the attention of the Houses to specific aspects of statutory instruments that have been laid before Parliament. As a joint committee, it draws its membership from both the Commons and the Lords. It meets weekly, and its reports can be found on Parliament's website.[95] JCSI operates under the Standing Orders of Parliament – Orders 74 (Lords) and 151 (Commons)[96] control its structure and governance.[97]

The basis for referring SIs to the special attention of both Houses includes:

- If it imposes a charge on the public revenues or contains powers to raise revenue for the government or any public authority
- If the measure is to be excluded from review by the courts
- That the SI seems to have retrospective effect and the parent Act does not provide for such effect
- That there has been an unjustifiable delay in publication of the SI
- That there has been an unjustifiable delay in informing Parliament of any measure that has been made without first having been laid before Parliament
- That there is doubt as to whether the measure is within the powers granted by the parent Act or where the use of powers is unusual or unexpected in light of the purpose of the parent Act

95 <www.parliament.uk/business/committees/committees-a-z/joint-select/statutory-instruments/news/new-committee-established>.

96 <www.publications.parliament.uk/pa/cm201314/cmstords/900/toc.htm>.

97 <www.publications.parliament.uk/pa/ld/ldstords/147/14701.htm>.

- That the measure requires further clarification
- Defective drafting – if JCSI notices that there are grammatical, typological or linguistically illogical aspects to the SI[98]

The preceding is not an exhaustive list, and the Committee can consider any other issues provided that they do not impinge upon the policy behind the measure. As such, the major limitation on the remit of JCSI is that it is **not** intended to review the *merits* of particular SIs but rather to highlight those that are likely to be controversial in terms of their material scope or the use to which the powers are intended to be put. This limitation significantly impacts upon JCSI's ability to scrutinise secondary legislation, but this should be viewed in light of the role of other committees in the scrutiny process.

MAKING CONNECTIONS – RETAINING A 'HOLISTIC' APPROACH

+++

When studying law, we must remember that the legal system is in fact a series of systems working alongside each other. When assessing how effectively a *particular* committee operates in relation to its task of scrutiny, it is important not to judge that committee in isolation but to look at the *whole system of scrutiny*. This means that you should read this particular section of the text on the JCSI in conjunction with the sections on the other parliamentary committees who *do* have the power to consider the merits of a secondary legislation.

The primary purpose of JCSI is to raise red flags against specific SIs for Parliament (and the department responsible for drafting) to examine. This is important in relation to securing effective protection of the rule of law, particularly where it is proposed that a measure is to have retrospective effect or where it seeks to exclude judicial review. It leaves substantive scrutiny of merits to other bodies and to the parliamentary processes outlined previously. Although separating the scrutiny of the *form* of the legislation (as JCSI does) from the *substance/merits* of that secondary legislation (functions performed by other committees) risks fragmentation, it also leads to a degree of specialisation. By having JCSI look only at the limited range of issues that are routinely within its somewhat superficial remit, an opportunity is missed to flag up content which might usefully be reconsidered by the relevant department.

If an SI is not required to be presented to both Houses, then the Commons has a Select Committee on Statutory Instruments that performs the same function as the JCSI and that draws its membership from the MPs who serve on JCSI.

DELEGATED LEGISLATION COMMITTEES (DLCS)

Delegated Legislation Committees are the mechanism through which most of the substance of secondary law is scrutinised by the House of Commons. In this regard, they have much in

98 These can be found in Standing Orders 74(2) and 151(1) for the Lords and Commons, respectively.

common with the Public Bill Committees that scrutinise primary law.[99] Unlike the JCSI and Select Committee on Statutory Instruments, the DLCs have the power to look at the substance, merit and policy underlying a particular piece of secondary legislation.

Much like Public Bill Committees, the rationale for having DLCs to consider secondary legislation is for reasons of efficiency. The time on the floor of the House is limited, and a committee structure allows the full detail of the legislation to be considered in a way that, for reasons of time, would not be otherwise possible. DLCs are composed of 17 members of the Commons, but any member may attend and speak. The members of the DLC vote on the principle of the piece of secondary legislation, which is then returned to the Commons. If the measure is to be passed using the affirmative resolution procedure, then there will be no further debate on the floor of the Commons and a vote will follow.

HOUSE OF LORDS SECONDARY LEGISLATION SCRUTINY COMMITTEE (SLSC)

The House of Lords Secondary Legislation Scrutiny Committee was previously known, from 2003 until the start of the 2010–2012 parliamentary session, as the Committee on the Merits of Statutory Instruments. It consists of 11 members and, unlike the Commons DLCs, has a fixed membership. Similarly to the DLCs of the House of Commons, the House of Lords SLSC looks at the merits and substance of measures and refers those that meet certain criteria to the main chamber of the Lords.[100] The Committee performs this role alongside ensuring that public body orders (discussed previously) satisfy the relevant statutory tests relating to improving efficiency, effectiveness and securing appropriate accountability of Ministers.[101]

The grounds for referring a piece of secondary legislation for special attention are laid out as follows:

1. That it is politically or legally important or gives rise to issues of public policy likely to be of interest to the House
2. That it may be inappropriate in view of changed circumstances since the enactment of the parent act
3. That it may imperfectly achieve its policy objectives
4. That the explanatory material laid in support provides insufficient information to gain a clear understanding about the instrument's policy objective and intended implementation
5. That there appear to be inadequacies in the consultation process which relates to the instrument[102]

99 Refer to Chapter 4 for more detail on the scrutiny of primary law.

100 <www.parliament.uk/business/committees/committees-a-z/lords-select/secondary-legislation-scrutiny-committee/role/tofref>.

101 The tests within Public Bodies Act 2011 s8.

102 <www.parliament.uk/business/committees/committees-a-z/lords-select/secondary-legislation-scrutiny-committee/role/tofref>.

In the annual report of the Committee for the session 2023–2024, it dealt with some 186 measures and brought around 9.0% of these to the attention of the House of Lords, predominantly on the basis that they were of great political importance or affected an important matter of public policy.[103] There remained, as ever, concerns about the quality of secondary legislation.[104]

The SLSC is seen as a particularly effective form of scrutiny, partly due to its fixed membership, including a number of cross-bench Lords. It has given, in recent times, some fairly strongly worded reports that are very critical of certain policies and of the approach of specific government departments to secondary law. One clear example of the strength of criticism can be seen in the 28th Report of the Committee in 2014 when it considered certain 'town and country' regulations that paved the way for highly controversial 'fracking'[105] operations.[106] The SLSC criticised the lack of time given to Parliament to consider such a contentious issue fully and the short period of consultation before the measure was laid.[107] The Committee also felt that the government's consideration of cost to the public sector was 'fragmentary and apparently inconsistent'.[108] It could be argued that the scrutiny in this case was ineffective as the measures under review still became law. However, the pressure of the SLSC led to more detailed guidance and information being provided by the government and further raised the profile of the issue amongst the public.[109]

The Committee does not restrict itself to commenting only on specific measures but has been known to comment on the general *quality* of secondary legislation. For example, in its 27th Report of Session 2023–2024, the Committee made comments relating to the continued rise in the number of correcting instruments (those measures that are passed to correct previous pieces of secondary legislation that were defectively drafted) and gave some rather scathing criticism of the *quality* of delegated legislation emanating from certain government departments.[110]

The Committee, in its interim report of 2022–2023, criticised:

- Overuse of urgent procedures
- Reactive legislation and failure to consider others' concerns
- Inadequate consultation
- Inadequate information on impact assessments

103 <https://publications.parliament.uk/pa/ld5804/ldselect/ldsecleg/125/125.pdf>.

104 ibid at [9].

105 Fracking is the alternative name for hydraulic fracturing, a controversial means of extracting natural gas for rocks.

106 Secondary Legislation Scrutiny Committee, *Twenty-Eighth Report* (HL 2010–2014, 28 January 2014).

107 ibid para 6. The Committee noted that the measure was given less time for consultation than government best practice would have suggested was necessary – 12 weeks as opposed to the 6 weeks actually given.

108 ibid para 13.

109 Emily Gosden, 'Pro-fracking Planning Reforms Rushed Through Despite Strong Opposition, Lords Warn' *The Telegraph* (London, 29 January 2014) <www.telegraph.co.uk/news/earth/energy/fracking/10605859/Pro-fracking-planning-reforms-rushed-through-despite-strong-opposition-Lords-warn.html>.

110 <https://publications.parliament.uk/pa/ld5804/ldselect/ldsecleg/125/125.pdf>.

- Poor quality explanation
- Number and type of corrections, which had continued to rise

This is important as the solution to each of these problems is in the gift of the government (i.e. those being subject to scrutiny), and yet such issues directly impact on the effectiveness of the working of the Committee in holding the government to account. The SLSC has not shied away from the issue and has been trying to hold the government to account not only for the substance of individual pieces of secondary legislation but also for the whole efficacy of the system of delegated legislation, indicating general examples of 'poor practice'.[111]

ANALYSING THE LAW – EFFECTIVENESS OF THE 'SYSTEM' OF SCRUTINY

Previously, this chapter warned against studying the work of individual committees in isolation. The SLSC also noted this reality by commenting on the number of correcting instruments used. They recognise that drafting errors are within the remit of the JCSI (discussed previously) but also noted that such errors led to great inconvenience for other committees, who may need to consider two or three versions of a statutory instrument.[112] The SLSC also commented that multiple versions (caused by corrections of poor drafting) are liable to reduce the clarity of information available for individuals who may be affected by the law.[113]

Despite the strong criticisms of the end-of-session report, in multiple sessions these problems recurred in 2022–2023 and were exacerbated by the pressures caused on resources as a result of the planning process for the UK leaving the European Union and the Covid-19 pandemic and seem equally prevalent in the 2023–2024 interim and final reports.

DEPARTMENTAL SELECT COMMITTEES (DSCS)

The work of government is, as was discussed in a previous chapter, split between different departments who have responsibility for various policy areas. The late 1970s saw a rise in demand for a stronger system of accountability of these departments to the House of Commons.[114] As a result of this demand, the 'Departmental Select Committees' were created in 1979. Although their remit is not restricted to (or even focussed on) scrutiny of delegated legislation, they have a broad remit to scrutinise the work of government. This includes the ability to examine the policies of the department, to look at the expenditure of the

111 <https://committees.parliament.uk/publications/40146/documents/196168/default/bid> at footnote 59, where it was noted that one SI was missing a commencement date!

112 Secondary Legislation Scrutiny Committee, *Forty Second Report* (HL 2013–2014, 13 May 2014) para 23, citing the measures emanating from the Home Office as being particularly problematic in this regard.

113 ibid para 22.

114 Select Committee on Procedure, *First Report* (HC 1977–1978, 588-I).

department, to examine the administration of the department and to produce reports for debate in the House of Commons.[115]

The Departmental Select Committees, because of their close work with the departments of government, have unparalleled knowledge of the workings of the central government and of the department to which they are aligned. They can call witnesses and often question Ministers. This complements the work of the other committees discussed and adds experience and expertise of policy areas. They are mentioned here not because they perform specific functions in relation to delegated legislation but rather because they have a more general role in relation to scrutinising the work of government. This could take the form of post-legislative reviews of how particular SIs are operating in practice and how well they are achieving their policy aims.

JUDICIAL SCRUTINY OF DELEGATED LEGISLATION

The analysis has so far focussed on the parliamentary process of scrutiny of delegated legislation. In addition to the committee structure of Parliament, the courts also play an important role in checking on the powers of the executive (normally the government) when they make law. Individuals are able to challenge measures on the basis that they are *ultra vires* – that is, that the measure is unlawful because the person passing it acted outside of the powers conferred by the parent/enabling act.

MAKING CONNECTIONS – THE INSTITUTIONAL BALANCE AND PUBLIC LAW

There are two interrelated connections to be made here that will enhance understanding of the role of judges in this area.

First, it is important to realise that judges have a constitutional responsibility to prevent abuse of power by the executive – it is a facet of both the separation of powers and the rule of law.[116] That constitutional duty finds its expression most clearly in the doctrines and principles of judicial review. For this reason, it is likely that any further study you may make of constitutional or administrative law will have a particular focus on judicial review.

Secondly, through judicial review, judges are supporting another constitutional principle, namely, parliamentary sovereignty. Delegated legislation, though often *proposed* by those holding ministerial posts, is *passed* under the *authority* of Parliament. Judges are therefore aiming to uphold the will and intention of Parliament when questioning secondary legislation.

115 Select Committee on the Modernisation of the House of Commons, *First Report* (HC 2001–2002, 224-II), para 35.
116 For more on the rule of law, see Tom Bingham, *The Rule of Law* (Penguin 2011).

When we take the preceding two points together, we can comment on the distinction between the courts' treatment of primary and secondary legislation. You should remember, from the previous chapter, that judges cannot question the validity of an Act of Parliament (i.e. primary legislation).[117] We can contrast this with the American legal system, where judges of the Supreme Court *can* challenge Acts of Congress.[118] This is because the courts recognise the sovereignty of Parliament within the legal system. Indeed, this is one of the core principles of the uncodified British Constitution. The same is not true of delegated legislation, which is often passed under parliamentary authority but proposed and executed by 'another'. This allows courts to question whether the person who was delegated powers has *exercised* those powers in compliance with parliamentary intent.

Scrutiny by judges, through the medium of judicial review, is an integral part of the complete *system* of monitoring secondary legislation. Much of the work of the parliamentary committees, discussed previously, is what may be termed *pre*-legislative scrutiny – this means that scrutiny happens in advance of the piece of secondary legislation being brought into force. Judicial review complements this by adding a system of *post*-legislative scrutiny – this means that scrutiny happens subsequent to the coming into force of the piece of secondary legislation.

An important point to note about judicial review is that it is not necessarily intended for judges to pass comment or judgment on the *quality* or *substance* of secondary law but rather to check whether it complies with the requirements of primary law. This has been expressed by Lord Donaldson with a football analogy in *ex parte Hammersmith and Fullham LBC*,[119] as follows:

> The referee is only involved when it is appears that some player has acted in breach of the rules. The referee may then stop the play and take some remedial action, but, tempting though it may be, it is not for him to express any view on the skill of the players or, how he would have acted in their position. Still less, following a breach of the rules does he take over one of the positions of the players.[120]

Judicial review is an excellent example of the multidimensional nature of law-making in the legal system of England and Wales as it shows the institutions interacting (Parliament, government Ministers and the judiciary) and how the various sources of law also interact (statute, secondary law and case law).

As mentioned previously, a judicial review claim can be launched on the basis of numerous grounds. Those of most relevance to a text on the English and Welsh legal system are:

117 *British Railways Board v Pickin* [1974] AC 765 (HL).

118 *Marbury v Madison* (1803) 5 US 137.

119 *R v Secretary of State for the Environment, ex parte Hammersmith and Fulham London Borough* Council and Others [1991] 1 AC 521 (HL).

120 ibid 561 (Lord Donaldson).

1. Procedural *ultra vires*
2. Substantive *ultra vires*

Procedural *ultra vires* refers to the idea that those exercising delegated powers should follow any mandatory procedures laid down in the enabling/parent act. This is illustrated in the *Aylesbury Mushroom*[121] case. In the case, the Industrial Training Act 1964 gave the Minister of Labour certain powers which were used to create, by order, the 'Agricultural, Horticultural and Forestry Industry Training Board'. However, the Act required that 'before making an industrial training order the Minister shall consult any organisation or association of organisations appearing to him to be representative of substantial numbers of employers engaging in the activities concerned'.[122] The Minister did not undertake such consultation and so had breached a fundamental procedural requirement of the primary legislation, and this led to a finding of *ultra vires* by the court.

Substantive *ultra vires*, on the other hand, relates to a situation whereby a person with delegated powers goes beyond the powers given by an enabling or parent act. In the *GCHQ*[123] case, Lord Diplock characterised an aspect of judicial review in the following terms: 'The decision-maker must understand correctly the law that regulates his decision-making power and must give effect to it.'[124] In practical terms, this means that a successful judicial review action may be launched when a Minister (or other decision-maker) abuses their discretion,[125] attempts to use their power for an improper or alternative purpose,[126] wrongly delegates their power[127] or simply acts beyond the powers conferred by the Act.[128]

ANALYSING THE LAW – THE COURTS AND SECONDARY LEGISLATION

The cases of *Reilly*[129] and *Reilly (No 2)*[130] demonstrate the importance of judicial review and how the grounds act as a safeguard on the risk inherent in Parliament delegating its law-making powers to members of the executive.

Partly as a result of public pressure over the size of the welfare bill, the coalition government passed the Jobseeker's Allowance (Employment, Skills and Enterprise

121 *Agricultural, Horticultural and Forestry Industry Training Board v Aylesbury Mushrooms Ltd* [1972] 1 WLR 190 (QBD).

122 Industrial Training Act 1964 s1(4).

123 *Council of Civil Service Unions v Minister for the Civil Service* [1985] AC 374 (HL).

124 ibid 410 (Lord Diplock).

125 *R v Somerset County Council, ex parte Fewings* [1995] 1 WLR 1037 (CA).

126 *Porter v Magill* [2001] UKHL 67, [2002] 2 AC 357.

127 *Carltona v Commissioners of Works* [1943] 2 All ER 560 (CA).

128 *Prescott v Birmingham Corp* [1954] Ch 210 (CA).

129 *R (Reilly) v Secretary of State for Work and Pensions* [2013] UKSC 68, [2014] AC 453.

130 *R (Reilly No 2) v Secretary of State for Work and Pensions* [2014] EWHC 2182 (Admin).

Scheme) Regulations 2011[131] based on powers under various enabling acts.[132] Under the Regulations, benefit payments could be sanctioned if an individual refused to participate in unpaid work schemes.

In *Reilly*, the applicant challenged the legality of the 2011 Regulations on the basis that they were *ultra vires*. Reilly had (effectively) been forced to give up unpaid work experience in her field of interest to take on a retail role with a national retail chain. She argued, in particular, that the Secretary of State for Work and Pensions had not adequately described the work scheme in the Regulation (as required by the enabling act) and had not published a policy describing the various schemes. As a result of the failure to comply with the requirements of the enabling act, the Supreme Court upheld the findings of the Court of Appeal to quash the decision, despite the fact that this would cost the government a great deal of money in claims for repayment of the unlawfully levied penalties.

The case of *Reilly* demonstrates the importance of post-legislative scrutiny in the form of judicial review. This point is reinforced when we consider that the House of Lords Committee on the Merits of Statutory Instruments[133] had already raised concerns during the legislative process about the lack of detail in the Regulations and how much power they transferred, without recourse to Parliament, to the executive.[134] Through this lens, it could be argued that judicial review acts as an additional safeguard where the parliamentary process of scrutiny is deficient. There is even a form of weak link between pre- and post-legislative scrutiny as Mr Justice Foskett made passing reference to the work of the Merits Committee when handing down his decision in *Reilly (No 1)* in the High Court.[135]

However, the effectiveness of the whole system of scrutiny can be called into question by the events that unfolded whilst the initial case in *Reilly* was still going through the judicial process. Before the decision by the Supreme Court was reached, the government passed (and in the face of strong opposition)[136] a new Act[137] that retrospectively validated decisions taken under the old regulations.

131 Jobseeker's Allowance (Employment, Skills and Enterprise Scheme) Regulations 2011, SI 2011/917.

132 Most importantly under s17 of the Jobseekers Act 1995.

133 Now known as the House of Lords Secondary Legislation Scrutiny Committee.

134 Merits of Statutory Instruments Committee, *Twenty-Ninth Report* (HL 2010–2012, 3 May 2011) [10]–[11].

135 *R (Reilly) v Secretary of State for Work and Pensions* [2012] EWHC 2292 (Admin), (2012) 156(32) SJLB 31 [44]–[48] (Foskett J).

136 For a flavour of the debate in the House of Commons, see the Third Reading debate – HC Deb 19 March 2013, vol 560 cols 855–96. In the Lords the language was less emotive but nonetheless critical. See HL Deb 25 March 2013, vol 744 col 945.

137 Jobseekers (Back to Work Schemes) Act 2013.

This had the effect of pre-empting and nullifying the effect of any Supreme Court decision and thus rendered the judicial review somewhat toothless. In the case it appeared that the government was able to free itself of the safeguards provided by judicial review. However, such retrospective legislation is both rare and controversial.[138]

Indeed, what followed was a further case, *Reilly (No 2)*, whereby the manner in which the government had acted was deemed to be incompatible with the right to a fair trial guaranteed by the European Convention on Human Rights. The courts also sounded a warning to Parliament about respect for the mechanisms of scrutiny provided by judicial review:

> Parliament's undoubted power to legislate to overrule the effect of court judgments generally ought not to take the form of retrospective legislation designed to favour the Executive in ongoing litigation in the courts brought against it by one of its citizens.[139]

As was discussed earlier in this chapter, the second half of the 20th century was characterised by an increase in the volume and scope of delegated legislation. This has put significant pressure on the existing system of parliamentary scrutiny and has led to a commensurate increase in the importance of judicial review as a post-legislative form of scrutiny. Despite the logical link between increased executive powers and the need for enhanced scrutiny, the government appears to be unhappy with such judicial 'interference'. When we consider the financial impact of cases like *Reilly* with estimates of costs of £130 million,[140] this is perhaps unsurprising.

ANALYSING THE LAW – THE RISE OF JUDICIAL REVIEW

There has been a steady increase in the number of judicial review applications, and this has led to some questioning whether the system is being used appropriately. In 2012,[141] the government launched a consultation paper with the intention of

138 One such instance was the War Damages Act 1965 which retrospectively overruled claims founded on the basis of *Burmah Oil Ltd v Lord Advocate* [1965] AC 75 (HL). For the controversies of retrospective legislation, see Geoffrey Loomer, 'Taxing Out of Time: Parliamentary Supremacy and Retroactive Tax Legislation' [2006] BTR 64.

139 *R (Reilly No 2) v Secretary of State for Work and Pensions* [2014] EWHC 2182 (Admin). [82].

140 Although this figure was questioned by the High Court in *Reilly* (ibid) [105]–[108].

141 Ministry of Justice, *Judicial Review: Proposals for Reform* (White Paper, Cm 25, 2012).

bringing forward reforms to the system of judicial review in an attempt to curb the 'significant growth'[142] in the number of judicial review applications. That report noted that the number of applications had risen from 160 in 1974 to over 11,000 by 2011. The government went on, in 2013, to make certain procedural changes that sought to limit the rights of those seeking judicial review.[143] However, and as noted in a response to the consultation paper, the government was not clear as to why this rise is particularly problematic and fails to take into account the significant developments in EU, human rights and immigration law that have partly prompted this rise.[144]

A further and latest review, led by an independent panel, was set up in 2020 to consider whether there needed to be reform to the grounds for judicial review, the range of executive decisions that could be reviewed, necessary changes to remedies and any procedural changes. The suggestions coming from the panel advocated for very limited change and underscored the importance of judicial review as a limit to abuse of power. The Judicial Review and Courts Act 2022 put these recommendations into force, primarily by limiting the ability of the Upper Tribunal to review certain decisions[145] and a change to a particular remedy to allow for more flexibility for judges to limit the impact of a finding of illegality.[146]

Governmental attempts to 'curb' judicial review should be treated with healthy suspicion. It should not be forgotten that it is often government Ministers who are *subject* to the judgments of the courts under judicial review. Thus, there is an inherent bias whereby government Ministers are keen to promote a narrative that increased litigation is 'judicial interference' rather than an important tool of accountability.

In summary, there is a tension between the need, on the one hand, for those upon whom public power is conferred to be able to act freely and, on the other, for those who have significant public powers to be held to account when passing and executing secondary legislation. Judicial review is intended not only to be a safety net, allowing for challenge to those SIs that unintentionally overstep parliamentary authority, but also to act as an important check on the power and authority of those exercising delegated law-making powers.

142 ibid para 25.

143 Alexander Home and Joanna Dawson, 'Judicial Review: Government Reforms' (House of Commons Library, 2013) <www.parliament.uk/briefing-papers/sn06616.pdf>.

144 ibid 5.

145 Judicial Review and Courts Act 2022 s2.

146 Judicial Review and Courts Act 2022 s1.

CONCLUSION

Secondary legislation, despite all its problems and difficulties, is a necessary tool of efficient governance. Secondary legislation is now a fact of life for the legal system. Without it, Parliament would be (even more) bogged down with debating primary legislation. For that reason, and although presented in distinct chapters within this work, it is important to read this chapter alongside the chapter on primary legislation (Acts of Parliament). Although Parliament is sovereign and, as a result, Acts of Parliament are at the apex of any hierarchy of norms within the UK, there is a danger that this underplays the importance of secondary legislation.

Secondary legislation is below primary legislation in hierarchy, but its impact can be significant. Understanding the symbiotic relationship between primary and secondary legislation is crucial to full and proper understanding of the English and Welsh legal system as a distinct subject. It is also important to understand the nature of secondary legislation and how it impacts on many other dimensions of legal study (e.g. contract law, public law and European Union law).

The advantages that secondary legislation brings in terms of efficiency, increased *local* decision-making and expertise are obvious. The public good behind the *principle* of secondary legislation in the legal system is, therefore, almost beyond question.

The problems come then not necessarily from the *principle* of secondary legislation but from how that principle is *executed* in practice. There are very real concerns over the volume of secondary legislation that is passed and, more crucially, how that legislation is scrutinised and controlled. The current patchwork system of scrutiny, with its many and disparate committees, can lead to a fragmented and ineffective system of scrutiny. Given the breadth of powers given to pass secondary legislation, an effective system of scrutiny is important to prevent the abuse of powers and to maintain the *quality* of such legislation.

TAKING THINGS FURTHER – PERSUASIVE AND IMPACTFUL LEGAL WRITING

In order to promote your critical awareness, it is important that you can do more than just state the relevant advantages and disadvantages of statutory instruments and the methods by which they are controlled and scrutinised. Students often present answers to questions about the nature of secondary law as a list of advantages and disadvantages of delegated legislation with a brief effort to evaluate the strength, and this often leads to bland, generic answers.[147] Better answers attempt to weigh the relevant arguments and link them together through a common theme.

147 This applies to all forms of legal essays and not just those relating to secondary law or even just a module on the legal system.

THE WEBSITE

The website that accompanies this textbook contains many useful resources that you can use to consolidate and further your knowledge of the law, to hone your skills of critical analysis and to test your knowledge.

6

CHAPTER 6
STATUTORY INTERPRETATION

INTRODUCTION

In an ideal world, Acts of Parliament would enter the legal system perfectly formed and drafted with such clarity and precision of language so as to raise no question over application. The world is far from ideal, and the English language is full of such nuance and flexibility that even the most straightforward of statutes can raise serious questions over interpretation. This is before we consider that some statutes may be drafted imperfectly or with intentional ambiguity.

The flexibility and ambiguity of words are not something unique to the field of law. Indeed, most disciplines struggle with the subtlety of the English language. However, in the legal field, words contained within legislation (particularly those in Acts of Parliament) take on an increased level of importance. The words themselves *are* the law; Acts of Parliament are viewed as the worldly manifestation of Parliament's sovereignty. The legal system requires trained people capable of interpreting the meaning of the words and applying them to the everyday situations of the subjects. That role falls primarily to the judiciary, and this chapter will explore how judges go about this task of interpreting the law found within statutes. In order to understand the approach(es) adopted by judges fully, the chapter will begin by exploring the importance of statutory interpretation, including some of the reasons that may lead to a need for such interpretations, as well as the inherent dangers of the principles of statutory interpretation itself.

AS YOU READ

This chapter broadly consists of two sections – the first of which deals with the need for statutory interpretation, and the second of which deals with the 'rules and approaches'. As you read, think about practical examples of how these principles may be applied.

By the end of the chapter, you should be able to **explain** the need for statutory interpretation and **discuss critically** the extent to which the rules affect the balance of power between the legislature and the judiciary.

In addition, you should be able to **evaluate** the strengths and weaknesses of, and relationships between, the legislature and the judiciary.

Also, you should be in a position to be able to **understand** the application of the approaches to statutory interpretation in a given hypothetical example.

DOI: 10.4324/9781032641829-6

THE IMPORTANCE OF STATUTORY INTERPRETATION

FOR THE LEGAL SYSTEM

The importance of statutory interpretation should not be understated. A great number of appeals that reach the Supreme Court are concerned with interpretation of statutes. Within the context of this textbook, statutory interpretation is one of the twin pillars (along with precedent, discussed in Chapter 9) of the judicial legal order (see Figure 6.1). It is also closely related to the issues discussed within Chapters 2, 4 and 5 on sources of law and the primary and secondary law-making process, respectively. As such, you should avoid reading these chapters (and, indeed, any of the chapters of this text) in isolation. Having this more holistic view of how topics fit together will lead you to a stronger critical understanding of the material. You should also try to see how different legal subjects fit together.

At its most basic level, statutory interpretation is important as it allows the legal system to function efficiently. Rather than have Parliament attempt to cover matters comprehensively in statutes, as may be the case in a civil law system, or force Parliament to a constant cycle of redrafting, judges are given jurisdiction to interpret the law in order to answer any questions of interpretation that arise in the application of the law. The majority of this chapter will be dedicated to this aspect of statutory interpretation.

The ability to attribute meaning to words is a very powerful tool. Much of the judiciary's time is taken with attempting to unravel the meaning of words as intended by Parliament. Andrew Burrows, in a public lecture, stated that he would 'estimate that over two thirds

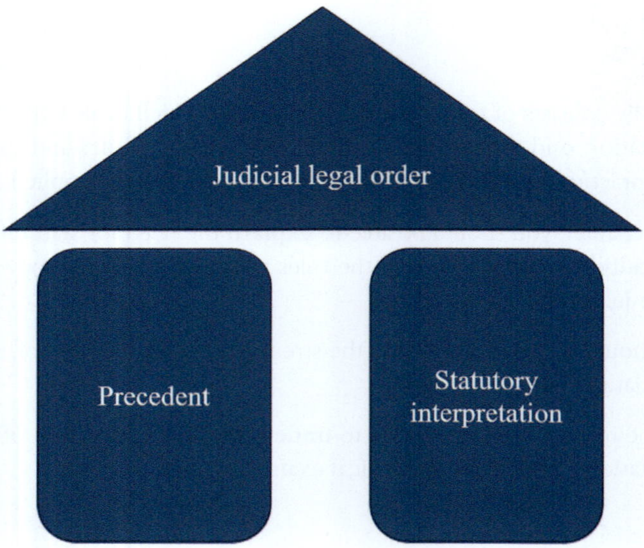

Figure 6.1 The twin pillars of the judicial legal order.

of the cases that I have sat on have involved some issue of legislative interpretation'.[1] While many cases raise new points of law, many more are concerned with the correct interpretation of statutory material. By allowing this power to be exercised by judges, the legal system of England and Wales has an added flexibility in that it is possible for poorly drafted measures to be 'saved' by the judiciary and for matters to develop more easily to match changes in society.

FOR STUDENTS (OF LAW AND OTHERWISE)

It is easy, amongst the technical rules discussed and the principles later, to lose sight of the practical, *educational* value of statutory interpretation to those undertaking legal study. The ability to read for meaning is one of the key skills of being a good law student. The obvious benefit is that it helps with understanding better the role of the judiciary and in analysing case law that may be required to be read during legal studies. Beyond this, it is important to understand how judges approach statutes so that accurate predictions can be made about the approach likely to be adopted in relation to new legislation. The law in a given area will almost certainly change over time, and sometimes the pace of change is staggeringly fast. Even where the pace of change is steadier, the amount of change can still be immensely significant. For example, the various acts governing company law have had incremental change over the last 150 years, but the number of sections has still grown by more than 510% in that time (from around 200 to the current 1,300 sections). Individual clients, or large organisations, may be interested in the likely impact of new statutes, and the ability to read beyond simple decoding of the meaning of words is a valued skill. Even when we are talking about legal documents other than statutes, such as contracts or collective agreements, the skills of interpretation are valuable.

Even outside formal legal education, in the form of a law degree or otherwise, the ability to read for purpose is a valuable skill both in terms of professional development and for academic reasons. Being able to understand the literal meaning of words is important, but it is also important to be able to determine the meaning of any piece of writing (a formal report, a company circular or even an email) not only from the literal meaning of the words but also from the other contextual factors (organisational or documentary) that surround them. Studying how judges approach the task of interpretation is helpful in this regard as it demonstrates the range of approaches that can be taken and can help construct alternative meanings that can be useful in an organisational environment.

By bringing together the strands discussed earlier, the importance of statutory interpretation becomes clear. It is vital to both the operation and the understanding of the legal system. Different approaches to interpretation can make a significant difference to the outcome in a particular case, and so formulating a set of principles that can be used to predict the various outcomes, and their likelihood of being adopted, is an important legal skill.

1 Lord Burrows, 'Seven Lessons from Inside the UK Supreme Court' (Neill Lecture, 2023) <Seven_Lessons_from_Inside_the_UK_Supreme_Court_Lord_Burrows_2725d87d66.pdf>.

ANALYSING THE LAW – DIFFERENT APPROACHES TO INTERPRETATION

The case of *Mandla v Lee*[2] aptly demonstrates the problems that can be caused by different approaches to statutory interpretation. The case concerned the interpretation of the Race Relations Act 1976.

The facts of the case are relatively straightforward. A father wished to place his son in a private school in Birmingham. As active members of the Sikh faith and community, the father and son wished for the boy to wear a turban in school. The headmaster of the school would not allow this as it violated the school's uniform policy. The legal issue was whether Sikh was within a 'racial or ethnic group' under the Race Relations Act 1976. If it was demonstrated that Sikhs were a racial or ethnic group, then the boy would be protected from discrimination, whereas if not, the school would not have unlawfully discriminated against him.

The Court of Appeal and the House of Lords came to radically different views over how to interpret the term 'racial or ethnic group'. Lord Denning in the Court of Appeal held that the word 'ethnic' was closely linked to the concept of race. In doing so, he relied upon the *Oxford English Dictionary* definition of the word. This had the result that Sikhs were not to be regarded as an ethnic group (and were not, therefore, covered by the prohibition from discrimination) as they did not share racial or ethnic characteristics, such as a distinct language or 'blood'. According to Denning, the only characteristic that separated Sikhs from other people was the religion of Sikhism, and religion was not a protected characteristic under the 1976 Act.[3] Lord Denning also had some words of criticism for the Commission of Racial Equality:

> I cannot pass from this case without expressing some regret that the Commission for Racial Equality thought it right to take up this case against the headmaster. . . . The statutes relating to race discrimination and sex discrimination are difficult enough to understand and apply anyway. They should not be used so as to interfere with the discretion of schools and colleges in the proper management of their affairs.

The House of Lords, and in particular Lord Fraser, did not find this an acceptable method of interpretation for this case and preferred a broader interpretation, indicating that to adopt a literal approach and to apply a dictionary definition to the term 'ethnic' (as Denning did), relying on scientific or biological evidence of racial characteristics would 'be absurd'. He also strongly disagreed with the view put forward about the Commission for Racial Equality, stating:

2 Mandla v Lee [1983] 1 All ER 1062. See Ian McKenna 'Racial Discrimination' (1983) 46 MLR 759.

3 Religion is now a protected characteristic; see Equality Act 2010 s4.

> The commission has a difficult task, and no doubts its inquiries will be resented by some and are liable to be regarded as objectionable and inquisitive. But the respondent in this case, who conducted his appeal with restraint and skill, made no complaint of his treatment at the hands of the commission.

It is interesting that two sets of senior judges applying the same law were able to come to opposite conclusions. This illustrates clearly the importance of understanding the different methods and approaches to interpretation and considering which is likely to be more persuasive in a case. As will become clearer as the chapter progresses, the fundamental task for courts in interpretation is to understand the intention of the Parliament that enacted them. You should start to reflect, given what you know of the legal system, on how a judge may go about achieving this purpose and which sources could be used.

THE NEED FOR STATUTORY INTERPRETATION

It is important not only to understand the mechanical processes or rules of statutory interpretation (which are discussed later) but also to understand *why* statutory interpretation is needed at all. Statutory interpretation is about attempting to discern Parliament's intent from, amongst other things, the words it uses in acts. This can be problematic because words can bear different meanings. Figure 6.2 demonstrates some (but not all) of the problems, caused in part by the problems of the English language, that lead to a need for judicial interpretation of statutes.

THE MULTIPLE OR UNCERTAIN MEANINGS OF WORDS

One of the most common problems that courts face when having to interpret statutory provisions relates to the fact that words can have wide, narrow, uncertain and even alternative meanings. The case of *R v Allen*[4] demonstrates this problem. Under s57 of the Offences Against the Person Act 1861, it was an offence to commit bigamy, that is, while married, if a person should 'marry any other person during the lifetime of the former husband or wife'. There was ambiguity in the word 'marry' within the Act, as a person committing bigamy did not marry the second person (i.e. the second marriage was void as it was not lawful). As such, if you were to adopt the *narrow* meaning of the word, the offence of bigamy was legally impossible to commit. However, if you were to adopt a *wider* meaning of the word, as the court did, so that it meant to go through a marriage ceremony, regardless of its legality, then the offence had been committed.

4 *Allen* (1872) LR1 CCR 367.

Figure 6.2 The need for interpretation.

A more technical example of this principle can be found in *Re Paramount Airways* (No2),[5] where the Court of Appeal had to consider whether the phrase 'any person' in s238 of the Insolvency Act 1986 was to be interpreted to mean any person within the UK, or whether it could be read more extensively to include people outside the jurisdiction. Despite the uncertainty and ambiguity of the phrase, the Court of Appeal held that 'the solution to the question of statutory interpretation raised by this appeal does not lie in retreating to a rigid and indefensible line. Trade takes place increasingly on an international basis. So does fraud'. This gave the Act extraterritorial application and demonstrates that even international forces can influence how a court will undertake its interpretative task.

POOR DRAFTING

In an ideal world, provisions of law would be perfectly drafted in such a way as to lead to only one possible, rational and just interpretation. However, and in addition to the other reasons identified earlier and later, it is sometimes necessary to interpret statutes because they are badly written. This is regrettable, but perhaps unavoidable, given the increase in legislative output over the past 70 years, both in terms of the number of distinct acts passed and in the length of these acts. The challenges posed by the proliferation of primary and secondary law in terms of distinct legislative instruments and page numbers were discussed in Chapters 4 (primary legislation) and 5 (secondary legislation), but this chapter considers the practical implications of poor drafting that makes it onto the statute book.

5 *Re Paramount Airways Limited* [1993] Ch 223, CA.

Badly written statutes put the courts in a difficult position as it is not clear what a judge should do when interpreting a defective statute, and this is a point returned to later in the chapter, when discussing interpretative approaches. In light of this difficulty, the judiciary tend to get impatient and vocalise their displeasure with poorly worded statutes. For example, the Landlord and Tenant Act 1987 has provided the judiciary with many opportunities for criticism of the drafting process and illustrates the difficulties that courts are faced with when ruling on unclear statutes.

Much of the purpose behind the Landlord and Tenant Act was to enable tenants in a mansion block to acquire certain powers to manage the disposal of their leases/property when the landlord wished to dispose of his interest in the building to a new potential landlord. The proposed mechanism was to give a right of first refusal to any tenant wishing to take up that opportunity. This was a noble and laudable proposal. However, there were a number of specific provisions within the Act that did not achieve this purpose and which, in light of the purpose, made little sense. For example, the prevention of the disposal of the protected interest in s6 applied to the original landlord. However, the duty not to dispose of the protected interest did not apply to the new landlord (whose conduct was governed by s12). If the purpose of the Act was to protect the interests of the tenants, then the absence of a s6 duty on the new landlord made little sense.

The provisions of the Landlord and Tenant Act 1987 were considered in numerous cases, and two judgments will be briefly mentioned to give a flavour of the problems caused by the Act and the reaction of the judiciary. In *Belvedere Court Management v Frogmore Development*,[6] Lord Bingham held that 'one could wish that the Act provided as many answers as it raised problems'.[7] He was sympathetic to the difficulties involved in drafting: 'I can readily appreciate the complexity of the task which confronted the draftsman in seeking to give legislative effect to this ambitious scheme.'[8] However, his criticism was more scathing in places:

> [T]he history of these proceedings is a dismal commentary on a measure intended to help tenants of mansion blocks, many of them of limited means. As it is, the legal profession would appear to be the main beneficiaries of this obscure statute.[9]

This criticism was an echo of earlier criticisms made by Browne-Wilkinson in *Denetower Ltd v Toop*,[10] where the Act was described as 'ill-drafted, complicated and confused'.[11]

THE DIFFICULTIES OF TURNING POLICY INTO 'LAW'

The problem of turning a policy into a law can be split into three distinct but interrelated issues. Firstly, what is a good idea in theory may simply be very difficult to implement into

6 [1997] QB 858 (CA).
7 ibid 881.
8 ibid 881.
9 ibid.
10 [1991] 1 WLR 945.
11 ibid 952.

practice. This may be because social problems, although readily recognised as such, do not present easy solutions. The development of the statutory law of harassment is a good example of this problem in action. The Protection from Harassment Act 1997 (PFHA) was passed in response to growing pressure to deal with the problem of stalking that was brought to public attention by high-profile instances of the damage stalking causes.

The Act sought to deal with problems by formulating a response in both civil and criminal law so that a victim of harassment could not only find satisfaction through the criminal justice system but also had a range of civil law remedies available. This, on the face of it, seems a sensible policy. Unfortunately, due to the mix of criminal and civil liability and the context of the Act itself, the courts have been faced with some interpretative problems.

For example, in *Thomas v News Group Newspapers*,[12] the court was asked to consider whether the meaning of 'harassment' should be interpreted so as to exclude a newspaper campaign directed at a particular person. It was clear that the meaning given in the Act was capable of including newspaper articles, but the question was whether it *should* include such articles given that Parliament had specifically been attempting to address the issue of stalking, that is, normally physically following, pestering and harassing a person. Given that it could not reasonably be denied that news articles could be within the meaning of 'harassment', the courts did not accept a narrow definition of the term. This case demonstrates that it is sometimes difficult to circumscribe the scope of the words in an Act so that they cover *only* the circumstances intended and no more.

Secondly, the precise basis of the need for the new law may not be very clear, and this level of uncertainty can feed through into the legislative proposal. This is also, in part, a consequence of the different interests that feed into the formulation of policy and legislative proposals. These interests can vary (from manifesto promises to international pressures to public or media pressure) and have already been discussed in Chapter 4, on law-making (Figure 6.3). It is not always the case that these interests pull in the same direction, and in an attempt not to wholly alienate different interest groups, proposals can often be watered down and/or compromised in order to satisfy different actors. As George Orwell noted, the use of language can sometimes disclose a tension between communicated and perceived intentions: 'The great enemy of clear language is insincerity. When there is a gap between one's real and one's declared aims, one turns, as it were, instinctively to long words and exhausted idioms, like a cuttlefish squirting out ink.'[13]

Finally, and more narrowly, the parliamentary process itself can create difficulties in concretising a policy into a clear, intelligible law. Sometimes, as part of the parliamentary process, the initial germ of a legislative 'idea' can end up very different to the final outcome that will be embodied within the Act of Parliament. While it is normally the government that forms the policy and is responsible for presenting a bill, it is Parliament that has the final 'say' over whether the policy

12 [2001] EWCA Civ 1233, CA.

13 George Orwell, *Politics and the English Language* (first published 1946, Penguin 2013).

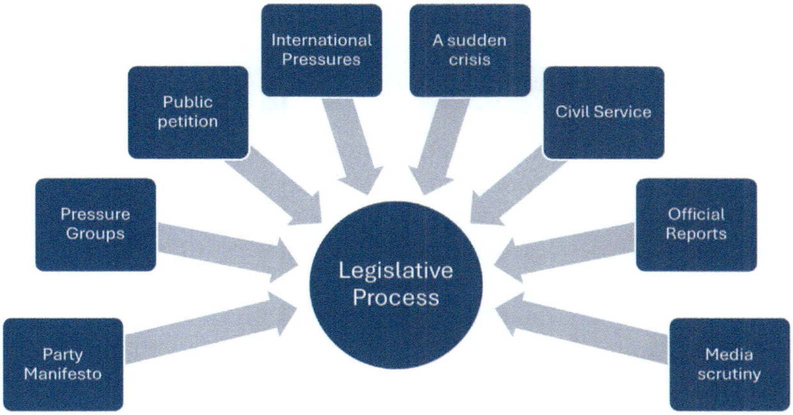

Figure 6.3 Summary of influences on law-making.

becomes law, and the precise form of words used. This means that other political parties in the Commons, or backbench MPs on the government side, or members of the House of Lords, might amend a bill so that its nature changes quite significantly.

It is also important to note that at each stage of the *legislative* process, the pressures identified earlier in Chapters 4 and 5 (or in some cases) persuade the political actors to change their view and make further amendments to the proposal. The three strands identified previously are, as already mentioned, interconnected and interrelated. They should not be viewed in isolation but as a system of pressures and influences that can influence the passage of law at all stages and in ways that can cause problems of interpretation.

NEW SITUATIONS

At times, technological or societal developments overtake a statute, and these result in pressure mounting on judges to reinterpret the law to include previously unconsidered situations. There are examples of this type of problem scattered throughout legislative history. This problem tends to affect, in particular, those areas which have seen drastic technological changes. One such area is that of protection of intellectual property by the law of copyright. The Copyright Designs and Patents Act 1988 sought to protect the rights of creators of, *inter alia*, artistic works (including literary, dramatic or musical works). Since that time, the age of the computer has developed, and computer software has become an important, and valuable, source of innovation and creativity. As such, the question arises whether software architecture and the code that generates the program can be protected by copyright. In the first instance, and in the absence of updating by Parliament, it was for the court to decide whether to extend the Act to cover this new situation.

Another, more emotive example of technological advances requiring changes to interpretation comes from the *Royal College of Nursing v DHSS*[14] case. The Abortion Act 1967

14 [1981] AC 800 (HL).

(s1) created a defence to the offence of child destruction where procedures were carried out by 'a registered medical practitioner'. Under the old law, there was only a common law defence for doctors. At the time of the passage of the Act, abortions were carried out through surgical means. The question raised by the Royal College of Nursing was whether the developments of non-surgical abortions (possible after significant scientific developments) called for an interpretation of the Act that allowed for nurses to also be involved in the process. In interpreting the Act, Lord Wilberforce considered it 'proper, and indeed necessary, to have regard to the state of affairs existing, and known by Parliament to be existing, at the time'.[15] He felt that a change to the meaning of the Act, due to its controversial nature, should be undertaken by Parliament even if such a change was seen as necessary and sensible. This was the minority view, with the majority of the House of Lords preferring a more pragmatic approach, focussing on the purpose of the Act (to allow women to have safe abortions). The court held, in a split court, that nurses working *under the direction of a doctor* were not acting unlawfully by virtue of their involvement with the abortion procedure since the doctor was in control of the non-surgical treatment when s/he directed that it should be administered.

ANALYSING THE LAW – RESPONDING TO TECHNOLOGICAL CHANGE

The two situations discussed previously boil down to fundamentally the same issue: should the Act be interpreted in such a way as to include later technological developments? Having said this, the interpretation applied to the Abortion Act 1967 was very much more controversial than that applied to the Copyright Designs and Patents Act. This is demonstrated by the sharp division in the House of Lords, with one dissenting judge suggesting that the approach adopted by the majority was 'redrafting with a vengeance'.[16]

This tension and its resolution in the approach adopted by the judiciary are discussed later when considering the notion that statutes are 'always speaking'.

APPROACHES TO PARLIAMENTARY DRAFTING

In formulating legal provisions, there are two extreme positions that could be taken in relation to drafting. On the one hand, provisions can be very loosely drafted in a way that invites judicial intervention and that allows judges to be involved in the process of developing the law; on the other hand, Acts of Parliament could attempt to be exhaustive and try to cover every possible situation through long and detailed provisions. Neither of those positions is necessarily preferable, and much will depend upon the specific context within which the Act of Parliament is drafted. However, both approaches to interpretation have inherent benefits and drawbacks. The flexible option is influenced to some extent by the approach in civil law

15 ibid 822.
16 ibid 831.

of countries which have a written constitution and a series of codes setting out the law, which is then drafted in such a way that it should rarely require amendment – unlike our statutes in England and Wales, which often have to have regular amendment.

At times it may be appropriate to draft provisions in such a way that they are flexible and adaptable. Although originally formulated outside the scope of the legal system of England and Wales, the European Convention on Human Rights, as incorporated by the Human Rights Act 1998, is an example of flexible drafting. The rights contained within the European Convention on Human Rights are not defined by the Convention and have been developed and interpreted by the European and domestic courts over more than 50 years. The more loosely drafted a legislative provision, the more heavily weighted judicial power is.

THE 'NATURAL' AS OPPOSED TO THE 'LEGAL' MEANING OF WORDS

As well as the rich diversity of everyday meanings that can attach to words, there is the added complication that words can sometimes carry a technical meaning, be it legal or otherwise. It is part of the job of the courts to distinguish between when Parliament is using a word in a technical sense and when the word is being used in its everyday form.

EXPLAINING THE LAW – DETERMINING TECHNICAL, LEGAL OR ORDINARY MEANING

This issue is demonstrated by the **Restriction of Offensive Weapons Act 1959**. Section 1 of the Act, as originally enacted, reads as follows:

s1 Penalties for offences

Any person who manufactures, sells or hires or offers for sale or hire, or lends to gives to any other person –

a) any knife which has a blade which opens automatically by hand pressure applied to a button . . . , sometimes known as a flick knife or flick gun, . . . shall be guilty of an offence and shall be liable on summary conviction to imprisonment for a term not exceeding six months.

A question arises as to how to interpret the phrase 'offers for sale'. There are (at least) two potential meanings that could attach to this phrase – an everyday/layman meaning or a technical legal meaning. It was precisely this issue that arose in the leading contract law case *Fisher v Bell*.[17]

17 [1961] 1 QB 394 (QB).

EXPLAINING THE LAW – *FISHER V BELL*

In the case, Bell was prosecuted under the Act outlined previously for offering for sale a flick knife. The facts were uncontroversial. Bell had placed a flick knife in the window of his shop, complete with a price ticket. He had been charged under the Act and subsequently argued that he was not, in the technical sense, offering for sale but that he was receptive to offers to buy.

Under the general law of contract, an offer, once accepted, becomes binding on the person making the offer. That is not how items displayed in shops are generally sold. It is normal that the *customer* makes the offer to buy the item, and the shopkeeper then chooses whether to accept the offer or not. Therefore, the display of an item in a shop is not an offer to sell but an indication that the shopkeeper may be receptive to offers. This type of situation has been deemed an 'invitation to treat' under the common law.

The difference, to a non-lawyer, may seem very small, but it is important to distinguish between the two situations, for practical reasons not relevant to the discussion here. The result was that Bell was not guilty of the offence as he had not made an offer for sale but, rather, an invitation to treat. The court had to make the assumption (even though it was clearly an oversight) that Parliament knew the technical meaning of 'offer for sale' and had chosen that phrase despite the loophole that it created.

Some would argue that the outcome of *Fisher v Bell* is unsatisfactory. If you think for a moment about the *purpose* of the Act, then it was clearly to prevent the sale of offensive weapons and to reduce the ability for people to acquire and subsequently use such offensive weapons. The outcome in *Fisher v Bell* did not achieve that aim and seemed to allow somebody to escape justice on the basis of a very narrow and technical distinction.

MAKING CONNECTIONS – CONTRACT LAW AND BEYOND

Having said this, it is important not to view the case in isolation. This is a danger when new to the study of law: judging the outcome of each case solely on its facts and losing sight of the 'bigger' picture. This is exacerbated when we are talking about the legal system as a subject, as it will invariably draw upon many areas of law.

This is a case that the reader will no doubt return to if undertaking the study of contract law. Think carefully about why the court was unwilling to apply a more 'common sense' approach to the term 'offer for sale' – although it might have led to a lack of justice in this particular case. Think, in particular, about the consistency that is needed within areas of law and how important the principle of legal certainty is to the legal system and how this may need to trump outcomes in particular circumstances. This is particularly so when discussing complex, but settled, legal principles, such as those found within the basic rules of contract.

The argument that the court in *Fisher v Bell* had been unable to achieve Parliament's intent is somewhat confirmed by later events. Following on from the case, Parliament passed the Restriction of Offensive Weapons Act 1961, which sought to cover the situation that arose in *Fisher v Bell* by inserting into the original Act the following phrase: 'or exposes or has in his possession for the purpose of sale or hire.' It could be argued that at a broader level, *Fisher v Bell* is an example of separation of powers in action (as discussed in Chapter 3 – Institutions of the Legal System) and of how statutory interpretation can promote better law-making. The court was not willing to go beyond their interpretative role and instead preferred to leave law-making to Parliament. The case highlighted a problem with the statute which was then 'solved' by the legislature. In this way, interpretation of statutes can be an efficient way of promoting and ensuring clearer drafting.

CONCLUSIONS ON THE NEED FOR STATUTORY INTERPRETATION

All the aforementioned reasons feed into the need for statutory interpretation within the legal system. The problems are not to be viewed as being mutually exclusive, but rather, they should be viewed as interacting and interrelated. For example, poor drafting can mean that the law is too vague or that it is not 'future-proofed' for subsequent developments. If we return, for a moment, to the Abortion Act 1967 and the case of *Royal College of Nursing v DHSS* we can see that some of the uncertainties created by the Act could have been resolved through clearer drafting: 'it lacks that style and consistency of draftsmanship both internal to the Act itself and in relation to other statutes which one would expect to find in legislation that had its origin in the office of parliamentary counsel.'[18]

The preceding gives a flavour of the wide-ranging issues that lead to a need for statutory interpretation. The list is not intended to be exhaustive and should be viewed as a starting point for future exploration. To put this differently, the aforementioned problems can require different approaches and solutions from the judiciary. Indeed, they are essential context, without which it will not be able to assess the merits of the different approaches to statutory interpretation. The next section will explore how the court goes about resolving, or at least reducing, some of these problems through adopting specific approaches to statutory interpretation.

THE DANGERS OF STATUTORY INTERPRETATION

In spite of the fact that statutory interpretation is of fundamental importance to the functioning of the legal system, it does come with inherent dangers. Foremost amongst those dangers is the power that it gives to the judiciary. Interpretation can, and does, change or determine the law and, in some circumstances, gives the courts a greater opportunity to *make* law.

18 *Royal College of Nursing* [1981] AC 800 (HL) 824 (Lord Diplock).

As a result of this, the principles of statutory interpretation also play a constitutional role, in that they determine an allocation of power between those who make the law (the legislature – Parliament) and those who apply the law (the judiciary – the courts). As was mentioned in Chapter 3, it is important that functions and powers of the different organs of the state are kept distinct, or at least that there are sufficient checks and balances on the powers of the judiciary (and, although less relevant for this chapter, Parliament). The principles of statutory interpretation seek, to an extent, to demonstrate self-restraint and deference being exercised by judges. In this way, statutory interpretation marks one of the key interactions between the legislature and the judiciary.

The judiciary readily accepts that there needs to be a separation of function between those who *interpret* the law and those who *apply* the law. This has been recognised by all levels of the judiciary over many years and in many different contexts where the interpretation of law is in question. The clearest expression of this principle comes from Lord Diplock in *Duport Steels Ltd v Sirs*:[19]

> Parliament makes the laws, the judiciary interpret them. . . . [T]he role of the judiciary is confined to ascertaining from the words that Parliament has approved as expressing its intention what that intention was, and to giving effect to it. Where the meaning of the statutory words is plain and unambiguous it is not for the judges to invent fancied ambiguities as an excuse for failing to give effect to its plain meaning because they themselves consider that the consequences of doing so would be inexpedient, or even unjust or immoral.

The preceding quotation tells us much about the attitude of some of the judiciary to the process of and rationale for statutory interpretation. Similar expressions can be found elsewhere within the case law. For example, in *Belvedere Court Management Limited*,[20] the court put the matter even more plainly when criticising the Landlord and Tenant Act 1987:

> Whilst the drafting of fully effective provisions would not be unduly difficult (and has been achieved in other legislation covering similar matters), it is not the role of the court to construct such provisions if they are not to be found expressly or implicitly in the Act as drafted. **The ease of the legislative task does not mean that the distinction between the roles of the courts and the legislature can be disregarded**. The solutions to the problems posed have to be found, if at all, within the scope of the interpretative tools open to the courts to uncover and give effect to the statutory intention.

The statement in this case is stronger than in *Duport Steels*, as it is a more direct warning against judicial law-making. Thus, even where judges could be fairly certain of getting the 'right' answer in creating new law, they should be mindful of the difference between the roles of the legislature and those of the judiciary. As a principle, it is, therefore, relatively uncontroversial to say that a large part of statutory interpretation is concerned with trying to determine the

19 [1980] 1 WLR 142 (HL) 157B–158C.
20 [1996] 1 All ER 312, [1997] QB 858 (CA).

intention of Parliament. This focus on intention is a method by which judges legitimise what they are doing. It can be argued that judges are strengthening the separation of powers by focussing on the intention of the legislature. In more recent times, the phrase 'parliamentary intent' has fallen out of such widespread use.

Although judges happily agree that separation of powers is an important safeguard in preventing judicial law-making, there is disagreement as to the extent to which different approaches achieve or threaten separation of powers. In this way, statutory interpretation also reveals some of the internal tensions that can exist as to the way in which judges go about their interpretative task. This tension is exemplified by the *Magor and St Mellons Rural District Council v Newport Corporation*[21] case. Within this case, a very liberal approach to interpretation was put forward by Lord Denning. He was unhappy simply to apply the intention of Parliament and wished to go further. In departing from the orthodox approach, he earned the reproof of Lord Simonds on appeal to the House of Lords, who held that Denning had been part of 'a naked usurpation of the legislative function under the thin guise of interpretation'.[22]

The exchange between Denning and Simonds demonstrates the significance of statutory interpretation in achieving the correct balance between the role and the powers of the judiciary and the legislature. On the other hand, Lord Denning, in the Court of Appeal, had put a strong case for a more purposive interpretation when he said:

> We do not sit here to pull the language of Parliament to pieces and make nonsense of it. We sit here to find out the intention of Parliament and carry it out and we do this better by filling in the gaps and making sense of the enactment than by opening it up to destructive analysis.[23]

This was but the beginning of a long-running collision of ideas and approaches between the House of Lords and the Court of Appeal, which lasted as long as Denning remained in the Court.[24] Statutory interpretation was not the only battleground between these two highest courts in the legal system of England and Wales. While Lord Diplock and others in the House of Lords generally spoke for the classic approach to established principle in the House of Lords, Lord Denning was ahead of his time in many ways, such as in respect of the purposive approach to statutory interpretation which did not become mainstream in domestic law until well after the UK joined the EU in 1973, although from that date it was used in interpreting the EU law, which then inevitably had an impact on our domestic law.

More recently, the dangers of judicial activism in interpretation have been brought to the fore by the European Court of Human Rights in the case of *Hirst*,[25] where the European Court held

21 [1952] AC 189 (HL).

22 ibid 190 (Lord Simonds).

23 *Magor and St Mellons Rural District Council v Newport Corporation* [1950] 2 All ER 1226 (CA) 1236 (Denning LJ).

24 Denning had previously sat in the House of Lords but returned to the Court of Appeal to assume the post of Master of the Rolls in the Court of Appeal.

25 *Hirst v UK (No 2)* [2005] ECHR 681.

that the UK's blanket ban on allowing prisoners to vote violated the European Convention on Human Rights. In doing so, they challenged a long-standing UK Act of Parliament and were accused of taking interpretation too far and were at risk of becoming quasi-legislators. Having considered both the reasons leading to the need for interpretation and the dangers that need to be avoided in construing legislation, it is now important to turn to the specific 'rules' or approaches of statutory interpretation.

TOOLS, RULES AND PRINCIPLES OF STATUTORY INTERPRETATION

In order to resolve specific cases that raise questions of interpretation, the judiciary has a varied toolbox comprising principles and methods that can be applied to different situations. What this text terms 'tools', others have labelled as 'approaches', 'canons' or even 'rules' of statutory interpretation. The fact that academics and judges use different terminology to describe what is, essentially, the same process further demonstrates the difficulties of the English language! Even judges vary the language used, preferring in more recent times the phrase 'statutory construction'. This text prefers 'tools' and 'principles', as opposed to 'rules' or 'canons', as it more accurately describes how judges use the various approaches to decide cases. This is because, to a large extent, the precise issue that gives rise to a need for interpretation (as discussed in the previous section) will be determinative of which 'approach' or 'tool' a judge uses to solve the case at hand. The Australian case *Cooper Brookes* sums up the position succinctly by stating that 'the rules [of statutory interpretation] . . . are no more than rules of common sense, designed to achieve this object. They are not rules of law'.[26]

THE ORTHODOX 'RULES' OF STATUTORY INTERPRETATION – A REJECTION

In an effort to explain and rationalise changing or evolving approaches or practices, academic textbooks[27] have come to rely on an orthodoxy surrounding statutory interpretation. This orthodox view takes the form of so-called 'rules' of statutory interpretation that are intended to classify different judicial approaches and to compare and contrast their merits and drawbacks. The 'literal', 'golden' and 'mischief' rules are no more than alternative legal lenses that can be applied to collections of cases so as to imperfectly explain potential reasoning. Standard and well-rehearsed cases are called upon to demonstrate the rules most colourfully and to show the unfairness that one 'rule' may evoke, or to present false alternatives should a different 'rule' be adopted. The attraction of the rules lies in their simplicity and their ease of application to *decided* cases.

26 *Cooper Brookes (Wollongong) Property Ltd v Federal Commissioner for Taxation* [1981] HCA 26 at 35.

27 The earlier edition of this textbook adopted this orthodox approach.

The challenge is that the provenance of these 'rules' cannot be found *expressly* within reported judgments. They are also less useful in helping judges and lawyers in *deciding* cases. Judges (speaking extra-judicially) and academics specialising in statutory construction are increasingly questioning their utility and are critical of a focus remaining on them to explain the modern method of statutory interpretation.[28]

The rules are mentioned here for the sake of completeness and because they have occupied, until now, a hallowed and special place in the academic scholarship on this topic. Also, practically, it may well be that the reader comes across these 'rules' in the texts that they read, and so it would be strange not to reference them. In outlining the following rules, the intention is not to give them exhaustive treatment but rather to highlight their key features. The intention is not to reinforce their legitimacy or to follow existing orthodox thought.

LITERAL RULE

The most commonly cited example of the principle underlying the literal rules comes from Lord Esher in the 19th century:

> If the words of an Act are clear, you must follow them, even though they lead to a manifest absurdity.[29]

Similar statements can be found in another 19th-century case, *The Sussex Peerage Case*,[30] where the court held thus:

> If the words of the statute are in themselves precise and unambiguous, then no more can be necessary than to expound those words in their natural and ordinary sense. The words themselves alone do, in such case, best declare the intention of the lawgiver.

The core principle of the literal approach is that judges look to the common and plain meaning of words in trying to determine what Parliament intended when passing the Act in question. Judges do not seek to go beyond the wording used by Parliament so as to consider extraneous material that would evidence an alternative or revised understanding beyond that which the clear meaning of the words suggests.

There are additional standard examples of the literal approach in action that further demonstrate how it operates. The following are just two examples and should not be taken as exhaustive:

1. *Whiteley v Chappell*.[31] Under the Act in question, it was an offence (punishable by up to three months in prison) to 'personate any person entitled to vote' at the election

28 Lord Burrow, 'Seven Lessons from Inside the UK Supreme Court' (Neill Lecture, 2023) <Seven_Lessons_from_Inside_the_UK_Supreme_Court_Lord_Burrows_2725d87d66.pdf> at p3.

29 Per Lord Esher in *R v Judge of the City of London Court* [1892] 1 QB 273 (CA).

30 (1844) 11 C; & Fin 85.

31 [1868] LR QB 147.

of guardians of the poor. The appellant had been accused of impersonating another person, who had died before the election. The court, with some reluctance, decided that the judges could not, 'without straining them, bring the case within the words of the enactment'. This may seem an odd result given that it allowed the appellant to escape justice for a clear wrong, but the judges in the case were worried that, should they do such violence to the words in order to convict, it would set an unwelcome precedent for judicial activism.

2. *IRC v Hinchy*.[32] When making an income tax return, Hinchy did not declare the full amount of interest that he had received and, as a result, underpaid income tax to the amount of around £15. He was charged a penalty payment under Section 25 of the Income Tax Act 1952, which required that where a person did not fully declare income, they would 'forfeit the sum of . . . treble the tax which he ought to be charged under this Act'. The IRC submitted that the penalty should treble his whole tax liability under the Act (totalling almost £440) and not just three times the amount he had underpaid (£15). Despite the extreme nature of imposing the higher penalty, the court felt unable to alter the natural and unambiguous meaning of the words of the Act.

GOLDEN RULE

The golden rule was said to owe its origin to the literal rule, slightly modified in order to take into account some other interpretation if an absurd result is produced by initially following the literal rule. Two 19th-century judges have contributed to this development: first, per Jervis CJ in *Mattison v Hart*,[33] who suggested sticking to 'the plain meaning' unless 'injustice or absurdity would result', adding that this was the 'golden rule for construction of statutes'; secondly, per Baron Parke in *Grey v Pearson*.[34]

The principles underpinning the so-called 'golden rule' are said to be evidenced in *Jones v DPP*,[35] in which it was held that a judge could not generally depart from the ordinary meaning of a statute, but if there was more than one meaning of the words in question, the judge could choose which one to follow, particularly if it avoided an absurdity.

The example typically given of this obviously undesirable result is the case of *Re Sigsworth*.[36] In this case, a son had murdered his mother and then committed suicide; since there was no will applicable, the statute to be interpreted was the Administration of Estates Act 1925, as the mother was intestate. As this meant the deceased son's family would inherit her property through him and there was a principle of public policy that a murderer should not profit from his crime, the Act was interpreted to avoid such a 'repugnant' result.

32 (1960) AC 748 (HL).
33 [1854] 14 CB 357.
34 [1857] 6 HL Cas 61.
35 [1962] AC 635 (HL).
36 [1935] Ch 89 (Ch).

A wider departure from the literal rule to avoid absurd consequences occurred in *Adler v George*.[37] In this case, the statute was the Official Secrets Act 1920, which protected certain of HM Forces bases by prosecuting anyone found 'in the vicinity of' such a place. The accused was found actually 'in' the base when he was apprehended, and the court considered that it would be absurd to be able to convict someone apprehended outside and not someone who had already gained entry, so interpreted 'in the vicinity of' to include actually within the prohibited place.

MISCHIEF RULE

The 'mischief rule' is said to date from the 16th-century *Heydon's Case*.[38] The court laid out four questions to answer questions of interpretation:

1. What was the common law before the passing of the Act?
2. What was the 'mischief' and 'defect' for which the common law did not provide (thus requiring the Act to be passed)?
3. What remedy had the Parliament 'resolved and appointed' to cure the defect?
4. What was the true reason of the remedy?

A fairly modern (and standard) example of the application of what is said to be the mischief rule is the case of *Smith v Hughes*;[39] the mischief in that case was prostitutes soliciting 'on the street', to the annoyance of the public, and the Act to be interpreted is the Street Offences Act 1959, s1(1) which prohibited common prostitutes from causing such annoyance, since it made it an offence to 'loiter or solicit in a street or public place for the purpose of prostitution'. The women were not in fact *in* the street itself but were on balconies or at open or closed windows at street level. Lord Parker LCJ pointed out the mischief was people being unable to walk along the street without being propositioned by prostitutes. Applying the mischief rule, the prostitutes were preventing the peaceful passing of people despite not actually being *in or on* the street as they were as much in or on it on the balconies and at the windows.

CONCLUDING REMARKS ON THE RULES

As said, the preceding rules are included in this chapter so that the reader can become familiar with them and understand how and why they became so prevalent in legal scholarship. In reality, the judiciary now adopts a modern, contextual and purposive approach to interpretation, and this will be explored in the following sections of the chapter. Despite the fact that the orthodox rules are losing their influence in legal education (and have never found particular favour with judges), they do still act as a way of understanding different approaches and articulating some of the challenges in the interpretative task.

37 [1964] 2 QB 7 (QB).

38 [1584] Co Rep 7a, that is, reported in Coke's Reports, those of Sir Edward Coke, a barrister later Chief Justice of England under Queen Elizabeth I and considered to be the greatest jurist of the Elizabethan and Jacobean ages.

39 [1960] 1 WLR 830 (QB).

One of the particular challenges of perpetuating the so-called 'rules' of statutory interpretation is treating them as competing visions of the 'truth', or suggesting that the rules are somehow in competition with each other. The reality is much more complex and nuanced. There are times that the rules would be in tension with each other. Equally true, there are times where both parties are arguing for a literal approach to the words but they disagree on what that literal approach means! It is also important to note that, at times, the different rules may actually support each other. Sometimes the literal approach seeks to address a mischief, whilst also being sound within a contextual and purposive interpretation. For this reason, amongst others, it is important to understand the unifying aim of statutory interpretation.

THE AIMS, PRINCIPLES AND PRESUMPTIONS OF STATUTORY INTERPRETATION IN THE MODERN CONTEXT

The overriding aim of statutory interpretation has found varying expressions over the centuries. Much of this change in how the aim of statutory interpretation has been described has little impact on the approach taken by judges. For many years, and still in many quarters, the aim was seen to be to understand the 'intention of Parliament'. This form of words found favour for many reasons, primarily because it legitimises the activity of the courts in forming an interpretation of the law. This legitimacy stems from the authority and sovereignty of Parliament and deflects from any suggestion that, in choosing a particular interpretation (where multiple may be tenable), judges are in fact developing the law or making policy decisions. It also pays due deference to Parliament as the body that authored or approved the legislative instrument.

At first blush it may seem a rather straightforward aim for those tasked with interpreting the law. However, the act of understanding what we mean by the 'intention of Parliament' is challenging, not least because of the competing voices and processes that lead to the adoption of legislation. There are also a host of political considerations that contribute to the compromises needed to pass legislation. In this way, the principle of divining legislative intent is a simple way of describing the purpose of statutory interpretation, but it is not terribly helpful beyond that.

THE AIM AND PURPOSE OF STATUTORY INTERPRETATION

One of the most powerful, recent articulations of the aim of statutory interpretation, which expands a little from the language of 'Parliament's intent', can be found in the judgment in R *(on the application of O)*,[40] where Lord Hodge states that:

> Statutory interpretation involves an objective assessment of the meaning which a reasonable legislature as a body would be seeking to convey in using the statutory words which are being considered. [31]

40 *R (on the application of O) v Secretary of State for the Home Department* [2022] UKSC 3, [2022] 2 WLR 343.

In this way, the act of statutory interpretation is to determine the *objective* meaning of the words used by Parliament. To be clear, those who speak of parliamentary intention are *not* speaking of the intention of the government in bringing forward legislation, the individual Minister who introduced the bill to Parliament, the drafters of the text or even the various MPs and members of the House of Lords who will have participated in debates or scrutiny.

The *meaning* of the words, according to Lord Hodge, is to be determined by the context within the Act. This approach carries a purposive (or purpose-based) dimension that may extend beyond literal and mechanical consideration of individual words. The meaning of the particular words is to be determined by reference to the context of the section, the other sections and the overall scheme of the Act of Parliament under consideration. By focussing on the meaning of the words *within* the legislation, Lord Hodge gives them primacy in the task of statutory interpretation.[41] This accords with principles of the rule of law, promoting clarity and accessibility of the law to citizens – or to put it differently, citizens should be able to understand their rights and obligations under statute law by reading the particular piece of legislation.

A consequence of the primacy of *intrinsic aids* is that things that may inform interpretation that are *outside* of the Act must take a secondary position.[42] This would include parliamentary material (such as Hansard or explanatory notes) and other *extrinsic* material (such as Law Commission reports or government consultations). Lord Hodge recognises that these can be helpful but cannot 'displace the meanings conveyed by the words of a statute that, after consideration of that context, are clear and unambiguous and which do not produce absurdity'.[43] Whilst Lord Hodge's judgment was met with approval by the other members of the Supreme Court, it is worth noting that Lady Arden was a little more cautious in downgrading certain extrinsic aids to interpretation, primarily pre-legislative materials.[44] She felt that such materials are not only helpful in casting a light on the history or mischief for which the statute was seen as the remedy but can also contribute (quite properly and constitutionally) to understanding the *meaning* of the words used.[45]

Having clearly laid out the aim of statutory interpretation, Lord Hodge also notes that the courts of England and Wales have developed assumptions around how Parliament can be presumed to have been acting in certain circumstances. The way in which these presumptions operate (and the impact that they have on interpretation) will vary with the circumstances of a given case. Some of these presumptions are explored in greater detail later in the chapter, along with the nature of intrinsic and extrinsic aids to interpretation and some of the common rules of language that are deployed by courts. These methods collectively act as a toolkit for judges to achieve the aim of statutory interpretation. As a toolkit, as opposed to a

41 ibid [29].
42 ibid [30].
43 ibid [30].
44 ibid [60].
45 ibid [70].

strict set of 'rules', they allow for flexibility but also a degree of consistency in completing the interpretative task.

In summary, when approaching statutory interpretation,

- the *aim* or *purpose* is to determine the objective meaning of the words used by Parliament;
- the *approach* is one of context and purpose, with primacy given to the words used within the statute; and
- the *method* is one of a mixed toolkit of presumptions, rules of language and use of intrinsic or extrinsic material to aid in interpretation.

Having considered in particular the aims and approach of statutory interpretation in this section, the remainder of the section will look at some overarching and interlinked considerations that govern the approach to statutory interpretation, before the remainder of the chapter looks at the methods and tools used by judges.

OVERARCHING CONSIDERATIONS

STATUTES ARE ALWAYS SPEAKING

The first principle to be considered is related to the ability of judges to apply statutes to circumstances that were not considered, or even could not possibly have been considered, by the parliaments that passed them. This is known as the 'always speaking' or 'updating' interpretation. It is generally applied where scientific or technological knowledge has advanced in ways not foreseen by Parliament. The requirement for 'updating' interpretation was touched upon earlier in this chapter when considering the need for interpretation, where the case of the *Royal College of Nursing* was considered.

A leading example of the principle in application is *Quintavalle*.[46] In the case, the House of Lords was asked to rule as to whether the definition of *embryos* for the purposes of the Human Fertilisation and Embryology Act 1990 included not only fertilised embryos but also cloned embryos. At the time of the Act's original passing, the procedure for cloning embryos was not known to science.

The court was faced with a choice of three approaches:

- Find that the use of cloned embryos was subject to licence (s3(1) of the Act) – this argument was put forward by the Human Fertilisation and Embryology Authority.
- Find that the use of cloned embryos was completely prohibited (s3(2) and 3(3) of the Act) – this argument was not brought forward by either party.
- Find that cloned embryos fell completely outside the scope of the Act and their use was neither prohibited nor subject to licence – the argument put forward by the Pro Life organisation bringing the claim.

46 *R (on the Application of Quintavalle) v Secretary of State for Health* [2003] UKHL 13, [2003] 2 AC 687 (HL).

In coming to the conclusion that the use of the cloned embryos should be governed by licence, the House of Lords adopted the 'always speaking' rule and sought to understand the policy of the Act. Lord Hoffmann held that the 'clear policy of the Act is to regulate the creation, keeping or use of embryos',[47] and so the logic would be that cloned embryos form part of the regulatory framework because they are embryos.

The approach of the courts is a nuanced one; they are not seeking to ask whether Parliament, if it knew of this *particular method* of creating embryos, would have regulated them, but rather what was Parliament's intention at the time of passing the Act. The interpretation given could be arrived at because the House of Lords were convinced that Parliament was trying to regulate all activities with embryos, regardless of how they had been created.

The Supreme Court in *News Corp*[48] – a case that involved determining whether the term 'newspapers' within the Value Added Tax Act 1994 included digital editions as well as print – speaks of the practical value of the 'always speaking' doctrine. It is used to 'prevent statutes becoming outdated'[49] and avoids the need for constant updating. However, there are clear limitations to its use. In *News Corp*, the court held that the defining features of 'newspapers' at the relevant time was that they were physical and could be accessed in their own right (as opposed to through a device).[50] On this basis, the 'always speaking' doctrine could not be applied because the term to be defined was of a different *type or kind* than the original term in the Act. Digital editions of newspapers were a form of *service*, whereas print newspapers were a form of *goods*.

THE PLACE OF MISCHIEF

Having earlier in this chapter debunked the use of the so-called 'mischief rule', it is important to note that judges do seek to understand the concept of 'mischief' in defining the meaning of legislation. This is because statutory interpretation is seeking to understand meaning within the context and purpose of the relevant legislation. The purpose of passing new legislation is often to deal with an emerging societal problem or with a problem in how existing law is being applied. If faced with questions of interpretation, it is legitimate for judges to consider the mischief and to give an interpretation that remedies that mischief. This theme is picked up further later when considering external aids to interpretation.

THE INTERPRETATION ACT 1978

The Interpretation Act 1978 defines, in statutory form, some common terms and gives an indication of how they should be understood in all other legislation. For example, references to masculine words or feminine words include the opposite gender. Equally, that words written in the plural would include the singular, and vice versa.[51] It also contains other forms of clarification, such as that distances in acts are to be understood to be in straight lines.[52] It

47 ibid [31].

48 *News Corp UK Ltd v Commissioners for HMRC* [2023] UKSC 7.

49 *News Corp UK Ltd v Commissioners for HMRC* [2023] UKSC 7 at [30].

50 ibid [53].

51 Interpretation Act 1978 s6.

52 Interpretation Act 1978 s8.

lays out definitions on time, on shorthand references to courts, to the meaning of 'person' and a whole set of other words that may regularly appear in Acts of Parliament and other legislation.

In this way, the Interpretation Act 1978 does not deal with methods or approaches to interpretation but rather creates a phrasebook of common words and how they are to be understood in legislation. Clearly, Parliament may wish in certain circumstances to adopt different meanings for terms included in the Interpretation Act 1978. For example, and contrary to the terms of the Act, it may be that Parliament will intend for gendered words to apply only to that gender. The use of clear words will indicate Parliament's intent and can displace application of the Interpretation Act 1978.

THE HUMAN RIGHTS ACT 1998 AND EUROPEAN INFLUENCE

The Human Rights Act 1998 is an innovative piece of legislation that intended to bring into English and Welsh law a framework for incorporation of the European Convention on Human Rights (ECHR). At its heart, the ECHR includes an international agreement to respect and enforce fundamental rights and freedoms. The Human Rights Act 1998 brings those rights into the domestic legal order.

As well as providing for the convention rights, the Act also places certain obligations on courts in how they interpret legislation. This interpretative obligation can be found in Section 3 of the Human Rights Act 1998:

> So far as it is possible to do so, primary legislation and subordinate legislation must be read and given effect in a way which is compatible with the Convention rights.

This obligation and what it means to go 'so far as it is possible' have been the subject of a long line of case law. This jurisprudence is complex. The fundamental point for this chapter is simply to note that this obligation shapes an understanding of all legislation when it impacts on the fundamental human rights enshrined in the Convention.

PRESUMPTIONS

Over time, judges have developed certain presumptions about what Parliament intends (and does not intend) by the words it uses. These help short-circuit what could otherwise be a very lengthy re-litigation of questions that could apply to very many statutes. The use of presumptions also helps parliamentary drafters and those proposing bills as they will have a sense of how judges will approach particular issues of general application. Beyond serving a practical purpose, these presumptions often underscore and help reinforce key constitutional messages related to the rule of law, such as the accessibility and availability of the courts.

It is important to reiterate that the following are *presumptions* and not hard rules. This means that clear statutory language that runs contrary to one of the presumptions will take priority. The approaches described in what follows are intended to be a non-exhaustive examination of the most significant presumptions in operation in the legal system.

AGAINST A CHANGE IN THE COMMON LAW

The common law and statute law are often painted as wholly distinct and separate areas of law. And indeed, for some purposes they are. It is also true that they seek to govern areas of law through their overlap and intersection. In order to deal with this, the courts have developed a presumption that any Act of Parliament will only alter the common law to the extent necessary to deal with the issue at hand. As Lord Reid once put it, Parliament

> can be presumed not to have altered the common law further than was necessary.[53]

A recent example will illustrate the point. In *Hassam*[54] the court had to deal with the differences of compensation available for whiplash injuries. The statutory scheme – governed by the Civil Liability Act 2018 – significantly reduced damages for the pain, suffering and loss of amenity (PSLA) related to whiplash injuries that had traditionally been available under the common law. The scheme did impact on damages available for PSLA for other injuries. The question to be resolved by the court was how to calculate damages for concurrent injuries (i.e. where there was whiplash *and* other injuries). Applying the presumption, the court held that the 2018 Act could not cut down the common law more than what was necessary and so could not adversely affect the calculation and award of damages for PSLA of non-whiplash injury where there was a concurrent whiplash injury.[55]

AGAINST OUSTING THE JURISDICTION OF THE COURT

Access to the courts is an important constitutional right and one that forms part of our understanding of the rule of law in England and Wales.[56] It is possible that Parliament will wish to exclude access to the courts under certain circumstances. This may be because there are alternative ways of individuals addressing and ensuring their rights (such as a statutory tribunal). In those circumstances, it is said that the jurisdiction of the court is 'ousted'. The presumption here is that Parliament, unless it uses express words, will not 'oust' the jurisdiction of the courts as Parliament will not have intended for unlawful decisions to remain unchallenged.[57]

AGAINST A VIOLATION OF INTERNATIONAL LAW

A contemporary understanding of the rule of law includes the need to respect and follow international law obligations. These take the form of treaties and other international agreements. It is not surprising, therefore, that the judiciary has developed a presumption that domestic law is to be read in ways that are in accordance with international law obligations. This has been described as a 'strong presumption',[58] and so it would require clear words to displace or rebut.

53 *Black-Clawson v Papierwerke* [1975] AC 591 (HL), 614.

54 *Hassam v Rabot* [2024] UKSC 11.

55 ibid [48].

56 *R (UNISON) v Lord Chancellor* [2015] UKSC 51 at [66].

57 For a case see *R (Oceana) v Upper Tribunal* [2023] EWHC 791 (Admin) at [52].

58 *Assange v The Swedish Prosecution Authority* [2012] UKSC 22, [115].

The fact that the presumption is strong does not mean that it is unassailable. Recently, in *R (on the application of FDA)*,[59] the court was faced with questions about the Conservative government's controversial 'Rwanda Scheme',[60] whereby they sought to remove immigrants who had arrived illegally (often following dangerous routes across the sea in small, unsuitable boats). The court had to decide whether Parliament had intended to give Ministers the power to act in such a way that was incompatible with international obligations under the European Convention on Human Rights. Despite noting the presumption of compliance with international law obligations, the court found that Parliament was clear in its intention by the words it used in allowing Ministers to act in a non-compliant way, and so the presumption was rebutted.[61]

AGAINST A VIOLATION OF FUNDAMENTAL RIGHTS OF INDIVIDUALS (THE PRESUMPTION OF LEGALITY)

In very many legal systems, there is a constitutional document that enshrines fundamental rights and liberties with which all legislation must comply. Legislation deemed not to respect those fundamental rights can be found to be unconstitutional and disapplied. No such document of higher law exists in the legal system of England and Wales. Partly to protect against violation of rights, the courts have developed a strong presumption that general words in legislation are intended to 'be subject to the basic rights of the individual'.[62] This is known as the presumption of legality, or non-interference. It would need the clearest and plainest of words to rebut this basic presumption.

Despite the high bar, there are public policy reasons that sometimes Parliament will rebut the presumption through the use of clear and plain language. In *Belhaj*[63] the Supreme Court did find that the Justice and Security Act 2013 did rebut the presumption in clear terms relating to the withholding of evidence for national security reasons.

THAT LEGISLATION APPLIES PROSPECTIVELY

It is a central tenet of the rule of law that legislation applies to future and not past events. The importance of this as a constitutional principle has found support through a presumption that legislation will be applied prospectively.[64] This to ensure that the law can be known (i.e. it brings certainty), and behaviour be modified accordingly (i.e. that it can be followed).

Despite it being an important presumption, Parliament can always choose clear and express words that displace the presumption, and courts would have little choice but to follow legislative intent. The War Damages Act 1965 is a(n infamous) example of retroactive legislation that removed the common law right to compensation for damage done during war regardless of whether the damage predated the Act. Similarly, in *Reilly (No 2)*[65] the Court of

59 *R (on the application of FDA) v Minister for the Cabinet Office* [2024] EWHC 1729 (Admin).

60 Safety of Rwanda (Immigration and Asylum) Act 2024.

61 *R (on the application of FDA) v Minister for the Cabinet Office* [2024] EWHC 1729 (Admin), [104].

62 *R v Secretary of State for the Home Department ex parte Simms* [2002] 2 AC 115 (HL), 131.

63 *Belhaj v DPP* [2018] UKSC 33.

64 *Walker v Innospec Ltd* [2017] UKSC 47.

65 *Reilly (No 2) v Secretary of State for Work and Pensions* [2016] EWCA Civ 413.

Appeal reiterated the existence of the presumption but found that it had been rebutted by the clarity of Parliament's intention.[66]

EXCLUSION OF THE CROWN

Given the peculiar history of the constitutional monarch in England and Wales, there are lots of questions about the role of the monarch and the relationship of the role to other parts of government and executive function in the loose notion of the 'Crown'.

It is a long-standing presumption that Acts of Parliament do not apply to the Crown.[67] Whilst this may seem slightly unusual to a modern reader, the relationship between the executive and the monarch is long-standing. The *Crown* is not a defined term but extends beyond the person who is the monarch, to include certain other arms of the state.[68]

An example will help illustrate the ongoing relevance (and difficulty) of this presumption. The case of *R (Black)*[69] concerned the question of whether the Crown was bound by the ban on smoking in enclosed public spaces and workplaces found within the Health Act 2006. In the case, a prisoner sought to take action to enforce the smoking ban at a prison (the management of which came under the Crown) through access to a confidential helpline to report on non-compliance. Despite testing the limits of the presumption, the Supreme Court felt unable to rebut the presumption that the Crown was not subject to the Act.[70] At various other points within the Act, the Crown was mentioned, and so the court concluded that had Parliament intended for the Crown to be subject to the restrictions of the smoking ban, then it would have made provision.

RULES OF LANGUAGE

The way in which language is used in acts follows standard patterns that help judges determine the meaning intended by Parliament. Despite a concerted effort on the part of the legal system to remove outdated legal Latin, this is one area where its use continues. The rules themselves are based on common sense and are straightforward to understand when accompanied by examples. It is also worth noting that they are based on general trends in the use of language and so are not strictly binding on the judiciary but may help inform how to approach questions of interpretation.

The overarching principle that meaning is contextual is captured by the phrase *noscitur a sociis* – 'known by its associates', or to put it differently, that words are understood by the other words

66 ibid [133].

67 *Bombay v Municipal Corporation* [1947] AC 58 (PC).

68 <https://researchbriefings.files.parliament.uk/documents/CBP-8885/CBP-8885.pdf>.

69 *R (Black) v Secretary of State for Justice* [2017] UKSC 81.

70 ibid [50].

that surround them. This has a number of dimensions that will be explored further in what follows.

EJUSDEM GENERIS ('OF THE SAME KIND')

This rule of language is a means for determining the relationship between specific and general words/categories. Where there is a list of classes of items that contain specific classes and general classes, the general classes are to be understood in light of the specific ones. For the sake of illustration, imagine an Act of Parliament that sought to regulate the ownership or management of the following: 'sheep, pigs, cattle and other animals'. The words 'sheep', 'pigs' and 'cattle' are all specific examples, whereas the phrase 'other animals' could be very broad, indeed. If a court was called upon to interpret the phrase 'other animals', then the *ejusdem generis* rule would mean that the judge should determine its meaning by reference to the specific categories of animal mentioned previously. As the specific classes of animals are all common *farmyard* animals, the phrase 'other animals' would include donkeys, chickens and horses but probably not include hamsters, tigers or bears. The use of specific classes followed by a general class is a typical drafting tool to ensure that the intention of a provision is clear without having to be concerned with listing every possible example.

In order for this rule to take effect, it must be clear from the specific words the common features joining them together into a single class or genus.[71] There are examples of application of the rule littered throughout the case law. One such example can be found in *DPP v Vivier*,[72] where the court was faced with a question of interpretation of the Road Traffic Act 1988. This Act applied 'on a road or other public place', and the question was whether the term 'other public place' included a private caravan park. The court held that the term 'public place' (the general) had to be interpreted in light of the specific term 'road' and so could include the caravan park.

EXPRESSIO UNIUS EST EXCLUSIO ALTERIUS ('EXPRESS MENTION OF ONE THING, EXCLUDES ANOTHER')

This rule holds that where a legislature mentions specific classes or categories, then it intends to exclude others not mentioned. For example, if statute specifically lists 'pigs, sheep and cattle' and makes no reference to any other animal, then it is to be taken that Parliament only intended for the Act to cover the animals listed.

The recent case of *Geddes*[73] powerfully demonstrates the potential impact of applying this rule of language, and also that it can apply not only to lists within a particular section but also to groups of sections within an Act of Parliament. The case concerned the deportation of a defendant to Jamaica following his conviction for the offence of wounding with intent to inflict grievous bodily harm. Legislation allowed for execution of the deportation to be 'stayed'

71 For a recent case where this failed, see *Cab Housing Ltd v The Secretary of State for Levelling Up* [2022] EWHC 208 (Admin), [2022] PTSR 1027.

72 *DPP v Vivier* [1991] 4 All ER 18 (QBD).

73 *Geddes v Secretary of State for the Home Department* [2024] EWHC 66 (Admin).

whilst final determination of appeals was ongoing. The Act[74] made reference to appeals in the Upper Tribunal and to the Court of Appeal. They did not reference other appeal routes. The defendant's appeal had been to the Supreme Court. Mr Justice Lane held that the *expressio unius est exclusio alterius* rule meant that Parliament 'must have intended to exclude other appellate situations'.[75]

EXPRESSUM FACIT CESSARE TACITUM ('STATEMENT ENDS IMPLICATION')

It is possible, in very many areas of law, to have both express and implied duties/powers/obligations. Various tests exist in order to suggest that a legal person has an implied right or duty. This rule seeks to govern the relationship between implied and express powers within legislation. It holds that where there is an *express* power (or duty or right) governing a subject or area, then the courts should not interpret an implied power (or duty or right) within the same area.

The Court of Appeal has recently considered this rule in the case of *Ball*.[76] The case concerned the variation of a noise abatement order issued by a local authority to a racing circuit under the powers granted by the Environment Protection Act 1980. The Act gave the local authority *express* powers to *issue* noise abatement orders. It did not specifically address whether the local authority had powers to *vary* the orders it had issued. Such a power of variation did lie with the Magistrates' Courts. The key question was whether it was possible to *imply* a power of variation in favour of the local authority. Following the *expressum facit cessare tacitum* rule, the court held that to *imply* a power would be inconsistent with the *express* powers given to the local authority and the Magistrates' Court under the Act.

INTERPRETATIVE AIDS – INTERNAL

There is a vast array of potential documentary sources that could be used to help understand the meaning of words in general and of words in legislation in particular. Bearing in mind what was said earlier, it is no surprise that courts focus on so-called 'intrinsic aids' to interpretation. These intrinsic aids are features of the Act (or secondary legislation) that are being interpreted in a given case. This is not surprising, given that the legislation as a whole is the crucial context for what Parliament intended when passing a given law.

OTHER SECTIONS WITHIN THE ACT, INCLUDING SCHEDULES

Perhaps most importantly, intrinsic aids would also include schedules within Acts of Parliament and sections or groups of section dealing with the same issue. There is no priority between schedules or sections in terms of the interpretative value they bring.

74 Nationality, Immigration and Asylum Act 2002 s104.

75 *Geddes v Secretary of State for the Home Department* [2024] EWHC 66 (Admin) [14].

76 *R (on the application of Ball) v Hinckley and Bosworth Council* [2024] EWCA Civ 433.

LONG AND SHORT TITLE

At its most obvious, the title of the Act (both long and short) will give a clue as to the meaning of the words it contains. By its nature, the short title will be of more limited value as it tends only to delineate the subject matter of the Act and goes no further.

The case of *Quintavalle*,[77] discussed elsewhere in this chapter, reinforces the value of long titles. In considering how widely to cast its interpretative net in terms of governing the use of embryos, the House of Lords found support in its approach from the long title of the Human Fertilisation and Embryology Act 1990. The long title read as follows: 'to make provision in connection with human embryos and any subsequent development of such embryos'.[78] As the long title spoke of 'any subsequent development', the court felt comfortable in ascribing to the word 'embryo' a wide meaning, to include activities related to new scientific approaches to their creation.

In some cases, the courts seem to suggest that the fact that the long title is amendable by Parliament as it passes through the system is a clear indication that it is intended to convey meaning to the words it contains.[79]

HEADINGS, MARGINAL OR SIDE NOTES

There is more complexity around headings and side or marginal notes within an Act of Parliament. This is because their nature has transformed over time. Before the turn of the 20th century, marginal notes (aimed at guiding and helping the reader navigate the law) were inserted *after* the passage of the Act and so were not viewed by Parliament before a bill became law and were not routinely prepared by parliamentary draftsmen. As their name suggests, they were inserted into the margins of the published versions of the Act. For this reason, they were not considered to be part of the Act, and there is clear case law against their use as a tool of interpretation of equal value to truly intrinsic aids.[80]

More recent practice has developed the position of 'marginal notes', and they now have an interpretative value, albeit more limited than other intrinsic aids. Marginal notes have now moved and no longer sit in the margins but are above the relevant sections and act as headings. These headings perform the same function as the old marginal notes but have different key characteristics. They are now, for most bills, drafted by parliamentary draftsmen and are prepared and published as an integral part of the legislation. This means that they are visible at all stages of the legislative process. For this reason, they can be used as an interpretative aid. The House of Lords in *Montila* held that they can be used by courts but that

> less weight can be attached to them than to the part of the Act that are open for consideration and debate.[81]

77 *R (on the Application of Quintavalle) v Secretary of State for Health* [2003] UKHL 13, [2003] 2 AC 687 (HL).

78 ibid [41].

79 Black-Clawson v Papierwerke [1975] AC 591 (HL).

80 See *R v Hare* [1934] 1 KB 354 (CA Crim), 355.

81 *R v Montila* [2004] UKHL 50.

This case demonstrates that even as between different interpretative aids, they intrinsically bring different value to the judicial toolkit.

INTRODUCTORY SECTIONS

In *R v (on the application of FDA)*,[82] the court noted the 'recent trend towards the inclusion of introductory provisions at the beginning of an Act which are designed to set its context and explain its purpose'.[83] This is a particularly useful innovation for courts faced with determining parliamentary intention.

INTERPRETATIVE AIDS – EXTERNAL

The value of components from within legislation to aid the interpretative task is clear. This section seeks to address the much thornier issue of the extent to which material from outside of the legislation in need of interpretation can and should be used as an aid to judges in determining what Parliament intended by the words it used.

The starting point is that which was expressed by Lord Hodge in *R (on the application of O)*, namely, that 'external aids to interpretation . . . must play a secondary role'[84] to internal aids. This position has a practical and a constitutional basis. On the practical side, there is a risk that litigation becomes much more costly if lawyers have to search and research things that sit outside the legislation under discussion (such as government White Papers, Law Commission reports or debates recorded in the pages of Hansard). On the constitutional side, there is an argument that citizens should be able to determine meaning themselves by reading the law and should not have to consult with other sources in order to understand their rights and obligations.

This has most clearly been stated in the *FDA* case referenced earlier, where the High Court held the following:

> It is . . . important to distinguish between two stages in the process of statutory interpretation. At the first stage, the court considers the words Parliament used, in context. If and only if this exercise yields a meaning which is ambiguous or uncertain, the court considers whether there are admissible external aids which can assist in resolving the ambiguity.[85]

By only having a secondary role, there is an argument that judges should only consult with external sources where ambiguity remains following use of internal aids. It should also be

82 *R (on the application of FDA) v Minister for the Cabinet Office* [2024] EWHC 1729 (Admin).

83 ibid [96].

84 *R (on the application of O) v Secretary of State for the Home Department* [2022] UKSC 3, [2022] 2 WLR 343.

85 *R (on the application of FDA) v Minister for the Cabinet Office* [2024] EWHC 1729 (Admin).

stated, by way of final introduction to this area, that the number of external sources is varied and diverse. Some external material may be of greater value and importance than others. Some material may be closer to the legislation in question. Some material may be parliamentary, and some may not. For this reason, although grouped together under the heading of 'external aids', the reader should keep in mind that they are themselves very different sources of information and may or may not be helpful to judges.

DICTIONARIES

The use of dictionaries to determine the ordinary and plain meaning of words has a certain simplistic attraction. It is an attraction to which judges sometimes submit. Discussed in the first half of this chapter was the case of *Mandla v Lee*,[86] where Lord Denning made extensive reference to various iterations and developments in different dictionaries of the word 'ethnic'. The attraction is superficial as it assumes that this is the approach Parliament takes to legislation, whereas often words are used in their everyday and not etymological sense. This point was made by one of Denning's fellow appeal judges in the case.[87] It is also clear that different dictionaries may well take different views on the meaning of words. For this reason, recourse to dictionary definitions has fallen out of favour with judges, and they are not seen as a particularly insightful aid to determining what Parliament intended by the words it uses.

LAW COMMISSION REPORTS AND OTHER PRE-LEGISLATIVE REPORTS

The Law Commission is an independent body that has a programme work to suggest reform to the law in various areas. Its role is discussed more fully in Chapter 3 as an influence on law-making. Given the express purpose of the Law Commission's reports to propose reform to the law, it is not surprising that judges, on occasion, find it useful to refer to the reports in understanding the meaning of legislation. The case law makes it clear that judges are free to refer to such reports, regardless of whether there is ambiguity in the legislation, as they form a key part of the historical context to the act. For example, in the recent case of *Nazir*,[88] the court made reference to examples within a Law Commission Report on Land Registration in determining the meaning of the Land Registration Act 2002.

There are often other reports commissioned by government that can inform the passage of legislation and are intended to explore social and legal issues. The case of *DPP v Bull*[89] demonstrates where these reports can clarify the mischief Parliament was intending to address.

The case involved considering whether the words 'a person' or 'anyone' within s1 Sexual Offences Act 1959 were intended to apply only to women for the purposes of the offence of loitering or soliciting for the purposes of prostitution, or whether Parliament had intended for this offence to apply also to men. The court was referred to a report (the Wolfenden Report) that was commissioned to look at the rise in prosecution of consensual homosexual

86 *Mandla v Lee* [1983] QB 1 (CA).
87 ibid, 15 (per Oliver LJ).
88 *Nazir v Begum* [2024] EWHC 378 (KB).
89 *DPP v Bull* [1995] QB 88.

acts and also the social issues arising from a growth of street prostitution. This report was commissioned by the government and led to the passage of the Act in question. It was clear from the report that they had considered only the mischief created by female prostitution and so construed the Act as to exclude male prostitution.

The court in *DPP v Bull* was also referred to Hansard (the record of parliamentary debate) but did not feel the need to use it as a form of interpretation, given how the Wolfenden Report resolved any ambiguity in the intention of Parliament. The rules around the use of Hansard are discussed later.

In a more general sense, *DPP* reveals a number of interesting points. Firstly, that courts can sometimes preference pre-parliamentary material (such as reports) over parliamentary material that was actually part of the passage of a bill (such as debates in Parliament). Second, that a purposive and contextual approach can lead to a narrower construction than a literal reading would suggest. In many textbooks, the literal rule is seen as narrowing or restricting judges, but this case shows that this is not always the case, as a 'literal' understanding of 'anyone' or 'a person', without further context, would almost inevitably be read so at to include men and women. Thirdly, and for the sake of completeness, the case shows how changing social attitudes influence the interpretation of the law, and male prostitution was brought within the definition of s1 by the Sexual Offences Act 2003.

CONSULTATION PAPERS

Before proceeding to propose legislation, the government may consult in a broad sense (on policy through a Green Paper) or in a narrow sense (with a White Paper). White Papers can sometimes contain draft versions of bills with elements of consultation. For this reason, they could be seen as useful to understanding the context of law and the intentions of the government in bringing forward legislation. They are permissible as aids to interpretation.[90]

The use of White Papers as aids to construction has not been without criticism or controversy. In *Milton*,[91] the court allowed an appeal where a judge had appeared to place too much reliance on words used in a White Paper to the extent that they lost sight of the words used in the actual Act under interpretation.

STATUTES IN *PARI MATERIA*

The legal system of England and Wales does not have an organised repository of legislation that governs similar areas of law. Civil law systems prefer 'codes' that bring together legislation on similar areas into a coherent whole. The closest English and Welsh law gets to this is where the government chooses to 'consolidate' multiple acts (and aspects of the common law) into a single Act. These consolidation Acts are not common and do not prevent subsequent developments taking place outside of the newly formed legislation.

90 *Phillips v The Secretary of State for Foreign, Commonwealth and Development Affairs* [2024] EWHC 32 (Admin).

91 *R (Milton) v Crown Prosecution Service* [2007] EWHC 532 (Admin).

As a result of the preceding, there may be fragments of law governing the same topic spanning over many Acts and many decades. These are known as statutes acting in *pari materia*. This leads to the perfectly reasonable question as to whether words used across Acts governing the same subject area should be given the same meaning. There is case law to suggest that there verges on a presumption that Parliament will have intended Acts governing the same area to have the same interpretation in order that an area of law will 'constitute a harmonious whole'.[92]

There are occasions where Acts will appear to restrict definitions so that they only apply to that particular Act. In *Marks*,[93] a case from Northern Ireland, the court had to consider whether the term 'terrorism' as defined in the Terrorism Act 2000 should hold the same meaning as the term 'terrorism' in the Northern Ireland Act 1998. The fact that a word is defined for the purposes of a specific Act does not mean that the *pari materia* rule should not apply. The court will have to look at the context. It is also true that there is not a *requirement* for judges to apply the same definition if they feel that consistency was not needed. In *Marks*, the court held that the nature of the two Acts was different – the Terrorism Act 2000 applied to the whole UK and was a criminal statute, whereas the Northern Ireland Act of 1998 had a limited territorial scope and was constitutional in nature.[94] *Marks* reinforces the notion that these are *aids* to interpretation that form part of a judicial toolkit. They are not 'rules' to be slavishly followed.

THE USE OF HANSARD AS AN AID TO INTERPRETATION – THE RULE IN *PEPPER V HART*[95]

The debates on legislation within Parliament may be thought to be a particularly useful source of aid to a judge seeking to understand the meaning of Acts of Parliament. These debates, since 1909, have been comprehensively reported and officially published by Parliament in Hansard. It is worth noting that before the 19th century, there was very little reporting,[96] and to report on a debate was a contempt of Parliament, and the author or publisher could face imprisonment or fine. Even in the early 19th century, only incomplete and selective reporting of debates was published.

With the full reporting of debates in Hansard in the 20th century, it became necessary to resolve the question as to, and the extent to which, judges may rely on those parliamentary debates in giving meaning to the words in statutes. In the early 1970s, the House of Lords decided that reference to parliamentary material (including Hansard) was not permitted.[97] This question was finally resolved in the case of *Pepper v Hart* in the early 1990s.

The case of *Pepper v Hart* concerned the interpretation of the Finance Act 1976 and how its tax provisions applied to a discounted fee charged by a private school for the children of its teachers. The dispute was whether, for the purpose of tax law, the 'cost' of the benefit was that of running the entire school divided by the total number of pupils (i.e. an average) or that the

92 *Commissioners for Her Majesty's Revenue and Customs v Lond Clubs Management* [2020] UKSC 49, [80].
93 *Marks v Minister of Justice* [2022] NIQB 57 (QBD).
94 *Marks v Minister of Justice* [2022] NIQB 57 (QBD) [35].
95 *Pepper (Inspector of Taxes) v Hart* [1993] AC 593 (HL).
96 Although newspapers found ways of unofficially reporting on debates.
97 *Davis v Johnson* [1979] AC 264 (HL).

'cost' was only any extra cost that would be incurred by educating those particular children in addition to other pupils (i.e. the marginal cost). That cost was crucial to determining the benefit to be taxed. The wording of the Finance Act 1976 was ambiguous, and so the courts had to determine between these alternative meanings. Both the High Court and the Court of Appeal, without reference to Hansard, found the words of the Finance Act to have meant the average of all costs and so found against the teachers. In the House of Lords, specific consideration was given to the question of whether or not the court should refer to Hansard in determining the meaning of the Act. The House of Lords did rely on the words of Hansard and, in particular, on comments from the Financial Secretary, who, in response to a question in Parliament on the very issue in dispute, made clear that the drafters of the legislation had intended a scheme that was in favour of the taxpayer.

In relying on the statements from Hansard, the House of Lords reversed the decisions of the lower courts and found in favour of the teachers and overruled its own previous authority in not allowing the use of parliamentary material (the 'exclusionary rule').[98] The House of Lords was keen to emphasise that this was only a partial relaxation of the rule, and Lord Browne-Wilkinson, giving the lead judgment, put it in these terms:

> [R]eference . . . should be permitted as an aid to the construction of legislation which is ambiguous or obscure or the literal meaning of which leads to an absurdity. Even in such cases references in court to Parliamentary material should only be permitted where such material clearly discloses the mischief aimed at or the legislative intention lying behind the ambiguous or obscure words. . . . I cannot foresee that any statement other than the statement of the Minister or other promoter of the Bill is likely to meet these criteria.[99]

This is the so-called 'rule in *Pepper v Hart*' and has the following requirements for when Hansard can be used to help the court determine meaning, usefully restated recently in *R (on the application of O)*, a case that was discussed earlier in this chapter:

1. Where the statute is ambiguous, obscure, *or* where a literal reading would lead to an absurdity
   and
2. Where the relevant passages relied upon in Hansard disclose the 'mischief' the legislation was aimed at resolving
   and
3. The relevant statement comes from the Minister or promoter of the bill[100]

The criteria were set out in a restrictive manner because there are dangers inherent in allowing too permissive an approach to including extraneous material not contained on the face of the legislation itself. These were articulated by the dissenting judgment of Lord Mackay in *Pepper v Hart* and even referenced by the majority.

98 Overruling *Davis v Johnson* [1979] AC 264 (HL) using the authority of the Practice Statement (Judicial Precedent) [1966] 1 WLR 1234.

99 *Pepper v Hart* [1993] AC 593, 634 (HL).

100 *R (on the application of O) v Secretary of State for the Home Department* [2022] UKSC 3, [2022] 2 WLR 343.

The primary concerns relate to certainty and accessibility of law. Citizens should not have to explore preparatory materials in order to understand and interpret the law. To do so is to place a burden upon them and is to threaten a key tenet of the rule of law. The rights and obligations of citizens should be plain on the face of the Act.

Secondary concerns relate to the prospects of cost and delay to the legal system. If lawyers were able to make liberal use of Hansard, then much time (and cost) would be devoted to exploring the debates of Parliament. The risk is that *all* cases involving statutory interpretation would require an exploration of Hansard. Given that, in many cases, the debates in Hansard are *not* of assistance in understanding the meaning of the words used by Parliament, there is a question of proportionality.

For these reasons, in subsequent cases, the test has been strictly applied. It is unusual for parties to be able to demonstrate that reference to Hansard is necessary, with courts either denying that the conditions for its inclusion are met, or finding that the same conclusion can be reached without reference to the rule in *Pepper v Hart*.[101]

In closing, it is worth reinforcing that when we refer to use of Hansard as an interpretative tool, we are specifically referring to the record of debates on the relevant legislation. As Hansard is a record of very many activities in Parliament, there is a risk that the rule in *Pepper v Hart* is seen in a broader way. The courts have been clear that it applies only to debates about the bill. This means that the work of other committees in commenting on the bill will not be admissible as an aid to statutory interpretation.[102]

EXPLANATORY NOTES

Modern government bills are always accompanied by a set of 'explanatory notes'. They are produced on behalf of government departments and are published alongside the bill and amended as bills move between the Houses of Parliament. They are intended to put the bill into its relevant context and to explain, in a less technical and more open manner, the intended operation of the bill. However, they do not form part of the bill and cannot be amended, nor are they endorsed by Parliament.

Given their curious and slightly unusual nature of being very close to the development of the bill but not officially part of it, questions have arisen as to the extent to which they can act as aids to interpretation. Fundamentally, should they be treated as more akin to pre-legislative material or subject to the same restrictions as Hansard.

The case of *Westminster City Council*[103] provides helpful clarity and a useful summary of the history of explanatory notes.[104] The case makes clear that explanatory notes are an admissible aid to statutory interpretation. It also held that they can be used even in the absence of

101 For example of the latter, see *Harding v Wealands* [2006] UKHL 32, [2007] 2 AC 1 (HL).

102 *Phillips v The Secretary of State for Foreign, Commonwealth and Development Affairs* [2024] EWHC 32 (Admin), [122].

103 *Westminster City Council v Asylum Support Service* [2002] UKHL 38.

104 *Westminster City Council v Asylum Support Service* [2002] UKHL 38, [5].

ambiguity on the face of the Act. The court indicated that, given their proximity to the bill as it passes through Parliament, explanatory notes may indeed be more useful as an aid to interpretation than Law Commission reports or government White Papers.

CONCLUSION

Amongst all the technical rules on the admissibility, or desirability, of using various aids to interpretation and the difficult choices over which 'approach' should gain priority, it is easy to lose sight of the core issues that underlie this whole area of law.

First and foremost, the English language will continue to cause problems of interpretation, no matter how well-drafted or exhaustive the discussion surrounding the passage of an Act of Parliament is. In fact, much of the beauty of the English language lies in its ambiguity, nuance and subtlety. If we accept this truth and wish to see a legal system capable of dealing with the increasing complexity of the world, then we must also accept that judges must play a central role in the interpretative process. This will, of necessity, involve judges making determinations about the meaning of words in statutes. Rather than expressing concerns over individual cases of statutory interpretation, it is more important to deal with the interaction between the myriad reasons requiring statutory interpretation and the specific approaches to such interpretation. The art of proper construction is predicated on achieving the balance between the need for statutory interpretation and the proper role of the court in the legal system of England and Wales. The tools of statutory interpretation act as a counterbalance (Figure 6.4)

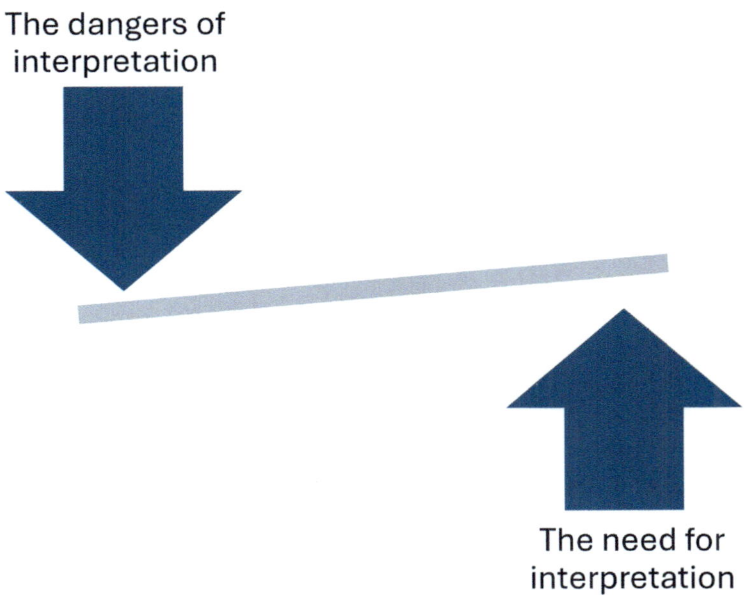

Figure 6.4 Tools of interpretation as a balancing force.

to prevent the courts from stepping into the shoes of the legislature while still allowing the judiciary to solve the problems provided by the written word in the cases they confront.

THE WEBSITE

The website that accompanies this textbook contains many useful resources that you can use to consolidate and further your knowledge of the law, to hone your skills of critical analysis and to test your knowledge. This includes a set of multiple-choice questions (MCQs) that can be used to test your knowledge and understanding of the material.

7

CHAPTER 7
THE JUDICIARY

INTRODUCTION

The judiciary is at the heart of our legal system, interpreting and applying the law that Parliament makes to individual cases. Additionally, judges make law through distillation of common law principles. As judges are responsible for recognising and giving life to 'the law', particularly through the common law, it is vitally important that they retain their authority and the trust of citizens. Maintaining independence and public trust is not always easy, but knowing the *nature* of the judicial task and the challenges that the structure of the judiciary poses will give a richer understanding of how the law operates on a day-to-day basis.

This chapter has two main aims. First to introduce the reader to the role of the judiciary and to explain (briefly) the different types of judicial office. Second, the chapter will explore some of the thornier issues (such as diversity in appointment and misconduct in judicial office) which jeopardise or threaten the attainment of one or more of the objectives of the legal system.

AS YOU READ

This chapter consists of a fairly dense set of (sometimes descriptive) information about various aspects of the judiciary. As you read, be sure to try to contextualise this information in light of the other chapters of the textbook and avoid reading it in isolation.

By the end of this chapter, you should be able to **identify the different levels of the judiciary** and **distinguish between senior and inferior** judicial office-holders.

In considering appointments to the judiciary, you should **think critically about diversity appointment** and **evaluate the effectiveness of changes to the process of judicial appointment**. Throughout the chapter, **consider the extent to which the independence of the judiciary is secured or undermined** by the points being discussed.

NATURE OF JUDGING AND ROLE OF THE JUDICIARY

Before exploring the different types of judicial office, it is important to give a brief account of the role of the judiciary in the legal system of England and Wales. This will add much-needed context and give an insight into the type of person who may be attracted to, and have aptitude for, judicial office.

DOI: 10.4324/9781032641829-7

MAKING CONNECTIONS – THE JUDICIARY AND THE LEGAL SYSTEM

++

There are important links to be made with other chapters in the textbook. The judiciary does not operate in isolation but forms an integral part of the overall system. For more on the core role of the judiciary, look at the chapters on **statutory interpretation (Chapter 6)** and judicial **precedent (Chapter 9)**. To explore the way in which the judiciary interacts with other parts of the legal system, look at the chapter on **sources of law (Chapter 2)** and the **institutions of law-making (Chapter 3)**. For a richer understanding of how judges contribute to particular areas of the justice system, refer to the **criminal justice (Chapter 11)** and **civil justice (Chapter 10)** parts of the textbook.

This section of the textbook focusses primarily on judicial office-holders and does not deal with the system of lay magistrates in any level of detail, despite the fact that since early medieval times, Magistrates' Courts have been the location of the start of both civil and criminal cases and every criminal case to this day begins in a Magistrates' Court (for which see Chapter 11).

The website that accompanies this text has a separate podcast dedicated to the magistracy and the role that they play in the legal system.

To talk of the 'judicial function' or the 'role of the judiciary' is to treat the 'judiciary' as if it is a single role or function, but this fundamentally misunderstands the nature of the judicial task. Any text seeking to differentiate the institutions of the legal system will claim that the judiciary 'applies' and 'interprets' the law and that they act as the 'resolvers of disputes'.[1] These three pillars of the judicial system risk oversimplifying what it is that judges do and how they do it. There are multiple roles within the judiciary, and different types of judges have responsibility not only for different areas of law and different types of dispute but also for different aspects of the justice system and for performing aspects of these overarching tasks of application and interpretation to varying degrees. The life of a judge in the County Court can be very different to that of a Court of Appeal judge, which is, again, very different to that of a judge sitting in the Crown Court. As such, the mix of functions that a particular member of the judiciary plays will also vary enormously.

It is also worth making the point that the role(s) of the judiciary incorporates a temporal dimension that has changed over time and that will continue to change in the future. Aspects of the role take on different degrees of importance at different times in the development of the legal system. As discussed in the chapters on law-making (Chapters 4 and 5) and sources of law (Chapter 2), the traditional role of the judiciary has focussed on the development of the common law. This was due to the fact that statutes were not as numerous prior to the mid-

1 For a provocative account of the judicial role, see John Griffith, *The Politics of the Judiciary* (5th edn, Fontana Press 2010).

20th century. The growth of statutory law, without necessary improvements to the *quality* of such law, has led to a greater need for judges to interpret Acts of Parliament. The interpretative role played by judges has therefore become a greater part of the judiciary's work than was once the case. The differing emphasis placed on alternative aspects of the judicial role over time is something that is even recognised by senior members of the judiciary. Lord Woolf once stated that it was 'one of the strengths of the common law that it enables the courts to vary the extent of their intervention to reflect current needs, and by this means it helps to maintain the delicate balance of a democratic society'.[2] The development of international (and domestic) fundamental rights protection has also affected the way in which the judiciary approaches its task.

Laid out (briefly) in Table 7.1 is a list of just some of the tasks faced by those who hold judicial office.

ANALYSING THE LAW – JUDGES BEYOND THE COURTS

In addition to the tasks (mentioned earlier) associated with their office, judges also fulfil a number of roles 'extrajudicially', and these can complement (or even jeopardise) their work. For example, judges can act as chancellors for universities, give lectures to various institutions[3] and also write commentaries on the law. This enhances the profile of the judiciary, and the authority of their office can add significant weight to these extrajudicial roles. Despite the qualities that judges undoubtedly bring to such tasks, it can be difficult (for the public) to disassociate the judicial from the non-judicial in some cases, and for judges to ensure that they maintain an impartiality compatible with their judicial role.

In particular, senior members of the judiciary are often selected to lead public inquiries into matters of public interest.[4] By doing so, they are acting on the appointment of the government in a non-judicial capacity and do not sit as a judge during the course of the inquiry. These inquiries can have an extremely high profile in the public consciousness, such as the Leveson Inquiry, and can lead to confrontations or close interactions with the government that blur the lines between when the judge is acting judicially and when he is not.[5]

The focus here has so far been on the role of the judiciary of England and Wales. It is important to remember that judges of England and Wales are now part of a broader

2 Where juries are used, it is the jurors' role to determine facts though the judge will give them helpful directions to assist them to focus on the issues to be determined. The role of juries is considered in greater detail in Chapter 12.

3 For a list of speeches given by the Justices of the Supreme Court, see <www.supremecourt.uk/news/speeches.html>.

4 Inquiries Act 2005 s10.

5 See the public disagreements between a government Minister (Michael Gove) and Lord Leveson during the inquiry chaired by the latter – <www.bbc.co.uk/news/uk-18256724>.

Table 7.1 The tasks of the judiciary

Role	*Description*
Fact-find	In the vast majority of civil and criminal cases, judges find the facts.[1] This means that they establish, where issues are contested, what the true facts of the case are. This is an important role as it is the material facts that give rise to the legal issue that needs to be resolved.
Give interpretation of the law	Where Acts of Parliament (or secondary law) are unclear or could bear multiple meanings, judges are called upon to determine the meaning of the law. In this sense, the judiciary gives an abstract interpretation of what the statutory provisions mean. Judges are also responsible, where juries are involved, for explaining the applicable law to the jury.
Apply the law	Once the facts have been established and an interpretation of the law is given, it is normally the judge's role to apply that interpretation to the specific facts in order to resolve the legal issue in question. They must also apply sentencing guidelines in the case of criminal trials.
Resolve disputes	It should not be forgotten that judges interpret or apply the law in cases where parties are in dispute. In this narrow sense, judges presiding over the courts to which applications are made provide a means of independently settling disputes. In a broader sense, and following the Woolf reforms to the civil justice system, judges are also there to encourage parties to engage with dispute resolution mechanisms short of litigation (such as mediation or arbitration), which are now at the core of dispensation of justice in all Westernised jurisdictions grappling with resolution of legal disputes.
Create law	Through the common law in particular, judges make law. Their interpretation of statutes can also be considered as a form of law-making. There are distinct chapters in this textbook on judges' interpretation of the law and on the case decision method by which judges make law. As Lord Denning put it, '[judges] every day make law, though it is almost heresy to say so'.[2]
Adjudicate on procedure	The civil and criminal courts have a sophisticated and complex body of rules relating to court procedure and a whole branch of law related to rules surrounding evidence. Judges must also adjudicate on these satellite issues as and when they arise in given cases.

1 Cited in Michael Zander, *The Law-Making Process* (7th edn, Bloomsbury Publishing 2015) 344.

2 *R (on the application of Reilly (No 2) and Hewstone v Secretary of State for Work and Pensions* [2014] EWHC 2182 (Admin), [2015] 2 WLR 309.

Role	*Description*
Check on executive powers	Judges can also be called upon to adjudicate on government action and act as a check that other branches of the state have not exceeded their powers. This is primarily achieved through the system of judicial review. This control of state power is a constitutional check that maintains the proper separation of powers and preserves the rule of law.
Safeguard the rule of law	In more recent years, partly prompted by the powers under the Human Rights Act 1998, judges have taken a more active role in safeguarding important constitutional principles, such as the rule of law. For example, in the case of *Reilly (No2)*,[3] the High Court was extremely critical of the way in which the government (and Parliament) had passed retrospective legislation to invalidate an ongoing legal dispute as this violated the principle of the rule of law.[4]
Manage cases	The judiciary now has an important part to play in an administrative and management sense. They control the court lists and the way in which the building housing the court itself operates. They must also actively manage cases and assign dates to hearings. This is important in reducing delays and preventing (or minimising) tactical applications designed to give one party an unfair advantage. Although some of these management tasks can be delegated to administrative staff, the responsibility tends to lie with more senior members at each level of the justice system.
Provoke changes	Judges are also in a position to influence the development of the law in a less direct way than mentioned previously under the title 'create law'. Where judges are unable to change the law (for example, where there is a binding precedent or there is a clear parliamentary intent contrary to the position that the judge wishes to take), they can still provoke changes. A well-reasoned judgment can influence higher courts to take a different view, and a convincing and powerful criticism of the current law may lead Parliament to rethink its position. This ability for judges to provoke reform has been strengthened by the passage of the Human Rights Act 1998 and the ability of judges to highlight where legislation is incompatible with fundamental rights.[5]

3 The prospect of retroactive legislation is an anathema to the English Legal System as it offends against the rule of law – see David Stott, '*Reilly and Hewstone v Secretary of State for Work and Pensions*' [2016] SLR 3.

4 Section 4 of the Human Rights Act 1998 gives judges the power to declare legislation to be incompatible with the European Convention on Human Rights and this triggers powers for the Government speedily to amend Acts of Parliament.

5 Lord Woolf, 'Droit Public – English Style' [1995] PL 57.

community of judges, and that has influenced both their role and their *approach* to their judicial function. For example, all English and Welsh judges were also European judges in the sense that they were, until 2020, part of the legal order of the European Union. Similarly, the European Court of Human Rights has had an influence (positive or negative, depending on your political hue) on judicial office-holders.

JUDICIAL OFFICE-HOLDERS

There is a variety of different levels and roles within the judiciary, and this section will attempt to summarise the different positions and, for the senior/superior[6] positions, give account of their place in the legal system. There are in excess of 5,000 judicial office-holders[7] and a further 13,000 lay magistrates. This chapter will focus on the judicial office-holders in the higher courts in the legal system. The tribunals are historically – and, to some extent, still functionally – distinct, and their judiciary has its own hierarchy, with rarely a crossover with the courts unless on appeal. The rationale for this separation of treatment will be obvious in the distinct sections on the lay magistrates and tribunals (Chapter 13).

The structure of the senior judiciary has gone through significant changes in the last 20 years. Most importantly, responsibility for the *leadership* of the judiciary has transferred from the Lord Chancellor to the Lord Chief Justice. This occurred through the Constitutional Reform Act 2005, which separated the office's former connections with the judiciary and profession from the core responsibility of the office as a member of the government, not least because (as head of the judiciary) this dual responsibility clearly fell foul of the doctrine of separation of powers, as discussed in Chapter 3. The Lord Chancellor is thus now merely a position in the government, held concurrently but not necessarily by the Secretary of State for Justice. This move is a significant shift made to ensure the ongoing independence of the judiciary, and it coincided with changes to the House of Lords.[8] The Lord Chancellor no longer needs to be legally qualified – s/he must instead be qualified 'by experience'[9] – as contemporary Lord Chancellors are no longer eligible to sit in any judicial capacity. Between 2012 and 2017, successive Lord Chancellors were not legally qualified. More recently, and to the time of writing, the post has been held again by those who are legally qualified.

Justices of the Supreme Court. The Supreme Court came into existence in 2009 and replaced the Appellate Committee of the House of Lords. The first Justices were drawn from the existing Lords of Appeal in Ordinary and have subsequently been appointed through ad hoc selection commissions (discussed later). There are 12 Justices, one of whom will serve as the President

6 Superior judges have unlimited jurisdiction (provided that jurisdiction has not been limited by statute) and so can theoretically sit anywhere and decide fully on aspects of procedure – see *Al Rawi v The Security Service* [2011] UKSC 34, [2012] 1 AC 531 [72].

7 <https://www.gov.uk/government/statistics/diversity-of-the-judiciary-2023-statistics>.

8 Whereby the judicial function of the Lords was transferred to the newly established Supreme Court.

9 Constitutional Reform Act 2005 s2(1).

(at the time of writing, Lord Reed), and another who will serve as the Deputy President (at the time of writing, Lord Sales). Sitting in the highest civil court in the United Kingdom and the highest criminal court in England, Wales and Northern Ireland[10] means that the Justices are the most high-profile judges in the legal system. By convention, two of the Justices will be senior Scottish judges, with a further Justice being selected from Northern Ireland. This is not a statutory requirement, but the Constitutional Reform Act 2005 does require that, when making appointments, consideration be given to the expertise of the judges (as a whole) and that there is adequate knowledge of the law of the constituent parts of the United Kingdom.[11]

Lord or Lady Chief Justice. The Lord or Lady Chief Justice (LCJ) is the most senior office-holder within the judiciary of England and Wales. As well as leading the judiciary as the President of the courts of England and Wales, they are also Head of Division,[12] leading the Criminal Division of the Court of Appeal. The LCJ also has the role of making representations to Parliament on matters that they deem to be of importance to the judiciary.[13] In October 2023, Dame Sue Carr became the first woman to be appointed to the role and took the title Lady Chief Justice.

Heads of Division. The next most senior judges are the Heads of Division. The Master of the Rolls leads the Civil Division of the Court of Appeal, while the President of the King's Bench Division,[14] the Chancellor of the High Court[15] and the President of the Family Division lead the respective Divisions of the High Court.

Lord and Lady Justices of Appeal. These are superior judges who sit ordinarily in the Court of Appeal. There are 38 such Justices.[16] When appointed to the Court of Appeal, Lord and Lady Justices become members of the Privy Council.

Puisne[17] *judges*. These are the least senior of the superior judges. They sit in the High Court and are given knighthoods when they take up their office.

Inferior judges. There is also a collection of inferior judges who usually sit at lower levels within the legal system. These can be summarised as following: circuit judges, who sit in the County Court, family court and Crown Court; district judges, who sit in the County Court; and recorders, who sit in the County Court and Crown Court. However, recorders must be distinguished from most of the other inferior judges since they – although at that level only part-time and fee paid – comprise the first rung of the judicial ladder towards

10 There is a separate criminal court system in Scotland.

11 Constitutional Reform Act 2005 s27(8).

12 Constitutional Reform Act 2005 s7(1).

13 Constitutional Reform Act 2005 ss 5(1) and (5)(a).

14 This post had previously also been held by the Lord Chief Justice, but the responsibility was passed to a new post, created in 2005, when the latter became head of the judiciary.

15 This was a post that had previously been undertaken by the Lord Chancellor.

16 Senior Courts Act 1981 s2.

17 Pronounced 'puny'.

permanent appointment in the High Court and above. There are also 'masters' (who are the equivalent of district judges in the County Court), who sit largely on interlocutory – interim administrative – matters in the King's Bench and Chancery Divisions of the High Court. The District Judges and Masters – although they form the hard working backbone of the superior courts – do not usually expect to be promoted to permanent appointments in the superior courts, although there are exceptions, for example, Dame Elizabeth Butler-Sloss, now Baroness Butler-Sloss, who began in the Tribunal Judiciary and was then a Registrar of the Family Division (equivalent of a Master of the King's Bench and Chancery Divisions, later becoming today's District Judges of the Family Division) before being appointed to the High Court (as only the fourth woman to reach that Court, after Elizabeth Lane, Rose Heilbron and Margaret Booth).

The superior judges have unlimited jurisdiction in the sense that their powers come from (and are limited by) statute rather than the common law. This means that the authority for their action comes from their judicial office rather than from the court in which they sit.[18] By contrast, the inferior judges have a statutory basis for their jurisdiction and must sit in a place that is designated as a court.

ANALYSING THE LAW – THE POWER OF JUDICIAL PERSONALITY

A reading of the two opening sections of this chapter could paint something of a bland picture of the judiciary of the legal system of England and Wales. However, judges are not raised in captivity away from all human influence. Indeed, judges will have had a distinct career (albeit one linked to the law) before taking up judicial office.

Judges have personalities and worldviews that are informed by, amongst other things, their education, employment and social backgrounds. This fact is important as it may affect (even subconsciously) the way in which they go about discharging the duties of their judicial offices. One of the great joys of studying the common law is to embrace this fact and to understand that judges have character strengths and flaws that help shape the life of the judiciary and the development of the law. That is not to say that judges are partisan or that they come to judgments not based on their understanding of the *law*; it is simply to note that their understanding of the law *and of the judicial function* may be coloured by their human experiences as much as by their legal experiences.[19]

If we look even at just the 20th and the 21st centuries, it is possible to study some of the notable characters of the legal system and to make some comment on their

18 See *Ipswich Board of Finance v Clark* [1973] Ch 323 (Ch) for a powerful example of this principle in action.

19 For a detailed discussion of this concept, see John Griffith, *The Politics of the Judiciary* (5th edn, Fontana Press 2010).

contribution to the judicial task. To take Lord Denning as just one, very famous, example, he has been described as being the 'best-known and best-loved judge in the whole of our history'.[20] He had a determination to drive forward development of the common law and was noted for his creativity, for example, resurrecting the long-dead concept of promissory estoppel in contract law.[21] This was a much more proactive approach to the judicial function of law creation than prevalent in many of his contemporaries. As Master of the Rolls, and through sheer force of character, Denning also convinced other members of the Court of Appeal to attempt to alter the very rules of binding precedent in *Davis v Johnson*.[22] The House of Lords, with rather sharp words for Denning, rejected this attempt by reaffirming 'expressly, unequivocally and unanimously'[23] the existing rules of precedent. Nonetheless, Lord Denning's attempts to free the Court of Appeal from the strict rules of precedent demonstrate the different way in which judges can view the judicial role.

As an example of background impacting on approach to the judicial function, we can look to Lord Atkin's Christian faith, which was a 'strong constant in his life'.[24] Lord Atkin was part of the majority that decided *Donoghue v Stevenson*,[25] and he based his judgment on the 'neighbour' principle, even alluding to the parable of the Good Samaritan.[26] It is almost beyond question that the correct decision was reached in *Donoghue* – that the manufacturer owed a duty to end users of its products – but the path to it for Lord Atkin was eased by his ability to relate the issue to his faith. Although the concept of a 'legal neighbour' is different to that of the Christian concept of 'neighbour', it is clear that Lord Atkin's Christian morality could have influenced his decision.

Lady Hale's dissent as the only female member of the court in *Radmarcher*[27] is also a notable example of the justices' backgrounds potentially influencing their approach to decision-making. Lady Hale also came to greater public attention due to her presiding over some significant judicial review cases, including the case which concluded that Boris Johnson's government had unlawfully prorogued Parliament.[28] Given her personal habit of wearing animal broaches, she became known as 'spider woman'.

20 Tom Bingham, *The Business of Judging: Selected Essays and Speeches 1985–1999* (OUP 2000) 409.

21 *Central London Property Trust v High Trees House* [1947] KB 130 (KB).

22 *Davis v Johnson* [1978] 1 All ER 841 (CA).

23 *Davis v Johnson* [1979] AC 264 (HL).

24 Geoffrey Lewis, *Lord Atkin* (Bloomsbury 1999) 20.

25 *Donoghue v Stevenson* [1932] AC 562 (HL).

26 ibid 580 (Lord Atkin).

27 *Radmarcher v Granatino* [2010] UKSC 42, [2011] 1 AC 534.

28 *R (on the application of Miller) v The Prime Minister* [2019] UKSC 41, [2019] 3 WLR 589.

APPOINTMENT OF JUDGES

CONTEXT

The appointment of judges, and particularly the most senior members of the judiciary, has long attracted criticism.[29] The history of judicial appointments is fascinating and rich but is largely beyond the scope of this text on the entire legal system of England and Wales.[30] Nonetheless, a flavour of that history is important to understanding the significance of the reform that has taken place in recent years.

In the dim and distant past, judicial appointments were solely in the gift of the Monarch and judges served at the 'King's Pleasure' as part of the King's Court. This meant that not only did potential judges need to find favour with the ruling monarch but that they had to maintain that favour in order to make a career in the judiciary and not be removed at the whim of the reigning monarch. This position was changed in the 18th century by the Act of Settlement 1701[31] which transformed judicial appointments to ones held indefinitely '*quamdiu se bene gesserint*' (during periods of good behaviour). This removed the stranglehold of ongoing patronage from the Monarch. The current wording for this principle can be found in the Senior Courts Act 1981 which states that senior judges will 'hold that office during good behaviour, subject to a power of removal by His Majesty on an address presented to His by both Houses of Parliament'.[32] This adds security of tenure for judicial office-holders, which is a fundamental part of securing the independence of the judiciary. Securing such a vote in both Houses of Parliament would be unprecedented for the modern judiciary.

Even with the passage of 300 years since the Act of Settlement, there has still been controversy as late as the 20th century over the secretive and overtly partisan way in which certain members of the judiciary have in the past been appointed. As recently as the 19th century, certain appointments were still seen to be politically motivated and not based wholly on merit.[33] This was because the Lord Chancellor was responsible for the appointments, and his office, as discussed elsewhere in this text, was overtly political. Even a Prime Minister of that time, Lord Salisbury, commented that 'party claims should always weigh very heavily in the disposal of the highest legal appointments. In dealing with them you cannot ignore the party system as you do in the choice of a general or an archbishop'.[34] These comments are revealing of the prevailing Conservative attitude of that time about the separation of powers and the independence of the judiciary. This links to the point made at the start of the chapter that the nature of the judicial role is not static and changes and evolves over time as *political* as

29 For a flavour of the debate, see Brenda Hale, 'Equality and the Judiciary: Why Should We Want More Women Judges?' [2001] PL 489 and Kate Malleson, 'Creating a Judicial Appointments Commission: Which Model Works Best?' [2004] PL 102 particularly at 103–9.

30 If you are interested in the history, then see John Griffith, *The Politics of the Judiciary* (5th edn, Fontana Press 2010).

31 Article 7.

32 Senior Courts Act 1981 s11(3).

33 For an extensive examination of the issue, see Adam Geary, Wayne Morrison and Robert Jago, *The Politics of the Common Law: Perspectives, Rights, Processes and Institutions* (2nd edn, Routledge 2013) 190.

34 Lord Salisbury, cited by Robert Stevens, *The English Judges: Their Role in the Changing Constitution* (Hart Publishing 2005) 14.

well as legal thought changes. It is also important to note that some systems around the world, including those like the USA that have a similar common law heritage, still maintain the political appointment of members of the judiciary.

The bench was equally seen to be reserved to barristers of long standing. Thus, solicitors were practically excluded from sitting in the senior courts of England and Wales. This was traditionally linked to the greater experience of the court process and of advocacy that went with being a member of the Bar. As rights of audience have expanded and a greater diversity of experience is seen as valuable for life on the bench, this qualification has slowly diminished.

The Courts and Legal Services Act 1990 significantly broadened the qualification requirements and allowed solicitors to be appointed to more senior judicial offices, although it is still perceived as easier to become a senior judge after a career at the Bar (due partly to the Inn structure for barristers).[35] In contrast to other judicial systems, a life on the bench is seen as a secondary career that follows on from a life in practice. This can exclude those who would have been suited to hold judicial office but who had not spent time as a solicitor or barrister. Lord Mackay as Lord Chancellor in the late 1980s was first to experiment in appointing academics as Recorders and, at that time, included Baroness Hale, later a full-time High Court and Court of Appeal Judge, and the President of the Supreme Court. Lord Irvine, as Lord Chancellor in the New Labour government of 1997, relaxed the family-unfriendly conditions for women in his encouragement of a wider pool of applicants, famously remembered for his mantra when announcing these changes: 'Don't be shy: apply.' The Tribunals, Courts and Enforcement Act 2007 sought to alter previously restricting frameworks to a degree, by lifting some of the restrictions on the holding of judicial office and to reduce the qualifying time period before a person can apply for certain forms of judicial office. For example, the Lord Chancellor has used the powers under s51 to extend the eligibility criteria for certain posts to include trademark attorneys and Fellows of the Chartered Institute of Legal Executives.[36]

While the preceding paints a somewhat closed picture for attaining judicial office, there are examples of the most senior appointments being made to those who had never previously held full-time judicial office. In modern times, the most notable of these is Lord Sumption, who had spent the majority of his legal career as a barrister and had not previously held a full-time judicial post. Lord Sumption was the first person to be appointed to the Supreme Court in this manner, but the situation was not unknown in the time of the House of Lords with Lords Reid, Carson and Radcliffe being other examples. More recently, Professor Andrew Burrows[37] took up a position in the Supreme Court in June 2020.

35 This led, indirectly, to Lord Collins becoming the first Lord of Appeal in Ordinary who had started a legal career as a solicitor.

36 Judicial Appointments Order 2008, SI 2008/2995 Schedule 1.

37 An honorary KC and Professor of English Law at the University of Oxford, who has also been a part-time Recorder, Deputy High Court Judge and Law Commissioner – <www.supremecourt.uk/news/lord-reed-appointed-next-president-of-supreme-court-alongside-three-new-justices.html>.

With the changes to the Lord Chancellor's office, brought about by the Constitutional Reform Act 2005, there were also significant changes made to the way in which certain judges were appointed. This was further to bolster the independence of the judiciary and to ensure greater transparency and diversity in the selection of judicial office-holders. The Constitutional Reform Act 2005 achieved this by establishing a new Judicial Appointments Commission (JAC), which has become an integral part of the appointments process. As we shall see, the final recommendation will still come in most cases from the Lord Chancellor, but their discretion has been severely limited to the extent that involvement in the process is more symbolic than substantive.

JUSTICES OF THE SUPREME COURT

A bespoke process exists for appointments to the Supreme Court. If a vacancy arises for a Justice of the Supreme Court, whether it is an ordinary judge or the President/Deputy President, then an *ad hoc* Selection Commission *must* be convened by the Lord Chancellor.[38] The Commission is required to select on the basis of merit[39] and will consult with senior members of the judiciary who are not part of the Commission, the Lord Chancellor and the First Ministers of the devolved regions.[40] The workings and composition of a Selection Commission for the Supreme Court is laid out in Schedule 8 of the Constitutional Reform Act 2005.

A selection committee for a Justice shall comprise of the President of the Supreme Court, the Deputy President, and one member from each of the appointment bodies in England and Wales,[41] Scotland[42] and Northern Ireland[43] who will be nominated by the Lord Chancellor. One of these members is required to be non-legally qualified. The special commissions are free to decide upon the most appropriate selection process[44] but the final recommendation of this Selection Commission is notified to the Prime Minister by the Lord Chancellor for recommendation to the King. This stage is of symbolic importance only as the Constitutional Reform Act 2005 compels the Prime Minister to recommend this person to the King[45] and they are expressly prohibited from recommending another person.[46]

JUDICIAL APPOINTMENTS COMMISSION

The governing provisions[47] of the JAC, found within the Constitutional Reform Act 2005, deal briefly with membership of the Commission, leaving the detail to a Schedule at the end of the Act.[48] Figure 7.1 summarises the governance structure of the JAC.

38 ibid s26(5).
39 ibid s27(5).
40 ibid s27(2).
41 Judicial Appointments Commission.
42 Judicial Appointments Board for Scotland.
43 Northern Ireland Judicial Appointments Commission.
44 Constitutional Reform Act s27(1).
45 ibid s26(3)(a).
46 ibid s26(3)(b).
47 Constitutional Reform Act 2005 s61.
48 Constitutional Reform Act 2005 Schedule 12.

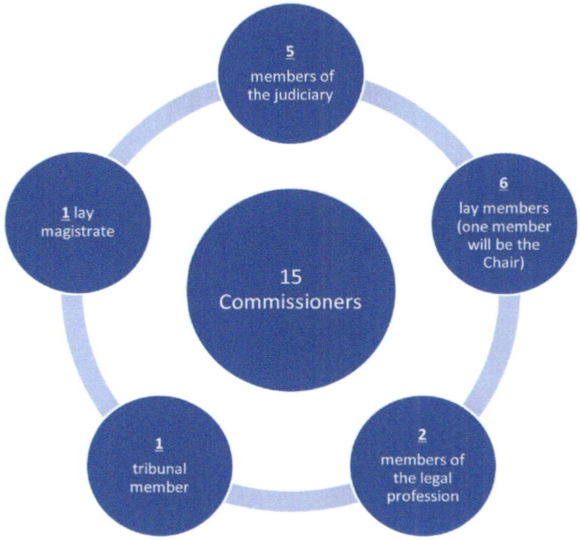

Figure 7.1 Membership of the Judicial Appointments Commission.

The vast majority of appointments to the superior levels of the judiciary within the legal system of England and Wales are made on the recommendation of JAC. The notable exception is the Supreme Court, which has a specific process by which new Justices are selected. The following section will seek to summarise the appointments process as it applies to those covered by the JAC scheme, have dealt previously with the Supreme Court process.

The establishment of the Judicial Appointments Commission has added significantly to the transparency and openness of appointments within England and Wales and is an important factor in maintaining trust in and respect for an independent judiciary. It may be convenient to talk of the 'system of judicial appointments', but there is not a single system for selecting judges. The system will vary (or at least the underlying provisions governing the appointment will be different) depending on the role and seniority of the judicial appointment in question. Distinct sections of the Constitutional Reform Act 2005 apply to different judicial office-holders and dictate the process by which the JAC should make its recommendations. The JAC system covers the appointment of the Lord Chief Justice and other Heads of Division,[49] Lords Justices of Appeal[50] and puisne judges of the High Court.[51]

Despite the fact that there are different structures in place for different groups of judges, all selections for appointments are subject to certain overriding requirements. A panel of the JAC cannot make a selection for appointment to a judicial office unless it is satisfied that the person

49 ibid ss66–75.

50 ibid ss76–84.

51 ibid ss85–94B.

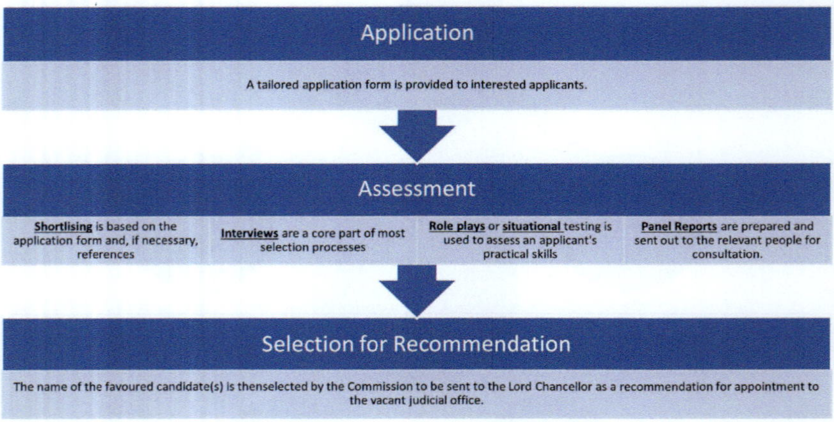

Figure 7.2 The process for selection and recommendation of judicial appointments.

is 'of good character'.[52] More importantly, the JAC must make all selections based solely on merit.[53] This last overriding requirement sends a powerful message about the future of judicial appointments and is an indication that although the Lord Chancellor is still involved in the process, *political* influence can no longer affect the outcome in any meaningful way. In taking its decisions, the JAC has developed certain competencies that guide its selection process. These are: *intellectual capacity; personal qualities; an ability to understand and deal fairly; authority and communication skills; and efficiency.*[54] The 'efficiency' criterion is of significant importance owing to the demands now made on judges of every level in disposing of business in a timely manner due to the stringency of the austerity cuts that have been made in His Majesty's Courts and Tribunal Service.

Figure 7.2 indicates the procedure that the JAC follows for making its selection and proposing its recommended candidates.

ANALYSING THE LAW – THE LORD CHANCELLOR AND JUDICIAL APPOINTMENTS

As has been seen throughout this section, there have been substantial changes to the way in which judicial appointments are made. From a secretive, insular and potentially politically driven process, we now have a system that is (more) open, transparent and subject to an overriding requirement for a meritocratic approach. Nonetheless, the final appointment is still made by the King on the advice of the Lord Chancellor or Prime Minister. It may seem, at first glance, unusual for the opportunity, provided by

52 ibid s63.

53 Constitutional Reform Act 2005 s63.

54 <https://jac.judiciary.gov.uk/925-qualities-and-abilities>.

the Constitutional Reform Act 2005, to remove the influence of the Lord Chancellor so completely from the appointments system to have been overlooked, but on reflection, this is not unusual as long as the UK has a monarchy which still nods to the long history of the development of the common law through the customs and culture of a thousand years.

To take a more radically modernising approach, as some had advocated, would be to ignore the continuing, but albeit more limited, role that the Lord Chancellor plays in the judicial system. The Lord Chancellor, despite in modern times neither a cleric (as in the Middle Ages) nor always a lawyer, as in the last few centuries, is under a statutory duty to ensure the independence of the judiciary.[55] It would be difficult for the Lord Chancellor to fulfil this role properly if they were not involved, even symbolically, in the judicial appointment process. In many ways, it is important that this duty lies with a political appointment rather than a judicial one. For example, this situation means that the Lord Chancellor can be held to account for this duty in Parliament.

Equally, during discussions of government policy in Cabinet, the Lord Chancellor can ensure at an early stage that planned policy does not jeopardise the independence of the judiciary, thus also bolstering the authority of the judiciary. It also means that any conflict between the judiciary and the government can potentially be neutralised from within the government, without the judiciary having to defend themselves publicly. In this respect, we can contrast the heavily criticised (non-)approach to this task taken by Liz Truss in the aftermath of the *Daily Mail*'s infamous and scandalous 'Enemies of the People' headline,[56] who failed to provide protection to the independence of the judiciary with that adopted by the later Lord Chancellor Robert Buckland following the prorogation case, who made prompt and public statements in support of the independence of the judiciary.[57] An overly formal approach to separation of powers would not allow this overlap to exist, but it is beneficial, in the whole, to the judiciary.

Some of the preceding analysis is reflected in the recent discussion within the House of Lords Constitution Committee which published a report in 2014 on the continuing role of the Lord Chancellor in the legal system.[58] A subsequent report in 2023 highlighted some of the challenges faced by the Lord Chancellor and advocated for bolstering the authority of the role.[59] Reading these reports will give you an additional insight into the reforms of the Office of the Lord Chancellor and the valuable contribution that the Office will continue to make to judicial appointments and the broader justice system in the future.

55 Constitutional Reform Act 2005 ss 3(1) and 3(6).

56 Which followed the High Court's initial decision in *R (Miller) v Secretary of State for Exiting the European Union* [2016] EWHC 2768 (Admin), [2017] 1 All ER 158. For comments of the Lord Chancellor, see Answers to Oral Questions on 8 October 2019 (Volume 664, 912599).

57 *R (Miller) v The Prime Minister and Cherry v Advocate General for Scotland* [2019] UKSC 41, [2019] 3 WLR 589.

58 Select Committee on the Constitution, *The Office of the Lord Chancellor* (HL 2014–15, I-75).

59 Select Committee on the Constitution, *The Roles of the Lord Chancellor and the Law Officers* (HL 2022–23, I-118).

PAY AND TRAINING

PAY

The rates of pay for salaried judges varies considerably and is based on 8 'groups' of judicial post-holders.[60] Generally speaking, the more senior the office, the greater the salary. The logic of this means that the Lord or Lady Chief Justice of England and Wales (as the most senior judicial off-holders) is in Salary Group 1 which for the year 2025/26 had a salary of £325,010). Towards the lower end of the scale, Employment Judges sit in Salary Group 7 and can expect a salary of £139,469. These are clearly high salaries and part of the justification for this is that they system is seeking to compete in a recruitment market when a senior member of the legal profession might expect to earn several times this amount in private practice.

Not all judicial post-holders are in salaried positions. Very much of the judicial function is discharged by fee-paid judges who are paid by the day or half-day to sit in court. The fees range from around £600 per day for a Judge of the First Tier Tribunal to just over £1,000 per day for a Deputy High Court Judge.[61] Persons acting as fee-paid judges often have alternative employment as members of the legal profession.

TRAINING

From 1979 to 2011, training for judges was provided by the Judicial Studies Board. This was replaced in 2011 by the Judicial College which now covers an expanded number of judicial office-holders, including those working in tribunals or coroners.[62] The LCJ is the person responsible, via section 7(2)(b) of the Constitutional Reform Act 2005, for the ongoing training of the judiciary and so plays an important role in the life of the Judicial College. The LCJ is supported in this aspect of their role by the Board of the Judicial College, which is its governing body. The current Chair of the Board is Lady Justice King.

As a permanent body, covering a significant number of judicial office-holders, the Judicial College now has a strategy[63] setting out its goals and immediate objectives. The overriding objective of the College is to provide training of the highest professional standard which

1. strengthens the capacity of those in judicial roles to discharge their functions effectively, including judgecraft skills, inclusive leadership and management;
2. helps leadership judges to promote professional development and career progression;
3. supports judges to thrive whatever their personal or professional background;
4. contributes to the efficiency and effectiveness of the administration of justice, in line with the wider ambitions of the senior judiciary; and

60 <https://assets.publishing.service.gov.uk/media/687e2c6a8adf4250705c96a0/judicial-salaries-2025-2026.pdf>.

61 <https://assets.publishing.service.gov.uk/media/66e82da8e4b40ed591881b6f/Judicial_Fees_2024_to_2025.pdf>.

62 From April 2013 coroners are also covered by the Judicial College, by virtue of regulations made under the Coroners and Justice Act 2009 s37.

63 Currently covering 2021–2025 <https://www.judiciary.uk/about-the-judiciary/training-support/judicial-college/judicial-college-strategy-2021-2025/>.

5. promotes and supports judges' ability to treat court and tribunal users, colleagues, and staff in an inclusive and fair manner.[64]

From the preceding it can be seen that the Judicial College has a function that extends beyond keeping judges updated with legal developments in their field of expertise. Rather, it is seen as a fundamental part of achieving the wider mission of the legal system and recognises the practical, administrative, public service and management aspects to the role of a judicial office-holder. This is reflected in the governing principles of the College, which signify that judicial training should focus on:

1. substantive law, evidence and procedure, and jurisdictional expertise delivered through induction into the judiciary, induction into new roles and continuation training which keeps judicial office-holders up to date on developments in their jurisdiction;
2. the acquisition and improvement of cross-jurisdictional judicial skills which support the wider development of the judiciary;
3. a better understanding of the social context within which judging occurs, as well as encouraging inclusivity, engagement and respect across the judiciary as it changes; and
4. learning that supports new ways of working and digital skills, preparing judicial office-holders for new technology, innovation and changes in the way justice is administered.[65]

The training includes induction to the role played by the judiciary, seminars on substantive and procedural law as well as sessions aimed at building softer skills. This reaffirms a commitment to life on the bench being an ongoing career choice, rather than simply a reward and path to retirement for illustrious barristers. The training provided by the Judicial College also acts as a mechanism by which a judicial office-holder can expand upon the range of cases that can be heard under any judge's initial or existing 'ticket'. Some of the courses offered are mandatory for those wishing to hear cases in new areas.

For the sake of giving some sense of the scope of activity undertaken by the Judicial College, in 2021–2023, it delivered more than 400 courses to almost 18,000 participants.[66]

COMPLAINTS, DISCIPLINE AND REMOVAL FROM JUDICIAL OFFICE

In order to ensure the independence of the judiciary, judicial office-holders have a certain security of tenure and the mechanisms for removing them from office are complex and rarely invoked. Outside of retirement and resignation,[67] senior judges can only be removed for serious failings in character and with the backing of both Houses of Parliament. Thus a judge in England and Wales has never been removed by this method. Judges of the inferior courts

64 ibid 5.

65 ibid 6.

66 <https://www.judiciary.uk/guidance-and-resources/judicial-college-review-of-activities-2021-22/>.

67 Judges rarely return to active practice after serving on the bench and some judiciary are prevented from doing so.

can be removed more easily than judges of the senior courts. Nonetheless, it is still relatively rare for judges to be removed from office. This section will deal firstly with issues of conduct before moving on to discuss the retirement of judges.

COMPLAINTS

The Lord Chancellor and Lady Chief Justice are responsible for discipline of the judiciary[68] and much of that work is undertaken by the Judicial Conduct Investigations Office (JCIO), which from 2013 replaced the Office for Judicial Complaints.[69] These complaints are about the conduct of judges and not about the quality of a particular judgment. This is an obvious but important point to make. Should a party to a case wish to challenge a decision or aspect of case management then they should do so through the appeals system.

As the JCIO can deal only with matters of conduct, the volume of complaints dealt with by the JCIO remains relatively low, with around 1,800 complaints in 2021–2022.[70] A large number of those complaints (68%) were regarded as inadmissible because they related to judicial decisions or case management issues.[71] Table 7.2 shows the categorisation of complaints in 2021–2022.

Of the 1,800 complaints there were 33 (1.8% of total) that were upheld. Table 7.3 describes the various sanctions and indicates the number of each in the reporting period (2021–2022).

Table 7.2 Categorisation of judicial complaints[72]

Complaint type	*Number*
Not specified	21
Inappropriate behaviour/comments	433
Delay	36
Judicial decision/case management	1,229
Conflict of interest	0
Failure to meet sitting requirements	14
Motoring offences	2
Misuse of judicial status	5
Civil proceedings	2
Financial fraud	0
Criminal convictions	0
TOTAL	1,817

68 Constitutional Reform Act s108.

69 The Judicial Discipline (Prescribed Procedures) Regulations (2014) SI 2014/1919 gives more details.

70 Judicial Conduct Investigations Office, *Annual Report* 2021–2022 <https://judicialconduct.judiciary.gov.uk/reports-publications>.

71 ibid 11.

72 ibid 13.

Table 7.3 Sanctions for judicial conduct[73]

Sanction	*Number*
Formal advice	12
Warning	10
Reprimand	4
Removed	7
Total	33

As can be seen from the preceding, only a very small proportion of complaints are either admissible or upheld. Also, if a judge leaves office before a complaint is heard then the conduct investigation will be set aside. This was the case for Justice Peter Smith (a High Court Judge) who retired days before facing a disciplinary hearing. Smith had something of a reputation for outspoken and potentially inappropriate conduct – he had threatened to withdraw support to a particular chambers in response to negative comments by one of its barristers; had used on-going litigation on which he was presiding to pursue a personal complaint about lost luggage; had been badly tempered with a partner from a firm in which he had failed to negotiate a salaried position; and had included a coded message in a judgment about a best-selling book *The Da Vinci Code*. Thankfully, such instances are rare.

PUBLIC PERCEPTION AND BEHAVIOUR OF THE JUDICIARY

It is easy to find examples of poor judgement, some amounting to serious misconduct, amongst members of the judiciary. These examples almost invariably end up in the popular press, regardless of whether they pass through the official complaints process. It should be borne in mind, however, that these represent little more than anecdotes, albeit ones which are salacious or scandalous enough to pique public attention. Although the scrutiny of judges has traditionally focussed on the substance of their judgments, increasing the lens of public perception is turning to individual comments made by judges during the course of proceedings. This has serious consequences for public trust in the judiciary.

EXPLAINING THE LAW – JUDGES DEMONSTRATING POOR JUDGEMENT

What follows is a selection of examples of what can, at best, be described as poor judgement on the part of members of the judiciary and, in some cases, amount to very serious misconduct. They are not intended to be extensive or exhaustive but merely show the way in which the press is able to bring judicial behaviour to the attention of the public. The cases range from misguided statements linked to judicial office to more serious cases of misconduct (either in the judge's private capacity or in their judicial office) to evidence of criminality.

73 ibid 17.

- In October 2012, a recorder (a part-time, fee-paid member of the lower judiciary) was arrested for perverting the course of justice and was subsequently jailed for 16 months in May 2014.[74] She was removed from the judiciary in August 2014 and also disbarred. She had lied to the police in witness statements and had even altered an earlier witness statement. What makes this case all the more extraordinary was that it involved the case of a Cabinet Minister (Chris Huhne) and his wife, who had been prosecuted for perverting the course of justice in relation to speeding tickets. This case demonstrates the sometimes uncomfortably close relationship between the judiciary and the executive.
- In March 2015, three judges (a part-time recorder, a part-time deputy district judge and a district judge) were removed and a further judge resigned after it came to light that they viewed pornography on computers provided for the purpose of their executing their judicial duties.[75] While the viewing of the material was not unlawful, the misuse of office equipment was deemed serious enough to warrant an investigation and removal from office.
- In January 2015, a circuit judge came under intense criticism for suggesting that a 16-year-old student had 'groomed' her 44-year-old teacher in a case against him. The judge's comments were used to justify a suspended jail sentence and were said to undermine the seriousness of the conviction for the offence.[76]
- In 2014, a judge resigned after making a racist comment about a victim of harassment. He is alleged to have said, 'With a name like Patel, and her ethnic background, she won't be working anywhere important where she can't get time off'.[77]
- In 2015, a High Court judge was subject to intense press scrutiny and criticism for saying that 'proper allowance must be made for what is, almost certainly, a different cultural context'[78] when considering an alleged situation of violence against a child. Sections of the press took this to mean that the judge was endorsing a different application of the law to newly arrived immigrants.[79] Focus was placed on this one comment in a 75-paragraph judgment which, if read in the whole, does not support some of the accusations made in the press that the judge was 'out of touch' with the modern world.

The preceding examples should not be treated as representing the conduct of the vast majority of judicial office-holders, and as with many of the other examples, poor

74 <www.bbc.co.uk/news/uk-28675376>.

75 <www.theguardian.com/law/2015/mar/17/three-judges-removed-and-a-fourth-resigns-for-viewing-pornography-at-work>.

76 <www.theguardian.com/uk-news/2015/jan/14/former-london-teacher-convicted-over-affair-with-teenager>.

77 <www.theguardian.com/law/2014/dec/07/judge-resigns-racist-remark-about-victim-richard-hollingworth>.

78 *A (Wardship: Fact Finding: Domestic Violence)* [2015] EWHC 1598 (Fam) [67].

79 <www.independent.co.uk/news/uk/home-news/judge-says-cultural-context-should-be-considered-when-investigating-allegations-of-parental-child-abuse-10308692.html>.

judgement should be placed into the full context before an assessment of poor conduct is made.[80] It could even be argued that these examples are notable because they are so few in number in a justice system that deals with such a volume of cases in a given year. These go to reinforce the high standards expected by those holding judicial office but also that some judges fall far below this expected standard.

The public's interest, or at least the interest of the popular press, in the unfortunate comments or actions of judges is explicable precisely because it goes to the heart of what society expects of its judges – good judgement. The comments may cause a moment of incredulity or outrage (or even amusement in some cases) but they do place at risk something of much greater value and that is public confidence in the authority of the judiciary. These remarks are doubly damaging when they confirm stereotypes of judges as 'out of touch' due to their social class or gender, a point discussed elsewhere in this chapter when considering the diversity of the judiciary. Moreover, these comments can sometimes be taken out of context and do not represent, in isolation, the full reasoning of the judge in a given case. Nonetheless, they are more high profile, particularly for the public, than the official complaints process and so should be given due consideration.

There are, of course, even more subtle ways for judges to be called to account for their conduct and behaviour, particularly as the official complaints process cannot be used to remedy incompetence or poor judgement in coming to their judicial decision in a particular case. Here, the appeals process itself can act as a form of rebuke where a judge does not live up to the high standards expected of the judiciary. This is evident in *Crinion v IG Markets*.[81]

ANALYSING THE LAW – PLAGIARISM AND JUDGES

In *Crinion*, the first instance judge had largely copied the submission(s) of one side of the dispute and passed it off as his judgment. The appeal was unrelated to the substance of the case and focussed almost entirely on the issue of whether the first instance judge should have simply copied the claimant's arguments in the way that he did. The extent of the copying was such that it appeared that the *original* document that described itself as the judgment was an amended electronic version of the submission from counsel.[82] The appeal was dismissed by the Court of Appeal, but contained within the judgment were some strong words of rebuke for the first instance

80 For an interesting and lively analysis of judicial behaviour, see Gary Slapper, 'The Judiciary – a Performance Review' (2015) 75 SLR 16.

81 *Crinion v IG Markets Ltd* [2013] EWCA Civ 587, [2014] 2 All ER (Comm) 55.

82 ibid [11].

judge. Sir Stephen Sedley gave the strongest criticism indicating that the approach taken by the judge was 'unacceptable'[83] and that he hoped that 'a judgment like the one now before us will not be encountered again'.[84] Lord Justice Longmore agreed, stating that he trusted that

> no judge in any future case will lift so much of a claimant's submissions into his own judgment as this judge has done and that, if substantial portions are to be lifted, it will be with proper acknowledgment and with a recitation of the defendant's case together with a reasoned rejection of it.[85]

In light of the fact that the appeal was *dismissed*, this seems like strong criticism for what the judge had done. This was not dealt with as a complaint and so would not have been recorded in the official statistics but is a clear sign that judgments of appeal courts can be used to rebuke members of the judiciary who have acted in questionable ways.

A different, but related, point can be seen in *ex parte BskyB v Essex Police*,[86] where a judge's formulaic approach to applying the law without justification was in issue. The judge had granted certain production orders for the police to gain footage held by broadcasters covering the Dale Farm evictions in 2011.[87] In dealing with the appeal, Lord Justice Moses noted that the judge involved had not adequately justified the need for such orders and the case 'affords a good example of the need for a judge to be scrupulous in specifying the evidence on the basis of which' he reaches his conclusions.[88]

This further demonstrates that the appeals system not only allows faulty judgments to be remedied but that it also can act as a way of reminding judges of important aspects of their role that may have been overlooked.

The website also contains a blog post on the *Serafin*[89] case where the extent of the first instance judge's behaviour towards the claimant fell so far below the expected standards of conduct that it rendered the trial unfair.

83 ibid [39].
84 ibid [40].
85 ibid [44].
86 *R (BskyB) v Chelmsford Crown Court* [2012] EWHC 1295 (Admin).
87 This involved reporting on the evictions of some 400 people from an illegal travellers' site in Essex.
88 ibid [33] (Moses LJ).
89 *Serafin v Malkiewicz* [2020] UKSC 23.

RETIREMENT

Judges for many years had a compulsory retirement age of 70.[90] The Pension Service Pensions and Judicial Offices Act 2022 increased this to the age of 75. The change to the retirement age meant that Lord Lloyd-Jones was able to return to the Supreme Court after retiring at the then compulsory age of 70 in January 2022 before being re-appointed when this age was changed to 75 in August 2022.

During their time in office, judges are also able to contribute to a generous[91] pension scheme that, after 20 years of eligible service, will pay an annual pension equivalent to half of the officer holder's pensionable pay.[92] Those members of the Supreme Court who are also members of the House of Lords will, when they retire, be able to return to the Lords and continue to vote, sit and serve on committees.[93]

JUDICIAL INDEPENDENCE AND NEUTRALITY

Judicial independence is one of the cornerstones of the legal system of England and Wales and is essential to ensure the authority and neutrality of the justice system. Public confidence in the justice system is predicated on the notion that judges make their decisions on the basis of the law and not on external pressures applied either by politicians or even other judges.

MAKING CONNECTIONS – PUBLIC LAW

The issue of judicial independence is a topic to which you will undoubtedly return if you are also studying constitutional law. It is the cornerstone of the separation of powers and certain conceptions of the rule of law.[94] These topics were briefly explored in earlier chapters, and the analysis there should be reconsidered here.

Not only is judicial independence paramount to these constitutional principles, but it is also vital to the way in which the judiciary is *perceived* by the public. Public confidence in the judiciary is reinforced if they are seen to be a separate entity to the executive, who enforces the law, and the legislature, who passes the law.

90 Judicial Pensions and Retirement Act 1993 s26(1) and Schedule 5, Senior Court Act 1981 s11.

91 Although, like many public sector pension schemes, the benefits have been decreased while the requirements for gaining a full pension have increased.

92 Judicial Pensions and Retirement Act 1993 s3(1).

93 Constitutional Reform Act 2005 s137.

94 Robert Stevens, 'A Loss of Innocence? Judicial Independence and the Separation of Powers (1999) 19 OJLS 365 or Roger Masterman, *The Separation of Powers in the Contemporary Constitution: Judicial Competence and Independence in the United Kingdom* (CUP 2010).

The Lord Chancellor is formally responsible for defending the independence of the judiciary. The contrasting effectiveness of different Lord Chancellors as they execute this function is discussed earlier. The duty was placed on a statutory footing in 2005 and the duty also extends to other Ministers of the Crown.[95] The Constitutional Reform Act 2005 requires an incoming Lord Chancellor to take an oath which reads as follows:

> I, [name], do swear that in the office of Lord High Chancellor of Great Britain I will respect the rule of law, defend the independence of the judiciary and discharge my duty to ensure the provision of resources for the efficient and effective support of the courts for which I am responsible. So help me God.[96]

The oath and the statutory duty may seem like little more than empty rhetoric but there is evidence that various Lord Chancellors have taken this duty extremely seriously and have tried to enforce it by heading off criticism of judges by other members of government. One example cited by Gee is where a written apology was issued after a junior government minister criticised the sentence handed down by a judge to a sex offender and was rebuked by the Lord Chancellor.[97]

It is in this area of the judiciary's interaction with the other institutions of the state that the independence of the judiciary takes on particular importance. By being independent from the legislature and executive, the senior judiciary has also been able to develop the rule of law as a way of balancing the powers between the different parts of the state. Overt recognition of the different functions that can be brought about because of this independence was given in the *Prolife*[98] case. In that case, Lord Hoffmann held that:

> Independence makes the courts more suited to deciding some kinds of questions and being elected makes the legislature or executive more suited to deciding others. The allocation of these decision-making responsibilities is based upon recognised principles. The principle that the independence of the courts is necessary for a proper decision of disputed legal rights or claims of violation of human rights is a legal principle.[99]

Lord Hoffmann's contribution suggests that judicial independence offers the judiciary not only protection from interference by Parliament and the government but also confers upon them additional duties within the constitution. The *Jackson*[100] case is an example of the courts taking this further and using rule of law to rebalance the constitution. In that case, albeit in non-binding *obiter* statements, several of the Law Lords took the radical view that the powers

95 Constitutional Reform Act 2005 s3.

96 Promissory Oaths Act 1868 s6A as amended by the Constitutional Reform Act 2005 s17.

97 <http://ukconstitutionallaw.org/2014/08/18/graham-gee-do-lord-chancellors-defend-judicial-independence>.

98 *R (Prolife) v British Broadcasting Corporation* [2003] UKHL 23, [2004] 1 AC 185.

99 ibid [76].

100 *R (Jackson) v Attorney General* [2005] UKHL 56, [2006] 1 AC 262.

of Parliament were limited by the principle of rule of law and that there could be a place for judges finding that an Act of Parliament was invalid if it interfered with constitutional principles in a significantly serious manner.[101]

As well as the need for government ministers to exercise caution in criticising judicial decisions, there are broader restrictions on the reporting and critical discussion of ongoing proceedings in court. These restrictions cover more than just the principle of judicial independence but they do have an element of preventing judges from being influenced by outside forces. This principle, known as the *sub judice* rule, is intended to insulate ongoing proceedings from outside influences. This principle is most commonly discussed in relation to Members of Parliament being precluded from debating ongoing cases but there is also the possibility of journalists committing the offence of contempt of court if their reports are seen to be interfering with the proper administration of justice.[102]

The view on the measures necessary to preserve judicial independence and neutrality has evolved over time and is by no means static. For example, it was once viewed as unacceptable for members of the judiciary to give interviews to the press or participate in documentaries. This view came most strongly from Lord Kilmuir (Lord Chancellor in the 1950s) who formulated what came to be known as the Kilmuir Rules which reiterated the 'importance of keeping the judiciary in this country insulated from the controversies of the day'.[103] Long since abandoned, the Kilmuir Rules add further evidence to the argument that the duty placed upon the Lord Chancellor to protect judicial independence is more than just symbolic and it is intended to enshrine pre-existing principles and practice. This practice is so much changed that the Supreme Court now hosts a collection of speeches given extra-judicially by its judges.[104]

JUDICIAL NEUTRALITY

As well as duties being placed on members of the government, the judiciary also has responsibility for safeguarding and self-regulating their conduct to avoid harming judicial independence. This is primarily achieved through the idea that no member of the judiciary should be a judge in his (or her) own cause. This means that judges who have an interest in a case to be decided should declare that interest and, if it would give rise to a danger of bias, recuse themselves from the case. The case law on this issue is voluminous and requires judges to consider both financial and non-financial interests before sitting on a case or they risk accusations of actual or perceived bias. Perhaps the most notable example of the principle in operation is of Lord Hoffman in a case involving General Pinochet.

101 For comment on the case, see James Allan, 'The Paradox of Sovereignty: Jackson and the Hunt for a New Rule of Recognition?' (2007) 18 KLJ 1.

102 Contempt of Court 1981 s1.

103 Cited in John Griffith, *The Politics of the Judiciary* (5th edn, Fontana Press 2010) 42.

104 <https://www.supremecourt.uk/speeches>.

EXPLAINING THE LAW – LORD HOFFMANN AND THE CHILEAN GENERAL

In the *Pinochet*, case the issue of judicial independence and the rule against bias came to the public's attention with accusations of bias levelled against Lord Hoffmann when sitting as a judge in an appeal in the House of Lords. The history of the case is complex but involved the extradition of General Pinochet, who had led a bloody military coupe in Chile. He subsequently came to the UK for medical treatment, and an extradition order to Spain was sought for him to answer alleged charges of murder and torture. The House of Lords ruled in favour of extradition by a narrow majority.

It was subsequently revealed that Lord Hoffmann (who had been in the majority) was a Director of a public interest group (Amnesty International) which had been permitted to intervene in the proceedings. Additionally, his wife also worked for Amnesty. Although there was no suggestion that Lord Hoffmann had acted in an improper manner in determining the case, there was a risk of the appearance of bias. The House of Lords was asked (in an unprecedented application) to review its decision with a different panel of judges. It took this opportunity to set aside the decision and to re-hear the case. The decision (but not the reasoning) was the same in the subsequent case, but it was one that excited public interest in the issue of judicial independence and neutrality and did a great deal to harm the reputation of the legal system.

The case demonstrates the importance of the principle in a very high-profile way. If we strip away the dreadful historical context of *Pinochet* we are left with a very simple principle. The underlying principle is that a person with an interest in a claim should *declare* that interest and recuse themselves from sitting in the case. This has been expressed in the Latin maxim: *nemo iudex in sua causa* (no person should be a judge in their own cause). Indeed, the cause supported by Lord Hoffmann was both charitable and largely beyond reproach and the criticism was not of his supporting such an organisation as Amnesty. Lord Hoffmann's failing, and it was a serious one, was in not *declaring* his interest and choosing not to step down from the case or to hear argument from the parties about his suitability to sit.

A more recent example of *personal* connections rendering a judge unsuitable to hear a case can be found in the Court of Appeal decision in *AWG v Morrison*.[105] The case concerned a potential witness in a fraud trial who was known, in a personal capacity, to the judge. The judge lived in a nearby village to the witness and their children knew each other and they had dined together. In the words of the judge: 'I would have the greatest difficulty in dealing with a case in which Mr Jewson was a witness where a challenge was to be made as to the truthfulness of his evidence.'[106] The independence of the judge was therefore not

105 *AWG v Morrison* [2006] EWCA Civ 6, [2006] 1 WLR 1163.
106 ibid [4].

only apparently in question but, through his own admission, *actually* in question. As the witness was not seen to be essential to the case, he was substituted and the judge did not recuse himself, against the wishes of the claimant (the appellant in the present case). The Court of Appeal reiterated the importance of judicial neutrality by emphasising that judicial impartiality 'is *the* fundamental principle of justice'.[107] The conclusion was that even though the witness was not called, there was a risk that the judge would be 'subconsciously biased by his long acquaintance with Mr Jewson'.[108]

This case highlights that judges must handle the question of apparent bias particularly carefully and consider recusing themselves if they have *any* connection with a case. This is in spite of any attempt by the judge to mitigate the risk. The strong message from the Court of Appeal was that inconvenience and cost to parties cannot be used to counteract claims of judicial neutrality.[109]

As well as *personal* interests, judges must ensure that their financial interests do not bring their independence or neutrality into question. The classic example of this was found in the circumstances regarding the *Dimes*[110] case which is less high profile (in non-legal circles) but no less important than the *Pinochet* case. In that case it was held that Lord Cottenham had been wrong to sit on a case involving a company in which he held shares as his financial interests would raise the potential for the appearance of bias.

JUDICIAL IMMUNITY

To ensure that judges are free to exercise their jurisdiction without fear of repercussions there is a form of judicial immunity for tasks carried out in furtherance of a judicial function. This immunity was reaffirmed by Lord Denning in *Sirros v Moore*.[111]

EXPLAINING THE LAW – JUDICIAL IMMUNITY

The case of *Sirros* involved an individual attempting to sue a judge (and police officers) for assault and false imprisonment after the judge ordered Sirros to be held in custody following on from a deportation appeal. Lord Denning had to rule on whether a judge could be held liable for things done in the course of discharging his judicial duties. Denning noted that since the 17th century, 'it has been accepted in our law that no action is maintainable against a judge for anything said or done by him in the exercise

107 ibid [6].
108 ibid [10].
109 ibid [30].
110 *Dimes v Grand Junction Canal Proprietors* (1852) 10 ER 301.
111 *Sirros v Moore* [1975] QB 118 (CA).

of a jurisdiction which belongs to him'.[112] He went on to hold, in the strongest possible terms, that the judicial immunity was absolute: 'No matter that the judge was under some gross error or ignorance, or was actuated by envy, hatred and malice, and all uncharitableness, he is not liable to an action.'[113] The remedy, according to Denning and the other Lords Justices, was to appeal against the decision of the judge. The position in *Sirros* was confirmed more recently in *Pius v Fearnley*.[114]

It may seem unjust to give judges too free a hand in how they deal with cases. However, it is a necessary requirement to ensure that judges are free to give judgment and to make the orders that they feel necessary. As well as the appeal system, as noted by Denning, there are other mechanisms by which judges can be held to account, not least the complaints system outlined previously.

Although judges cannot be held *personally* liable for actions taken while acting judicially, it should be noted that the immunity in *Sirros v Moore* does not preclude the potential of a civil suit against the government for errors of law committed by the judiciary in certain areas of law. For example, a member of the judiciary who committed a sufficiently serious breach of European Union law may have rendered the UK Government liable in damages – the so-called state liability principle.[115]One of the key arguments put forward against such liability in *Kobler v Austria* related to the independence of the judiciary. The response of the Court of Justice of the European Union was that the liability was not personally attached to the judge and so there is no prospect of independence being called into question.[116]

DIVERSITY IN THE JUDICIARY

THE PROBLEM

There has been long-standing recognition from both within and outside of the judiciary that more could be done to ensure that there is a greater diversity in the range of people appointed to judicial office.[117] This recognition has come in the form of multiple (critical) reviews of diversity in the judiciary and has even found expression within decided cases.

112 ibid 132 (Lord Denning MR).

113 ibid.

114 *Pius v Fearnley* [2013] EWHC 2216 (Ch).

115 For the seminal case on judicial error, see Case C-224/01 *Kobler v Austria* [2003] ECR I-10239, and for the issue being discussed in the UK context, see *AG v Cooper* [2010] EWCA Civ 464, [2011] QB 976.

116 ibid [42].

117 Brenda Hale, 'Diversity and Inclusion in the Judiciary' (2022) 78 Magistrate 24.

EXPLAINING THE LAW – LADY HALE AND THE CASE OF FINANCIAL PROVISION

The case of *Radmacher*[118] was a high-profile family law case concerning financial provision on the breakdown of a marriage. The couple concerned had made an 'ante-nuptial agreement',[119] and the Supreme Court had to consider the weight to attach to such an agreement when granting financial revision. It was an important case in terms of substantive family law and was made all the more interesting by the fact that the Supreme Court was split down gender lines, with the all-male majority against very strong dissent from the sole female voice in the court. During the course of her judgment, Lady Hale noted that '[i]n short, there is a gender dimension to the issue which some may think ill-suited to decision by a court consisting of eight men and one woman'.[120]

While the issue of diversity has been recognised, and great strides have been made to redress the balance, the problem has proved extremely difficult to address. In 2009 Jack Straw (the then Lord Chancellor) established an Advisory Panel on Judicial Diversity that found, in 2010, that previous attempts had not led to significant progress with judicial diversity.[121] After more than a decade of activity and supported by the Judicial Diversity Committee, a Judicial Diversity and Inclusion Strategy was launched in 2020, covering the period until 2025.[122] At the time of writing, no new strategy from 2026 has been announced or published, with the last update being in January 2025.[123]

Moreover, becoming a member of the judiciary has not traditionally been seen as a primary career path but rather one that follows on from a career in legal practice and, in particular, from being a barrister and – mostly in the lower judicial ranks – a solicitor or chartered legal executive. This means that well-established problems with diversity in legal practice will have significantly narrowed the pool of applicants eligible to be considered for judicial office.

The lack of diversity in the judiciary is multifaceted in that there are a number of groups that are currently (or have historically been) underrepresented. Particular focus has, in the past, been on the lack of women in the judiciary, whereas more recent focus has been about lack of diversity in terms of ethnicity and socio-economic groupings.

It is interesting to note that despite an emerging concept of intersectionality – the notion that characteristics such as race, gender and social class can 'intersect' to heighten inequality –

118 *Radmacher v Granatino* [2010] UKSC 42, [2011] 1 AC 534.

119 That is an agreement on the division of assets on separation that is entered into *before* the marriage takes place.

120 *Radmacher v Granatino* [2010] UKSC 42, [2011] 1 AC 534, [137] (Lady Hale).

121 <https://www.judiciary.uk/publications/advisory-panel-recommendations/>.

122 <www.gov.uk/government/news/progress-on-judicial-diversity-but-more-to-do>.

123 <https://www.judiciary.uk/guidance-and-resources/message-from-lcj-and-spt-judicial-diversity-and-inclusion-update-2024/>.

within discrimination, this is not something about which much is written or discussed within the judiciary. Intersectionality and its impact on diversity in the judiciary is not discussed by the 2020–2025 strategy and the academic literature on the subject is sparse.[124] Outside of discussions of gender and ethnicity, there has been more limited discussion on other forms of diversity and other factors of disadvantage.

To return to gender, the lack of presence of women judges was not simply a matter of circumstance but was, to an extent, embedded within the framework of the legal system of England and Wales. For example, reference was made only to the title of 'Lord Justice of Appeal' in the Senior Courts Act 1981.[125] This caused considerable practical problems when Elizabeth Butler-Sloss was elevated from the High Court[126] to the Court of Appeal in 1988. As an interesting aside, she was only the fourth woman judge of the High Court and was, as were the other women judges, assigned to the Family Division. This automatic assignment to the Family Division is further evidence of the institutional assumptions made about women in the judiciary, even as recently as the 1980s. An even more striking example of this was Dame Rose Heilbron, who had made a particular name in high-profile murder trials,[127] who was also assigned to the Family Division of the High Court.

The defect with Dame Elizabeth Butler-Sloss's title was not *formally* remedied until the early years of the new millennium when the 1981 Act was amended to include the title 'Lady Justice of Appeal' alongside the masculine version of the title.[128] In her early years, she was accordingly officially referred to as a Lord Justice of Appeal, although counsel had come to refer to her in the rather tortuous manner of 'My Lady, Lord Justice Butler-Sloss' in court. As Master of the Rolls, and to end this 'plainly absurd' usage, Lord Bingham issued a Practice Direction which encouraged counsel to use either 'My Lady' or 'Lady Justice Butler-Sloss' in court, even if her formal title would need to be changed by statute.[129]

Similarly, the route for progression to senior posts used to come either through direct appointment of leading KCs or occasionally through promotion from the Circuit Bench. The 'circuits' are 6 broad geographical areas in which judges sit. Given the size of the circuits, it can be that circuit judges need to spend long periods away from home while sitting full-time 'on-circuit' trying crime at Assizes and later in the Crown Court. As women have typically been primary care givers the structure of the circuits disproportionately impacted on the progression of women judges. Lord Irvine, Lord Chancellor in the New Labour government of Tony Blair in 1997, attempted to address the circuit sitting problem by offering potentially more flexible arrangements to suitable candidates and by encouraging more women to apply from both the Association of Women Barristers and from women solicitors.

124 There is an interesting study based on the US judiciary and the impact that intersectionality has on judicial decision making: Lee Epstein and Jack Knight, 'How Social Identity and Social Diversity Affect Judging' [2022] LJIL 897.

125 Senior Courts Act 1981 s2(3).

126 She had been only the fourth woman judge of the High Court.

127 Having been the first woman to be leading counsel in a murder trial.

128 Courts Act 2003 s63(1).

129 Practice Note (Mode of Address: Lord Justice Butler-Sloss) [1994] 1 FLR 866.

Table 7.4 Gender and ethnicity split amongst the judiciary as of 2025

Judicial office	*Female – NB (%)*	*BAME – NB (%)*
Justice of the Supreme Court	2 (17%)	0 (0%)
Heads of Division	2 (40%)	0 (0%)
Court of Appeal Judges	9 (23%)	1 (3%)
High Court Judges	32 (30%)	9 (8%)
Deputy High Court Judges	30 (25%)	14 (13%)

Table 7.4 summarises the position in relation to different groups of people within the more senior ranks of the judiciary. Clearly, this is a very fluid picture, but further updates can be found online.[130]

The picture painted by this data is (depressingly) consistent with a paucity of representation for women in the highest levels of the judiciary. The situation is particularly stark in terms of representation of minority ethnic groups. The next section will discuss the ways in which the judiciary has sought to remedy the imbalance and to promote greater diversity.

THE SOLUTION

The JAC is under a statutory duty, when executing all aspects of its work, to consider how to 'encourage diversity in the range of persons available for selection for appointments'.[131] It is important to note that this push for diversity is subject to the overriding requirement for selection to be on the basis of merit.[132] Thus, although there is statutory recognition of the problems with the lack of diversity in the judiciary, this will not mean that those from underrepresented groups will be selected for appointment without also demonstrating that they have the aptitude and ability to be a successful member of the judiciary. In this way equality is achieved alongside, and not instead of, merit.

By changing the eligibility criteria for holding judicial office, the system has broadened the category of persons who can be selected and this will, in turn, lead to greater diversity in the judiciary. Lord Collins (as the first solicitor) and Lady Hale (as the first woman, and who had served a long spell in academia, including initially a short period in part time practice at the Bar and as a Law Commissioner) are contemporary examples at the very highest level of the Supreme Court of how diversity has improved in more recent years, culminating in her since having been the first woman Deputy President and also the first woman President of

130 For appointments below the Supreme Court, data was found from – <https://www.gov.uk/government/collections/judicial-diversity-statistics> which includes a helpful dashboard.

131 Constitutional Reform Act 2005 s64(1).

132 ibid s64(2).

the Supreme Court. Meanwhile there have been two BAME appointments to the High Court, Dame Linda Dobbs (who was also the first such appointment) and Sir Rabinder Singh, who has recently been promoted to the Court of Appeal as its first Lord Justice from a BAME background.

A consequence of the changes to eligibility is a greater freedom to recruit potential judges from a wider field than was previously possible. For example, the High Court has been subject to a recent pilot under the banner of the 'Diversity Support Initiative'.[133] The pilot offered a structured support programme of work shadowing and mentoring for those who had never held judicial office. The pilot was designed to prepare those from non-traditional backgrounds (i.e. non-judicial office-holders) for the JAC selection exercise to be appointed to the High Court. The pilot was restricted to certain categories of person currently underrepresented in the High Court.[134] Those taking part in the programme were not guaranteed to be selected, due to all selections being made on merit, but the programme was designed to encourage diversity and to allow those from a non-judicial background to compete more effectively with those applicants who were more familiar with the court process.

THE WEBSITE

The website that accompanies this textbook contains many useful resources that you can use to consolidate and further your knowledge of the law, to hone your skills of critical analysis and to test your knowledge. This includes a set of multiple-choice questions (MCQs) that can be used to test your knowledge and understanding of the material.

133 Launched jointly by the Lord Chief Justice and the Lord Chancellor, who are also under a statutory duty to encourage diversity – Constitutional Reform Act 2005 s137A.

134 Women, BME and those from a less-privileged background.

8

CHAPTER 8
THE COURT STRUCTURE

INTRODUCTION

Courts dealing with the law of England Wales are structured in a somewhat confusing way and classifying them can be challenging. The structure is a consequence of the social, political and unique legal history of the jurisdiction and the structure continues to evolve to deal with the fresh challenges faced by the modern world. Whilst England and Wales has a unified system of courts, the precise role a particular court adopts can vary depending on the subject matter or particular issue it is asked to consider.

At the most straightforward and simplistic level courts can be divided along the lines of whether they are senior or inferior courts. They can also be categorised on the basis of whether they are courts of first instance or those that are exercising appellate jurisdiction. Or even whether they hear civil or criminal matters. As with many aspects of the legal system, even these straightforward categories can be problematic in their application and do not paint the fully rich picture of the court system.

At the top of the hierarchy sits the Supreme Court of the United Kingdom.[1] It also acts as the final court for civil matters from Scotland and Northern Ireland. This means that the present-day Supreme Court applies two separate systems of law in relation to appeals from Scotland and from England and Wales, which is sometimes very noticeable within the same subject area. An example of this is the completely different approaches to the breakdown of cohabitation relationships in the two jurisdictions, where Scotland has a statutory system to be found in the Family Law (Scotland) Act 2007, exemplified in the Scottish appeal of *Gow v Grant*,[2] while England and Wales have no such statutory provision, so that the applicable law is that of constructive trusts, as in the English appeal of *Jones v Kernott*.[3] For the purposes of this chapter, we will be focussing on the courts that apply the law of England and Wales but will note in relevant places where there is overlap and shared functions.

The courts system has not been immune from the challenging economic environment and decisions around the funding of the legal system has impacted significantly on the court estate. Towards the end of this chapter there are some reflections on the need to modernise and reform the court estate with some critical analysis of the implications of the physical estate for the administration of justice.

1 Which is neither a senior nor inferior court!

2 [2012] UKSC 29, [2013] SC (UKSC) 1.

3 [2011] UKSC 53, [2012] 1 AC 776.

DOI: 10.4324/9781032641829-8

AS YOU READ

Much of this chapter is concerned with the way in which cases heard by our judges are distributed amongst our various courts and with giving detailed information on the process by which this is done and how the system works in general.

It is important that, as you read, **you do more than just memorise** this information. Attempt to **synthesise** what was said about the judiciary in Chapter 7, as this will breathe life into the court structure. Think **critically** about the implications of the structure of the court system that has been arrived at in the legal system, and **reflect** and **compare** with the structures adopted in different jurisdictions. A particular area of focus ought to be on the reforms to the highest court in England and Wales, with some **critical thought** given to what the change has meant for the wider legal system.

THE FRAMEWORK OF SENIOR AND INFERIOR COURTS

This chapter explores the framework of the courts in England and Wales, from the Magistrates at the bottom to the Supreme Court at the top. This building understanding from the bottom to the top is important as the Supreme Court hears only appeals[4] whereas the vast majority of cases will start in one of the two inferior courts, the Magistrates' which have both civil and criminal jurisdiction, or the County Court, which is exclusively civil.

Above this lowest level are the senior courts. These comprise the High Court and Court of Appeal, as well as the Crown Court. The former two have both civil and criminal jurisdiction, whilst the Crown Court sits exclusively on criminal matters. The Crown Court sits both in London and regionally.

These senior courts include courts of both civil and criminal jurisdiction, which have their origins (in the distant early Middle Ages) in the King's Council, the 'Curia Regis' out of which all subsequent courts evolved, either organically out of the Council itself when convenience dictated, or by statutory creation: thus all courts are still HM the King's Courts, and judges of every level sit under the Royal Arms, which are prominently displayed on the wall behind them as they sit on the bench.

These judges now include those of the relatively newly unified Tribunal Service,[5] and the entire courts and tribunal system is now known as HM Courts and Tribunal Service, or 'HMCTS',

4 There is one exception where the Supreme Court has first instance jurisdiction to hear specific matters about the competence of the devolved institutions to make law.

5 The Tribunal Service was created by the Tribunals Court and Enforcement Act 2007, but not all tribunals were in practice transferred in immediately (most in the following three to four years, though some, for example, the Residential

thus still distinguishing between courts and tribunals. This chapter will therefore not address the tribunals, although the courts and tribunals have now been joined up in HMCTS, as the tribunals have a separate identity and function, and thus a separate chapter (Chapter 13).

TAKING THINGS FURTHER – VISITING COURTS

While reading about the court system is very important, nothing brings home the workings of the system quite so clearly as a visit to an actual court. Making some actual court visits will allow you to think more critically about how the courts work in dealing with the cases before them and thus facilitate evaluation of the systems that you observe there. You can see the administration of justice in its realist sense and also experience the system as a direct observer.

A much-needed skill for any student of law is the ability to draw out themes that cross different areas of study. As you read the distinct sections, you should attempt to synthesise the information so as to make connections: for example, you may be studying both criminal law and contract law, the first of which you will encounter in your local Magistrates' Court, and the second in your local County Court. If you live and/or study in London, you can go to the High Court as well, and in most parts of the country, there will be an accessible Crown Court for attending more significant criminal trials than the initial appearances and trials of petty crime that characterise the Magistrates.

Finally, in Parliament Square at Westminster, the Supreme Court welcomes the public, providing helpful summary sheets at reception for each of the cases heard in the building – usually one in the Supreme Court room, which has a number of rows for public seating at the rear of the room, to which there is free access, and one in the Privy Council jurisdiction, which sits in their secondary court. Thus, although these cases are, by definition, complex and probably involve both unfamiliar topics and more recondite points than those early in their studies may normally be used to, which is why they are on appeal in the Supreme Court or Privy Council, a visit affords a unique opportunity to see leading advocates in action and to hear the Justices questioning them as they argue their cases. Moreover, a video of every day's full hearing is always uploaded onto the Court website the next day, for further perusal at leisure.

So when you visit these courts, always look for cases in their lists which you will best understand, perhaps because you will have been studying the substantive content of the law to which they relate.

However, to begin with, your court visits are bound to be informative whether or not you understand much of the content of the cases you are observing, as to start with you will be noticing routine features of the court itself and of the personnel involved, which you

Property Tribunal not until after 2011). The amalgamation within the Ministry of Justice as HMCTS was in 2011, following a consultation in 2010.

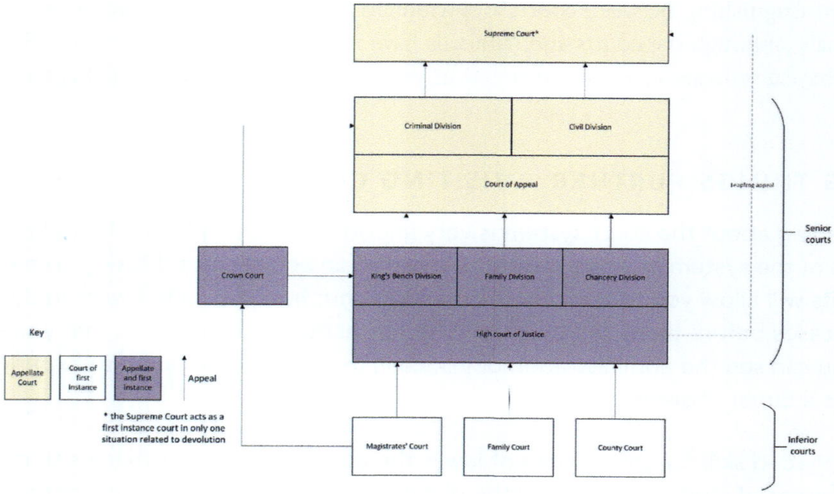

Figure 8.1 The court structure of England and Wales.

will then recognise as either much the same or similar, but with some variations in the next court that you go to, although as time goes on and your visits progress, you will get more out of the visit in actually understanding the content of the case for each side.

Meanwhile Figure 8.1 shows the complete court structure (excluding the tribunals, which we will follow in Chapter 13).

THE INFERIOR COURTS

Before the arrival of the essentially Norman 'Curia Regis' through which the early Norman Kings dispensed justice after the Conquest of 1066, there was a well-developed Saxon system of low-level local justice administered through regional law enforcement by royal officials.

From this pervasive rural network of local courts around England and Wales eventually grew the formally organised regional magistracy, dealing with minor cases in both civil and criminal law, a system which has come down to us today. Thus, for example, 200 years after Henry II, the magistrates were so well established that they were given the job of enforcing agricultural wages under the Statute of Labourers 1351, passed to control the wages of the depleted agricultural workforce, which had been halved in the Black Death of 1349, but on which the medieval kingdom depended for sufficient labour, both to farm the land for food and to work in the lucrative wool trade, the country's most crucial financial resource.

It was out of this rich legal history grew the system of inferior courts. The inferior courts tend to have some shared characteristics that distinguish them from the senior courts. It is important to note that these distinctions are not universally applicable and over time some of the orthodox means of distinguishing courts has become less clear.

The key distinguishing features of inferior courts are thus:

- Typically subject to the supervisory jurisdiction of the High Court, which means that their decisions can be judicially reviewed as well as being appealed
- Typically have a narrow and tightly defined jurisdiction
- Typically are independent courts that have jurisdiction over a limited geographical area

As an example of the evolution of the legal system, the changes to the County Court demonstrates the difficulty of definitively categorising courts. Since 2014, the contemporary County Court has become a national court sitting both in the capital and locally in regional centres. This is in contrast to the former system of county courts', which acted as a network of individual courts in appropriately spread geographical locations. This is why the County Court is now referred to in the singular as opposed to the plural county courts. It is one court that can sit in multiple locations as opposed to a series of independent courts. It is this precision of language and understanding that exemplifies the nuances of the legal system. Regardless of the new identity as a national court, this has not changed the modern County Court's location in the framework as an inferior court.

THE SENIOR COURTS

Similarly, from the itinerant Curia Regis of the medieval kings were eventually developed the senior courts. This was partially a practical concern as the old structures could not then have indefinitely accommodated all the judicial functions into which they had been expanded by Henry II, known as 'the Lion of Justice', and his successors. There was also a developing sense of intersecting (and thereby conflicting) jurisdictions amongst the different judicial bodies that had developed organically over time. This included different remedies and procedures for the different courts.

The Supreme Court of Judicature Acts 1873 and 1875 sought to rationalise the fragmented the court system and unite the common law courts with those that had developed out of principles of equity. Notably, it brought together a number of different courts into the Supreme Court of Judicature, including the High Court (with its then 5 divisions, now 3) and the Court of Appeal. The Crown Court was later created by the Courts Act 1971 in a further exercise of consolidation of specialist courts. These three courts were collectively referred to as 'The Supreme Court of England and Wales' and older literature will still term them in this way. However, with the transfer of the judicial functions of the House of Lords to a newly established 'Supreme Court of the United Kingdom' in 2009[6] necessitated a change of name to those courts and they are now referred to as 'senior courts'.

The most recent articulation of the position can be found in the Senior Courts Act 1981, which names the Crown Court, the High Court of Justice and the Court of Appeal as the 'senior' courts of England and Wales. The Act also explains the composition of the various courts and denotes their jurisdiction and particular powers that they can exercise.

6 By means of the Constitutional Reform Act 2004 s23.

The chapter will proceed by examining the courts with jurisdiction to hear civil cases before progressing to those with jurisdiction to hear criminal cases. Let us start with the Magistrates since the first distinction that we need to make is between civil and criminal law, and the Magistrates do both, so this is as good a place as any to jump in at the deep end. Following initial coverage of the Magistrates, in this part of the chapter we shall concentrate on the flow of the Civil Court structure, mentioning where there is a criminal jurisdiction alongside, but leaving a similar, more detailed account of the Criminal Court structure until after completing that for the Civil Courts.

MAGISTRATES' COURTS – CIVIL AND CRIMINAL JURISDICTION

The Magistrates are amongst the oldest of courts, having had their origins in small local jurisdiction in the early Middle Ages. By the mid-14th century, they were sufficiently established to be entrusted with the enforcement of the Statute of Labourers, leading to their being progressively used to keep local order in various ways. This explains from where their formal title as 'Justices of the Peace' came. The fact that they mostly now do appeals from licensing authorities and used until recently to deal with small domestic issues in family law indicates their provincial nature.

Every town of sufficient size not to be called a village will probably have a Magistrates' Court.[7] In larger towns it will probably share buildings in a Court Centre with the County Court. The Magistrates section of a court centre will also sometimes be called the 'Youth Court', a division of the Magistrates which deals with youth justice and is not supposed to sit at the same time as the (adult) Magistrates' Court is in session. The intention behind this practice is to keep youth justice separate from adult crime, and thus the young and impressionable offenders away from potentially hardened criminals. The Magistrates' Court is much better known for its criminal jurisdiction but it is important to note that it also hears limited civil matters. Given the lack of expensive juries or salaries, the Magistrates' Court provides deals with a significant volume of cases in a cost-effective way.

CRIMINAL JURISDICTION

All criminal cases commence in the Magistrates' Court, where a person charged with a crime must be brought before the magistrates and either tried or committed for trial elsewhere. For more serious crimes transfer will be to the Crown Court. As will be discussed in the chapter concerned with the criminal justice system, there are some offences that can be tried in either court. The venue of these 'either-way offences' will be determined by whether

- the magistrates consider the Crown Court would be the more appropriate venue due to the particular and unusual features of a case, or

7 A complete list of courts can be found here – <https://courttribunalfinder.service.gov.uk/courts>.

- the Crown Court penalty would be more suitable than the more limited powers of punishment available to magistrates, or
- where the accused elects for trial by jury.

Magistrates' courts are mostly presided over by unqualified and unsalaried Justices of the Peace appointed from the local area for which that court dispenses justice and who usually sit in benches of 2 or 3, though a single magistrate may try a summary offence not punishable by imprisonment, for example, driving without insurance, non-payment of TV licences. The relevant statutes are the Magistrates Courts Act 1980 as amended by the Criminal Justice and Courts Act 2015. As they are mostly not legally qualified and voluntary, though trained and able to claim expenses, lay magistrates are advised on the law by a Legal Advisor, formerly known as a Magistrates' Courts Clerk. However there is also a class of salaried and qualified magistrates,[8] formerly called Stipendiaries, and now styled 'District Judges (Magistrates' Courts)' who, while having the same jurisdiction, can sit alone and are often found in busy urban courts.

CIVIL CASES

The Magistrates used to have more substantial civil law jurisdiction. This was notable through its Family Law jurisdiction, but since the inauguration of the Family Court in 2014 the magistrates who used to sit in the Magistrates' Court as a domestic court – dealing with small financial claims between spouses and in respect of maintenance of children – have gone to sit at the lowest level of the Family Court where they are called 'Judges of the Family Court'.

There still remains, however, some small first instance civil jurisdiction, predominantly licensing, and recovery of some civil debts, for example in relation to income tax as well as non-payment of council tax.

THE COUNTY COURT – CIVIL JURISDICTION ONLY

As explained earlier, the County Court is (since 2014) a single national court (similar in status to the Family Court which determines all family cases that do not need specifically to go to the High Court). However, despite now being classified as a single national court with its own seal which sits in many different locations around the country as the national Crown Court does, the contemporary County Court is still technically the inferior court it has always been since the first network of county courts was set up in 1846. This is to say it is a creature of statute in which its governing legislation sets out its jurisdiction, which is first instance civil only, but concurrent with the High Court.

8 These salaried magistrates must have been barristers or solicitors for at least seven years: Courts and Legal Services Act 1990, Access to Justice Act 1999. There are about 30,000 lay magistrates and about 100 district judges (Magistrates' Courts).

The relevant statutes are the County Court Act 1984 as amended by the Crime and Courts Act 2013, s17 and Schedule 9, which created the single national County Court in place of the former system of individual county courts to hear small cases originally set up in 1846. The judiciary are principally Circuit Judges, assisted by District Judges and Deputy District Judges, but any High Court or Court of Appeal judge, and also any Recorder, may also sit there. The Court's great relevance to students of law is that it tries contract and tort cases[9] thus affording a suitable diet of subject matter of relatively simple cases for court hearings to be observed by those studying the legal system.

The County Court is thus subject to the supervisory prerogative jurisdiction of the High Court and the orders of *mandamus, certiorari* and prohibition, and pursuant to the Senior Courts Act 1981 s29(3), the High Court can quash any decision of the County Court if it has exceeded its jurisdiction. The contemporary County Court therefore has no inherent jurisdiction and it has the character of providing local access to a civil jurisdiction similar to the High Court but more cost effectively. The County Court is thus likely to be found in a larger town with a Civil or Combined Court Centre, and there are currently many locations, usually to be found in precisely the same buildings as the former county courts sat in. It is a court of record although classified as an inferior rather than senior court.

The original 19th-century county court concept was based on the old county sheriff's courts, namely summary justice in a local court, and the contemporary statutory creation was aimed at saving money following Sir Henry Brooke's 2008 Report *Should the Civil Courts Be Unified?*[10] This resulted in a recommendation *not* to make this change (as had however already happened in other common law jurisdictions, for example, Ontario in Canada) but also for the closure of a number of court buildings, the introduction of more online and electronic handling of cases, together with the implementation of two new specialist centres – the County Court Money Claims Centre at Salford[11] and the County Court Business Centre in Nottingham.[12] These are designed to save money by improving case management.

The County Court now automatically tries most lower value civil claims unless there is some reason for starting or trying a case in the High Court, which will usually be more expensive in every way (not least in court fees and the cost of representation) although both courts use the same Civil Procedure Rules (CPR) 1998 and the same fast track and multi-track approach, introduced by the Woolf Reforms (see later in this chapter). There are some exceptions to the general principle of starting low value claims in the County Court as some cases must be started in the High Court, for example, in Defamation.

The other significant feature of the County Court is its small claims jurisdiction. This usually involves contract, tort (especially personal injury), landlord and tenant and perhaps probate

9 Subjects normally encountered early on in the study of law.

10 Brooke, LJ, Judicial Office, August 2008.

11 Issuing claims and offering an online determination for claims for fixed amounts under £100,000; see <https://www.gov.uk/make-money-claim>.

12 This facilitates removing repetitive, staff-intensive cases from the County Court to a computer-supported environment.

claims. The small claims procedure is simple, conducted by a District Judge, and should allow parties to appear without legal representation, with the consequence that costs are not normally awarded. This should lead to quicker, cheaper and less stressful outcomes. Dispute resolution other than by means of litigation is encouraged and most courts will have some dispute resolution service available.

APPELLATE JURISDICTION OF THE COUNTY COURT

There is a limited appeal system whereby District Judges' decisions may be appealed to a Circuit Judge of the same court. Such appeals have their origins in the analysis of civil appeals by Brooke LJ in the case of *Tanfern Ltd v Gregor Cameron-Macdonald*,[13] in which it was established that in civil cases an appeal lies to the next judge in the hierarchy.

THE HIGH COURT – CIVIL JURISDICTION

This, in its modern dress, is the direct descendant of the medieval King's Court, which morphed into the Court of King's Bench now represented by the King's Bench Division of the High Court of Justice. In the intervening hundreds of years there have been various other Divisions of the High Court, but today the principal ones are the King's Bench Division, Chancery Division and Family Division. There was a suggestion by the Heilbron-Hodge Committee (which in 1993 produced one of the reform reports prior to the Woolf Reforms 1994–1998) that the King's Bench and Chancery Divisions should be merged, but this was never seriously considered, as to do so would have created unnecessary complexity and lost the best features of both Divisions.

The King's Bench Division (KBD) deals predominantly with contract and tort claims, that is, the original common law diet of common law courts, as opposed to the traditional Chancery topics (see text under Chancery Division) although the Division can take a variety of other cases if it wishes. However, the KBD also has three subdivisions:

- The Commercial Court, with specialist judges to deal with insurance, banking and similar topics connected with city financial business, such as Lloyds[14] 'names' losses caused by high insurance claims; they also use expedited procedures, make determinations on documents in some cases without a hearing and promote out-of-court dispute resolution, for example, through the City Disputes Panel.
- The Admiralty Court, a specialist maritime law court dealing with losses to cargo and ship collisions, with a specialist judge sitting with two assessors from the Masters of Trinity House[15] to advise on seamanship and navigation.

13 [2000] 2 All ER 801 (CA).

14 Lloyds of London being the underwriters for many policies and a historic core city business.

15 Founded in 1514, Trinity House is an ancient maritime authority responsible for all lighthouses and navigational aids in England, Wales, the Channel Islands and Gibraltar, and also a deep-sea pilotage authority in relation to ships sailing in Northern European waters, clearly providing specialist expertise in maritime matters.

- The Technology and Construction Court, which deals with any cases involving technical complexity, such as building and construction generally, engineering and computer technology, including cases of any such complexity referred to it by the Chancery or King's Bench Division.

There is also the Divisional Court of the King's Bench Division, distinct from the three KBD Divisions mentioned previously, which is an important court for the purpose of hearing applications for judicial review, statutory appeals and *habeas corpus*, and when it exercises these functions, it is known as the 'Administrative Court'.

The Chancery Division traditionally deals with corporate and personal insolvency, mortgages, leases, property generally, partnership, intellectual property, patents, trademarks, copyright, disputes relating to trusts and settlements, inheritance and administration of estates, wills and specialist company law matters, for which there is a specialist Companies Court within the Division. Another specialist court within the Division is the Patents Court. However, in recent decades the Division has also undertaken much heavy commercial litigation and less of the traditional old Chancery documentation work in connection with trusts and settlements owing to the diminution of volume of such work. Cases are determined by a single judge and juries are never used.

The Family Division deals with cases in relation to adult relationships such as marriage, civil partnership and their dissolution; child law generally including child protection for which the state[16] is responsible; wardship and cases involving children's rights to determine their own medical treatment, in respect of which the High Court has an inherent jurisdiction. However, there are many provisions in the governing statutes and in the Family Procedure Rules 2010 as amended that deal with transfers to and from the High Court to the Family Court which now has High Court judges sitting in it along with Circuit Judges and Magistrates owing to the various levels at which the Family Court is designed to operate. This last point is important as it avoids the former necessity to apply to different courts, thus introducing more flexibility and saving the Family Division of the High Court for cases that really require the expertise of the judges normally sitting there.

The Division also deals with international child abduction under the Hague Convention to which the UK is a signatory, and this is an example of the specialist expertise for which the Family Division of the High Court is most conveniently reserved.

The more routine work, such as under the Marriage Acts, Matrimonial Causes Act 1973 and associated legislation, Civil Partnership Act 2004, Gender Recognition Act 2004, Children Act 1989 is now allocated to the Family Court. This brings all levels of Family Justice into one court where possible in order to reduce the necessity for transfers between levels, although sometimes geographic or other reasons still require a transfer to another location of the Family

16 Through the local authority.

Court, or indeed to the High Court. This will most typically be due to the sensitivity of a case requiring superior security, which a local Family Court might not be able to provide due to local resourcing limitations.

TAKING THINGS FURTHER – THE RELATIONSHIP BETWEEN THE HIGH COURT AND THE COUNTY COURT

Despite the 2008 Brooke Report's recommendation that the High Court and County Court should not be unified, and although the High Court is a senior court and the County Court an inferior court, that is not to say that the two courts do not work together in some ways to provide a holistic system of first instance civil justice. Besides the possibilities of transfer between the two courts, they both share the same Civil Procedure Rules (CPR) 1998, which were a key product of the Woolf Reforms 1994–1998

In addition to using the same CPR for procedure, both County Court and High Court use the same tracking and proactive judicial case management systems that were a key Woolf innovation (and which are discussed in more detail in Chapter 10).

THE TRACKS SYSTEM AND CASE MANAGEMENT

The track system was inspired by the long-established small claims court originally in use in the old-style county courts. Here low value cases were heard in consumer disputes, housing and even personal injury, and procedure was flexible so that the judge could run hearings in whatever way appeared most suitable, including when parties might not be professionally represented. However in addition to small claims two other tracks were added by the CPR – a fast track and a multi-track – so that cases over a small claims limit but still of relatively low value could be fast tracked, whereas those over such low value or of greater complexity or both could be allocated to a multi-track. This enabled fast track cases to be heard relatively quickly, and in no more than a day, with fixed costs and a limitation on experts. Those apparently more suitable to the multi-track could be consigned to the proactive hands of judicial case management, which enabled a creative case management judge to set up pre-trial reviews, preliminary hearings, time limits and other directions, thus controlling both costs and delay.

Allocation to the appropriate track is achieved by issue to both parties of an allocation questionnaire which the parties complete with sufficient information for the case management judge to form a view as to the appropriate track. This includes information intended to elicit value, complexity, likely length of the hearing and also adding the parties' preferences, to which the court may or may not accede as the case may dictate. This is because the object of these systems is to use only a proportionate amount of the resources of the court rather than to allow cases to run for a disproportionately long time for the value of the case. This aim is dictated by the overriding objective in the CPR r1.1, which requires that cases are dealt with justly and that the parties are on an equal footing. Since the introduction of the CPR the aim has also always been to encourage dispute resolution (DR) at all stages, including adjournment wherever possible to enable the parties to try one other form of DR – these alternative forms of DR are discussed in Chapter 14.

The CPR also introduced the concept of 'pre-action protocols' to ensure that the defendant fully understands the claim and has a chance to consider settlement and that neither party is embarking on litigation unnecessarily. As the pre-action protocols are required by the Rules, failure to observe them is likely to be penalised in costs.

THE COURT OF APPEAL – CIVIL JURISDICTION

The next court in the hierarchy above the High Court is the Court of Appeal. It has two divisions, the Civil Division and the Criminal Division: this section of the chapter however deals largely with its civil business; for the criminal aspects see later. It is, as the name suggests, an appellate court and so does not hear cases at first instance.

The Court of Appeal (Civil Division) is presided over by the Master of the Rolls (MR) who is also Head of Civil Justice. The title of this office had its origin in the Middle Ages when this judge did indeed keep the 'rolls' on which were recorded decisions of the King's Courts, and in modern times he (there has not yet been a woman judge as Master of the Rolls) is also responsible for some aspects of the regulation of solicitors, for example, he determines the cost of solicitors' practising certificates.[17]

Permission to appeal is almost always required for an appeal to this court.[18] The contemporary rationalisation of appeals requires that there should generally only be one appeal, rather than a case going from court to court up to the Supreme Court, so many appeals will not progress further than the Court of Appeal. Some may never go to the Court of Appeal but directly to the Supreme Court, the final UK appellate court, by the 'leap-frog' process provided by the Administration of Justice Act 1969 ss12–15.

Where a second appeal is required beyond one already made from the judge of first instance (what is known as 'a second-tier appeal') there must be an important point of principle or practice or some other compelling reason for the appeal sought, and the Court of Appeal must consider this to be the case.

All the senior judges who hold offices identified in the Constitutional Reform Act 2005 sit in the Court of Appeal, that is, the Lord Chief Justice (LCJ), Chancellor (formerly called the 'Vice-Chancellor') of the Chancery Division, the Master of the Rolls and the President of the Family Division. There are also up to a maximum of 39[19] Lords Justices of Appeal and some High Court judges (and sometimes retired High Court judges) are invited to sit, since there are

17 Solicitors Act 1974 s11(1).

18 Access to Justice Act 1999 s54 and CPR Part 52.

19 Dictated by Senior Courts Act 1981 s2(1)(b).

usually several courts of either three or five judges required daily. In recent times the court has much increased its capacity, now hearing as many as nearly 4,000 cases in a year.

THE SUPREME COURT

Appeals from the Court of Appeal go to this final UK appellate court, which replaced the Appellate Committee of the House of Lords in October 2009, alongside others from the Court of Session in Edinburgh,[20] and the courts of Northern Ireland. There are 12 Justices of the Supreme Court, who are no longer given a peerage as when they were elevated to the House of Lords Appellate Committee, though they may already have one, for example, Baroness Hale was appointed to the House of Lords Appellate Committee before 2009. Either the Court of Appeal or the Supreme Court must give leave for an appeal to the Supreme Court; it is usual to ask the Court of Appeal first and then if the application is refused the appellant may apply to the Supreme Court.

Appeals are usually on questions of law, and of a complex nature, although an appeal on a question of fact is possible in civil cases (unlike in the case of criminal appeals). Now that the Court has been operational for more than ten years, there has been an interesting article on its judicial leadership in an issue of the academic journal Legal Studies[21] which analyses the way in which its Justices have worked together in all cases heard so far.

THE JUDICIAL COMMITTEE OF THE PRIVY COUNCIL

The Privy Council is a body that advises the UK monarch and carries out important functions on their behalf. In this context there is a Judicial Committee of the Privy Council. Its role in the legal system of England and Wales is fairly limited, and it hears appeals on certain matters, for example, from within the Church of England, from the Court of Admiralty and on disputes over heraldry.

Beyond its limited *domestic* jurisdiction, appeals go to the Judicial Committee of the Privy Council if from outside the UK, for example, the British Overseas Territory of Bermuda and certain Caribbean jurisdictions which have not abolished this appellate channel. Dependant on the jurisdiction of origin, these appeals can reach the Privy Council directly or are referred to the Committee after appeal his made to 'His Majesty in Council'. In this way, aspects of the Privy Council's work are not part of the court system for the legal system but are mentioned here for completeness and to show the interaction.

The Justices are the same as those who sit in the Supreme Court with the addition of some Commonwealth judiciary members who sit on cases from their own jurisdictions. It is also the final appellate court for the Channel Islands and the Isle of Man, where some English and Welsh judiciary sit on those islands' appeals (in the Channel Islands as Deputy Bailiffs and in the Isle of Man as a Judge of Appeal).

20 On civil matters only.

21 Rosemary Hunter and Erika Rackley, 'Judicial Leadership on the UK Supreme Court' (2018) 38 LS 191–220.

THE CRIMINAL COURT SYSTEM

Beginning at the bottom, as with the civil process, the first level in the criminal courts is the Magistrates. This court system has a much more extensive role than as at the bottom rung of the civil ladder, since all criminal cases begin in the Magistrates' Court.[22] This court, together with the Crown Court, comprise the launch pad for first instance criminal hearings.

The Magistrates have both a relatively limited first instance trial role, for less serious crimes ('summary offences'[23] and some offences which can be tried 'either way', that is, in the Magistrates' or the Crown Court)[24] and also a committal role, to decide preliminary matters (such as 'bail' and 'remand') and to send more serious crimes ('indictable offences')[25] for trial at the Crown Court, which also has an appellate role in determining appeals from the Magistrates. No criminal cases actually start in the Crown Court without going before the Magistrates first for committal if not being tried there.

From first instance, criminal courts have their own appellate ladder similar to civil cases, to the Court of Appeal (Criminal Division) and then to the Supreme Court. In some rara circumstances, the High Court's Administrative Court (in the King's Bench Division) also has a special role in hearing a particular class of appeals on point of law from the Magistrates, by way of 'case stated'. It will be remembered that the bench of magistrates unless a stipendiary magistrate sitting alone – now called a 'District Judge (Magistrates' Courts) – would not be legally qualified so this 'case stated' appeal route was originally created to enable a more complex point of law to be considered by the qualified and infinitely more experienced High Court judiciary in the KBD, and in documentary form. Hence the origin of the term 'case stated', since the Magistrates' Court could be asked to 'state a case' for the High Court judiciary to consider on this special form of appeal.

THE MAGISTRATES' CRIMINAL JURISDICTION

Crimes are investigated and, where appropriate, charged by the police and then prosecuted by the Crown Prosecution Service, a statutory body set up for the purpose in 1986.[26] The CPS then takes over the offence charged and prosecutes it, since as in most common law systems the criminal court process is adversarial. In adversarial systems the two parties, prosecution and defence, present their opposing cases, the prosecution in order to put the case for the state which has charged the accused with the relevant crime and the defence for the accused, who will have access to both solicitors to prepare the case for his defence and barristers to present

22 Magistrates Courts Act 1980 s18A, as amended by the Criminal Justice Act 2003.

23 For example, driving offences under the Road Traffic Acts, and many other statutory offences.

24 For example, less serious assaults, criminal damage, less serious offences under the Theft Act 1968.

25 For example, treason, murder, attempted murder, manslaughter, rape, serious assaults, aggravated burglary, that is, cases too serious for trial by the magistrates but needing a professional judge and a jury. Judges are 'ticketed' for these cases within four classes of seriousness of indictable offences, the most serious being allocated to a High Court Judge, and the less serious to a Circuit Judge or Recorder.

26 Prosecution of Offences Act 1985 s3(2). A case may sometimes come to them from other sources as well, for example, from the local authority in relation to prosecutions for trading standards breaches.

it and to challenge the prosecution's case as presented by the prosecution witnesses called to give evidence in support of the charge. In the Magistrates' Court, where there is never a jury, the magistrates then decide on guilt on the basis of the evidence called. They then also decide on the sentence, for which there is structured guidance according to the type of case and a number of other variables.[27]

MAKING CONNECTIONS – ADVERSARIAL AND INQUISITORIAL DIFFERENCES

This adversarial system is completely different from the civil law system's approach, which is inquisitorial. Another feature of the adversarial system is that the prosecution has a duty to disclose all material evidence to the defence, whereas the defence is under no duty to disprove the prosecution's allegations, since on the contrary (except in very limited circumstances) the prosecution must prove its case or the accused cannot be convicted.

If the offence is serious ('indictable', that is, must be tried on indictment in the Crown Court) the accused will only make his/her first brief appearance before the magistrates, who will formally commit for trial by the Crown Court. The Court will also grant legal aid and bail if appropriate or remand the defendant in custody if not. There is otherwise no hearing at this level, and the accused will not enter a plea until the Crown Court, where a judge will hold a Plea and Case Management Hearing (PCMH).

If the offence is an 'either-way' offence (also called a 'hybrid offence') the accused will have to enter a plea at the Magistrates' Court, whereupon if the plea is guilty the magistrates may sentence straight away, or they may elect to commit to the Crown Court for sentence. Magistrates will commit for sentence if they consider their powers of sentencing are inadequate. If the plea is not guilty the magistrates will hold an allocation hearing[28] to decide where the case will be heard[29] although some cases involving children and serious or complex fraud cases are usually sent straight to the Crown Court.[30] The magistrates have published guidelines to help them to decide whether a case is suitable for summary or Crown Court trial.[31]

If the offence is 'summary' only the accused is not entitled to trial in the Crown Court and trial will take place before the magistrates without a jury. This is the main diet of the Magistrates' Court. Appeals against conviction and/or sentence go to the Crown Court or to the Administrative Court of the King's Bench Division, by way of case stated.

27 <www.sentencingcouncil.org.uk>.

28 Criminal Justice Act 2003.

29 This is determined under the Magistrates Courts Act 1980 s19. It is only a mode of trial hearing, not to determine guilt or innocence. If the magistrates decide the case is suitable for summary trial, the accused will be told he can choose whether to be tried by the magistrates or by the Crown Court with a jury: s20.

30 Crime and Disorder Act 1998 ss 51B and 51C.

31 Criminal Justice Act 2003 s170.

Of the overall proportion of criminal cases only a very small number (less than 5%) are indictable offences going to the Crown Court. The remaining 95% or more are less serious and are disposed of by the Magistrates.

THE CROWN COURT

Crown Court procedure is completely different from the Magistrates' Court, since the findings of fact (by the jury) and the direction on the law to the jury (which is in the hands of the judge) are separated. There is a clear delineation of function since the judge has no say in the jury's decision (outside of specific judicial directions) and the jury has no say in the sentence (which is up to the judge, albeit in accordance with structured guidance). The role of the jury is considered further in Chapter 12.

Since the Crown Court is a national court which also sits regionally around the country it will be the centre for criminal trials in its regional location. This is the same in London, where the Central Criminal Court (the Old Bailey) is the main London Crown Court. Given the size and population density of London there are others, for example Southwark Crown Court, Snaresbrook Crown Court and Croydon Crown Court. As the Court is a national court it has jurisdiction to hear all criminal trials wherever committed, although mostly cases will be tried regionally unless of such notoriety that a fair trial might not be easily available locally in which case it is usual to hear such a case at the Old Bailey.

In this sense, judges of the High Court still go out 'on circuit' to hear cases in regional locations of the Crown Court, since owing to the ticketing system for Crown Court cases High Court judiciary will be needed who will otherwise normally be sitting in London at the Royal Courts of Justice in the Strand. Although some lesser indictable offences can be heard by Circuit Judges and Recorders who may be available locally, the top two classes of seriousness amongst the indictable offences will require High Court judges.

APPELLATE JURISDICTION OF THE CROWN COURT

The Crown Court also hears appeals from the Magistrates, against conviction and sentence. No permission is required and only the convicted accused can appeal. The prosecution has no right to appeal to the Crown Court against a decision of the Magistrates. An appeal to the Crown Court will be a complete rehearing 'de novo', with witnesses but without a jury, and the Crown Court can vary the decision or confirm it, but it cannot increase the sentence beyond the magistrates' limits.

Alternatively the prosecution and defence can each appeal to the Administrative Court of the KBD on the grounds that the magistrates' decision was wrong in law, which is not a rehearing, but an appeal by way of case stated on the basis of legal argument, and if that is not successful a further appeal can be made to the Supreme Court, provided it is on the basis of a point of law of general public importance and leave must be obtained from either the Administrative Court or the Supreme Court.

COURT OF APPEAL – CRIMINAL JURISDICTION

The Court of Appeal has a particular division dedicated to criminal appeals. This Court was created in 1966 to replace the old Court of Criminal Appeal, created in 1907, to hear criminal appeals only. The Court of Appeal (Criminal Division) is presided over by the Lord Chief Justice, the most senior criminal judge.

The Court hears appeals against conviction or sentence in the Crown Court but does not entertain further appeals from the Divisional Court of the King's Bench Division which go directly to the Supreme Court.

There are also special requirements provided by the Criminal Appeal Act 1968 as amended by the Criminal Appeal Act 1995, s2 about the way in which the Court of Appeal (Criminal Division) is to approach the appeal. The Act provides that the Court *shall* allow an appeal if the judges hearing the appeal feel that the conviction is '*unsafe*', and in all other cases, they shall dismiss the appeal.

The judges of the Court of Appeal (Criminal Division) are the Lords Justices of Appeal of the Court of Appeal and are not restricted to former purely criminal specialists. Some High Court judges also sit periodically, and it has become a custom to invite retired High Court judges to sit especially when there are not enough judiciary to go round when listing is particularly busy. It is easy to identify such sittings since the Court of Appeal judges still in office are always referred to in Law Reports by their Lord Justice's designation, for example, as Smith LJ, whereas a retired High Court judge would be referred to by his out of office title, namely his knighthood, as, for example, Sir Jeremiah Smith. Lords Justices of Appeal promoted from the High Court will already have a knighthood, traditionally given on their elevation to the Bench, so it was agreed at the time of the Judicature Acts 1873–5 that to distinguish Court of Appeal judges from those of the High Court, the Lords Justices would also be created Privy Councillors, thus obtaining the suffix 'PC'.

SUPREME COURT

Like the Court of Appeal, the Supreme Court requires permission to be granted before an appeal can be accepted, either by the Court itself or by the Court of Appeal. It is usual to seek permission first from the Court of Appeal and if that is refused application is made to the Supreme Court. There is also a statutory requirement[32] that the Court of Appeal must certify that the case involves a point of law of general public importance and that it appears that it is one which should be considered by the Supreme Court. Either the Court of Appeal or the Supreme Court must also give leave to appeal.

32 Criminal Appeal Act 1968 s33.

THE JUDICIAL COMMITTEE OF THE PRIVY COUNCIL

This 'alter ego' of the Supreme Court hears criminal appeals from some Commonwealth and British Overseas Territories that have retained this appeal channel as in the case of civil appeals. In the case of appeals to the Privy Council, special leave must be given for a criminal appeal, which will not be given unless there are exceptional circumstances, for example, a substantial injustice has occurred and the accused has potentially not had a fair trial.

THE CRIMINAL CASES REVIEW COMMISSION (CCRC)

This is not actually a court but an alternative channel for a review of appeals in order to avoid a miscarriage of justice. Established by the Criminal Appeal Act 1995, the Criminal Cases Review Commission has investigatory powers to help determine whether there has potentially been a miscarriage of justice. If it determines that this is likely, it can refer the case back to the appeal courts for a fresh hearing. In determining whether to support a review there normally needs to be substantial new evidence or a new legal argument that was not tested in the original trial or subsequent appeals. Sometimes such miscarriages of justice are only actioned long after the actual conviction, for example, in the case of Derek Bentley, convicted and executed for the murder of a policeman in 1953, pardoned in 1995 and his conviction for murder finally quashed in 1999.[33]

More recently, in 2023 and 2024, following a technology scandal (the Horizon Scandal) within the Post Office, the CCRC has been involved in referring the cases of sub-postmasters who were wrongfully convicted of fraud.

TAKING THINGS FURTHER – VISITS TO THE CRIMINAL COURTS

Criminal Courts are particularly worth visiting since it is usual to be simultaneously studying the legal system, legal method and criminal law, thus affording an ideal opportunity to attend court hearings in a subject area in which you will have already acquired some subject knowledge. After the Magistrates' Court, the next most accessible is likely to be a local Crown Court sitting, where attendance in the public gallery is usually not a problem (as it may be in London, where, for example, the Old Bailey often has queues for admission).

33 *R v Derek William Bentley (deceased)* [2001] 1 Cr App R 21 (CA). Per Lord Bingham, LCJ, in introducing the referral from the CCRC, treated as an appeal to the Court of Appeal, 'rarely has a court been called upon to review the safety of a conviction recorded over 45 years ago' but finding the summing up of the trial judge so prejudicial as to make the conviction unsafe, so that 'the summing up in the present case had been such as to deny the appellant that fair trial which was the birth right of every British Citizen'.

Another opportunity for obtaining some hands-on experience of criminal court hearings is to seek a 'marshalling' placement with a criminal judge (i.e. 'shadowing' a judge in a local Crown Court) or a 'mini-pupillage' with a barrister or set of Chambers, or vacation placement with a firm of solicitors, in both cases with a practitioner who has a predominantly criminal practice. More information about this can be found on the accompanying website, where it is more convenient to address ways of obtaining such useful experience.

THE INFLUENCE OF EUROPEAN COURTS

Until the end of January 2020, the UK was a member of the institutions of the European Union, including the Court of Justice. The UK provided a judge to sit in the main court and a further two in the so-called General Court. Although those judges have now left the CJEU, the English and Welsh legal system will remain connected to the jurisdiction of the European courts for many years to come. Even after the end of the transition period, the case law of the Court of Justice of the European Union will remain relevant in understanding the interpretation of law that originated from our membership. The CJEU has jurisdiction to hear questions on the interpretation of EU law referred to it by the domestic courts and this previously included those courts of the English and Welsh legal system. During the UK's membership, this was achieved by means of the 'preliminary reference procedure' detailed in Article 267 TFEU. It should be made clear that the CJEU was never an *appellate* court within the legal system of England and Wales, even during the time that the UK was a member state of the EU. In this way the CJEU has always sat slightly outside the formal court structure, but its binding judgments of interpretation have had a significant impact within that structure. Whilst this impact is changing as the time since our departure increases, the cases of the CJEU remain an important guidance point when understanding law passed during our membership of the European Union.

Distinct from the European Union, the UK remains a signatory to the European Convention on Human Rights (ECHR). The ECHR is a long-standing international agreement that seeks to govern human rights protection amongst its 46 member states. As part of that framework there is a judicial body called the European Court of Human Rights (ECrtHR). Individuals are able to seek a judgment from the ECrtHR against their state once they have exhausted all domestic court processes. The court sits outside of the formal legal system of England and Wales but is an influential (and, in some cases or from some perspectives, controversial) judicial body. Its judgments are binding on the member states who are signatories and the judgments can also be influential as domestic courts wrestle with interpretation and application of the Convention rights. This aspect of the influence of the ECRtHR is picked up and discussed more fully when considering the doctrine of precedent in a subsequent chapter.

A CRITICAL APPROACH TO THE COURT STRUCTURE

Both the civil and criminal courts have been the subject of extensive reports and suggestions for reform but, except in the case of the civil courts (where a suggestion to amalgamate the County and High Courts was rejected by the Brooke Report in 2008) there has been no suggested reform to alter the structure of the criminal courts since the last major recast of their systems by the Courts Act 1971 which abolished much historic framework[34] not really suitable to modern times. Such research and reform as there have been in the criminal system has been targeted towards criminal process rather than the courts as such and are addressed in Chapter 11, on criminal justice, where it sits more appropriately.

Contemporary reform in respect of both the civil and criminal courts has therefore more recently focussed on court buildings and on the practicalities of adapting procedure to the increased use of digital solutions than on any changes in what appears to be the now firmly established court framework, despite the fact that projected reform repeatedly refers to 'the digital court'. Whilst it is natural to focus on process, it should not be understated the impact that the court estate has on the administration of justice. Through promise of new digital services, more than half the courts in England and Wales were closed over the past 20 years. It is not at all clear that the increase in use of technology has mitigated the impact of such a scale of closure. This significant reduction in the size of the court estate has a real consequence for access to justice. Distances that parties, witnesses and legal professionals have to travel has increased. This is likely to have a sharper impact on those with disabilities, those at the bottom of the income distribution and those with caring responsibilities.

There is some limited research, now a little dated, on the potential impacts on locally administered justice.[35] Equally, in response to a government consultation on the future of the court estate, the Chair of the Justice Committee in Parliament outlined concerns around further closures and the risks of valuing financial savings above access to justice.[36] The government's response to the consultation sought to 'provide greater assurance that, when we make changes to our estate, we maintain effective access to justice, provide value for money to the taxpayer and make sure that our courts and tribunals are as efficient as possible'.[37] This has resulted in new and stronger principles that will inform any future plans for rationalisation of the court estate. There is also a concern that the deterioration of the court estate has an impact on court users' perceptions of the quality of justice being administered.

34 Such as the historic assizes, where, from 1559 to 1971, High Court judiciary toured the country to try major crime (replaced by the national, regionally sitting Crown Court with four different levels of judicial 'ticketing') and the Quarter Sessions (replaced by the constantly sitting modern Magistrates' Court).

35 Lord Phillips of Sudbury, '"To No Man Will We Deny, Delay or Sell Justice" – a Perspective on Court Closure' (2015/16) 71 Magistrate 13.

36 <https://www.parliament.uk/globalassets/documents/commons-committees/Justice/correspondence/20180227-Letter-Lucy-Frazer-court-tribunal-estate.pdf> and the consultation can be found at the following link:

37 <https://consult.justice.gov.uk/digital-communications/transforming-court-tribunal-estate/results/fit-for-future-consultation-fullpage.pdf>.

CONCLUSION

Beyond the text and diagrams of this chapter, it is important to note some of the broader themes that arise out of the essential information set out. First, the framework of courts is not exclusively either civil or criminal in either set of courts involved in their apparent specialisms. Despite the framework of the specialist divisions of the High Court, at Court of Appeal level and above in the Supreme Court, our top judiciary are generalists rather than narrow specialists. They are steeped in the general principles of English and Welsh law and of the application of it in our unique ways of statutory interpretation and application of judicial precedent, as they were in their rudimentary first inception as members of the medieval King's Council. This is regularly made clear when it is evident from reports of decided cases that whatever their previous background in practice and on the Bench, the Lords Justices of the Court of Appeal and the judiciary of the Supreme Court are expected to sit on both civil and criminal appeals in accordance with the demands of the service.

Secondly, that the structure of the courts of England and Wales is closely linked to the legal history and development of the substantive law. The jurisdiction has reflected the diverse needs of areas of law, whilst seeking a unified set of processes and venues. At times, such as the Judicature Acts 1873 and 1875, the Courts Act 1971 and the Constitutional Reform Act 2005, there is more of a fundamental reform to the system of courts, but this appetite for structural reform has waned in more recent years, to be replaced with a desire to make the courts more digitally accessible.

Thirdly, the court system is a very visible facet of the legal system. The historical focus on distributed, local justice means that (at least historically) the local courts are a familiar sight to citizens and operate as a civic space and window into the law. As the system pushes, through court closure and consolidation, for efficiencies and greater use of technology, there is a risk of a physical, emotional and psychological distance growing between the citizen and the administration of justice. This is in addition to the very real concerns around access to justice for court users.

THE WEBSITE

The website that accompanies this textbook contains many useful resources that you can use to consolidate and further your knowledge of the law, to hone your skills of critical analysis and to test your knowledge. This includes a set of multiple-choice questions (MCQs) that can be used to test your knowledge and understanding of the material.

9

CHAPTER 9
PRECEDENT

INTRODUCTION

Courts dealing with law in the jurisdiction of England and Wales employ systems of statutory interpretation[1] and the use of precedent, which are radically different from those of the civil justice systems. In England and Wales, we have no codified constitution; the law is partly statutory and partly 'case law',[2] that is, previous determinations of judges, which have been collected together in the various series of 'law reports' since the Middle Ages. Out of this developed the original common law of the land, the principles of which have given English and Welsh law its unique flavour.[3] In this way, statutory interpretation and principles of binding precedent give the law of the courts legitimacy and authority and thus form the two pillars of the judicial legal order in England and Wales.

It is important to understand the interrelationship between statutory interpretation and precedent. They are neither fully overlapping nor mutually exclusive. Precedent had traditionally been fetishised by academics of the common law, and there is recognition that the common law is increasingly being 'swallowed up'.[4] Nonetheless, precedent is still one of the twin pillars of the judicial legal order in the legal system of England and Wales.

AS YOU READ

Much of this chapter is concerned with the mechanics of the use of precedent in English and Welsh courts and, in particular, how precedent is used in the hierarchy of courts and how the system works in general. It is important that, as you read, **you do more than just memorise** this information. It is particularly important when studying precedent that you **understand the terminology** deployed in discussions about cases. As with learning about the courts themselves, you need also to **practise reading case reports** in the various series of law reports and to find *ratios* and *obiter dicta* yourself. This will help you develop your skills of **critical analysis** and will help you in **applying the law** to new situations. Much of the time of all those involved in the legal system is devoted to decoding and discerning the principles applied in a given case.

While reading such cases, you should begin to **think critically about how the courts work in dealing with the doctrine of precedent in cases before them** and thus to be able to **evaluate the system**.

1 See Chapter 6, on statutory interpretation.

2 And NB case law, as in reported cases, in the various series of law reports, is always written 'case law' (never 'case *laws*'), as *case law* is a generic term, like the 'common law', which is another name for the law that comes from reported cases.

3 See Chapter 2, Sources of Law.

4 Lord Burrows, 'Seven Lessons from Inside the Supreme Court' (Neill Lecture, 2023) <https://supremecourt.uk/uploads/Seven_Lessons_from_Inside_the_UK_Supreme_Court_Lord_Burrows_2725d87d66.pdf> at 1.

DOI: 10.4324/9781032641829-9

THE RATIONALE AND PRACTICAL CONSIDERATIONS FOR PRECEDENT

THE RATIONALE

The underlying rationale and principle of precedent is straightforward – that cases which raise similar or identical legal issues should be decided in a similar way. This brings certainty to the law and to those subject to it. Unfortunately, the practical realities of precedent are much more complex. As we shall see, the doctrine of precedent is steeped in difficult language and operates within a hierarchy of courts and is subject to underlying rules and principles. It would be sensible to discuss first the rationale for precedent before explaining how it finds expression in the common law and then considering the rules and principles that govern its exercise.

Given that the legal system of England and Wales is a *common law* jurisdiction[5] we already know that case law has a particular importance for the development of the law. In the absence of a fully codified constitution or comprehensive civil code, judges are left to 'fill the gaps' in the law through the cases that come before them. Although Parliament is now a keen legislator, it has not always been so and prior to the 19th century the volume of legislation was low meaning that the courts had bigger gaps to fill. For example, in the areas of contract and crime in particular the legislative landscape was fairly barren. Even at a time of greatly increased activity from Parliament, courts are required to continue to operate within the 'gaps' and to consider how abstract legislation is to be applied in particular cases. This puts case law front and centre in not only *interpreting* statutory law but also in creating, developing and refining legal principle. For this law to have the confidence of its citizens there must be a degree of certainty.

ANALYSING THE LAW – LEGAL CERTAINTY

It is to be remembered from Chapter 1 that one of the functions of law is to regulate relationships between individuals and between individuals and the state. Thus, there needs to be a degree of certainty not only about the principle but also as to how it will be applied in particular cases. This is part of the doctrine of 'legal certainty', which is a core requirement of the rule of law.[6] The natural consequence of legal certainty in the context of case law is that it provides a compelling argument for the *binding nature* of legal judgments. By this we mean that decisions taken should be binding on future courts.

5 As discussed in Chapter 1.

6 For a nuanced consideration of the principle of 'legal certainty' in English and Welsh law, see Lord Mance, 'Should the Law Be Certain?' (The Oxford Shrieval Lecture, 11 October 2011) <www.supremecourt.uk/docs/speech_111011.pdf>.

In this way, the doctrine of precedent should be treated with particular care. It is much more than just a set of technical rules that govern how judges arrive at outcomes. Precedent is achieving one of law's most fundamental purposes – giving people certainty as to their rights and obligations.

The corollary, and sometimes contrasting, principle that arises from legal certainty is that of *res judicata*.[7] This principle requires there to be a degree of *finality* to judicial decision-making and prevents parties, other than by appeal, from continuing to seek redress for the same issue within the courts. When all appeals have been exhausted, the decision, whatever its merits, is final as between the parties. This gives certainty on an individual level to the parties to a case.

In this way, precedent provides certainty in the law for *all*, and *res judicata* provides certainty to the parties in a given case.[8] The court in *Cassell*[9] put the matter rather well when holding that 'some degree of certainty is at least as valuable a part of justice as perfection'.

Precedent, and its attendant rules, allows the legal system to achieve a mix of certainty and flexibility. The certainty has been discussed previously but the flexibility is also important. There are conditions, that we will come to, that allow for the common law to evolve through the doctrine of precedent. Principles are set and followed but may also be *refined* over time by subtle judgments that distinguish themselves from one another, or more senior courts can overturn earlier precedents that are deemed inappropriate. In this way, precedent achieves a balance between *certainty, justice* and *progress*.

The language of this doctrine of precedent which exists in English and Welsh law is also known as *stare decisis*, which is Latin[10] for 'let it stand' (Latin having first been the language of English law in the early Middle Ages). More widespread use of Latin endured until the period of the Woolf Reforms (1995–1998) by which time English was officially promoted for use in court as part of an overall policy of simplification of court practice. One of the areas in which Latin has doggedly survived is in describing the doctrine of precedent.

In this way the principle of *stare decisis* is deceptively straightforward – decisions that resolve legal issues in particular cases will be binding on future courts when the same legal issue

7 Meaning that a decision, when taken, will be final.

8 Even if the principles of *res judicata* themselves are still the subject of litigation! Most recently in *Peter Farrar v Leongreen Limited* [2017] EWCA Civ 2211, [2018] 1 P&CR 17.

9 *Cassell v Broome* [1972] AC 1027 (HL) at 1054.

10 Books of Latin legal phrases were still being published at the turn of the 20th century – E Hilton Jackson, *Latin for Lawyers* (Sweet and Maxwell 1915).

arises. As will be clear as you read further, this is straightforward in principle, but much less so in its practical application.

TAKING THINGS FURTHER

The companion website that accompanies this textbook contains resources to help understand the structure of a case and guidance on how to analyse it.

PRACTICAL CONSIDERATIONS

With ready acceptance of the *concept* or *principle* of precedent, we turn now to some of the thornier practical and theoretical issues that flow from that principle. It is here that we start to come across some difficulties and challenges that need to be overcome in order to establish an effective and workable system of precedent.

THE REPORTING OF CASES

The first practical consideration is that if judgments are to be binding statements of principle, then those judgments that create or develop principles need to be available for reference by lawyers and citizens. This is not only a practical concern but a core aspect of the accessibility of the law under the principle of the rule of law.[11] What follows is a brief history of case reporting that is intended to explain why there are often numerous citations of cases and to explain why it is important to consider the 'most authoritative' case report in legal writing and research.

In the medieval times, collections of cases were gathered into 'year books' that were published at infrequent intervals. With the advent of the printing press, the 16th and 17th centuries saw a rise of commercially available 'law reports'. These were not governed by the court system or state and were a creation of (normally) high profile lawyers whose account of the case could be relied upon. The reliability and weight placed upon those reports by lawyers and the courts was largely dependent on the reputation of the lawyer involved and so these reports – known as nominate reports – would often carry the name of the Barrister (e.g. Burrow or Plowden Reports). These reports were not consistently formatted, nor were all cases of importance necessarily reported, and some were of questionable quality.[12] Newspapers took up the mantle in the mid-1800s with the advent of, amongst others, the *Law Times* reports. Again, the quality of these was variable in part because judges still gave judgment only orally, and so the accuracy could be difficult to monitor.

By 1865 there were a number of commercial law reports and commoditising the judgments of courts was seen to be problematic, particularly because of the risks of inaccuracy and

11 Sebastian Lewis, 'Precedent and the Rule of Law' 41(4) *Oxford Journal of Legal Studies* (2021) 873.

12 For example, the reporter Espinasse, of whom a judge said that he was not going to rely on the reports of Espinasse 'or any other ass'.

the infrequency of the publications. The solution was the creation of the not-for-profit[13] Incorporated Council of Law Reporting that would produce 'authorised' law reports – known as the Law Reports. These are considered the most authoritative reports of cases and *must* be cited in court if available[14] and will contain all cases that introduce or modify principles or which settle questions over uncertain areas of law. This may all seem rather technical and distant and may have a whiff of pedantry and awkwardness about it. However, the Court of Appeal issued a stern (and potentially costly) reminder to lawyers about the importance of adhering to the practice of citing the most authoritative case reports and expressed its 'deep regret' with non-compliance with the procedures on the presentation of authorities:[15]

> [J]udges of this court have limited time for pre-reading in advance of an appeal. Adherence to the practice directions means that that limited time can be more productively spent. Parties can expect that the cost of preparing a non-compliant bundle of authorities is at risk of being disallowed.

This makes clear that the judiciary may even penalise those who ignore the Practice Direction on the citation of authorities in the costs that they are able to recover!

Any selection of cases for publication involves a risk in that an important case may be overlooked but the alternative of publishing *every* judgment of the courts would be unsustainable. This means that any number of cases are not 'captured' within the official, authoritative Law Reports. Such cases, when cited, are denoted by 'unreported' after the party names. This sort of case may have come to notice through having been reported briefly in a monthly journal noting developments in the main fields of law (such as Current Law, which is bound and kept in that form in most practitioner and some academic libraries) or a specialist or general professional journal (such as *Solicitors' Journal, New Law Journal, Family Law*) or even an academic journal (such as *Law Quarterly Review, The Conveyancer*).

A diagram of the major series of the official Law Reports can be found in Figure 9.1.

In addition to the main series, the ICLR also publish several other (mostly specialist) series of reports that seek to gather together important judgments and may be cited where a Law Report version is unavailable – for example, the Weekly Law Reports (WLR),[16] the Business Law Reports and the Industrial Cases Reports (ICR).

13 On establishing the ICLR, the Bar Committee rejected the notion that the government should fund the publication of reports, and this remains true to this day. Unofficial but perfectly acceptable reports still exist today, with the All England Reports probably being the most significant, recording as they do cases from the Supreme Court, Court of Appeal and High Court.

14 Practice Direction (Citation of Authorities) [2012] 1 WLR 780.

15 *Parry v Keystone Healthcare* [2019] EWCA Civ 1246, [2019] 4 WLR 99 [26]–[27].

16 'The Weeklies' are an ICLR series of all but one WLR that go into the annual bound volumes cited in the normal way as [2019] AC etc.

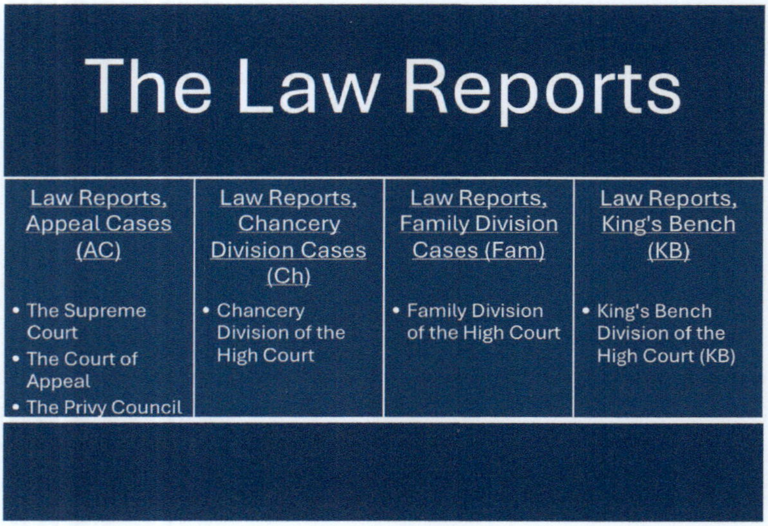

Figure 9.1 The Law Reports.

In 2001 the courts took a further step forward in terms of the accessibility of their judgments through the issuing of a Practice Direction on the use of 'neutral citation'.[17] This was a recognition of the increasing digitisation of both reports and judgments. Neutral citation involves identifying the judgment rather than a law report. Each judgment is coded according to the court and is then given a sequential number when it is handed down, and each paragraph of the judgment is also numbered. The format of such neutral citations is as follows:

> [YEAR] | COURT CODE | JUDGMENT NUMBER and, if relevant, [PARA NUMBER]

And so the fourth paragraph of the 1,246th case of the Civil Division of the Court of Appeal in 2019 would be as follows:

> [2019] EWCA Civ 1246 at [4]

TAKING THINGS FURTHER – DEVELOPING LEGAL WRITING SKILLS

Coming for the first time to these citations can be challenging. Over time these references to cases will become second nature. At the earlier states, they can be confusing and difficult to navigate. The companion website gives some examples of how to construct references to cases and some exercises to test your understanding of this important area of legal writing. As you read other texts, pay particular attention to the footnotes and consider how the author has constructed their reference and what it tells you about the authorities cited.

17 Practice Direction *Judgments: Form and Citation* [2001] 1 WLR 194.

The major developments in case reporting have been precipitated and encouraged by technological advances – the advent of the printing press and electronic case reports are just two examples. This process of technology influencing and driving forward the law and the processes of the legal system is apparent not only in this chapter but also elsewhere.

DISCERNING THE 'VALUE' OF JUDGMENTS

It should be clear from the study of the court structure in Chapter 8 that there are different levels of court – for example the inferior and senior courts – and it would not make sense for inferior courts to bind all courts in the system. This means that there need to be rules by which we establish the 'precedential value' of the different tiers of the court system and consider the extent to which those tiers are bound by their own judgments. Another practical consideration is the extent to which judgments from outside of the jurisdiction influence the judgment of an English or Welsh court. Both of these considerations are discussed in more detail in the following sections.

ESTABLISHING THE BINDING ELEMENT

As we shall shortly discover, not *all* aspects of a judgment are binding. The binding element is, in short, that principle which was necessary to resolve the legal issue. Unfortunately, judgments do not always make clear which parts are intended to be binding and, when multiple judges sit, the task of unearthing the binding element of the case can be challenging.

THE ELEMENTS OF A CASE

A judgment will contain a great number of 'statements'. Some of those statements will be elucidation of the facts, some will be points of new principle, some will be speculation about issues outside of the present dispute, some will be relevant only to the parties (such as cost orders) and some will be purely 'ornamentation'. Being able to identify the various central elements of a case is an essential legal skill.

THE MATERIAL FACTS

A judgment will include a summary of the facts – material or otherwise. The material facts are those that give rise to the question of principle that the court must resolve in order to settle a case. Whether a fact is 'material' will depend upon the principle in issue. Some facts are clearly just part of the parties' 'stories', and judges sometimes have the air of a frustrated author in how they articulate those facts. Most prominent amongst these was Lord Denning, who was known for his ability to bring to life the facts of cases, introducing one case about a traffic accident with the now-famous line 'It was bluebell time in Kent'[18] and, in another case, painted the scene of a village cricket pitch as the backdrop to a case about the law of nuisance:

18 *Hinz v Berry* [1970] 2 QB 40 (CA).

> In summertime village cricket is the delight of everyone. Nearly every village has its own cricket field where the young men play and the old men watch. In the village of Lintz in County Durham they have their own ground, where they have played these last seventy years. They tend it well. The wicket area is well rolled and mown. The outfield is kept short. It has a good club-house for the players and seats for the onlookers.[19]

RATIO DECIDENDI

A very large part of the study and practice of law is in the scouring of the case reports to separate the crucial, binding point of principle from 'the rest'. Or in convincing the court that a particular case raises *different* issues to that in the authority cited by the opposing side. Or in persuading the senior courts that they should reconsider and potentially overrule decided cases. In order to achieve *any* of these purposes, it is important to first be able to *discover* the principle that led to the court making a particular determination.

This is often referred to as the binding principle of the case. The use of the word 'binding' can be a little problematic when you take into account the nuances of other aspects of the case. The binding principle that leads to the resolution of the legal issue is called the *ratio decidendi*.[20] Lawyers often simply call this the '*ratio*'.

An example, although a difficult one, of this might be the famous case of *Donoghue v Stevenson*,[21] that of the decomposing snail found in a ginger beer bottle, which laid the foundations of the law of negligence and of the duty of care. The main issue in this case, which was decided on 26 May 1932, was whether the manufacturer of the drink within the bottle (along with the snail's remains) owed a duty of care in tort to the eventual consumer of the beverage, since the central issue was that a duty of care was owed to one's neighbour. There was a distinguished Bench including Lords Buckmaster and Atkin; the result of the judges' deliberations on the factual matrix and the evidence in support was that the manufacturer did owe a duty of care to anyone who came in contact with the contaminated drink as it was reasonably foreseeable that anyone might drink it and 'everyone' was that manufacturer's neighbour for this purpose, so such a duty is therefore owed in those circumstances. Therefore, such a product should be fit for its anticipated use. What was not clear from the case was the extent or scope of this 'neighbour' principle. It took subsequent cases to establish what was the *ratio* in *Donoghue* and what the limits of the concept of duty of care were. To demonstrate the other point made earlier in this chapter, *Donoghue* was a landmark case in itself, but it also led to further developments of the law of tort as it was refined and applied to new circumstances (where the material facts led to a dispute based on the same legal principles).[22]

19 *Miller v Jackson* [1977] QB 966 (CA) at 976.

20 The Latin roughly translates to 'reason for the decision'.

21 [1932] AC 562 (HL).

22 See *Hedley Byrne v Heller* [1964] AC 465 (HL) for an express acceptance that *Donoghue* was to be the first in a number of cases that would develop and extend the 'neighbour' principle.

TAKING THINGS FURTHER – IDENTIFYING THE RATIO

The case of *Youngsam*[23] (discussed later in relation to the power of the Supreme Court to depart from its own decisions) gives a sensible account of the nature of both *ratio* and *obiter*. It is worth reading this case in full, given that it is rare for the judiciary overtly to enter into an analysis of these terms that are so important to the doctrine of precedent.

OBITER DICTA

By way of contrast, the judge in any reported case may have said other things about other principles which were not central to the case or the decision, and these *cannot* form part of the *ratio decidendi*. Such statements are known instead as *obiter dicta*, which is Latin for 'things said by the way' or 'outside' the central issue. It is worth noting that even the judiciary acknowledge that the 'the border between the *ratio decidendi* of a case and judicial *obiter dicta* is not always easy to chart. . . . However, every judicial decision in relation to a given set of facts should (or ought to) have a *ratio*.'[24]

It may be tempting to dismiss the value of such *obiter*, but this would overlook the value that it can bring to the legal system. The most useful *obiter* can be split into three categories.

First, statements of law made during the course of a judgment that are not based on the material facts or are based on hypothetical situations. Denning's (J) judgment in *High Trees House*[25] is a famous example of the power of *obiter*. In this case, and speaking *obiter*, Denning postulated that on alternative facts the law would have *estopped* the behaviour of the respondents and this would have had the effect of re-animating the long-neglected doctrine of promissory estoppel. In later cases,[26] relying on Denning's persuasive reasoning (which was not, in any way, legally binding), the courts did, in fact, resurrect the principles of promissory estoppel. In this way, *obiter* in early cases can inform *ratio* in later case.

Second, statements of law that *are* based on the material facts of the case but which do not form the basis of the decision (for example a dissenting judgment).[27] These are equally useful because, as said elsewhere, the law is not static. Thus dissenting judgments can be useful in the future, should a court with the ability to overturn existing precedent wish to call upon the logic of those judges who earlier formed a minority.

23 *R (Youngsam) v The Parole Board* [2017] EWHC 729 (Admin), [2017] 1 WLR 2848.

24 *L, M and P v Devon County Council* [2021] EWCA Civ 358 [69].

25 *Central London Property Trust Ltd v High Trees House* [1947] KB 130 (KB).

26 *Total Metal Manufacturing v Tungsten* [1955] 1 WLR 761.

27 Judges in the legal system of England and Wales do not always agree within a case, which is why the most senior courts always have an odd number sitting on a case to ensure that an outcome can be reached. Those judgments in the majority form the binding legal precedent, whilst the comments of the minority (in dissent) do not form part of the binding aspects of the case.

Third, particular attention should be given to *obiter dicta* that comes from the most senior courts and especially the Supreme Court. The Supreme Court has little control over the cases that it hears and will be involved in only a very small proportion of the cases brought within the legal system. It's opportunity to shape the law is therefore constrained by its appellate and generalist characteristic. The cases it hears will all raise issues of significant legal importance, but those principles will need resolution within the facts of the case. This means that whilst the Supreme Court will have to resolve the dispute at hand, its Justices may wish to make broader observations on the law (by their very nature, *obiter*) that are meant to signal their individual or collective view on the law in a given area.

What we can conclude from the preceding is that the label *obiter dicta* is a broad one that is helpful to a degree but one which must be handled with caution. The future impact of *obiter dicta* and how it is treated in subsequent litigation will depend on a number of factors, including the stability of the law in a given area, the seniority of the judge or court making the decision and the degree to which the *dicta* in question was subject to detailed argument.

CONCLUDING THOUGHTS ON *RATIO* AND *OBITER*

Before turning to the hierarchy of courts and the precedents they set, it is worth reflecting on the relationship between *ratio* and *obiter*. The previous analysis is based on a fairly orthodox view of the doctrine of precedent. The challenge, according to that orthodoxy, is in discovering the *ratio* of a case. This is indeed challenging and will not only be the core of the dispute in a given case but is often also the source of legal analysis and academic dispute long after the case has been decided. Once the challenge of identifying the *ratio* is complete, then orthodox thinking draws bright lines between the 'binding' (*ratio*) and 'non-binding' (*obiter*) elements of the case. *Ratios* are binding on courts considering the same legal issue in the future (subject to the precedential hierarchy discussed later), and *obiter* is not.

This orthodox position is one that you will find in much legal writing and commentary on the doctrine of *stare decisis*. It does, however, neglect the evolving and dynamic nature of the 'rules' and principles of precedent and risks oversimplifying a complex relationship between *ratio* and *obiter*. The case of *Barton*[28] demonstrates the limits of the orthodox position and the flexibility of the common law. The Court of Appeal in this case had to rule upon whether statements made in *obiter* by the Supreme Court in the case of *Ivey*[29] bound them in *Barton*. Given the strength of the *obiter* and its unanimous acceptance in the Supreme Court case, the Court of Appeal felt formally bound to adopt it in resolving the case before it even though the statements of law were strictly *obiter*.

TAKING THINGS FURTHER

A more detailed account of *Barton* and its implications for the doctrine of precedent can be found in a blog post on the website that accompanies this text. This case is one of

28 *R v Barton* [2020] EWCA Crim 575.
29 *Ivey v Genting Casinos* [2017] UKSC 67.

a series that shows the orthodox view of what is 'binding' to be flawed and lacking the necessary nuance.

Whilst there are specific conditions – for example, the unanimity in the Supreme Court around the statements made in *obiter* – that apply in situations such as *Barton*, there is a broader point that is being made for the purposes of this text. *Precedent* is a creation of the common law and so will adapt and evolve to the changing needs of the legal system. The degree of flexibility and change is likely to remain at the margins of the doctrine because of the overriding need for legal certainty. Nonetheless, the ability for the doctrine to evolve is something often overlooked. Readers of and commentators on the law of *stare decisis* should keep this more sophisticated understanding at the front of their mind.

THE PRECEDENTIAL HIERARCHY

This, however, is not the end of the story as far as the use of such binding precedents are concerned. A decision which qualifies for the doctrine of *stare decisis* must also fit within the hierarchy of courts which must (or need not) accept the decision as binding on them. The basic principle in relation to this issue is that all courts below that in which the decision was made are bound and must follow the decision made in the relevant case, whereas those above do not have to and, in any case, may overrule it in a later case. Within this hierarchy, not all courts are capable of setting binding precedent.

Thus, a decision made in the Court of Appeal is binding on all lower courts except the Supreme Court; however, it is also binding on the Court of Appeal itself, subject to some exceptions (see later in this chapter). Depending on the nature of the case and composition of the Court of Appeal, the Supreme Court might also find such a Court of Appeal judgment 'persuasive'. The following table lays out the formal hierarchy of courts in the English and Welsh legal system. What follows after is an account of the specific rules that apply to each court.

Table 9.1 gives some indication of the various courts and their relationships.

THE SUPREME COURT

It will be remembered that the Supreme Court (formerly the House of Lords) is the highest appellate court in the legal system of England and Wales. It ought to be no surprise that its decisions are binding on all courts that are, necessarily, lower than it in the hierarchy. It also has the power to overrule decisions made by courts lower in the hierarchy.

Traditionally the House of Lords decisions were even binding on itself, with an inability to be able to overturn its own earlier judgments. This was made clear in the *London Tramways*[30] case,

30 *London Street Tramways v London County Council* [1898] AC 375 (HL).

Table 9.1 The precedential hierarchy

Court	*Bound by others*	*Self-binding*	*Binds others*
Supreme Court (SC)	No	Yes – subject to Practice Direction of 1966	All other courts
Court of Appeal (Civil) (CA)	SC	Yes – subject to the *Young* criteria	HC; CC; inferior courts
Court of Appeal (Crim) (CA)	SC	Yes – subject to the *Young* criteria and an exception where individual liberty is at stake	HC; CC; inferior courts
High Court (HC) – Appellate Jurisdiction	SC; CA	Yes – subject to the *Young* criteria and an exception when considering criminal cases where individual liberty is at stake	CC; inferior courts
High Court (HC) – Supervisory Jurisdiction	SC; CA	No	Inferior courts
High Court (HC) – First Instance Jurisdiction	SC; CA; HC – Divisional Courts	No	Inferior courts
The Crown Court	SC; CA; HC;	No	No
The Inferior Courts	All other courts	No	No

where the House of Lords unanimously declined to overturn its own previous decision on the basis that to do so would lead to

> the disastrous inconvenience – of having each question subject to being reargued and the dealings of mankind rendered doubtful by reason of different decisions, so that in truth and in fact there would be no real final Court of Appeal.[31]

Essentially this was an argument based on legal certainty and *res judicata*, the principle that at some point there should be a final and definitive ruling on an issue.

31 ibid 379.

The present situation, since 1966, has been a complete change of heart in that the House of Lords (and now the Supreme Court) *can* overrule its own decisions. This principle is articulated in a Practice Direction.[32] It is interesting that the House of Lords chose to make this statement and change the rules of precedent in a practice direction, rather than taking the opportunity of stating this change of approach in a case. This only goes to underscore the need to maintain legal certainty in this area and to demonstrate that this was a deliberate and significant change not motivated by argument in a given case.

The Supreme Court, having taken over seamlessly from the House of Lords as the final appellate court of the United Kingdom, has not thought it necessary to re-issue the 1966 Practice Statement.[33] This means that the Supreme Court can depart from its own previous decisions when necessary, on the same basis as the 1966 Direction.

The 1966 statement referred to the fundamental value of precedent to developing legal certainty and providing 'at least some degree of certainty' for individuals.[34] Against this the Law Lords had weighed the injustice that can be caused by an overly rigid adherence to the rules of precedent.

The power to overrule its own judgments is used sparingly and, normally, with express reference to the balancing exercise within the Direction. Perhaps its most famous use was in its *Shivpuri*[35] case on the potential criminal liability for attempting to commit a crime that was, in fact, impossible to commit where it overruled its judgment in *Anderton*[36] from the previous year.

The use of the 1966 Direction is also more likely to be used in relation to questions around the application of the common law than in terms of construction or interpretation of a particular statute.[37]

Nonetheless, there are more recent examples that demonstrate the genuine balancing that needs to happen before the Supreme Court should depart from one of its previous rulings. In *Knauer*,[38] the Supreme Court – without criticising – found the reasoning in two House of Lords cases to be flawed, but this, of itself, did not persuade the judges to invoke the 1966 Practice Statement, something that the justices held should be very 'circumspect'[39] in doing. The Court relied on three factors in coming to its decision to depart from its own prior judgments in this case:

---

32 Practice Direction *Judicial Precedent* [1966] 1 WLR 1234.

33 And has judicially made reference to the fact that the Court will continue to rely upon the Direction, which is 'part of the established jurisprudence relating to the conduct of appeals'; *Austin v Mayor and Burgesses of the London Borough of Southwark* [2010] UKSC 28, [2011] 1 AC 355 at [24].

34 Practice Direction *Judicial Precedent* [1966] 1 WLR 1234.

35 *R v Shivpuri* [1987] AC 1 (HL).

36 *Anderton v Ryan* [1985] AC 560 (HL).

37 *R v National Insurance Commissioner, Ex parte Hudson* [1972] AC 944 (HL) 966.

38 *Knauer v Ministry of Justice* [2016] UKSC 9, [2016] AC 908.

39 ibid [23].

1. The prior judgments were illogical and causing unfairness.
2. The lower courts were avoiding the effects of then judgments through artificial use of 'distinguishing', which meant that legal certainty was already being undermined; thus, the advantages of precedent in this case were already being eroded.
3. There had 'been a material change in the relevant legal landscape since the earlier decisions'.[40]

Despite the passage of time, there is still development of the principles of application of the Practice Direction, as can be seen in *Youngsam*.[41]

ANALYSING THE LAW – OVERRULING THROUGH *OBITER*

In *Youngsam,* the High Court was faced with a novel and thorny question – could the Supreme Court overrule its own previous decisions by comments made *obiter* and without express reference to the Practice Direction? The instinctive answer may be that this ought not to be possible because *obiter* is not part of the binding *ratio* of the case.

The question arose because of the Supreme Court's ruling in *Whiston,*[42] where members of the Court had made statements about how the case would have been resolved in other circumstances. On one reading, the *obiter* would have supported the departure from a previous decision of the House of Lords in *West.*[43] The High Court in *Youngsam* undertook a detailed analysis of the Practice Direction and noted a number of things.

First, that the text itself does not say that departure can only happen when the Practice Direction is 'invoked' expressly. Second, it does not require that departure is based on unanimous agreement of the Justices. Third, it does not require that the *ratio* in the case in which the Practice Direction is operative to be the same as the *ratio* in the case seeking to depart – that is, the power to overrule can be exercised through *obiter.*

The position was helpfully summarised as follows:

> Where a majority of the Justices have in the clearest possible terms decided that one or more of its previous decisions are not to be followed then it is not for this court to seek to emasculate the later decision by reanalysing the earlier case law and reaching a contrary view.[44]

40 ibid.

41 R (Youngsam) v The Parole Board [2017] EWHC 729 (Admin) [2017] 1 WLR 2848.

42 R (Whiston) v Secretary of State for Justice [2014] UKSC 39, [2015] AC 176.

43 R (West) v Parole Board [2005] UKHL 1, [2005] 1 WLR 350.

44 R (Youngsam) v The Parole Board [2017] EWHC 729 (Admin) [2017] 1 WLR 2848 [39].

The Supreme Court as recently as 2023 demonstrated that it is not enough to demonstrate that a previous judgment was merely incorrect to invoke the use of the Practice Direction.[45] It takes an undefined further quality – such as the authority is preventing the proper development of the law, or that it is contrary to public policy – before the Court will use it.

THE SENIOR COURTS

The senior courts are all bound by the judgments of the Supreme Court and their effect amongst themselves varies.

COURT OF APPEAL (CIVIL DIVISION)

The Court of Appeal's decisions bind all inferior courts, and the Court is bound by its own decisions, unless some exception applies to this 'self-binding' rule. The case of *Young v Bristol Aeroplane Co Ltd*[46] lays out the exceptions, but they are fairly narrowly understood. The exceptions are:

1. Where previous Court of Appeal decisions conflict with each other, when they usually follow the latest but need not do so.[47]
2. Where a previous Court of Appeal decision – that has not been formally overruled – conflicts with a later decision of the House of Lords or Supreme Court, when it must follow the superior court's decision even if it believes it to be wrong!
3. Where a previous CA decision appears to have been made *per incuriam*.[48] In 1985, *in Williams v Fawcett*,[49] the Court attempted to get the traditionally accepted *per incuriam* rule extended (as it was, at that stage, quite narrow) so as to give themselves a better chance to correct the error, which Sir John Donaldson, in that case, considered 'a manifest slip or error'.

This list is the most commonly used of the 'exceptions' to the self-binding rule but there are others, including the fact that the Court of Appeal may be free of the rules of precedent if the earlier judgment is incompatible with EU law. What is clear is that there is no *generalised* power for the Court of Appeal to depart from its own previous judgment.

Following the introduction of the Practice Statement of 1966, in relation to the House of Lords power to depart from its own judgments, Lord Denning as Master of the Rolls attempted to extend this power to the Supreme Court. At first, this did not find favour amongst his contemporaries in the Court of Appeal, with them rejecting the extension and saying that Denning had 'sought to wield a broom labelled "For the use of the House of Lords only"'.[50] Eventually, Denning did find support from within the Court of Appeal, but the House of Lords itself was quick to quash the attempt to establish such a power. In rejecting Denning's

45 See *Jti Polska v Jakubowski* [2023] UKSC 19 at para [40]–[44] for a case that declined to use the Practice Direction.

46 *Young v Bristol Aeroplane Co Ltd* [1944] KB 718, [1944] 2 All ER 293 (CA) per Lord Greene MR.

47 *Great Peace Shipping v Tsavliris Salvage* [2002] EWCA Civ 1407, [2002] 4 All ER 689.

48 As discussed previously.

49 [1986] QB 604 (CA) Donaldson MR.

50 *Gallie v Lee* [1969] 2 Ch 17 (CA) 41.

approach, the House of Lords affirmed 'expressly, unequivocably and unanimously that the rule laid down in the [*Bristol Aeroplane Case*] as to *stare decisis* is still binding on the Court of Appeal'.[51]

The reasons for keeping the self-binding rule (with limited exceptions) are clear. The need for legal certainty is paramount. And, in contrast with the Supreme Court, it is possible to appeal and put right errors in that way. Also, the number of judges and sittings within the Court of Appeal is very different to that of the Supreme Court, and there is a greater risk to certainty as a result of any exception.

COURT OF APPEAL (CRIMINAL DIVISION)

In theory, the two divisions operate the same system, but in fact, the self-binding rule works in a slightly different and more flexible way in the Criminal Division. This has come about through two causes: (1) case law and (2) the impact of the liberty of the subject being at stake in criminal appeals, thought to be more important than rigid consistency. This leads to a slightly different view being taken of precedent because of the danger of a wrongful conviction going unaddressed. Lord Woolf also contributed to this debate in *R v Simpson*[52] when he suggested that the Criminal Division had a residual discretion to treat one of its previous decisions as not binding when there were grounds to consider the decision was wrong, pointing out that a wrong decision in such a case could do much more harm than a wrong decision in the Civil Division. Considering the decisions that have turned out to be wrong in recent years, this seems to be a very sensible approach; see, for example, *R v Derek William Bentley (Deceased)*[53] *per* Lord Bingham of Cornhill.

HIGH COURT (APPELLATE AND FIRST INSTANCE JURISDICTION)

The lowest court which creates a precedent potentially binding is the High Court and its Divisional Courts. Precedents are only a small proportion of all the cases decided in any year, and those which are potentially precedents are usually found to come from the High Court, Court of Appeal and Supreme Court.

The High Court is bound by courts superior to it in the hierarchy, that is, the Supreme Court, the House of Lords and the Court of Appeal, but is not bound by its own previous decisions. However, the Divisional Courts of the KBD, including the powerful Administrative Court, is bound by its own decisions, unless a *Young v Bristol Aeroplane Co* exception applies to them.

When the Administrative Court is considering criminal cases there may be more flexibility by analogy with the Criminal Division of the Court of Appeal.

THE CROWN COURT

This court, being a national criminal court, is bound by decisions of superior courts. However, as it is a national court sitting regionally, there are other judges of this court who are making

51 *Davis v Johnson* [1979] AC 264 (HL).

52 [2003] EWCA Crim 1499, [2004] QB 118, per Woolf CJ.

53 [1998] 1 Cr App 21 (CA).

decisions in parallel, and so decisions are persuasive but not binding authority as between the various courts sitting as Crown Courts around the country.

THE INFERIOR COURTS

These courts – including the County Court and Magistrates' Court – are bound by all superior court decisions but their own decisions bind no one, not even other courts at the same level in the hierarchy.

THE EUROPEAN COURTS

Having considered the precedential hierarchy in the legal system of England and Wales, it is important to point to the influence of the European courts – particularly the Court of Justice of the European Union and the European Court of Human Rights – on the domestic principles of precedent.

Each has traditionally exerted a significant influence over the rulings of English and Welsh courts and has had a disruptive effect on the orthodox rules of precedent. As the UK has now left the EU, the influence of the CJEU will continue to evolve, diminish and change over time.

As you read the next two sections consider how the legal system has evolved to incorporate judgments of courts that sit slightly outside of the formal court hierarchy. Consider the challenges, to consistency, certainty and legitimacy, caused by the accommodation of judgments of these courts into domestic law and practice. Also consider the potential advantages of accommodating different systems in this way and what it says about the potential flexibility and adaptability of the legal system of England and Wales.

COURT OF JUSTICE OF THE EUROPEAN UNION (CJEU)

As between the Court of Justice of the European Union and the European Court of Human Rights, arguably the former has had the most dramatic impact on the system of precedent in the legal system of England and Wales. Whilst this was certainly the case during the UK's membership of the EU, it is still true since the UK's departure. Its own prior decisions do not bind the CJEU, but it is rare for the court to depart from its own case law. In this way there is a type of *jus commune* (or common law) precedent within the European Union. Its judgments were, during the UK's membership of the EU, thought to be binding on all domestic courts. Membership of the EU also meant that courts lower in the hierarchy discussed previously could potentially disapply the decision of a higher court (including the Supreme Court) if it conflicted with EU law.[54] This was a rather remarkable power and one that risked upsetting orthodox understanding of the doctrine and rules of precedent. With the UK now having now left the European Union, the situation has changed in some significant ways.

Most courts in England and Wales will continue to be bound in perpetuity by decisions of the CJEU given before the end of the transition period (31 December 2020) by virtue of the European Union (Withdrawal) Act 2018.

54 *Ivnov Elchinov* [2010] ECR I-8889.

The Supreme Court is not bound and is able to depart from CJEU judgments on the same terms as it can currently depart from its own judgments (i.e. through the use of the principles established by the 1966 Practice Direction).[55] At the time of the passage of the EU Withdrawal Act, it was only the Supreme Court that had such power. Following a consultation, the possibility of extending this power was inserted into the Act and can be brought into force by virtue of secondary legislation. Such secondary legislation has been enacted and (most notably), the Court of Appeal can now also depart from CJEU judgments on the same terms as the Supreme Court.[56]

The Court of Appeal had opportunity to consider this newfound power in *TuneIn*,[57] where the judgment articulated the factors to be taken into account, including whether there had been changes to the domestic or legal framework since departure from the EU. Ultimately, it felt that there were no compelling reasons to depart from the retained EU case law in that case. In a further case, *Industrial Cleaning Equipment*,[58] the Court of Appeal first used this newfound power in a dispute involving the law of trademarks.

At the time of writing the Supreme Court has not made use of the powers under the 2018 Act to depart from CJEU judgments. However, in rather powerful *obiter*, the court has made clear that these powers will apply not only to cases involving events *after* the transition period but could and should apply to events that happened *before* the end of the transition period.[59] This is a significant extension of what was widely understood to be the situation and gives much greater flexibility to the Supreme Court and Court of Appeal.

Judgments handed down after the end of the transition period are not binding at all on any part of the hierarchy but courts, according to s6(1) of the European Union (Withdrawal Act) 2018, may 'have regard' to them. In this way, they will form non-binding, or persuasive, precedent into the future.

As can be seen from this relatively short section, the untangling of the relationship between the UK and EU is complex and will continue to evolve over time.

DECISIONS OF THE EUROPEAN COURT OF HUMAN RIGHTS

Having considered the relationship between the CJEU and domestic courts, it would be sensible to briefly consider the impact that the European Court of Human Rights has on the domestic system of precedent.

The ECrtHR is a body of the Council of Europe, and it has responsibility for the interpretation of the European Convention on Human Rights. That Convention is incorporated into the law of England and Wales by the Human Rights Act 1998. The Convention is binding on its contracting parties, and the Human Rights Act 1998 was a pivotal piece of Labour legislation

55 European Union (Withdrawal) Act 2018 s6(4)(a).

56 The European Union (Withdrawal) Act 2018 (Relevant Court) (Retained EU Case Law) Regulations 2020, SI 2020/1525, Reg 3.

57 *TuneIn v Warner Music UK Ltd* [2021] EWCA Civ 441.

58 *Industrial Cleaning Equipment v Intelligent Cleaning Equipment & Another* [2023] EWCA Civ 1451.

59 *Lipton v BA Cityflyer* [2024] UKSC 24.

intended to bring the rights closer to individuals and allow them to enforce those rights in UK courts. Two sections of the Human Rights Act 1998 have an impact on our understanding of the doctrine of precedent: s2, regarding the interpretation of the Convention Rights, and s3, concerning interpretation of domestic legislation.

THE HUMAN RIGHTS ACT 1998: SECTION 2(1)

s2(1) requires that 'a court or tribunal **must** take into account' judgments, decisions, declarations or advisory opinions of the European Court of Human Rights (ECtHR). In this sense, Parliament has given, through the words it has chosen, a relatively clear instruction to courts. Case law of the ECtHR should be considered when determining the interpretation of Convention rights, but they are not to be taken as binding. For this reason, they will form the role of a non-binding or persuasive sort of precedent. This seems a compromise between allowing domestic courts to operate according to their own rules and hierarchy whilst also limiting divergence amongst the contracting members. From a pragmatic perspective, there is also a heightened risk that the UK would eventually lose in increasing numbers of cases before the Strasbourg court if the judiciary were not taking into account relevant cases law.

We might anticipate that as a result of s2, courts in England and Wales would typically follow and be persuaded by the judgments of the ECrtHR, but that this would not be universally so. The position the English and Welsh courts themselves adopt is pragmatic and sensible and best encapsulated by a judgment given by Lord Neuberger in *Pinnock*[60] at [48]:

> This court is not bound to follow every decision of the European court. Not only would it be impractical to do so: it would sometimes be inappropriate, as it would destroy the ability of the court to engage in the constructive dialogue with the European court which is of value to the development of Convention law. Of course, we should usually follow a clear and constant line of decisions by the European court. But we are not actually bound to do so or (in theory, at least) to follow a decision of the Grand Chamber.

Lord Neuberger cites *Horncastle*[61] as a notable example of when the courts of England and Wales declined to follow the jurisprudence of the ECtHR. The ability of the domestic courts to take a different path than the European court is useful as a check on the development of European human rights norms and allows for a more local and contextual development.

THE HUMAN RIGHTS ACT 1998: SECTION 3

The second influence on precedent stemming from the Human Rights Act 1998 comes in the form of s3. This is an instruction from Parliament as to how courts ought to interpret domestic legislation when cases raise issues relating Convention rights. S3(1) reads as follows:

> So far as it is possible to do so, primary legislation and subordinate legislation must be read and given effect in a way which is compatible with the Convention rights.

60 *Manchester City Council v Pinnck* [2010] UKSC 45, [2011] 2 AC 104.

61 *R v Horncastle* [2009] UKSC 14.

This makes clear that courts are intended to provide domestic law with a conforming interpretation with Convention rights *as far as it is possible* to do so.

STATUTORY INTERPRETATION

Although we are discussing precedent in the present chapter, it is important to consider the impact and influence of s3 on the process of statutory interpretation. S3 adds a further device in the judicial toolbox of interpretation. It also demonstrates the link between the twin pillars of the judicial legal order – statutory interpretation and judicial precedent.

By placing a strong conforming interpretative duty on the domestic courts, s3 has the potential to disrupt the precedential hierarchy. This is the case where previous case law, perhaps decided before the coming into force of the Human Rights Act 1998, has historically interpreted legislation in a way that is not in conformity with Convention rights. S3 would potentially give courts a wide-ranging power to disapply that former interpretation and apply a new and conforming interpretation.

MECHANISMS FOR AVOIDING OR CORRECTING PRECEDENT

Precedent is about providing legal certainty for settled principles of law. It allows individuals and their legal representatives to understand how cases raising similar issues will be decided. However, there are still times when the law and its legal principles need flexibility to be able to develop. This tension between certainty and flexibility is at the core of an adversarial common law legal system. There may be arguments as to the applicability of a certain decided case to new facts or fresh legal arguments as to the 'correctness' of a prior decision. It may be that counsel have very different interpretations of the outcomes in a legal case. These are the types of issues that are debated in the courts daily. For this reason, there may be sound justification for not wishing to follow a specific decision which would be otherwise binding on the court in question.

In these circumstances there are four possible ways of achieving this: distinguishing the precedent on the facts, so it does not apply; reversing of the decision by a higher court in the same litigation; declaring that the decision was made *per incuriam*; or overruling by a higher court in a later case involving a different legal dispute.

DISTINGUISHING

In the adversarial system that is in operation in England and Wales, opposing legal representatives will provide to the court their 'skeleton argument', including a list of authorities upon which they will seek to rely. It could be that it would be fatal to one side's case if the court accepted the reading of the law put forward by the opposing side. For this reason an advocate may wish to argue that the precedent does not apply.

One way of achieving this is by arguing that the present case should be 'distinguished' from the authority in question. This involves persuading the judge that *the material facts* of the instant case are different from those of the precedent to the extent that the same legal issue does not apply or that the legal issue ought to be resolved differently.

This must, of course, be done with care as there is a duty on an advocate not to mislead the court, and even if the judge accepts the advocate's argument, the ultimate decision might still be reversed on appeal. If the judge successfully accepts the distinguishing arguments, then the judge will be developing the law in deciding that that precedent does not apply in the circumstances of the case before the court on that occasion.

REVERSING

This will only occur if there is a successful appeal against the applicability of the precedent at an earlier hearing on the basis of *the law*, for example, the Court of Appeal's decision is reversed by the Supreme Court because the precedent should not have been applied. Reversing therefore happens *within* the history of a single case and prevents the lower court's error from becoming part of binding precedent in the future.

OVERRULING

This occurs when the Court of Appeal or Supreme Court finds that an earlier case was wrongly decided. The most famous case of this type is probably the 1992 attempted marital rape and assault prosecution of *R v R (Marital Exemption)*.[62] The appeal arose because there was a long-standing principle of English and Welsh law that a husband could not be guilty of raping his wife since, on marriage, she had irrevocably consented to sexual intercourse with the husband. In this case the parties had separated, and the wife was living with her parents. The husband nevertheless took an opportunity to attempt to have intercourse with her against her will and was charged with attempted rape. His defence relied on Sir Matthew Hale's *Pleas of the Crown* (1736), which stated that 'the husband cannot be guilty of rape committed by himself upon his lawful wife, for by their mutual matrimonial consent and contract the wife has given herself up to him in this kind unto her husband which she cannot retract'. The husband was convicted and appealed on the basis that, as he could not be convicted of rape, he could not be convicted of the attempt either.

The House of Lords unanimously rejected his defence, overruling the previous common law, in a decision of Lord Keith of the Kinkel, to the effect that Hale might have been right about the state of the common law in 1736 but that, in 1992, this could no longer be claimed, owing to the change in the nature of marriage (in 1992, a partnership of equals, with remedies available for ill treatment of the wife being no longer a subservient partner, or as Lord Keith stated, 'a chattel'). This was really inevitable in view of the changes that

62 [1992] 1 AC 599 (HL).

had taken place in divorce law[63] and in generally understood developments in the law around equality,[64] and despite the long standing nature of the common law principle Hale referred to, which was itself based in a long past concept of matrimony which, by 1992, was no longer rooted in religion or the practices of the Church in relation to matrimony and its dissolution.

It is more common for the Supreme Court to overrule the decision of a lower court than to reconsider its own earlier cases,[65] but there are recent examples of the Supreme Court overruling its own precedents.[66]

PER INCURIAM

This is a somewhat limited form for avoiding what would otherwise be a binding precedent. It can only be used where it can be demonstrated that the previous case was decided without reference to a statutory provision or other case that would have changed the outcome. To put it differently, and to use the meaning of *per incuriam*, that the case was decided carelessly or in ignorance of relevant authority. The Court of Appeal described *per incuriam* as those

> decisions given in ignorance or forgetfulness of some inconsistent statutory provision or of some authority binding on the court concerned: so that in such cases some part of the decision or some step in the reasoning on which it is based is found, on that account, to be demonstrably wrong.[67]

Given the quality of advocates and the judiciary in the senior courts, such occurrences ought to be rare and exceptional. Indeed, although this method of avoiding precedent is frequently pleaded, it is rarely successful. A recent example of an unsuccessful attempt at a *per incuriam* argument can be found from the Supreme Court.[68]

PERSUASIVE OR NON-BINDING PRECEDENT

The term used to describe this section is a little challenging as, by its very nature, *precedent* is binding. What we mean by *'non-binding' precedent* is sources that may be persuasive to courts considering legal issues. These persuasive precedents can take very many forms, and those described later are not intended to be exhaustive.

63 Divorce Reform Act 1969, Matrimonial Causes Act 1973.

64 Equal Pay Act 1970, Race Relations Act 1976.

65 The circumstances in which the Supreme Court is able to depart from its own judgments are dictated by the Practice Statement, *House of Lords: Judicial Precedent* [1966] 1 WLR 1234 and is discussed earlier in greater detail.

66 See, for example, *Knauer v Ministry of Justice* [2016] UKSC 9, [2016] AC 908, where the court overruled its previous decisions in *Cookson v Knowles* [1979] AC 556 (HL) and *Graham v Dodds* [1983] 1 WLR 808 (HL).

67 *Morelle v Wakeling* [1955] 2 QB 379 (CA).

68 See *QX v Secretary of State for the Home Department* [2024] UKSC 26.

RATIO OF A COURT LOWER IN THE HIERARCHY

A court in the lower ranks of the judicial hierarchy must be the first to decide new principles of law. Such cases start often in the High Court or Crown Court. If these cases raise new and interesting points of law, then judges in those cases will need to come to a view as to the correct legal principle to be applied or the case could not be resolved. In doing so, they will adopt a particular *ratio*. It may be that this aspect of the case is or is not appealed. Judges deciding the same point of principle (either in that particular case or another) in a higher court would not be bound by the rules of precedent to apply that *ratio* due to their superior position in the precedential hierarchy. Nonetheless, it may be that the superior court is fully convinced by the *ratio* of the lower court and choose to adopt it themselves.

In this way, the well-reasoned judgments of lower courts may inform and persuade the reasoning of higher courts and so can act as an important persuasive form of precedent.

DISSENTING JUDGMENTS IN PREVIOUS CASES

At certain levels of the court system, judges sit in panels of different numbers ranging from the typical 3 panel bench to the Supreme Court, which can sit with 11 of the 12 justices on a case. Where panels are used, it is possible for *each* judge to give their own judgment on how the case should be resolved. Whilst it is typical for one judge to give a leading judgment with the rest simply agreeing, this is not universally true. This is in contrast to very many other legal systems where judges who sit in panels are required to come to a single, agreed judgment.

Judges in England and Wales, sitting on the same case may disagree on the outcome of the case or the reasoning leading to the outcome of a case. Where they disagree with the outcome of the case and apply a different legal principle in doing so, this is known as a 'dissenting' judgment. These are, of course, not binding as they do not form the legal basis for how the case was resolved and so can be described only as 'persuasive'. They are things said *obiter dictum*. Nonetheless, it may be that, in time, understanding of the law changes and senior courts become convinced of the logic that was once found in dissenting judgments and overrule the majority view.

MINORITY JUDGMENTS IN PREVIOUS CASES

If a judge on a panel would agree with outcome of a case proposed by the majority but would do so for different reasons, they would be described as providing a 'minority' judgment. In much the same way as dissenting judgments, such minority judgments are not 'binding' as they do not contain the *ratio* that helped dispose of the case. Again, these would be comments made *obiter dictum*. They can, however, be put forward as persuasive precedent that may convince a superior court in the hierarchy to depart from the majority view.

DECISIONS OF COURTS OUTSIDE OF ENGLAND AND WALES

Clearly courts that sit outside of the legal system cannot produce judgments that are binding on the courts of England and Wales. This is manifestly sensible and to be expected. However, courts all around the world are dealing and grappling with similar legal issues. There are also systems, such as those in Australia or Canada or New Zealand, that adopt a common law approach influenced by and developed from the common law tradition of England and Wales. For this reason, it may be that English and Welsh judges find it helpful to see how other jurisdictions have dealt with complex legal problems. In this way, the judgments of courts outside of the English and Welsh legal system can provide persuasive authority for how the law should be developed.

Slightly more complicated is the position of the Judicial Committee of the Privy Council. This is the highest court for some Commonwealth countries, the British Overseas Territories and the Crown Dependencies. It sits in mixed panels of members of the UK Supreme Court and senior members of the judiciary from the relevant country from which a dispute has arisen. Generally speaking, its judgments are only persuasive for the purposes of English and Welsh law, but the presence of serving members of the Supreme Court adds additional weight to that persuasive function. It should be noted that there are *certain limited circumstances* when the judgments of the Privy Council can be seen as binding within England and Wales, but *generally* speaking, they provide persuasive precedent only.[69]

ACADEMIC THINKING AND LAW REFORM

The views of academic and distinguished practitioner writers can be influential on judicial thinking, as can speeches given by judges but not in a judicial capacity. As such writing is not made in the context or hearing of a particular case, it cannot be regarded as binding. The orthodox position has been to consider the comments of jurists and academic writers very rarely,[70] but there is increasing reference to the viewpoints of academic in understanding criticism of the law and alternative views on how the law should be developed.

Equally, the views taken by law reform bodies (such as the Law Commission) can act as a form of persuasive precedent in helping judges to resolve cases.

FINAL THOUGHT

The preceding demonstrates that outside of the framework established for dealing with the binding rules of precedent, judges have a variety of tools available to inform their decision-making. These will be used in different cases in different ways and there is no form of hierarchy of these forms of persuasive precedent. To put this differently, the extent of *how* persuasive something is will vary considerably. In broad terms, points found in minority arguments that had been fully argued in the case may be more persuasive than points that had not been argued at all. Equally, the comments made by a Supreme Court Justice in a dissenting judgment may be more persuasive than comments made by a judge lower down in the judicial hierarchy.

69 See *R v James* [2006] EWCA Crim 14, [2006] QB 588 at [43] for an explanation of the highly unusual situation of when the judgments of the Privy Council may be seen to be binding.

70 See The Hon Mr Justice Beatson, Inner Temple Reader's Lecture Series, 'Legal Academics: Forgotten Players or Interlopers', 12 November 2012, in the series 'Academics and Practitioners: Friends or Foes' <www.judiciary.uk/wp-content/uploads/JCO/Documents/Speeches/justice-beatson-inner-temple-lecture-12112012.pdf>, in which he explains that while the work of jurists has always been a source of law, in civil law systems they have, when still living, in the past been regarded as *not* such an appropriate source in English and Welsh law until relatively recently, prior to which the rule was 'better read when dead'!

CONCLUSION

Beyond the text and graphics of this chapter, it is important to note some of the broader themes that arise out of the essential information set out.

First, the framework of the application of the doctrine of precedent is not exclusively either civil or criminal, and there are variations in how the doctrine applies in the different courts in the civil and criminal systems. There is a particular form of flexibility encouraged by some leading judges in criminal cases where the liberty of the subject is at stake. This also seems to be some explanation for the flexibility that has occurred in relation to the hierarchy of courts where human rights are involved. This demonstrates that courts are often dealing with competing principles – in this instance, of providing legal certainty against ensuring justice for individuals whose liberty may be in jeopardy.

Secondly, despite the framework of the specialist divisions of the High Court, at Court of Appeal level and above in the Supreme Court, our top judiciary are generalists rather than narrow specialists, steeped in the general principles of English and Welsh law and of the application of it in our unique ways of statutory interpretation and application of judicial precedent. This is regularly made clear when it is evident from reports of decided cases that whatever their previous background in practice and on the Bench, the Lords Justices of the Court of Appeal and the judiciary of the Supreme Court are expected to sit on both civil and criminal appeals in accordance with the demands of the service.

Thirdly, and most importantly, you should recognise that whilst many present the rules of precedent as inflexible with stark, bright lines between *ratio* and *obiter*, this is overly simplistic. Many of those lines only find their brightness in retrospect (i.e. after a case has been decided). The job of an advocate is to persuade and convince judges that their line of argument is the correct one and that a particular precedent should or should not apply. In this way, the rules are dynamic tools for understanding the disputes before our courts and for resolving them. Equally, the rules themselves are not cast in stone in the manner presented by many legal commentators. The 'rules' of precedent are creatures of the common law and have shown a subtle ability to evolve and develop as needed by the judiciary.

THE WEBSITE

The website that accompanies this textbook contains many useful resources that you can use to consolidate and further your knowledge of the law, to hone your skills of critical analysis and to test your knowledge. This includes a set of multiple-choice questions (MCQs) that can be used to test your knowledge and understanding of the material.

10

CHAPTER 10
CIVIL JUSTICE

INTRODUCTION

Early in your legal studies, you will start to read about a number of cases decided by judges in the civil court system. It is the civil courts that deal with disputes in areas of law dealing with the rights and obligations which individuals, and businesses, owe to each other in areas such as contract, tort, family and company law. Thus, civil cases happen as between private parties disputing their legal rights and obligations. This is in sharp contrast to criminal cases where the state is prosecuting an individual for a criminal offence. It is in the operation of these two justice systems that we see the administration of justice most clearly.

Where an individual or business believes that one or more of its legal rights has been affected, there is usually a desire to enforce those rights in the civil courts. Once a successful court suit has concluded, the court staff, including judges, generally does not take any action without prompting by one of the parties, so many people still see more court action as the way forward, but in recent times, there has been much more emphasis on out-of-court settlement, which can still be enforced through the courts if necessary as a legally binding agreement.

The purpose of this chapter is to provide an understanding of the steps that a party has to take to ensure that it wins its claim at court. This process has developed over many years. The courts have to deal with a wide range of claims, broadly applying the same steps and requirements about the format of evidence whatever the value, including in low value claims, perhaps by a builder for some works to a house where the work was unsatisfactory, or possibly not even completed so that the householder had to employ someone else to finish the job properly and this is the routine stuff of small cases in the County Court. These cases lack *some* of the notoriety of their criminal counterparts – with some notable exceptions – but make up a significant part of legal practice both for solicitors and barristers. From the very highest-valued contract or personal injury claim to the smallest of small claims, the civil justice system provides a pathway to justice. Indeed, civil cases make up a significant portion of the workload of cases dealt with by courts in England and Wales with around half a million claims per quarter and around 15,000 of those making it to trial. As a result, the civil justice system more than pulls its weight in terms of the administration of justice, and by examining its features, it will be possible to learn much about the legal system 'in action' and the challenges of delivering 'justice' in the current environment.

AS YOU READ

It is well worth referring back to the chapter on the court structure[1] while reading this one so you are clear about how cases progress through the system. For most lawyers involved in the

1 Chapter 8.

DOI: 10.4324/9781032641829-10

civil justice system, much of their time will be spent dealing with cases in the High Court or the County Court, the two civil trial courts also known as the **courts of first instance**. It is in one of these courts that a claim will start. If a case involves either an important legal principle or a great deal of money, one of the parties might be unhappy with the judgment given by the High Court or County Court judge so decide to appeal. Sometimes those appeals will be heard by judges in the Court of Appeal and, possibly, the Supreme Court (formerly the House of Lords). These are the **appellate courts** for civil justice.

As you read, **consider critically** the structures and processes being described and reflect on how they impact on the ability of individuals to access justice. As you contemplate the Civil Procedure Rules, **evaluate** whether they strike the right balance between certainty and flexibility. Finally, **compare** this area of the legal system, driven as it is by process, with some of the more principle-based chapters that came before it.

The purpose of this chapter is *not* to hope to give you a full understanding of the complex and technical rules of civil justice but, rather, to highlight to you the key features and to start to get you to think about how those processes shape justice.

TERMINOLOGY AND A LITTLE HISTORY

Before we move on to consider the detailed rules that apply it is important to come to terms with some of the basic terminology of the civil justice system, primarily how the main protagonists are termed. Civil justice is fundamentally a dispute between individuals.[2] Those individuals and businesses are referred to as 'parties' to a dispute, perhaps an unfortunate term as even the winning party rarely has a great time. The costs of resolving the dispute in court, the work involved in complying with the court rules, the expense of legal advice and representation, often the delay in getting a hearing, the unpredictability of the outcome, the time taken away from other day-to-day activity (whether in a business or in a party's personal life) and the fact that, even if the case is won, it is very unlikely that all the costs of the litigation, both financial and non-financial will be recovered, make it often a stressful experience.

The person bringing the civil law claim is deemed the 'claimant',[3] and the person defending the claim is called the 'defendant'. For most[4] civil law claims, the *claimant* has the *burden* of proving that alleged events took place and must discharge that burden to the civil law *standard* – on the so-called *balance of probabilities*. This means that the claimant must adduce evidence that *proves* his claim on the basis that the things alleged are more likely than not to be true.[5] To take

2 Whether those are 'natural' individuals or 'legal' individuals (such as businesses).

3 Until 1998 the equivalent term used was the 'plaintiff'.

4 There are some exceptions to this principle or times when this burden is 'reversed', such as involving cases of discrimination in the workplace by virtue of the Equality Act 2010 s136.

5 This is in sharp contrast to the criminal standard which requires proof 'beyond all reasonable doubt'.

an allegation of breach of contract as a starting point, the party who brought the allegation of breach of contract has the burden of proof, to prove the existence of the contract, its terms, how the other party is in breach and the loss that has been suffered. That party needs to prove each of those elements to the civil standard in order to be successful.

Having dealt with basic terminology we move to consider the history of the reforms to the civil justice system, in particular its recent history. We do this not because of a great desire to chart out this history of the legal system, as interesting as that is, but rather to give the context necessary for understanding the modern civil justice rules. The history of civil justice has been far from straightforward with multiple rounds of reforms (successful and unsuccessful) over the past 20 years amid a growth in cost, delay and complexity of process. Much has been done to streamline the process of civil justice but there is still some way to go. This pressure to reform and innovate to meet the challenges of demands on the court service has been matched with a government policy of reducing the cost of justice. Money has been removed directly from the court estate and also in support for those seeking justice through legal aid. This has led to a rise in 'litigants in person' that the legal system is having to deal with. For the purposes of this chapter, we will look at the history of civil justice both pre- and post-1998, when a seismic shift in the rules was achieved, precipitated by the Woolf Report.[6]

CIVIL JUSTICE PRE-LORD WOOLF

Coming to the nub of the issue, by the mid-1990s, the civil justice system was creaking from the weight of its own processes and the volume of cases it was supposed to be processing but, in fact, failing to do so. The rules were complex and found spread over multiple sources, with different rules applying in the different courts. This, along with the parties having to manage and navigate the court processes with only very light judicial case management, meant that faith and trust in the ability of the law to deliver justice were in question. It was expensive to bring an action (with the cost often outweighing the damages sought) and the length and outcome of proceedings was too uncertain. Even if a judgment was reached, enforcing that judgment could be very difficult and often led to 'hollow' victories.

Against this backdrop, the Lord Chancellor commissioned then Master of the Rolls Lord Woolf to prepare a report on access to justice and to recommend reform to the civil justice system. Lord Woolf duly prepared his interim and final reports. In his interim report, Lord Woolf highlighted the following as core to an effective civil justice system. He found that civil justice should

1. be *just* in the results it delivers;
2. be *fair* in the way it treats litigants;
3. offer appropriate procedures at a reasonable *cost*;
4. deal with cases with reasonable *speed*;
5. be *understandable* to those who use it;

6 Lord Woolf, *Access to Justice Reports* (Interim Report 1996 and Final Report 1997) <http://webarchive.nationalarchives.gov.uk/20060213205513/www.dca.gov.uk/civil/final/contents.htm>.

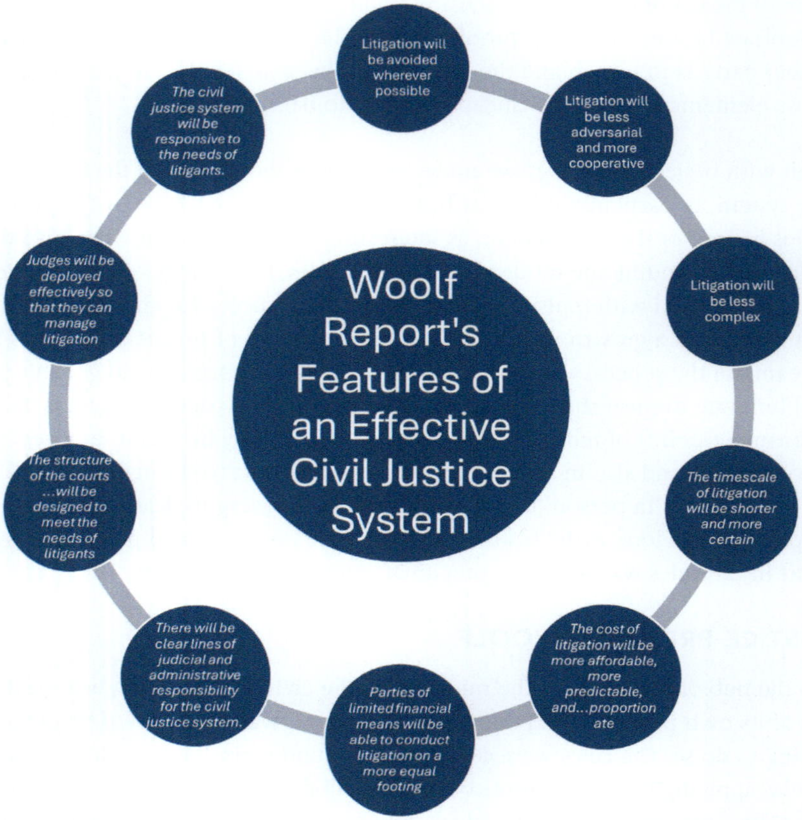

Figure 10.1 Woolf Report: features of an effective civil justice system.

6. be *responsive* to the needs of those who use it;
7. provide as much *certainty* as the nature of particular cases allows; and
8. be *effective*, adequately resourced and organised.[7]

In order to achieve this, he proposed a new landscape of civil justice based around the features shown in Figure 10.1.

These features eventually led to an overhaul of civil justice through the adoption of the Civil Procedure Rules (discussed in greater detail later), which revolutionised the way in which civil claims are issued, resolved and managed.

7 Lord Woolf, *Access to Justice Reports* (Interim Report 1996 and Final Report 1997) <http://webarchive.nationalarchives.gov.uk/20060213205513/www.dca.gov.uk/civil/final/contents.htm> at para 1.

CIVIL JUSTICE POST–LORD WOOLF

As we shall see later in this chapter, the Civil Procedure Rules (with some modifications), which were the result of the Woolf Report, are still in place today. They fundamentally changed the civil process within the legal system. However, things have not stopped there, and over the nearly 30 years following on from the Woolf Report and its reforms, there have been further attempts at dealing with the issues generated by such high levels of demand for civil justice.

THE JACKSON REPORT

Almost ten years on from the Woolf Report in 2009, the Master of the Rolls ordered a review of the *costs* of civil litigation amid fears that such costs were spiralling out of control. Lord Justice Jackson was commissioned and produced a 557-page report in 2010 with 109 recommendations. Amongst the many recommendations that were taken up, the following have the potential, in particular, to cut the cost of litigating:

- Those who were successful could no longer recover certain items in costs.[8]
- A cap was placed on certain types of fees in personal injury cases.[9]
- An extended category of fees was made available.[10]

This was coupled with a greater push, as was evident in the Woolf Report, for settlement and alternatives to litigation.

THE BRIGGS REPORT

The year 2015 saw another Master of the Rolls (this time joined by the Lord Chief Justice) commission another review into civil justice, this time by Lord Justice Briggs, and in particular the structure of the civil courts. He reported in 2016 and identified five weaknesses in the system:[11]

- Problems with access to justice caused by excessive costs and cost risks in claims involving moderate sums
- What Briggs LJ termed the 'tyranny of paper' and the 'obsolete and inadequate IT facilities in most of the civil court system'[12]
- Unacceptable delays in the Court of Appeal
- Underinvestment in provision of civil justice outside of London
- Problems in the processes for enforcing judgments and orders

8 'After the event insurance' and 'conditional fee arrangement' success fees. These are discussed later in the chapter when considering award of cost.

9 Success fees limited to 25% of damages in personal injury cases.

10 Contingency fees (discussed later) were made available for a wider range of claims.

11 Lord Justice Briggs, *Civil Courts Structure Review* (Final Report, 2016) <www.judiciary.uk/wp-content/uploads/2016/07/civil-courts-structure-review-final-report-jul-16-final-1.pdf>.

12 ibid 115.

Many of these recommendations have not been adopted and put into practice, due in part for financial reasons and also due to the Covid-19 pandemic, which put other significant pressures on the civil justice system. However, aspects are starting to be taken-up, most notably one of the major recommendations around the piloting and introduction in 2018 of the 'Online Money Service' for making certain low value claims (up to £10,000) in the County Court.[13] This system saves the need for paper forms and replaces a very outdated online system that was in use from 2002. The pilot ran successfully and has now been adopted as a mainstream method for low-value recoveries.

TAKING THINGS FURTHER – KEEPING UP WITH DEVELOPMENTS

Many of the recommendations of Briggs and Jackson are still being considered, piloted and implemented. It is important that you keep on top of these developments in order to keep your knowledge and understanding of the legal system current. Subscribing to blogs and updating websites can be a good way of keeping abreast of these developments. The companion website for this textbook will also contain regular updates on matters impacting on the legal system.

One of the themes that emerges from all the preceding reports is the centrality of effective dispute resolution outside of the court system – that is, settling claims in ways that do not involve litigation. This is one reason this textbook has a chapter devoted to alternative methods for resolving disputes.[14] That chapter considers the ways in which those methods are integrated and complementary to litigation rather than the 'bolt on' it once was.[15]

The remainder of this chapter will consider a civil action from claim to resolution and takes an approach that splits the civil process broadly into three phases:

- Before trial – including pre-action protocols, issuing, disclosure and track allocation
- At trial – including the typical process, remedies and costs
- After trial – enforcement and appeals

FROM DISPUTE TO TRIAL

Disputes arise continually. The vast majority are resolved informally, perhaps using businesses or organisations set up to help resolve claims, or through discussion by those involved. Let us

13 <www.gov.uk/make-money-claim>.

14 See Chapter 14.

15 See the Introduction by David Gauke, the then Lord Chancellor and Secretary of State for Justice, to the 2019 Review of the contentious 'LASPO' Act (the Legal Aid, Sentencing and Punishment of Offenders Act 2012), which made stringent cuts in the provision of legal aid, particularly in family law. <https://assets.publishing.service.gov.uk/government/uploads/system/uploads/attachment_data/file/777038/post-implementation-review-of-part-1-of-laspo.pdf>.

look at some typical cases so as to pick one that might actually fail to resolve out of court and so go into the court process.

Many people involved in road traffic accidents contact their insurance company, which helps arrange for repairs to a damaged car and, perhaps, supplies a hired car whilst the damaged car is repaired. Most of those people do not understand the legal basis of any claim that they may have and do not need that understanding. It is unusual that such a case goes to court, unless it might be to a criminal court – the Magistrates[16] – if one or both parties in the accident were in breach of a provision of the Road Traffic Acts or for a breach of Construction and Use Regulations, for example, not having adequately maintained one of the cars involved, so that lights, brakes or tyres or some other part of the vehicle was found to be defective and possibly contributed to the accident, or – worst of all – one party was not insured. Mostly the ordinary road traffic accident does not result in a civil suit as there will usually be a settlement between insurers although as explained there may be associated criminal proceedings for one of, or both, the drivers. Equally, problems with contracts can often be resolved between the parties.

However, not every dispute can be resolved informally like this. For those cases, the person who believes that s/he has suffered a wrong will have to use the civil courts. In those situations, the first step for the potential claimant is to identify the legal basis of the claim. In some cases, it is simple, so for example, where a customer of a business fails to pay for the goods he receives, the business may argue that the customer breached the contract between them and the customer. The next step is then to identify the terms of the contract. Some terms will be agreed, such as the amount of goods and the price. Other terms might be imposed by laws passed by Parliament, such as the Consumer Rights Act 2015, which requires the goods to be fit for purpose and of a satisfactory quality and others yet may be implied into the contract as a matter of business necessity.

Another example might be a claim by a person injured whilst driving a van. The injury occurs when another car hits the van from behind whilst the van is stationary in traffic. The aggrieved party may describe the other driver as 'negligent' without understanding the legal term they are using. If there is a dispute that cannot be resolved by negotiation then someone, usually a lawyer paid for by the insurers, will have to consider precisely what 'negligence' means in that context and to decide whether to issue a claim in court, which in this case would be a tort claim.

Whilst those two cases are, in legal terms, relatively simple the civil courts also have to deal with multi-million-pound disputes perhaps involving complex issues in company law or an alleged breach of trust, which are more challenging legal subjects.

PAYING FOR LEGAL SERVICES

A potential client seeing a solicitor for the first time has a number of worries, about how soon they will recover from his injury (if at all) in the case of an accident or how they will receive

16 See Chapter 8, The Court Structure, and Chapter 11, Criminal Justice.

goods that were not delivered or were dangerously defective. For almost all clients, one of the first questions they ask their solicitors is what a claim is going to cost them. It is a sensible and reasonable question.

Traditionally, legal costs were a simple matter, for the solicitor at least. The client would instruct the solicitor who would raise a bill at the end of the work that the client had to pay. Sometimes the client might be provided with a quotation, or estimate, indicating the fee that would have to be paid. More commonly, particularly for civil disputes, the client would be provided with some information about the hourly rate that the solicitor would charge, but usually with no indication of the number of hours of work involved. Perhaps understandably, clients and others argued that such an approach was an encouragement for solicitors to be inefficient.

The Access to Justice Act 1999 made some significant changes to the legal market in England and Wales. Amongst other things, it introduced conditional fee agreements ('CFAs'), popularly known as 'no win, no fee agreements'. As they currently operate, generally a client is not liable to pay the client's own solicitor for the work done if the claim is lost.[17] Importantly, the losing client remains liable for their opponent's costs but may be able to purchase an insurance policy to cover those fees, if they can afford the premium.[18] If the claim is successful, the client must pay their solicitor's legal costs which are usually recovered from the losing party. The client may also have to pay the solicitor a further sum, known as a success fee (which can be up to 100% of the regular fee).[19]

Solicitors can also act on the basis of 'damages-based agreements' (DBAs) that are sometimes known as contingency fees.[20] Under such an agreement the solicitor takes a share of any damages awarded rather than being paid a set hourly fee.

Otherwise, if there is no CFA and no fixed costs agreement (which some solicitors operate for common suits likely not to be complex or problematical), a client will be paying on an hourly rate, which the solicitor is obliged to detail in writing to the client at the start of the case, together with other 'client care' information set out by the Law Society in its Code of Conduct, including who will have overall charge of the client's matter and who is to do the day-to-day work (this may usually mean two to three people in all), what position that lawyer holds in the firm, to whom to make complaints, etc., and this has to be a best estimate if the hourly rate of one or more of the lawyers involved and the overall likely costs cannot be precisely detailed. This information also has to be updated regularly.

17 These encourage solicitors only to take on those cases where there is a good prospect of success.

18 The cost of this 'after the event' insurance policy is not recoverable if the claimant is successful. This was a revolution of the Jackson Reforms.

19 Again, not recoverable from the other side even if successful.

20 These used to be fairly restricted (e.g. to employment matters), but the Jackson Reforms liberalised them and made them available for more mainstream litigation.

ANALYSING THE LAW – THE REALITY OF THE COSTS OF LEGAL ADVICE

In English and Welsh law, the normal rule is that the loser of a case pays the other side's legal costs, the costs that the other side has paid its solicitors, barristers and other advisers in pursuing its claim. Do not forget that the losing party has also to pay its own legal costs in many cases, sometimes doubling its legal bill. Costs can be considerable, in some cases running into hundreds of thousands of pounds, and sometimes over a dispute in which the value is very much less. There has been much publicity recently, for example, over the amount that some people spend over 'boundary disputes' – that is, about a few feet of garden where it is claimed that, for some reason or another, a neighbour has sited a fence or wall incorrectly, but the actual monetary value of that little strip of garden is many times less than the legal costs of even one side of the argument, and a small fraction of the legal costs bill for both sides. As a result, a mediation service has been set up involving specialist surveyors from the Royal Institution of Chartered Surveyors (RICS), who are trained mediators, to resolve such disputes, which generally results in the parties saving a substantial amount of money, especially if the parties are able to obtain a fixed fee quotation from the surveyor-mediator and thus to avoid the expense of litigation.

Legal aid may be available in certain, limited circumstances. This allows for government funded support for legal actions. This applies beyond just civil cases and finds its latest incarnation in the Legal Aid, Sentencing and Punishment of Offenders Act 2012.

TAKING THINGS FURTHER – LEGAL AID AND ITS REFORM

Legal aid has proved a difficult topic for political actors, with significant 'savings' being made by cutting spending on government-assisted legal action. These reforms have been deeply controversial amongst the legal profession, as the amount invested in this area has fallen drastically, with fewer areas being subject to the regime. As legal aid applies to civil and criminal cases, the website that accompanies this text contains additional information about the legal aid scheme as it used to apply, and also the most recent developments in the reform of legal aid.

CIVIL PROCEDURE RULES (CPR)

The Woolf Report (discussed earlier) led to the introduction of the Civil Procedure Rules as we know them today. These Rules, known as the 'CPR', have been continuously amended and can be found in full at www.justice.gov.uk/courts/procedure-rules or in the 'White Book', the practitioners' book published annually. Each edition of the White Book also has a 'service' of periodic supplements on recent changes in practice and amendments to the Rules and associated Practice Directions. Should individuals wish to pursue claims, then they will be subject to the rules and processes of the CPR.

Introducing the reader at this stage to the CPR does not intend or encourage them to remember or learn the *detail* of the CPR[21] but only to introduce them to the processes, rules and procedures of the administration of civil justice. From this we will be able to draw out certain themes or principles that highlight important issues for the legal system. The purpose of the CPR, like any set of court rules, is to try to ensure that evidence is put before the court in a sensible, coherent form that allows for the efficient distribution of justice and to reduce the opportunities to cheat or abuse the court.

The CPR is divided into different parts, each dealing with different aspects of the court procedure. There are currently 89 Parts of the CPR. Many of those parts have a subsection, known as a Practice Direction, giving further details on the Court's approach to that part. The CPR is reviewed and updated regularly, with more than 193 updates at the time of writing. It is worth considering some parts in a little more detail, particularly those that apply across the proceedings. Other parts will be explored as we look more closely at the stages of litigation.

OVERRIDING OBJECTIVE (PART 1)

Part 1 of the CPR is the overriding objective, a new policy statement which was not articulated in the Rules of the Supreme Court[22] or the County Court Rules, which preceded the CPR. This rule requires courts to deal with cases 'justly and at proportionate cost'. Amongst other things, the overriding objective seeks to ensure that the parties are on an equal footing and to assist the judge to deal with the case in ways which are proportionate. Proportionality requires the court to consider the amount of money in dispute, the importance of the case and its complexity as well as the parties' finances. Importantly, the parties are required to help the court achieve the overriding objective (Figure 10.2), a slightly challenging concept for some clients who might be willing to spend considerable sums of money on legal costs to defeat their opponent.

PRE-ACTION STEPS

It is a commonly held belief that over 95% of legal cases do not go to a trial before a judge. There are many reasons that legal disputes never go to trial. It is widely appreciated that disputes can be resolved more easily if attempts are made soon after the dispute arises. Certainly, once parties have spent considerable amounts of money on lawyers, it becomes harder to resolve disputes as the stakes get higher.

21 Which could well be the subject of a textbook all of its own!

22 This was *not* the Supreme Court brought into existence by the Constitutional Reform Act 2005 but, rather, the 'old' name for the Senior Courts, notably for our purposes the High Court and the Court of Appeal.

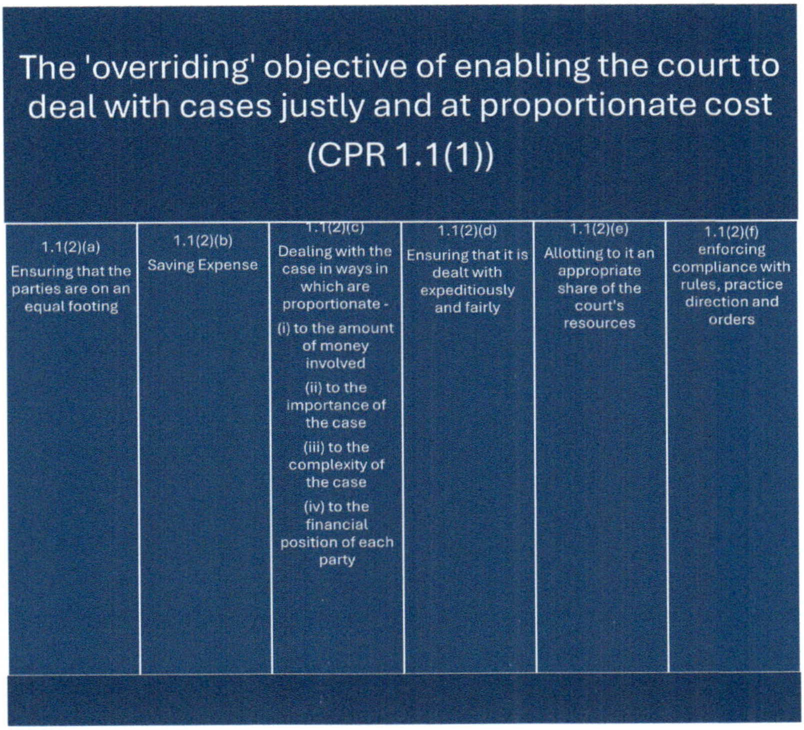

Figure 10.2 The overriding objective.

The CPR were written to try to encourage parties to resolve claims without court proceedings. At first sight, it seems illogical that the court can affect behaviour before it becomes involved. The CPR, however, achieves this in two ways. Firstly, it uses the Practice Directions on pre-action conduct and protocols. Those set out certain steps the parties are expected to carry out before commencing proceedings, such as writing detailed letters setting out the legal basis of a claim and sending with them copies of any supporting evidence, such as a copy of a contract.

In fact, the Practice Directions set out situations where rather more information must be provided in certain types of cases, so-called protocols. There are protocols for, amongst other things, personal injury claims, housing disrepair, defamation and debt claims. All these protocols are designed to encourage the parties to take steps that ought to be taken in that type of claim. So for example, the personal injury protocol requires the claimant to write a detailed letter of claim. The letter must set out the legal basis of the claim, summarise the relevant facts and detail the losses suffered by the claimant, supplying supporting documents where possible.

Claimants have to detail their loss of earnings, if any, special expense in relation to treating the injury and provide further detail of her likely recovery time.

The protocol requires the defendant to reply, within set time limits, allowing a period for the defendant to investigate the claim, and to put forward its version of events, if different. It should also supply documents where it has any applicable to the dispute. In personal injury cases, the insurer will often write these documents, as it is usually a condition of the insurance cover that any claim against an insured person is handled by the insurance company.

Importantly, the Practice Direction and all the protocols emphasise the need for the parties to use litigation as a *last resort*, using some form of alternative dispute resolution where possible. The variety of alternative methods is discussed in detail in Chapter 14. The Practice Direction suggests negotiation, mediation and early neutral evaluation as forms of resolution that might be tried.

APPLYING THE LAW – LOOKING BEYOND THE LAW

When studying law, it is easy to become focussed on legal rights. It is important to understand that people and businesses have a wider perspective. For example, many shops will provide refunds to customers even if there is no legal requirement to do so but as a gesture of goodwill and/or to avoid adverse publicity. In other situations, the parties to a dispute might reach a compromise by negotiation, perhaps having discussed the problem by telephone or in an exchange of emails. Sometimes, if the dispute is between two parties with an existing business relationship, they will wish to avoid 'souring' that relationship through court action. Other people will not take any action to enforce their legal rights because they do not understand the law or the court system and cannot afford a lawyer to help them. This means that whilst the legal provides a court system for the resolution of disputes, many will not proceed for good or bad reasons.

The Practice Direction and protocols are to be used *before* court proceedings commence and are not part of the *court process*. There seems no obvious reason why the parties would not necessarily follow them assuming a claimant hires a lawyer to file the court paperwork and to handle pre-court stages required by the protocol. They *are* part of the CPR as the CPR gives the court the power to penalise parties for their behaviour before proceedings were commenced. So, if a claimant who suffered a personal injury did not follow the protocol and send a letter of claim, the court might prevent that party from pursuing the claim further until they have followed the steps the protocol required, and the same for a party who did not consider an offer to mediate or follow some other form of dispute resolution.

One of the main ways in which the courts seek to ensure that parties comply with the CPR is by imposing costs penalties. Normally, if the claimant is successful in its claim, the defendant would have to pay the bulk of its legal costs. If it ignored a step in the Practice Direction, the court might order the claimant to carry out that step but order that it cannot recover the costs of the step from the other side, even if it wins the claim. Parties have even been penalised from the early 2000s, as already mentioned, for not considering any dispute resolution process because of thinking they had strong cases so need not. The point is that the court is not supposed to be used if some other resolution is available! – though it may make a difference what actual strength of case is demonstrable and whether there is a need for a decision that the claimant is right about a point of law.

Figure 10.3 shows the overall court process for a standard case.

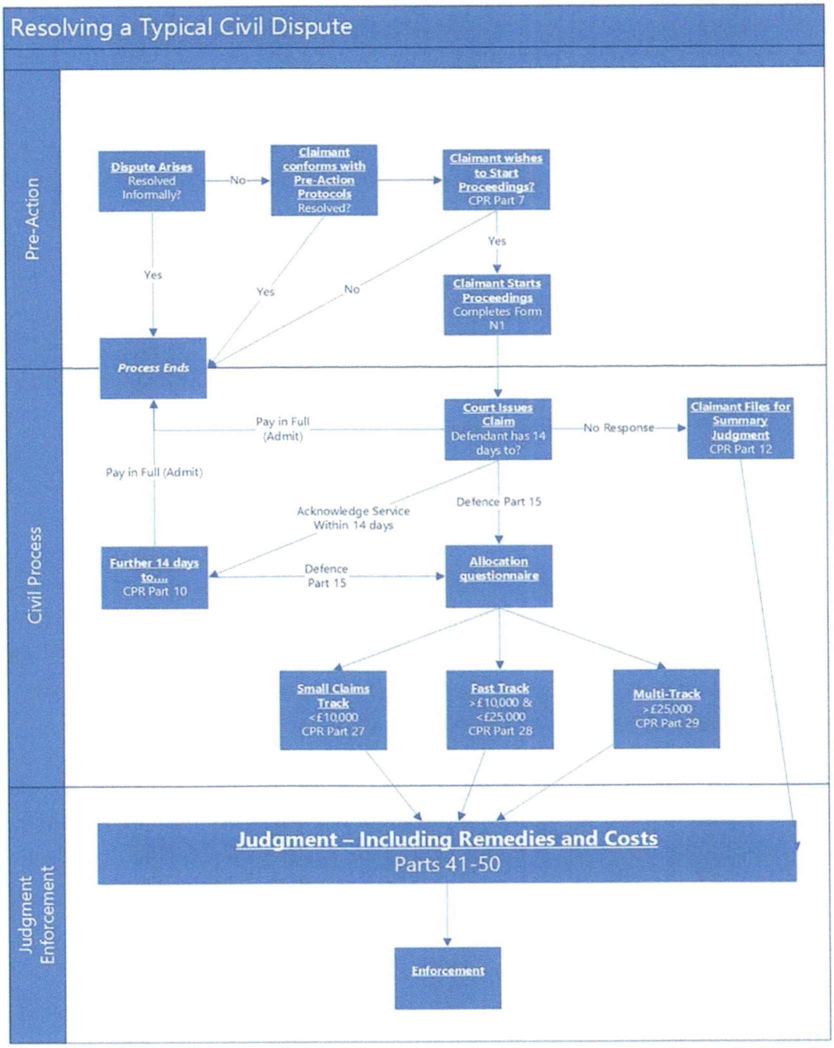

Figure 10.3 Resolving a civil dispute.

ISSUE AND THE TRACKS

A dispute cannot be resolved in all circumstances. Sometimes the parties' valuations are too far apart, or one (or both) of the parties might simply be unreasonable. In other cases, whilst the claimant or the claimant's solicitor writes a letter of claim, the intended defendant simply ignores it. Once an impasse has been reached, or the letter of claim ignored, the claimant has a decision to make – whether or not to issue proceedings at court to start the claim. This is a critical decision for a claimant, for if later deciding to end the claim, the claimant would be the one who would have to pay the bulk of the legal costs that the defendant had incurred to that time. The claimant would, of course, also have to pay the claimant's lawyer's costs, whether the claimant is an individual or a company.

STARTING PROCEEDINGS (PART 7)

Assuming the claimant wishes to bring a claim, that party would draft a claim form. For certain claims, particularly of very low value, there is a new online process. This is a standard court document (Form N1)[23] requiring certain essential details, such as the names and addresses of the parties, brief details of the claim and its value.[24] In some cases, the particulars of claim would be set out on page 2 of the claim form. In other cases, the details would be in a separate document, called the Particulars of Claim. These documents, with copies for the court and for each defendant, are sent (usually, although not always, electronically) to court with the appropriate court fee. The fee is paid to the court to commence proceedings. These fees vary according to the expected value of the claim and can escalate quite quickly – for claims worth over £200,000, the court fee is £10,000![25]

APPLYING THE LAW – A SUMMARY OF STARTING OF PROCEEDINGS

The particulars of claim are referred to as statements of case, as they state the parties' legal cases. Statements of case used to be referred to as 'pleadings', a term used by some older textbooks (and lawyers!). This old term is still useful for students to know when reading older cases which still have force and appear in subject specialism texts – so when you see this term, statements of case are what they are now.

All statements of case, as well as witness statements and experts' reports, must contain a statement of truth. This is a standard form of words, required by Part 22 of the CPR, confirming that the facts contained in that specific document are true. If a person signs

23 Form N1, the universal claim form, can be found on the internet. See <www.gov.uk/government/publications/form-n1-claim-form-cpr-part-7>.

24 Covered by CPR Part 16 (Statement of Case).

25 For a list of fees for civil cases, see <https://www.gov.uk/government/publications/fees-in-the-civil-and-family-courts-main-fees-ex50/civil-court-fees-ex50>.

a statement of truth without an honest belief that the facts are true, then that person is committing contempt of court (and that is the same if signing on behalf of a limited company). Contempt is a criminal offence, so a person found guilty could face an unlimited fine, a prison sentence of up to two years or both. In *R. (on the application of Accident Exchange Ltd) v Broom*,[26] seven defendants were found to be in contempt of court, having signed documents in a previous case where they knew the facts set out in the documents to be false. Each defendant was sentenced to prison for around a year.

COURTS' POWER OF CASE MANAGEMENT (PARTS 1 AND 3)

Another cross-cutting theme that emerges from the Woolf Reforms and the overriding objective of Part 1 is the changing role of the court in managing the court processes. Courts must adopt an 'active' approach to case management to ensure that justice is delivered quickly and in a cost-effective manner. The courts' responsibility in this respect is to, amongst other things, encourage cooperation between the parties, encourage the use of ADR and give directions that ensure that the trial of a case proceeds quickly and efficiently. From 2015, this may include the court using Early Neutral Evaluation to assess the merits of a particular claim. The parties are *expected* to take such actions that support the court's role in this endeavour. The powers of the court to achieve this aim can be found in Part 3 of the CPR and are fairly wide-ranging.

ISSUING

Once the court has received the papers and fee, it issues the claim. Issuing is the formal step when the court proceedings begin. It may involve little more than the papers being stamped but is important as many deadlines start or end on the date the claim is issued. For example, under section 11 of the Limitation Act, all personal injury claims have to be *issued* within three years of the injury occurring (there are very limited exceptions to this rule). If the claim is issued after that time, the defendant has an absolute defence to the claim. This means that the claimant would not receive compensation from the defendant, however strong the claim may be.

RESPONDING TO PARTICULARS (PART 9)

Once the claim is issued, it is then for the defendant to respond to the claim. There are strict time limits that apply to the response.

The options open to a defendant are to file or serve thus:

- An *admission* (CPR 14)
- A *defence* (with or without counterclaim) where he wishes to contest the claim (CPR 15)
- An *acknowledgment of service*

26 [2017] EWHC 1530 (Admin).

If the defendant disputes the claim, then that party will file a defence, within 28 days of the claim being received from the court. If the defendant misses the deadline, then the claimant sends a form to the court to enter default judgment.[27] To give a sense of scale, of the 252,000 judgments given between October and December 2023 around 234,000 (some 93%) were default judgments.[28] Around 11,000 cases went to trial in the same period. This shows that a great number of claims do not receive a response, and an even smaller fraction of those claims make it through to the court (many that do not end in default judgment are therefore either settled or withdrawn).

OFFERS TO SETTLE (PART 36 OFFERS)

At any point during the proceedings, one party may make a formal[29] offer to settle, and these offers are known as 'Part 36 Offers' because they are governed by Part 36 of the CPR. Such offers are made 'without prejudice' (i.e. with no acceptance of liability).

These offers are an important strategic tool for parties because a refusal of a Part 36 Offer can result in negative consequences in terms of the award made on success. This is all part of the culture and incentives of the court in trying to get parties to settle their disputes without going through to a trial. A party has 21 days in which to consider and accept or reject such an offer.

An insurer acting on behalf of a claimant may well weigh up the prospects of success and the likely cost of the litigation and make an Offer to Settle under Part 36. Equally, those responding to a claim may wish not to go through with a trial after initially serving a defence and could make a Part 36 Offer in order to try to bring the process to a close.

ALLOCATIONS

If the case is defended and no Offer to Settle is made or accepted, then the case will be allocated for trial. When the court receives the defence, it sends the parties a form (known as an allocation questionnaire – Form N150) asking them to supply information about the claim and the steps they consider necessary for the claim to go to trial. The court will consider this information, but by issuing the claim, the parties at that stage lose control of the claim as the court begins its case management (now, as mentioned previously, a proactive feature of civil justice included by Lord Woolf in his suggestions in the *Access to Justice* reports for modernising civil justice and adopted in all cases since the CPR 1998 was brought into force in 1999). This means it considers the steps required taking account of the value of the claim, its legal and evidential complexity and similar matters which were another feature of Lord Woolf's reforms in allocating cases to 'tracks', so that they could be managed more efficiently.

The court then sends out a document setting out the steps that the parties must take with a deadline for each step. As is discussed later, the steps normally involve the exchange of

27 CPR Part 12.

28 <https://www.gov.uk/government/statistics/civil-justice-statistics-quarterly-october-to-december-2023/civil-justice-statistics-quarterly-october-to-december-2023>.

29 Or any number of *informal* offers.

evidence. Thus, the order might require the parties to send each other copies of all relevant documents, by a specific date. This document is usually referred to as 'Directions', as it directs the parties as to what to do and when.

The starting point when considering the steps required is the value of the claim. It is on this basis that the court decides which of the three available tracks the case is allocated to and which thereafter the claim will follow. There are small claims, fast and multi-tracks.

SMALL CLAIMS TRACK (PART 27)

The small claims track applies to claims for less than £10,000, save for some personal injury and housing claims, where the limit is £1,000. The small claims track is designed to be less formal than the other tracks. In part, this is because the winning party does not ordinarily recover its legal costs from the losing party, save for the fee it paid to the court to start the claim. As a result, it is relatively rare for parties to use (or instruct) lawyers to represent them in such a claim.

Part 27 of the CPR deals with small claims track cases. Its Practice Direction provides further details, including some standard Directions for use in most circumstances, set out in Appendix B. The standard Directions provide that:

1. The parties must deliver to every other party and to the court office copies of all documents on which they intend to rely at the hearing no later than 14 days before the hearing. (These should include the letter making the claim and the reply.)
2. The original documents must be taken to the hearing.
3. The date of the trial is then fixed, and the court gives an estimate of how long the trial will take, perhaps two hours.
4. The Directions encourage the parties to contact each other with a view to trying to settle the case or narrow the issues. However, the court must be informed immediately if the case is settled by agreement before the trial date.
5. The Directions prevent the parties from relying on any report from an expert unless express permission has been granted by the court beforehand. Anyone wishing to rely on an expert must write to the court immediately on receipt of this Directions Order to seek permission, giving an explanation why the assistance of an expert is necessary.

The judge who hears the trial is often more likely to intervene than judges in fast and multi-track trials, perhaps by asking more questions of witnesses to ensure that evidence is brought out and allegations made by witnesses are challenged.

FAST TRACK (PART 28)

The fast track is for those cases that are worth more than £10,000 (i.e. the small claims limit) but less than £25,000 (i.e. the multi-track lower limit). Part 26 of the CPR, which explains which track applies to cases, states that the fast track applies thus:

- Only if the trial is likely to last for no longer than one day
- If oral expert evidence at trial will be limited to (1) one expert per party in relation to any expert field, and (2) expert evidence in two expert fields

Part 28 of the CPR deals specifically with the fast track. On allocating a case to the fast track, the court is expected to set Directions to take the case to a trial, no more than 30 weeks later. Ensuring that a case is ready for trial in just over half a year does not seem that challenging, until you appreciate that some lawyers are responsible for more than 100 client files.

The court Directions set out the further steps required, again using some information provided by the parties. The timeline runs from the date that the court allocates the track and normally requires parties to disclose documents within four weeks. Ten weeks after allocation, the parties must exchange witness statements, and four weeks later, they must exchange experts' reports (if any have been obtained and not been agreed). Twenty-two weeks after the case was allocated, the parties must return completed pre-trial checklists (also known as listing questionnaires) to the court. These are standard forms and ask a series of questions to establish whether the case is now ready for trial.

MULTI-TRACK (PART 29)

The multi-track is used for the most valuable claims of over £25,000. Some lower-value claims can be dealt with on the multi-track, but only in limited circumstances, such as when the case involves complex factual, legal or evidential issues; has a large number of parties; or involves a great deal of oral evidence. Importantly, such claims are still being dealt with in the County Court. The High Court only covers claims worth £100,000 or more.

As with the other tracks, once the case has been allocated to the multi-track, the court will want to set some Directions, setting out the steps that the parties need to take to progress the case to trial. The big difference is that, generally, the parties can have a greater say in the timetable and the steps needed. Indeed, in multi-track cases, the parties would be expected to work together to agree on some Directions. There are some standard Directions and even a menu of model paragraphs that the court makes available online for the parties to use.[30]

THE CIVIL TRIAL PROCESS

Despite the pre-action steps and the push for parties to use non-court means to resolve disputes, some cases still go to trial. Having dealt with disclosure as well as preparing and exchanging witness and expert evidence, it may seem like there is little left to do to prepare for trial. Cases that do not involve minors will be likely to be heard in public.[31] The trial will take place before a judge, sitting alone, who will have probably previously worked as a solicitor or barrister, although since the Judicial Appointments Commission was established in 2006, the pool has widened somewhat (see Chapter 7).

30 <https://www.justice.gov.uk/courts/procedure-rules/civil/standard-directions/list-of-cases-of-common-occurrence/menu-of-sd-paragraphs>.

31 CPR Part 9.

Having what seems like a strong legal claim is not enough for success at court. A party may consider, for example, that it has a strong claim that the other party is in breach of contract. However, it will need to prove that claim. There are, broadly, three evidential aspects that the parties have to deal with after the case has been issued through to trial. They are disclosure, witness evidence and expert evidence.

Disclosure relates to documents, with the requirements set out in Part 31 of the CPR. Each party has to gather the documents over which it has control that are relevant to the claim, then prepare a list of them. This list is sent to the other side, which can request copies of any documents that it wishes to see. Importantly, parties are required to disclose not only the documents on which they rely (to prove their own case) but also documents that harm their case and those that assist the other side. Before the CPR, this process used to be called 'discovery', where the parties 'discovered' what documents the other side had that might be relevant. In theory, if the parties have complied with the pre-action steps just discussed, there should be little more to 'discover' at this stage.

Discovery used to be one of the most expensive steps of the litigation process, as lawyers considered many documents, perhaps thousands, to see whether they were relevant to the dispute. For fear of missing the one document that might be the 'smoking gun', the lawyers would then ask to see all the documents disclosed by the other side. A similar trick was used to hide documents that a party did not want the other side to find. You were obliged to disclose every qualifying item, but it was not necessary to make it easy for an opponent to find! Litigants would then bury a document of this sort in a large category of uninteresting looking documents in the hope that the unlucky legal clerk going through all this relatively boring documentation would not persevere and would give up after no more than a cursory glance at a few documents near the start of that particular list. The Jackson reforms have changed the rules of disclosure to make them much more limited for all cases other than those involving personal injury.

Once the parties have all the relevant documents, they can then finalise their witness evidence. It can be unwise to do this earlier, in case a document is disclosed that can undermine a carefully crafted legal argument. The witness evidence must be set out in detailed form, as required by Part 32 of the CPR, that is, in a statement, which becomes that witnesses' evidence at the hearing.

Historically, the first time that a party would know what a witness for the other side was going to say was when they gave evidence (known as evidence-in-chief) at the trial. Such an approach was referred to as 'trial by ambush'. The lawyer representing the other side then put questions to that witness, known as cross-examination, to try to undermine the evidence given, a challenging task for the lawyer who had no advance knowledge of what was going to be said. The approach rarely suited clients, although the lawyers, who were paid whether or not their clients won the trial, had little incentive to change the system.

The CPR now requires that parties should prepare detailed statements, in paper form, setting out the evidence that each person will give if the case goes to trial.[32] Importantly, those statements are exchanged with the other side weeks or months before the trial. The 'cards on the table' approach to litigation encouraged by the CPR, including the pre-action steps, means that the witnesses and the gist of the evidence they will give ought not to be a great surprise to the party receiving them. If the case still progresses to trial, there is a further change – the witness will not give evidence-in-chief, as the court will normally rely entirely on the contents of the statement, so the witness will go straight into being cross-examined.

The final piece of the evidential puzzle is that of expert evidence. Before the CPR, expert evidence was a growing area. In personal injury claims, both sides would have medical experts dealing with the range of injuries suffered and there might also be employment experts, giving evidence on the type of work that the injured person could do, and nursing experts, explaining how the type and extent of the ongoing nursing care that a permanently injured person would require, amongst others.

In terms of ordering, the party bringing the claim will start. Traditionally, the party's lawyer would give an opening speech, explaining the basis of the claim and how the evidence would prove it. The witnesses would be cross examined by counsel for the claimant and then the defence repeats the process. The parties' counsel then 'sum up' their cases, giving a final speech, defence first, claimant last of all, then the judge gives the decision with an explanatory judgment on the reasons.

REMEDIES

At the end of the case, the judge will, on the basis of the evidence, find for the claimant or defendant. If the defendant wins, then the claimant's case is dismissed and the court will make an order as to costs. If there was a (successful) counterclaim, then the court may issue one of the following remedies. Equally, if the claimant wins, then the court will award a remedy and costs.

There are three main forms of remedies that the court may award:

- Interim relief
- Damages
- Equitable remedy

INTERIM RELIEF

These are included in this section for completeness but, as their name suggests, will have been granted at an earlier stage in the proceedings. They are governed by CPR Parts 23 and 25 and include, amongst others, all interim injunctions, freezing injunctions and search orders.

32 CPR Part 32.

DAMAGES

The most typical remedy in a civil case will be damages. These are a common law remedy that are available as of *right* – that is, if the case has been proved and loss has been suffered then damages will be awarded. The CPR Part 41 governs the award of such damages. They can be *compensatory, aggravated, nominal, contemptuous* or *exemplary*.

The principles on which damages are calculated will vary according to the area of law covered by the substantive dispute. For example, in a breach of contract claim, the aim of the court will be to put the claimant in the same position as if the contract had been fulfilled. This is to be contrasted with claims based on the law of torts (such as a negligence claim for personal injury), where damages are designed to put the claimant back in the position *as if the tort had not happened*. This means that someone suffering a personal injury would be able to claim for economic loss arising out of that injury. The judge would refer to existing judicial practice in calculating that loss.

ANALYSING THE LAW – ARE DAMAGES AWARDED OR WON?

Civil cases are often presented in quite a strange way in the public press. Cases are often described, in quite sensational terms, as resulting in 'bumper' or 'large' or 'record-breaking' damages, with a large number of £000,000 involved. Damages are often described as being 'won' rather than 'awarded'. Having considered the complex and time-consuming nature of civil process, it is important to reflect critically on these reports and their impact on the public perception of civil justice. Also reflect on the *nature* of damages in English and Welsh law, which are firmly based on concepts of *loss* rather than on principles of *gain*.

EQUITABLE REMEDY

It may be remembered from Chapter 2 – 'Sources of Law' – that many of the principles of equity find expression in *remedies* that are *discretionary* in nature. These include thus:

- *Specific performance.* Rather than award damages, the court may insist upon performance of a contractual obligation. The court *could* issue an order of specific performance, but these are rare and normally reserved for cases where damages would prove inadequate, such as a contract for the transfer of a unique asset or piece of land.
- *Injunctions.* These take the shape of *prohibitory* (to refrain from doing something) or *mandatory* (to make someone do something) orders.
- *Rescission.* The setting aside of a contract in its entirety.

COSTS (PARTS 43–47)

Costs is a complex subject, with burgeoning litigation happening on this point alone (i.e. arguments over the award and calculation of costs). The courts' treatment of costs is contained within Parts 43–47. In short terms, costs are paid by the losing side, who bears not only their own costs but also those of the other side.[33]

This can be modified and adverse costs findings made if the behaviour of the winning party has been unreasonable. The Court of Appeal has recently ruled in *Dammermann*[34] that it will not provide general guidance as to what constitutes unreasonable behaviour but cited the judgment in *Ridehalgh* of Lord Bingham,[35] who said, 'The acid test is whether the conduct permits of a reasonable explanation'. This has included, amongst other things, an unreasonable refusal to undertake mediation and failure to follow practice directions.[36] The Jackson reforms also changed the rules regarding the recovery of ' success fees' and the 'after the event insurance' that often go along with personal injury claims.

TAKING THINGS FURTHER – THE LIFE OF A COSTS LAWYER

Even to those who work full-time in the law, legal costs are rarely a thrilling topic. However, solicitors' firms and barristers have to make a profit or they cease to trade. An understanding of how lawyers charge their clients will improve your understanding of the area and your employability since this is an area of high-volume work in which paralegals are often essential to a firm's ability to deal with that volume. See Chapter 15 for an understanding of the opportunities for law graduates to work in the law without qualifying as a solicitor or barrister.

ENFORCEMENT (PARTS 70–74)

Unfortunately, obtaining a judgment for a sum of money does not force the losing party to pay anything. When the losing party is backed by an insurance company, payment is made relatively soon after judgment is given. In other cases, the losing party may not pay, because either they have no funds or they do not wish to do so. At that point, the winning party has a range of options. All methods of enforcement, forcing the debtor to pay, require steps to be taken by the winning party, as they are not automatically carried out by the court. Depending on the nature of the dispute and the financial situation of the defendant, careful consideration should be given as to the means of enforcement.

33 Subject to some reform that came about from the Jackson Report and the advent of Qualified One-way Costs Shifting (QOCS) in certain personal injury cases.

34 *Dammermann v Lanyon Bowdler LLP* [2017] EWCA Civ 269.

35 *Ridehalgh v Horsfield* [1994] Ch 205 (CA).

36 *Parr v Keystone Healthcare Ltd* [2019] EWCA Civ 1246.

Successful claimants can consider trying to enforce the judgment by seeking control over the defendant's assets,[37] salary,[38] bank balance[39] or goods.[40]

APPEALS

If a party is unhappy with the outcome of a civil case, then they may be in a position to be able to appeal. Such appeals are governed by Part 52 of the Civil Procedure Rules. The practice and process of appeals is complex and beyond the scope of a text intended to introduce the reader to the legal system of England Wales. Nonetheless, there are a few underpinning principles that are worth noting here for completeness.

Typically, there will only be one opportunity for one level of appeal, and the precise routes can be determined by the Lord Chancellor through secondary legislation. There are limited opportunities for a second appeal, and this will normally only be granted where an important legal principle is at stake. The other important principle to note is that there needs to be permission granted either by the original court or from the appellate court. This filter is important, and permission will only be granted if there is a real prosect of success or there is some other important principle at stake.

BUT WILL THERE BE A TRIAL AT ALL?

What has gone before in this section highlights the main features and processes of civil justice from start to finish. The CPR is a vast improvement on the situation that subsisted prior to 1999, but the process is still complex and generates additional cost.

In fact, it is statistically unlikely that a dispute will go to trial. So while lawyers might be instructed initially it is very likely that the case will be resolved through settlement, withdrawal or by some other means of dispute resolution (such as mediation).

It is also common for a defendant's public liability insurers to attend mediation with the injured person's lawyer(s) in order to achieve a settlement since they prefer not to waste time and money on litigation unless essential.

In this way, it is important to understand the civil process but also to realise that much negotiation happens, as intended in the multiple reviews of civil justice, outside the courtroom door rather than inside it.

37 A charging order under CPR Part 79.
38 An attachment of earnings order under CPR Part 89.
39 A third-party debt order under CPR Part 72.
40 A warrant of control under CPR Part 83.

THE WEBSITE

The website that accompanies this textbook contains many useful resources that you can use to consolidate and further your knowledge of the law, to hone your skills of critical analysis and to test your knowledge.

11

CHAPTER 11
CRIMINAL JUSTICE

INTRODUCTION

Many students new to law immediately connect any mention of 'criminal justice' with major criminal trials in the Crown Court, even if their mental picture does not then also jump immediately to trial at the Old Bailey in London, the most famous of these courts. However, there is a lot more to the system of criminal justice than the sort of trial for which members of the public, as well as law students, queue for a seat in the Old Bailey public gallery. The criminal justice system involves a whole host of other 'actors', including the police, the Crown Prosecution Service and an army of other legal professionals involved in the administration of criminal justice. Equally, a great deal of the criminal justice system takes place outside the courts, in the community and in the more than 1,000 police stations of England and Wales.

This chapter seeks to demystify and decode some of the major structures and processes of the criminal justice system and criminal trials. The intention is to give the reader an overview of how the system fits together and to describe how it sits within the broader legal system.

AS YOU READ

Think **critically** about the different stages in the criminal justice system, from initial investigation through charge and prosecution to full trial and conviction. By taking a holistic view of this part of the legal system, it is possible to gain a greater understanding of the principles that underpin criminal justice. The police have a great number of powers, and you should **assess** whether these aid in the administration of justice.

This criminal justice system contains a great deal of procedural law, and it is important that you have an **understanding** of the basic processes that govern the gathering and presentation of evidence. Also, you should **think critically** about the *people* involved in the criminal justice system and the roles that they play here and elsewhere in the legal system. As you read the sections on governing the trial process, try to think of the benefits and drawbacks of the trial process.

Finally, be sure to **consider** the similarities and differences between criminal justice, civil justice (already considered in Chapter 10) and administrative justice (to be considered in Chapter 13). Where there are, in particular, differences, consider whether they are there for *principled* or merely *historical* reasons.

DOI: 10.4324/9781032641829-11

THE CRIMINAL JUSTICE SYSTEM IN SUMMARY AND SOME TERMINOLOGY

It is important to note, as we did for civil justice, that there is a lot of terminology that has specific meaning within the context of the criminal justice system. The body bringing the action is called the *prosecution* and, for most offences, are doing so in the name of the King. The person responding to the accusation is known as the *defendant*, and the person against whom the offence is committed is known as the *victim*.

The prosecution holds the *burden of proof* in criminal matters, meaning that they must demonstrate that the necessary ingredients of the offence have been proven. They must do this to the necessary *standard of proof*, which for criminal trials is *beyond all reasonable doubt*. The burden and standard of proof combine to put into practice the general principle within the criminal justice system that there is a *presumption of innocence*.

In the law of England and Wales, there are two verdicts.[1] If the prosecution has discharged its burden of proof to the necessary standard, then the relevant decision-maker (either the judge or the jury) can find the defendant *guilty*. If the prosecution fails to discharge the burden of proof and so there is at least a reasonable doubt as to guilt or the defence successfully argue a legal defence (such as insanity or duress), then the decision-maker must find the defendant *not-guilty*.

From the outset it is important to dispel certain of the myths and assumptions that have grown up around the criminal justice system, which is often portrayed in dramatic, glamourous and exaggerated form in popular culture. First, 98% of criminal cases are dealt with in the Magistrates' Court and never reach a Crown Court. Secondly, some never even reach a court as they are never 'tried' at all, for example, the more minor road traffic offences, where the accused pleads guilty by post, so the magistrates only decide the penalty; those charged with these offences usually need not even attend. Thirdly, there is much to process behind the scenes before an accused can even be brought before any court, and this underlying work is done either by the police or by the Crown Prosecution Service (CPS) or both, one of whom will initially need to define the charge on which the accused would be taken to court. Fourthly, as seen in Chapter 8 on the court structure in England and Wales, all criminal cases *begin* in the Magistrates' Court, whatever happens after that stage.

Fifthly, while the police can prosecute minor crime before the Magistrates where the accused is going to plead guilty, the CPS will have to be involved once an accused decides to defend a charge, which means that, depending on its seriousness, the case might still be tried in the Magistrates' Court, or it may or must go to the Crown Court.

1 In other jurisdictions, including Scotland, there have been alternatives available, such as the controversial 'not proven' verdict. In September 2025, the Scottish Parliament voted to abolish this verdict.

Which court a specific defendant is tried within will depend on whether it is a 'summary offence' (tried on a summons before the Magistrates) or an 'indictable offence' (tried on indictment[2] in the Crown Court) or an 'either-way offence' (i.e. one which can be tried in either court, depending on which form of trial the accused chooses). However, where an indictable offence is to be tried in the Crown Court, a summary offence (which would normally go for trial to the Magistrates) can be added to the indictment, and the two offences tried together there: this is not as complicated as it sounds, since clearly one charging document, one court and one trial are obviously both a more efficient pathway and also cost-effective; see further later in the chapter.

This apparently complex system, in which the police deal with charging the simpler and undefended cases and the CPS deals with charging more complex and defended cases, is in place because the CPS is the government body set up in 1986 to take most prosecutions out of the hands of the police, who (prior to that date) used both to investigate and initially to prosecute crimes which they detected. The Head of the CPS is the Director of Public Prosecutions (DPP) a government appointment and is responsible to the chief government law officer, the Attorney General (AG), who is also the government's chief legal advisor. The AG sometimes acts as counsel for the government in very important cases, in which the AG may personally take over or bring the prosecution. In some cases a prosecution cannot be brought without the AG's consent or that of the DPP.[3]

There are still other bodies which can investigate offences against the law and initiate prosecutions, for example, local government departments dealing with weights and measures and other local regulatory matters such as breaches of environmental provisions, or the Health and Safety Executive which can prosecute for breaches of Health and Safety regulations; the police can also still initiate prosecutions for some low level offences such as under the Road Traffic Acts. However, generally speaking, the CPS is now involved in most *defended* cases because of the principle that there should be a central, specialist and independent prosecuting authority to ensure appropriate enforcement of the criminal law, which the police clearly are not if they are also the investigating authority.

TAKING THINGS FURTHER – THE POST OFFICER AS PROSECUTOR

The challenges posed by prosecutions other than by the CPS are exemplified by the recent Post Office Horizon scandal that came to light in the 2020s. The Post Office retained private prosecutorial powers dating back to the 17th century, and it used these powers, over a period of more than 15 years, to pursue around 700 sub-postmasters for fraud and theft. The Post Office did so on the basis of evidence of accounting

2 An indictment is only a more complex form of charge sheet for the Crown Court than that used in the Magistrates' Court for summary offences. There is a certain amount of technicality involved in drafting an indictment, so this is normally done by the CPS, or the prosecuting counsel from the Criminal Bar instructed by the CPS, a necessary precaution so as to avoid the defence counsel taking some point about invalidity of the indictment.

3 See <www.cps.gov.uk/legal-guidance/consents-prosecute>.

discrepancies highlighted by its adoption of new accounting software called 'Horizon'. Many sub-postmasters had raised complaints about the new software, but these reports were supressed as the Post Office initiated its private prosecutions. Some 200 sub-postmasters were sentenced to prison on the basis of this evidence.

Eventually, defects with the software, including the Post Office's attempts to cover these up, came to light, as did failings in the execution of the prosecutions (including around duties of disclosure). At the time of writing, a growing number of the prosecutions have been overturned as unsafe, and Parliament is considering a blanket scheme to overturn the remaining convictions.

This scandal has renewed calls to review the remaining powers of private prosecution.

There are two separate stages of prosecuting someone for an offence – first, detection and investigation and, secondly, formulation of the charge on which an accused will be tried. The keen student of criminal justice must understand this process before taking a decision on which trial court to attend: before embarking on a first court visit, the prior practical decision at that stage will be as between the probably very *local* Magistrates or the nearest Crown Court. Thus, this decision must be taken before deciding whether it is really worth travelling to the Old Bailey public gallery queue in London when a similar trial may be observed in a Crown Court nearer home or place of study. Once before a court it is, in most cases, for the prosecution to prove its case. This placing of the responsibility for demonstrating that an offence has been committed is a cornerstone of the criminal justice system of England and Wales.

So let us begin at the beginning, with the detection and investigation of offences by the police or other bodies, following which, unless the police are dealing with the simpler prosecuting work before the Magistrates, the criminal activity established must be drawn to the attention of the CPS so that its specialist personnel may decide whether there is evidence sufficient to secure a conviction and to follow that up with a prosecution.

DETECTING CRIME AND KEEPING ORDER: POLICE ORGANISATION AND INVESTIGATION POWERS AND SAFEGUARDS FOR THE CITIZEN

The maintenance of public order was one the principal purpose of the law that was discussed in Chapter 1 of this text. For many, it is the most important function of law and the legal system, as without public order, the state cannot function. In this context the criminal justice system plays an important role not just in relation to specific public order offences (for example, riot, violent disorder or affray) but also in terms of the general confidence and consent of the people to be governed. Whilst most textbooks covering the legal system would start with the courts, this one places particular importance on the pre-court process. This starts with consideration of the police and their place in getting criminal offences prosecuted and criminals convicted. Given the centrality of the police to the criminal justice system, maintaining faith and confidence in the police is important for the whole of the legal system. Recent events involving police officers have done much to rock that confidence.[4]

Surprisingly, in modern times, there is still no national police force as such in England and Wales. Instead, a number of different regional forces remain locally based, mostly defined by counties, though in Greater London the local force is called the Metropolitan Police. There are very many parallels here with other structures explored earlier in this text, notably of locally based justice and a network of different actors.

These distinctions between the London and regional policing authorities are important since some police powers are only exercisable by senior officers of certain ranks whereas these two historic London forces have different titles for the ranks of their police from those of the regional forces in the remaining policing locations around the country. The heads of the two London forces are called 'Commissioners' whereas in the regional forces their most senior officers are 'Chief Constables'.

It should be noted that not all uniformed and 'plain clothes' staff supporting a force will actually be police officers but might instead be, for example, 'Police Community Support Officers' ('PCSOs', who are civilians wearing a different but similar uniform to police officers' and whose purpose is a 'visible' patrolling role) or 'Special Constables' who have police support roles, first developed in times of shortage of staff in wartime but now a feature of contemporary policing. Nevertheless, these PCSOs do have certain defined powers, such as to issue fixed penalty tickets for littering, dog fouling, cycling on footpaths and other minor anti-social activity, and to ask for identification, seize goods and detain members of the public when an offence has been committed. However, although their respective Chief Constables or Commissioners may grant these subsidiary officers further discretionary powers, this does not usually include investigating offences, because extension of their routine powers is generally criticised on the basis that these personnel lack sufficient training to perform more than the purpose for which they were originally appointed, since they are not regular police officers and are paid at a lower rate. For one thing, in the highly technical context of modern criminal justice such lack of specific experience and specialist training at the investigation stage could prevent otherwise entirely deserved convictions.

In view of the continued national fragmentation of forces, it is perhaps surprising that nothing has been done to create a more nationally integrated force at the regular police officer level; for example, the Crime and Courts Act 2013 created a National Crime Agency (NCA), the rationale for which was addressing both organised crime and the UK's international response to certain

4 This includes the murder of Sarah Everard by a serving police officer who had a history of offending behaviour and where clear institutional failings allowed him to continue in his role. Further criticism of the police came from their inappropriate handling of women who had gathered, in contravention of Covid-19 rules, for a peaceful vigil for Sarah Everard.

types of crime. As a result, the personnel who operate in this serious organised crime field combine the powers of police constables, immigration officers and customs officers.

Nevertheless, the importance of the role of the police in preserving law and order as well as supporting the rule of law is recognised today in their progressive professionalisation, in the course of which the police have recently become a graduate profession with a defined career structure designed to serve the need for appropriate detection of crime and gathering of evidence for its prosecution. This means that even the lower ranks of the regular police forces, who are routinely involved in initial questioning of suspects, now need to understand the complexities of how to collect evidence in such a way that it will be admissible in a potential prosecution rather than excluded for unfairness or other flaw not compliant with the concept of human rights, which now play such an important role in the implementation of the rule of law. This is because in a liberal democracy it is recognised that, in an era of serious organised crime, there must be a balance between effective policing and individuals' rights and freedoms which may inevitably be infringed in the process of detection of offences.

This professionalisation of the police has more recently been supported by the appointment of elected regional police and crime commissioners,[5] who are supposed to monitor police resources in their areas so as to ensure that the force for which they are responsible is efficient: thus, their work includes setting police budgets and, if necessary, hiring or dismissing Chief Constables. There has, however, been much criticism of their role and its performance, as well as the value to the taxpayer.[6] The government announced on 13 November 2025 its intention to abolish the role as a failed experiment.[7]

Complaints about the police are still handled by the police themselves although in theory this is by an Independent Police Complaints Commission (IPCC) established by the Police Reform Act 2002 but funded by the Home Office. However, as it is substantially staffed by former police officers its actual independence, or any definable difference from the former system of investigation by senior officers, has inevitably been questioned.

THE POLICE ROLE IN GETTING THE ACCUSED TO COURT

This section of the chapter explores the mechanics of investigation of crime, that is, police powers to stop and question people; to search persons and vehicles; to enter and search premises; to arrest, detain and question suspects; to take samples, photographs and impressions; and to hold identity parades.

Since the Police and Criminal Evidence Act (PACE) 1984 this has become yet another complex area of police contribution to criminal justice, so it is easy to see why the police has had to be

5 Under the Police Reform and Social Responsibility Act 2011. This only applies to regional forces outside London, since in Greater London the PCC function is undertaken by the Mayor of London (i.e. not the Lord Mayor of the City of London or the individual Borough Mayors).

6 See Simon Cooper's paper at the annual conference of the Society of Legal Scholars, 4–7 September 2018, 'Police and Crime Commissioners: A Corrosive Exercise of Power Which Destabilises Police Accountability'.

7 <https://www.gov.uk/government/news/police-and-crime-commissioners-to-be-scrapped>

Table 11.1 The PACE codes

Code	*Last updated*	*Power covered*
A	2023	The exercise of police powers to 'stop and search' people and vehicles
B	2023	The exercise of police powers to search premises and seize property
C	2023	Requirements for the detention, treatment and questioning of people in police custody not suspected of involvement with terrorism
D	2023	Identification
E	2018	Audio recordings at police stations
F	2018	Visual recordings at police stations
G	2012	The police powers of arrest
H	2023	The detention, treatment and questioning of persons in police custody who are suspected of involvement with terrorism
I	2023	Detention, treatment and questioning under the National Security Act 2023

professionalised. Since 1984 the restrictions on what police can do when at first investigating crime and gathering evidence are contained in PACE 1984 and the Codes A to I made under it:[8] these relate to 'Stop and Search' (including the obligation to record encounters with the public) 'Search of Premises and Seizure of Property' and 'Powers of Arrest'. This power, contained in PACE s24 as amended,[9] even enables arrest to ascertain a person's identity, when a potential suspect or a witness might disappear, hindering the investigation or prosecution of the crime: s24(5). It is worth noting that the PACE Codes are regularly updated to reflect modern policing practice which goes some way to explain why the codes themselves are not statutory as the present approach allows them to develop more easily over time.

The full codes of PACE are shown in Table 11.1.

8 The codes are not actually part of the PACE statute but have indicative rather than statutory force, meaning, that they should be observed by police officers, but if there is a breach, that does not necessarily mean that evidence gathered in contravention of any provision is necessarily inadmissible in later criminal proceedings. Inevitably, this means there is a respectable case for arguing that they should be part of the statute, but the contrary argument is, of course, that the police face enough difficulties in gathering evidence for the prosecution of crime and that PACE 1984 itself was intended to strike a balance between crime prevention and its prosecution so as to protect the public and the recognition and preservation of traditional liberties and guarantees of human rights. Also, the flexibility inherent in the 'Code' model is worth preserving and fits with the discussion of secondary legislation in Chapter 5.

9 By the Serious Organised Crime and Police Act 2005.

Thus, the role of the police in relation to offences that may later be prosecuted often begins in the street or elsewhere in public, or even at a person's house or other premises, long before any court is reached. PACE has been statutorily updated several times since 1984.

Initially the prosecution can still use evidence obtained unlawfully, improperly or even unfairly[10] but this can have adverse consequences.[11] In the Crown Court where there will be a jury, the judge will decide whether such evidence is admissible and if not will prevent the jury hearing it at all; however in the Magistrates' Court (where there is no jury as the magistrates are the judges of both fact and law) it is up to the Bench of Magistrates with assistance from their Legal Advisor, or the salaried or part time fee paid District Judge (Magistrates' Courts)[12] sitting alone, to decide whether such evidence is admissible or not, and to disregard it in making their decision if it is inadmissible.

For the police to use any of these PACE-controlled 'Stop and Search' or 'Search and Seize' powers, the officers concerned must mostly have a reasonable suspicion that they are going to find prohibited articles for which the search is being conducted, for example, blades or other offensive weapons.[13] They can also search, for example, for fireworks carried in contravention of fireworks regulations.

In addition there are other restrictions: the search must take place in a location to which the public have access, the person searched must only be required to take off outer clothing[14] and stopped for search must be told what is being searched for;[15] but if the item(s) searched for are found those can be seized as evidence.[16] However the Equality Act 2010 also has an impact here, as Code A now includes a provision (called a 'reminder') that there shall be no stereotypical discrimination against any of the protected characteristics addressed in that Act. There has, over a number of years, been significant controversy over the use of 'stop and search' powers and whether it has a discriminatory dimension either in design or through application, principally against those from minority ethnic backgrounds.[17]

10 *Kuruma v R* [1955] AC 197 (PC).

11 A warning to the jury by the judge to disregard such tainted material if such evidence is wrongly admitted following a breach of PACE or the Codes; a 'stay of the proceedings' for abuse of process, that is, proceedings ended; police disciplinary proceedings; civil or criminal proceedings against the officer concerned.

12 Formerly called stipendiary magistrates.

13 PACE, s24 provides that a police officer can arrest anyone committing or about to commit an offence when an officer reasonably suspects this is the case or that an offence has already been committed by such a person; thus, the officer need not be sure, so that the test is partly objective and partly subjective: *O'Hara v Chief Constable of the Ulster Constabulary* [1997] AC 286 (HL).

14 PACE 1984 s2.

15 Code A.

16 ibid s1(6).

17 Ben Bowling and Coretta Phillips, 'Disproportionate and Discriminatory: Reviewing the Evidence on Police Stop and Search' (2007) 70 MLR 936.

THE POLICE STATION, DETENTION, QUESTIONING AND ASSOCIATED POWERS

Taking anyone to a police station against their will deprives them of liberty when that is a fundamental human right, and Article 5 of the European Convention on Human Rights (ECHR) guarantees that liberty. Thus, a police officer acting in this way must *objectively and reasonably* believe that this action is necessary[18] so that an officer always needs to consider whether asking a suspect to come to the police station voluntarily might be a practical alternative to arresting such a person, as if arrested such a suspect will have no choice.

There are strict rules as to the treatment of suspects at the police station, and as to questioning both on the way to the station and once there. Code C provides that suspects *must not be questioned* except at a police station or other authorised place of detention, since this would deprive them of rights under PACE and Codes C, E and F[19] to which they are entitled, for example, legal advice.

When suspects arrive at the police station, the next step depends on whether they have gone voluntarily or have been arrested. If attending voluntarily, under PACE s29, they can leave at any time, unless then arrested to prevent such a departure. If already under arrest, they must be brought before the Custody Officer as soon as possible. This is an officer of at least the rank of sergeant who is not involved in the investigation concerning the suspect and who is thus independent. The Custody Officer must open a record which details the offence for which the accused is arrested, the grounds for detention and whether legal advice has been requested; the record must also include various regular checks on the suspects' appropriate treatment. For example, suspects have a right to regular meals at recognised mealtimes (two light ones and one main meal to be offered every 24 hours, plus drinks at meals and on reasonable request) and sleep (8 hours uninterrupted, usually at night). By virtue of PACE ss56 and 58, and the Annex B to Code C, there is a right to inform someone of their whereabouts as soon as possible. The notification of whereabouts and legal advice rights are only to be delayed on the authority of a senior officer (a superintendent in the case of legal advice and an inspector in the case of notification to a third party of the suspect's whereabouts on detention).

Detained persons may also make one telephone call, and if they request legal advice no interview should take place until that legal advice is received. Detainees should be checked every hour, be placed in a space which is habitable (i.e. not damp, ill lit or not lit at all, also properly ventilated); they must also have clean bedding and toilet facilities and clinical attention if appearing to need it, for all of which the Custody Officer is responsible.

The Custody Officer's job is therefore a very responsible one, pro-active rather than reactive. Thus, that officer must actually alert any detainee brought to his or her attention on arrival at

18 *Hayes v Chief Constable of Merseyside* [2011] EWCA Civ 911, [2012] 1 WLR 517; *Richardson v Chief Constable of Essex* [2011] EWHC 773 (QB), [2011] 2 Cr App R 1 where the Court held that 'necessary' is an ordinary English word so no need to go into what it means.

19 Code C (Detention, Treatment and Questioning of Persons by Police Officers); Code E (Audio Recording of Interviews With Suspects); Code F (Visual Recording With Sound of Interviews With Suspects).

the station to the right to legal advice and also to the services of the designated Duty Solicitor and must monitor and review the length of any custody, which is limited to 72 hours.

Moreover where a detainee is mentally disordered or 'a juvenile' (under 17) the Custody Officer must ask an 'appropriate adult' to come to the police station to give the person concerned detailed advice and assistance. This third party is normally a parent, guardian or social worker, and in any case not anyone employed by the police. Moreover, s11 of the Children Act 2004 requires chief police officers (and some other bodies) to ensure that in the discharge of their functions they have regard to the need to safeguard and promote the welfare of all persons under the age of 18.

DETENTION, TREATMENT AND QUESTIONING

As set out previously, detainees at the police station, whether on arrest or merely voluntarily there, 'helping the police with their enquiries', have certain basic rights to humane treatment, police detainees must have a cell to sleep in but must also have proper bedding, undisturbed sleep and meals at appropriate hours.

Rights while at the police station extend further: whether under arrest or voluntarily there during a police investigation, it might seem that no one is obliged actually to answer any questions at all, since questioning is usually the purpose of such police station attendance. This choice simply not to respond at all is known as 'the right to silence', one of the key freedoms under English and Welsh criminal law, which except in specific circumstances requires that guilt is 'proved beyond reasonable doubt', rather than that an accused should prove innocence. This might seem really odd when a case has reached a formal investigation stage, since the purpose of police investigation is to detect crime and process its investigation.

However, there is, of course, a downside to this for the suspect, since although the right to silence and the principle of innocence till proved guilty are absolute, 'inferences' (i.e. common sense conclusions) can be drawn if reasonable explanations that might have been given at the investigation stage are not offered when they might have been but instead saved till a later stage – when there would have been time and opportunity for a guilty person to think them up. There are therefore more rules which have to be complied with during this key investigation stage.

First, any questioning at any stage is an 'interview' and Code C states that this must be at the police station, so not in the street or on the journey to the station. Secondly, on arrival at the police station, that important official, the Custody Officer, must assess any person suspected of involvement in an offence as to fitness for interview. Thirdly, before an interview can commence the interviewee must be formally 'cautioned'. This, too, comes from Code C, and the formal wording is as follows:

> You do not have to say anything. But it may harm your defence if you do not mention when questioned something which you later rely on in court. Anything which you do say may be relied on in evidence.

Fourthly, Code C requires that interviews must be recorded. If the suspected offence is a summary one, there is a choice of method, which can be a written record, a sound recording or a video recording. If it is for an indictable offence, then Codes E and F require an audio or visual recording with sound, and the recording medium used must be unwrapped and resealed in the interviewee's presence. Moreover, the record must audibly include the interviewing officers' identities and those of any others present (e.g. a health professional, the station duty solicitor or any lawyer that the detainee or voluntary attendee has chosen to call upon) and contain a repeat of the caution and reminder of the right to free legal advice. In addition to the regular meals already mentioned, interviews also require regular breaks, for example, every two hours, a properly lit and ventilated interview room, no requirement of the interviewee to stand, and it should be ended as soon as, in the opinion of the officer in charge, enough information has been gathered for a viable prosecution.

Of course, sometimes the interview will gain no information at all if the interviewee declines to answer any questions, possibly on the advice of the solicitor present. One result that might be hoped for is a confession or admission of some sort, for which there are more rules under sections 76 and 82. According to s82(3) a confession is any statement wholly or partly adverse to the interviewee; it does not merely mean an admission of the offence, for example, where s/he admits being present or in the neighbourhood of the offence but denies committing any offence. Such admissions are only admissible in evidence if not obtained by 'oppression' (s76(2)(a), for example, interrogation involving repeated shouting or bullying over a long period until the interviewee gives up and agrees to the interviewers' suggestions)[20] or by inducements (s76(2)(b), defined as 'anything said or done which is likely, in the circumstances, to render any confession unreliable', for example, offering quick and easy bail from the police station in return for admissions of guilt which the interviewee has pressing reasons to accept).[21] In these circumstances, the prosecution at a trial would have to prove that the resulting admissions were not tainted in this way, a submission which for obvious reasons trial courts tend to have reservations in accepting as they did in these cases.

TAKING SAMPLES

If questioning has not produced the evidence required to justify prosecution, the police do have power to collect other potentially useful information in some cases, whether or not the detainee agrees to it; for example, they can take a photograph (s64A and Code D)[22] but can only use or disclose it for a purpose in connection of investigation, detection or prevention of offences or for prosecutions or sentences. Such photographs may be retained after the purpose in question but only used again for like purposes. Obviously, such a photograph may be very useful for a variety of permitted purposes.

20 *R v Miller* [1993] 97 Cr App R 99 (CA) (13 hours questioning on suspicion of murder, 300 denials by the accused before eventually confessing).

21 *R v Barry* [1992] 95 Crim App R 384 (CA) (sole carer father of nine-year-old son induced to confess in return for bail to enable him to return as soon as possible to the boy).

22 Which details the information which must be given to the detainee before such samples are collected.

More useful are likely to be fingerprints, although these may be taken without the subject's consent only where the detainee has been arrested or charged with a 'recordable' offence (i.e. recordable in police records – though this would include a 'caution'[23] or warning as well as a conviction: s61). More useful still might be an imprint of footwear, which can be taken under the same conditions as fingerprints: s61A, or a 'non-intimate sample' (hair or a scraping from under a nail) which is also subject to the same conditions.

'Intimate samples',[24] if not agreed to by the detainee, may only be taken with the permission of an inspector or officer of superior rank, who has to have the same 'reasonable belief' of the subject's involvement in a recordable offence, as in most cases where this objective belief is required, and if the subject refuses consent, a judge or jury may later draw inferences.

The police can now retain these samples whether or not the subject is charged or convicted, except for footwear impressions which have to be destroyed after six months from their being 'necessary' for detection, investigation, prosecution etc.: s63S, though the DNA sample itself has to be destroyed as soon as the DNA profile has been extracted.

Thus, the contemporary police have a good deal of scientific assistance at their disposal.

SEARCH OF PREMISES

For search of premises a warrant issued by a Justice of the Peace (Magistrate) is usually required. Such a warrant will be issued if there are reasonable grounds to believe that an indictable offence[25] has been committed and that there is material on the premises that is likely to be of substantial importance to investigation of the offence. On certain occasions, pursuant to PACE s17, it is sometimes justified for police to search without a warrant. This would include when they have a warrant of arrest to arrest a person for an indictable offence or for a number of summary offences (e.g. driving under the influence of drink or drugs) in any of which cases they must reasonably believe that the person to be arrested is in the premises.

There are other exceptions to the need for a warrant, such as where the search is necessary to save life or limb or prevent serious damage to property, and there is also a power under s18 if the premises are owned or controlled by a person under arrest for an indictable offence, although in that case the police must reasonably believe that there is evidence on the premises relating to the indictable offence – or another indictable offence which is connected or similar – *and*, in that case, the officer(s) concerned have the authority of an inspector or more senior police officer.

23 A *caution* is a formal process where the offender admits guilt but the police or CPS prosecutors decide to engage in this process (which will still remain on the police national computer) rather than to prosecute. This usually applies to minor offences, as it cannot be used for an indictable offence or certain either-way offences: Criminal Justice and Courts Act 2015 s117.

24 Blood, semen, urine, dental impressions.

25 This means an offence that is triable on indictment in the Crown Court rather than a less serious (summary) offence triable by the magistrates: see Chapter 8, on the court structure.

Otherwise it is true that a citizen's 'house is his castle' and it cannot be entered by force unless the aforementioned conditions apply (and even if they do any force used must be proportionate). However if any relevant material is found on premises to which the police have correctly obtained access, they can seize it as evidence.

CHARGING THE ACCUSED

With the exception of those charges brought directly by the CPS or other prosecuting agencies with the power to do so under certain statutes, the usual channel into the trial process will be from the police station to the Magistrates' Court, whether or not the case is then tried there.

Once it is clear that there is sufficient evidence to charge an offender, which pursuant to PACE s37 will be the decision of the Custody Officer, s37A requires that officer to have regard to guidance issued by the Director of Public Prosecutions in deciding whether to charge the accused, and with what offence, or whether to pass this matter to Crown Prosecutors, who are employed by the CPS and available within police stations to provide charging advice; this service includes a duty prosecutor out of hours. There is thus a strong link between the police station and the CPS for the purpose of settling the *correct* charge with a view to bringing prosecutions which do not waste everyone's time by collapsing at the trial stage.

In theory, this system should work to ensure that only sound cases are pursued (and the citizen thus not harassed by speculative charges), since the rules also distinguish between the minor 'summary' offences which can be *tried* by the Magistrates' Court (which may include 'either-way' offences, where the accused will plead guilty and sentencing by the Magistrates is likely to be suitable) and the more serious 'indictable' offences which will start in the Magistrates but be tried in the Crown Court. The Custody Officer may make charging decisions only in the case of the summary or either-way offences in the first category and *not* in relation to indictable offences, where the charging decision must be made by the CPS.

Moreover, if the initial investigation stage has been properly conducted, evidence should have been appropriately gathered: however there are other options open since apart from a charge a case could be disposed of in an appropriate context by a warning or caution, or the accused could be released on police bail to enable the CPS to make a charging decision at a later date: s37B.

Taking a decision of this sort can be quite complex so that such a delay might be justified. There is a Code for Crown Prosecutors which sets out specific tests to be applied: Prosecution of Offenders Act 1985, s10. Clearly, the first test is whether the evidence is sufficient, but the second requires the Prosecutor dealing with the case to consider whether prosecution is in the public interest, in which context the age, health, etc. of the perpetrator, the seriousness of the crime and the likelihood of repetition if the offence is not prosecuted together with the impact on the victim are all relevant, and as to which the Prosecutor must form an overall view.[26]

26 See <www.cps.gov.uk/cps/news/publication-revised-code-crown-prosecutors>.

Once an accused has been charged no further questioning is allowed other than in exceptional circumstances: Code C 16.5, and by PACE s38 the Custody Officer must order the detainee's release unless further detention is necessary, for example, where the charge is murder or some other reason to believe that s/he will fail to appear in court to answer to bail. So we may now move on to look at how a case progresses through the criminal justice system.

THE CRIMINAL COURT PROCESS

Where an accused is not charged at the police station (because it is not a charge within the police powers but for the CPS to handle, or for other reasons), the CPS process is to issue a written charge together with a requisition for the accused to appear before a Magistrates' Court to answer the charge. These documents are then served on the accused. The former process, still seen in some old black-and-white films, of laying an information before a Justice of the Peace (Magistrate) is now only available for private prosecutions, that is, that the CPS is not prosecuting or has discontinued, which members of the public discontented with the outcome of a public prosecution sometimes avail themselves.

THE SUMMARY TRIAL PROCESS

In view of all the attention to detail and professionalism required of the police in the investigation stage it might be thought that this would automatically get the accused into court for a trial without further delay. In practice this only tends to happen in the Magistrates' Court on summary only offences where the accused can decide whether to plead guilty or not guilty and if the former for the court to proceed to sentence, though there might be an adjournment for a pre-sentence report to be prepared.

The trial will either be by three lay magistrates with the assistance of their legal advisor or of a single professional magistrate, a district judge (Magistrates' Courts).[27] A notable exception to this is for minor crimes that are uncontested and which are not subject to imprisonment, where a single magistrate can set alone. In such circumstances, the case could also be determined only on the papers and also in the absence of the accused and counsel for prosecution and defence.

However, normally the accused should be present and plead to the charge. The magistrate(s) will decide both facts and law, though with regard to the law the bench has the advice of the Legal Advisor whose advice must be given in the presence of the prosecution and defence so that they may make submissions on any points which arise.

27 Criminal Justice and Courts Act 2015 ss 46–50.

The Magistrates will be trying either summary or either-way offences, and the trial will proceed in the same way as in the Crown Court, save that there is no jury and a majority verdict of two magistrates is sufficient. However, the Magistrates also have the option of not sentencing themselves but remitting the accused to the Crown Court for sentence in the case of serious or sexual offences.[28]

EITHER-WAY OFFENCES BEFORE THE MAGISTRATES AND/OR THE CROWN COURT

Either-way offences in the Magistrates' Court are more complicated and here there is inevitably more pre-trial work to be done, not least because if an offence is either way it is necessary to decide where it will be tried for which there is an 'allocation procedure'.[29] If the decision is to send the case to the Crown Court it will be sent there forthwith pursuant to the Crime and Disorder Act 1998 s51.[30] Both the court and the accused have an interest in having a say as to the location of the trial. This is effected by a process called 'Plea Before Venue' in which the accused is asked if s/he would plead guilty or not guilty when the case comes to be tried.[31] If the plea is guilty the Magistrates must then decide whether their powers are sufficient to sentence the accused for the offence in question (Magistrates having only the power to award a maximum six-month custodial sentence or 12-month if two or more either-way offences are involved) or whether the case should be sent to the Crown Court for sentence, where that Court's powers are usually up to the maximum or statutory limit for the offence(s) in question. Clearly the accused will also be bearing this discrepancy in sentencing powers in mind when deciding whether to go for a quick decision before the Magistrates with a lesser maximum sentence available or whether to go for a Crown Court trial before a jury where s/he might have been advised that s/he would be more likely to get off altogether, and in fact statistically acquittal is more likely in the Crown Court where the jury decides on guilt or innocence.

If the accused either says that s/he will plead not guilty or does not say what the plea will be, then the Magistrates must follow the Allocation Procedure in ss19–23 of the Magistrates Courts Act 1980 as amended by the Criminal Justice Act 2003 (CJA 2003). In accordance with the Criminal Procedure Rules 2025 Part 9 (CrimPR 2025, Part 9),[32] this means that before the Allocation Procedure can commence, the prosecution must serve on the accused details of the prosecution case – otherwise, since *they* must prove their case, not the accused disprove it, it would not be fair for the accused to have to say which way s/he would plead until the strength of the prosecution's case could be assessed by the defence team.

---

28 Powers of Criminal Courts (Sentencing) Act 2000.

29 In old reports, this is called 'mode of trial' procedure.

30 The 'committal proceedings' found in old reports are now replaced by the contemporary allocation procedure.

31 Magistrates Courts Act 1980 s17A.

32 To distinguish the Criminal Procedure Rules from the comparable civil set, the CPR 1998, the Criminal Procedure Rules are usually abbreviated CrimPR 2025. See the rules in full at <https://www.legislation.gov.uk/uksi/2025/909/contents>.

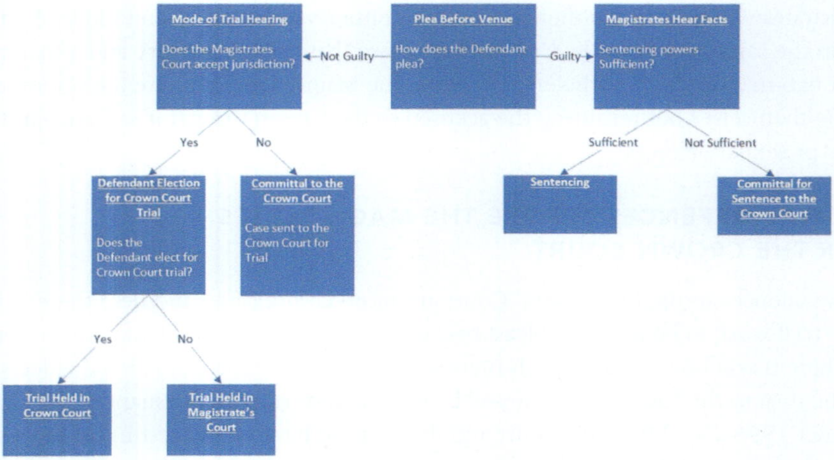

Figure 11.1 Criminal trials in either-way offences.

Thus, it is seen that criminal justice in English and Welsh law is as adversarial as the civil process and is regulated by rules of court very similar in format to the CPR 1998 as amended, which have reformed civil justice. Like the CPR they have numbered Parts (50 corresponding to the stages of a criminal case, preliminary hearings to appeals, last updated in 2025),[33] are supplemented by Criminal Practice Directions (CPDs) and have an 'overriding objective', which is thus:

- Acquit innocent defendants
- Deal with the parties fairly
- Recognise the defendant's rights (especially the ECHR Article 6 right to a fair trial)
- Respect the interests of witnesses, victims and jurors
- Deal with cases efficiently and expeditiously
- Deal with cases in ways which take into account the gravity of offences, complexity of issues, severity of consequences and needs of other cases

The wording clearly echoes the objectives and resource issues which are articulated in the CPR 1998, and the parties are also expected to conduct the case in accordance with the overriding objective which seeks to balance the interests of both prosecution and defence just as in the CPR 1998 as amended and (in the Family Court) the FPR 2010 as amended those rules of court attempt to balance the interests of all parties as a whole (including those of HMCTS who must administer the courts so as to deliver justice and to achieve these respective overriding objectives).

ALLOCATION PROCEDURE

First, the Magistrates must decide if the case is suitable for trial by them. If they decide it is not, for example, inherently too serious, then the accused will be sent for trial at the Crown Court and has no say in the matter (see Figure 11.1).

33 <https://www.legislation.gov.uk/uksi/2025/909/contents>.

There are several factors the Magistrates must take into account before making their decision apart from the seriousness of the offence: nature of the case, their sentencing powers and any other relevant circumstances: they need to be told about the accused's previous convictions as this would affect sentencing. The parties, that is, prosecution and defence, may make representations on suitability for one trial venue or the other.

If the Magistrates decide the case could be tried by them, then the accused must decide if he will elect trial by jury in the Crown Court or if he prefers to be tried by the Magistrates, and that is the accused's decision entirely, no doubt with the assistance of the defence team. Before deciding, the accused can ask the Magistrates for an indication of whether they would be likely to give a custodial or non-custodial sentence on a plea of guilty, and though they do not have to answer this question, they may do so.

To the accused, there is a balancing exercise that will need to be done in order to determine whether they would prefer to have their case heard in the Crown Court, or to remain in the Magistrates' Court. In terms of the attraction to the Crown Court:

- A judge will usually keep prejudicial evidence from the jury, unlike in a Magistrates' Court, who may not be able to forget it.
- A Crown Court judge may be better able to deal with the law.
- A jury may be sympathetic to the factual context in which the alleged offence took place.

In terms of weighting towards the Magistrates' Court:

- The Crown Court's greater sentencing powers.
- The Crown Court is more expensive, and convicted, the accused may have to pay part of the prosecution costs.
- It may take longer to get a court hearing, which may matter to an accused.

There are Allocation Guidelines issued by the Sentencing Council to help inform any decision of the magistrates.[34]

INDICTABLE OFFENCES

Since these must go straight to the Crown Court pursuant to the Crime and Disorder Act 1998 s51, it might be thought that that would mean these cases reached trial without more ado. However these cases have a Plea and Trial Preparation Hearing (PTPH) which must be set by the Magistrates when sending the case to the Crown Court and this must be within 28 days of despatch by the Magistrates to the Crown Court. The reason for this is that the accused must be 'arraigned' in the Crown Court, that is, the charge must be read out to the accused who must then plead to the charge, guilty or not guilty, since the plea is taken there and not at the Magistrates. Obviously if the accused then pleads guilty there will be no need for a trial and as in the same circumstances in the Magistrates' Court, the court (i.e. the Judge in the Crown

34 <https://www.sentencingcouncil.org.uk/wp-content/uploads/Allocation-definitive-guideline-Web.pdf>.

Court) will proceed immediately to sentence, unless an adjournment is needed for a pre-sentence report to be prepared.

Where the accused pleads not guilty, there will be more pre-trial preparatory work to do so that information will need to be gathered from the parties in order that the PTPH judge can set a timetable for the trial, and as for a more complex civil trial, since this will concern thus:

- The issues in the case
- Witnesses to be called
- Expert evidence to be relied upon

But also since this is a criminal trial:

- Whether there is any 'bad character' evidence, the subject of complex rules pursuant to the Criminal Justice Act 2003, or other applications.

The judge should then be able to set a date for the trial but sometimes a case might be so complex that a further PTPH will be required, called a Further Case Management Hearing (FCMH), for example, if the case is particularly serious, includes a vulnerable witness, the accused is a child or unrepresented, or there is some other complexity such as a lengthy trial, but the Crim PR PD3A indicates that there should not be a further hearing other than in exceptional circumstances, another indication of how the Crim PR have followed the civil and Family Courts' rules in encouraging expedition and efficiency. Nonetheless, at the time of writing there remained something of a crisis in the delays of criminal prosecutions with trials being listed, in some cases, *years* after the alleged offence took place.

TRIAL ON INDICTMENT IN THE CROWN COURT

After the pre-trial hearings, are we ready to begin the actual trial? Not necessarily! There may be a stage called 'plea bargaining' to deal with, and there may be issues about 'disclosure', and these may happen right up to or even on the day of the trial, including at the door of the court, and either could hold up the trial or even prevent its taking place at all.

The object of plea bargaining is to encourage pleas of guilty in return for a sentence benefit for the accused so that, for example, the accused might plead guilty to a lesser charge on the same facts in return for a lesser sentence. It might be thought that this is unethical since if the police and CPS have done their job properly the accused should be coming to court on the right charge already. However, a guilty plea to a lesser charge in these circumstances can also benefit the victim as well as the administration of criminal justice, in addition to the accused: the victim because s/he will not have to give evidence of what may have been traumatic circumstances, the administration of criminal justice as a guilty plea will free up court time and resources in a system which is overloaded, and the accused who may then have a lesser sentence since there is a discount for a guilty plea (up to a third, and the more discount the earlier in the process the plea of guilty occurs).

Disclosure issues which might arise at the last minute might be because of some argument about what is known as 'unused material'. The prosecution will already have given the accused all material on which it intends to rely at the trial under the initial disclosure rules, which required disclosure of anything that might reasonably undermine the prosecution case or assist the defence, and in response, the accused is to provide a 'defence statement' which sets out the main points of the defence, for example, whether there is an alibi claimed, and of witnesses who are to be called: Criminal Procedure and Investigations Act 1996, s6. However, the prosecution also has a duty to keep disclosure under review,[35] particularly in light of the defence statement, including material they do not intend to use but which may be necessary to disclose to ensure a fair trial, that is, the unused material, and if the accused who has given a defence statement suspects that there is material that the prosecution has which should have been disclosed, disclosure of that material can be applied for under s8 of the Act.

THE CROWN COURT TRIAL PROCESS

Finally, we have arrived at the trial as such. This may be many months or even years after the facts that lead to the charging of the accused with the offence. This is an adversarial process, as in civil cases but the one major difference between a civil trial in the County or High Court and the criminal process in the Crown Court is the role of the jury in the Crown Court. The first stage of a Crown Court trial is to empanel and swear in a jury (see Chapter 12). The accused is then 'given in charge to the jury' which means they are then told that it is for them, having heard all the evidence, to determine whether the accused is guilty or not guilty. The only role of the judge in relation to this crucial issue in the trial is to direct the jury as to whether there is sufficient evidence in law for them to find the accused guilty, and if not that they must acquit him.

The trial then commences, usually in public and with the accused present, though there is power to hear the case in private[36] or in the accused's absence; for example, if an accused has absconded, this will not prevent the trial being held.

THE ORDER OF SPEECHES AND EVIDENCE

A Crown Court case is carefully choreographed with a specific running order that ensures that cases have a consistency of approach as between them and that both sides get the opportunity to put their case.

THE PROSECUTION CASE

The case for the prosecution is first, beginning with an opening speech by prosecution counsel, who outlines the evidence in simple form, so the jury understands what the case is

35 s7A.

36 For example, where the offence is under the Official Secrets Acts and to admit the public might be prejudicial to national safety.

about. Prosecuting counsel will then call the witnesses against the accused, who will then be 'examined in chief' (which means asking them to give their evidence, in practice asking them if they stand by the evidence that they have already given when making the signed statement, called their 'proof of evidence'). These witnesses are then cross-examined by defence counsel. If there are several co-defendants tried together, defence counsel for each is entitled to cross-examine separately. Prosecution counsel may then 're-examine' to clarify the evidence that has been given before passing on to the next witness. At this stage of giving evidence-in-chief, the prosecution may not generally ask 'leading questions' (i.e. those to which the question suggests the answer), and in most cases, witnesses must give evidence personally, though if any evidence is not disputed, the statement may be read out instead of the witness attending personally.

At this stage, the prosecution has provided its case and so there is an opportunity to assess whether it is *possible* to demonstrate that the relevant standard of proof – beyond reasonable doubt – can be established even if all prosecution evidence is accepted. This is a question of law – that is, whether it is *possible* for the prosecution case to be proved to the requisite standard – and so it is for the judge alone to make this determination on application by the defence.[37] Although the judge finding 'no case to answer' is rare, it is an important feature of criminal justice as it reinforces the fact that it is for the *prosecution* to discharge the burden of proof to the requisite standard. If this is, in law, impossible then the trial should be halted through a direction from the judge to acquit.[38]

THE DEFENCE CASE

Following the prosecution case, the defence counsel goes through the same process, unless following the conclusion of the prosecution evidence the defence team considers that the prosecution has not established a sufficient case on which to convict the accused of the offence(s) charged, in which case they will make a submission of 'no case to answer'. This, of course, is because of the principle that, with certain specific exceptions, it is for the prosecution to establish its case, not for the defence to establish the innocence of the accused. Thus, if the submission is successful, the judge will direct the jury that they must acquit the accused. The case must be proved by the criminal standard of 'beyond reasonable doubt', and the prosecution bears the burden of proof throughout, including disproving any defences, with rare exceptions, for example, the defence must prove the common law defence of insanity, and some statutes require the defence to assume the burden of proof, for example, the Homicide Act 1957 s2 in relation to diminished responsibility.[39]

There are also certain other specific rules which might change the process described previously, for example, where the accused is acting in person (without legal representation) s/he will not be permitted to cross-examine a 'victim' or 'vulnerable person',[40] that is, a sexual

---

37 The jury are not informed of this application for fear that it will prejudice the defendant should the trial proceed.

38 It was put in *R v Galbraith* [1981] 1 WLR 1039 (CA) that it was a judge's *duty* to stop a case in these circumstances.

39 See *M'Naghten's case* (1843) 10 CI and Finn 200; *Woolmington v DPP* [1935] AC 462 (HL); *Mancini v DPP* [1942] AC 1 (HL).

40 Youth Justice and Criminal Evidence Act 1999.

offence complainant or a child witness, whereupon such questions may only be put through the judge.

The case for the defence then follows in the same way, with an opening speech by defence counsel and all witnesses, including the accused, examined in chief by the defence counsel. If the accused is acting without legal representation, s/he can still make an opening speech outlining the case for the jury and the evidence to be called, providing s/he is going to give evidence and call other witnesses. However, if the accused is the only witness or is not going to give evidence, there is no entitlement to an opening speech. If there are several co-defendants, their evidence is given in the order in which they appear on the indictment, and they are cross-examined in the same order, with each witness also being cross-examined by counsel for the other co-defendants. Nevertheless, this is normally the limit of the prosecution's opportunity to challenge defence evidence, as prosecution counsel cannot normally introduce any further evidence unless in rebuttal of any evidence given by the defence; for example, if the accused gives evidence of good character, the prosecution can then introduce evidence to the contrary.

CLOSING SPEECHES

There are then final speeches from each side. The prosecution goes first here, and the defence last,[41] usually a significant advantage as 'having the last word' means the defence's case is last in the jury's memory before they hear from the judge in his summing up.

SUMMING UP

Next, the judge will 'sum up', explaining to the jury the elements of the offence(s), the burden and the standard of proof. The judge will also consider some more technical points, such as 'inferences' that may be drawn from certain matters, such as silence at certain points when an explanation could have been given, and also the impact of an accused's good or bad character. Given the technical nature of some of the rules or principles and their central importance to the jury's determination, it is important that judges undertake this activity with particular care. There is also regular training on summing up that is provided by the Judicial College.

VERDICT

Following the summing up, the jury will 'retire' to consider its verdict. They are first encouraged to try to reach a unanimous verdict and only if this is not possible (after a period of at least two hours) will the judge direct them that the court will accept a majority[42] verdict. The jury can ask, normally through their foreperson,[43] for clarification as to the law or the evidence. The jurors would traditionally be sequestered to a hotel if deliberations lasted more than a day, but the Criminal Justice and Public Order Act 1994 altered the position and the jury may now, unless the judge directs otherwise, return home between days of deliberation.

41 Criminal Procedure (Right of Reply) Act 1964 s1.

42 Most typically 10–12.

43 The jury will elect a foreperson from within their number, and this person is responsible for structuring the discussions and will typically be the person who communicates with the judge and who speaks in court to confirm the verdict.

If no majority can be reached and it seems that this will not change, then proceedings will end with a *Watson*[44] direction, and it will be for the CPS to consider whether there is merit in a retrial.

Verdicts will be either 'guilty' or 'not guilty'.[45] If guilty, the judge will either proceed immediately to sentence or alternatively fix another date for sentence, for example, if a pre-sentence report is required which cannot be provided immediately.

SENTENCING

Sentencing takes place against the backdrop of s142 of the Criminal Justice Act 2003, which lays out the factors to which the court must 'have regard'. These include the *punishment* of offenders, the reduction in crime, the reform and rehabilitation of offenders, the protection of the public and the making of reparation of offenders to persons affected by their offences.

The courts can, depending on the offence, issue a range of sentences, including discharge,[46] a fine, community sentence[47] or custodial (prison) sentence.[48] Therefore a sentence can range from no particular punishment (an unconditional discharge) to a 'whole life term' which will involve a sentence with no end. There are a range of factors that will help a judge in determining the appropriate sentence; chief amongst these are the sentencing guidelines produced by the Sentencing Council[49] and any guidance issued by the Court of Appeal.

TAKING THINGS FURTHER

The website that accompanies this text contains some practical examples of how sentencing is applied in the courts. It considers very serious and less serious criminal offences and uses hypothetical situations to demonstrate how judges go about balancing the various factors that must be taken into account when calculating a sentence.

APPEALS

Criminal appeals are more complex than those considered for civil matters. The stakes in terms of individual liberty are clearly much higher.

In the most general of terms, defence appeals can be against conviction or against sentence. At the level of the Magistrates' Court, appeals against sentence or conviction will go to the Crown

44 *R v Watson* [1988] QB 690 (CA).

45 In Scotland, there is a second route to acquittal with a verdict of 'not proven'.

46 Complete or conditional.

47 There is a wide range of community sentences, from curfew and tagging to unpaid work in the community to drug and alcohol courses.

48 Suspended, of determinate period or of an indeterminate period.

49 Governed by the Coroners and Justice Act 2009.

Court where a new hearing of the entire case will be heard.[50] Appeals from the Crown Court will go to the Court of Appeal (Criminal Division).

There are also a number of routes of appeal for the prosecution, including the ability for the Attorney General to refer questions of law to the Court of Appeal[51] and also to refer sentences where they are regarded as unduly lenient.

As discussed in the chapter relating to the court structure, there are also limited mechanisms for resolving miscarriages of justice when new evidence or new legal argument come to light after all routes of appeal have been exhausted. This requires reference back to the Court of Appeal by the Criminal Cases Review Commission.

THE WEBSITE

The website that accompanies this textbook contains many useful resources that you can use to consolidate and further your knowledge of the law, to hone your skills of critical analysis and to test your knowledge. This includes a set of multiple-choice questions (MCQs) that can be used to test your knowledge and understanding of the material.

50 There is also an appeal by way of case stated that would go to the High Court where magistrates have exceeded their jurisdiction or to consider a point of law.

51 These do not affect the outcome of a particular case.

12

CHAPTER 12
THE JURY

INTRODUCTION

Trial by jury is an iconic and long-standing feature of the legal system of England and Wales. It is also amongst the most easily recognisable and identifiable parts of the justice system. The ability to serve on a jury is one of the few opportunities that citizens have to be intimately and directly involved in the *administration* of justice in the legal system. Equally, being tried by a jury of one's peers is an important safeguard in preventing the abuse of state power. In this way, trial by jury takes on a constitutional significance for both jurors and parties and is elevated above many other aspects of the legal system. Despite this recognition and importance, or perhaps because of it, there is also an air of mystery to the role of juror and a fair amount of wrongful perception about how widespread jury trials are and how they operate. Although seen by some as an antiquated and creaking part of the system, the concept of trial by jury is faced with some very modern problems, including the rise of social media and increased press coverage of the behaviour of parties and jurors.

The purpose of this chapter is to unpick the law and policy surrounding jury trials and to assess the contribution that they make to the legal system. This analysis will involve looking at the development, use and function of jury trials, as well as tackling some of the problems caused by trial by jury. The chapter will also briefly consider potential reforms of the system of jury trials.

AS YOU READ

By the end of this chapter you should be able to **describe** the origin and function of the jury in criminal and civil trials. In addition, you will be able to **explain** the qualification requirements for being called for jury service and the grounds on which a person may be disqualified, excused or deferred from jury service.

Turning to higher-order skills, as you read, **consider critically** the merits (and problems) of maintaining the system of jury trials, and try to **evaluate** recent changes and proposals for reform of the jury system. By doing this, you should begin to form a view of what future, if any, jury trials have in the legal system.

In order to try to unify the diverse strands of analysis in this chapter, **consider** the development of technology as both a challenge to jury service and a way of achieving greater efficiency in the selection for and implementation of jury trials.

DOI: 10.4324/9781032641829-12

THE IMPORTANCE OF THE JURY

ORIGINS

Within the legal system, the origin of juries can be traced back at least to the 11th century. However, it is important to note that the juries of Saxon and Norman times are almost unrecognisable compared to the juries in use today.[1] Originally, jurors of the early and late Middle Ages had an *investigatory* role outside of a formal trial and jurors were drawn from a narrow class of persons. This extended beyond criminal matters and jurors were also involved in resolving private land disputes. The common understanding of juries today relates to criminal trials, but they were (and still are) also used in civil matters. The key unifying factor was the independent investigatory nature of the role of a juror, coupled with the highly restricted eligibility criteria to act as one.

The 13th century started to see a change in the function of jurors from evidence gatherers and witnesses of good standing towards the role that they occupy today as triers of fact and as those that determine guilt or innocence, since it is the jury, *not* the judge, who decides, on the evidence before the court, whether the case against the accused has been *proved*, on the criminal standard of 'beyond reasonable doubt'.

This 13th century, early medieval, time in the development of the legal system of England and Wales was one of some upheaval with the right to jury trial being enshrined in Magna Carta[2] after the turmoil between the barons, the Church and the King and trial by ordeal[3] losing the support of the Church. Nonetheless, juries still retained evidence gathering functions for a further 400 years. During this time, and as procedural/evidential rules developed in the common law courts, the assumption that jurors ought to have some connection with the facts of the case (an almost witness-like role) diminished and was replaced with the contrary assumption that jurors ought to have *no* connection with the parties or facts of the case before the trial. As we shall see later in this chapter, it is now of vital importance that a juror has no prior knowledge of the parties and that research by jurors into the circumstances of the case may lead to a conviction being unsafe. This is a clear example of how a legal system can develop as it matures and in such a process even accepted understandings can be overturned.

Thus, like many features of the legal system of England and Wales, the role of the jury has developed over time with the very function changing significantly. And yet at the core, the principle of involving citizens in the *administration* of justice has remained.

1 It is of interest to note that one thing that has stood the test of time is the *number* of jurors typically used (12). This quirk (found in jury systems around the world) is discussed in Gary Slapper, *How the Law Works* (2nd edn, Routledge 2011) Ch 8.

2 Article 39 of Magna Carta 1215 states: 'No free man is to be arrested, or imprisoned, or disseised, or outlawed, or exiled, or in any other way ruined, nor will we go against him or send against him, except by the lawful judgment of his peers or by the law of the land.'

3 Ended by Pope Innocent III in 1215 and recognised in England by Henry III in 1219, although the practice continued in Europe for many years after that and, indeed, was still prevalent in England in the Civil War and also even later in the American Colonies.

THE RATIONALE FOR JURY TRIAL

There is a great deal of legal and political rhetoric surrounding jury trial. Its place in Magna Carta has ascribed to it a constitutional value that is difficult to displace. Despite its inherent weaknesses and costs to maintain, support for jury trial is still high amongst the legal professions, the judiciary, politicians and citizens.

The emotive nature of trial by one's peers can make it difficult to pinpoint the underlying rationale for retaining the jury system. The most vocal and persuasive reason given for maintaining trial by jury relates to ensuring freedom and liberty for citizens. Perhaps most famously, Lord Devlin held that the principle of trial by jury is 'more than an instrument of justice and more than one wheel of the constitution; it is the lamp that shows that freedom lives'.[4] This had added weight when it is remembered that traditionally many crimes that would have required jury trials had the death penalty as the ultimate punishment. In those cases, the need to protect the citizen from potential abuse by the state was particularly important.[5] By removing judges as the sole arbiter of fact and guilt, the potential for an accusation of state bias is reduced.

ANALYSING THE LAW – SEPARATION OF POWERS

The principle of separation of powers, and particularly the independence of the judiciary, is considered elsewhere in this text and is a theme that will be explored if you study constitutional law in any level of detail. Given that there is a well-established appeals system that is distinct from any executive interference, it is unclear whether the additional safeguard of trial by jury is still necessary. Jury trials are used in a minority of cases (both civil and criminal).

Abuses of the legal process by the state are pernicious and deleterious to public confidence in the justice system. Nonetheless, are arguments in favour of jury trial that rely on the risk of 'state' or 'establishment' bias compelling? Are there examples of times where jury trials have equally led to unsatisfactory results or miscarriages of justice?

Although discussed in greater detail later, it is worth noting that the principle of 'jury equity' could also be cited as a reason for supporting jury trials. In criminal trials, juries are entitled to acquit on the basis of conscience and against the compelling evidence that the legal 'ingredients' of an offence have been satisfied.

4 Lord Delvin, *Trial by Jury* (Stevens & Son 1956) 164.

5 In the words of Lord Justice Cassels '[Juries] stand between the Crown and the subject, and they are still one of the main defences of personal liberty.' *R v McKenna (William James)* [1960] 1 QB 411 (CA) 329 where a judge threatened to keep a jury overnight if they could not reach a speedy verdict.

The issues discussed so far focus on the reasons that one of the *parties* may support the use of juries. Lord Denning noted that jury service gives 'ordinary folk their finest lesson in citizenship'.[6] The public duty aspect and sense of civic responsibility are an additional reason for jury trial. This may be a slightly romanticised view (particularly given the attempts that citizens go to in order to *avoid* jury service) of modern citizenship, but it is a timely reminder that the justice system is as much about *cultural* and *societal* identity as it is about strict legal rules. This cultural heritage is fuelled by powerful jury scenes that are portrayed in the media and popular culture within the UK and beyond.[7]

None of the preceding is to say that juries are not without their detractors. In a direct response to Lord Delvin's *statement*, Professor Darbyshire wrote a scathing but well-reasoned attack on jury trials, arguing that they led to 'erratic and secret decisions [that] run counter to the rule of law'.[8]

TAKING THINGS FURTHER AND ANALYSING THE LAW – JURIES AROUND THE WORLD

It is easy to become absorbed in the particular legal culture under study and to forget that there are alternative approaches taken elsewhere in the world. Given the prominence accorded to jury trial in the news and in popular fiction (particularly those emanating from high-profile common law jurisdictions like the USA, which dominate the film-making industry), a student new to the study of law may be forgiven for thinking that all legal orders adopt the jury system in an extensive manner. This is far from the truth, and certain jurisdictions adopt a more restrictive system of trial by jury than that in operation in England and Wales or do not operate jury trials at all.

Different legal cultures attach different levels of importance to the various advantages and disadvantages of trial by jury. The proponents of jury trial often point to the ability of juries to acquit in the face of the law as a distinct advantage. This ability to judge according to a juror's conscience can, however, spark unease and, it is argued, led to the removal of trial by jury in India from the 1960s. On the other hand, the lack of a jury for the high-profile murder trial of athlete Oscar Pistorius has also led to calls for a reconsideration of the system in South Africa.

6 See more in Alfred Denning, *What Next in the Law* (Butterworths 1982) 33.

7 Some of the most memorable court scenes in major films and literature involve speeches to the jury. One of the most famous of such speeches to the jury is that of Atticus Finch, defence counsel in Harper Lee's Pulitzer Prize–winning novel *To Kill a Mockingbird*, filmed with Gregory Peck in the role in 1962, as he defends a Black man accused of raping a White girl, at the height of Southern United States race discrimination unrest, which still has considerable impact in both film and literature, despite the passage of time.

8 Penny Darbyshire, 'What Can We Learn from Published Jury Research' [2001] Crim LR 970. Later research (by Cheryl Thomas *Are Juries Fair?* February 2010, Ministry of Justice Research Series 1/10) seems to suggest that some of the criticisms of jury trials were based on assumption rather than fact, as the report (described in the media as 'groundbreaking' – inevitably as little or no research has been done) found that they were fair and 'effective', but also that 31% of jurors did not understand the instructions they were given.

Although jury trial is a fundamental right under the British constitution,[9] it is not regarded as a facet of the basic human right to a fair trial under the European Convention on Human Rights.[10] This means that within Europe there is no common approach to jury trials. Some countries use them for a range of offences (e.g. England and Wales), others save them for extremely serious criminal offences (e.g. France), some use them only in very particular circumstances (e.g. Sweden)[11] and others do not use jury trials at all (e.g. the Netherlands).[12]

Equally, when studying legal systems, it is important to note that even core features can (and will) evolve over time. Japan has, within the last two decades, introduced a limited form of jury trial. Similar moves have been made in Mexico – a state which has the *potential* for jury trials mentioned in its Constitution but which has not applied extensive trial by jury since the 1930s.

Not only is understanding the way other jurisdictions choose to do things an important way of better understanding the legal system; it can also be a way of enriching assessment answers. The same is true when considering the reasons that a legal system chooses to change a core feature. By including, in a meaningful way, commentary on other legal systems, you can demonstrate to an examiner a wider understanding of how the law operates within the legal system and how (and why) things might be done differently elsewhere. This involves more than just commenting that things are done differently, and an effort should be made to explain *why* things may be done differently and to assess whether the alternative is more or less effective than the approach taken by the English legal system.

Having explored briefly the origins and potential rationale(s) for the system of trial by jury, the chapter will now turn to the different purposes to which jury trials may be put.

THE FUNCTION AND FORMS OF JURY TRIAL

Given the important constitutional value placed on jury trial, it is of interest to note that the *use* of jury trial is now fairly limited in the legal system of England and Wales. The trend, over the past 300 years, has been for a reduction in the types of cases that are given a jury trial. Jury trials are now predominantly reserved for serious criminal matters but still have a place in both the system of coroners' courts and in certain (albeit very limited) civil matters. As this chapter will explore at its end, that reform and narrowing continues today.

9 As evidenced by its inclusion in Magna Carta 1215.

10 The right is to an independent tribunal – this requirement can be met by a trial by judge alone (a bench trial), as found in *Twomey* [2013] ECHR 577, which is discussed later.

11 Jury trials are only for highly particular situations, such as in defamation trials.

12 Jury trials were used for a few years during the 19th century, whilst the Netherlands was under French occupation.

FUNCTION OF A JURY

In addition to the symbolic and historical importance attached to jury trial, the jury performs a set of practical functions.

Chief, and common, amongst the functions of a jury trial is that of determining the true facts of the case, where these are in dispute. The judge will determine matters of law and procedure and will direct the jury as to the relevant legal tests and will explain core concepts such as the burden and standard of proof. This separation of functions between the judge (determines the law) and jury (determines the facts) is of particular importance for criminal trials. A judge can direct the jury to acquit the defendant where the *legal* test cannot be satisfied even if the jury were to accept as true *all* of the facts presented by the prosecution.

In certain criminal trials, the jury also gives a verdict as to guilt. It is probably here that a jury's work is best known by the public and by law students. However, the dramatisation and widespread reporting of high-profile criminal trials lead to a distorted perception as to the use of jury trial even for criminal matters. Over 95% of criminal cases are heard, without juries, in the Magistrates' Court. It is only more serious crimes that are tried in front of a jury in the Crown Court.[13] As almost two-thirds of defendants plead guilty when they reach the Crown Court, the number of cases that are determined with a jury is a very small proportion of all trials.

Although the jury in a criminal trial will normally determine both factual matters *and* produce the verdict, this is not always the case. If a defendant is unfit to be tried then the jury may still go on to determine the facts – that is, whether the accused 'did the act or made the omission charged against him as the offence'[14] but does not determine guilt.[15] In this way, juries are sometimes involved simply to find the facts. A relatively recent example will serve to illustrate this principle. In 2015, the CPS announced that Lord Janner – a prominent politician and barrister – would not be charged for historic allegations of sexual offences against children. The CPS decided that, although there was sufficient evidence to pursue a prosecution, it was not in the public interest to do so as Lord Janner was suffering from the advanced stages of dementia. This decision was subject to a review and a 'trial of the facts' was ordered for April 2016 with the intention of determining whether Janner had committed the alleged acts.[16]

CRIMINAL TRIALS

In the criminal justice system, juries are only used in trials that take place in the Crown Court. As is discussed in Chapter 11, there are two types of criminal trial – a trial on indictment and a summary trial.

---

13 <www.judiciary.gov.uk/about-the-judiciary/the-justice-system/jurisdictions/criminal-jurisdiction>.

14 Criminal Procedure (Insanity) Act 1964 s4A(2).

15 *R v Antoine* [2001] 1 AC 340 (HL). Interestingly, the test for fitness to plead, which still depends on the ruling in the 1836 case of *R v Prichard* (1836) 7 C&P 303, includes whether the accused understands that s/he may challenge jurors.

16 His death in December 2015 effectively put an end to any proceedings.

Indictable offences are amongst the most serious known to the law of the England and Wales and will take place in the Crown Court with a judge and jury.[17] Summary offences are tried in a Magistrates' Court, involve less serious offences[18] and do not involve a jury.

There is also a category of offences known as 'either-way' offences.[19] These, as the name suggests, can be settled by a trial on indictment or summarily. The initial decision as to venue is made by the Magistrates' Court in a 'mode of trial' or 'allocation' hearing.[20] If that court feels that, amongst other things, they have insufficient sentencing powers then they can commit the trial to the Crown Court. If the Magistrates' Court decides to hear the case themselves then the defendant charged with an 'either-way' offence can choose instead to have the case heard by a jury in the Crown Court. It is often written that the defendant has a 'choice' in either-way cases, but this is not quite true.[21] A defendant can elect for a Crown Court trial if the lower court feels it can effectively exercise its jurisdiction, *but* a defendant **cannot** elect for a trial in the Magistrates' Court if the case is committed to the Crown Court. In reality, very few defendants elect for a jury trial at such allocation hearings.

As the vast majority of criminal trials start and end in the Magistrates' Court the proportion of proceedings *eligible* for trial by jury is small. Over time, offences have been reclassified so that more are classed as summary or triable 'either way' further reducing the remit of trial by jury. For example, the Criminal Law Act 1977 made the majority of driving offences summary offences. Equally, by increasing the sentencing powers of magistrates,[22] fewer cases are committed in circumstances where the lower court is of the view that it has insufficient powers as to sentence. It is also easy to overlook the fact that even if a defendant is due to be tried in the Crown Court, it does not necessarily follow that a jury trial will happen. If a defendant pleads guilty, as is often the case,[23] then a jury will not be used.

The combination of preceding factors means that the proportion of trials that end up involving a jury is very small. Despite the incremental reduction in jury trials and their *statistical* insignificance, there is still a hesitation in removing jury trial altogether, particularly for more serious offences. Successive governments have publicly declared their respect for and commitment to retaining the remit of jury trials.[24]

17 Most common indictable offences are such as murder and robbery (triable *only* on indictment).

18 Most common summary offences are the less serious driving offences, for example, careless driving and a raft of construction and use offences under the Road Traffic Acts.

19 A common either-way offence example is most Theft Act 1968 varieties of stealing, including burglary, which in one sense is serious, particularly because if such forced entry is committed in residential premises at night, there is clear danger to the residents, so might be tried in the Crown Court if associated circumstances, for example, amount and methodology, are also serious or might, for various reasons, be categorised as less serious, so the procedure as between Crown Court trial and summary hearing in the Magistrates' Court is decided on the basis of the associated circumstances.

20 For the allocation hearing, see Chapter 11, Criminal Justice.

21 For advice to the accused on choice at the allocation hearing, see Chapter 11, on criminal justice.

22 For sentencing in either-way cases, see Chapter 11, Criminal Justice.

23 Due to the potential benefits of a more lenient sentence for an early guilty plea.

24 For example, the Deputy Prime Minister made positive comments and commitments as part of a response to a government consultation on a Modern Bill of Rights intended to replace the Human Rights Act 1998 – <https://www.

BENCH TRIALS IN CRIMINAL MATTERS

Through the combination of magistrates and jurors, the vast majority of criminal trials are determined by lay persons rather than by a member of the judiciary. This reinforces the fundamental principle identified earlier in this chapter, namely that criminal liability should be established whilst minimising the possibility for abuse by the state. This may help explain why any suggestion of removing jury trials, even in very particular circumstances, tends to be treated with suspicion and attracts considerable controversy.[25] The (Labour) government sought to introduce, via ss 43 and 44 of the Criminal Justice Act 2003, restrictions on jury trials in two circumstances – where the case concerned serious/complex frauds and where there was evidence of jury tampering, respectively. This would have led to a new practice of 'bench trials' (i.e. a trial with a judge but no jury) for these categories of criminal activity. The life of these sections is discussed later.

SERIOUS OR COMPLEX FRAUD CASES

There has been concern in the past about jurors' ability to deal with and fully to understand complex fraud issues.[26] As the suffrage for jury service has expanded and financial transactions have become more complex, the criticism of using a standard jury for this type of case has increased. This is not a new criticism and is something that even staunch supporters of the use of jury trials have commented upon.

Lord Denning, for example, supported the use of a 'special panel' of jurors in such cases or, in the alternative, proposed the use of a trial with a judge and expert assessors.[27] Denning makes the powerful point that the use of ordinary jury members in cases involving complex financial information may frustrate the oath taken in which the juror commits to understanding and using the evidence in order to come to a verdict.[28] Equally, the Roskill Report in 1986 recommended that jury trials be dispensed with in fraud cases, but this recommendation was not taken forward by the then Conservative Government of the time.

The Labour government of 2001 sought to implement the possibility for a bench trial where the case concerned complex frauds. The proposal was even put on statutory footing in the form of s43 of the Criminal Justice Act 2003. However, the provision required an affirmative vote in both Houses of Parliament before it would come into force. The Labour government tried on two occasions to bring into force this provision but was frustrated by the House of Lords on both occasions. Eventually the coalition government of 2010 brought forward legislation to repeal s43 of the Criminal Justice

---

gov.uk/government/consultations/human-rights-act-reform-a-modern-bill-of-rights/outcome/human-rights-act-reform-a-modern-bill-of-rights-consultation-response>.

25 See later, for example, where the Labour government tried to do this in the Criminal Justice Act 2003 ss 43 and 44.

26 See, for example, Law Now in Canada, Charles Davison, *Jury Trials; Cost, Controversy and Secret Powers* (3 January 2019) <www.lawnow.org/jury-trials-cost-controversy-and-secret-powers>.

27 Alfred Denning, *What Next in the Law* (Butterworths 1982) 71.

28 ibid 72.

Act 2003 before it was ever commenced.[29] In typical public policy cycles, the Leveson Independent Review of the Criminal Courts in 2025 suggested the removal again of trial by jury in complex fraud cases as way of saving court time and increasing the effectiveness of justice.[30]

SERIOUS RISK OF JURY TAMPERING

As well as trying to abolish jury trials in cases of serious fraud, the Labour government also made provision, by s44 Criminal Justice Act 2003, for the use of bench trials where there was a *serious* risk of jury tampering. In contrast to the section on fraud trials, this measure *was* brought into force in 2007.

The initiative for invoking s44 lies with the prosecution,[31] and the judge has no discretion in whether or not to order a trial without a jury if two conditions are satisfied.[32] The conditions are as follows:

- First, 'that there is **evidence of a real and present danger that jury tampering** would take place'.[33]
- Second, 'that, notwithstanding any steps (including the provision of police protection) which might **reasonably be taken to prevent jury tampering**, the likelihood that it would take place **would be so substantial** as to make it **necessary in the interests of justice** for the trial to be conducted without a jury'.[34]

As is obvious from the preceding extract, a risk of jury tampering is not enough for a judge to order a trial without jury. There must also be a consideration of proportionality, that is to say are there any measures that could be taken to *reduce* the risk of jury tampering and it is only where the risk would remain substantial that it would be in the 'interests of justice' to deny a jury trial. This is a reflection, built into the statute itself, of the importance attached to jury trials. It is clear that such a bench trial should only happen as a last resort. The justification for the provision, and its fairly high threshold conditions, was given in the *JSM*[35] case. Lord Judge, the Lord Chief Justice, noted that 'any defendant who is responsible for abusing the principle . . . has no justified complaint that he has been deprived of a right . . . which he himself has spurned'.[36] While Lord Judge recognises the public policy concerns underpinning s44 (i.e. that those who denigrate or abuse their rights can have

29 Protection of Freedoms Act 2012 s113.

30 <https://assets.publishing.service.gov.uk/media/686be85d81dd8f70f5de3c1f/35.49_MOJ_Ind_Review_Criminal_Courts_v8b_FINAL_WEB.pdf> [51]–[102].

31 Criminal Justice Act 2003 s44(2).

32 ibid s44(3).

33 ibid s44(4), emphasis added.

34 ibid s44(5), emphasis added.

35 *J, S, M v R* [2010] EWCA Crim 1755, [2011] 1 Cr App R 5.

36 ibid per Lord Judge.

them removed), there is also the protection of innocent citizens who may be subjected to intimidation should they act as jurors.

EXPLAINING THE LAW – JURY TAMPERING

The provisions on jury tampering were first applied and tested in the trial of John Twomey. The *Twomey*[37] case involved a high-profile armed robbery from Heathrow Airport in 2004. Trials were held in 2005, 2007 and 2009. John Twomey was unable to give evidence in the first, the jury failed to reach a verdict in the second and the third collapsed amidst allegations of jury tampering. It is estimated that the aborted trials cost in the region £25 million and that it would cost at least £6 million for protective measures to be put in place to prevent further tampering in a fourth trial, and even then there would be a risk of tampering with the jurors through intimidation of their families. It was against this background that the s44 of the Criminal Justice Act was invoked. The subsequent conviction was challenged on appeal before the Court of Appeal[38] and the European Court of Human Rights.[39]

Before the Court of Appeal, it was argued that the powers under the Criminal Justice Act 2003 interfered with Twomey's right to a fair trial under Article 6 of the European Convention on Human Rights. If we cast our minds back to the early sections of this chapter, then it is worth noting that not all signatories to the ECHR operate jury trials, and so it could not be successfully argued that access to trial by jury was a condition of having a fair trial. This logic was followed by the Court of Appeal and the European Court in dismissing the appeals.

The importance of the balancing exercise involved in the application of s44 was reinforced *R v J, S, M*,[40] where there was a successful appeal against a decision to order a bench trial in a case involving a conspiracy to pervert the course of justice. The appeal was based on the incorrect application by the trial judge of the *necessity* criterion in s44(5). The Court of Appeal held that a judge had to be sure that other methods of mitigating the risk of jury tampering were not effective before ordering a bench trial. In the case it was held that measures to mitigate the risk of jury tampering could be sustained for the relatively short period (two weeks) that it was expected that the trial would take place. In this way, the Court of Appeal reasserted that the provision of juryless trials was a measure of 'last resort'.[41]

37 *R v Twomey, Blake, Hibberd and Cameron* [2011] EWCA Crim 8, [2011] 1 WLR 1681.

38 ibid 8. Appeal against conviction lost before Lord Judge, CJ, Rafferty J and Roderick Evans J, sitting at the Old Bailey for security reasons.

39 [2013] 57 EHRR SE15 appeals on basis of an unfair trial without a jury unanimously rejected.

40 [2010] EWCA Crim 1755, [2011] 1 Cr App R 5.

41 ibid.

CIVIL

Jury trials used to be common for civil matters (i.e. those disputes between private parties). Land disputes and cases involving defamation[42] were commonly heard before a jury. The function of a jury was similar to that in criminal trials.

The Common Law Procedure Act 1854 marked the start of a sharp decline in the use of jury trials for purely civil matters. Section 1 of the Act allowed the parties to consent, in writing, to forgo a jury trial and to have all issues of fact and the calculation of damages to be determined solely by a judge. Thus, even in the mid-19th century, more control was given to the parties in deciding whether to have their private dispute settled with or without a jury. This was taken further over the coming century by the Administration of Justice (Miscellaneous Provisions) Act 1933[43] which abolished the *right* to a jury trial in most civil cases. By the 1980s, the right to jury trial in civil cases was retained in relation to a minority of actions, including thus:[44]

- Defamation
- Malicious prosecution
- False imprisonment
- Fraud

A judge could only refuse to order a jury trial in the preceding cases if the trial would involve 'prolonged examination of documents or accounts or any scientific or local investigation which cannot conveniently be made with a jury'.[45]

Outside these areas, there was no right to a jury trial, but a court could, in its discretion, allow one for other types of cases. In *Ward v James (No2)*[46] – a road traffic case – Lord Denning noted that there had been a steady decline in jury trials in personal injury cases, partly as a result of parties not *asking* the court to exercise its discretion.[47] Denning also noted that, in such cases where a request for jury trial is made, there is a suspicion that it is done because the party concerned has a 'weak case, or desires to appeal to sympathy'.[48] Moreover, Denning noted that juries were not accustomed or well-equipped to deal with the question of damages in certain categories of very serious personal injuries and was strongly of the view that uniformity and consistency of award were needed.[49] Therefore, the difficulties in assessing *damages* led Denning to comment that so 'important is it [calculation of damages]

42 Untrue statements of fact, either in written (libel) or spoken (slander) form, that damage the reputation of a real or legal person.

43 s6 (now repealed).

44 For cases in the High Court, this requirement can be found in the Senior Courts Act 1981 s69(1). A similar provision is in place for actions brought in the County Court, which can be found in the County Court Act 1981 s66(3).

45 ibid.

46 [1966] 1 QB (CA) 273.

47 ibid 296 (Lord Denning).

48 ibid.

49 ibid 300. Denning also made the comparison to sentencing, which is not left to the jury in criminal matters.

that the judge ought not, in a personal injury case, to order trial by jury save in exceptional circumstances'.[50]

Where they are used, civil juries decide by a simple majority.

Retaining civil jury trials, particularly, for defamation cases became increasingly problematic as the consistency of outcomes was questionable and juror involvement in the setting of damages was highly controversial. Although the criticisms have been long-standing, it was only in 2013 that real change was brought about with the passage of the Defamation Act 2013. This new Act removes the presumption of jury trial in defamation cases.[51] As such, slander and libel cases will now be heard in the same way as other civil cases, unless a judge specifically orders a jury trial.

ANALYSING THE LAW – DEFAMATION AND JURIES

The Defamation Act 2013 was considered in the *Yeo*[52] case involving MP Tim Yeo and a defamation suit against the *Sunday Times*. The *Times* made an application for the trial to be heard by a jury, and that application was refused in 2014. Citing an earlier statement by Lord Denning, Mr Justice Warby noted that the right to a jury trial is 'of the highest importance, especially when the defendant has ventured to criticise the government of the day, or those who hold authority or power in the state'.[53] In rejecting the application, however, the judge went on to say, 'Parliament no longer regards jury trial as a right of "the highest importance" in defamation cases. It is no longer a right at all'.[54]

In refusing a jury trial, the High Court not only recognises the change in the law but also dispenses with prior interpretation of the right to a jury trial in cases involving defamation. The interpretation of law that existed prior to Defamation Act 2013 had weighed *in favour* of permitting a jury trial, particularly in cases involving the reputation of politicians.[55] The High Court in *Yeo* took the opportunity to revisit this reasoning and found that having a *reasoned judgment* – that is, one delivered by a judge and that is absent in cases involving a jury – was more beneficial than involving the public in cases involving public figures.[56] The court also noted that, despite Mr Yeo's prominence

50 ibid 303.

51 Defamation Act 2013 s11.

52 *Yeo MP v Times Newspaper Ltd* [2014] EWHC 2853 (QB), [2015] 1 WLR 971.

53 ibid [20].

54 ibid [47].

55 See *Rothermere v Times Newspapers Ltd* [1973] 1 WLR 448 (CA). It should be noted that although Tim Yeo was in an influential position, he was not a member of the Government.

56 'There are real risks of a jury verdict being unclear or misunderstood or both.' *Yeo MP v Times Newspaper Ltd* [2014] EWHC 2853 (QB), [2015] 1 WLR 971.

in the public eye, he was not a member of the government. There is merit in these arguments, but the High Court also went on to rely on a more dubious proportionality argument, noting the increased delay and cost involved in a jury trial needed to be taken into account when considering granting a jury trial (s11 of the Defamation Act 2013).

The judgment in *Yeo* marks a significant change in the direction of the law. Not only does it apply rigorously the new presumption against jury trials for defamation cases; it also confirms the high hurdles necessary in order to convince a court that such a mode of trial is necessary. In this way, the classic 'special' treatment given to defamation cases is being brought more in line with other areas of law, such as negligence.

CORONERS' COURTS

For the sake of completeness, it is necessary to mention that a jury is sometimes used in inquests conducted by coroners.[57] An inquest is necessary in limited circumstances surrounding certain deaths. The vast majority of such inquests are held by the coroner acting alone as finder of fact and law. However, in very limited circumstances, an inquest may involve a jury. These circumstances include the following:

- Deaths that result from accidents in the workplace
- Deaths in prison
- Deaths that were the result of injuries caused by police officers[58]

The role of jury in such inquests is to establish certain of the key facts, such as the identity of the person who has died and the circumstances surrounding their death.[59] Juries used in inquests are permitted to give a range of verdicts, but these do not, in any way, settle criminal or civil liability.[60] There is no definitive list of verdicts, but commonly used verdicts include thus:

- Natural causes
- Accident/misadventure
- Neglect
- Suicide

57 The coroner being a local judicial official who inquires into certain deaths and also has functions under the Treasure Act 1996 in respect of items of buried treasure (gold, silver and potentially some other artefacts). It is a very old office dating from at least the 11th century and is normally held by lawyers or certain members of the medical professions and others such as the police.

58 The precise form of wording can be found in the Coroners and Justice Act 2009 s7(2).

59 Coroners Act 1988 s11(5).

60 Inquest conclusions must **not** even appear to determine such matters – Coroners and Justice Act 2009 s10(2) in force since 2013. The Act largely repeals the 1988 Act.

- Unlawful killing
- Dependency on drugs
- Industrial disease
- Open verdict (used where there is not enough evidence to establish a definitive verdict)

JURY SELECTION

Having discussed the nature, origins and form of jury trials in the legal system in the previous section, this part of the chapter will turn to the more practical principles and processes that underpin the *selection* of potential jurors. Although the rules surrounding the eligibility, excusal and summoning of jurors could appear to be mechanical and overly formalistic, it is nonetheless a crucially important part of the legal system. How juries are selected determines the composition of the final jury and, if conducted improperly or erroneously, could potentially influence the outcome of a given case. Also, improperly constituted juries could damage the public perception of this historic institution.

This section will look at the process of summoning a jury, eligibility criteria for selection, the jury in waiting, challenges and swearing-in. The focus will be on the method of selection in criminal trials.

SUMMONING

The summoning of potential jurors is undertaken by the Central Summoning Bureau (CSB) but formal responsibility for the summons lies with the Lord Chancellor.[61] The CSB uses a method of random selection based on the *eligible* entries contained on the electoral register.

It is an important point to note that there are no restrictions as to where a person may be required to report in order to discharge their duty as a juror,[62] but the Lord Chancellor is required to be mindful of the 'convenience of the persons summoned and to their respective places of residence, and in particular to the desirability of selecting jurors within reasonable daily travelling distance of the place where they are to attend'.[63]

The Juries Act 1974 also allows the court to make additional 'exceptional' summons if a jury is likely to be incomplete. This power permits the court to make summons, without the normal formal written notice, to those in the court or in the vicinity[64] of the court at that time.[65] Jury service is compulsory and a failure to serve when summoned is an offence and can be punished by a fine.[66]

61 Juries Act 1974 s2(1).
62 ibid s2(3).
63 ibid s2(2).
64 This could include those passing in the street on which the court building is located.
65 Juries Act 1974 s6(1).
66 Juries Act 1974 s20.

ELIGIBILITY

The eligibility criteria for serving on a jury have been simplified over time and are relatively straightforward to understand.[67] A person is qualified to serve, according to s1 of the Juries Act 1974, provided that they:

- Are registered as an elector for local or parliamentary elections
- Are aged between 18 and 75[68]
- Have been ordinarily resident in the UK, Channel Islands or Isle of Man for five years or more since the age of 13
- Are not ineligible or disqualified

Partly in order to widen the potential pool of jurors, there is a statutory basis – in s68 of the Criminal Justice and Courts Act 2015 – for increasing the upper age limit for those serving on a jury to 76.[69] At the time of writing, the provision has yet to be brought into force.

INELIGIBILITY

Despite the wide scope of s1 of the Juries Act 1974, there has traditionally been reluctance for the legal system to allow those in certain professions to sit on a jury. Thus, barristers, solicitors, judges, magistrates, police officers and members of the clergy were, until 2004, ineligible to serve on a jury (along with peers, criminals and lunatics). The Criminal Justice Act 2003 s321 swept away this whole category of ineligible persons and now only those who are 'mentally disordered' are ineligible for service.[70]

The reform of the law to increase the numbers eligible for jury service has not been without controversy. More particularly, the extension of eligibility to police officers, lawyers and others involved in the administration of justice has been subject to close judicial consideration and reconsideration in a number of subsequent cases. It is important to understand that the inclusion of the preceding, previously ineligible categories was without statutory caveat or condition and so it would appear that Parliament had intended to include these jurors without reservation. As we shall see, the courts have developed a more nuanced approach that looks very closely at the personal circumstances of certain jurors in assessing whether there is a risk of bias.

APPLYING AND ANALYSING THE LAW – ELIGIBILITY TO SIT

The issue of the interpretation of s321 of the Criminal Justice Act 2003 came to the fore in the conjoined cases heard on appeal under the name of the lead appellant *Abdroikov*.[71] The case concerned three defendants who had been convicted by

67 Prior to 1972, a juror also had to be a homeowner, with the consequence that around 95% of women were ineligible to serve on a jury.

68 The upper age limit was changed from 70 to 75 by s68 Criminal Justice and Courts Act 2015.

69 The provisions of the new CJCA 2015 would further amend the Juries Act 1974.

70 This change was the result of a recommendation out of Auld LJ in the *Review of Criminal Courts* (2001) Stationary Office.

71 *R v Abdroikov* [2007] UKHL 37, [2007] 1 WLR 3538.

separate juries, each of which had included a person involved in the administration of justice. The jurors had been a solicitor directly employed by the Crown Prosecution Service, a serving police officer with no prior involvement in or connection with the case being tried and, finally, a police officer who had served for a short period with another officer who was the victim in the case, but there was no suggestion that they knew each other.

When the case reached the House of Lords on appeal against conviction, a split decision was reached. The majority allowed the appeal in the first and final case outlined previously. For the police officer who had served alongside the victim, the majority found that, because the evidence was in dispute, there was a real risk of the appearance of bias.[72] In the case of the CPS employee, it was held that being a salaried employee of the prosecutor would call into question the appearance of an impartial jury.

The outcome in *Abdroikov* demonstrates that even unambiguous changes to the law, brought about by statute, do not automatically equate to certainty in the law. The development of the law has been controversial amongst academics and members of the judiciary. In *Abdroikov* itself, Lord Rodger's dissent was critical of the majority view, going so far as saying that the decisions would 'drive a coach and horses through Parliament's legislation'.[73] His view was that Parliament had acted unequivocally in extending the eligibility criteria and that the courts should follow this intention. Academic criticism has also focussed on the lack of certainty that *Abdroikov* has created following Parliament's attempt to extend the eligibility criteria.[74]

DISQUALIFICATION

In addition to those who are ineligible to serve on a jury, there are also those who are disqualified from sitting on one. If such a person knows that s/he is disqualified but still sits on a jury then that person will have committed a criminal offence, punishable by a fine.[75] Table 12.1[76] contains details of those who are disqualified for life and those who are disqualified for ten years following certain events.

72 Applying the standard *Porter v Magill* [2001] UKHL 67, [2002] 2 AC 357 test for bias, namely 'the question is whether the fair-minded and informed observer, having considered the facts, would conclude that there was a real possibility that the tribunal was biased'.

73 Lord Rodger's dissenting judgment starts at [28] and continues to [43] of the *Abdroikof* judgment.

74 Nicola Lacey, Celia Wells and Oliver Quick, *Reconstructing Criminal Law* (4th edn CUP 2003); Terence Morris and Louis Blom-Cooper, *Fine Lines and Distinctions: Murder, Manslaughter and the Unlawful Taking of Human Life* (Waterside Press 2011).

75 Juries Act 1974 s20(5)(d).

76 Drawn from the Juries Act 1974 Schedule 1.

Table 12.1 Those disqualified from jury service

Disqualified for life	*Disqualified for ten years*
A person who is on bail in criminal proceedings	Convicted of an offence under section 20A, 20B, 20C or 20D of the Juries Act 1974
Sentenced to imprisonment for life	Convicted of an offence under paragraph 5A, 5B, 5C or 5D of Schedule 6 to the Coroners and Justice Act 2009 (equivalent offences relating to jurors at inquests)
Sentenced to detention during Her Majesty's pleasure or during the pleasure of the Secretary of State	Convicted of an offence under paragraph 2, 3, 4 or 5 of Schedule 2A to the Armed Forces Act 2006 (equivalent offences relating to members of the Court Martial)
Sentenced to imprisonment or detention for public protection	Served any part of a sentence of imprisonment or a sentence of detention
Sentenced to an extended sentence under section 226A, 226B, 227 or 228 of the Criminal Justice Act 2003 (including such a sentence imposed as a result of section 219A, 220, 221A or 222 of the Armed Forces Act 2006) or s210A of the Criminal Procedure (Scotland) Act 1995	Had passed on him a suspended sentence of imprisonment or had made in respect of him a suspended order for detention
Sentenced to a term of imprisonment of five years or more or a term of detention of five years or more	Had made in respect of him a community order under section 177 of the Criminal Justice Act 2003, a community rehabilitation order, a community punishment order, a community punishment and rehabilitation order, a drug treatment and testing order or a drug abstinence
A person for the time being liable to be detained under the Mental Health Act 1983	
A person for the time being resident in a hospital on account of mental disorder as defined by the Mental Health Act 1983	
A person for the time being under guardianship under section 7 of the Mental Health Act 1983 or subject to a community treatment order under section 17A of that Act	
A person who lacks capacity, within the meaning of the Mental Capacity Act 2005, to serve as a juror	

GROUNDS FOR EXCUSAL OR DEFERRAL

If an eligible person is called for jury service, then that person is under a strict obligation to obey the summons. In the past, there were broad and generous grounds for being excused from jury service, as of right. Members of Parliament, those aged over 65 and doctors were amongst those who would be granted automatic excusal if they so requested.[77] This system was changed by the Criminal Justice Act 2003, and now (limited provision for the armed forces aside)[78] the right to excusal is limited to those who have previously served in juries within the past two years.[79] The Central Summoning Bureau is also able to defer or offer *discretionary* excusal if a person can show that they have 'good reason'.[80]

The Lord Chancellor has issued statutory guidance, under s9AA of the Juries Act 1974, on the application of principle of excusal and deferral.[81] The opening paragraph makes it clear that applications for excusal or deferral must be considered 'carefully, sympathetically and with regard to the individual circumstances of the applicant', but perhaps more strikingly, the CSB should 'not hesitate to refuse a request if no "good reason" is given'.[82] This statement, so early in the guidance notes, reinforces the message that excusal should be exceptional. The guidance notes go on to say that deferral should be considered before excusal is granted, thereby ensuring that all selected persons have the opportunity to be summoned. This not only ensures that citizens are involved (irrespective of their initial wishes) but also means that they can be excused service for good reason.

The guidelines go on to give some indication of the sorts of application that would justify different responses. The following list outlines these situations and the responses:

- Insufficient understanding of English – *excusal* (para 6)
- Caring responsibilities – *deferral* in first instance (para 7)
- Beliefs (religious or secular) that are incompatible with jury service – *excusal* (para 8)
- Participation in religious festivals – *deferral* (para 8)
- Geographical difficulties in getting to the court building – *an alternative court to be considered* (para 9)
- Holiday – *deferral* (para 10)
- Business reasons – will be 'looked at closely', but *excusal* only granted for 'unusual hardship' (e.g. small businesses) (para 11)
- Shift workers – *excusal* or *deferral*, depending on context (para 12)
- Students and hardship for vacation workers – application to be treated *'sympathetically'* (para 13)

77 Juries Act 1974 s9(1) (now repealed).

78 According to the government website, www.gov.uk, members of the armed forces (all three services) are ineligible for service if on full pay. However, it appears that there is also an excusal provision which would cover other circumstances, for example, reserve if jury service would interfere with duties.

79 Juries Act 1974 s8(1).

80 Juries Act 1974 ss 9A and 9AA.

81 HMCS, *Guidance for Summoning Officers When Considering Deferral and Excusal Applications* (2009).

82 ibid [1].

- Teachers and students during term time/during exam periods – *deferral* in first instance (para 14)
- Conflicting with other public duties – *deferral* (para 15)
- Members of Parliament and conflict parliamentary duties – *deferral* (para 16)
- Speaker of the House of Commons – *deferral* to a time when Parliament is not sitting (para 17)
- Those involved in the administration of justice and the judiciary on the basis that they might be known to the parties – *deferral* or relocation to another court in the first instance (para 18)
- Additional consideration made to granting *excusal* when the application is from an employee of the prosecuting authorities, serving police officers in locality or serving prison officers (para 18)
- Members of the Armed Forces where the Commanding Officer certifies that the absence would affect operational efficiency – *excusal* or *deferral* to be considered (para 19)
- Work commitments – *deferral* in the first instance (para 20)
- Physical disability making attendance difficult – treated *sympathetically for excusal* (para 21)

The very detailed guidance, just touched upon, makes it very clear that every effort will be made to accommodate jury service through deferral before an excusal is to be considered. The normal position is that a person should apply in advance of appearing at court, but it is possible for a person to request excusal or deferral at the court in person.[83]

FROM SUMMONS TO SERVING

Once at the court building, the potential jurors are split into groups of between 15 and 50. There is no set number to this part of the process, but larger groups are often used where a case is likely to take more than two weeks, as this gives plenty of scope for non-selection on the basis of other commitments. If a trial is likely to take many weeks or months, then the judge will question the availability of the jury for this period of time.[84] An official of the court will then randomly select, via names written on paper, 12 persons to sit in that particular case and the remaining people are returned to the pool for selection in another case.[85] The prosecution and, in more limited circumstances, defence then have the opportunity to challenge the selection of the jury as a whole or of individual jurors. The jurors are then sworn in (by oath or affirmation) to 'try the defendant and give a true verdict according to the evidence'.[86]

CHALLENGES

During the process of jury selection, and before the jurors are sworn in, both the defence and prosecution have the opportunity to challenge membership of a particular jury under the conditions that follow.

83 The Consolidated Criminal Practice Direction – Criminal Procedure Rules IV.42.1.

84 Criminal Practice Direction IV.42.2.

85 Twelve is the normal size of the jury, but a trial may continue with a lesser number, provided that number does not fall below nine.

86 The Consolidated Criminal Practice Direction – Criminal Procedure Rules IV.42.4.

CHALLENGING THE ARRAY

Under a challenge to the array, it is possible for the membership of the *whole panel of jurors* in a particular case to be put in question. The Juries Act 1974 permits such a challenge on the basis that the person responsible for summoning the jurors is biased or has acted in an improper way in the execution of this duty.[87] Given that the selection is now largely produced centrally by random selection from a database, the scope for bias or improper conduct is greatly reduced. The effect of this is that challenges on this ground are very rare.[88]

CHALLENGE FOR CAUSE

The Juries Act 1974 gives both the prosecution and the defence the opportunity to challenge individual jurors for cause. The Act indicates that alleging that a juror is disqualified is a potential ground for review but otherwise is silent on the potential other 'causes' that may apply, stating only that 'nothing in this Act affects the law relating to challenge of jurors'.[89]

In addition to disqualification, the other major ground for establishing 'cause' to challenge is that the juror is biased. The test for bias is that which is well-established in public law by Lord Hope's statement in *Porter v Magill*: 'The question is whether the fair-minded and informed observer, having considered the facts, would conclude that there was a real possibility that the tribunal was biased.'[90] As the *deliberations* of the jury are not admissible evidence in an appeal, determining whether there is a real possibility that a juror (or entire jury) is biased can be difficult. As a challenge for cause must happen before a juror is sworn in, it is unlikely that a challenge for cause on the basis of bias will be successful unless such bias is manifest and obvious from the outset.

ANALYSING THE LAW – DEALING WITH BIAS

Based solely on the preceding reasoning, it is possible to criticise the legal system's approach to challenge for cause as being too restrictive. By considering challenges for cause *in isolation*, it would appear that there is the opportunity for biased, or even disqualified, jurors to sit and taint the whole process of jury trial.

However, when a broader view is given to the criminal justice system, it soon becomes apparent that there are *other* safeguards to prevent this injustice from happening. This is because challenge for cause is only *one step* in the trial process. It is more common, but that does not mean that it happens frequently, that potential for bias becomes

87 Juries Act 1974 s12(6).

88 For example, the most recent but ultimately unsuccessful attempt at such a challenge came from the British Virgin Islands in *Director of Public Prosecutions of the Virgin Islands v William Penn* [2008] UKPC 29. There has not been a reported challenge to the array from within the English Legal System for more than 20 years.

89 Juries Act 1974 s12(4).

90 *Porter v Magill* [2001] UKHL 67, [2002] 2 AC 357 [103] (Lord Hope).

apparent during the course of a trial. For example, in *Pintori*,[91] it was emphasised that a juror working with officers called as witnesses in a case may have the appearance of bias and should not have sat on the jury.[92] This meant that the conviction was unsafe and the appeal was allowed.

It is possible to draw out from the preceding an important lesson of more general application when studying the legal system. It is often easy to take a single element of the system, such as 'the jury', or even an aspect of that element 'challenges to the jury' and to subject it to intense scrutiny. Indeed, any form of legal study will encourage this sort of critical analysis. However, it is always important to remember the 'bigger picture' (i.e. where this 'piece' fits in the broader machinery of the legal system). One of the hallmarks of success is to take an issue or area of law and balance the detailed analysis against a more general framework. Achieving that balance well provides for more convincing and sophisticated assessment answers.

There is a further important qualification on a challenge for cause. This is that neither party is entitled to ask questions of the jurors before making the challenge. This means that unless a juror is known to the defence or prosecution, it will be extremely difficult to know whether there is or is not cause. In this regard, the prosecution sometimes has a distinct advantage over the defendant due to the (controversial) practice of jury vetting.

STANDBY (AND JURY VETTING)

Standby is available to the prosecution only. Technically, this is a completely open challenge but is, in reality, reserved to cases where 'jury vetting' has occurred. As such, it is subject to tight controls from the Attorney General.

As a point of principle, and to qualify the discussion that follows, it is important that some form of 'vetting' of potential jurors is possible. For example, it is now routine for there to be a Disclosure and Barring Service (DBS) check of all jurors to ensure that they are not disqualified by virtue of their own past criminality.[93] This saves relying on the potential jurors' own assessment as to eligibility to serve and prevents trials from taking place that include disqualified jurors. This is perfectly acceptable and is part of administering justice in an efficient manner. It is investigations conducted by the state into jurors that go *beyond* a DBS check that are anathema to the principles of jury trial.

In the 1970s, it became clear that certain additional checks had, in certain cases, been taking place into the backgrounds of particular jurors to ensure that they did not hold views that would make them unsuitable for jury service. This came to light following the so-called ABC

91 [2007] EWCA Crim 1700, [2007] Crim LR 997.

92 ibid [24].

93 A process that has received judicial endorsement – *Mason* [1981] QB 881 (CA).

trial concerning the Official Secrets Act 1911. These additional, and covert, checks were controversial because one of the core principles of trial by jury is that state interference was reduced by selecting from a large and open pool of jurors and that the grounds for ineligibility had been set down by statute.[94]

Again, we see the legal system attempting to balance competing interests, as an argument could be made that additional checks are conducive to the administration of justice in certain cases, for example, ones concerning national security or terrorist activities. To allow for proper accountability for the use of additional checks, the process of jury vetting is now subject to guidance and personal approval from the Attorney General following a request of the Director of Public Prosecutions.[95] The cases in which the Attorney General would authorise a challenge as a result of vetting are restricted to those cases of great public importance (i.e. not routine cases). The justification for cases of national security is that the evidence may be given *in camera*[96] and that certain jurors may put at risk the sensitive nature of the material. The second justification is that, in such cases, there is a real risk to the administration of justice if a juror were themselves to hold extreme views that created such bias that they could jeopardise the case.

UNDERPINNING PRINCIPLES

In executing their duty to try a defendant and to give a verdict based on the evidence, there are some general principles that underpin *how* a jury trial operates. The most important of these principles are the requirement for **majority decisions**, the concept of '**jury equity**' and the **duty of confidentiality**.

MAJORITY DECISIONS

In criminal trials, the normal number of jurors is 12. This number can, as a result of jurors being dismissed by the judge during the course of a trial, be as low as nine. The Criminal Justice Act 1967 abolished the long-standing tradition of unanimous judgments, where all jurors had to agree to a verdict. This was a principle of long-standing with Lord Denning discussing a rather extreme example from the 14th century where a judge initially threatened a juror with imprisonment unless he agreed with the other 11 jurors.[97] It was not uncommon for jurors to be kept without basic necessities ('without meat, drink, fire or candle')[98] to ensure that a majority be reached. The current position, contained in s17 Juries Act 1974, is that majority verdicts are acceptable. A minimum of ten with juries of 11 or 12 members.

94 Lord Denning was particularly scathing of any attempt to 'vet' jurors beyond the basic statutory grounds of disqualification in *R v Sheffield Crown Court Ex parte Brownlow* [1980] QB 530 (CA) holding that, in his view it was 'unconstitutional for the police authorities to engage in "jury vetting"' at 542.

95 Issued first in 1989 as 'Attorney General's Guidelines on Exercise by the Crown of Its Right of Stand-by' (1989) 88 Cr App R 123 and updated in 2012 – <https://www.gov.uk/guidance/jury-vetting-right-of-stand-by-guidelines--2>.

96 In private and not as part of an open, public process.

97 Alfred Denning, *What Next in the Law?* (Butterworths 1982) 36.

98 ibid 37 citing Blackstone's Commentaries III, 375.

In cases of ten jurors, nine must agree. The change to majority decisions has led to the more efficient administration of justice but also sought to mitigate the risk of jury tampering (dealt with elsewhere in this chapter) and of juror bias.

The underlying rationale of a jury *deliberating* is now secured in criminal proceedings by the requirement that majority, as opposed to unanimous, verdicts can only be accepted by the Crown Court where there have been at least two hours of deliberation.[99] In the case of a guilty verdict, the numbers in agreement and in dissent must be read out in open court.[100] The removal of the requirement of unanimous verdicts was a significant change in policy and further demonstrates the significant evolution of the legal system over time.

'JURY EQUITY'

As has been mentioned previously, jury trials are still justified as a means of involving citizens in the administration of justice. The principle of 'jury equity' seeks to balance the administration of justice with individual conscience. The principle allows a jury to acquit a defendant despite the fact that the necessary *legal* ingredients of an offence is made out *or* despite the fact that a defence that is pleaded is not technically available to the defendant. In this way, and for more serious criminal offences, the cold law is injected with some sense of community morality, albeit the morality of a small proportion of society. The principle finds favour as early as the 17th century in *Bushel's Case*[101] where it was held that jurors, as sole finders of fact, could not be *punished* on the basis that they exercised judgement in coming to a conclusion (i.e. verdict) on those facts. It later developed into a more sophisticated ability for the jury to come to so-called perverse verdicts to acquit.

The principle of jury equity affords the rigidity of the law a certain degree of flexibility but only where that flexibility favours the defendant. This means that a judge can order an acquittal where a *legal* test necessary for conviction cannot be made out on the facts but cannot order a conviction. This has been recently reaffirmed in *Brandford*[102] with the Court of Appeal making it clear that any attempt to withdraw a defence from the jury should be handled carefully so as not to violate the principle that a judge cannot direct a jury to convict.

EXPLAINING AND ANALYSING THE LAW – JURY CONSCIENCE

Discovering the *actual* motives of a jury in acquitting (or convicting) a defendant is almost impossible due to the requirement of confidentiality in deliberations. However, it may be that the use of 'jury equity' is more likely to occur in two categories of case –

99 Juries Act 1974 s17(4).

100 Juries Act 1974 s17(3).

101 *Bushel's Case* (1670) 124 ER 1006.

102 *R v Brandford* [2016] EWCA Crim 1794, [2017] 4 WLR 17 [49] citing *R v Wang (Cheong)* [2005] UKHL 9, [2005] 1 WLR 661.

where the case has a *political* dimension or where the jury is *empathetic* to the position of the defendant.

On the political side, the case of *R v Ponting*[103] is often cited as the leading example of a political acquittal in the face of overwhelming evidence of guilt. The sinking of the Argentinian warship the *Belgrano* was a particularly controversial development in the Falklands Crisis of the 1980s. Clive Ponting, a senior civil servant at the Ministry of Defence, sent governmental documents concerning the sinking of the *Belgrano* to a Labour MP. He was subsequently charged with an offence under the Official Secrets Act 1911. During the trial, the judge made it clear to the jury that the elements of the offence had been made out (and were not in dispute) and that Ponting's attempt to rely upon a defence under the OSA was doomed to fail. Nonetheless, the jury refused to convict and acquitted Ponting of the charge.

Jury equity also allows the law to be applied compassionately. For example, the case of Dr Biezanek[104] demonstrates how a jury can inject empathy into the rigid application of the law. Dr Biezanek was charged with various drugs offences – primarily possession with intent to supply and supply of cannabis (a controlled drug). At no point did Dr Biezanek deny the facts, and so a conviction may be assumed to have been inevitable. However, the jury acquitted her of all charges. She had been supplying the drugs to her daughter to help manage a serious illness. Although we cannot know the basis of the acquittal, it is widely believed (and reported by the press at that time) that in this case, as in others involving the provision of drugs for medical purposes, the jury were sympathetic to the actions of a parent attempting to alleviate the suffering of a child.

When looked at from an *individual* level, the principle of jury equity, as applied in the preceding cases, seems, at the least, understandable and, at the most, laudable. It softens the hard edges of the law. However, it can cause confusion in the public's understanding of the purpose of a jury trial and also in the reporting of the outcomes of particular cases.

CONFIDENTIALITY OF DELIBERATION

In order to protect the discussions of jurors it is important that their deliberations are confidential. Equally, jurors ought to decide cases based on the evidence presented and not on matters (or prejudices) extraneous to the case.

103 *R v Ponting* [2015] Crim LR 318 (CA).

104 Reported in the public press – <www.independent.co.uk/news/uk/drug-case-doctor-is-cleared-solicitor-calls-for-legal-reform-to-enable-gps-to-supply-cannabis-1511893.html>.

The matter was traditionally governed by s8 of the Contempt of Court Act 1981 which stated that it was 'a contempt of court to obtain, disclose or solicit any particulars of statements made, opinions expressed, arguments advanced or votes cast by members of a jury in the course of their deliberations in any legal proceedings'. This served to protect juror deliberations, but it also acted as a barrier to investigating jury deliberations and could make appealing against convictions on the basis of improper conduct by jurors very difficult.[105] There were a number of cases where it became increasingly difficult to justify the harsh line that s8 drew in balancing juror and defendant rights, despite the efforts of the judiciary to distinguish between matters that fell within deliberations (which were covered by s8) and those that were extraneous to it (which were not covered by s8). The situation led some to question whether s8 was compatible with Article 6 of the European Convention on Human Rights, which seeks to ensure that all accused are given a fair trial.

Advances in technology and the advent of social media have led to increased access to information and this presents two particular challenges for jury trials. First, the internet can be a tempting place for jurors to perform additional 'research' into either the law or the lives of those who are subject to judicial proceedings. This challenge, which comes *at the time* of the trial, can lead jurors to try the case other than on the evidence admitted and presented to court. Second, social media in particular presents *post-trial* risks in that jurors may be tempted to share information about the deliberations that they, and their fellow jurors, engaged in on online platforms.

Within the context of a rise of jurors investigating and researching the cases on which they sat, the Law Commission published a report in 2013.[106] The recommendations of this report were adopted and enacted via the Criminal Justice and Courts Act 2015, which created a range of new criminal offences within the Juries Act 1974, including thus:

- Jury research during the trial period[107]
- Sharing research with another juror[108]
- Jurors engaging in other prohibited conduct[109]
- Disclosing jury's deliberations[110] (other than in limited circumstances)[111]

In this way the legal position has sought to evolve to be responsive to changes in technology, but this has not prevented some jurors from still acting in ways incompatible with their important role.

105 *R v Mizra; R v Connor and Rollock* [2004] UKHL 2, [2004] 1 AC 1118.

106 Law Commission, *Contempt of Court: Juror Misconduct* (Law Comm No 340, 2013).

107 Juries Act 1974 s20A.

108 Juries Act 1974 s20B.

109 Juries Act 1974 s20C – *prohibited conduct* means 'conduct from which it may reasonably be concluded that the person intends to try the issue otherwise than on the basis of the evidence presented in the proceedings on the issue'.

110 Juries Act 1974 s20D.

111 Governed by ss 20E-G, which essentially allows for disclosure to certain named bodies for the furtherance of justice.

This is again evidence of the legal system operating in a way that is dynamic with solutions to new problems finding their way into the law through a mix of technological advancement and real-life cases. In this instance, the law is seeking to ensure the integrity of the system and to secure rights to a fair trial for those accused of serious crime, while punishing (or deterring) behaviours incompatible with these aims.

JUROR BEHAVIOUR

Before departing from the jury it is important to consider juror behaviour in a slightly broader sense. Lord Denning – speaking extrajudicially – once harked back to the 19th century as 'the golden age of trial by jury'[112] and lamented the wider selection in place during his time on the bench, going so far as to suggest that jury service should require an interview and references.[113] This is very far away from a random, peer-based system intended to generate the absolute minimum of 'state interference' necessary for the proper administration of justice.[114]

Jurors doing strange or inappropriate things as part of the trial process is rare but not unknown. Most trials are conducted entirely appropriately and with a jury acting with the propriety and earnestness we would expect.[115] However, there are occasions where the behaviour of jurors lays bare the broader criticism of involving ordinary citizens in the most serious criminal trials.[116] The brief examples that follow are intended to highlight some of the challenges faced by the justice system but should not be 'over read' as requiring, of themselves, a fundamental rethink of the role of juries.

The case of *Young*[117] provides a startlingly bleak examination of the challenges posed by jury trials. Stephen Young had been convicted on two counts of murder. He appealed against his conviction when it came to light that four jurors, in the hotel accommodation provided between two days of their deliberations, had constructed and consulted a Ouija board in order to commune with the spirit world and speak with one of the deceased victims. He alleged that this demonstrated that his conviction had not been based on the evidence presented and was successful in his appeal. The case also demonstrates the difficulties caused by the old s8 of the Contempt of Court Act 1981 inasmuch as the court could only investigate the claim because it had not happened in the jury room as part of the deliberations but in the hotel between sessions. Had the jurors undertaken this course of action *during* deliberations in the jury room,

112 Alfred Denning, *What Next in the Law* (Butterworths 1982) 46. It is worth noting that all jurors at that time were male, middle-class and householders.

113 ibid 76 where he said – 'Nowadays virtually every member of the population is qualified to sit as a juror. No matter how illiterate or uneducated or unsuitable he may be. And where the changes, by sheer weight of numbers, are loaded heavily against the jurors being the sensible and responsible members of the community.'

114 And could be said to be inconsistent with his strong (judicial) criticism of state interference in the selection of jurors in *Ex parte Brownlow*, discussed earlier in relation to jury vetting.

115 And as discussed in Chapter 7, the judiciary itself is not immune from lapses in judgement.

116 Including the juror who was jailed for feigning illness on the fifth day of a trial when, in truth, they had gone to watch a theatre production – <www.bbc.co.uk/news/uk-england-manchester-16288257>.

117 *R v Young* [1995] QB 324 (CA).

then s8 would have prevented an investigation of the conduct of the jury by the Court of Appeal.

ANALYSING THE LAW – JUROR BEHAVIOUR AND THE INTERNET

There is no doubt that advancements in technology (as discussed previously) bring with them new forms of idiocy and challenge. What might once have been private folly[118] can now be laid bare for all to see. This takes two distinct forms – the use of social media and the use of the internet to search for material relating to the case.[119]

To take an example of the first, in the case of *Fraill*,[120] the juror communicated with an acquitted defendant over text message, despite the fact that they were still hearing the trial of a co-defendant. Whilst some instances of juror impropriety are a result of naïve ignorance, this juror was well aware of the risks to the trial that they were posing as the following was admitted in evidence in her contempt hearing: 'pleeeeeese dont say anyhting cause jamie they could call mmiss trial and i will get 4cked to0.'[121] Social media also proved to be the undoing of Kasim Davey, who expressed inappropriate views about his role as a juror in a child sex offence case and was sentenced to two months in prison.[122]

For an example of the second, the new range of offences relating to jury research (discussed previously) has started to bite in more recent times. The first case to consider these new offences involved the conviction for contempt of Theodora Dallas for sharing information with other jurors about the defendant's prior involvement in a rape case when hearing a case about grievous bodily harm. The case eventually made its way to the European Court of Human Rights, where the UK was found not to have violated Dr Dallas's rights by prosecuting her for contempt.[123] A more recent example came in the form of *Stoddart*,[124] where a juror was convicted of contempt for researching the previous criminal history of a defendant in a burglary trial.

Most recently, in 2023, and striking as a case involving a solicitor serving on a jury, a juror caused the abandonment of a trial of historical sexual abuse allegations by undertaking research outside of the trial process and discussing it with other jurors.

118 But not more acceptable for it.

119 Littered throughout the case reports, there are plenty of examples of such conduct – *R v Thompson* [2010] EWCA Crim 1623, [2011] 1 WLR 200;

120 *Attorney General v Fraill* [2011] EWHC 1629 (Admin), [2011] 2 Cr App R 21.

121 ibid [16].

122 *Attorney General v Davey* [2013] EWHC 2317 (Admin), [2014] 1 Cr App R 1 where Davey had said: 'Woooow I wasn't expecting to be in a jury Deciding a paedophile's fate, I've always wanted to Fuck up a paedophile & now I'm within the law!' at [6].

123 *Dallas v United Kingdom* (2016) 63 EHRR 13.

124 *Solicitor General v Stoddart* [2017] EWHC 1361 (QB).

The juror had sought to research the dimensions of the house where the alleged abuse took place to determine whether she could resolve the disputed question of whether the complainant had a room of their own or whether they shared it with their brother. The research had been conducted through the website Rightmove. The solicitor was sentenced to two months in prison and also suspended from practice for eight years as a result of this jury research.[125]

PROPOSED REFORMS TO THE JURY SYSTEM – THE LEVESON REVIEW

As has been demonstrated throughout the rest of the chapter, there have been iterative and constant changes to the system of jury trial in England and Wales over the decades and centuries. Most recently Sir Brian Leveson was commissioned to conduct a review of the Criminal Courts. This was precipitated by the increased backlog of more than 70,000 pending Crown Court proceedings and listing of trials more than four years into the future. This consistent pressure was caused primarily by a lack of investment in criminal justice and the increasing complexity of cases that are put before juries. The review report (Part I)[126] was published in July 2025.[127] The report tackles very many issues beyond the scope of this chapter in its 388 pages and 45 recommendations.

The recommendations for reform of the system of jury trial in England and Wales are transformative and have proved highly contentious. Principal amongst the recommendations impacting on jury trials are as follows:

- The establishment of a new Crown Court Bench Division within the Crown Court. The purpose of the new division would be to hear certain either-way offences with a judge and two magistrates in place of a jury.
- To reinvigorate the abandoned attempt to allocate certain offences for consideration by a judge alone. These would most likely be serious fraud cases, cases of significant complexity or where a defendant elects for a judge-only trial (subject to certain procedural safeguards.
- To reclassify some either-way offences as summary offences and to remove the right to elect a Crown Court trial in other circumstances.

125 A summary of the disciplinary action taken by the regulator (which includes a summary of the facts) can be found at the following link – <https://solicitorstribunal.org.uk/wp-content/uploads/2023/10/12473.2023.Mitchell.pdf>.

126 The scope of the second part of the review is less likely to have direct implications for trial by jury.

127 A copy of the report can be located here: <https://assets.publishing.service.gov.uk/media/686be85d81dd8f70f-5de3c1f/35.49_MOJ_Ind_Review_Criminal_Courts_v8b_FINAL_WEB.pdf>.

- To broaden the use of 'out-of-court resolutions' (such as penalty notices or cautions) to ease the burden on the criminal justice system.

If the recommendations of the report are carried forward, there would be a significant change to deployment of the use of jury trials in England and Wales. There remain open questions and criticisms of the report, with concerns around the further dismantling of what has seen to be a core fundamental right within England and Wales. As was discussed at the opening of the chapter, a healthy system of jury trial can build trust in the justice system and some of the proposals may put that further in jeopardy whilst also not dealing with chronic underinvestment in criminal justice.

At the time of writing, the government has announced its intention to significantly curtail the right to trial by jury in relation to a whole series of offences.[128] This, if implemented, would significantly narrow the use of jury trials in England and Wales. The days following the announcement have generated concern about the proposals from the criminal bar and members of the judiciary as well as politicians. The website will seek to keep pace with these proposals, which feel likely to be watered down in the face of such vociferous concern from the profession and parts of civil society.

THE WEBSITE

The website that accompanies this textbook contains many useful resources that you can use to consolidate and further your knowledge of the law, to hone your skills of critical analysis and to test your knowledge. This includes a set of multiple-choice questions (MCQs) that can be used to test your knowledge and understanding of the material.

128 <https://www.lawgazette.co.uk/news/lammy-to-reveal-future-of-jury-trials-today/5125300.article>.

13

CHAPTER 13
ADMINISTRATIVE JUSTICE AND THE TRIBUNAL SYSTEM

INTRODUCTION

Administrative justice unfortunately seldom has the same appeal to the average student of legal systems as criminal justice. Even civil justice casts more rays of glamour where defamation may be found in the King's Bench and celebrity divorce in the Family Court. However, administrative justice is of fundamental importance to the proper functioning of the legal system and provides access to less expensive forms of specialist justice (in the form of tribunals) *and* allows individuals to challenge the unlawful actions of the government and its agencies. Administrative justice reinforces the separation of powers by allowing the judiciary to perform an important check on executive action.

Many of the most significant judgments to be handed down in English and Welsh courts over the last 100 years have been on the basis of the processes and principles of administrative law. Although generally it is the criminal cases that are raised in the public consciousness through the press, the ruling by the Supreme Court in September 2019 that the Prime Minister had acted unlawfully in advising the Queen to prorogue Parliament gained widespread coverage and was a product of administrative justice.[1]

AS YOU READ

Much of this chapter is concerned with the different ways in which cases heard by our judges are distributed between the Administrative Court and the Tribunals Service, and in giving more detailed information on the process by which this is done and how the system works in general. Particular attention is given in relation to the Tribunals Service, which is likely to have a closer relationship to the life of the student than the Administrative Court, in which it is unlikely that many will be quickly going for judicial review or requiring *habeas corpus*.

As you read, **consider critically** the purpose of the structures that you read about and **compare** how they contrast with other court-based actions. Also **evaluate** the distribution of power that results from administrative justice.

It is also important that you view administrative law in action, and you can achieve this by visiting the tribunals and **comparing** the descriptions here with the real-life workings. A visit

1 *R (on the application of Miller) v The Prime Minister; Cherry and Others (Respondents) v Advocate General for Scotland* [2019] UKSC 41, [2019] 3 WLR 589.

DOI: 10.4324/9781032641829-13

to the Employment Tribunal is a good place to start as the subject matter of the cases is often relatable and easy to follow.

ADMINISTRATIVE LAW AND JUSTICE

Administrative law is the field of law that a trainee or newly qualified solicitor might be likely to come into contact with even more so than with either of the mainstream areas of civil or criminal justice, since 'administrative justice' refers to areas of law which are more common in the lives of the individual citizen than either civil or criminal justice. This is because the term 'administrative justice' has several meanings:

- The mechanisms for reviewing the decisions of those who exercise public powers, in order to ensure that they are lawful. The most obvious of these mechanisms are judicial review and the prerogative writs (now called 'orders'), such as *habeas corpus* (an ancient remedy requiring production and/or release from any form of potentially unjustified detention). These actions were historically assigned to the Administrative Court and are thus a contemporary function of the Divisional Court of the King's Bench Division.[2]
- The work of the 70-plus administrative tribunals on which the Leggatt Review reported in 2001, and which have since been reformed and their work enlarged by the Tribunals, Courts and Enforcement Act 2007. In this sense, the term covers a huge field of law administered in tribunals by a much greater number of judges than populate the mainstream courts.
- The other mechanisms for administrative accountability, including the work of ombudsmen and inquiries.

These overlapping forms for raising and resolving disputes between individuals and the state all have – at their heart – the same core purpose of attempting to hold an increasingly large range of public bodies to account for their exercise of public powers (see Figure 13.2). When taken together they provide an effective and robust system of accountability that is stronger and more effective than would be possible in a system based entirely on court action.

Judicial review is the most formal and legalistic of the methods of accountability and can incur great cost (emotional and financial) and take a long time to resolve. The tribunals were intended to provide (less) formal methods for resolving disputes within specialised tribunals that can deal with often technical decisions within cognate subject areas. The tribunals are expected to deal with cases at pace and at such volume that would prove difficult for the generalist courts. It is important to recognise that the Courts Service and Tribunals are part of a unified system of His Majesty's Courts and Tribunals Service (HMCTS) but within which courts and tribunals still keep their distinct functions: whereby judges in the courts always *determine* cases and their role is exclusively *judicial*, but technically it seems the tribunal

2 See Chapter 8, on court structure.

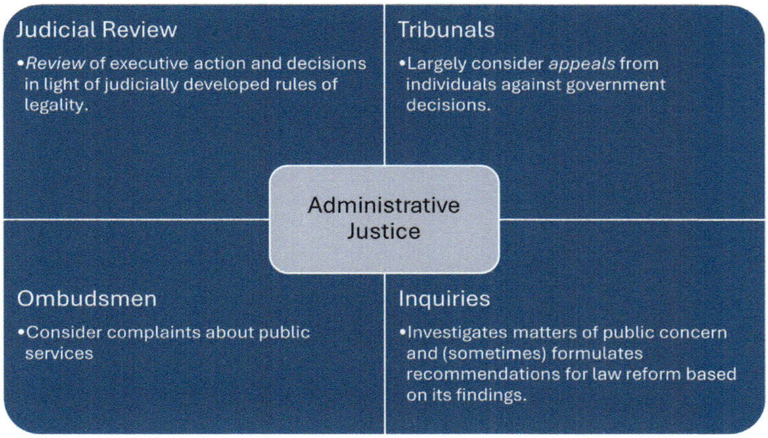

Figure 13.1 The elements of administrative justice.

judiciary's functions are partly judicial and partly administrative, which is why the separate tribunal system was set up in the first place, because their partly administrative functions were considered unsuitable for the court process.

In the course of this 2007 reorganisation, the numbers and remits of the various pre-2007 tribunals have been expanded to around 100 tribunals dealing with ever more numerous jurisdictions, resolving disputes between government ministries and the citizen and between other non-government organisations and the individual. Accordingly, while the distinguished 19th-century jurist A. V. Dicey considered[3] that there was no such thing as a separate corpus of administrative justice outside the common law (which was arguably incorrect even at that time, since there were still the first category of cases heard by the KBD Divisional Court), this could not logically be said now, in view of the wide and more recently expanded tribunals' jurisdiction.

Ombudsmen are used widely and where the questions are not necessarily *legal* or in need of 'determination' by a court and are often linked to levels and quality of 'service' provided by important public bodies, such as the Parliamentary and Health Service Ombudsmen, or private service Ombudsman like the Pensions Ombudsman or the Legal Services Ombudsman. The use of an Ombudsman is important where actions falling below a certain quality standard may not necessarily be *unlawful* but, nonetheless, should be capable of redress – this is often termed 'maladministration'. The present Ombudsman service in the UK had its origins in an influential 1961 report of the All Party law reform society JUSTICE, The Citizen and His Council, which when followed by three further reports not only resulted in the establishment of UK Ombudsman services, but facilitated the developing dispute resolution services which generated the spread of mediation in the 1990s; the importance of such key Ombudsman influence was recognised by the judicial mediation movement in Europe (founded as the

3 Albert Dicey, *Introduction to the Study of the Law of the Constitution* (1885) (10th edn. Macmillan 1959).

European Association of Judges for Mediation (GEMME) in 2003), of which the Ombudsman of the three Scandinavian countries were early members.

Finally, inquiries can be used to ensure that 'public scandals' or 'public tragedies' can be properly investigated and *recommendations* made to prevent recurrence.

MAKING CONNECTIONS – PUBLIC LAW

+++++++++++++++++++++++++++

This chapter only sketches out the main institutions, functions and principles of administrative justice and does not seek to subject them to a comprehensive or exhaustive treatment. This is because this area of law properly falls under the label of 'public law', being concerned as it is with the control of exercise of state power. If you go on to study 'public law' in greater detail, then you will need to consider these institutions and structures more fully. Our purpose here is simply to draw attention to the features of administrative justice, as they appear most relevant to the legal system of England and Wales.

The remainder of this chapter will explain the structures of each of these methods of achieving 'administrative justice' and some consideration will be given to their effectiveness.

COURTS AND TRIBUNALS

The post-2007 reforms and the unified HMCTS have in no way sought to blur the distinction between the courts and the tribunals but merely to bring both forms of formal dispute resolution under the umbrella of one government department, that of the Ministry of Justice. While in general terms the civil and criminal courts continue to deal with court based civil and criminal justice, the tribunals deal with decisions in the fields of central and local government administration and regulation, which have always been regarded as less suited to the court process: such as decisions in relation to social security and welfare benefits, housing and town and country planning, education, employment and numerous other everyday concerns likely to touch a citizen's life, even down to the detail of the regulation of buses, coaches and heavy goods vehicles and of estate agents and consumer credit, all of which have their post-2007 slot in the Tribunals Service.

There are thus, as identified previously, two distinct types of administrative justice for us to examine that are based on the exercise of a judicial function: (1) the classic public law element which is an extension of the courts' jurisdiction and is dealt with in the Administrative Court, which includes judicial review of actions of public bodies and officials, including inferior courts (such as appeals on cases stated in Magistrates' Courts and use of the prerogative writs) and of the decisions of local councils and members of the executive, and even including those of individual government *ministers*,[4] although the prerogative writs cannot be used against *the Crown*, and (2) the numerous specialised government agencies and other organisations which deal through the Tribunals Service with all these everyday sectors of the framework of modern life which the citizen usually calls our personal 'admin'.

Category (1) has already been encountered in the chapters on civil and criminal justice and the court structure, which is why the reader is signposted back to those chapters.

Category (2), dealt with in the tribunals, which have existed for around 200 years, is therefore probably more deserving of the name 'administrative justice' than (1). The tribunals were originally set up to deal specifically with administrative matters in relation to the public, thus providing greater accessibility for the public than to the courts which were not originally created or later adapted to deal with the public other than through their lawyers.[5] Unfortunately, the general public often thinks that hearings in the 'Tribunals Service' are as much 'courts' as those in the 'Courts Service', especially since the two have been unified within the MOJ as 'HMCTS'.

The first tribunals were, however, set up for dealing with such technical matters as tax (late 18th and early 19th century) and, later in the 19th century, to deal with issues in connection with the industrial revolution and the development of railways and canals. Nowadays, the successors to these original tribunals still have a place in the post-2007 tribunals system, which now provides a modern tax jurisdiction, serviced by Tax Judges, in the Tax Chamber, whereas the successors to the 19th-century tribunal regulating the canal and railway workers are to be found in the Transport lists, serviced by Transport Judges, in the General Regulatory Chamber of the First Tier of the Tribunals Service and the Administrative Appeals Chamber of the Upper Tier. These two chambers deal with appeals from the national network of Traffic Commissioners who regulate the road haulage and bus and coach industries and also allied jurisdictions such as appeals in relation to driving instructors' qualifications, which go to the First Tier General Regulatory Chamber.

Disputes in employment of all sorts have now achieved their own tribunal, the Employment Tribunal which has its own Employment Appeal Tribunal. These two tribunals sit under what is called a 'separate pillar', distinct from the main framework of the rest of the Tribunals Service. The Employment Tribunal is mentioned here for the sake of completeness but is not (formally) part of the system of administrative justice, concerned as it is with the private

4 For example, *R v Secretary of State for the Home Office ex p Fire Brigades Union* [1995] 2 AC 513, [1995] 2 WLR 464 (HL), where the Home Secretary changed the payment rates for criminal injuries by introducing a new tariff when he should have replaced the former non-statutory scheme by legislation as intended by Parliament in the Criminal Justice Act 1988 and not to do so was an abuse of power.

5 Which is one reason the present influx of litigants in person (LIPs) causes so many problems for both LIPs and court judiciary, see, for example, per Black LJ in *Lindner v Rawlins* [2015] EWCA Civ 61, where the respondent husband, a businessman who was not a lawyer, got the law wrong, leaving the court to research the law he should have relied on, and which counsel representing him would have known and already submitted to the court.

disputes of labour disputes. Employment Tribunals share many of the *features or perceived benefits* of the other tribunals – such as ease of access, ability to deal effectively with high volumes of cases while maintaining specialism and all in a (relatively) inexpensive and less formal way than is possible from within the court environment.

DISTINCTION BETWEEN COURTS AND TRIBUNALS

Despite the formal unification of courts and tribunals within HMCTS, courts and tribunals do thus remain distinct, and although originally tribunals were intended to be sufficiently informal[6] (providing accessibility to the public without lawyers) this has not really been maintained since many tribunals have become formalistic and technical. Moreover, all tribunals now have some rules, formal or informal, plus some recognised 'practices' which bring their processes ever closer to those of the courts.

The word 'tribunal' is also sometimes used in a general dictionary definition sense in relation not to a tribunal in the Tribunals Service sense but to a *court*, and the reader must look out for this meaning in other contexts. Sometimes *tribunal* is used in an even broader sense, as a body established to resolve disputes. This would clearly cover courts as well as tribunals, also, for example, professional conduct committees and, indeed, arguably, many other self-regulatory committees, whether having a judicial or administrative function. This is compounded by the fact that some tribunals (such as the one dealing with immigration and asylum) sit in places that look very much like courts, while others are much less formal. Thus, 'tribunal' has both a general and a legal definition, in the latter case defining its position in relation to the framework of the legal system of England and Wales.

Some cases may be found in the reports where the distinction between courts and tribunals has been debated, and it seems that does not depend on the name given to the body in question, for example, *AG v BBC*[7] where the House of Lords decided that a 'local valuation court' was not a court, even though it had the word 'court' in its title. Equally, in *General Medical Council v BBC*[8] the Court of Appeal held that the Professional Conduct Committee of the GMC was not a court (the point of these decisions being that generally for a person to be found 'in contempt of court' within the meaning of the Contempt of Court Act 1981, they must have been in a *court*). Rather confusingly the Employment Appeal Tribunal (EAT) is a *court* for the purpose of the Contempt of Court Act 1981. This is a good example of the well-known maxim that Parliament is 'supreme' and can enact anything it decides to – in detailing the composition and functions of the modern Employment Tribunals in the Employment Tribunals Act 1996 as amended it, *inter alia*, decided the EAT was a *court*. This can make the study of this area quite difficult, but one of the features of the legal system is its constant evolution and readiness to accept bodies for what they *are* rather than just what they are labelled to be.

6 Particularly in relation to processes and rules of evidence.

7 [1980] 3 All ER 161 (HL).

8 [1998] 3 All ER 426 (CA).

THE ADMINISTRATIVE COURT

It will be remembered from perusal of the chapters on the court structure[9] and criminal justice[10] that the Divisional Court of the King's Bench Division has one important distinctive function as a court for hearing of judicial review, certain statutory appeals and cases of *habeas corpus* and other historic remedies, and as such is the most important of the Divisional Courts of the KBD. It is based in London, besides in other major provincial cities, that is, Birmingham, Cardiff, Leeds and Manchester.

The Divisional Court of the King's Bench Division is thus distinct from the other three KBD Divisional Courts already mentioned in the chapter on court structure (Chapter 8), as it is *the* court for the purpose of hearing applications for judicial review, statutory appeals and *habeas corpus* and similar suits protective of the liberty of the subject. When it exercises these functions, it is known by the separate name of the 'Administrative Court', and you will sometimes see reports of cases heard in it in *The Times* Law Reports or, of course, in other reports series.

SUPERVISORY JURISDICTION OVER OTHER COURTS, TRIBUNALS AND AUTHORITIES

The Senior Courts Act 1981 s28A gives the court jurisdiction in 'case stated' on points of law from the Magistrates' Court, and both Magistrates' Court and County Court are subject to the supervisory prerogative[11]jurisdiction of the High Court. These cases and use of the orders of *mandamus* (now called a 'mandatory order'), *certiorari* (now called a 'quashing order') and prohibition (now called a 'prohibiting order') are normally heard in the Administrative Court. Also, for example, pursuant to the Senior Courts Act 1981 s29(3), the High Court can quash any decision of the County Court if it has exceeded its jurisdiction and the same is true of Magistrates' decisions. These functions may be carried out by a single judge or by a divisional court of two or three judges, and if such a court is constituted the chair of the three justices is likely to be a Lord Justice of Appeal who normally sits in the Court of Appeal. The court also has some supervisory jurisdiction over coroners under the Coroners Act 1988.

JUDICIAL REVIEW

This used to be a prime function of the Administrative Court when judicial review became a growth industry from the late 1980s, for example, in human rights, immigration and asylum, which produced a large number of such reviews, particularly in the field of immigration and asylum. These have more recently reduced significantly since immigration appeals were transferred to the Upper Tribunal Chamber for Immigration and Asylum in November 2013.

9 Chapter 8.

10 Chapter 11.

11 So called as they used to be the way that sovereigns controlled the actions of their officials, which is why they cannot be used against the Crown but can be against individual Ministers who are servants of the Crown.

Grounds for judicial review enable a person with a sufficient interest in the matter to be brought to the court to ask a judge to review the lawfulness of the following:

- Any enactment short of an Act of Parliament[12]
- A decision, action or failure to act by someone with responsibility to exercise a public function

MAKING CONNECTIONS – SEPARATION OF POWERS

+++++++++++++++++++++++++++++++++++++

Judicial review is not about assessing the *merits* of the original decision but of its *lawfulness*. It is also not an *appeal* against the decision but, as the name suggests, a *review*. It will be remembered that a core theme of this text is about the distribution of powers within the legal system of England and Wales, something that was explored in Chapter 3 in terms of the institutions. Judicial review distributes powers towards the judiciary (and legislature)[13] at the expense of the executive. This helps to explain why the government is keen to curb the powers of the court in relation to judicial review, often under the guise of cost savings or the burden of judicial review to public services.[14]

By not entering into discussions about the *merits* of decisions and restricting the analysis to lawfulness, we can see that the court is attempting to abide by the principles of separation of powers by not *becoming* the decision-maker but, rather, adjudicating on the lawful basis of the decision. This is an important 'check' on the powers of the executive and not only bolsters the courts' position within the legal system but ensures that Parliament's will in passing legislation enabling the use of public powers is not misused.

The fault or flaw complained of may be either procedural or substantive. 'Procedural' in this instance means not following an appropriate procedure set down for the purpose or context, or failure to observe natural justice, for example, not allowing one side to make representations. 'Substantive' means doing something unauthorised but also includes making an unreasonable decision, such as in *Associate Provincial Picture House v Wednesbury Corporation*,[15] the case which gave its name to the principle of '*Wednesbury* unreasonableness' because of the fact

12 In the legal system, it is impossible for the court to review the lawfulness of an Act of Parliament, which is to be contrasted with other jurisdictions (such as the United States of America), where courts may be able to call into question the legality of primary legislation.

13 The court is often keen to stress that it is undertaking its judicial review function in a way that is compatible with and protective and respectful of parliamentary sovereignty – see *R (on the application of Miller) v The Prime Minister; Cherry and Others v Advocate General for Scotland* [2019] UKSC 41, [2019] 3 WLR 589 [41] and *R (on the application of UNISON) v Lord Chancellor* [2017] UKSC 51, [2017] 3 WLR 409 at [68].

14 <https://consult.justice.gov.uk/digital-communications/judicial-review>.

15 [1947] 1 KB 223 (HL).

that in that case Lord Greene established the potential for challenging a discretionary decision because it was plainly unreasonable.

This was later confirmed by Lord Diplock in *Council of Civil Service Union v Minister for the Civil Service*[16] where he took Lord Greene's concept further, articulating the grounds more clearly – to include illegality, irrationality and procedural *impropriety*, rather than simply not following an appropriate procedure – and also including *proportionality* between the decision challenged and the purpose for which it is made.

It seems that overactive use of JR may have had some contribution to make to the decision to expand the Tribunals Service jurisdictions; see next section. However, the judiciary has been keen to preserve their control over both courts and tribunals, and attempts in drafting to exclude JR have not succeeded as they tend to have been interpreted to exclude other appeals (where, for example, a provision states that a decision shall be 'final and conclusive') as the courts have interpreted such phrases narrowly, as meaning that other appeals are excluded but not JR. An early case in this category was *R v Medical Appeal Tribunal ex p Gilmore*,[17] where Lord Denning said, 'The word "final". . . does not mean without recourse to *certiorari*' (now a quashing order), and in s*E Asian Fire Bricks Sdn Bvd v Non-Metallic Mineral Products Manufacturing Employees Union*,[18] where the drafting did manage to exclude *certiorari* for error of law on the face of the record; the Privy Council noted that that did not exclude JR if there had been action which was *ultra vires* or in breach of natural justice.

THE TRIBUNALS SERVICE – REFORMED FRAMEWORK OF THE TRIBUNALS

The expansion of tribunals in fact began before the Leggatt Report and the Tribunals, Courts and Enforcement Act 2007, and was much earlier generated by the 1945 Labour government whose reforming zeal itself generated the modern welfare state. In passing a number of Acts creating the welfare state, there was inevitable creation of opportunity for the state to come into conflict with its citizens. This necessitated a forum for dealing with those disputes and the need for a tribunal system slowly became apparent. The courts were clearly unsuitable for this task, and thus it was not long before the tribunals were obliged to shoulder the burden. Conceptually, the Franks Committee[19] thought that their role was adjudicative rather than administrative, but it seems now to be generally agreed that their role is more administrative than adjudicative though inevitably they also make determinations in a quasi-judicial role. To this end, the current chairs of their chambers and of the committees into which they are

16 [1985] AC 374 (HL).

17 [1957] 1 QB 574 (CA).

18 [1981] AC 363 (PC).

19 Appointed on 1 November 1955, their report on Administrative Tribunals and Enquiries was published in 1957, Cmnd 218.

formed to make these determinations are classed, and addressed as, judiciary, although the specialist 'wing' members who sit alongside the judicial chairpersons are usually not 'judges; but 'tribunal members'.

One purpose of the creation of tribunals was to relieve the pressure on overloaded courts. The original supervisory body was the Council on Tribunals, but this was replaced by the Administrative Justice and Tribunals Council, which was then itself abolished under the Public Bodies Act 2011,[20] was briefly replaced by an Administrative Justice Advisory Group in 2012, and then in 2013 by an Administrative Justice Forum, an independent body sponsored by the MOJ whose job it was to 'gauge how the administrative justice and tribunals system is working . . . to identify any areas of concern or good practice and to provide early, informal testing of policy initiatives'. This organisation was itself replaced in 2017 by a new supervisory body hosted by the law reform society JUSTICE.

Development over the first fifteen years of the 21st century since the Labour Government decided to work on the tribunal system was extensive. In 2001, the then Lord Chancellor, Lord Irvine, appointed Sir Andrew Leggatt, a retired judge,[21] to review the administrative tribunals which were then dealing with nearly a million cases a year although only three had very substantial work (social security and child support – which did the bulk of the work – employment and immigration and asylum, while of the rest many had little work and some were virtually defunct). He recommended creating a unified tribunal system, thus making them independent of their sponsoring government departments, providing a coherent and unified appeal system, and overhauling the position of the lay members so that no members actually sat on any tribunal unless they had a function to fulfil.

These recommendations were adopted in 2003; the new Tribunals Service was inaugurated in 2005 and began to operate in 2006–2007 when the Tribunals, Courts and Enforcement Act 2007 was passed. In 2011 the new Tribunals Service amalgamated with the courts (up to and including the Court of Appeal) to form HMCTS, becoming an agency sponsored by the MOJ. Gradually the former separate tribunals were inducted into the new systems, except for the Employment Tribunal and its appeal body, the EAT, which was planned to remain as a 'separate pillar' alongside the framework of the First and Upper Tiers of the unified Tribunals. Both tiers were divided into chambers which usually housed more than one tribunal of similar or at least non-conflicting fields of operation, and the Tribunals Service was headed by a Senior President of Tribunals (currently Sir James Dingermans, from the Court of Appeal).

Appeals go from the First Tier to the relevant Chamber of the Upper Tribunal, and with permission an appeal may go from there to the Court of Appeal, on point of law only. The Senior President of Tribunals is responsible for training, guidance and welfare, and for representing the views of the tribunal judiciary to the government and to Parliament. The Lord

20 This Act is discussed in greater detail in Chapter 4, on primary legislation.

21 Not to be confused with George Leggatt, his son, who was appointed to the Supreme Court.

Chief Justice has also delegated some of his powers under the Constitutional Reform Act 2005 to the Senior President, mainly concerning discipline of the tribunal judiciary.

THE FIRST TIER AND UPPER TRIBUNAL

Figure 13.2 captures the complexity of the system of tribunals and their interrelationship. The following section will seek to explain, in outline, the work of each of the chambers.

FIRST-TIER TRIBUNAL

The First-tier Tribunal has seven chambers.

THE GENERAL REGULATORY CHAMBER (GRC)

This has nearly 20 subject lists which are now brought together to continue the regulatory work that used to be done in separate tribunals before the GRC was established in 2006. Details of their work can be found on the HMCTS website which now provides one destination to go to for information. These separate areas of GRC responsibility include (in alphabetical order) charities, claims management services, community rights to bid, copyright licensing, electronic communications and postal services, environment, estate agents, examination boards, food, gambling, immigration services, information rights, letting and managing agents, microchipping dogs, pensions regulation, professional regulation and transport. Two of the commonest here are regulation of estate agents under the Estate Agents Act, and of HGVs and buses and coaches by the Traffic Commissioners.

THE SOCIAL ENTITLEMENT CHAMBER (SEC)

This deals with asylum support (but not with asylum claims or with other immigration matters) as it has in effect a welfare benefits focus. It also deals with Criminal Injuries

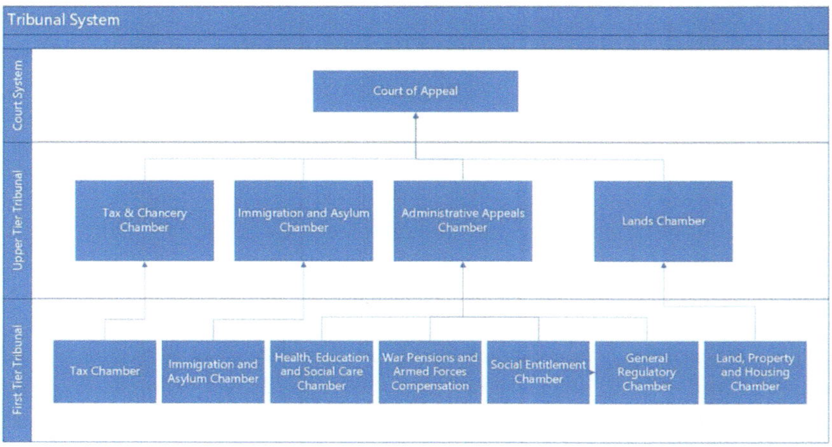

Figure 13.2 The tribunal system.

Compensation and Social Security and Child Support. This Chamber is very busy and has a heavy workload for obvious reasons. (The bulk of the work here is welfare benefits under numerous such Acts as child support under the Child Support Acts 1991–1995 and the Child Maintenance and Other Payments Act 2008.)

HEALTH, EDUCATION AND SOCIAL CARE CHAMBER

This one deals with care standards (that is, appeals against decisions from organisations concerned with children and vulnerable adults, and those regulating social, personal and healthcare); special educational needs and disability; mental health review; and primary health lists (that is, appeals and applications from decisions made by Primary Care Trusts as part of the local management of such lists concerning medical practitioners).

IMMIGRATION AND ASYLUM CHAMBER

This is the Chamber that deals with appeals from immigration and asylum applications and decisions made by the Home Office (in connection with which the SEC deals only with provision for applicants' and appellants' support). The Appeals concern decisions which refuse asylum in the UK, refuse entry or leave to remain, or to deport someone who is already in the UK.

PROPERTY CHAMBER

This is a busy Chamber dealing with residential property disputes, such as under the Leasehold Reform, Housing and Urban Development Act 1993; Commonhold and Leasehold Reform Act 2002 (CLARA 2002); land registration under the Land Registration Act 2002; and agricultural land and drainage matters.

TAX CHAMBER

Two main areas of work are done by this Chamber: any tax appeals from decisions of HM Revenue and Customs (HMRC) and MPs' expenses where the decisions are made by a Compliance Officer appointed by the Independent Parliamentary Standards Authority (IPSA). The Compliance Office is responsible for determining and paying MPs' expenses and appeals are made under the Parliamentary Standards Act 2009.

WAR PENSIONS AND ARMED FORCES COMPENSATION CHAMBER

This Chamber hears appeals against refusal of war pensions refused by the Secretary of State for Defence.

THE UPPER TRIBUNAL

The Upper Tribunal has four chambers: Administrative Appeals, Tax and Chancery, Lands, and Immigration and Asylum.

ADMINISTRATIVE APPEALS CHAMBER

This is a busy Chamber which hears appeals from the First-tier chambers, unless there is a more specialist chamber in the upper tier to hear their appeals, for example, Transport appeals will go automatically to the Administrative Appeals Chamber as this is a regulatory jurisdiction which fits perfectly with the Administrative Appeals diet, but appeals from First-tier Tax Chamber will of course go to the Upper Tribunal Tax and Chancery Chamber; likewise, appeals from the First-tier Property Chamber will fit with the Upper Tribunal Lands Chamber, and First-tier Immigration and Asylum appeals go to the Upper Tribunal Immigration and Asylum Chamber.

TAX AND CHANCERY CHAMBER

This and the First-tier have brought together four previous tribunals to hear the full range of direct and indirect tax cases, replacing other variously named tribunals.

LANDS CHAMBER

This Chamber hears appeals from the First-tier Property Chamber but also continues the work of the pre–Tribunals, Courts and Enforcement Act 2007 Lands Tribunal, which joined the Tribunals Service in 2009. The Chamber is often still called the Lands Tribunal!

IMMIGRATION AND ASYLUM CHAMBER

This Chamber hears appeals from the First-tier Chamber of the same name; both chambers at First-tier and Upper Tribunal levels were established in 2010, and as the Upper Tribunal is a superior court of record it, seems that this Chamber can hear appeals from both the First-tier and its own Asylum Chamber decisions.

HOW CASES ARE HEARD IN TRIBUNALS

This adversarial system used in the courts is somewhat different from the Tribunal Law Systems' approach which is not only more informal than a court hearing but also inquisitorial and has more similarity to the inquisitorial system in civil law systems. Whilst this is the design principle underpinning tribunal justice, much adversarial style has made its way into tribunal hearings as the law they administer has become more technical. This is true in the Property Tribunals, where, for example, expert valuation in property cases may be needed because under, for example, the LRHUDA 1996 and the Leasehold Enfranchisement Act 1967 technical calculations and professional judgement are required to determine what figure should be paid to the lessor by the lessee. However, the tribunals system as a whole is still built on the original tribunal ethos, that is, that lawyers are not needed, although this may not be the situation for optimum results in some specialist cases. In theory it should also cost less than in the court system.

The judges of the **Tribunals Service** are of three types: (1) the lawyers, (2) the specialist wing members and (3) the lay members, who are no longer used in some jurisdictions, owing to the need for economy. All are appointed by the Lord Chancellor and take a judicial oath though appointment is through the Judicial Appointments Commission (JAC) as with judges for the courts, and some will already have been inducted into other jurisdictions in the courts, for example, existing magistrates who sit as lay members. Some of the wing members are also appointed by the Lord Chancellor as judges in the same way as the lawyers, in the same way as when in pre-2007 days, they were called Lawyer and Valuer Chairs respectively, rather than judges.

EMPLOYMENT TRIBUNALS AND OTHER 'DIFFERENT' TRIBUNALS

Before departing from discussion of the system of tribunals in the context of *administrative law*, it is important to note again the existence and role of the Employment Tribunal. Employment Tribunals (ETs) and the Employment Appeal Tribunal (EAT) are governed by the Employment Tribunals Act 1996. The ET and EAT consider statutory claims arising from employment law – such as unfair dismissal, redundancy, unlawful deduction of wages and a whole raft of discrimination-based claims.[22] The regular courts retain jurisdiction to deal with certain matters arising out of employment disputes, largely those concerned with common law claims – such as wrongful dismissal. The vast bulk of the work of the Employment Tribunal is focussed on the private law disputes between workers/employees and employers.

Along with the Employment Tribunals in their separate pillar, there are some other tribunals which do not belong to the Tribunal Service framework, for example, the Special Immigration Appeals Commission (SIAC) established under the Special Immigration Appeals Act 1997. This is the special 'secret' jurisdiction that deals with some cases with such high national security risks that the person before the Commission may not even know what risk he is alleged to present and the issue is usually whether s/he should be allowed into the UK or if s/he should be deported for security reasons. Curiously, it is sometimes possible for the public to attend such hearings although even the parties and their lawyers are also warned that they may have to leave the hearing at some point because of the secrecy, in national security interests, of the evidence to be heard.

OMBUDSMEN

Turning away from essentially adjudicative forms of administrative law, the Ombudsmen schemes in operation provide a useful alternative when individuals wish to complain about the *quality* of service received from public bodies as opposed to making allegations of unlawful behaviour. Ombudsmen are deemed 'representatives of the people' and are given specific remits to consider complaints brought to their attention. It is important to note that here we are concerned with Ombudsmen schemes as they apply to *public* bodies and not the Ombudsmen who act as consumer and service watchdogs for a whole host of *private* services. The Ombudsmen responsible for public services include:

- Parliamentary and Health Service Ombudsman
- Local Government and Social Care Ombudsman
- Housing Ombudsman Service

22 Employment Rights Act 1996; Equality Act 2010.

The primary administrative Ombudsman in England and Wales is the Parliamentary and Health Service Ombudsman who considers complaints about public authorities, the National Health Service and UK Government Departments. This allows for citizens to resolve complaints in a single, accessible way. There are several practical factors that undermine the effectiveness of the Ombudsman. First, in respect of issues about the NHS, the Ombudsmen can receive direct complaints from members of the public but concerns about government departments must come from an MP. This hinders the effectiveness of administrative justice and essentially places additional hurdles in the way of bringing justice to wronged individuals. Secondly, complaints must be about 'maladministration' – a rather hazy concept – that can be best described as 'bad governance'.[23] By having such uncertain terms as part of the core activity of the Ombudsman, it may dissuade people from calling upon the service. Finally, whilst the Parliamentary and Health Service Ombudsman has a wide-ranging remit, the Ombudsmen cannot accept complaints about government policy.

The Local Government and Social Care Ombudsman receives complaints about adult social care and councils. The Ombudsman can hear and resolve complaints about council services even if they have been contracted out to a private provider. This is an important extension of the remit of the Ombudsman and ensures that those who are responsible for public services, even if third parties deliver them, can be held to account.

The Housing Ombudsman Service is interesting in that it provides a service for tenants of social housing and local authorities on a mandatory basis and is also open to private landlords on a voluntary basis. The Ombudsman considers disputes around charges, repairs and property condition as well as considering how complaints to the landlord have been addressed.

In this way, the Ombudsman scheme provides a small but important piece in the overall puzzle that is administrative justice in the legal system of England and Wales. It provides both *direct* and *indirect* means of addressing the public use of power but in a way that is not related to the *lawfulness* of that use.

INQUIRIES

Inquiries were briefly mentioned in relation to the institutions of the legal system in Chapter 3. They play an important role in terms of administrative justice as they allow for failings of public bodies or the law to be brought to light and for suggestions for changes to the legal position to be made in response. Inquiries can also act as the 'lightning rod' for the public's anger and the call for an inquiry can be a way that governments diffuse public disquiet or as a political weapon used by politicians to criticise the incumbent government.

23 For the difficulties in defining the term, see *R (Liverpool City Council) v Local Commissioner for Local Government* [2001] 1 All ER 462 (CA).

The Inquiries Act 2005 lays down a specific statutory basis for Ministers to establish an inquiry. The purpose of such inquiries is to *find facts* and, in some cases, make recommendation. Inquiries, according to s1, can be held when it appears to a Minister that

1. particular events have caused, or are capable of causing, public concern, or
2. there is public concern that particular events may have occurred.[24]

Such inquiries are often held in haste following a public scandal. There is often a 'muddying' of the role of inquiries with the judicial role performed in courts. This misconception should be dispelled from the outset. They do not have the power to 'punish' any wrongdoing and, generally, any obvious criminal charges should be dealt with through the courts before an inquiry is launched.[25] Inquiries are intended to be *fact finding* and may (but do not have to) make recommendations as to law or political reform. The Francis Inquiry published an incredible 290 recommendations following its investigation into the failing at Mid Staffordshire NHS Foundation Trust.

EXPLAINING THE LAW

For example, following the disastrous fire at the Grenfell Tower that killed 72 people, a public inquiry was launched by the (then) Prime Minister Theresa May and chaired by Sir Martin Moore-Bick (a retired judge of the Court of Appeal).[26] The remit of the inquiry was to examine the circumstances of the fire and to make recommendations. The Phase II final report was published in September 2024.

Further recent examples of public inquiries are focussed on the Post Office IT failings that led to wrongful prosecution of sub-postmasters[27] and the high-profile inquiry into the UK's preparedness and response to the Covid-19 pandemic.[28]

As was mentioned in Chapter 3, inquiries can be led by judges provided certain formalities are followed, including consultation with senior members of the judiciary.[29] Judges have been used in a number of high-profile inquiries.[30] The advantages of utilising the skills of a judge (or a retired judge) to lead such an inquiry are clear:

24 Inquiries Act 2005 s1(1)(a)–(b).

25 This happened in the Bichard Inquiry (into the murder of two young girls that eventually led to a reform of the system of criminal record checks) but did not happen in relation to the Leveson Inquiry (into Press Standards), and this caused significant disruption to the workings of the inquiry.

26 <https://www.grenfelltowerinquiry.org.uk>.

27 <https://www.postofficehorizoninquiry.org.uk/>.

28 <https://covid19.public-inquiry.uk/>.

29 Inquiries Act 2005 s10.

30 Including – the Leveson Inquiry into press standards, Lord Saville's Inquiry into Bloody Sunday, the Hutton Inquiry into the death of Dr David Kelly.

- They may well have expertise in the subject matter considered.
- They will carry authority with those involved, including senior politicians.
- They will have credibility with the public.
- They will be used to dealing with complex (and, at times, distressing) evidence.
- They may have the ability to understand the practical consequences of any recommendations.

One of the issues of using judges is that it further 'muddies', in the public's mind, the role and purpose of inquiries and how they are intended to be distinct from court proceedings. This is not helped by the fact that the involvement of judges often ends up with a more formalised approach to the giving of evidence and the involvement of additional KCs to ask questions of the witnesses.

ANALYSING THE LAW – MAKING LAW IN HASTE

There is no question that public inquiries are an important aspect of administrative justice and the legal system. They allow a very public light to be shone on the innermost workings of the legal system and can identify gaps in the legislative landscape. However, such a public and sometimes emotional way of generating law reform can be problematic. The Bichard Inquiry is a good example of this. It was set up following the murder of two young girls by a man known to them and who had had police involvement in the past, before he gained a job at the girls' school.

The inquiry (rightly) identified failings in the system of criminal checks for those working in certain roles that brought them into close proximity with children. Out of the recommendations were rapidly born the Criminal Records Bureau (CRB) and a system of 'enhanced' and 'basic' criminal checks. The legislation had been ill thought through and was passed too quickly. These CRB checks grew in volume and became a significant administrative burden that was out of proportion with the *actual* protections that they gave against former criminals (and those accused of certain crimes) gaining access to vulnerable people. The CRB system was very wide and left it to individual police forces to decide the extent to which historic (and, in some cases, very historic) criminal offences could be revealed.

Eventually, the CRB system was replaced with the Disclosure and Barring Service (DBS) – which set time limits on the sharing of certain minor offences and established specific rules for young offenders – following a successful challenge to the scheme on the basis that it breached human rights.[31] Even the new DBS scheme was not improved enough to avoid a declaration from the Supreme Court upholding the issuing of a declaration of incompatibility by the Court of Appeal in January 2019.[32]

31 *R (T) v Chief Constable of Greater Manchester Police* [2014] UKSC 35, [2015] AC 49.

32 *R (P, G and W) v Secretary of State for the Home Department and Another* [2019] UKSC 3, [2019] 2 WLR 509.

CONCLUDING THOUGHTS ON ADMINISTRATIVE JUSTICE

From the preceding text it is clear that administrative justice is delivered through a patchwork of different systems, institutions, personnel and processes. The uniting principle is one of ensuring that those with public powers exercise those powers lawfully and appropriately. The administrative justice system allows for individuals to hold to account and seek redress for decisions taken about them by those wielding public powers. Given that public powers touch upon the lives of all citizens, the legal system in this area is intended to provide fast and effective resolution of disputes. In this area (whether that's via Ombudsmen or Tribunals but not involving judicial review), there is less reliance on formal legal process and on legal representation, and this is intended to make justice more accessible and more affordable. Administrative justice can also manifest on a collective level with the use of public inquiries to investigate and make recommendations.

Also coming out of the preceding text is a clear sense of creeping 'legalism' within administrative justice that pushes back on the aim for a less formal form of justice. This is clear in increasing representation in the tribunals, an increase in the use of judicial review and the appointment of leading figures in law as chairs of public tribunals.

THE WEBSITE

The website that accompanies this textbook contains many useful resources that you can use to consolidate and further your knowledge of the law, to hone your skills of critical analysis and to test your knowledge. This includes a set of multiple-choice questions (MCQs) that can be used to test your knowledge and understanding of the material.

14

CHAPTER 14
DISPUTE RESOLUTION (DR)

INTRODUCTION

Having spent the last seven chapters discussing the various facets and intricacies of the formal judicial system, one could be forgiven for believing that every dispute involving legal rights or obligations will inevitably end up being resolved through formal court proceedings in the form of litigation. That, indeed, used to be the orthodox way of viewing the legal system of England and Wales, but now a broader focus has been given to the notion of resolving disputes by means other than litigation.

Any protracted study of the legal system of England and Wales is likely to skew perception about the extent of use of litigation. The natural tendency of legal academics and practitioners in a common law system is to focus on court proceedings. In reality, very many legal issues had only end up in litigation when other, less formal, methods of resolving disputes prove unsuccessful. The very organisation of the legal system had certainly, by 1990, for some time, been predicated on the notion that early settlement and resolution of disputes is preferable, both for the parties concerned and for society more generally. Nonetheless, it has been a challenge to view alternative forms of dispute resolution as an equal and integral part of the legal system as litigation, rather than a 'bolt on' or set of satellite processes. Both the Woolf Reforms[1] and the Jackson Reports[2] (discussed in Chapter 10) attempted to promote and encourage the use of alternative forms of resolving disputes.

This chapter will explore the meaning of these 'alternative' forms of dispute resolution and how they now operate not as adjuncts or satellites to litigation but as an *integral part* of civil justice in the legal system. The chapter will explain the rationale for dispute resolution (DR) and explore its operation in detail through the processes of arbitration and mediation.

AS YOU READ

As you read this chapter, it is important that you gain an **understanding** of the rationale and principles of dispute resolution. This will allow you to be able to **describe** and **assess critically** the different types of DR that operate within the legal system of England and Wales.

Consider critically the benefits to the parties and the legal system of facilitating effective DR. As you read, try to **compare and contrast** the mechanisms here with the more formal concepts of litigation that are discussed elsewhere in this textbook.

1 The final report was published in 1996 and with recommendations implemented in the Civil Procedure Rules in 1998.

2 Preliminary report in 2009 and final report in 2010.

DOI: 10.4324/9781032641829-14

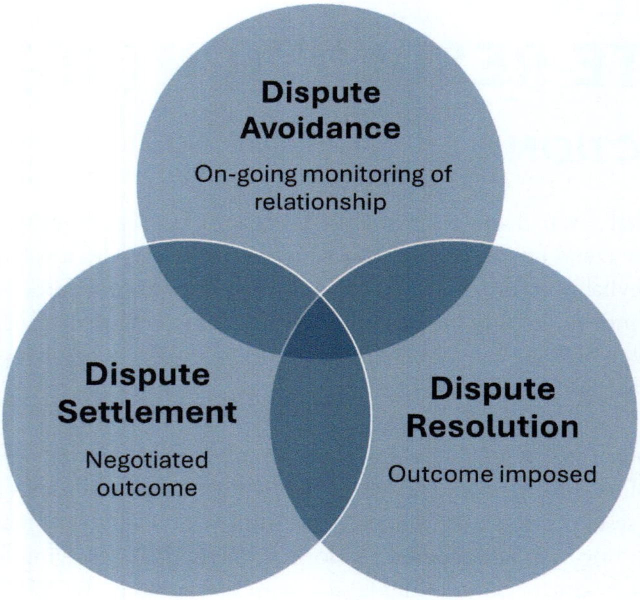

Figure 14.1 The different understandings of DR.

PRINCIPLES OF DISPUTE RESOLUTION (DR)

The problem encountered in Chapter 6 on statutory interpretation, in terms of the flexibility of words, is also present in trying to determine what is (and what is not) covered by the phrase dispute resolution (DR), particularly as an alternative to litigation. It is a notoriously flexible term that has different meanings to different people (see Figure 14.1). In the broadest sense, the term could be applied to any form of procedure (formal or informal) that seeks to provide an alternative to resolving disputes through litigation. This would include arbitration, negotiation, mediation, conciliation and a range of other methods discussed later. A narrower construction of DR is that it applies to forms of dispute resolution that do not involve the **outcome** of the process being determined by a **third party** (i.e. methods that are not adjudicative in nature).

This chapter takes a very broad view of the term, similar to that taken by Parliament in its Standard Note on DR:

> Dispute resolution (DR) is the collective term for settling civil disputes with the help of an independent third party and without the need for a formal court hearing.[3]

3 Diana Douse, 'Mediation and Other Alternatives to Court' (House of Commons Library, 2013) <www.parliament.uk/briefing-papers/SN04176/mediation-and-other-alternatives-to-court>.

This would therefore include both mediation and arbitration. This broad understanding of DR is chosen because the current chapter comes at the end of a series of chapters that are mainly linked to litigation and a broad understanding of DR will act as a counterpoint to that discussion. There are those in the academic world who would argue that this is too broad a conception and that the focus of DR should be on the *parties* resolving the dispute *themselves* with or without the aid of a third party, rather than including more adjudicative methods of dispute resolution which involve the issue being *determined* by a third party.[4]

The chapter could have taken the even broader view of DR adopted in the Practice Direction (Pre-Action Protocol) as the 'collective description of methods of resolving disputes otherwise than through the normal trial process'.[5] However, this view would include an almost unmanageable number of extremely informal dispute resolution methods that are only tangentially linked to the more formal legal system. It would also include methods of resolution already discussed elsewhere in the textbook – particularly Chapter 13 on the administrative justice system – such as ombudsmen and tribunals. Again, we are wrestling with the fluidity of language and its impact on our understanding of the legal system. Many of the principles discussed later apply in relation to mediation and arbitration.

ANALYSING THE LAW – JUST 'DISPUTE RESOLUTION'?

In order to draw the distinction between litigation and other forms of dispute resolution, it is tempting to adopt the nomenclature *alternative dispute resolution* (ADR), and it is a common term used in other textbooks.

There is an inherent danger, sought to be avoided in this text, in using the term 'ADR' that relates to the word 'alternative'. In this context, the word should not be misunderstood. It does not mean unusual or unorthodox. It does not mean a different choice to the normal or regular way of resolving disputes. It is not an inferior term to 'litigation'. It is simply being used to describe methods other than litigation. This is an important issue as it goes to both the credibility and attractiveness of 'ADR' as a way of resolving disputes.

Methods of 'ADR' were traditionally viewed as stemming from the failings of the court system (a point explored in Table 14.1) and so as some kind of second choice. In many ways, the opposite situation is true. Litigation is the alternative that arises when formal or informal forms of dispute resolution fail and the parties are left turning to the law and formal court structure to resolve disputes that they could not themselves resolve. As is explored throughout this chapter, far from being 'alternative' in the pejorative

4 For the difficulties in language surrounding DR, see Sir Laurence Street, 'The Language of ADR' (1992) 58(2) Arbitration 17.

5 PDPAC 3.1(3).

sense, DR is a mainstream device for resolving disputes. The legal system itself – through the rules of civil procedure in particular – now more formally recognises and supports DR even within the system of litigation. This process began with the new CPR 1998, which introduced a concept of 'hands on case management' in which the judiciary were charged with the task of 'actively managing' cases listed before them for interlocutory appointments, which were for the first time intended to be the subject of a proactive stocktaking of the optimum handling of a claim, whether by traditional litigation or by DR or a combination of the two.

Judges have powers to adjourn at any time for ADR to be considered and attempted, and some have used such powers more energetically, persuasively and determinedly than others, with open questions about the extent to which they may compel parties to use it. In addition, case law (as discussed later) has developed a well-defined cost penalty system suitable for complete failure by a party even to consider DR when it might be appropriate.

Table 14.1 lays out some of the problems that parties face when using traditional court-based litigation, and these may go some way to explaining the enthusiastic adoption of DR in some quarters.

TYPES OF DR

Figure 14.2 gives an indication of the major forms of dispute resolution and gives a brief description of how they normally operate. The figure is not intended to be exhaustive but rather to give a flavour of the variety of methods that are available to parties to resolve their disputes. The contents of the figure are based on the guidance notes accompanying the government's Dispute Resolution Commitment.[6] The nature and implications of this Commitment are discussed later in the chapter.

MUTUALLY EXCLUSIVE OR HYBRID FORMS OF DR?

It is also very tempting to separate out the different types of DR completely and to laud the advantages and decry the disadvantages of each. This typology risks ignoring the fact that, quite often, the different forms of dispute resolution interact with each other and can form part of a *system* of methods of resolving disputes that escalates, normally, towards arbitration or litigation. However, that escalation can be cyclical with several attempts at different forms of DR. To put this differently, the methods of ADR are not *intended* to be mutually exclusive. In some jurisdictions there is an accepted process called 'Med-Arb', where if a mediation does not settle all outstanding issues, the mediator may act as an arbitrator to make an award on the outstanding issue(s). It is still possible, however, for a mediator to settle as many issues

6 Ministry of Justice, 'The Dispute Resolution Commitment: Guidance for Government Departments and Agencies' (May 2011) <www.justice.gov.uk/courts/mediation/dispute-resolution-commitment>.

Table 14.1 Problems with litigation

Delays
From lodging initial applications to final judgment, the court system is by no means quick. Although things have improved following on from the Woolf and Jackon Reforms and ongoing routine CPR amendments, the court is still not an attractive option if parties wish to settle disputes quickly.
The delay is often caused by the specific and technical procedures used by English and Welsh courts.
Costs
It is a banal truism (though one worth repeating) to point to the high cost of litigation. There is also increased risk in litigation as the losing party will normally need to pay not only his own costs but also the costs of the other side.
Public hearings and reporting
Court hearings are (generally) open, and so parties can have their commercial transactions exposed to competitors. Parties may also be reluctant to have the fact that they are in dispute made public.
Lack of technical expertise
Although there are divisions within the High Court, there is a risk that generalist judges are not well-equipped to deal with certain technical subjects, and the calling of expert witnesses and the writing of expert reports will only add to the costs of the proceedings.
Adversarial
The adversarial nature of the common law legal system has many benefits, but it can be unsuitable for certain types of dispute, including those involving families, although family justice has enthusiastically absorbed arbitration because of its faster and cheaper delivery of an award, which there is confidence the court will enforce if made by a trained professional family arbitrator.
Lack of party control (process and outcome)
Parties must follow the procedural rules laid down by the legal system and may not opt for procedures of their own creation when a case is heard in court under court rules. Another reason parties seeking a family justice determination will often opt with confidence for family arbitration by a member of the Institute of Family Law Arbitrators, which can enable a dispute to be determined within a more flexible and less costly system - into which they can have much more case management input into setting up the arbitration than within the confines of court rules on evidence and procedure.

(Continued)

Table 14.1 (*Continued*)

ADR also enables the parties to pick their own arbitrator, whereas they cannot pick their own judge since the court will list cases in accordance with its own gatekeeping system, when and before whom they decide.
As an adjudicated outcome, a court decision is one that is imposed on the parties with only the potential for appeal if the result is unwelcome. While this notionally means that there will be a 'winner' in the case, it could well be that neither party is happy with the outcome.

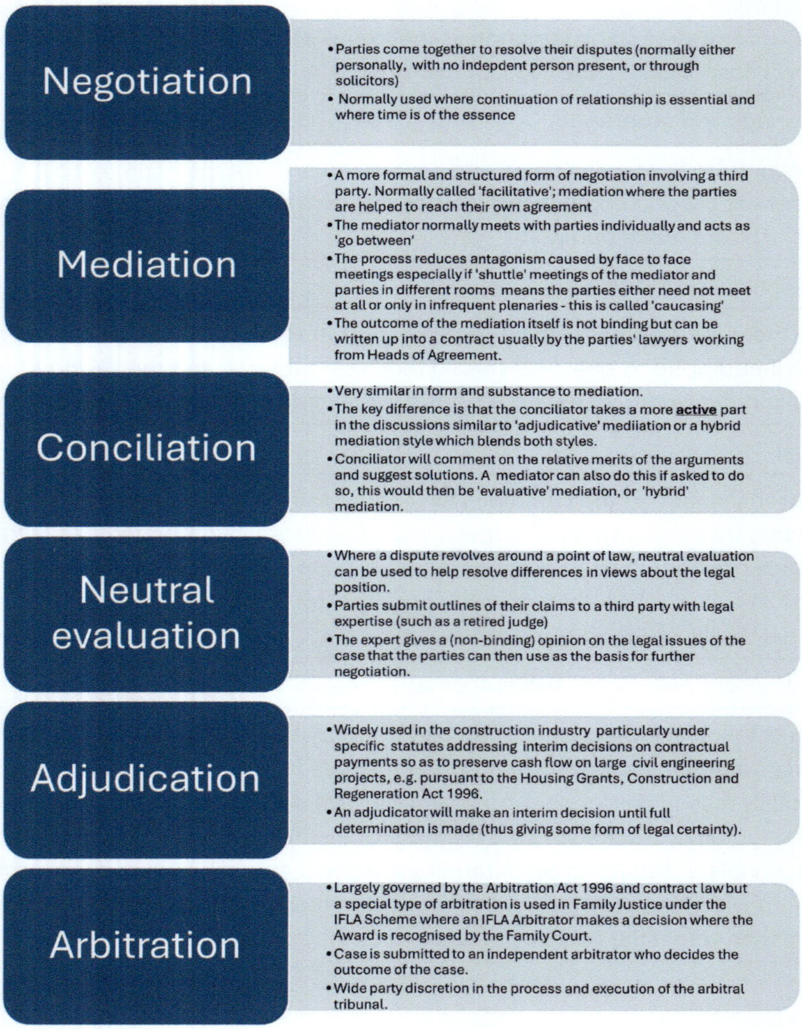

Figure 14.2 Forms of dispute resolution.

as possible in mediation and to refer the outstanding issues to another arbitrator who comes fresh to the case, and this is sometimes done.

EXPLAINING THE LAW AND TAKING THINGS FURTHER – HYBRID DISPUTE RESOLUTION

The most common type of hybrid process is Med-Arb. This method combines mediation and arbitration into a single dispute resolution process. This type of process is common in construction agreements, particularly in the USA and also in Canada, which has refined the hybrid system. It is also used in family matters.

Under Med-Arb the parties, when they have exhausted their informal efforts to resolve their disputes, first enter into mediation. If the mediation process is successful, then the agreement can be transposed into a contract that would then bind the parties. If the mediation fails outright to resolve the dispute, the process progresses to a full arbitration, with either a new arbitrator appointed (essential in England and Wales) or, in other jurisdictions, the mediator 'stepping into the shoes' of an arbitrator.

During the mediation (or after it), parties are free to enter into further rounds of negotiation before progressing to arbitration if there is no prospect of settlement. The whole idea of Med-Arb allows parties to have certainty of process without progressing straight to adversarial proceedings. However, having knowledge that, should the cooperative fail, there is the prospect of an adjudicated solution can be very attractive and can focus negotiations at earlier stages. Figure 14.3 indicates the flow of a potential cyclical 'hybrid' form of DR.

RATIONALE FOR DISPUTE RESOLUTION (DR)

The desire to resolve disputes through methods other than litigation can arise for a number of reasons and some of these reasons are explored during the following section of the chapter. In analysing these multiple rationales, you should bear in mind that certain forms of dispute resolution achieve these different purposes to varying degrees. It should also be remembered that stakeholders within the process may have different reasons for wishing to encourage the use of DR that cannot be so easily classified and categorised. For example, some disputants are suspicious of forms of dispute resolution that do not lead to binding results as they can just prolong what they see to be the inevitability of court action. Equally, some disputants may have preference for a form of DR (whether it is appropriate to a particular dispute) because of familiarity and successes with that form in the past.

PARTY CONTROL OF THE PROCESS

One of the primary reasons for supporting DR within a legal system relates to its ability to respect party choice and party control over the process. The concept of party choice being a central plank of the English and Welsh Legal System's incorporation of DR is recognised

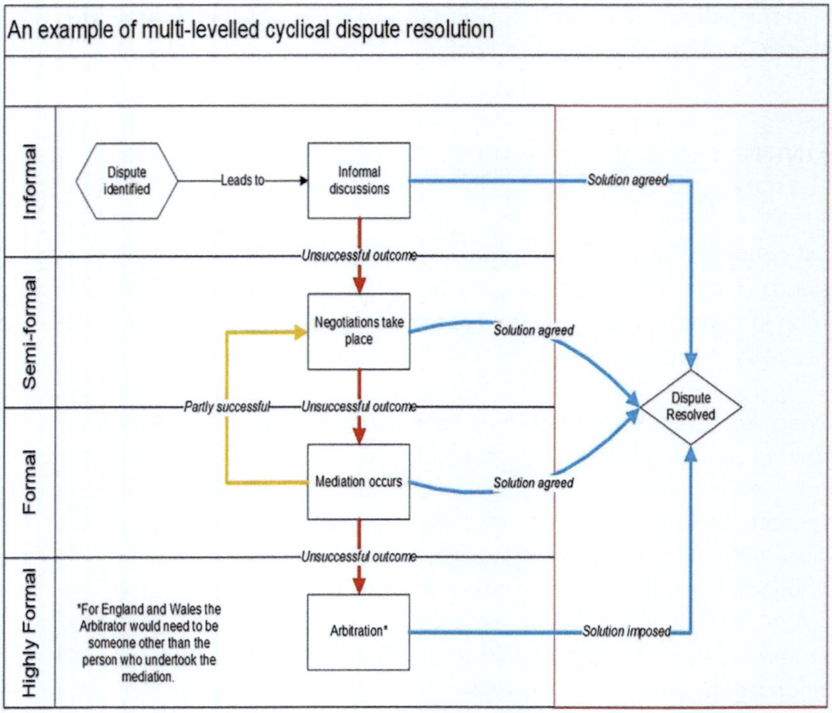

Figure 14.3 Hybrid Forms of dispute resolution.

both in the case law[7] and in statutory form.[8] Although party choice is often treated as a single principle, it can actually be split into two (or possibly more) sub-principles: party choice over *outcome* and party choice over *process*.

The former is most easily demonstrated when talking about mediation and conciliation where the independent third party is not determining a given dispute but facilitating the parties in coming to an *agreed* solution. This is particularly useful in family disputes, where the parties are thought more likely to abide by, and feel satisfied with, outcomes which they are involved in creating. Party choice as to *process* is more evident in arbitration where the outcome is imposed by the arbitrator (and so is adjudicative) but the whole process, including issues of evidence and even choice of arbitrator, can be controlled by the parties. For one thing, the parties to an arbitration will sign an agreement to arbitrate and to be bound by the arbitrator's award, and (assuming there is no issue about jurisdiction), the court will enforce this in the absence of error of law or procedural irregularity. This is a major advantage to parties privy

7 *Lloyd v Wright* [1983] QB 1065 (CA) 1072, where it was held that 'the court does not claim a monopoly in deciding disputes between parties. It does not, of its own initiative, seek to interfere when citizens have recourse to other tribunals'.

8 Arbitration Act 1996 s1(b) reads as follows: 'the parties should be free to agree how their disputes are resolved, subject only to such safeguards necessary in the public interest'.

to international commercial relations who wish to settle any dispute according to the law of England and Wales but without having to use the court system.

COSTS

Like party choice, the issue of cost is multifaceted. While discourse normally focusses on the benefits to the individual in terms of cost,[9] it must also be remembered that the legal system itself saves money and time when disputes are resolved other than at court through litigation. This can occur due to 'settlement at the courtroom door', where those in dispute only avoid litigation late on in proceedings and thereby waste court time in the case management process. The Woolf Report[10] and the Jackson Report[11] on the costs of civil litigation both advocate the use of DR as a method of avoiding spiralling costs. As was discussed in Chapter 10, the Access to Justice Act 1999[12] and changes to the Civil Procedure Rules (also discussed later) encourage and support the use of DR.

Generally, the costs of using certain forms of DR are lower for disputants than the costs of litigation. Some jurisdictions take this idea much further, particularly where there are perceived problems in relation to access to justice. As just one example, the Legal Services Authority Act 1987 of India regularises the concept of Lok Adalat (the People's Court), where retired judges, amongst others, sit in public in order to resolve disputes through compromise, sitting on up to 150 cases in one day.[13] As such, it is a quick and efficient form of dispute resolution that attracts no fees whatsoever. Although this could be accused of being second-class justice, it does allow those who would otherwise struggle to afford court fees to have access to justice. However, within the legal system of England and Wales, this idea that DR leads to highly reduced costs should not be taken too far. Although it is true that the services of a skilled mediator are likely to be less expensive than the sum cost of pursuing a case through litigation, it should be remembered that not all mediations are successful. Where a particular mediation fails outright, the parties are likely to revert back to pursuing the action through the courts. The total cost would be greater than if litigation on its own had been pursued. Similarly, the fees for arbiter can be significant, particularly in relation to complex commercial contracts and disputes (e.g. involving shipping or construction).

APPROPRIATE FORUM FOR DISCUSSION

Much of the growth of the use of DR is linked to an acceptance that different disputes raise different issues and so may require different solutions. In this regard, two distinct but interrelated factors (in addition to costs) should be taken into account when considering the processes of dispute resolution (including whether to progress to litigation): *the relationship of the parties and the importance of the issue*.

---

9 In one case, for example, the costs of litigation far outstripped the amount recovered: *Seventh Earl of Malmesbury v Strutt* [2008] EWHC 424 (QB), [2008] 5 Costs LR 736 [6] – this was described as 'a horrendous figure' by Jack J.

10 Lord Woolf Final Report 'Access to Justice' (HMSO July 1996).

11 Lord Justice Jackson Final Report 'Review of Civil Litigation Costs' (HMSO Jan 2010).

12 Access to Justice Act 1999 s4(4)(c), for example, requires those administering legal aid to take decisions to 'achieve the swift and fair resolution of disputes without unnecessary or unduly protracted proceedings in court'.

13 For a brief description of the operation of Lok Adalat, see Soumita Majmundar, 'Lok Adalats (People's Courts) in State of Gujarat' (1991) 9(2) Commonw Jud J 18.

Determining the relationship of the parties is an important step in selecting the *appropriate* form of dispute resolution. If the relationship is familial in nature, then the importance of both maintaining a continuing relationship and of the parties' feeling ownership over the final outcome is paramount. This is why family law disputes are often dealt with via mediation, which is seen as less confrontational than a court hearing and has the advantage of being an agreed, as opposed to imposed, solution. Similarly, if the relationship is one of equal commercial actors in an industry that requires a high level of technical knowledge, or where transactions take place over multiple countries, and especially where the particular industry involves a small circle of principal companies and individuals. Therefore, many disputes concerning international commercial contracts are settled via arbitration. If there is significant imbalance in the power relationship between the parties then, depending on the skill and gravitas of the mediator, mediation may not adequately protect the weaker party, and so conciliation may be a better option. This is why ACAS is often involved in conciliation in employment situations.

Finally, if the relationship is one of consumer and provider of services that are of low value, a progressive 'complaints' system that incorporates multiple methods of dispute resolution may prove sensible as court action is likely to be prohibitive in terms of costs. This is the system that is operated in relation to disputes between members of the Association of British Travel Agents (ABTA) and consumers who have booked holidays through ABTA members.

Similarly, determining the importance of the issue is a key step in assessing which is the most appropriate form of dispute resolution for a particular dispute. For example, if the outcome is likely to govern future relationships, then an adjudicated solution (or a neutral evaluation) that can be relied upon in the future will be the most desirable outcome, as opposed to a negotiation that could be re-opened the next time the dispute is made. Equally, if the legal position is extremely unclear, there may be a *strategic* advantage in avoiding litigation that may settle the point against a party. Similarly, if determination of *legal rights* is unimportant then a negotiated settlement may be better as it allows for strategic bargaining to occur with low-cost risks.

The following sections of the chapter will focus on two methods of dispute resolution: arbitration and mediation. These are chosen as they are the most prevalent forms of dispute resolution and represent the dispute resolution (arbitration) and dispute settlement (mediation) forms of DR. As a result, the discussion contained in the following sections will reveal some of the principles of the broad categories of dispute resolution, as well as their strengths and weaknesses. However, in focussing on the principal methods of DR, other, less prevalent forms should not be overlooked or forgotten and are more briefly explored at the end of this section.

ARBITRATION

The nature of arbitration is adjudicative. The parties submit their case to an independent third party (or panel of such people) sitting as an arbitral tribunal. The arbitral tribunal determines the outcome and whose findings, called 'awards', are normally legally binding and can be enforced as if they were ordered by a court. Arbitrators act in a judicial manner and follow the rules of natural justice[14] but do not have to follow the strict procedural rules of litigation in the civil courts. The arbitrator normally has specialist expertise in the subject matter of the dispute that is far beyond that which could be expected from a judge sitting in a generalist court. Quality of arbitrator can be assured through using one listed by professional bodies, such as the Chartered Institute of Arbitrators (CIArb).[15] Arbitration is attractive to those dealing with sensitive commercial information as confidentiality can be assured.

Being adjudicative and adversarial in nature, arbitration is the method of DR that bears the greatest resemblance to litigation. However, there is a danger of confusing the two. Lord Scarman gave a concise and accurate statement of the similarities and differences in *Bremer Vulcan*:[16]

> **Litigation . . . is a compulsory process** available as of right to anyone who issues a writ: it is not to be compared with the process of arbitration, which arises from **consent** and is **conducted according to terms agreed, expressly or impliedly by the parties**. Arbitration is, of course, subject to a measure of statutory control: but this control in no way detracts from the **essentially contractual nature of arbitration**. . . . But arbitration, while consensual, **is also an adversarial process**. There is a dispute, the parties having failed to settle their difference by negotiation. Though they choose a tribunal, agree its procedure and agree to accept its award as final, the process is adversarial. **Embedded in the adversarial process is a right that each party shall have a fair hearing, that each should have a fair opportunity of presenting and developing his case**. In this respect, there is a comparability between litigation and arbitration. In each **delay can mean justice denied** (See Figure 14.4).[17]

ARBITRATION ACT 1996 (AS AMENDED BY THE ARBITRATION ACT 2025)

Much of the law surrounding the conduct and principles of arbitration within the legal system of England and Wales can be found within the Arbitration Act 1996. The Act has recently been amended by the Arbitration Act 2025, which institutes some changes and reform to the area, both to bring further clarity and to amend certain developments that had come about through interpretation of the original Act. These changes were suggested as part of the work of the Law Commission.

The 1996 Act arose in the wake of the UNCITRAL Model Arbitration Law of 1985, which the UN provided in order to promote greater consistency in the arbitration laws of the various member countries. In response to the Model Law, Lord Justice Mustill, who chaired the UK Departmental Advisory Committee on Arbitration Law, suggested that the legal system of

14 A point recently reinforced by the Privy Council in *Cukurova v Sonera* [2014] UKPC 15, [2015] 2 All ER 1061 [31].
15 www.ciarb.org.
16 *Bremer Vulkan v South India Shipping Corporation* [1981] AC 909 (HL).
17 ibid 999 (Lord Scarman).

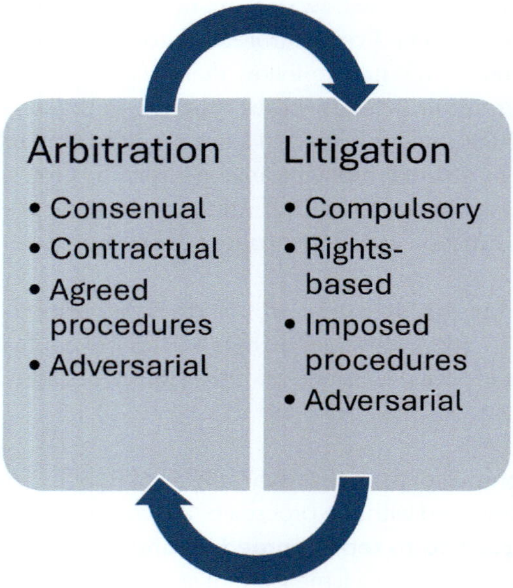

Figure 14.4 The relationship between arbitration and litigation.

England and Wales should not fully adopt the Model Law.[18] It was felt that to adopt the Model Law would be to harm the existing, highly developed principles of arbitration law that had arisen via common law and statute. Instead, Lord Mustill's Committee reported in 1989 that an attempt should be made to lay down 'in statutory form . . . the more important principles of the English and Welsh Law of arbitration, statutory and (to the extent practicable) common law'.[19] Out of this, and some seven years later, came the Arbitration Act 1996.

RATIONALE OF THE ARBITRATION ACT 1996

The purpose of the Arbitration Act 1996 was and remains twofold. Firstly, and as noted previously, it was about consolidating the existing statutory framework and the existing case law. As you will recall from Chapter 4 on primary law-making, this type of Act is a partly consolidating act. Secondly, the aim was further to increase the attractiveness of England and Wales as the seat and, more particularly, London as the location for international commercial arbitration. This was a process which had already begun at the time owing to the reputation of the judiciary and of international commercial arbitrators, many of whom were retired judges of the Commercial Court, other High Court judges and Court of Appeal and House of Lords judiciary.

In many ways, the first aim arises out of the second, with a codified set of principles reducing uncertainty for those who wish to use English and Welsh commercial law to settle their

18 Departmental Advisory Committee on Arbitration Law, 'A Report on the UNCITRAL Model Law on International Commercial Arbitration' (HMSO 1989).

19 ibid [108].

disputes. This reveals one of the most important motivations for using arbitration as opposed to litigation, namely that parties sometimes wish to utilise the *legal principles* of a system without having to pursue those principles through the formal system of courts. If you cast your mind back to Chapter 1 of this textbook, you will recall that a distinction was drawn between the 'law' and the 'system' of laws that govern a nation. Arbitration allows parties to use, for example, the legal principles of English and Welsh commercial law to settle their disputes without having to be at the mercy of English and Welsh judges sitting in the courts of England and Wales applying the court procedures of that jurisdiction. Arbitration can, therefore, be law without a legal system, but reinforced by the international reach of the CIArb and its regulatory framework.

It is important to note from the outset that the Arbitration Act 1996 applies only to written agreements to arbitrate.[20] These written agreements will usually be found in contracts and so formal arbitration happens most commonly where the parties have a contractual relationship. The underlying contract, which will normally give rise to the dispute, need not be written itself providing that the agreement to arbitrate is in written form. The agreement to arbitrate is classed as a distinct agreement even if it forms part of the contract.[21] This doctrine of separability is particularly important as it means that if the validity of the contract itself is called into question during the arbitration proceedings, then the legitimacy of the arbitration cannot itself be questioned for that reason.

Much of the Act applies only where the seat of arbitration is England and Wales.[22] The seat of arbitration relates to the law that governs the actual arbitration procedure and the way in which, and where, an award can be enforced. Some sections of the Act apply where the seat is elsewhere, but the law of England and Wales has been selected to settle the dispute.[23]Finally, some provisions apply regardless of the law chosen to settle the dispute or the seat of arbitration.[24] It should, therefore, be recognised that the Arbitration Act 1996 can apply, to varying degrees, in a wide range of circumstances where arbitration has been selected as the method to settle the dispute.

As will be discussed in greater detail later, the Arbitration Act 1996 can be viewed through a number of lenses: the powers it gives to arbitral tribunals, the powers it gives (or reserves) to courts and the matters it leaves to parties' choice. Figure 14.5 attempts to illustrate these different aspects of the Arbitration Act 1996 through categorising some (but not all) of its provisions.

20 Arbitration Act 1996 s5 – 'The provisions of this Part apply only where the arbitration agreement is in writing, and any other agreement between the parties as to any matter is effective for the purposes of this Part only if in writing.'

21 Arbitration Act 1996 s7.

22 Arbitration Act 1996 s2(1).

23 For example, Arbitration Act s7, on separability of the agreement to arbitrate, and s8, on the death of a party. These requirements are laid down in the Arbitration Act 1996 s2(3). Some clauses of an agreement to arbitrate are therefore non-negotiable and must be included.

24 Most notably, the Arbitration Act ss9–11, on the ability of the court to stay proceedings, and s66, on enforcement of awards. These requirements are laid down in the Arbitration Act 1996 s2(2).

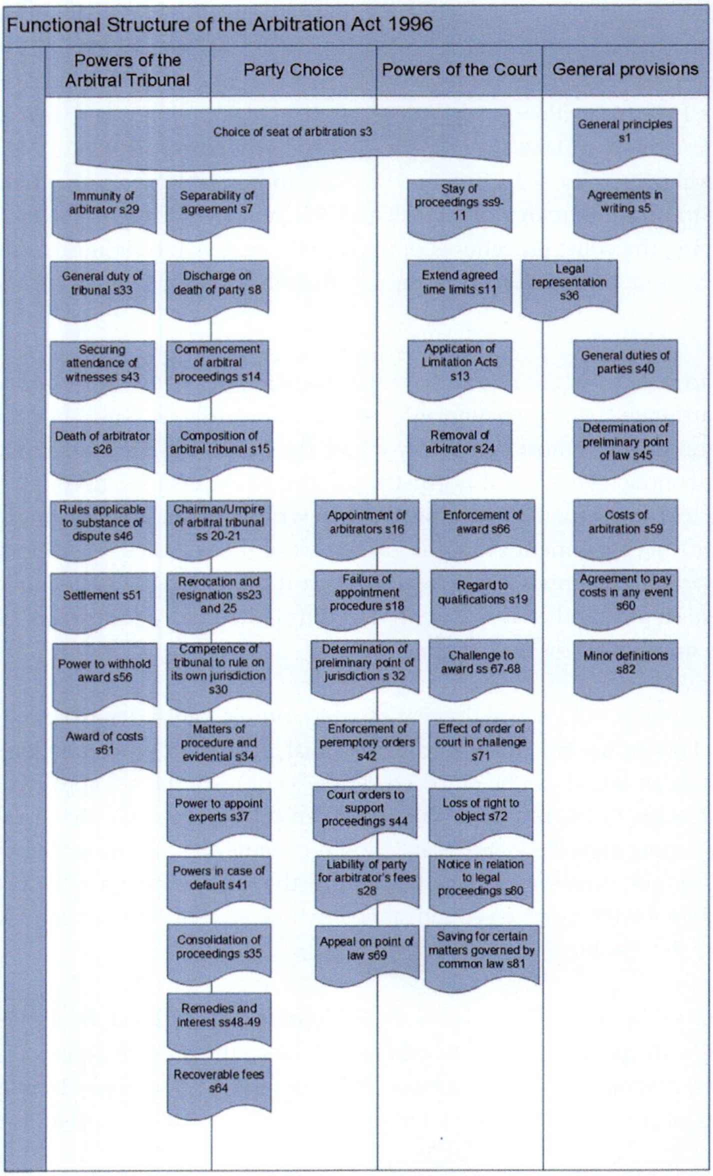

Figure 14.5 Structure of the Arbitration Act 1996.

A note of caution should be applied to Figure 14.5. It is unlikely, in a study of the legal system, that you will need to know all the listed provisions in any level of detail. Instead, the diagram should be used only as a way of understanding that the Act is sculpted around these broad themes, with particular emphasis on party choice. Where a provision straddles a line in the diagram it represents a situation where parties *can* decide what happens in that situation, but there is a default position if the parties do not deal with the issue in their agreement to arbitrate.

GENERAL PROVISIONS OF THE ARBITRATION ACT 1996

The wording of the Arbitration Act 1996 is unusual for an Act of Parliament in that it opens with very 'principle-based' sections. This is likely to indicate the importance of the second purpose of the Act, as described previously – to improve the attractiveness of London as a centre of worldwide arbitration. It is a 'sales pitch', intending to explain what place arbitration holds in the legal system of England and Wales and is particularly useful in international arbitration. The more important sections of the Arbitration Act 1996 are laid out later, starting with those that reinforce the idea of party choice before moving on to discuss the powers that are granted to the arbitrators under the Act and ending with a discussion of the role of the courts under the Act. It is clearly a positive feature of the Act that, while some sections of the Act must be followed and cannot be changed by the parties, any not so designated are optional.

EXPLAINING THE LAW – ARBITRATION ACT 1996

Section 1 of the Act transcends these themes and lays down the following principles:

S1: a. The object of arbitration is to obtain the fair resolution of disputes by an impartial tribunal without unnecessary delay or expense.
b. The parties should be free to agree how their disputes are resolved, subject only to such safeguards, as are necessary in the public interest.
c. In matters governed by this part, the court should not intervene except as provided by this part.

Section 1 gives out a number of important messages about the nature of arbitration in the legal system. Firstly, it explicitly recognises one of the perceived advantages of arbitration in cutting cost and delay (s1(a)). Secondly, it emphasises party choice in the process (s1(b)). Thirdly, it expressly and unequivocally limits the jurisdiction of the ordinary courts in becoming involved where an arbitration agreement exists (s1(c)). This is a clear indication of support for DR as a matter of public policy. Rather than reading as the opening section to an important and very technical Act of Parliament, it reads as an open advertisement on the benefits of using England and Wales as the seat for arbitration. It strongly reinforces the three key benefits of arbitration as a method of DR: avoidance of cost and delay, the importance of party choice and the limited involvement of the formal institutions of the legal system.

The desire for arbitration to be an expeditious method for parties to resolve their disputes is reinforced by the case law. In *Bremer Vulcan*,[25] the House of Lords held that excessive and unreasonable delay to answer a claim of arbitration may lead to a repudiatory breach of the

25 *Bremer Vulkan v South India Shipping Corporation* [1981] AC 909 (HL).

arbitration agreement, entitling the other party to treat the requirement to refer disputes for arbitration as void. This is because excessive delays prejudice a right to a fair hearing. As Lord Denning reminisced in the Court of Appeal:

> When I was young, a sandwich-man wearing a top-hat used to parade outside these courts with his boards back and front, proclaiming 'Arbitrate, don't litigate.' It was very good advice so long as arbitrations were conducted speedily: as many still are in the City of London. But it is not so good when arbitrations drag on forever.[26]

PARTY CHOICE

The Arbitration Act 1996 gives the parties involved a large amount of autonomy over not only the choice of arbitration as a method of dispute resolution but also over how the Arbitration Tribunal conducts itself. Schedule I of the Act lists the *mandatory* provisions that apply notwithstanding any agreement between the parties. These are minimum standards that provide some level of consistency and certainty to the disputants. Aside from this, the parties can determine whether other sections of the Act apply. In most instances, each issue is left to the arbitration agreement, but the Act gives default positions, should the parties not cater for the particular issue in their agreement. The following is subject to an overriding duty on the arbitrator to

> act fairly and impartially as between the parties, giving each party a reasonable opportunity of putting his case and dealing with that of his opponent, and adopt procedures suitable to the circumstances of the particular case, avoiding unnecessary delay or expense, so as to provide a fair means for the resolution of the matters falling to be determined.[27]

The parties have the power to determine, amongst other things, the following aspects of the arbitration:

1. The seat of arbitration (s3)
2. The date on which arbitral proceedings are commenced (s14)
3. The number, identity and process of appointment for the arbitrator (s15 and s16)
4. The function of any chairperson (s20)
5. The revocation of the authority of a particular arbitrator (s23)[28]
6. The procedures of the tribunal and any rules of evidence that will apply (s34)

In the absence of agreement on any of the preceding points, the Arbitration Act 1996 details within the relevant section how the matter is to be resolved.

26 *Bremer Vulcan v South India Shipping* [1980] 2 WLR 905 (CA) 933 (Lord Denning MR).

27 Arbitration Act 1996 s33.

28 This power must be exercised by both parties acting jointly (s23(1)) and in writing (s23(4)), unless they have a different procedure detailed in their arbitration agreement.

EXPLAINING THE LAW – PARTY CHOICE

Given the prominence of party choice in the Arbitration Act 1996, it is not surprising to find the courts placing similar emphasis on its importance. Thus, in the *Channel Tunnel*[29] case, Lord Mustill was keen to emphasise the following when parties have chosen a form of dispute resolution, such as arbitration, to settle their contractual disputes:

> Having made this choice I believe that it is in accordance . . . with the interests of the orderly regulation of international commerce, that having promised to take their complaints to the experts and if necessary to the arbitrators, that is where the appellants should go. The fact that the appellants now find their chosen method too slow to suit their purpose, is to my way of thinking quite beside the point.[30]

POWERS OF COURT

Although s1 of the Act makes it clear that courts should not lightly intervene in the arbitral process, that same section does make clear that the court itself is given powers under the Act. A court, for example, has the power to stay proceedings under s9(1) of the Act where one of the parties tries to bring a legal action before the arbitration is allowed to run its course. This power ensures that the courts are not used to bypass the agreement of the parties to settle their dispute by arbitration and helps to achieve the rationale of s1(c) Arbitration Act 1996, namely, of non-interference by the court in private agreements. s9(4) creates a presumption that the court will grant such a stay unless it is satisfied that the agreement to arbitrate is 'null and void, inoperative, or incapable of being performed'. The court also has a power to extend any time limits within the arbitration.[31] In order to invoke this power, the court must be satisfied that either it would be unjust, due to the behaviour of one of the parties, to hold the other party to the time limit or where the delay was due to circumstances outside of the 'reasonable contemplation' of the parties.

The previous subsection of this chapter dealt with the appointment of a suitable arbitrator or arbitrators and noted that this was left to party choice. The courts are only permitted to intervene, by virtue of ss166 and 18, where this process fails or where there is nothing in the arbitration agreement pertaining to appointment.

The courts maintain jurisdiction to remove an arbitrator in the following circumstances:

- Where there are doubts as to impartiality[32]
- Where the arbitrator does not hold qualifications stipulated by the arbitration agreement[33]

29 *Channel Tunnel Group v Balfour Beatty Construction* [1993] AC 334 (HL).
30 ibid 353 (Lord Mustill).
31 Arbitration Act 1996 s12.
32 Arbitration Act 1996 s24(1)(a).
33 Arbitration Act 1996 s24(1)(b).

- Where there are doubts as to mental or physical capacity to conduct the proceedings[34]
- Where the arbitrator has failed to conduct the hearing properly *and* where 'substantial injustice has been or will be caused' to the person applying for the court's intervention[35]
- Courts can also order enforcement of the award, which will be treated in the same manner as enforcement of a court order[36]

The preceding powers of the court in the case of arbitration are largely about ensuring that there are procedural safeguards in place so that parties feel confident in electing arbitration as their method of DR and to govern situations where party choice fails.

In addition to the aforementioned powers, the courts have a role in ensuring that arbitral awards are fairly arrived at and managing the process of challenge to an award. It is here that we see an inherent tension between the stated aims of arbitration. By this we mean that the legal system has to try to balance the wants of the parties in avoiding litigation and in ensuring that awards made are fair and do not distort the established law. Thus, even after the completion of an arbitral hearing, the parties may still end up in court. Due to the wish of the legal system to make the UK an attractive choice for international commercial arbitration the circumstances for challenging an award of an arbitral tribunal through the court system are extremely limited.

The following circumstances give rise to potential for challenge:

- If the substantive jurisdiction of the tribunal is in issue (s67)
- If there were serious irregularities that risk causing injustice to the applicant (s68)[37]
- If there is an alleged error of law (s69)

The possibility for appeal on a point of law has proved to be controversial as it risks undermining the speed and efficiency of the arbitration process and introducing many of the pitfalls of litigation. To prevent recourse to the 'error of law' becoming too frequent the Act lay down a strict test for the courts to apply. In exercising this jurisdiction and granting leave for an appeal, the courts must follow strict guidelines of s69(3), which have their origin in the common law test of *The Nema*:[38]

1. That the determination of the question will substantially affect the rights of one or more of the parties
2. That the question is one which the tribunal was asked to determine
3. That, on the basis of the findings of fact in the award,

34 Arbitration Act 1996 s24(1)(c).

35 Arbitration Act 1996 s24(1)(d).

36 Arbitration Act 1996 s66.

37 This can include failure of the tribunal to comply with its duties, where the tribunal acts outside of its agreed powers or where the tribunal has failed to act according to the procedures agreed by the parties.

38 *Pioneer Shipping v BTP Tioxide (The Nema)* [1982] AC 724 (HL) 742 (Lord Diplock).

a. the decision of the tribunal on the question is obviously wrong, or
b. the question is one of general public importance and the decision of the tribunal is at least open to serious doubt

4. That, despite the agreement of the parties to resolve the matter by arbitration, it is just and proper in all the circumstances for the court to determine the question

Parties can even attempt, through agreement, to circumvent the potential of challenge to an arbitral award. This attempt to oust the jurisdiction of the court is controversial as it runs the risk of violating fundamental rights, such as the right to a fair trial/hearing. This very issue was raised in the *Sumukan*[39] case.

The Arbitration Act 2025 has sought to limit further challenges to jurisdiction under s67 of the Arbitration Act 1996. A line of case law, culminating in the Supreme Court's judgment in *Dallah*[40] had led to increased diversion to court to rehear matters that were considered or to be considered by the arbitral tribunal. The changes brought about by the Arbitration Act 2025 are premised on excluding additional areas of challenge to jurisdiction.

MAKING CONNECTIONS AND ANALYSING THE LAW – OUSTING THE JURISDICTION OF THE COURT

+++

The legal system of England and Wales protects certain fundamental rights. One of those rights is the right to a fair trial under Article 6 of the European Convention on Human Rights. In the *Sumukan* case, a contract contained, by reference to a statutory scheme, an arbitration agreement that itself excluded the possibility of appeal on a point of law. In essence, the arbitration agreement wished to exclude the court's jurisdiction under s69 of the Arbitration Act 1996.

Although s69 of the Act states that an appeal on a point of law is possible '[u] nless otherwise agreed by the parties', in *Sumukan* the question was whether the exclusion of s69 jurisdiction needed to be expressly stated, rather than incorporated by reference. The line of argument was that to exclude the jurisdiction of the court was a serious issue that should only be used where parties expressly agreed to it. To decide otherwise, the claimants argued, would violate the right to a fair trial. The court disagreed, holding that excluding appeal by reference was not a violation of the ECHR.

The reasoning of the High Court here is interesting as it based on the purpose of arbitration as preserving 'privacy and confidentiality'[41] and 'to reflect and preserve the twin objectives of finality and party autonomy'.[42] In doing so, the court has

39 *Sumukan v Commonwealth Secretariat* [2006] EWHC 1148 (Comm), [2006] 1 All ER (Comm) 621.
40 *Dallah v Pakistan* [2010] UKSC 46.
41 ibid [16].
42 ibid.

placed great emphasis on contract, as opposed to public law, principles. Indeed, in supporting the finding, Mr Justice Colman made express reference to the general law of contract on exclusion agreements.[43] He went further in saying that, in comparison to a contract law issue on excluding *liability*, the exclusion of a right to appeal did not go to substantive rights but went '**only** to the ancillary dispute resolution machinery'.[44]

What is clear from the *Sumukan* case is that in the balance between procedural rights and contractual freedom, the court will place special emphasis on the latter due to the policy objectives – party freedom and independence from the courts – where arbitration is involved.

POWERS AND DUTIES OF ARBITRATORS AND THE ARBITRAL TRIBUNAL

Although not appearing until the mid-portion of the Arbitration Act 1996, it is important to note that each individual arbitration tribunal is under an overarching duty to

> act fairly and impartially as between the parties, giving each party a reasonable opportunity of putting his case and dealing with that of his opponent, and adopt procedures suitable to the circumstances of the particular case, avoiding unnecessary delay or expense, so as to provide a fair means for the resolution of the matters falling to be determined.[45]

The preceding general duty reiterates the points made at the start of this section of the chapter, namely that the Arbitration Act 1996 has a dual purpose of achieving a fair and just outcome according to the wishes of the parties and of allowing for an expedient and cost-effective resolution of the dispute. The arbitral tribunal is under a duty to decide the dispute according to the law chosen by the parties and/or any other considerations that the parties may agree.[46]

As well as the general duty to act fairly, the arbitral tribunal has general powers in relation to the organisation of arbitration proceedings. Amongst these general powers is the ability to require and administer oaths and affirmations.[47] The arbitrator(s) has important powers in relation to the jurisdiction of the arbitration tribunal. This power extends to determining the validity of the arbitration agreement itself and to the subject matter of the dispute to be determined.[48]

In addition, and if the parties do not agree otherwise, the tribunal can determine evidential and procedural issues from basic decisions such as the location of the arbitration proceedings to more complex rules on disclosure of documents and whether the proceedings will be

43 ibid [19] (Colman J) citing Lord Justice Bingham in *Circle Freight International Ltd v Medeast Gulf Exports Ltd* [1988] 2 Lloyd's Rep 427 (CA), 433 (Bingham LJ).

44 ibid [20] (Colman J).

45 Arbitration Act 1996 s33.

46 Arbitration Act 1996 s46.

47 Arbitration Act 1996 s38.

48 Arbitration Act 1996 s30.

Figure 14.6 Common forms of arbitration.

through written statements only or whether oral arguments would be heard.[49] These powers include the determination of admissibility of evidence and any weight that will attach to particular types or pieces of evidence.

The arbitrator has a very strong immunity for acts done in discharge of his or her duty. This extends beyond acts undertaken negligently, and s29 makes arbitrators only liable for acts or omissions made in bad faith. Should a party cause 'inordinate and inexcusable delay', then the tribunal has the power to make an award dismissing the case.[50] In relation to remedies, the tribunal, agreement notwithstanding, has powers to issue a range of remedies that are broadly similar to those available to an ordinary court. The arbitral tribunal can order a payment of money (akin to damages) and order things similar to injunctions and specific performance.[51] The arbitral tribunal can also order an award of costs.[52]

COMMON EXAMPLES OF ARBITRATION

The principles of arbitration, as they now find expression in the Arbitration Act 1996, that apply within the legal system have developed largely in the context of commercial law. The importance of freedom of contract/party choice, confidentiality and speed of process has therefore dominated the understanding of formal arbitration as a dispute resolution mechanism. As a result, much of what is talked about in relation to the Arbitration Act 1996 is directly relevant for and related to commercial arbitration.

Nonetheless, and more recently, the Arbitration Act 1996 has increasingly been used by a wider range of disputants to settle their disagreements. This has been complemented with statutory schemes of arbitration. The forms of arbitration discussed in this section are summarised in Figure 14.6. They are not mutually exclusive, and one notable overlap is that many faith-based arbitration frameworks are established to deal with matters relating to family disputes.

COMMERCIAL ARBITRATION

Even within the ill-defined arena of 'commercial law' certain transactions and relationships lend themselves more to arbitration than others. For example, arbitration agreements (and adjudication) are common in construction contracts. This is due primarily to the need for disputes to be dealt with swiftly and with relevant expertise over costs when construction projects overrun on time or budget or require significant amendments. This was evident with

49 Arbitration Act 1996 s34.

50 Arbitration Act 1996 s41(3).

51 Arbitration Act 1996 s48(4)–(5).

52 Arbitration Act 1996 s61.

the *Channel Tunnel* case just discussed. The case involved the valuation of changes to the original agreed work. As well as being a construction case, *Channel Tunnel* also demonstrates the other major area where arbitration is used and that relates to relationships that take place, or operate, in the international arena – in the case of the Channel Tunnel project, primarily between companies and governments in the UK and France.

The term 'international commercial arbitration' is often used when describing the use of the Arbitration Act 1996. The term has connotations that suggest resolution at the international level but as there is no supranational system of arbitration this has to have a national context. We are talking about *international disputes* that take place in a *national jurisdiction* according to *domestic* rules of the chosen jurisdiction.

The lack of a supranational forum or of a fully harmonised set of international rules for settling arbitrations results in competition between jurisdictions to become the seat of individual arbitrations. It is from this competition that the 'sales pitch' of s1 of the Arbitration Act 1996 arises. Consequently, commercial contracts involving cross-border activity often contain arbitration clauses. This adds a great deal of certainty to proceedings and prevents 'forum shopping' – a practice by which a party in dispute will pick the most advantageous jurisdiction within which to launch an action. Where a contract is to be executed by parties in different countries or where goods are to be shipped across many territorial waters it can lead to a great deal of uncertainty. Arbitration can help strip away that uncertainty and allows parties to dictate, before a dispute even arises, where and by which law their disagreement is to be resolved.

FAITH-BASED ARBITRATION

Traditional textbook discourse on the legal system of England and Wales tends to focus on commercial arbitration and will analyse the merits and disadvantages of arbitration as a whole in relation to the commercial world. That presents a very narrow view of the role of arbitration (and DR more generally) in society. This chapter takes a broader view and will consider the use of faith-based arbitration as a mechanism of resolving disputes. This is seen as a growing and contentious area of DR within the legal system of England and Wales. For example, in 2007, the Muslim Arbitration Tribunal (MAT) was established. It allows Muslims to have certain types of dispute determined in accordance with Schools of Islamic Sacred Law. The tribunal sits with at least two members: one a scholar of Islamic Law and the other a qualified solicitor or barrister. The integration of faith into the DR system is a highly charged political issue and also tells us a great deal about the flexibility of the legal system and of acceptance of faith considerations within that system. The degree of sensitivity over the issue of faith-based dispute resolution was drawn into sharp focus by the comments of the Archbishop of Canterbury in 2008, when he appeared to advocate the adoption of religious law within the legal system of England and Wales.[53] His comments found some support from Lord Phillips, speaking extrajudicially.[54]

53 For academic comment, see Julian Rivers, 'The Secularisation of the British Constitution' (2012) 14(3) Ecc LJ 371, 391 <https://www.cambridge.org/core/journals/ecclesiastical-law-journal/article/secularisation-of-the-british-constitution/40886A0AB7A0E649D2AC109EFCA01A75>.

54 <http://news.bbc.co.uk/1/hi/uk/7488790.stm>.

The critique of the perceived rise of 'Sharia Law' has also been of significant discussion and interest in more recent political discourse, with the rise of the Reform Party in the UK. The party's major gains since the 2024 General Election were fuelled by concerns over immigration and this has manifested in a mistaken belief that a *separate system of law is in operation*. The truth of the matter is that application of DR to religious contexts happen in the framework provided by the legal system of England and Wales.

EXPLAINING THE LAW – FAITH-BASED ARBITRATION

The judgment in *AI v MT*[55] is revealing as to the approach of the courts to faith-based arbitration. The case concerned an orthodox Jewish couple whose marriage ran into difficulties, and as a result, the British-born mother refused to return to Canada with her children. Initially, the father sought an order from the English and Welsh courts requiring the return of the children. The parties then agreed that their dispute be resolved using a specific Jewish religious arbitration tribunal whose decision they would respect – that of the Beth Din in New York.

In the case at hand, the courts of England and Wales were asked to dismiss the father's initial claim, given the agreement of the parties to proceed to a binding religious tribunal through the New York Beth Din. The court refused to make the order on this basis, but after examining the principles that would be used in the religious tribunal, Mr Justice Baker indicated that the award of the New York Beth Din would be 'likely to carry considerable weight with the court . . . [but] . . . would not be binding and would not preclude either party from pursuing applications to this court in respect of any of the matters in issue'.[56] On this basis, a consent order was granted, and the father's initial claim dismissed. When the matter returned to court after the completion of the Beth Din hearing, Mr Justice Baker endorsed the findings of the Beth Din and transferred them into an order.

In this case, the legal system managed to accommodate the wishes of the parties, based on their deeply held religious views, while not threatening the consistency of the legal system. As a result, the faith-based tribunal was respected within a secular court system. This was possible because the principles by which the New York Beth Din came to its conclusions were equivalent to those that would have been followed by an English and Welsh court. However, and unlike a commercial arbitration, the Beth Din award could not be binding and enforced in the legal system of England and Wales without final approval from a court. As the interests of the children were paramount to the determination of the Beth Din, the court felt able (cautiously) to respect the choice of the party. However, Mr Justice Baker made it clear that if he was 'independently of the view that it was not in the child's best interests [he] would

55 *AI v MT (Alternative Dispute Resolution)* [2013] EWHC 100 (Fam), [2013] 2 FLR 371.
56 ibid [15] (Baker J).

unhesitatingly say so and refuse to order it, notwithstanding the very great respect this Court has for the deliberations of the Beth Din'.[57]

Although mediation is a more prevalent form of dispute resolution in this area, it is clear from this case that many of the perceived benefits of commercial arbitration can extend into the realm of family law. It is worth noting that Mr Justice Baker made particular reference to the benefits of speed, cost and the ability of the parties to choose the specific arbitrator who will settle their dispute.[58] The 2011 judgment of the Supreme Court in *Jivraj*,[59] marks an important step in the recognition of faith-based arbitration as an integral part of the legal system. In the case, Lord Mance's comments are particularly enlightening in that he held that arbitrator's contracts are of a *sui generis* nature which means that arbitrators are not employees and are not subject to discrimination rules.[60] This, contrary to the judgment of the Court of Appeal in this case,[61] means that it is lawful for those of faith to have a contractual requirement that an arbitrator be drawn from a particular faith without breaching the rules surrounding discrimination on the basis of religious beliefs.

Turning back to *AI v MT*, Baker J went even further so as to suggest that party autonomy, even in sensitive family law disputes, underpins both the Children Act 1989[62] and Article 8 of the ECHR.[63] However, and as demonstrated by the case, due to public policy issues surrounding the welfare and protection of children the benefits of arbitration must be hemmed in with additional safeguards. Thus, parties are unable to oust the jurisdiction of the court through agreement in certain matrimonial and family matters.[64] The *quid pro quo* being that the court will give significant weight to the award given by a tribunal that follows principles common to English and Welsh law. The judgment in *AI v MT* is of particular importance in debunking the assumption that recent trends in the growth of DR have been traced to the 'waning role of some of society's traditional [dispute resolving] institutions – the family, the church and the community'.[65] The case demonstrates that religion, dispute resolution and the legal system, can not only co-exist but also have a meaningful and beneficial relationship.

While *AI v MT* represents a seemingly satisfactory accommodation of belief and party autonomy within the legal system, the principle is not without controversy. Concerns have been expressed about the practice of certain faith-based arbitration tribunals where (1) the principles adopted to resolve disputes are not in accordance with English and Welsh law and

57 ibid [18] (Baker J).

58 ibid [32] (Baker J).

59 *Jivraj v Hashwani* [2011] UKSC 40, [2011] 1 WLR 1872.

60 ibid [77]–[78] (Lord Mance).

61 *Jivraj v Hashwani* [2010] EWCA Civ 712, [2011] 1 All ER 50.

62 Which vests, via s2, responsibility for the welfare of children primarily with the parents.

63 Which secures the right to a family life.

64 A principle laid down as long ago as the 1920s in *Hyman v Hyman* [1929] AC 601 (HL) 613 – a case concerning an agreement of a wife not to petition the court for maintenance on the ending of her marriage.

65 Frank Sander, 'Alternative Dispute Resolution in the United States: An Overview' in Julio Betancourt and Jason Crook (eds), *ADR, Arbitration, and Mediation* (AuthorHouse 2014) 2.

(2) where certain tribunals are falsely claiming jurisdiction to adjudicate on matters (including certain family and criminal matters) that they should not be deciding.

MAKING CONNECTIONS AND ANALYSING THE LAW – LEGISLATIVE REACTION TO FAITH-BASED ARBITRATION

Chapter 4 examined the process by which legislation is passed. The chapter discussed the prospect of non-government bills being introduced into Parliament, particularly on sensitive matters. In order to address the concerns over false claims of jurisdiction and threats to equality, Baroness Cox introduced a private members' bill – the Arbitration and Mediation Services (Equality) Bill – in the 2012–2013 session.

The Bill sought to criminalise false claims of jurisdiction and to ensure equality (particularly in relation to sex) in execution of arbitration proceedings and other proceedings available under English and Welsh law based on faith. Baroness Cox made an impassioned speech on the introduction of the Bill to the House of Lords, indicating existing problems in relation to certain Sharia 'courts' and community pressure on Muslim women not to resort to the more formal legal proceedings.[66] These issues range from problems over substantive differences in treatment of men and women to those relating to evidence and procedure.[67]

While the concerns were aimed at parts of the Muslim Arbitration Tribunal, the vast majority of problems seem to arise in less formal fora, where women are led to believe that the Sharia 'court' has binding powers. During the second reading of the Bill, Baroness Donaghy noted that the problems caused by certain forms of faith-based dispute resolution risk bringing the whole system of DR into disrepute.[68] As was mentioned in the second reading stage of the Bill in the House of Lords, certain faith-based dispute settlement processes are questionable because women often suffer 'a language barrier, huge cultural or family pressure, ignorance of the law, a misplaced faith in the system or a threat of complete isolation', which means that the process is 'as consensual as rape'.[69] While the Bill ultimately did not make it through the process to become an Act of Parliament, it is indicative of the strength of feeling and concerns around faith-based arbitration. The Bill was re-introduced in subsequent sessions, most recently in 2016–2017, but again failed to progress and become law.

Indeed, the immediate misunderstanding and later equally misunderstood backlash in the media against the eminently sensible judgment in *AI v MT* demonstrates that separating out the 'appropriate' DR from the 'inappropriate' DR is by no means easy.

66 HL Deb 19 October 2012, col 1683.
67 ibid col 1693.
68 ibid col 1687.
69 ibid col 1687.

FAMILY LAW ARBITRATIONS

Family law issues have since the early 1980s been more traditionally resolved by conciliation or mediation, partly due to the need for party engagement in forming the solution and in an effort to reduce the antagonism that goes along with adjudicative, adversarial processes. Nonetheless, in February 2012, the Institute of Family Law Arbitrators (IFLA)[70] was able to establish a scheme of family law arbitration. This was not based on any statutory framework. The IFLA creation, however, demonstrates the growing popularity of arbitration in a growing number of fields. Although certain issues (such as divorce) cannot be definitively determined by such arbitration, other issues such as financial arrangements and inheritances could be resolved using this new scheme, and the accompanying private child law issues were added in 2016, so as to enable an 'all issues' determination by an arbitrator qualified under both sets of rules.[71]

Most recently, arbitration has been extended outside the civil and commercial context to family law, both in determining financial and property cases and issues in the private law relating to children. This initiative was undertaken by a pan professional group of stakeholders centred on the Chartered Institute of Arbitrators, which was guided by the Family Law Bar Association and Resolution. The entire scheme was inspired and brought to life by an academic and practitioners' research committee known as the Centre for Child and Family Law reform, usually chaired by a specialist Family judge, and sponsored by City University of London. The scheme was launched, originally only for financial and property cases, in 2012; is administered by Resolution; and its regulatory board initially chaired by the former Labour Lord Chancellor, Lord Falconer of Thoroton. The current Chairman is Lord Neuberger of Abbotsbury, recently retired President of the Supreme Court, and the scheme was extended to include private child law cases in 2016. Training of new arbitrators continues annually, and the scheme is already gathering sufficient momentum to provide significant assistance to the Family Court in addressing its volume of work and, in particular, reducing delay in awaiting hearings for disposal of their cases, since a study by one arbitrator[72] has shown that an arbitration can be completed within three or four months, half the time that might otherwise be spent in awaiting a hearing date at the Family Court.

ROLE OF ABTA

Before departing from specific examples of arbitration in action, a final example of the process will be considered. This time it comes from the distinct arena of consumer relations. The Association of British Travel Agents (ABTA)[73] is, as the name suggests, a trade association for tour operators and travel agents. As part of its remit it operates an escalating complaints procedure for consumers.[74] This starts with a consumer complaining to a company that is an ABTA member. If the complaint cannot be settled using the internal complaints procedure

70 <http://ifla.org.uk>.

71 The IFLA Rules (two separate sets for the Financial Scheme and the Children Scheme) can be obtained from the IFLA website, <www.ifla.org>, or the website <www.familyarbitrator.com>, or Frances Burton, *Core Statutes on Family Law 2020–2021* (Palgrave Macmillan, published August 2020).

72 Dennis Sheridan and Suzanne Kingston, *Family Arbitration: Practice and Precedents* (2nd edn, Law Society 2017).

73 <http://abta.com>.

74 <http://abta.com/go-travel/travel-clinic/complaints>.

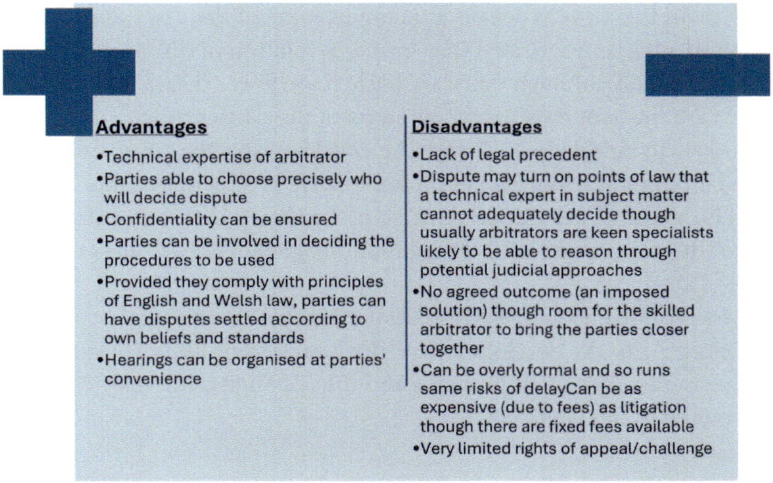

Figure 14.7 Advantages and disadvantages of arbitration.

of the company, then the matter can be referred to ABTA, who will advise on options for the consumer. If no solution is forthcoming, then at the apex of the scheme is a system of arbitration. To put this differently, if a complaint cannot be settled using ABTA's complaints procedure there is the option to have the matter referred to binding and independent arbitration. Again, the important point is not the precise process of the ABTA scheme but rather what it tells us about the nature and extent of arbitration in the legal system of England and Wales. The ABTA scheme is designed to offer consumer protection to those booking services with ABTA members and a certain and defined dispute resolution scheme for the companies who are members. The collapse of Thomas Cook in September 2019 has brought greater public attention to the work of ABTA.[75]

ADVANTAGES AND DISADVANTAGES OF ARBITRATION

The brief set of examples of arbitration discussed in this section has revealed, or at least alluded to, both the advantages and disadvantages of arbitration when compared to litigation and other forms of DR. These advantages and disadvantages are detailed in Figure 14.7.

Due to the adversarial nature of arbitration, you will notice that some of the drawbacks of arbitration are the same as the drawbacks of litigation. It is similarly adjudicative and adversarial in nature. Indeed, many would argue that some of the problems of the court system, such as delay, are now equally ingrained in the system of arbitration, though this is likely to apply only to the largest arbitrations where the scale is in itself the problem.

While Figure 14.7 is useful to get a snapshot of the merits of arbitration, one must not lose sight of the fact that many arbitral tribunals proceed in a less than perfect way and we

75 And ATOL.

should not view them in an overly idealised manner. Some of the cases discussed previously demonstrate this. *AI v MT* demonstrated that speedy resolution of disputes is not always possible within arbitration although there are likely to be fewer delays than within the court system since the case focusses only on the interests of the parties to which the plentiful supply of arbitrators is likely to be able to conform. The concerns over the treatment of women within some faith-based arbitration tribunals question the fairness of certain tribunals. While party choice is said to be a core of arbitration the case of *Sumukan* demonstrates that some parties are not fully aware of the consequences of the arbitration agreements that they enter into.[76]

There is also a risk that by encouraging resolution of disputes outside of court in particular areas that it is damaging to the development of the legal system itself. The common law survives on the cases that come before courts and the (often incremental) development of the law by way of cases heard and decided.

MEDIATION

PRINCIPLES OF MEDIATION

Mediation differs from arbitration in that it is not *adjudicative* in nature, which is to say that the outcome is not determined by an independent third party. Rather, the role of the mediator is to facilitate the parties in coming to a mutually agreed outcome. The theory behind mediation is that parties are placed in a 'win-win' situation where each side is involved in creating the 'solution'. This is to be contrasted with litigation (or, indeed, arbitration) where a solution is imposed on the parties, leading to a 'win-lose' situation.

Having the parties actively engaged in the process of creating the solution is of particular importance to disputes that will have a continuing impact on the relationship of the parties. For this reason, mediation is frequently the 'best solution' where the parties are likely to have or have had an ongoing relationship and where differences may be exacerbated by litigation. Thus, it is often the case that mediation is used in family disputes (such as divorce) or those involving an employment relationship.

The other significant difference between arbitration and mediation is that while arbitration is regulated, both by statute and the courts and by the professional organisations, such as the globally active CIArb, mediation is generally *not* regulated. However, there are operative codes for mediation, such as that of the EU, and international organisations which offer 'certification'. In the UK, the Civil Mediation Council, which requires members to do annual CPD (continuing professional development), makes one qualified through a recognised providers' course. The CMC also provides a complaints procedure.

76 Although this is affecting the court system as well with the significant rise in litigants in person who may have little understanding of the process or potential outcomes.

MAKING CONNECTIONS – OTHER JURISDICTIONS

++++++++++++++++++++++++++++++++++

Chapter 1 discussed how cultural identity can help shape the way in which the legal system operates. This is evident in the emphasis (or lack of it) that is placed on the use of mediation in legal systems around the world. One of the core principles or aims of mediation is to avoid conflict and to promote consensus as a method of dispute resolution.

This helps explain why certain legal cultures emphasise the importance of mediation over litigation or arbitration. For example, in China, with its strong basis in Confucian (and Communist) moral philosophy, there has traditionally been a focus on mediation as it allows parties to 'save face' due to its 'win–win' nature.[77]

As well as being its major strength, having to reach a consensual decision is also the greatest weakness of mediation. This is because there will, inevitably, be times when the parties are unable to come to an agreement. To this end, the statement of Lord Justice Thorpe in *Marsy*[78] that 'there is no case, however conflicted, which is not potentially open to successful mediation, even if mediation has not been attempted or has failed during the trial process',[79] is perhaps a little optimistic. Where parties fail to come to agreement in their mediation, the option for litigation is still available and the parties will have spent time and money on the services of a mediator. As such, while successful mediation is normally less costly than litigation, a failed mediation will only add to the cost and delay of the process, although it may have narrowed the issues and solved others.

Mediation also offers a wider range of remedies that cannot be ordered by a court. As the Court of Appeal in *Halsey* stated, 'for example, an apology; an explanation; the continuation of an existing professional or business relationship perhaps on new terms; and an agreement by one party to do something without any existing legal obligation to do so'.[80] The very nature of these remedies is different to those available to a court. This is an important point because it demonstrates that not only is the *process* of dispute resolution different for certain methods of DR but also are the *outcomes*. This further reinforces the idea that selection of the correct forum for deciding disputes is crucial to obtaining the 'appropriate' solution.

The use of mediation is not a panacea for all disputes. Manifestly, there will be cases that are unsuitable for mediation. These include where the case raises a point of law that is of general interest to a particular sector or market and that is likely to arise again in the future. In that instance, the benefits of having a binding precedent may outweigh the additional costs

77 Gabrielle Kaufmann-Kohler and Fan Kun, 'Integrating Mediation into Arbitration: Why it Works in China' (2008) 25(4) J Intl Arb 479, 479.

78 *Al Khatib v Masry* [2004] EWCA Civ 1353, [2005] 1 FLR 381.

79 ibid [17] (Thorpe LJ).

80 *Halsey v Milton Keynes General NHS Trust* [2004] EWCA Civ 576, [2004] 1 WLR 3002 [15].

involved in litigation. Similarly, where a party is likely to need interim relief or where there are allegations of malpractice by one of the parties, litigation may be the better option.

EXAMPLES OF MEDIATION IN THE LEGAL SYSTEM OF ENGLAND AND WALES

MEDIATION IN FAMILY CASES

Given the consensual nature of mediation, it is not surprising to find that mediation is prevalent in relation to family matters and particularly used in settling issues around divorce. The Family Act 1996 sought to promote the use of mediation in family disputes. It then became compulsory under the FPR 2010 for divorcing couples relying on public funding to attend a mediation information and assessment meeting (MIAM) before starting proceedings. This meeting, which is not itself mediation, sought to explain and, in appropriate cases, recommend mediation to all divorcing couples. The Children and Families Act 2014 addressed this issue statutorily by requiring all applicants (with the exception of those in cases alleging domestic abuse) to attend an MIAM meeting. This obviously goes a long way towards encouraging mediation, especially now that the form the mediator must sign is incorporated into the form of application to commence proceedings, so the MIAM cannot now be dodged except in exceptional circumstances, for example, the other party will not come.

COURT-BASED SCHEMES

Many of the courts of the legal system of England and Wales have been involved in developing the use of DR, including mediation. Some of these are outlined here, just to give a flavour of how the courts are involved in the process of mediation. There is a great deal of experimentation within the legal system and, in particular, the courts in relation to DR. What is described here represents the most well-known of those experiments. While there are often good reasons to characterise the legal system as archaic and slow-moving, we must also remember that there are good examples of innovation from the within the system.

COURT OF APPEAL MEDIATION SCHEME (CAMS)

The Court of Appeal has jurisdiction to recommend mediation when it is dealing with permission to appeal on certain areas of law. The scheme has been in operation since 2000 and applies to all non-family cases that come to the Civil Division of the court, unless they are claims of a very high value (over £250,000). From 2012, the CAMS entered a pilot system where *all* eligible cases involving sums less than £100,000 are automatically referred for mediation through the Centre for Effective Dispute Resolution (CEDR, already mentioned previously).[81] CEDR, the original not for profit DR centre to be set up in the UK, is now probably the leading dispute resolution consultancy centre in the world, and its members (retired judges as well as leading barrister and solicitor commercial DR specialists) are independent of the courts, and unlike the court based mediation schemes set up by the Ministry of Justice, this means the CAMS scheme is not manned by court staff or Ministry of Justice appointed mediators. This independence is crucial because if the mediation process fails then the disputants will return to the Court of Appeal, which should have no knowledge

81 <www.judiciary.gov.uk/announcements/news-release-mediation-pilot-court-of-appeal>.

of the discussions that took place during the mediation. Another advantage of this scheme is that CEDR is probably also the largest and most diverse global source of expertise in conflict resolution so that the service has access to both the best theoretical expertise and practical experience available anywhere. Thus, if mediation cannot fix a dispute at this level, it probably is an exceptionally difficult one to settle though that may not mean that some other choice of third-party neutral could not facilitate a settlement, as the *Masry* case has already shown.

The Commercial Court (part of the new Business Courts group) also promotes DR, though not through a specific reference to CEDR neutrals but via its specifically proactive case management systems, through which it will, if necessary, nominate a neutral or panel of neutrals suitable for any particular case.

SMALL CLAIMS TRACK MEDIATION

The small claims track mediation scheme has gained widespread approval within the various court areas of England and Wales. The major benefit of the scheme is that, in comparison to the other schemes detailed previously, it is free for parties to use. The system is funded by HMCTS. The mediation is usually operated using the telephone and a face-to-face meeting is not necessary.

By considering (albeit briefly) the different schemes of mediation on offer from within the formal structures of the legal system of England and Wales, it should become clear that there is evidence of growing reliance on DR as an integral part of the process of litigation. Mediation is an important element of the whole picture of dispute resolution both within and outside the formal structure of litigation (see Figure 14.8 for the advantages and disadvantages of mediation). The courts have been central in ensuring the growth of mediation, and further developments (such as the introduction of a small claims track to the Patent Court) suggest that this will continue in the future. Meanwhile, the government has been keen to promote the use of the term 'dispute resolution' rather than 'Alternative dispute resolution', in order to

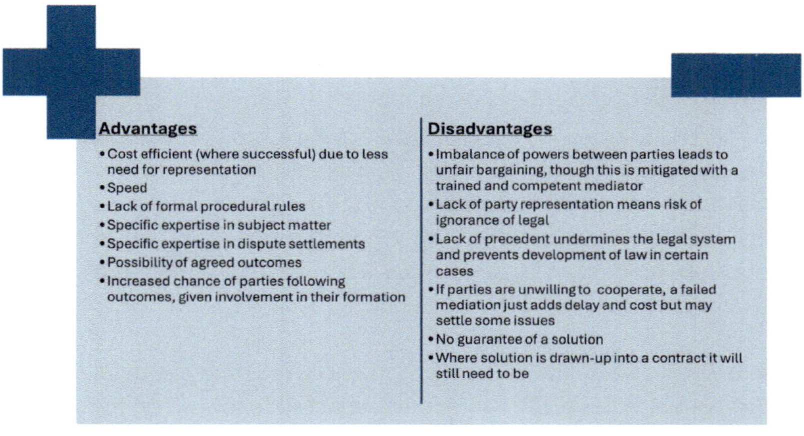

Figure 14.8 Advantages and disadvantages of mediation.

erase (if it can) the unfortunate dependence on the word 'alternative' to suggest that DR is a mere option as an alternative to litigation which disputants can ignore at will.

OTHER FORMS OF DISPUTE RESOLUTION

Whilst mediation and arbitration are the two major forms of DR other than litigation in the courts, there are other schemes and models of dispute resolution. These include early neutral evaluation and negotiation.

TAKING THINGS FURTHER

The website that accompanies this textbook contains short explanations of each of the major forms of dispute resolution as a summary to help paint the picture of the DR landscape in England and Wales.

ENCOURAGING THE USE OF DISPUTE RESOLUTION

When we talk of alternatives to litigation it is an easy assumption to make that this also means that the formal court structure will not be involved in the resolution of DR-based disputes. As has been demonstrated previously, in relation to mediation, this is simply not true and the courts have an important dual role of encouraging the use and managing certain aspects of DR as well as in reducing mediated settlement terms to consent orders to end disputes on terms agreed in Heads of Agreement with the help of the mediator who acted as third party neutral to facilitate the agreement. Indeed, many of the innovations of the legal system's treatment of DR can trace their roots to actions of the courts. Alternative forms of dispute resolution also have support from the government in the form of a commitment to settle their own disputes using DR, where appropriate. The implications and content of that commitment are discussed later in further detail.

MAKING CONNECTIONS – WOOLF REFORMS

++++++++++++++++++++++++++++++++

As was discussed in Chapter 10, the civil justice system has been (re)designed in such a way as to encourage parties to consider DR. The reforms of Lord Woolf marked a turning point for the use of DR in the civil courts. New powers and procedures were introduced to help facilitate the use of DR. When this is coupled with changes to the way in which public funding of legal disputes is administered, there is a strong impetus and incentive for parties to use DR.

Some of the powers and duties of the court to encourage the use of DR can be found in the Civil Procedure Rules (CPR), which were enacted following on from the Woolf Report. Part 1 of the CPR is concerned with the overriding imperative of empowering the courts to manage cases 'justly and at proportionate cost'. As part of the changes brought about by the Woolf Reforms, courts are under a duty actively to manage cases.[82] In particular, under CPR 1.4(2)(e), the court must '[encourage] the parties to use an alternative dispute resolution procedure if the court considers that appropriate and [facilitate] the use of such procedure'. In order to fulfil the duty of facilitating DR, courts are empowered to 'stay' proceedings so that the parties can explore the possibility of using an alternative method of resolving their dispute.[83] This can either be where the parties request a stay[84] or where the court of its own motion thinks it would be appropriate to order a stay.[85]

The case of *Cowl*[86] demonstrates the strength of feeling that the courts should use their case management powers in a way that strongly encourages DR. In that case, Lord Woolf held that '[t]he courts should not permit, except for good reason, proceedings for judicial review to proceed if a significant part of the issues between the parties could be resolved outside the litigation process'.[87] Although his comments can be applied very broadly, he was of the view that where public funds were concerned an attempt to use mediation as a cost saving measure was of paramount importance: 'Today sufficient should be known about alternative dispute resolution to make the failure to adopt it, in particular when public money is involved, indefensible.'[88]

COMPULSION

One of the major questions arising, particularly but not solely in relation to mediation, is the *extent* to which the courts should 'encourage' the use of alternative methods of dispute resolution when the parties are reluctant to do so. Here we have something of a continuum from the courts having no role at all in the promotion of DR to the very different position of courts *forcing* parties into attempting a form of dispute resolution when they are reluctant to do so (Figure 14.9).

In relation to mediation, the courts initially settled on something of a halfway house, falling short of compulsion but by no means allowing parties freely to disregard the prospect of mediating their dispute, and without penalties. More recent case law has, however, confirmed the option for courts to compel DR. An analysis of the case law will demonstrate the approach that has been taken to forcing disputants to use DR.

82 CPR 1.4.

83 CPR 26.4.

84 CPR 26.4(2).

85 CPR 26.4(2A).

86 *Cowl v Plymouth City Council* [2001] EWCA Civ 1935, [2002] 1 WLR 803.

87 ibid [14] (Lord Woolf CJ).

88 ibid [25] (Lord Woolf CJ).

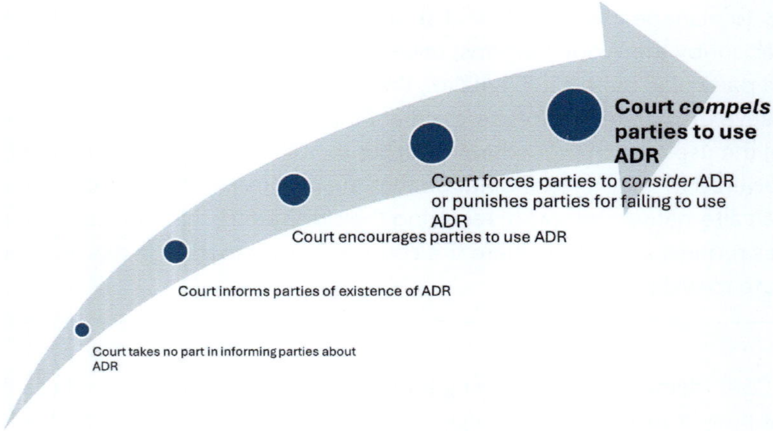

Figure 14.9 The continuum of compulsion.

The case of *Dunnett*[89] continued the progress, started by *Cowl*, towards cost sanctions for refusals to mediate. The court in *Dunnett* specifically sought to raise the profile of mediation and the consequences for parties for failing to engage with DR:

> It is to be hoped that any publicity given to this part of the judgment of the court will draw the attention of lawyers to their duties to further the overriding objective in the way that is set out in CPR Part 1 and to the possibility that, if they turn down out of hand the chance of alternative dispute resolution when suggested by the court, as happened on this occasion, they may have to face uncomfortable costs consequence.[90]

The consequences alluded to in *Dunnett* of parties refusing to consider DR (in this case, mediation) were fully considered in the *Halsey* case, where useful clarification of the preceding cases was given. It is important to note that the statements around compulsion in *Halsey* have been put into doubt by subsequent case law.

To put it simply, in *Halsey* the Court of Appeal held that a party should not be compelled to use a form of DR against his will, but *unreasonable refusal* to mediate could lead to an adverse costs order. It is important to note that subsequent case law has displaced the *Halsey* position some 20 years later.

Halsey was a joined case where the appellants sought a cost sanction against the defendants for refusing to participate in mediation. Mrs Halsey had made a claim against Milton Keynes NHS Trust under the Fatal Accidents Act 1976 on the basis that the death of her husband was caused by alleged medical negligence. Mrs Halsey was happy to mediate (and accept a very small sum of money), but the Trust persistently refused her offer on many occasions. The Court held that the Trust had not acted unreasonably in refusing the offers to mediate and refused to make an

89 *Dunnett v Railtrack Plc* [2002] EWCA Civ 303, [2002] 1 WLR 2434.
90 ibid [15].

adverse costs order. In coming to its conclusion the court made general points about the role of DR and gave more detailed guidance on the circumstances under which a court would make an adverse costs order.

On encouraging the use of DR, the court held thus:

> It is one thing to encourage the parties to agree to mediation, even to encourage them in the strongest terms. It is another to order them to do so. It seems to us that to oblige truly unwilling parties to refer their disputes to mediation would be to impose an unacceptable obstruction on their right of access to the court.[91]

The court went on to say that an order compelling parties to mediate would potentially breach the parties' right to access to the court and thus be a violation of Article 6 of the European Convention on Human Rights.[92]

When discerning who should prove or disprove the reasonableness of the refusal to follow through with DR, the Court of Appeal noted that as this was a departure from the general rule that costs should follow the event 'the burden is on the unsuccessful party to show why there should be a departure from the general rule'.[93] In other words, it is for the party who offered to mediate, and not the party refusing, to prove that the refusal is unreasonable. The desirability of the burden of proof being decided in this way will be discussed further later in the chapter.

The Court of Appeal in *Halsey* put forward a number of (non-exhaustive) factors that will help future courts determine whether a party has acted reasonably in refusing an offer to decide the matter by DR:

1. The nature of the dispute
2. The merits of the case
3. The extent to which other settlement methods have been attempted
4. Whether the costs of the DR would be disproportionately high
5. Whether any delay in setting up and attending the DR session would have been prejudicial
6. Whether the DR attempt had a reasonable prospect of success[94]

As mentioned previously, this is not compulsion but encouragement of the strongest possible form. The threat of a costs sanction could, if applied liberally, be akin to a requirement to mediate when one party so requests. The principles laid down in *Halsey* were applied in a number of subsequent cases before falling out of favour.[95]

91 [2004] EWCA Civ 576, [2004] 1 WLR 3002.

92 ibid [9].

93 ibid [13].

94 ibid [16].

95 *Reed Executive Plc v Reed Business Information Ltd (No 2)* [2004] EWCA Civ 887, [2004] 1 WLR 3026; *Burchell v Bullard* [2005] EWCA Civ 358, [2005] BLR 330.

The Court of Appeal has commented upon the application of *Halsey* in cases where one party wishes 'to have his day in court'. The court in *Rolf*[96] noted that this was one of the reasons that the court in *Halsey* fell short of *compelling* parties to enter into a process of DR. However, the court went on to state that wanting one's day in court does not seem to be 'an adequate response to a proper judicial concern that parties should respond reasonably to offers to mediate or settle and that their conduct in this respect can be taken into account in awarding costs'.[97] In concluding, Lord Justice Rix noted that the rationale of a *Halsey* sanction on costs is not to give the impression that mediation will always be successful but that it can be a useful exercise in potentially saving the parties time, money and frustration:

> It is possible of course that settlement discussions, or even mediation, would not have produced a solution; or would have produced one satisfactory enough to the parties to have enabled them to reach agreement but which [the Defendant] might now, with his hindsight of the judge's judgment, have been able to say did him less than justice.[98]

Returning to the *Halsey* case, the safeguards (or, as some would have them, obstacles) laid down in that case may water down what would otherwise be a very strong incentive to consider mediation. Two aspects of *Halsey* have troubled the minds of academics and judges since the decision was handed down. These relate to the assertion that the burden for proving that refusal to mediate was unreasonable falls not on the person refusing the mediation but on the person seeking an adverse costs order and that compulsory orders for mediation would breach the European Convention of Human Rights. By placing the obligation to prove unreasonableness not on the person who has refused, the court in *Halsey* introduced evidential difficulties for those willing to mediate.[99] It would have been much more conducive to the encouragement of DR if the party unwilling to enter into dispute resolution (particularly when recommended by the courts) had the burden of demonstrating that their behaviour was reasonable.

The proposition regarding Article 6 of the ECHR put forward in *Halsey* has been largely discredited by academics[100] and subsequent developments outside the courts of England and Wales and more recently by the Court of Appeal. Although initially finding passing domestic support in *Hickman v Blake*,[101] the judgment of the Court of Justice of the European Union in *Alassini*[102] would seem to settle the issue that, on the face of it, an order to mediate would not necessarily impinge upon a party's right to access to justice.[103] The finding that Article 6 is

96 *Rolf v de Guerin* [2011] EWCA Civ 78, [2011] CP Rep 24.

97 ibid [41].

98 ibid [48] (Rix LJ).

99 For a response to the criticism, see Lord Dyson, 'A Word on *Halsey v Milton Keynes*' (2011) 77(3) *Arbitration* 337.

100 Brenda Tronson, 'Mediation Orders: Do the Arguments Against them Make Sense?' (2006) 25 CJQ 412.

101 [2006] EWHC 12 (QB), [2006] 3 Costs LR 452 [21].

102 Joined Cases C-317–320 *Alassini v Telecom Italia* [2010] ECR I-2213.

103 Having said this, it should be noted that the facts of *Alassini* are slightly different given that the scheme of mediation would not have cost the parties anything and had an extremely limited time frame of operation.

not, as a matter of course, violated if a party is ordered to mediate is further strengthened when looking at legislation emanating from European Union provisions[104] and the fact that other jurisdictions have automatic referral to mediation, although they take care not to refer to this as 'compulsory mediation'.[105] Despite this, the reluctance in *Halsey* to compel parties to enter into DR appears to have stultified discussions about moving from encouragement to compulsion.

Furthermore, on one construction of the Civil Procedure Rules, it is possible to argue that the courts are already able to order parties to use DR to resolve their dispute. It should not be forgotten that just because a court *could* order mediation, it would not be the case that the court *would* order mediation. As part of the general duties of the court towards good case management, it could be argued that the court should have the *discretion* to order mediation in cases where the facts suggest that it would have some prospect of success. Indeed, it can be argued that, despite the reticence shown in *Halsey*, the court already has the power to order ADR through a combination of CPR 1.4(2)(e) (on the duty to encourage DR) and CPR 3.1(2)(m) (on the power of the court to 'take any other step or make any other order for the purpose of managing the case and furthering the overriding objective'). This would safeguard parties from having to mediate in every case, particularly where there is no prospect for success.

The *Halsey* position has been extended to cover not only outright refusals to mediate but also where a party ignores an offer to mediate[106] or where a party acts unreasonably *during* mediation. The case of *Strutt*[107] is the leading case on the latter development.

EXPLAINING THE LAW AND ANALYSING THE LAW – UNREASONABLE BEHAVIOUR IN MEDIATION

In the case of *Strutt*, James Carleton Harris (7th Earl of Malmesbury) pursued a negligence claim against surveyors for failing adequately to negotiate a commercial lease of the claimant's land to be used as a car park for Bournemouth International Airport. It was common for such leases to include 'turnover' clauses that were heavily in favour of the landowner. Such a clause was not negotiated at the time of the original lease.

104 Directive 2008/52/EC on certain aspects of mediation in civil and commercial matters [2008] OJ L136/3. Article 3(a), for example, talks of mitigation that is 'ordered by a court or prescribed by the law of a Member State'.

105 For example, Italy and Canada, as set out at the 2017 Academics' Conference of the CMC and FMC in London on 13 October 2017, where it was revealed that Italy had done 80,000 automatic referral mediations in the previous year, and that in Ontario, Canada, the level of hearings had been reduced by successful automatic referral to 2% of previous volume.

106 *PGF II v OMFS* [2013] EWCA Civ 1288, [2014] 1 WLR 1386.

107 *Seventh Earl of Malmesbury v Strutt* [2008] EWHC 424 (QB), [2008] 5 Costs LR 736.

The parties entered into mediation, with the claimants wishing to settle originally at a figure of around £100 million. By the time of the trial, this had reduced to some £5 million. They eventually won the case and were awarded just short of £1 million. As such, their position during mediation had been greatly exaggerated, and so the behaviour during the mediation was unreasonable. The court therefore severely restricted (but did not completely remove) their ability to recover costs 'by reason of their attitude in mediation'.[108]

In coming to a judgment, Mr Justice Jack held that unreasonable behaviour during a mediation was similar, in effect, to unreasonable refusal to mediate. The court held that

> a party who agrees to mediation but then causes the mediation to fail by his reason of unreasonable position in the mediation is in reality in the same position as a party who unreasonably refuses to mediate. In my view it is something which the court can and should take account of in the costs order in accordance with the principles considered in *Halsey*.[109]

On first blush, the outcome in *Strutt* seems sensible, but it is not without dangers. By continuing formally to integrate forms of DR into the legal system, the courts risk ending up acting in a supervisory role, and the result is likely to delay the process as the 'conduct' of the parties is examined. As the court is not party to the actual mediation, this may prove difficult, and an overly interventionist court would detract from some of the perceived benefits of the process of mediation. It also goes expressly against part of the rationale in *Halsey* (at paragraph 14) when discussing the issue of failed mediations more generally: 'if the integrity and confidentiality of the process is to be respected, the court should not know, and therefore should not investigate, why the process did not result in agreement.'

If one looks at the case from the perspective not of the substantive issues but from the point of costs alone, then the decision may seem more reasonable. Costs had risen to some £5.3 million and were 'wholly disproportionate to the sum actually recovered by the claimants',[110] which was in the order of £1 million. As such, the issue of who should bear the costs of the litigation was as materially important as the question of liability.

The most recent case law has turned again to consider whether the *Halsey* position of non-compulsion was still the correct interpretation of the law. In *Churchill*[111] the Court of Appeal considered whether courts could in fact compel parties to use DR. The first question was

108 ibid [88].
109 ibid [72] (Jack J).
110 ibid [6].
111 *Churchill v Merthyr Tydfil CBC* [2023] EWCA Civ 1416.

whether the County Court was bound by *Halsey* as a matter of precedent. The Court of Appeal found that the statements in *Halsey* around compulsion were in fact *obiter dictum*. This means that they were not binding.

In considering whether the *obiter* was nonetheless the correct statement of the law, the Court of Appeal in *Churchill* did not follow the same logic as that found in *Halsey*. In *Churchill* it was held that a court could lawfully compel a party to participate in various DR mechanisms before turning to judicial determination through litigation. Providing such compulsion would be proportionate to the interests of settling matters justly and at reasonable cost, courts are able to order it. The Court of Appeal intentionally did not lay down a detailed list of criteria to be applied but left it open for courts to consider the issue in the following terms: 'whether a particular process is or is not likely or appropriate for the purpose of . . . a fair, speedy and cost-effective solution.'[112]

Before departing from the issue of compulsion, a more general observation should be made. *Halsey* was unpopular from the outset but was considered settled law for the best part of two decades. It took a bold Court of Appeal to clarify the decision and reinforces the nuanced way in which the law can develop and how clever arguments about basic legal principles (such as the difference between *ratio* and *obiter*) can be helpful in courts correcting wrongful steps in the common law.

ENCOURAGEMENT FROM WITHIN THE FORMAL LEGAL SYSTEM

The previous section of this chapter dealt with some of the court-based mediation schemes that exist within the legal system. However, there are other schemes that are in operation outside mediation but that happen within the courts. In addition, the government has committed itself to pursuing DR within the disputes that arise in the operation of Departmental Business.

SMALL CLAIMS TRACK

Perhaps the most notable innovation of DR *within* the civil justice system was the development of the small claims track of the County Court.

> MAKING CONNECTIONS – THE COURT STRUCTURE
>
> +++++++++++++++++++++++++++++++++++++
>
> More detailed examination of the 'track system' of the County Court can be found in the chapter (Chapter 8) concerned with the court structure of England and Wales.

The majority of cases dealt with by the small track are of low value. Recent changes mean that non-personal injury cases of up to £10,000 are likely to be allocated to the small claims track.

112 ibid [66].

Consultation is underway, at the time of writing, to increase further the value of claims that will be automatically allocated to the small claims track.

Where the small claims track is used, the procedures of the court are simplified and costs are rarely awarded meaning that most people allocated to this track will appear without legal representation. The intention behind this simplification of the small claims track was to remove the formality and overly legalistic processes of the County Court where cases were relatively straightforward and of low value. This, it should be noted, is a similar aim to that of certain forms of DR. By adopting a more flexible approach to these claims, the Woolf Reforms hoped to encourage a greater range of claimant to gain access to the justice system in a way that did not have prohibitive costs.

THE COMMERCIAL COURT

In 1993, following a Practice Statement,[113] the Commercial Court began issuing DR orders in appropriate cases. If the court issues a DR order, then the parties must inform the court of the method of DR attempted and, where unsuccessful, why the DR failed. This helps to focus the mind of those involved but falls short of compulsion. Such strong support of DR coming from the Commercial Court is unsurprising given that it is familiar with the process of arbitration as many cases that come before it will contain arbitration agreements. As was noted in *Halsey*, the Commercial Court scheme 'is the strongest form of encouragement. . . . It is to be noted, however, that this form of order stops short of actually compelling the parties to undertake an ADR'.[114]

GOVERNMENT ENCOURAGEMENT

As well as the court system embracing the principles of DR, central government has also had an important role in facilitating the spread and 'normalisation' of DR. In 2001, in the wake of the Woolf Reforms and the Access to Justice Act 1999, the Lord Chancellor Lord Irvine made a 'Pledge' committing government departments to use DR to settle their own disputes wherever appropriate. The importance of this step should not be underplayed given that this will cover many high-value contracts awarded through procurement.

In 2011, the Ministry of Justice reconfirmed the commitment of central government to the process of DR.[115] The new Dispute Resolution Commitment was launched and sought to build on the work of the DR Pledge. The Commitment aims 'at encouraging the increased use of flexible, creative and constructive approach to dispute resolution'.[116] It is interesting to note that the original Pledge was launched shortly after the Woolf Reforms came into force and the new Commitment came shortly after the Jackson Report on the costs of civil litigation. The restatement and further development of the Pledge is hardly surprising given that the Ministry of Justice estimate that the Pledge saved almost £400 million of litigation costs in the

113 [1994] 1 WLR 14 (QB).

114 *Halsey v Milton Keynes General NHS Trust* [2004] EWCA Civ 576, [2004] 1 WLR 3002 [30].

115 <www.gov.uk/government/news/djanogly-more-efficient-dispute-resolution-needed>.

116 ibid.

ten years of operation.[117] Given the high success rate of governmental settlements, this would seem a sensible approach both as a matter of public policy and as a matter of cost saving. The government Pledge/Commitment neatly demonstrates the benefits of DR both to the legal/political system and to the individual parties involved.

Alongside the Commitment, the Ministry of Justice has published detailed guidance on how the Commitment will work in practice.[118] The guidance makes it clear that procurement contracts for goods and services will include clauses that require DR (as appropriate) to be used before litigation is considered. Government contracts will therefore have 'a full framework for the escalation of disputes beginning with a reference to the project board, followed by negotiation between named representatives of the parties and thereafter, if necessary, recourse to a non-binding DR procedure (primarily mediation) and, in the event of failure to agree a settlement, ultimate resort to litigation in the courts or, if preferred, arbitration'.[119]

ANALYSING THE LAW – THE GOVERNMENT PLEDGE IN ACTION

Despite the government Pledge to use DR in the settlement of disputes that may arise in departments, a question remained as to whether this Pledge was enforceable in court. The issue of the enforceability of the pledge arose in *Royal Bank of Canada v Ministry of Defence*.[120] The case concerned the construction of a lease, with the Secretary of State as the defendant. The Ministry of Defence, despite the Pledge, turned down offers by the claimant to mediate the dispute. When it came to the issue of costs, the court was swayed to issue a *Halsey*-type costs sanction because of the refusal.

Mr Justice Lewison gave an extremely strong judgment, stating, '[T]he formal pledge given on behalf of all government departments is something which I must take into account and to which I ought to attach great weight'.[121] By talking about the weight of the Pledge in determining costs, Mr Justice Lewison is implying that the Pledge itself is not legally binding but forms a persuasive factor that courts should bear in mind. In concluding, he found that the Pledge was 'the most important'[122] feature in determining costs.

What is particularly interesting from the extracts of the case just given is that the court did not focus (at all) on the *reasonableness* of the refusal of the MoD to countenance mediation. To this end, *Halsey* was not mentioned at all in the costs judgment. Thus, it is unclear whether the same types of factor are relevant when considering government

117 ibid.
118 ibid.
119 ibid.
120 *Royal Bank of Canada v Ministry of Defence* [2003] EWHC 1841 (Ch).
121 ibid [10] (Lewison J).
122 ibid [12] (Lewison J).

refusal to attempt DR. The preceding clearly indicates that the Lord Chancellor's department has not advised the government to consider DR whenever it is offered. This would appear to place government departments in a more restricted position, even where they are acting in a private capacity.

One suggestion could be that the public declaration/pledge will reverse the burden of proof issue of *Halsey* with the government department having to justify a choice not to enter into DR.

SUMMARY OF USE OF DR *WITHIN* THE FORMAL LEGAL SYSTEM

Figure 14.10 attempts to summarise some of the different forms of DR that are used at various points in the formal institutions of the legal system. This will help to consolidate knowledge of the points discussed previously and also to set them into the broader institutional context. Given the strong emphasis on early settlement in the CPR it is not surprising that many of the schemes developed so far occur in the lower levels of the court structure.

CONCLUSION

There are two dangers involved in adopting, as this chapter has done, a very liberal understanding of DR. Firstly, we create the impression that there is 'litigation' on the one hand

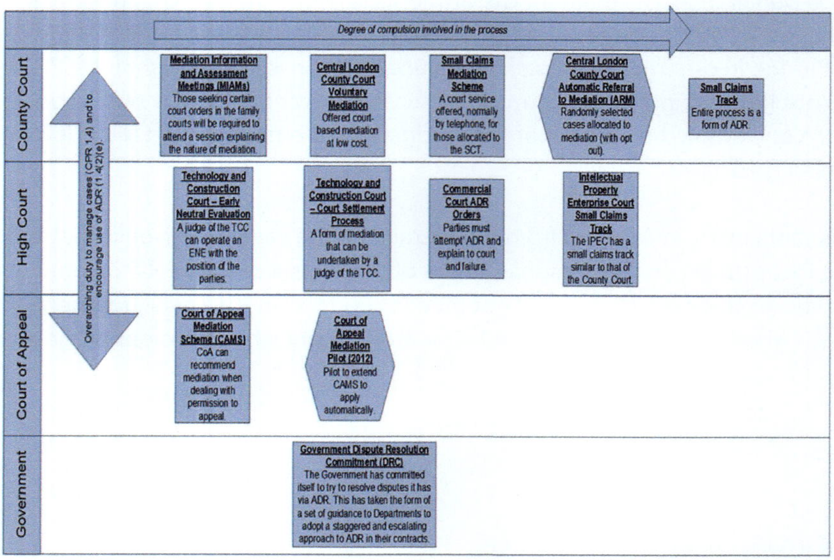

Figure 14.10 Summary of the use of ADR in the legal system.

and 'everything else' on the other. The implication of that would be that litigation is the gold standard and everything else is second class justice. This is simply untrue since the time has now come to make it clear that DR is *part* of litigation, not a bolt on. Moreover, the methods described previously should already now be viewed as part of a suite of options that can be used by disputants in addition to or in place of litigation.

The second risk is that by discussing the forms of DR (be it arbitration, adjudication, mediation, conciliation, early neutral evaluation or med-arb) within a single chapter it could create the impression that each is designed to deal with the same issues. This is equally untrue. Fundamentally, methods of alternative dispute resolution should be used when they are appropriate for the dispute – both objectively in terms of the *type* of dispute and subjectively for the needs of the *particular* parties in dispute.

With such strong and growing support from the judiciary and the government, the prospects for DR seem very strong within the legal system of England and Wales. When this is coupled with the changes to legal aid, particularly in family disputes, the incentive for increased use of DR seems particularly strong. While this may be beneficial in terms of government spending and for 'balancing the books' of civil justice, one should not ignore the law of unintended circumstances. A Marxist analysis of the current drive to cut costs of the legal system could suggest that, where there is significant imbalance of power between the parties, alternative dispute resolution turns into inferior dispute resolution, with litigation remaining the domain of the wealthy and powerful.

THE WEBSITE

The website that accompanies this textbook contains many useful resources that you can use to consolidate and further your knowledge of the law, to hone your skills of critical analysis and to test your knowledge.

15

15

CHAPTER 15
LEGAL PROFESSIONALS

INTRODUCTION

The reader may be surprised by the title of this chapter since it might well be thought by the average non-lawyer that there is basically only one legal profession in England and Wales, that of a 'lawyer' (as in most jurisdictions in the world). Those who know something of the legal system will probably think that there are two – 'solicitor' and 'barrister'. For at least the past three or four decades, this has no longer been the case, as the breadth of people involved in the provision of legal services has increased.

This chapter will explore the different roles of the fully qualified, as well as the variously partly or wholly unqualified, sectors of the workforce, which together process English and Welsh law through the justice system. This variegated workforce, which deals with the cases which end up in law reports and textbooks but which set out as just someone's dispute, is now operated in as many as eight distinct legal professional specialisms, each supervised by their specific regulators (or by none).

The chapter will also consider the strengths and weaknesses of the training and regulation of the professions and explore some of the emerging and long-standing issues facing those providing legal services.

AS YOU READ

Think about the wider picture of contemporary British life and the roles and functions of the working population, and to what extent the law touches their lives and occupations if they are not themselves lawyers.

Consider the different roles of the practising barrister or solicitor; the chartered legal executive; the partly qualified 'paralegal', the **'in-house' lawyer** working in the law department of a company or of local or central government; **the specialist lawyers** – dealing with **trademarks and patents**, or **wills, inheritances and property** transactions.

The focus of this chapter will be on the two dominant branches of the legal profession – that of solicitor and barrister. There is a myriad of other legal professions that will be discussed much more lightly. Understanding the modern legal profession does involve a certain amount of historical analysis that led us to the current position.

DOI: 10.4324/9781032641829-15

A HISTORICAL PERSPECTIVE ON THE LEGAL PROFESSIONS (11TH–20TH CENTURY)

This section will consider the emergence of the concept of a legal profession. A very detailed account is beyond the scope of this textbook but can provide further extra reading for those interested in the history of law and legal traditions. A detailed historical analysis[1] is also interesting as it can demonstrate how the division of work between solicitors and barristers came about and which remains relevant today. What follows is a brief sketch of some of the key milestones in arriving at the modern legal profession that we have today. The first point to note is that Justice has been served and administered in different ways across the centuries and pinpointing the emergence of an organised legal profession is not straightforward.

Prior to the 12th century the administration of justice was diverse and diffuse. Justice was extremely local and based on customary law and local practice. Feudal lords oversaw the system and groups of lords coordinated in so called 'hundreds' or 'shire courts'. There were no organised judiciary and no formalised legal profession. Individuals largely represented themselves or called upon community elders or spokespeople to represent their interests.

Through the late 11th (following the Norman Conquest) to the middle of the 12th century, we see the emergence of a more coordinated justice system in England under the authority of the King. This is early development of the 'common law', administered by the Royal Courts and with travelling judges. These judges were often members of the clergy. At this time, there is still no formalised legal profession but towards the end of this period we start to see emerge a class of 'clerks' who can provide advice.

Through the next two centuries (13th and 14th), the common law develops and spreads in a more consistent manner through England. Law becomes more complex and difficult for lay litigants to understand and so the 'legal professions' begin to emerge. There are 'serjeants at law' who have the right to plead cases and provide advocacy and also attorneys who would deal with increasingly technical matters of legal process and help to prepare cases for trial. In many ways the 'Serjeants at law' are the early iteration of barristers and 'attorneys' are a forerunner of solicitors with different roles in the administration of justice. It is also worth noting that during this period the emergence of a legal profession had impact on the judiciary. Following the time of feudal lords, the judiciary had been dominated by the clergy, but this often meant that the emerging legal profession were better informed on the law than the judges hearing the cases. By the end of the 14th century, it was required that judges were selected from amongst members of the emerging legal profession. This is a practice that largely continues today, despite efforts to widen the pool of those who can take judicial office.[2]

1 Such as found in James Brundage, *The Medieval Origins of the Legal Profession – Cannonists, Civilians, and Courts: Canonists, Civilians, and Courts* (U of Chicago P 2008).

2 And in contrast to some systems where a role in the judiciary is seen as career path of itself, rather than as a natural progression from a role in the legal professions.

With a growing and increasingly complex set of courts, judiciary and legal profession, it was inevitable that legal education, training and regulation would follow. We can see the early self-regulation of the profession through the establishment of the Inns of Court and the Inns of Chancery in the 14th century. Much like other guilds for other skilled professions, these became places of community and education. The Inns of Chancery did preparatory education activities and fed through to the four main Inns of Court (Lincoln's Inn, Gray's Inn, Inner Temple and Middle Temple) and became the training ground for the emergence of barristers who took the place of serjeants at law. For those wishing to become barristers, the four Inns of Court remain essential and are described further in what follows.

There was much rationalisation of the common law and of the professions in the 16th-18th centuries with the creation of King's Counsel to signify the most senior barristers and the use of the term 'solicitor' became more common.

The 19th century saw significant steps in the professionalisation of barristers and solicitors with the establishment of representative organisations. The General Council of the Bar was established in 1894, and the Law Society was founded in 1825, to represent the interests of barristers and solicitors respectively. The unification of the common law and the courts of equity by the Judicature Acts 1873–1875 also had the practical and legal effect of merging attorneys into the broader category of solicitor.[3] At the turn of the 20th century, women were able to join both parts of the legal profession by virtue of the Sex Disqualification (Removal) Act 1919.

THE MODERN DEVELOPMENT OF THE LEGAL PROFESSIONS

As the preceding narrative shows, the start of the 20th-century England and Wales had established two complementary strands of legal profession – barristers, whose principal job it was to provide specialist advice and advocate representing clients in court, and solicitors, who were to be more general advisors who prepared work for court. Although there were many further changes that impacted on the development of the professions, the position remained largely structurally unchanged throughout the first half of the 20th century.

THE 1970S AND THE BENSON REPORT

During the 1970s there was growing public disquiet about the costs of legal services exacerbated by the need to sometimes engage the services of both a barrister and solicitor. The Conservative Government of the time also had concerns about competition within the sector and the dangers of an almost wholly self-regulated set of professions. The government

3 The Supreme Court of Judicature Act 1873 s87.

established a Royal Commission, under the chairmanship of Henry Benson[4] with the remit of exploring:

> 'The organisation, management and regulation of the legal profession in England and Wales, and the provision of legal services to the public.'[5]

The report when published in 1979 did not propose major change. It voiced strong support for retaining the existing distinctions between solicitors and barristers and did not propose radical change to the system of regulation of barristers or solicitors. It made some modest suggestions around legal education and the process of complaint that were implemented by the government (and both of which are picked up later in the chapter). It also rejected calls to liberalise the market and allow further competition from non-lawyers into previously reserved matters of legal service provision.

1980S TO THE MID-1990S: THE PUSH FOR LIBERALISATION

As noted earlier, the Benson Report did little to quell growing public dissatisfaction with the provision of legal services in England and Wales. Pressure for reform, albeit limited, continued to grow through the 1980s at a time of significant market liberalisation and globalisation.

Given much of the public encountered solicitors when purchasing or selling a home, it is not surprising that in the mid-1980s there was a modest change to the regulatory environment that opened up competition in this space as home ownership became a reality for more people. The Administration of Justice Act 1985, as well as more tightly regulating complaints about solicitors, also introduced by virtue of Part II of the Act a new category of legal professional – the Licensed Conveyancer. These could undertake and manage certain property transactions that had previously been the sole purview of solicitors. The impact was to increase competition and drive down cost.

TAKING THINGS FURTHER

It is important to remember that political and societal change can influence heavily on the regulation and work of the professions. The changes and debates around increasing competition and opening the professions were happening at the time of the Thatcher government. Many key public services were privatised, exposed to the realities of the market and also encouraged to promote competitive practices. In addition, home ownership was increasingly seen as an indicator of success and social status, and this was driving demand in the property market. It is hardly surprising, therefore, that the area of reform that was supported by government related to property transactions.

4 Interestingly himself not a solicitor or barrister but accountant.

5 <https://archive.org/details/royalcommissiono0000grea/mode/2up>.

The clear distinction between solicitors and barristers remained in place over this period but came under increased pressure. Modest reforms to rights of audience blurred the previously quite clear lines between the professions. Historically solicitors only had rights of audience in the lower courts. The Courts and Legal Services Act 1990 also enabled professional bodies to grant rights of audience in the higher courts to their suitably qualified members:[6] accordingly, from 1993 the Law Society was able to grant Higher Rights certificates to solicitors to appear in the higher courts. This had an impact of also opening the higher ranks of the judiciary to solicitors.[7] It also paved the way for a sub-branch of the solicitor profession known as 'solicitor advocates'.

THE 2000S AND THE CLEMENTI REVIEW

The pressures for significant reform of the regulation of solicitors and barristers gained pace throughout the late 1990s and early 2000s with a critical Office of Fair Trading report[8] on 'Competition in Professions' noting the closed nature of market for the provision of legal services (amongst other professions). Flowing from this conclusion, and based on prevailing competition theory, this would have a detrimental effect on consumer protection, access to the market and price.

As a result of these concerns, the Secretary of State for Constitutional Affairs appointed Sir Clementi in 2003 to undertake a comprehensive review of the regulatory framework for legal services in England and Wales. The report had the following terms of reference:

> To consider what regulatory framework would best promote competition, innovation and the public and consumer interest in an efficient, effective and independent legal sector. To recommend a framework which will be independent in representing the public and consumer interest, comprehensive, accountable, consistent, flexible, transparent, and no more restrictive or burdensome than is clearly' justified.

It should be clear that this is a broad ranging terms of reference that led to an extensive report in 2004, which in turn proposed significant changes to the structure of the market for the provision of legal services. The report identified three areas of concern in recommending change:

1. A concern that the regulatory framework was outdated, lacking transparency or flexibility and with insufficient degrees of accountability
2. A concern that the current complaints system left consumers exposed and that there was insufficient independence in the current approach
3. That the business structures through which legal practice had operated (predominantly

6 Courts and Legal Services Act 1990 s27.

7 A distinguished solicitor led the way into the higher judiciary and up the ladder of the judicial hierarchy in establishing this norm: first, as Mr Justice Collins (2000–2007), then in the Court of Appeal and Supreme Court. Formerly Lawrence Collins, he was a partner in the well-known city firm of Herbert Smith, now Herbert Smith Freehills.

8 <https://webarchive.nationalarchives.gov.uk/ukgwa/20140402132426/>; <http://www.oft.gov.uk/shared_oft/reports/professional_bodies/oft328.pdf>.

for solicitors, the traditional law firm owned and managed by solicitors) were too restrictive

The Clementi Review led to widescale recommendations for fundamental change to the system of regulation and structure within the provision of legal services. These recommendations centred on: regulation and oversight; making consumer/client interests much more central to the system; overhauling the system of complaints; instituting the possibility of different business structures. The bulk of the recommendations of the Clementi Review found implementation through the Legal Services Act 2007, which is discussed in greater detail in the section of this chapter dedicated to the regulation of the professions.

THE REGULATION OF THE PROFESSIONS AND LEGAL SERVICES

Regulation of the legal professions is complex and involved. It is not the intention of this textbook to cover all the nuances or to provide a comprehensive account of such regulation. Instead, the following section will highlight some key features and principles, as well as innovations brought about to modernise and further competition relating to the market in legal services through the Legal Services Act 2007. Much of the following analysis will be made in the context of the work of barristers and solicitors, but the Act has a broader and deeper remit.

CONTEMPORARY LEGAL PROFESSIONALS

In addition to barristers and solicitors there are a number of other professionals who provide legal services. Most notably, in the category of generalist practitioners (i.e. those who have a general license to practice) are legal executives. They have succeeded in gaining recognition of their own organisation, the Institute of Legal Executives (dating in that format from 1963 but originating in the Solicitors' Managing Clerks Association of 1892). This was achieved in 2012 by their obtaining a Royal Charter, thus becoming the Chartered Institute of Legal Executives and finally establishing themselves alongside both solicitors and barristers as the third major group of law professionals. This organisation of legal executives is now known as CILEx and its members are identified by grade up to Chartered Legal Executive (Fellow)[9] and recognised as potentially qualifying to apply for judicial office, along with solicitors and barristers.[10]

Joining these generalist practitioners are groups of specialist providers of legal services and these include licensed conveyancers, notaries, costs lawyers, patent attorneys and trademark

9 Other levels include student, affiliate, associate and graduate member.

10 There are a number of members of the judiciary who come from a CILEx background, including the first woman member of CILEx to become a judge – Elizabeth Johnson, as a fee-paid judge of the first-tier tribunal (Social Entitlement Chamber).

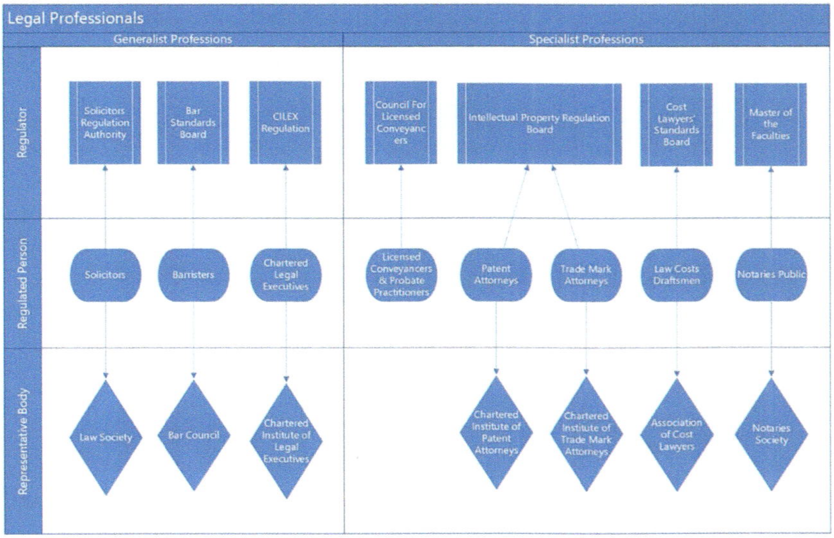

Figure 15.1 The legal professionals.

attorneys. Thus, along with the smaller specialist lawyers' groups which also have their own regulator, we achieved *eight* regulated legal services professions.[11]

Figure 15.1 provides a diagram that lays out the following:

1. The three main groups of generalist[12] legal professionals
2. The five groups of specialist legal professionals

THE LEGAL SERVICES ACT 2007

The Legal Services Act 2007 created a new framework for the regulation of legal services and made significant changes to the structure of the professions and created some new organising principles. The Act opens with a list of 9 (originally 8) regulatory objectives:[13]

1. Protecting and promoting the public interest
2. Supporting the constitutional principle of the rule of law
3. Improving access to justice
4. Protecting and promoting the interests of consumers
5. Promoting competition in the provision of services within subsection
6. Encouraging an independent, strong, diverse and effective legal profession

11 Excluded from this list are those chartered accountants who perform particular probate services.

12 Which is not to say that these groups will not 'specialise' in particular areas but rather that they have a general license to practice.

13 Legal Services Act 2007 s1.

7. Increasing public understanding of the citizen's legal rights and duties
8. Promoting and maintaining adherence to the professional principles
9. Promoting the prevention and detection of economic crime[14]

It can be seen from this list that the regulatory purview created by this Act is very wide. This marked a significant shift of focus towards *independence* and *protection of the public*, including consumers as well as defining professional principles for those authorised to provide legal services authorised persons.[15]

THE REGULATORY FRAMEWORK

A particular innovation of the Legal Services Act 2007 was to inject significant new and independent regulation into what was a highly self-regulated profession.

Historically, the self-regulation of barristers and solicitors had been undertaken by the body that also represented their interests. As part of a response to the Clementi Review and the development of the Legal Services Act 2007 the regulatory and representative functions of these bodies were ripped asunder. Now, the General Council of the Bar Council represents and promotes barristers, and the Law Society of England and Wales represents and promotes the profession related to solicitors.[16]

Having separated out the representative function, we are left to consider the independent regulators of the professions. There are essentially two layers of regulators – the oversight regulator and the professional regulator(s). The former has oversight of the individual regulators, whilst the latter directly regulate the professions for which they are responsible.

THE LEGAL SERVICES BOARD

Sitting at the apex of the regulatory structure is the Legal Services Board.[17] It does not regulate individuals or corporate structures (such as law firms) but rather acts as a 'super-regulator' and has oversight of each of the approved regulators associated with a branch of the legal profession.

The Board has a Chair, a Chief Executive and at least 7 but no more than 10 other members.[18] In an effort to ensure its independence the majority of the Board, including the Chair, must be 'lay members' (i.e. those who have never undertaken regulated activity) and the rest must not perform a reserved legal activity during the term of their appointment. It is independent of government and funded by the professions through a charge to the professional regulators. Nonetheless, it is required to provide reports to the Lord Chancellor, who lays them before Parliament, and so its work is subject to parliamentary scrutiny and public accountability. This

14 This final objective was inserted by the Economic Crime and Corporate Transparency Act 2023.

15 s(1)(3)(a)–(e).

16 For brevity, we will not list the representative organisations of the other branches of the legal profession, but their names are readily available online.

17 Established in accordance with s2 Legal Services Act 2007.

18 Legal Services Act 2007 Schedule 2.

link through to the democratic institutions is also confirmed by the fact that its members are formally appointed by the Lord Chancellor.

The statutory purpose of the Board is to promote the regulatory objectives[19] and to assist the professional regulators it oversees in developing and maintain standards and in the developing of education/training of authorised persons.[20]

THE INDEPENDENT PROFESSIONAL REGULATORS

The Legal Services Board has oversight of an approved list of regulators,[21] and each profession has an independent regulator that is distinct from its representative body who fulfil the regulatory function. This creates a slightly complex interrelationship of regulator and representative. An example of this nexus of relationships might help to explain.

TAKING THINGS FURTHER

The Law Society of England and Wales is the approved regulator for the purposes of the Legal Services Act 2007. However, as it is also the representative body for solicitors, there is a risk that there would not be sufficient independence. For this reason, the regulatory functions of the Law Society are fully *delegated* to an independent regulator. This independent regulator is the Solicitors Regulation Authority. The Legal Services Board has responsibility for oversight of the Law Society as the approved regulator and also to ensure that the Law Society does not interfere with the regulatory independence of the Solicitors Regulation Authority. Equally, the Legal Services Board cannot interfere with the *representative* function of the approved regulator (in this example the Law Society).

This pattern is repeated across the legal professions with the following acting as the independent professional regulators:

- Bar Standards Board – Barristers
- CILEx Regulation – Chartered Legal Executives
- Intellectual Property Regulation Board – Trademark Attorneys and Patent Attorneys
- Council of Licensed Conveyancers – Licensed Conveyancers
- Costs Lawyers Standards Board – Costs Lawyers
- Master of the Faculties – Notaries
- Institute of Chartered Accountants in England and Wales – Probate Practitioners

Although regulating very different individuals, there is some commonality amongst these regulators. First and foremost is their independence from representative bodies. Second is the shared requirement to be guided by the regulatory objectives. Third is a focus on public

19 This duty is confirmed by Legal Services Act 2007 s3.

20 This principle of assistance of the professional regulators can be found in s4.

21 Found in Schedule 4.

Figure 15.2 Powers of the regulator.

interest and not the interests of the profession. Fourth is the structure of the Boards of these independent regulators, each of which populated by a majority of lay members. These all relate in some way to core mission and structure. There are also commonalities in their powers and functions, which are summarised in Figure 15.2.

RESERVED LEGAL ACTIVITY AND AUTHORISED PERSONS

The Legal Services Act 2007 also created the concept of the 'reserved legal activity' (s12) as a core category of activities which can only be carried out by 'authorised persons' (s18) or 'exempt persons' (s19).

The list of reserved legal activities is exhaustive and comprises the following:

1. The exercise of a right of audience
2. The conduct of litigation
3. Reserved instrument activities
4. Probate activities
5. Notarial activities
6. The administration of oaths

Schedule 2 fleshes out the meaning of each of these activities for the purposes of the Act. Different branches of the profession will only be allowed to undertake categories of reserved legal activities in accordance with their authorisation from their independent regulator.

Authorised persons will, by and large, be the various groups of legal professionals identified early in the chapter.

Those authorised by a regulator will have a clear understanding and responsibility to maintain that understanding of when they are engaged with reserved legal activity and the limits that come with this. Nonetheless, even almost 20 years on from the passage of the Legal Services Act 2007, some uncertainty and ambiguity remain. The recent case of *Mazur*[22] shows the nuances of the Act.

ANALYSING THE LAW

In *Mazur*, the High Court had to consider whether a non-authorised person could conduct litigation – a reserved legal activity – where they were employed by an authorised firm and undertaking the work under the supervision of an authorised person. The High Court was clear that being an employee of an authorised firm was not enough to satisfy the requirements of the Legal Services Act 2007. The court reinforced the basic and unarguable point that reserved legal activity (including conducting litigation) could not be undertaken by non-authorised people.[23] The court was also clear that a non-authorised person can assist and support an authorised person in the conduct of litigation.[24]

What is perhaps unhelpful in the case was that the judge did not, for understandable reasons, give guidance of the boundaries between support and assistance and where this transgresses to the non-authorised person undertaking a reserved legal activity (even under supervision).[25]

It is worth noting that this case has caused significant disquiet amongst solicitors' firms where practices of supervised work had been common.[26] Not having clear guidelines will mean it is not completely straightforward in determining how far 'assistance' to an authorised person can go. The case, at the time of writing, was on appeal and so should be treated with some caution. Nonetheless, it shows the importance of knowing the limits to which non-authorised persons are subject in relation to reserved legal activity.

22 *Mazur v Charles Russell Speechlys LLP* [2025] EWHC 2341 (KB),

23 ibid at [63].

24 ibid at [64].

25 ibid at [65].

26 The Law Society has produced a practice note: <https://www.lawsociety.org.uk/topics/regulation/mazur-and-the-conduct-of-litigation to support solicitors in responding to the case>.

The stakes of conducting a reserved legal activity as a non-authorised person are high as to do so amounts to a criminal offence,[27] as is pretending to be entitled to undertake such work.[28]

A significant amount of work done by legal professionals (and those that support them) is of a legal nature but is not a reserved legal activity. For example, anyone can undertake legal research or write a will as these are not covered by the reserved areas. It may be those that are legal qualified and properly authorised will provide better quality outcomes but it is important to distinguish that from the legal necessity to be authorised to do the work.

THE UNREGULATED LEGAL PROFESSION

Legal professionals often work alongside a whole range of unregulated individuals who help to support the provision of regulated activity. These are varied and are mentioned here for the sake of completeness and not to give the impression that all work undertaken in a legal environment is conducted by authorised persons.

In this regard there are a large number of 'paralegals' who are not qualified as barristers, solicitors or other authorised person but may be, and often are, law or non-law graduates or indeed qualified as a member of some other profession. Their distinguishing characteristic is to have obtained work in a law firm or other legal context so as to learn 'on the job', often to have obtained expertise in particular areas of work which can be performed to a high specialist standard but then their 'billable hours' charged to clients at a lower rate than the services of the qualified solicitors who supervise them. Some law graduates also choose the paralegal route with a view to completing qualification as a solicitor later (see further the section on Education and Training) or simply with a view to gaining experience before deciding on a permanent career path. Moreover in whatever way such 'paralegals' have come to work in a firm of solicitors, the SRA Code of Conduct, which regulates solicitors' professional work, is satisfied if the firm's paralegals are supervised by a qualified solicitor, thus explaining the vast expansion of this business model for delivering a firm's time intensive but less lucrative workload. Paralegals provide a cost-effective way of delivering a high volume of low value legal work (for example in relation to rental disputes or road traffic accident insurance work).

School leavers can also choose to adopt alternative ways of becoming a solicitor through an 'on the job' type approach. This follows the introduction of law apprenticeships pursuant to the government's apprenticeship levy, collected as a tax by HMRC from 6 April 2017, through which law firms with a wage or salary bill of £3 million or over are obliged to pay this apprenticeship levy exacted by the government. Firms can then best amortise this expense by sending staff on day release to complete such courses.

27 Legal Services Act 2007 s14.

28 Legal Services Act 2007 s17.

Figure 15.3 Legal apprenticeships.

Figure 15.3 illustrates the legal apprenticeships available at the time of writing.

A more recent addition to the legal workforce is the Legal Technologist. These may be current or formerly authorised legal professional but can also be someone with a completely different and more technical background. The growth and impact of legal technology on the work of the professions is discussed later in the chapter, but its advent has led to those with experience of how to make law firms more efficient and effective through technology to be highly valued.

To add to this mix of non-authorised legal person are those that interact with the justice system in other ways. One example will suffice. For those litigants in person[29] for whom the process can be overwhelming the court has confirmed that they may have support from a friend or some other individual. These supporters are termed McKenzie Friends after a case involving parties of that name.[30] Such individuals provide a variety of functions such as emotional support, note-taking and helping the individual prepare their case. There are strict limits to the support that can be provided, for example as they lack rights of audience they should not speak (without the judge's express permission, which is really given) or act as the litigant's representative. Whilst historically the person acting as a McKenzie friend would be a family member or friend there has been the (controversial)[31] development of *paid* McKenzie friends.

29 Those who do not have the support of an authorised person to represent them.

30 *McKenzie v McKenzie* [1970] 3 All ER 1034.

31 Kerry-Ann Barry, 'Unregulated Legal Advisers and Negligence Liability: A Timely Warning for McKenzie Friends' (2019) 35(3) PN 185; Leanne Smith and Emma Hitchings 'Professionals and Partisans: Lessons for Family Lawyers from a Study of Fee-Charging McKenzie Friends' (2019) 31(4) CFLQ 343.

THE WORK OF THE PROFESSIONS

Clearly a significant portion of a legal professional's life is taken up undertaking reserved legal activity as an authorised or exempt person. However, there is a significant amount of work (and often the majority of time in a week) that is ancillary or preparatory to undertaking a reserved legal activity.

THE WORK OF SOLICITORS

Solicitors potentially undertake a wide range of work, but it is only those 'reserved activities' that are subject to the greatest degree of regulation and control. They can also work in a wide range of environments – from partnerships to sole practitioners to Limited Liability Partnerships and Alternative Business Structures. These ABS's were an innovation of the Legal Services Act 2007 which encouraged a greater diversity of business structure, whereas law firms could previously only be owned and run by solicitors. This opening up of new forms of business structure has introduced new competition and greater flexibility into the sorts of firm that exist. There are also differences in terms of location (which has an impact on work undertaken) such as between the City, the regions and high street practice.

A solicitor must maintain a practising certificate in order to undertake reserved activities.[32] Solicitors are licensed for a general practice[33] and so whilst people may specialise in areas of law or on particular types of reserved activity, they must maintain competency in all areas. Although there is no regulatory reason to prevent practising across the whole range of activity and subject areas, solicitors who improperly provide advice or perform legal work in areas where they have little expertise risk being sued in the general law of negligence.

The nature of the work of solicitors includes, but is not limited to, the following:

- Offering legal advice to private clients – on relationships (personal and commercial), on land transactions, on the administration of their estates
- Offering legal advice to corporate clients – advice on commercial transactions, company form etc.
- Offering legal advice in public law environments – such as in relation to the work of solicitors employed by local authorities
- Offering legal advice and supervision in pro bono[34] situations – such as at law clinics and law centres
- Preparing cases for trial – such as completing and submitting court forms and preparing bundles for use by barristers

32 SRA Practice Framework Rules 2011.

33 That is, there is no formal concept of 'specialisation' in terms of regulation, outside of some quite niche areas – such as advising at police stations or gaining higher rights of audience.

34 Unpaid work that is still regulated to the same standard as for work attracting a fee.

Solicitors are divided in the SRA statistics into the total of those on the Roll (around 210,000 currently) and those with practising certificates (currently just over 176,000). There has been a sharp rise in the numbers in both categories with an additional 50,000 of each since 2011.[35] There has also been significant growth in registered foreign lawyers over the same period. Thus, despite the widening of the range of professions able to undertake reserved activity, there remains a healthy and buoyant market for solicitors.

Solicitors practise either individually or in partnerships in firms of solicitors (in which they may be remunerated as a partner with a share of profits depending on their partnership agreement, or as salaried partners or associates). They also work in employed practice for other companies as general counsel, or in the new alternative business structure entities in partnership or employment with other non-solicitor professionals. There are also two forms of partnership available, if a solicitor is in a partnership rather than employed as an associate or consultant, namely a traditional partnership under the Partnership Act 1890 or under the more recent LLP entity under the Limited Liability Partnerships Act 2000, introduced in 2001. In both cases there will be a partnership deed setting out the solicitor's rights and obligations.

It is worth noting that solicitors registered and authorised by the Solicitors Regulation Authority have rights of audience to appear in certain inferior courts such as the County Court and Magistrates' Court. Should they wish to exercise higher rights of audience (for example, to appear before the Crown Court, Court of Appeal or Supreme Court then they must demonstrate their competence in advocacy and be approved for such work by the Solicitors Regulation Authority. Those with higher rights of audience are known as solicitor advocates. At the time of the growth of such solicitors, there were some criticisms that they were not of the same standard as barristers (including unfortunate comments from the then Lord Chancellor Michael Gove).[36] The rise of solicitor advocates shows the innovations brought about by liberalisation of the market and of the increasing cross-over between the professions at the margins of their activities.

THE WORK OF BARRISTERS

Barristers are either self-employed (practising most typically from sets of Chambers sharing administration and expenses as tenants) or may be employed by a company, local or central government (which operates a government legal service) or even by a law firm. When self-employed by a corporate entity as their 'in-house' lawyer, a barrister is often referred to as the company's 'General Counsel'.

The largest employer of salaried barristers is the Crown Prosecution Service. Employed barristers are all now equally regarded as 'practising' although this was not always the case, since until the reconstitution of the Bar Council now nearly 20 years ago, so as to give employed barristers a seat on it, employed barristers were not regarded as 'practising'.

35 <https://www.sra.org.uk/sra/research-publications/regulated-community-statistics/data/population_solicitors/>.

36 A robust defence of the position followed, see Jeremy Robson, 'Gove's Nonsense: Barristers vs Solicitor Advocates' (2016) 160 Sol J 19.

When in practice as self-employed, barristers are subject to the 'cab rank rule' which means that they cannot refuse a case in their area of work and before their regular court(s) and for their regular fee. This rule exists to ensure that no unpopular case is ever left without a barrister for representation in court, for example, in the case of a terrible crime which might disgust every normal person.[37] This is a central plank of access to justice in England and Wales. The cab rank rule and the need for even those accused of the most awful crimes to be represented, can be difficult for the public and press to understanding. For example, current Prime Minister Keir Starmer came under criticism ahead of the 2024 General Election for having previously represented Abu Qatada, a high-profile suspected terrorist.

Barristers[38] undertake a range of work, most visible the advocacy that defines them in the eyes of the public. Barristers have rights of audience in all courts in the legal system of England and Wales. When appearing in criminal matters in the Crown Court and higher they will be wearing the wig and gown that has become such a part of our shared cultural heritage. Another big section of work is the giving of expert opinion on legal issues, normally at the request of a solicitor. This use of 'Counsel's Opinion' can be used not only to assess complex legal issues but as part of the decision-making on whether to litigate by providing the instructing solicitor with an idea about potential success.

The vast majority of work for barristers comes from solicitors via 'instructions'. The most important relationship here is between the solicitor and the barrister with whom the client then takes a lesser role in receiving their advice and deciding whether to act on it. Barristers may now also accept direct access work pursuant either to the Bar's licensed access route whereby certain organisations, for example, firms of accountants or specific individuals may apply to the Bar Council to be licensed to instruct barristers directly owing to their expertise in such work, or pursuant to the Bar's Direct Access Rules 2004

There were in 2025 (most recent figures on the Bar Council website[39]) almost 18,500 practising barristers, of whom around 2,100 were King's Counsel (KCs or 'Silks' – called thus as they wear a silk gown). Thus, the number of practising barristers is small when compared to that of solicitors. KCs are regarded as the pre-eminent advocates of the legal system. Since 2005, KCs have been selected by an independent nine-member King's Counsel Selection Panel established by the Bar Council and the Law Society, assisted by the Ministry of Justice, and which comprises two solicitors, two barristers, a judge, three lay members and a lay chair. They select on the basis of competence criteria: integrity, understanding and use of the law, oral and written advocacy, working with others and diversity.[40]

There is also an employed version of Honorary Silk, open to solicitors as well as non-practising barristers and academics who are not members of the practising Bar, for which an annual

37 <www.barstandardsboard.org.uk/media/1460590/bsb_-_cab_rank_rule-paper_28_2_13_v6_final_.pdf>.

38 Here we are talking primarily about the self-employed Bar as opposed to the employed Bar, where work is organised and requested by the 'employer'.

39 <https://www.barcouncil.org.uk/policy-representation/dashboards/demographics-dashboard.html>.

40 <www.kcappointments.org>.

announcement invites nominations, which must be on a specified form, and cannot be sent in personally by the nominee. This has revived the former practice of granting the honorary KC rank to employed barristers who have performed distinguished work contributing to the development of the law (such as to Baroness Hale, when as Professor Brenda Hoggett she was a Law Commissioner in the 1980s, and to her husband, Professor Julian Farrand, also a Law Commissioner and later also Pensions Ombudsman and Insurance Ombudsman). In logic, this system (which prior to 2005 also depended on the former patronage of the Lord Chancellor) probably did not survive the recasting of Silk appointments from 2005 when the King's Counsel Selection Panel was instituted, but the recent system has acknowledged some significant contributions outside the practising Bar, such as Professor Lorne Crerar and the work of Dawson and Cornwell solicitor Anne-Marie Hutchinson OBE in the development of family law, in particular through her work for the charity Reunite on international child abduction and forced marriage.

EDUCATION AND TRAINING FOR LEGAL PROFESSIONALS

As the professions have evolved, so have the routes to training and education. You need not be aware of the detail of this evolution but being aware of it can help you to better understand how we have come to the current position. The phases of legal education and training reveal a tension as to the mix of *academic* and *vocational* skills necessary to produce the best possible lawyers. That mix, and where the current system sits has caused significant disquiet, particularly around recent reforms of the route to become a solicitor. A taste of the 20th century history may be helpful.

Training of legal professionals in more recent times used to be fairly straightforward – qualification was for many years obtained either by an undergraduate degree, in law or a non-law subject, which was taken first and then supplemented by the centrally set and marked written Final Examination of the Law Society for solicitors, or the Bar Final Examination for intending barristers; either of these was able originally to be studied for separately from a degree so that the candidate proceeded directly to the relevant examinations, a degree not being essential until 1982. Thus, a non-graduate would take a Part I covering the subjects otherwise already studied and passed by a graduate, who would be exempt from Part I if the degree transcript revealed that a sufficient standard had already been obtained in the subjects for which exemption could be sought. Part II then covered further heads central to general practice either as a barrister or solicitor, including the more important specialist subjects ranging from company law to family law. Only black letter law, and no vocational knowledge, skills or aptitude was required for these examinations which did not differ greatly from those under university syllabuses although they were supposed to be somewhat more vocationally orientated.

Examination preparation (including for the Part I Examinations for those without a degree, or for which a candidate had not obtained a sufficient standard for exemption) was historically undertaken by private endeavour, with the aid of specialist instruction if required: this was done either in class at specialist law tutors, by distance learning (in those days a hard copy or postal course) or on the candidate's own. Part II usually required a little more study, either through a postal course or in a specialist class, a system still in use for most State Bar Examinations in the USA, where self-study is usual because the candidate will already have completed a law degree which will in any case have involved a graduate course undertaken following a foundation first degree as in all states within the USA, law is only available as a graduate course.

Up to the 1960s the Law Society ran such classes for solicitors in its own School of Law, and the Inns of Court School of Law in Gray's Inn ran those for the Bar. Inevitably private enterprise meant that commercial tutors eventually offered targeted tuition courses, the best known up to the 1980s for both Law Society and Bar students being that of long established law tutors, Gibson and Weldon, originally in Chancery Lane, which amalgamated with the Law Society's School of Law in 1964, whereupon a new name, 'the College of Law', was assumed and the entire framework of preparation for the (centrally set and marked) solicitors' qualifying examinations were devolved to the College and a number of universities. The name has been kept, although for a short time it was re-badged as 'the College of Law of England and Wales', until more recently it obtained university status and is now known as 'the University of Law'.

At this time formal pupillage was not required of barristers though solicitors were obliged to enter practical training within formal 'articles of clerkship' with a qualified solicitor.

There matters rested until 1979 when the Inns of Court School of Law (ICSL) designed and implemented a genuine Bar Vocational Course (BVC) for barristers intending to practise in England and Wales, a course which included both knowledge of law and practice and vocational skills such as advocacy and other interpersonal competences closely allied to a barristers' work. It was also decided to make both Bar and Law Society qualification a graduate course, either through candidates obtaining a Qualifying Law Degree (QLD) encompassing what were seen as the agreed 'foundations of legal knowledge' required by either Bar or Law Society, or a non-law degree plus fast track conversion course for non-law graduates, called at first a Common Professional Examination (CPE) or later a Graduate Diploma in Law (GDL).

The former Bar Examinations were initially retained for barristers not intending to practise in England and Wales and for overseas students, but then phased out in the 1990s, and the ICSL's original monopoly devolved to a handful of universities and similar institutions. In the meantime, the Law Society had followed the style of the BVC with a Legal Practice Course (LPC) implemented in 1993, which required both much the same black letter knowledge of the law and range of vocational skills as the BVC.

There matters again rested, with a stage of training (a QLD or non-law degree + GDL, supervised by a joint committee of Bar and Law Society called the Joint Academic Stage Board, the JASB) until the end of the first decade of the 21st century, when once again the BVC and LPC duo were subjected to further modernisation, in the process of which the BVC also became the Bar Practical Training Course (BPTC).

In summary, the position for solicitors (other than apprenticeship, which was noted earlier) had been, until most recently, as described in Figure 15.4. It is important to note, particularly for solicitors, that this figure represents the *old* route to qualification and will not be available to any as a pathway now, with the 'SQE' (Solicitors Qualifying Examination) route (discussed later) becoming the dominant way of becoming qualified.

In Figure 15.5 you can see the position as it related to qualification as a barrister. These have remained less changed by recent reform

Figure 15.4 The pre-SQE route to qualification as a solicitor.

Figure 15.5 The routes to qualification as a barrister.

In 2011, it was decided to conduct a Legal Education and Training Review (LETR) in order, in summary, to study in further detail whether existing training was appropriate and/or whether other associated aims, such as achieving wider access to the profession especially at less cost to students, and/or greater satisfaction of clients could be better served. It was the first major review since the Ormrod Report 1971. The Review reported in 2013 recommending the development of 5- to 7-year apprenticeships and further attention to the quality of diversity in pathways into the regulated professions. In the meantime, the Joint Academic Stage Board was discontinued, and Bar and Law Society training went their separate ways.

At this point, it seems that both the SRA and the BSB decided to treat the entire era of the expensive LPC and BVC/BPTC as a mistake and to find ways of reverting to the old, cost-saving system of centrally set qualifying examinations which students could prepare for how they pleased, plus (in the Bar's case) specialist Advocacy Teaching. There is some doubt as to whether the cost savings, particularly for the Solicitors Regulation Authority, will have been achieved when the cost of preparation for the new scheme is factored in. From 2015, the Solicitors Regulation Authority consulted on significant changes to the system of qualification, including a return to centrally administered exams, and these are laid out in what follows. Having an understanding of the routes in Figure 15.4 remains important as there is a long transition period through to the early 2030s to ensure that those who embarked on the 'old' route' were able to qualify and not be prejudiced by the changes.

Whilst there have also been more recent changes to the route to qualification for barristers (discussed later), these are less significant a change than faced by those wishing to become a solicitor.

SOLICITORS – THE CURRENT ROUTE TO QUALIFICATION

The Solicitors Regulation Authority spent time during the late 2010s (beginning in 2016) consulting on new pathways to qualification.[41] The reasons for this wish to review and replace the current routes to qualification were primarily around thus:

- A lack of regulatory assurance as to the consistency of outcome produced by so many universities offering the LPC
- A lack of consistency of approach to the delivery of the LPC and variation in the standard of assessment
- Overly complex routes to qualification
- A lack of integration of academic and professional competencies
- The rising costs pressures of the LPC for those wishing to qualify
- A lack of confidence that the 'training contract' model of sign-off assuring professional competency
- A lack of transparency as to the 'quality' of providers of legal education
- Widening access to the professions

41 For the full consultation, see: <https://news.sra.org.uk/globalassets/documents/sra/consultations/solicitors-qualifying-examination-2-consultation.pdf>.

The thrust of the SRA's concerns were around consistency of outcome.[42]

The new route contains the following four stages, which can notionally be undertaken in any order:

1. Obtaining a degree in *any* subject or have equivalent experience (such as gained through an apprenticeship
2. Successfully completing both stages of the Solicitors Qualifying Examination
3. Having undertaken the equivalent of two years' full-time work experience
4. Meeting the character and suitability requirements

DEGREE-LEVEL STUDY

Traditionally, someone wishing to demonstrate that they met the academic requirements to become a solicitor would take a Qualifying Law Degree or a non-law degree followed by the Graduate Diploma in Law, which covered the foundations of legal knowledge. This would satisfy the academic stage of training and so such applicants would be exempt from further examination of their knowledge of the law. The changes in 2021 now means that there is no requirement to complete any formal legal study to become a solicitor. There are also no exemptions for the centrally assessed Solicitors Qualifying Examination for those who have studied for a law degree. One would hope that taking a programme of legal study would assist in preparation for the central examinations, but it is not a necessary requirement.

THE SOLICITORS QUALIFYING EXAMINATION (SQE)

Perhaps the most significant change brought about by the reform of the routes to qualification is the introduction of the centralised set of assessments known as the Solicitors Qualifying Examination (SQE). There are two parts to the assessment, and both must be completed in order to pass the SQE overall.

The first part of the assessment (SQE1) tests functioning legal knowledge across a large number of subjects, many of which will be familiar to those studying a law degree (such as contract, tort and criminal law) and some of which are more focussed on practice (such as the administration of estates, legal services and solicitors accounts. These subjects are spread over two papers totalling 360 multiple-choice 'single best answer' questions. The papers are taken over a two-day period and must both be passed in order to pass the assessment overall. In July 2025, the pass rate for the SQE1 had dropped to around 40%. The second part of the examination (SQE2) is more practically focussed and contains four oral (in the context of interview and note attendance and advocacy) and 12 written (in the context of case and matter analysis, legal drafting, legal writing and legal research) assessments. Candidates must secure an overall pass mark for SQE2 and there is no separate measure of oral or written skills. The pass rate for the SQE2 was, in January 2025, 77%.[43]

42 It is worth noting that there was a significant opposition to the proposals that were voiced throughout the consultation and implementation of the proposed changes.

43 It is perhaps not surprising that the pass mark is stronger for SQE2, as only those who pass SQE1 will have progressed to take the more practically focussed assessments.

Statistical analysis is used to determine the 'cut point', and so the pass mark will vary by cohort, to take into account variation in question setting. The SQE assessments are delivered nationally by Kaplan SQE Limited. Despite cost being a significant barrier of entry to the profession, the cost of taking SQE1, as of September 2025 was £1,934 and SQE2 had a cost of £2,974. Those cover the cost of taking the assessment but not any costs associated with preparation.

QUALIFYING WORK EXPERIENCE (QWE)

The concept of Qualifying Work Experience (QWE) replaced the former notion of Period of Recognised Training (PRT). The traditional two-year training contract was the traditional method of satisfying the requirements of PRT, where a trainee solicitor typically worked on rotation in different areas of the firm and had a supervising solicitor who signed off on their overall competency to practice.

The introduction of QWE brings with it much greater flexibility. There is still a requirement to gain at least the equivalent of 2 years' work experience, but this need not be in the context of a training contract. QWE is now portable and can be gained at any stage, not just following the completion of an LPC. Aspiring solicitors can now complete this work experience in a variety of contexts with up to four different organisations. This significant liberalisation means that paralegals are able to build up QWE, as are those who spend time supporting law clinics or law centres.

The period of QWE must be signed off by a solicitor.[44] In a very marked change from the old system of PRT, the person signing off on the experience is not asked to comment on the *competence* of the individual or their standards of work. They are simply being asked to confirm the length of time of the experience, that there was opportunity to develop at least two of the competencies required of solicitors (but not that the candidate actually developed those competencies!) and that there were no concerns that would be relevant to the test of character and suitability.

THE TEST OF CHARACTER AND SUITABILITY

Finally, a person must have the required character and suitability to instil in the public trust and confidence in the profession. For this purpose those wishing to apply for admission as a solicitor must declare anything that could call into question their suitability. This includes matters relating to criminal activity, conduct of their finances, academic offences related to integrity or other disciplinary matters.

CONCLUDING COMMENTS ON THE ROUTE TO QUALIFICATION

Following confirmation of all the aforementioned conditions, someone may be admitted to the Roll, meaning essentially that they register themselves as a solicitor.

In closing, whether these changes to education and training, which are, according to the SRA, built on the goal of saving students the escalating cost of the LPC, are a sound development remains to be seen. Since its adoption, there have been a number of high-profile errors

44 Or Compliance Office for Legal Practice (COLP).

in the assessment process, a declining pass rate and a growing concern about differential performance by those from particular ethnic and socio-economic groupings, as well as lingering worries about its ability to properly assess legal knowledge.[45]

Some universities have made changes to their degree programmes to address the lack of student capacity or willingness to undertake much further study or expense in addressing the new arrangements. These programmes integrate, to a larger or lesser extent, the requirements of the SQE. Other universities have taken a different approach and have not linked explicitly their curricula to preparation for the SQE. This can be because they do not have staff with the relevant practical experience or because there is a worry that the academic content of a law degree (particularly through its electives) would be squeezed out of the curriculum if an attempt was made to make the programme SQE compliant.

BARRISTERS – THE CURRENT ROUTE TO QUALIFICATION

Much less has changed in recent years in relation to the routes to qualification as a barrister but there have been some subtle changes. There are broadly three stages to complete:

1. The academic stage
2. The vocational stage
3. Pupillage

ACADEMIC STAGE – DEGREE-LEVEL STUDY AND LEGAL KNOWLEDGE

In order to satisfy the academic requirement, a candidate must hold a degree of at least a 2:2 standard either in law or by completion of a conversion course (such as a Postgraduate Diploma in Law commonly known as PGDL). An aspiring barrister must study the 7 foundations of legal knowledge subjects and also gain an appreciation of legal research.

VOCATIONAL STAGE

Before embarking on the vocational stage, a student must join one of the 'Inns of Court' – the honourable societies of which every barrister must become a member. The Inns of Court are Lincoln's Inn,[46] Inner Temple,[47] Middle Temple[48] and Gay's Inn, and it will be remembered from earlier in this chapter that they play an important community and training function in the life of a barrister.[49]

Students then progress to the Bar Professional Training Course (BPTC) of the Bar Training Course (BTC). This is a formal course of study that normally lasts for a year. During the BPTC, students will be given instruction in skills and knowledge and will need to study advocacy; ethics; opinion writing; resolution of disputes out of court; civil litigation, evidence and remedies; criminal litigation, evidence and remedies; conference skills; and drafting.

45 Anthony Bradney, 'The Sound of Silence: The SRA and the SQE' (2024) 58 Law Teach 150.

46 <www.lincolnsinn.org.uk>.

47 <www.innertemple.org.uk>.

48 <www.middletemple.org.uk>.

49 <www.graysinn.org.uk>.

On competition of the vocational stage, students may then be called 'to the bar' by their Inn, provided that they have also completed their 10 (down from 12 in 2021) 'qualifying sessions'. These qualifying sessions are a mixture of lectures, moots, debates, training and dining. Each student must attend at least one session related to each of the following themes: ethics, standards and values; preparation for pupillage, career development and well-being; equality, diversity and inclusion; advocacy skills; and legal knowledge, justice and the rule of law. Being 'called to the bar' entitles a person to use the title of barrister but not yet practice independently.

PUPILLAGE

Students must then obtain a pupillage of a total of 12 months, or two of six months each,[50] with a pupil supervisor. The 'first six' is a non-practising period that is then followed by a 'second six' where the pupil barrister takes on work independently but still under the supervision of the pupil supervisor. There used to be prescriptive rules of eligibility to become a pupil supervisor, but the Bar Standards Board have significantly reduced the regulatory requirements in this area.

There is no right of audience during the first six months, but in the second, a pupil may conduct his or her own cases under the supervision of the pupil supervisor, whose professional indemnity insurance covers the pupil's work as well as the supervisor's own. Pupillages have been paid since 2000 and the pupil is now to be guaranteed a living wage,[51] assuming that the newly called barrister has managed to obtain a pupillage since there are only around 550 pupillages available annually, approximately a third of the number of those taking the BPTC who are likely to want to try for one. Just over half of those on the BPTC are now women, and women also score as highly, if not slightly higher, in obtaining pupillage as men; however, the comparative figures fall sharply when it comes to retention after the initial few years in practice, as the retention figures on the Bar Council website unfortunately indicate.[52]

QUALIFICATION

Upon completing pupillage, a barrister will need to find 'Tenancy' with a Chambers or otherwise 'squat' in their existing Chambers without Tenancy. A barrister must then complete the 'New Practitioners' Programme' which is a form of continuing professional development that takes place during the first three years post qualifications and that has a total required commitment of 45 hours.

Thus there are still some challenges in qualifying for the Bar, which is expensive to achieve, even if a scholarship is obtained, and even if a further scholarship is obtained from Chambers where the student will be a pupil, some of which can be drawn down for the BPTC year before the promised 'living wage' is available for the pupillage year.

50 If not offered 'tenancy' at the end of a pupillage, a pupil barrister can continue to take an additional 'sixth' known as a 'Third Six Pupillage'.

51 *The Lawyer* (30 May 2018).

52 *Women at the Bar* (BSB Report, 16 July 2016) <www.barstandardsboard.org.uk>.

COMPLAINTS

Complaints systems are a feature of modern life. Every well-run business of whatever size now tends to have an internal complaints system which is the consumer's first port of call. This has been much influenced by the consumer rights legislation which has impacted on English and Welsh law owing to influence from the EU. The change in regulatory focus prompted by the Legal Services Act 2007 and the separation of regulator from representative means that the interests of the consumer of legal services is much more central than it has been at any other point in history. Underscoring this point is that two of the regulatory objectives, to which the LSB, SRA and BSB must commit, mention the public interest and the interest of consumers.

Complaints against legal professionals are particularly important given the central role solicitors and barristers play in the administration of justice. They are often the public's only conscious interaction with the legal system and a breach of trust or falling public confidence in the *professions* may lead to a fall in confidence in the law and the legal system.

COMPLAINTS AND DISCIPLINE AGAINST SOLICITORS

The first level of complaint is in house at a solicitors' firm and this is regulated by the Solicitors Code of Conduct 2011 which requires observation of the ten core principles which were written into the new version of the code published in that year and which addressed principles and behaviours which were to be pervasive within a solicitor's performance rather than, in the style of the previous edition of the code, requiring certain positive actions and prohibiting certain negative ones. This change is because it is now considered that no completely comprehensive code can be provided to address every context individually; thus, an *approach* to a solicitor's work is now the preferred system.

The core principles are that a solicitor must do thus:

1. Uphold the rule of law and the proper administration of justice
2. Act with integrity
3. Act in the best interest of each client
4. Not allow independence to be compromised
5. Provide a proper standard of service to each client
6. Behave in a way that maintains the trust that the public places in a solicitor and in the provision of legal services
7. Comply with legal and regulatory obligations and deal with regulators and ombudsmen in an open and timely manner
8. Run the firm's business/carry out the solicitor's role in the business effectively and in accordance with proper governance and sound financial and risk management principles
9. Encourage equality of opportunity and respect for diversity
10. Protect client money and assets

Solicitors, whether individual practitioners or working in a firm, should have a formal complaints procedure and this should be brought to clients' attention at the outset of any matter. It must be easy to understand and enable clients to complain by any reasonable means. It must be responsive to individual clients, for example, those who are vulnerable in some way. Complaints must be dealt with promptly and fairly, enabling them to be investigated sufficiently. There must be appropriate remedies, and no charge must be made for handling a complaint. This is normally addressed by the issue of a client care letter when instructions are first taken, indicating who will handle the client's matter and to whom in the firm any complaint should be made.

The SRA, being the regulator, deals with compliance with the code in respect of conduct issues and, if the complaint is not resolved in house, can take regulatory action, for example, issuing a reprimand or closing the practice in extreme circumstances.

Reference can also be made to the Solicitors' Disciplinary Tribunal,[53] a statutory tribunal which decides cases of professional misconduct and has powers arising under the Solicitors Act 1974, which include striking off the Roll, suspension, reprimand and (under SA 1974 s43) prohibiting any solicitors' employee from working in a law practice without the consent of the Law Society. The SDT can also issue fines and order the costs to be paid to the investigating authority (normally the SRA on behalf of the Law Society). Direct applications can be made to the SDT, but all evidence and investigation will have to have been submitted at that time (i.e. the SDT does not have power to investigate or gather evidence about any matter). The SRA also holds the Compensation Fund used to compensate for the activities or omissions of dishonest solicitors and every solicitor makes an annual contribution to this fund. There is a right to appeal from the SDT to the High Court. If the various methods of redress are deemed insufficient, then the complainant can still sue the solicitor for professional negligence, which will engage the solicitor's professional negligence insurance, and the insurers will take over the solicitor's defence and pay any damages awarded by the court.

If a complaint does not relate to misconduct but rather to the service provided, then reference can be made to the Legal Ombudsman (described in more detail later).

COMPLAINTS AGAINST BARRISTERS

This is regulated by the Code of Conduct of the Bar of England and Wales, which similarly to the SRA's for solicitors puts up some general flags against unacceptable behaviour but does not go into as much detail as to what positive behaviour is expected. Basically, it expressly forbids a barrister to do thus:

1. Engage in conduct, whether in pursuit of his profession or otherwise, which is

    a. dishonest or otherwise discreditable to a barrister,
    b. prejudicial to the administration of justice, or
    c. likely to diminish public confidence in the legal profession or the administration of justice or otherwise bring the legal profession into disrepute

53 <www.solicitorstribunal.org.uk>.

2. Engage directly or indirectly in any occupation if his association with that occupation may adversely affect the reputation of the Bar or, in the case of a practising barrister, prejudice his ability to attend properly to his practice[54]

However, as the Bar is largely a referral profession the first step in a complaint will usually be to the instructing solicitor, before raising the issue with the barrister and then, if the complaint is still unresolved, with the BSB, which can address either professional misconduct, for example, dishonesty or incompetence, or alternatively inadequate professional service, which means service falling significantly below the norm expected of a barrister. The BSB can disbar the barrister (similar to striking off a solicitor from the Roll), suspend them for a period, impose a fine or require repayment of fees, or simply requiring the barrister to apologise to the client.

Barristers can now in the last resort be sued for professional negligence and like solicitors will have professional negligence insurance in place to handle the case and to pay any damages awarded. It was not always the case that barristers could be sued, originally because the barrister did not enter into any contract with either the solicitor or the lay client as the fee paid was an honorarium, to which there was no contractual entitlement (hence the little pouch sewn into the pleats at the back of the barrister's gown for the honorarium discreetly to be paid!). This concept of a barrister's fee being only some sort of glorified 'tip' dated originally right back to Roman times. Immunity from suit lasted into the 20th century when the CLSA 1990 s62 confirmed the immunity and extended it to solicitor advocates, but in 2003, in the case of *Hall*,[55] it was decided that the immunity was an anomaly, since no other profession had any such privilege, so a barrister is now as liable to be sued in negligence as any other professional.

THE LEGAL OMBUDSMAN

The Legal Ombudsman Service, set up in 2010, is independent and impartial and can deal with complaints about the service provided by a wide range of lawyers, including solicitors but not barristers. It has a Board is known as the Office for Legal Complaints It publishes an annual review, providing a single, free gateway for consumers' complaints which it then analyses so as to provide feedback to the profession in order to enable improvement in accordance with the regulatory objectives of the Legal Services Act 2007 as set out in s1(1). The Ombudsman can direct that a faulty service can be put right, for example, by apologising, doing remedial work, reducing or refunding unlimited fees or paying compensation up to £50,000. Outcome statistics are available and published regularly.[56]

Figure 15.6 shows the complaints process up to the Legal Ombudsman and, if the consumer is still dissatisfied, to the ultimate remedy of a civil suit for professional negligence.

54 <www.barstandardsboard.org.uk/for-barristers/bsb-handbook-and-code-guidance/the-bsb-handbook.html>.

55 *Hall v Simons* [2003] 3 All ER 673 (HL).

56 <https://www.legalombudsman.org.uk/information-centre/data-centre/complaints-data/>.

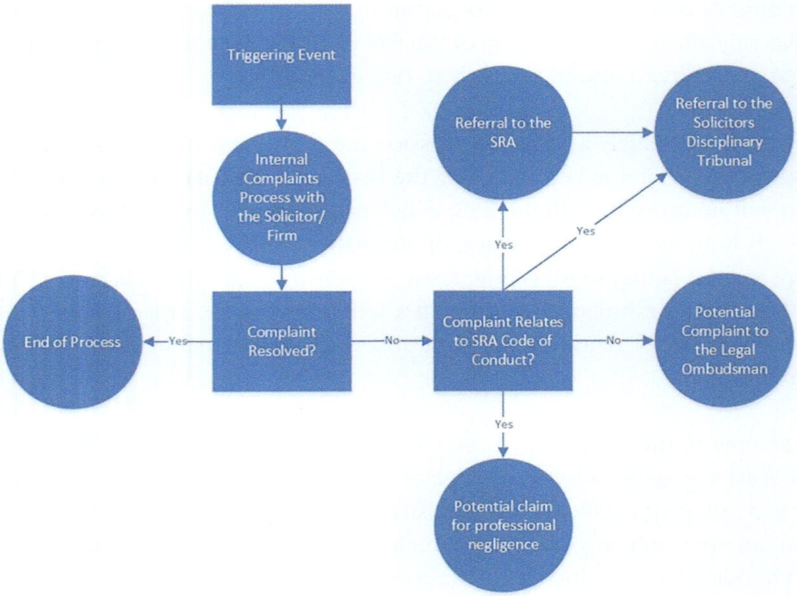

Figure 15.6 Procedure for complaints against solicitors.

THE FUTURE OF THE LEGAL PROFESSION

As we are now more than halfway through the third decade of the 21st century, it would be easy to think – if one watches the barristers decant from the Crown Court robed with wig box under arm – that the system that governs the profession remains the same as it did 200 years ago. However, looking beyond some of the imagery, symbolism and pageantry of the law, we do see evolution. This evolution comes in terms of the regulation and conduct of the professions, and technology would seem to be putting pressure on the professions to go further in reforming the ways of working of barristers and solicitors.

TAKING THINGS FURTHER

The website that accompanies this textbook contains a podcast about the concept of 'legal tech' and its implications for the work of solicitors. It is a concept that concerns both the regulation of new technologies (such as cryptocurrencies) and also the way in which legal practice engages with the technological revolutions of the 21st century. It considers the impact of artificial intelligence and machine learning on the development of law and legal practice. An awareness of the future shape of the professions as they embrace these changes will help gain a better understanding of the 'modern' legal professions.

Fusion of the professions – a discussion of significant pedigree – now seems a dead topic with all the change that has occurred to widen access, increase diversity and expand cost effective services. The Bar Council insists that

> [t]he existence and structure of the Bar has . . . very substantial public advantages. Barristers develop expertise in advocacy and in specialist areas of the law which enables them to provide expert advice and services to solicitors and other professional clients.[57]

Besides coming from the Bar Council itself, which should know the strengths of its own profession as well as anyone, this is manifestly only another way of putting the point that the Bar has the facilities to provide an elite referral service to solicitors which saves both the smallest firms without extensive in-house expertise in recondite areas of law, and even medium- and large-size firms which cannot cover every specialism, from having to allocate precious research time to specialist subject areas of which a specific barrister or set of Chambers may be experiencing day-to-day up-to-date familiarity in the course of advocacy in the higher courts.

Cautiously, one may opine that for the first time in nearly 70 years, the use to which a lawyer's education, training and skills can be put is relatively extensive. The qualified barrister now has a choice of practising in Chambers or as an employed barrister, the growth of the use of paralegals has meant that there is an alternative to going directly to the Bar and there may be further advantages of starting work in the solicitors' side of the profession. Another alternative is to be a legal executive, now fully recognised as a third branch of the profession alongside solicitors and barristers. From this position, it is possible to qualify as a practitioner through CILEx[58] and ultimately even as a solicitor if the firm in which a paralegal has worked satisfactorily as a legal executive is willing to provide a training contract. From the solicitors' office it is then possible to transfer to the Bar which is a pathway regulated by the Bar Standards Board,[59] and as the Bar remains a referral profession except for the few who have trained to receive direct access from clients, inevitably a former solicitor is welcome along with his or her contacts.

This chapter has covered in significant detail a wide range of matters concerning the evolution of the legal professions and has sought to do so with a critical eye. Nonetheless, there is much that it has not been possible to tackle in this chapter, without it running to an unwieldly length. A stubborn and long-lasting challenge has been access to the professions from those with protected characteristics or from certain backgrounds.

57 The Bar Council response to the 2004 Consultation Paper 'Review of the Regulatory Framework for Legal Services in England and Wales'.

58 See <www.CILEx.org.uk>, CILEx runs its own law school and examinations so that a paralegal may qualify first as a legal executive and then later as a solicitor.

59 <www.barstandardsboard.org.uk>, there is a special information section for transferring solicitors.

TAKING THINGS FURTHER

The website that accompanies this textbook contains further detail on the challenges of maintaining and improving the diversity of the sector and of access to the professions. The website helps to further understand the nature of the challenge – particularly for women, those from minority ethnic backgrounds and those with disabilities – as well as the efforts of the professions to deal with what is a long-standing and slow moving issue.

CONCLUSION

The preceding account of the contemporary professionals can only be a snapshot within the limited chapter length. For a genuine understanding of the profession and how it works today, some limited fieldwork will be necessary. This is one of the benefits of joining an Inn if you intend to go to the Bar, as this can be combined with applying for the valuable scholarships which are awarded to potential candidates for a career at the Bar at that stage. In the meantime, the best thing you could do to familiarise yourself with the profession is to apply for a mini-pupillage at the Bar (two or three days, or possibly a week, shadowing a barrister in Chambers practising in a field of law which interests you) or a summer placement at a firm of solicitors, again in an area of practice in which you might wish to specialise.

TAKING THINGS FURTHER

In order to promote your critical awareness, it is important that you can do more than simply setting down a descriptive account of how the legal profession, in all its contemporary sectors, actually works. You must be able also to identify the relevant advantages and disadvantages of the changes in structure of the profession and the methods by which they are regulated, as well as being able to take a critical view of whether the current systems are likely to work or, indeed, actually working, which may be difficult unless there has been some empirical evaluation. It is not enough to present answers to such questions as a list of advantages and disadvantages followed by a brief effort to evaluate the strength of the arguments in favour of or against the changes made in the conclusion. As commented elsewhere in this book, this is an overly simplistic way of approaching legal essays and often leads to bland, generic answers.[60] Better answers attempt to consider the rationale for the changes and to relate them to contemporary life in a practical manner.

To be able to do this, you need to keep in touch with changes in policy and its implementation, which inevitably requires some regular reading about current affairs and also about current affairs in the profession. A good source of the former are the

60 This applies to all forms of legal essays and not just those relating simply to a module on the English and Welsh legal system.

broadsheet newspapers *The Times, Telegraph, Guardian* and *Independent*, including *The I*, the *Independent* digest, which is supported by its website, www.inews.co.uk (website edition is free). The latter can be read in the Law Society's publication, *Law Society Gazette*, the weekly newspaper for solicitors since 1903, www.lawgazette.co.uk, and/or in the Bar Council's monthly publication since 1985, *Counsel* magazine, https://counselmagazine.co.uk, published by Lexis Nexis. All these publications should be available in any law library. Alternatively, you can use *The Lawyer* website, which is read by the entire profession, https://thelawyer.com.

There are also many blogs which address the Bar, for example, www.thesecretbarrister.com, and see the book of the same name also reviewed by *The Guardian*, on 28 April 2018, in which it is said that the author writes engagingly on various current topics interesting students of law.

THE WEBSITE

The website that accompanies this textbook contains many useful resources that you can use to consolidate and further your knowledge of the law, to hone your skills of critical analysis and to test your knowledge. This includes a set of multiple-choice questions (MCQs) that can be used to test your knowledge and understanding of the material.

16

CHAPTER 16
SKILLS FOR LEGAL STUDY

INTRODUCTION

It is an overlooked truth that *how* you study is as important a determinant of success as *what* you study. Investing some time and thought into how you can be *efficient* and *effective* in your study of legal subjects can create far greater returns than simply reading more cases or studying more journal articles or analysing yet more legislation. This chapter seeks to unpick some of the considerations to which those studying legal subjects should set their minds. Study is a deeply personal matter, and strategies that work for one person will be ineffective for another. This chapter should not be read as a 'series of instructions' but rather as a toolkit that should be actively considered as you embark on your studies. There are some tips, some strategies but mostly some points for reflection. By articulating things to consider in your own study, the chapter seeks to prompt the reader to *reflect* on what successful study means to them.

This chapter achieves three interconnected purposes. First, it considers some tips and strategies in forming good study habits that could be applied to any field of study. Second, it will equip you with some of the technical skills needed to be an effective student of law. This includes looking at strategies for reading, writing, researching and communicating your knowledge and understanding. It combines those skills in such a way as to make a critically informed student of law. Third, it seeks to give an indication of those skills that go beyond the traditional core academic skills. These include non-written forms of communication and other people-centred or soft skills.

ESTABLISHING GOOD STUDY ENVIRONMENTS AND STUDY HABITS

Legal study involves developing the technical and general skills necessary for success. Being mindful of and purposeful about your study environment and study habits is a factor of that success. This section seeks to highlight some of the issues that you should consider before and during any form of legal study. The degree to which these habits and your environment detract from or enhance your legal study is deeply personal. For some, silence is a necessary condition for success, whereas for others that silence is oppressive and induces anxiety.

STUDY ENVIRONMENT(S)

It would be overly simplistic to talk of *a* study environment. Most of those studying law will do so in a variety of places and spaces. These can range from formal study environments, over which a student may have little control, such as a lecture theatre or seminar room, to those born of necessity, such as a library or communal study space between classes, or at home

DOI: 10.4324/9781032641829-16

or on public transport during a commute; to those of choice, such as cafés, parks or other public spaces. Study environments therefore take different forms, and each can be more or less effective depending on what works best for the person studying.

Study environments will be likely to take a physical, digital and emotional form, and so consider *where* you study most effectively as well as *how* you study. Think about the *space you have*, the *noise levels* you can tolerate,[1] the *temperature* and the general comfort of where you sit (or stand or lie!) to study. Also pay attention to *distractions* that appear in certain physical environments.

In the 21st century, you should also be conscious of the digital environment(s) in which you are working and studying. These bring with them their own sets of challenges and opportunities. Having the entire world at your fingertips is incredibly powerful as a learning opportunity but can also come with an endless array of distractions and notifications or the ever-present temptations of social media.

Something that is rarely discussed in study skills sections of textbooks is the importance of the emotional environment in which you are working. This can be impacted by a whole range of factors, including diet, general well-being, exercise and the things that are happening in your life that are not related to your study. The time of day you study, for example, will influence the level of productivity and level of distractions. Being aware and mindful of these factors can help you study in a way that is most conducive to good health and well-being, as well as ensure the most effective learning environment.

TAKING THINGS FURTHER

It can be helpful to consider actively your study environment and improve it where you can.[2] The website that accompanies this textbook contains a helpful pro forma to support you in understanding the environments available to you and whether they are supporting your learning.

STUDY HABITS

A crucial part of forming a healthy and enthusiastic relationship with study is what might be termed 'study habits'. These are the routines and techniques that we use to manage study, to make the most effective use of the human, digital and physical resources available and to balance study against competing interests in life, be they social, familial or work priorities.

SCHEDULE AND ROUTINE

Establishing a healthy study schedule and developing routines can help move one towards more effective learning. If you are studying for a degree in law, then there will be both

1 For some, study can only be effective in complete silence, whilst others are more productive with background or white noise.

2 It is well understood that not everybody has the ability to alter the environment in which they work.

structured and unstructured time. Structured time, such as lectures or workshops or seminars, will give a certain shape and rhythm to your week. However, the study of law involves much unstructured, independent study. Making the most of this time can be challenging. Planning your time well is important. Reflect on the gaps in your schedule and how they might be most productively used. Plan time to consolidate knowledge and understanding from lectures and seminars, as well as time to develop new knowledge and understanding or to prepare for assessments or seminars. Having a plan and completing a schedule will ensure that you use your time for the greatest effect. Consider the environment you will have to study in and also the relative importance of the tasks that require completion.

Invest time in understanding proper project management as these are skills that you can apply also in other contexts. Plan breaks and treats so that you feel that your progress is rewarded and that you are suitably refreshed. Consider the intensity of the task; often, consolidating understanding is more straightforward and less intense than generating new knowledge and understanding. Therefore, schedule tasks according to when you feel you may be most productive. These personal study preferences are important to keep in mind. For some, consolidating knowledge immediately after a lecture is more effective, whilst for others allowing some time before revisiting materials leads to better outcomes. Similarly, some feel more productive and alert at particular times of the day.

NOTE-TAKING

If you are enrolled on a formal programme of study, then being able to take notes effectively is a crucial skill. There is a tendency, amongst those new to the study of law, to treat note-taking as a form of transcription. Students will try to capture every word spoken by their lecturer. This is often unnecessary, not least because many lectures are now recorded for future reference, and ineffective. It can distract from active listening and detract from the meaning and point being made by the speaker. Equally, taking notes from cases or academic journal articles may necessitate a different method (as the information may be well-structured) than that deployed for lectures and videos.

Investing time in exploring different forms of note-taking for different purposes can be beneficial. From simple bullet point and indented lists, moving from big picture to points of detail can be a good starting point. However, there is a risk that this is difficult to keep pace with lectures that are dense with information that may not appear in a linear fashion. This method is much more likely to be helpful when you are summarising information contained in journal articles or other written materials.

One popular type of note-taking is the Cornell method. It is helpful as it encourages greater clarity in note-taking and also engages skills of synthesis and reflection. Each page is split into three parts, with two columns of unequal width, with the first taking up 25% of the page and the remainder being taken up by the second. There is then a horizontal line blocking off 5–7 lines at the foot of the page. The wide column is used in making the actual notes, picking out important points and recording information. The narrow column is then used to record key words and prompts, such as questions intended to help you recall the substantive material. The space at the foot of the page is then used to summarise the main points on the rest of the page.

There are lots of templates available online that you can use to understand how this method works.

The Cornell method may be a popular form of note-taking that helps engage and re-engage with the substantive material covered in lectures, but it is not the only one. You should explore and experiment with different methods and deploy them in different contexts. This will help you develop good habits for note-taking and also allow you to find the method that most helps you to study effectively.

FINDING SUPPORT

Study can be a solitary experience, but this need not be the case. There are lots of sources of support to which you can turn to enrich the experience. It is important to reflect on the sources of support that may be available to you and to think about which forms of support you may need at different times. The following section highlights three groups of people who may be able to support your studies.

If you are studying law as part of a formal course, such as through a degree programme, then academics are a primary source of support. Those teaching the formal subjects are there to help you achieve your best work, and so making the most use of their expertise and guidance can be transformative to your understanding. It is typical for academics to hold 'student hours', or 'office hours' or 'consultation hours'. These are time put aside, normally every week, to discuss concerns about your study or even to take further discussions started in the more formal classroom setting. These are hours dedicated to you as a student and give you unparalleled access to one-to-one academic time.

Before making use of office hours, you should think about what you may think is most useful for you to discuss. Arriving with some pre-thought-out questions can help structure the discussion and ensure you cover everything that will help you. If you are visiting an academic because you are struggling with the content, then try to think through the precise things with which you are struggling and make note of the things you understand well. Equally, time spent with academics can be used to further your understanding and hone your critical thinking skills. It is possible to test out arguments or your own thinking about legal problems/issues and to enter into a discussion with an informed thinker who can help you develop your own critical thinking.

Academics can also signpost you to appropriate support if your personal circumstances are impacting on your ability to study. Many universities offer 'personal tutors' who can help guide and support you through university processes or advise you on policy. For those studying on formal programmes, such as degree programmes, there will also be members of university/college professional services teams who can help you. These are often arranged into portfolios of service – such as finance or well-being teams. These teams can help with a whole host of things that are impacting your ability to study. Other members of professional service teams may be able to give more direct support to your study. Library teams often offer support for academic writing and other core skills, discussed later.

The third group of people who can provide support are fellow students. Peer-assisted learning and study can be exceptionally effective. To talk with those who have shared challenges and experiences can be very helpful. Some universities offer formal schemes of peer mentoring, but for those that do not, they can also be achieved informally by networking. Talking with fellow students about the challenges you face and engaging in debates about the legal issues you identify not only can further your knowledge and understanding of the technical aspects of law but also sharpen your other critical skills, such as communication, persuasion and analysis.

In summary, it is important to make the most of the human capital associated with study. Academics, professional service teams and peers all have a shared interest in your success. It can be easy to become a 'lone scholar' – and to be clear, this works for some – but students often thrive most through collaboration and discussion with others.

UNDERSTANDING LEARNING RESOURCES

As well as the human/social capital that can enrich your experience, there are other learning resources that may be available to you. These can include physical resources in libraries and databases available digitally. In orienting yourself for your legal studies, you should take note of the range of materials and resources available, how to locate them and what means are used for their access. There is a temptation to review resources only at the start of your studies, but this should be resisted. Regular review of the resources available should become part of your study habits. Familiarising and re-familiarising yourself with the legal databases will mean that you will be able to make more effective use of them.

PREPARING FOR ASSESSMENTS AND MAKING THE MOST OF FEEDBACK

TAKING THINGS FURTHER

This textbook is not intended to provide specific advice or guidance on how to undertake assessments. The text is designed to be of use both to those who are learning the law as part of a formal qualification or programme of study and to those who may just be interested in understanding better the legal system of England and Wales. However, there are some tips that may be useful to share. The website that accompanies this textbook has some resources intended to help prepare for assessments and some advice on how to make the most of feedback on assessments.

THE SKILL AND IMPORTANCE OF CRITICAL THINKING

Most law schools in England and Wales will quite rightly claim that one of the skills developed by a law degree is that of 'critical thinking'. Many will claim that the development and mastery of this skill is the primary objective of such a degree,[3] and it will feature prominently in programme, course and module paperwork. Despite this revered prominence, it is often a concept with which those studying law struggle to engage. The purpose of this section is to demystify the concept and unpack what it might mean and to think of practical ways in which the skill can be developed and refined.

Given that many academics struggle to articulate the features of critical thinking and there is no shared or single understanding of the concept, it is important that students in particular gain a sense of their own institution's interpretation and definition of *critical thinking*. The authors of this textbook take the view that at its heart critical thinking in a legal context is the ability to

- form logical judgements on propositions of law, fact or opinion (reasoned conclusions)
- through the consideration of arguments/evidence (evaluation),
- including application and interpretation of legal sources (synthesis)
- relating to a sound understanding of the area of law (purposeful knowledge).

We decided to start our description of *critical thinking* with the desired *output* – an ability to form reasoned judgements on propositions of law, fact or opinion. This includes the application of those reasoned conclusions. This is because it is the *output* of critical thinking that is the desired skill. In this regard, critical thinking is a set of interconnected cognitive processes that we are then required to communicate to the world in various ways (for example, through a written assessment highlighting a contentious topic within the law). Equally, we could have started with the acquisition of knowledge as the first step towards the desired outcome.

In truth, critical thinking is an accumulation of very many different skills that operate at different levels. This accumulation of skills can be challenging to develop, and given their interconnections, a deficiency in one area (for example, the ability to evaluate arguments or incomplete knowledge) can have a significant impact on the overall process of critical thought. Faulty knowledge will lead to faulty thinking. Flawed application or interpretation of legal principle will impact analysis and evaluation.

Layered through these stages of critical thinking from knowledge to synthesis to evaluation to reasoned conclusions is a recognition that a highly developed critical thinker will recognise the internal and external biases in weighting and considering evidence. Additionally, critical *thinking* is a set of internal cognitive processes that happen within the confines of a person's mind. For this reason, the ability to be able to communicate – orally, or in writing – your reasoning and the steps of your analysis is an aligned but crucial skill.

Given the primacy of critical thinking, much of the remainder of this section will be devoted to unpicking the various aspects of legal and study competences that will help you refine this

3 Schools of law are by no means unique in this claim, with it featuring heavily in the discourse around the benefits of humanities and social science subjects more broadly.

crucial skill. Whilst critical thinking can feel a little amorphous in the academic environment, we exercise critical thinking on a daily basis, and a real-world example may help reveal the complexity and value of critical thinking.

TAKING THINGS FURTHER – THE MOBILE PHONE RECOMMENDATION

Before reading further, consider the example of giving a recommendation to a friend or family member as to which mobile phone they should purchase. Think about how you would go about this task and what skills you may need and what process you would go through in forming the recommendation. Before progressing further, write down the steps you would go through and any sources you might use. The next section of the chapter will then walk through this with the skills of critical thinking in mind.

Imagine that you are asked to give a recommendation on the *best* mobile phone someone should buy. This is not an uncommon request, but it is one, to satisfy effectively, to which we would instinctively and without conscious thought apply the skills of critical thinking. This example will be stretched a little and unpacked to explore the various facets of critical thinking.

A recommendation informed by critical thinking would start with some questions to consider. Who is asking for the recommendation, and why? What preferences or prejudices might be embedded in the request, and how should they be dealt with? Are there any known parameters in which to work, such as affordability? What is meant by 'best' in this regard; is it 'best price' or 'best functionality' or 'best aesthetic'? Good critical thinking will consider how to weigh the various understanding of 'best' in this context as the key tool of evaluating the recommendations. In this regard, the critical thinker spends some time understanding the context of the problem whilst assessing any implicit or explicit parameters. This will set a framework or standard by which to approach the problem. In this regard, *effective planning*, is a crucial precursor to critical thinking.

A good critical thinker would then assess the state of their existing knowledge and attempt to surface any biases (conscious or unconscious) that their current state of knowledge brings. Most people own a mobile phone and will have personal preferences and views that may inform or prejudice the recommendation given. The critical thinker reflects and acknowledges the extent and limitations of their existing knowledge as well as their biases.

It may be that following the assessment of current knowledge, gaps are identified. In our example, this may be around the current state of mobile phone technology or about pricing structures or the different features that may be available. The critical thinker addresses these knowledge deficits in a discriminate way by reading or gathering or researching *information* that fills the deficit. In doing so, the critical thinker would likely focus on building their knowledge in a way that is not linked to particular products or mobile phones in the first instance. In this way, they are understanding the field of knowledge. The danger here is that there will be a bewildering amount of knowledge to be acquired, and so it is necessary to filter that information in such a way that is going to be useful for the task at hand. The person asking for a recommendation for a new mobile phone is not going to be interested in the whole history of telecommunications or of the very technical way in which mobile phones work. The critical thinker therefore needs to be careful that they do not overwhelm themselves with knowledge and are able to determine the proportionate knowledge that is *necessary* and *appropriate* for them to make informed recommendations.

The sources of research will be important to a critical thinker. They will explore a variety of source materials, assessing for relevance, authority and bias. It may be that, at the knowledge stage, they are interested only in factual commentary in peer-reviewed sources (e.g. textbooks or industry magazines or information articles). Even where seeking 'facts', it is important that attention is paid to potential biases. When the critical thinker feels that they have enough knowledge, they would move on to consider other sources of information that they can interpret and apply in order to answer the recommendation. Someone exercising effective self-management in this task might test their understanding of their knowledge by exploring different sources that explain the same points and synthesising this information into a coherent and applicable knowledge base.

A person with underdeveloped skills of critical thinking may just, at this stage, regurgitate the knowledge gained and not address the core requirement of giving a recommendation on given parameters. Stopping at 'repeating knowledge' is a common approach adopted by those early in their legal study. It is not helpful and does not do the thing that was asked – to make a recommendation. A person with well-developed skills of critical thinking would wish to put forward arguments and analysis based on evidence that satisfies the requirements set.

The next stage of research, when there is a secure base of knowledge and understanding,[4] is to explore the evidence that forms the basis of various arguments about which mobile phone might be 'best'. Different, more analytical research skills would be deployed to identify *relevant* material, filtering out things that may well be interesting but do not help answer the request for a recommendation. In this context, those 'arguments' about which might be the 'best' mobile phone could come from different sources. The websites of the different mobile phone producers would likely feature, as might expert opinions and consumer reviews. It may be that broader quantitative data is available for consideration, such as purchasing habits.

At this stage, where we are essentially exploring different potential arguments that nudge us towards or away from a particular recommendation, we must be especially mindful of bias. This includes confirmation bias, which is the phenomenon of us seeking, favouring and putting forward evidence that supports our own existing beliefs. Equally, a strong critical thinker will assess the potential bias, reliability and authority of the sources. It is trite but true

4 Recognising that knowledge can never be complete and that further research and analysis will bolster and change understanding.

to note that some sources are more reliable than others. A company website is likely to paint a wholly positive picture of the products they market. An 'expert' opinion may be influenced by their own ideology or by whom they are paid. Consumer reviews can be difficult to verify. When assessing sources and evidence, an effective critical thinker will consider:

- The purpose and audience for which the content was created
- The author of the argument and whether they have expertise or conflicts of interest
- The source of the information and whether it is independent and peer-reviewed
- The time at which the information was published and whether this affects its currency or applicability[5]
- Whether the argument can be confirmed or verified by other sources of information

As well as being the stage most susceptible to bias, this is a delicate stage of critical thinking for other reasons as we are moving away from knowledge towards synthesis of that knowledge into a set of arguments for evaluation. This is a higher-order skill than simply gaining knowledge. Here you would *start* the process of evaluating each mobile phone applying insights gained from analysing and interpreting these arguments against the base knowledge and the various yardsticks of what constitutes 'best'. This is likely to be multi-layered and cyclical but would likely involve:

- *Factual comparisons and analysis.* For example, which phone has the highest-resolution camera or the fastest processor or integrates with product Y or service Z.
- *Consideration of the views and arguments of others.* For example, how satisfied consumers are or the view of expert users.

It is important at all times to not become distracted from the task, in this case to form a *recommendation*. For complex tasks, it is sometimes the case that our attention wanders and we lose purpose. Information rarely presents itself in neat parcels that are fully relevant to the task at hand. Things may end up being interesting but not relevant! Being able to filter out irrelevant information is a key part of forming a convincing and focussed narrative. This is why determining the parameters and their relative important/weighting from the outset is important. These form the 'yardsticks' for measuring and weighting different arguments.

Having assessed the various sources of information and distilled their relevant arguments, it would be time to bring those together into a coherent narrative. For the task at hand, we would consider, for each mobile phone, the merits and demerits we have discovered and analysed and attempt to weight them against a particular mobile phone and between different mobile phones. This weighting will be as to the extent to which each of the arguments helps us determine which is the 'best' mobile phone.

Having satisfied ourselves as to the best recommendation of a new phone, we have exercised and explored the skills of critical thinking. However, this is not enough. If we just say 'iPhone'

5 This is especially true in a legal context!

or 'Google Pixel' or 'Samsung Galaxy', then this is not likely to satisfy the person requesting the recommendation. They will likely wish to know why. We now need to articulate that recommendation in a way that is acceptable to the person asking us and which demonstrates in a logical, reasoned and persuasive manner *how* we formed this view. Depending on the circumstances, it may well be that we need to *explain* the recommendation. This will involve skills of communication and persuasion. At heart the recommendation should be not only the *outcome* of the critical thinking process but also an account of the *process* that led to the outcome. The most compelling recommendation will be one that inspires confidence as to the recommender's knowledge, that articulates the sources that form the basis of the arguments relied upon, that evaluates the relevant strengths and weaknesses of those arguments as they relate to the parameters established and that comes to a clear and evidenced conclusion.

The detailed example presented earlier seeks to ground the abstract concept of 'critical thinking' in the real world. It gives insight into the process and outcomes, as well as some of the pitfalls.

ACADEMIC STUDY SKILLS

There are a range of core academic skills that come together to provide for effective study. They are interconnected and interdependent, but each needs to be acquired, developed and mastered. The rest of this section will touch upon the various academic study skills that you should actively seek to utilise as you study substantive legal subjects. The focus here will be on developing knowledge, understanding the language of the law, researching, demonstrating academic integrity, reading and writing.

KEEPING YOUR KNOWLEDGE UP TO DATE

For much of the time, the law follows an orderly process of development, with careful planning and policy papers and structured calls for reform. Equally, the law sometimes moves rapidly, sometimes unpredictably and often at times when you least expect it. Textbooks go to print at fixed points in the year, putting in concrete terms the law as understood at that time. Judgments are given in cases without a knowledge of how future courts will use the principles concerned to expand or contract the law. Parliament passes legislation without a full understanding of how the laws they make will be interpreted by the judiciary. New technologies may pose new challenges to existing legal principles. For this reason, being able to keep abreast of what is happening with the law is an important skill.

Without intending for the reader to become paranoid or unduly worried, it is a good practice to consider at all times that what is being read in a journal or a case may already be out of date. For comfort, every academic, at some point in their career, has been slightly embarrassed to learn that they have missed a development in the law that has been picked up by a bright and enthusiastic law student. Perhaps more worryingly, the legal system itself has at times become ensnared in its own complexities.

There are, however, some strategies for keeping on top of developments in the law and the legal system and thereby avoiding academic or professional embarrassment. The days of seeking out paper corrections and updating inserts into ring binders is thankfully no longer such a necessity, and the digitisation of the legal system has helped make this process less painful and more effective.

The best and first resource for understanding the law is to go to the primary source for legislation or case law. For the former, you should visit legislation.gov.uk[6] as this generally keeps pace with changes in a relatively short period of time. The website also contains the amended content of legislation, removes outdated text and links, through to amending legislation. In addition, there is the possibility of just browsing new legislation. For case law, and outside of the commercial databases, you can browse the National Archives[7] for judgments from 2001 and BAILII[8] for older judgments. Both will provide links also to recent judgments if you are just seeking to chart the development of the law rather than searching for a specific case.

If you are seeking to understand better the most significant questions of statutory interpretation or of development of the common law, then you should be a frequent visitor to the Supreme Court's website.[9] Unlike the advice of 'general browsing' earlier, the listings for the Supreme Court are manageable to revisit weekly, and easily understandable press releases are available for decided cases. This provides for a straightforward understanding of the matters occupying the most senior judicial offices in the UK.

The second approach to updating relates to understanding the potential future shape of the law in a given area. Understanding the policy landscape and upcoming changes to legislation can give a sense of the direction of particular areas of law and enhance your critical thinking and analysis of the law as it stands. The UK Parliament website[10] lists bills in process during the current session of Parliament and provides links to various committee reports and hearings. This can provide fruitful ground for understanding the context in which legislation is proceeding. The Law Commission website[11] also provides a strong indication of the areas of law that are thought to be in need of reform or clarification, and it contains many useful reports and summaries of the case for change.

The third approach is to seek out and read only the most recent *analysis* of the law. When researching, balance looking for seminal and timeless pieces of academic writing with those that contain the most recent exposition and analysis of the law. This will ensure that you have not missed more recent developments. The major legal journals all provide updating emails and alerts that help you keep on top of developments in the law. Just periodically browsing

6 <www.legislation.gov.uk>.

7 <https://caselaw.nationalarchives.gov.uk/>.

8 <https://www.bailii.org/>.

9 <https://www.supremecourt.uk/>.

10 <https://bills.parliament.uk/>.

11 <https://lawcom.gov.uk/>.

the article titles and abstracts from the generalist journals (such as *Legal Studies*,[12] *Cambridge Law Journal*,[13] *Modern Law Review*[14]) will help give a sense of the dynamism of the law, as will doing the same for more specialist journals. You can also consider academic blogs as a source of useful information, often published more rapidly and in close proximity to legal developments.[15] Equally useful, but perhaps to be treated with more caution,[16] are the many leading social media accounts that provide a very current analysis of the law and legal developments.

Fourthly, seek out *professional* (as opposed to academic) commentary on the law. This will help give you a sense of the practical impact of developments in the law. These tend to follow on closely from legal development, as opposed to academic journals that are published some months after developments happen. To this end, very many of the leading law firms or chambers provide commentary on new case law and legislation. This is often intended to promote themselves to new clients and so are not aimed at those studying law and are written in an accessible style.

Fifthly, and finally, commercial databases such as Westlaw also contain various 'updating' functions whereby you can sign up for email notifications when new developments in the law happen, such as decided cases or new legislation. These can be used to gain insights into particular topics but also can be used more broadly to keep abreast of developments within the principles of the legal system.

DEPLOYING LEGAL TERMINOLOGY

As a discipline, law has its own language. The rest of this textbook has introduced the reader to a number of new terms. There are specialist terms that are peculiar to legal study (such as *ratio* or *obiter* or *tort*), and there are general words that have a particular meaning in the legal context (such as 'judgment' or 'obligation'). Even at a sub-discipline level, each branch of law has its own language, with which it is important to become familiar.

The misuse and misunderstanding of legal terminology is a particular danger for those new to legal study, and it can be fatally undermining to others' confidence in your knowledge and understanding. The challenge here is that it is not always possible to know the things you don't know!

TAKING THINGS FURTHER – THE LANGUAGE OF THE LAW

The website that accompanies this textbook has some of the most common mistakes of students in relation to the use of legal terminology. This list has been compiled from

12 <https://www.cambridge.org/core/journals/legal-studies>.

13 <https://www.cambridge.org/core/journals/cambridge-law-journal>.

14 <https://www.modernlawreview.co.uk/>.

15 For example, see <https://ukconstitutionallaw.org/> for a good example of a reliable and authoritative blog that is regularly updated with information relevant to the study of the legal system of England and Wales.

16 Not because of their quality but partly as they are not peer-reviewed or subject to professional editing or verification.

university academics in an attempt to help put you on the front foot in relation to the appropriate use of legal terminology.

The best method for ensuring the appropriate use of legal terminology is to read widely. The more you read, the more you will become familiar with the language of the law. Keeping a general list of definitional terms can be helpful at the early stages of legal study. This can then be supplemented and added to in relation to the various sub-domains and disciplines within law.

RESEARCHING

Whether you intend to progress to legal practice or otherwise, the skills of legal research cannot be overlooked. They are the bedrock of success in legal study and involve synthesising and combining skills of reading, writing and analysis. Research is often presented as part of a linear process: you do the research, you read the outputs of that research and then you write up the findings. This textbook is at risk of perpetuating that view by the structure of this chapter. The research process is much more dynamic and cyclical than this linear structure suggests. Research should continue through all stages of a project, including during any writing process. There is an iterative cycle of refining and redefining the basic question that is seeking to be answered. This more cyclical view of research is likely to lead to more sophisticated and refined outcomes and helps make each stage more manageable (and enjoyable!).

As with other legal skills, research can be used for different purposes, and thinking about the sources used and the methodology deployed can be transformational in how you go about undertaking legal research. As will be discussed shortly, defining the research problem/question will influence what research needs to be done and the methods deployed. For example, and at a rather superficial level, the sources and weighting given to surveys and sources may greatly enhance empirical research but may prove a distraction to the doctrinal/black letter researcher. Understanding cases from other jurisdictions may inform the comparative researcher but may do little to further the work of the interdisciplinary lawyer attempting to understand the interface between law and other disciplines, such as business or engineering.

TAKING THINGS FURTHER

When using legal databases, the searches you perform can have a big impact on the results produced. The website that accompanies this textbook also contains some advice on how to conduct effective searches.

The diagram in Figure 16.1 seeks to capture the essence of the legal research process once an initial research question has been defined. You can see from the diagram that there are several points in the research process where the research question or problem is revisited, refined and re-understood. As you create your own knowledge and understanding, it is important to keep

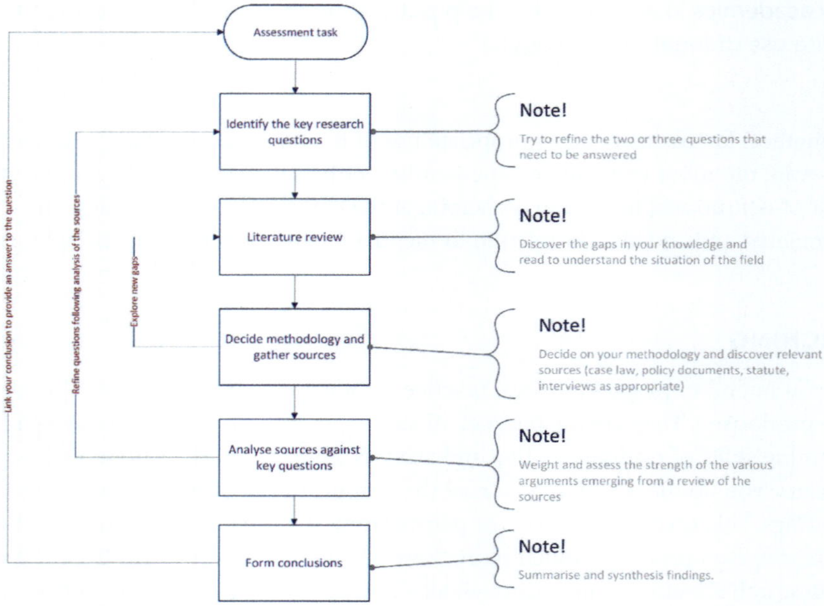

Figure 16.1 The research process.

coming back to the research question(s). This will ensure you remain focused and also allow you to take a fresh perspective on work you may have already completed.

REFERENCING, ACADEMIC INTEGRITY AND ETHICS

Having undertaken significant research, it is important to remember to keep track of where ideas have come from and of the thoughts of others that have influenced your work. For this reason, tracking and recording your references is important. If you are using a footnote system (such as the one deployed in this textbook), then proper referencing adds weight and authority to the points you are making. Use of referencing also makes clear to others those ideas that are your own and those of others on which you are choosing to rely. For the legal scholar, commenting on the law, it is also important to be able to indicate through referencing an understanding of from where a legal principle has been extracted (be that a case or statute or piece of delegated legislation).

TAKING THINGS FURTHER

The website that accompanies this textbook contains an exercise of correct referencing using the OSCOLA system of referencing.

ACADEMIC INTEGRITY AND ETHICS

Behaving and learning in an ethical manner and acting with integrity in your studies are of primary importance. If you wish to pursue a career in practice, then maintaining integrity and strong ethical standards is crucial. The regulators of legal service providers and the general public have high expectations of the standards of lawyers given their central role in the administration of justice. Learning ethical behaviours through legal study is an excellent preparation to meet those expectations. Being able to demonstrate the steps taken to reference the work of others correctly, for example, shows you as an ethical researcher.

GENERATIVE ARTIFICIAL INTELLIGENCE FOR LEGAL STUDY

In the same way that the law and its practice are being transformed by the advent of artificial intelligence, so is the study of law and other disciplines. This is no new phenomenon, and technological advancement has challenged lawyers and those studying law over the centuries, from the advent of the printing press to the birth of the internet to the growth of social media and, more recently, the progress of generative artificial intelligence. In summary, generative AI creates new content or responses based on patterns in large data sets. It is a truly transformative technology and one that provides both opportunities and challenges. Generative AI has application to both legal study and legal practice but should be used with caution.

TAKING THINGS FURTHER – THE BENEFITS OF GENERATIVE AI

To demonstrate the power of generative AI, the text that follows within this box was generated wholly by the use of generative AI.[17] The results on the benefits of AI are as follows:

> Generative AI is transforming the study of law by enhancing research, writing, analysis, and practical training. Its greatest value lies in helping law students learn more efficiently, think more critically, and prepare for a technology-driven legal profession.
>
> AI tools can quickly summarize case law, statutes, and judgments, allowing students to focus on interpretation rather than data gathering. They can generate arguments for and against legal positions, simulate judicial reasoning, and provide instant feedback on writing, improving both analytical and drafting skills. In legal writing, AI assists with structure, tone, and clarity, while also offering model examples of memos, briefs, and essays that help students master professional communication.
>
> Beyond research and writing, generative AI creates immersive learning experiences. It can simulate judges, clients, or opposing counsel in virtual moot courts and interviews, allowing students to practice advocacy, negotiation, and client communication in realistic settings. AI tutors also provide personalized learning, adapting to each student's pace and offering customized exercises and quizzes that reinforce understanding.
>
> Generative AI also supports theoretical and policy exploration. It allows students to test hypothetical legal scenarios and explore the ethical, regulatory, and philosophical

17 Using ChatGPT with the prompt "Write a short narrative explaining the benefits of AI to the study of law."

implications of AI itself – issues that are increasingly central to modern law. Furthermore, by automating tasks like citation checking and document summarization, AI improves productivity and accessibility, especially for non-native speakers and students with disabilities.

Exposure to these tools prepares students for legal workplaces where AI is already used for contract review, compliance, and predictive analytics. At the same time, it raises vital concerns about accuracy, bias, confidentiality, and overreliance – challenges that future lawyers must learn to navigate responsibly.

In essence, generative AI is not a replacement for human reasoning but a partner in legal education. It bridges theory and practice, enabling law students to become more efficient researchers, clearer writers, and more adaptive professionals ready to shape the future of law and technology.

The preceding shows an idealised view of the benefits of generative AI to legal study. There are clear benefits to summarising complex information, bringing stylistic support to writing and helping sharpen skills of critical thinking. Whilst useful as a tool, it does come with a number of pitfalls.

TAKING THINGS FURTHER – THE PITFALLS OF GENERATIVE AI

To demonstrate the equal and opposite power of generative AI, the text that follows within this box was generated wholly by the use of generative AI.[18] The results on the dangers of AI are as follows:

While generative AI offers powerful advantages to the study of law, it also presents serious drawbacks and dangers that must be managed carefully. One of the most significant concerns is inaccuracy. AI tools can produce text that appears convincing but contains factual or legal errors – a phenomenon known as "hallucination." For example, they may invent case citations, misstate legal principles, or confuse jurisdictions. Because accuracy is essential in legal education, students who rely on AI without verifying its outputs risk misunderstanding or misapplying the law. Compounding this issue is the lack of transparency in how most AI systems source their information.

Another major drawback is the issue of bias and fairness. AI systems learn from existing data, including legal texts and social materials that may reflect historical or systemic inequalities. As a result, they can unintentionally reinforce racial, gender, or socioeconomic biases in the examples or analyses they generate. If used uncritically, such tools can distort students' understanding of justice and equality under the law.

18 Using ChatGPT with the prompt "Write a short narrative explaining the dangers and drawbacks of AI to the study of law."

There are also serious academic integrity concerns. When students use AI to write essays or draft legal documents, it becomes harder to distinguish between genuine learning and mechanical assistance. Overreliance on AI can discourage original thought, weaken research and writing skills, and even encourage plagiarism. Legal education is designed to cultivate independent reasoning, so excessive dependence on technology can undermine the very skills that make effective lawyers.

Finally, there are ethical and professional risks associated with relying on AI in a discipline grounded in human judgement and moral reasoning. Students must grapple with questions about accountability for AI-generated errors, appropriate citation practices, and the role of technology in shaping legal outcomes. Overuse of AI can also narrow the learning experience, focusing students on answers rather than the interpretive, argumentative, and empathetic dimensions of law that define good advocacy and judgement.

In summary, while AI can enhance legal education, it also carries dangers – such as inaccuracy, bias, plagiarism, privacy breaches, and ethical confusion – that can weaken the quality of legal learning if left unchecked. To use AI responsibly, law students must learn not only how to benefit from its efficiency but also how to question, verify, and limit its use. In legal study, as in practice, technology should remain a tool that supports human reasoning – not one that replaces it.

Given this mix of benefits and real challenges, it is not surprising that providers of legal education (and indeed all forms of education) have struggled in recent years in giving good advice to students on the ethical and appropriate use of generative AI. If you are on a formal programme of study, it would be useful to acquaint yourself with the approach taken by your institution as some do not permit the use of AI at all in the preparation of assessments, and to us it would constitute academic misconduct or an academic integrity offence.

Where institutions do allow the use of AI, it should be used responsibly and ethically as a tool to augment and help you build the skills you need to succeed. This can involve adopting a critical thinking approach (described in detail earlier in this chapter) to the inputs and outputs of AI. Finding independent corroboration of material generated by AI is essential, particularly checking for bias and hallucinations. Much like any other source of information, students should use it as a tool to enhance their own understanding and critical awareness and not as a shortcut or replacement for the development of independent skills.

GENERATIVE ARTIFICIAL FOR PRACTICE

For those wishing to join the legal profession following a period of legal study, getting into good and ethical behaviours around AI is important as it will set you up for the rest of your professional career. Falling into poor ethical habits or using AI as a shortcut to proper research and preparation can have significant impacts on careers. The obligations that come with being a member of the legal profession(s) include obligations not to mislead the court. An emerging set of cases serves as a powerful warning in this regard.

In *Ayinde*,[19] a barrister was accused of including non-existent case law within a bundle submitted to the other party and before the court. There were case names and citations throughout the skeleton that, on closer examination, could not be found in any law report. The barrister was unable to provide, under close scrutiny from the judge, a convincing explanation of how this happened. They had also been deeply unprofessional in correspondence when challenged by the solicitors of the other side. A suggestion was made that these could have been 'hallucinations' created by the use of AI to research the area of law. The judge in this case was not capable of finding that the barrister had used generative AI as they had not been sworn in or cross-examined. Nonetheless, an interesting observation was made in *obiter*. The judge held that 'it would have been negligent for this barrister, if she used AI and did not check it, to put that text into her pleading'.[20] The potential negligence does not arise merely from the use of AI but, rather, where it has been used uncritically and without proper verification or where a legal professional does not put their mind to the risks of using AI at all. Given the very public censure, and the regulatory consequences, it is important that practitioners treat AI with caution and with an ethical framework. The judge also required a transcript of judgment to be sent to the Bar Standards Board and Solicitors Regulation Authority under the duty to self-report.[21] Whilst *Ayinde* is not an isolated case and is part of a growing pattern of suspicion of unethical use of AI by the professions,[22] there is no evidence of systematic abuse of AI by the legal professions.

The Courts and Tribunals Service has also issued recent and refreshed guidance to members of the judiciary on their own use of AI in preparing judgments and discharging the requirements of their judicial office.[23] There is evidence that some judges are using AI to help them summarise and draft sections of judgment. In 2024, Lord Justice Birss stated that AI had been 'jolly useful' in helping him summarise an area of law. Although contentious at that time, it seemed to be an ethical use with appropriate verification from his extensive understanding of the area of law. Whilst judges ought to be able to rely on the professional standards of those appearing before them, they will need to be particularly mindful of litigants in person who will be preparing cases themselves and will not necessarily know how to verify information they find online, including through the use of AI.[24]

TAKING THINGS FURTHER

The website that accompanies this textbook has further information about how technology is changing the world of legal practice. This is broader than, but incorporates, the use of AI to streamline and automate very many legal tasks. This is an area known as LawTech.

19 *Ayinde v London Borough of Haringey* [2025] EWHC 1040 (Admin).

20 ibid at [65].

21 ibid at [78].

22 See the postscript to the very recent immigration tribunal judgment *AK v The Secretary of State for the Home Department* [decision number UI-2025-002918].

23 <https://www.judiciary.uk/wp-content/uploads/2025/04/Refreshed-AI-Guidance-published-version.pdf>.

24 For a recent example of just such an occurrence, see *Harber v HMRC* [2023] UKFTT 1007 (TC).

READING

Reading is one of the fundamental skills necessary for success in legal study and legal practice, as well as for effective critical thinking. From the outset, when confronted with any piece of text, the reader should consider carefully *why* they are reading it and *what* they hope to gain by doing so. Aimless reading has its place in developing a general understanding of the law, but the volume of material available on even the most niche legal topics means that there needs to be a method to reading when it is directed to a specific task. The rest of this section attempts to outline the different purposes for which people may read and to give some advice on how to do each successfully. There is then a consideration of different types of legal text and how best to tackle them.

READING WITH PURPOSE

Whatever the text, it is important always to read with purpose. Before reading anything, consideration should be given to the reasons for identifying the text as relevant and also the intended outcomes. The three primary 'purposes' identified in this textbook are reading *for context*, reading *for knowledge*, and reading *for analysis*. All the aforementioned reasons for reading have their place and should be deployed to varying degrees depending on the *purpose of the reading*. They are strategies and tools that should be expressly thought about before reading takes place and are not intended to be mutually exclusive.

READING FOR CONTEXT

By this term we mean reading to get a general understanding of the shape of the area of law. This is not a detailed examination of the part most relevant but rather to get an understanding of how various aspects of the law knit together into a coherent whole. For example, reading solely about unfair dismissal law may give a detailed understanding of that area of employment law, but it will not give an understanding of how it fits with the other potentially fair reasons for dismissal. There is clearly a danger of 'overreading' and its becoming unmanageable, but equally there is a danger of 'underreading' and it becoming too narrow in scope too early. Often, being able to 'join the dots' between different areas is revealing of more general principles that underpin the law in a particular area.

READING FOR SPECIFIC KNOWLEDGE

Any scheme of legal learning (whether from a textbook or a module or a degree programme) is intended to give a basic understanding of an area of law. Reading for knowledge can enrich that basic framework and can help you understand better an area of law. This is achieved through furthering your knowledge and also reinforcing what you may have been taught on a module through a different perspective or lens. Quite often, a formal series of lectures can only give so much information and is intended to give a rough shape to a subject that is then refined and defined through reading around the subject for specific knowledge.

The second reason for reading for knowledge relates to law being an applied discipline. It may be that someone needs to read to understand what was decided in a particular case in order to determine whether that principle could or should be applied in another case (as in a hypothetical problem question or a real-life dispute). In this scenario, the reader should be focusing on the articulation of the legal principle and any legal tests established or explained.

Any analysis in the text, for example, commentary on what the law *should be* or its deficiencies, should be treated more cautiously. A client or party to a dispute is generally less interested in what the law *should* be than they are in what the law *is*, unless there is a reasonable chance that a well-argued point may change the law. Of course, analysis that reveals uncertainty in the law or that may persuade a judge in the higher courts that a previous case was wrongly decided is helpful in some circumstances but less so where you are simply trying to understand the principle in question and its application to the facts of the case.

READING FOR ANALYSIS

Alongside sketching either a general or detailed picture of the extent and application of the law, it is often necessary to read to understand arguments about the law and legal principles. This reading for analysis or to inform evaluations is a higher-order skill that will take some time to acquire and master. It is not always possible to separate out analysis from knowledge.

Evaluating the strength of various arguments will help enrich your understanding and allow you to form reasoned conclusions on propositions of law. When considering a question of whether the law in a particular area is *effective* or in need of reform, analytical reading helps determine and marshal your arguments. Reading academic commentary in journal articles would be at the heart of this type of analytical reading.

In approaching such reading, the critical thinker will have formed some thoughts as to what factors or features may help determine what *effective* might mean in these circumstances. These are the 'intellectual yardsticks' by which we measure the question of effectiveness. It may be that we are considering 'effective' to mean a number of things – for example, whether the law is cost-effective *or* whether the law is certain *or* whether the law fits a coherent picture of a principle *or* whether it meets a specific policy aim/outcome. Critical reading may shape the number of these yardsticks you use in your argument, or they can simply build the weight of evidence for the argument you are seeking to demonstrate. Read not only to follow the argument of the author but also to dissect those arguments, and gather them for a purpose. Avoid making notes 'about' a journal article. As you read, identify the main arguments being made, assess them for relevance and then weight them based on the strength of the analysis presented.

This approach of focussing less on the individual content piece you are reading and more on the arguments it contains can be especially powerful if you have undertaken thorough research. This is likely to have generated a number of pieces that argue the same point. Having different perspectives that support your analysis can make your argument stronger and more compelling. It may also be the case that your reading reveals tensions and contradictions between various authors on the same topic. This is typical in many legal areas. Try to understand the *evidence* that various authors have used to make their points and assess the relative strength and authority of the analysis.

As an effective critical thinker, you should also spend some time understanding the broader context in which a particular piece of analysis has been written. In the same way as you should be mindful of your own biases and influences, so should you be aware of the biases and influences of others. Reflect on the time at which a particular piece of work was authored and how the social, economic or political realities of that time may have influenced the writer. Assessing the jurisprudential lens through which an author has assessed a legal argument can be revealing. It can also give you the opportunity to consider alternative perspectives by applying different jurisprudential ideas and theories to the problem at hand. Theoretical frameworks and locating authors within those frameworks can make for sophisticated argument and can bolster the authority of the arguments you are making. Or help to explain why you might disagree with the findings of a particular author.

Seek, in your reading, diverse voices who may bring alternative perspectives. Much of the early literature about legal issues is written by White, Western men (pale, male and stale!). Consider how this can influence the perspectives that are taken and whether a broader and more diverse literature can provide different insights.

READING STRATEGICALLY

Even when someone has undertaken sensible, measured and meaningful research into a legal topic, it can still feel rather overwhelming to look at the assortment of journal articles, cases, statutes and policy documents that need to be considered. For this reason, it is important to be ruthless and strategic in reading and keep in mind always the purpose. This involves as much a consideration of what is **not** read as what is.

When seeking to tackle a curated reading list of researched texts, the first thing to do is to think about the *order* of reading materials. This is important as reading different texts in different orders can influence your understanding. Lots of factors can influence the order in which you tackle materials, including your level of familiarity of the area and its complexity. There is no 'correct' approach to this question, and quite often there is a need to return to early reading in light of changed perspectives by things read later!

Generally, being able to place specific topics within their broader context is helpful, and so starting by reading for *context* can be helpful. This would suggest textbooks and introductory texts make a good starting place. For areas heavily dominated by policy uncertainty or the prospect of reform, reading policy documents can be a useful starting point as well.

There often comes a point when researching a legal topic where the researcher must make a choice as to read *analysis of the law* (largely academic writing in journals) or the *primary materials* (cases and legislation) first. Again, there is no 'most effective' way of making this choice, and those studying should experiment with what leads them to their most effective arguments and outcomes. The researcher just needs to make an active decision on whether they wish to come to the primary materials (i.e. the law) with or without knowledge of how it has been analysed. This can be helpful in forming a core understanding of the material and allowing the researcher to form their own views. Equally, on technical or complex matters, it may make sense to be 'guided' through the material by an author with specific expertise.

Anyone with an interest in studying law and the legal system will quickly come to understand that being able to identify and read different sources is an indicator of success. Recognising that different sources can provide different insights into the same legal topic or issue is an important step in being more strategic in your reading.

READING DIFFERENT SOURCES

One of the most challenging dimensions of legal study is in reading, understanding and analysing different primary and secondary sources. Each source, whether its legislation or case law or journal articles, presents different challenges and opportunities. The task can feel intimidating to those new to legal study. As with all skills, the more you do, the more you understand!

TAKING THINGS FURTHER

The website that accompanies this textbook includes videos exploring the main features of a case in the jurisdiction of England and Wales and further videos exploring the features of primary and secondary legislation.

In addition, there are resources on the website that explain some of the challenges and strategies for reading the following sources: case law, legislation, policy documents, academic writing.

CONCLUSION ON READING

Reading is a skill that develops with repetition, and the more widely and deeply you read, the more compelling your arguments and the sharper your analysis will become. Focussed reading, with a clear understanding of the purpose and aims of looking at a particular piece of material, will also help. Over time you will become more proficient at reading and be able to both skim for key words and read for deep thought.

WRITING

Writing for legal purposes is another of the centrally important skills that are developed through the study of law. Clearly, the limited space in this text cannot give definitive and exhaustive advice on all approaches to writing.[25]

THE MECHANICS OF WRITING

First and foremost, understand the basics of written English. Rules of grammar are important as they allow you to best and most persuasively put forward your argument. Improvement, following many years of formal education can be a challenge, but the more clearly you can articulate your argument, the more persuasive it is likely to be. Very many universities offer generalised support (not linked to a particular discipline) for writing, and it would be beneficial to explore what is available and what might help.

Breaking text with paragraphs can help properly marshal your argument and ensure a proper flow. A reader can better understand when you are moving to new points or building upon

25 There are very many study skills books that have more extensive guides to legal writing or writing for legal study.

existing ones if the sections and paragraphs are of a reasonable length. Equally, particularly for long-form essays, headings can also neatly and concisely guide the reader through the text. This should be balanced against the need to maintain a natural flow, and so too many headings or subheadings can end up being confusing or make the text more difficult to follow.

Communicating your critical analysis or critical application of the law is a skill that is best developed not through the reading of textbooks but rather through practical endeavours. Take all opportunities presented to put into action your learning and the advice given in what follows. Summarise and synthesise your notes into new written forms. Undertake all opportunities to write, including completing formative assessments where they are available. Write for legal essay competitions. Write for legal blogs or other media. These will all allow you to build and develop your skills and proficiency.

Reflect carefully on any feedback that you are given on written style and structure. Feedback on summative work is intended to help you improve your writing skills, and so look for patterns of feedback that you are given and make a plan to act on those patterns. If structure is something with which you struggle, then read general study materials around structure and think carefully about writers who seem to be able to convey an argument in a clear and logical way and seek to deploy the structural devices that they use.

For legal work, adopting a fairly formal tone of writing is important, and slang references and abbreviations should be avoided where possible. In this way, having a keen sense of the purpose of the task and the intended audience is important. A different style, and tone, is likely to be adopted when writing a blog post for the general public as opposed to a skeleton argument for a moot or a policy report or traditional legal essay.

Once a written artefact has been created, it is important to properly proofread the work. This is task that is often overlooked or is executed poorly in the preparation of written assignments. Proofreading takes time and a sense of purpose. Read through work several times, each time adopting a different focus. You should read thinking about grammar and flow; you should read thinking about structure; you should read thinking about substantive content (i.e. is there a coherent argument?) and you should read to ensure all propositions or statements of law are properly supported with references to case law or statute.

Part of writing for different purposes and understanding your audience is to think carefully about the precise task that has been set. In the course of legal study, this will most typically be a legal essay or a hypothetical scenario or problem question.[26] The preceding advice applies equally to both types of legal problem. What follows is a little more tailored advice in relation to essays and problem questions.

ESSAYS

Legal essays are a staple of legal education. Whether they set out a thesis to be considered or invite a more general critical evaluation, there are some common features of strong responses.

26 There are, of course, a whole host of other assessment types.

Before beginning work on an essay, it is important to understand fully the criteria by which it will be assessed. Understanding the measures by which your written work will be assessed is crucial to success. There is a typical suite of assessment criteria that are used, but making reference to those in use by your university would be helpful. Obvious examples would include:

- Knowledge and understanding
- Critical analysis or evaluation
- Synthesis of argument
- Structure
- Use of evidence/sources or evidence of research
- Relevance or focus
- Reference

Having established *what* will be assessed, it is important to plan *how* best to go about answering a particular question. Constructing a legal argument is much like any essay in that it will have a short introduction, a hefty middle section and a short conclusion.

The introduction to a legal essay should demonstrate an understanding of the task that has been set. General introductions to the whole area of law are unnecessary and do not show the required focus. After demonstrating to the reader that you have a strong understanding of the precise question set, the introduction should also be a means of 'sign-posting' the rest of your essay. You should be clear with the reader about the journey on which you will be taking them and the main pillars of our argument. Having conducted your research and having read widely and deeply, you should be able to signal to the reader the main stages of your argument and its progression over the course of the rest of your essay.

The main bulk of the essay will deal with the legal reasoning necessary to address the question asked. This will be done by deploying the skills of critical analysis (discussed earlier). In planning the essay, consider what might make for a sensible and flowing argument. Do you start with the strongest argument in favour of your position and work your way down, before considering arguments that do not support your position? Or is it best to deal with matters in a thematic way, considering both the things that support and do not support your argument at the same time? These are matters of judgement and will vary on the nature of the task.

Each paragraph should provide a different but related piece of the puzzle and should not be so short as to disrupt the 'flow' of the essay, but equally not so lengthy as to lose the thread and focus of the argument. Paragraphs should be linked, and it should be clear to the reader as to whether the present paragraph links to or distances itself from the previous paragraph or, indeed, whether it deals with a wholly different issue. Phrases such as 'moreover', 'in addition', 'building on this argument' or 'this is further evidenced by' can indicate that you are seeking to *build* on the existing point.[27] Phrases such as 'by contrast', 'on the other hand' or 'however'

27 These phrases and the ones that follow are not intended to be indicative rather than exhaustive. Do consider referring to

can indicate to a reader that you recognise a *different* but *conflicting* point to the one that you have just addressed. Phrases such 'now considering the second of my three principal arguments', 'moving on to consider x' or 'the next part of the essay will analyse y' can help the reader understand that you are moving on to an entirely new point. This can really help navigate through your argument, allow for a good flow and prevent abrupt changes in direction within the essay. You should use a variety of these phrases so that your essay does not appear formulaic.

Strong legal essays make judicious use of supporting authority. All propositions or statements of the law should be supported with adequate authority to support that proposition. This can be case law or legislation. In terms of case law, it is often prudent to cite the case establishing a legal principle and, if research is important, to consider any recent examples of case law where this principle has been applied or critiqued. Long expositions of the facts of case law are *less* likely to be relevant to essays with strict word limits.[28] Case law is there to help support the argument you are making or validate statements about the law.

A crucial skill for writing legal essays relates to the *weighting* of evidence or argument. Through reading and research, you will likely have gathered a sizeable number of arguments or potential approaches to the question set. It is important that, through application of critical analysis, you are able to properly *weight* these arguments. The first thing is to decide on their relevance and importance to the question asked. Are they central to your argument or peripheral? Are they major contributors to your answer, or are they minor? From reading about these arguments, how persuaded are you by them? As you develop your notes, it is most sensible to keep track of how persuasive the argument is and why you feel persuaded. This will help you, in turn, to construct the most persuasive argument to the question.

As you then write, you should not present the arguments blandly but indicate to the reader which are the most persuasive and why. You can use language to help with this. Phrases such as 'compelling', 'there is overwhelming evidence to support', 'most convincing' can help, when supported by literature or judicial analysis, to show the reader the strength of that argument. Equally, and referring back to the section on 'linking' arguments, you can show more sophisticated skills of critical analysis by *comparing* and *contrasting* the relevant weight of arguments. Phrases like 'this argument, while still persuasive, is less convincing than X', 'the position put forward by X is less convincing because of Y', 'there is less merit in the argument that X should be the overriding leal principle applied' bring home to the reader the relative and comparative importance of your arguments. Equally, you can use phrases such as 'this is the least convincing reasoning', 'there is little evidence in the case law to support the position taken by X' or 'the argument put forward by X is undermined because it does not give sufficient attention to legal principle Y' to show you do not find the arguments compelling. This weighting of arguments will not only help you clarify your response but also demonstrate to the reader that you have used your skills of legal analysis and evaluation.

'academic phrase banks', such as the one found here – <https://www.phrasebank.manchester.ac.uk/> – can help to give you a sense of good writing style.

28 There may be some occasions when the use of facts is necessary, but generally, this is not the case for legal essays.

The strongest legal essays, whilst maintaining flow and direction, do make 'callbacks' to the question asked. Peppering your answer with the words of the question will make sure that you maintain focus and will also ensure that the reader is persuaded that you are attempting to answer the precise question that you have been asked, rather than a generic answer to any question on this topic. Whenever you have completed your consideration of a cognate set of arguments or points, it is worth summarising what piece of the puzzle they have provided in answering the question set.

Concluding your answer is important. Conclusions should be short and focussed. They should summarise the main findings of the essay, based on the arguments presented throughout. A good conclusion will provide a direct answer to the question that has been set. Whilst it may be tempting to treat conclusions as an opportunity to reveal a new, compelling and overwhelming argument, this temptation should be resisted. Legal essays are not murder mystery novels, and nothing in the conclusion should come as a surprise to the reader. By having considered the main body of the essay, the reader should be able to anticipate how the essay will conclude. The purpose of the conclusion is to summarise, synthesise and bring together all that has gone before into a concise response to the question.

TAKING THINGS FURTHER

The website that accompanies this textbook contains an example essay question based on the legal system of England and Wales. The website contains step-by-step instructions on how to consider and tackle such a question with an annotated solution.

PROBLEM/HYPOTHETICAL QUESTIONS

Much of the study of law is characterised by the application of legal principles to hypothetical, factual scenarios. We will refer to these as 'problem questions'. Given their prevalence in law school assessment and their link to the real world of advising clients on the law applicable to their situation, it is important that the right approach is taken. Although it is unlikely that such 'problem questions' will emerge in your study of the *legal system* of England and Wales,[29] understanding the skills utilised will be helpful to your ability to solve problems.

The first thing to keep in mind when answering problem questions is to reflect on the precise nature of the task set. Quite often, you will be asked to advise a particular party as to their legal rights, obligations or liability. Paying close attention to this as a form of audience and purpose is very important. In an employment dispute, to take one example, it may require a different approach whether you have been tasked with advising an employer or an employee as to their legal rights.

29 They are much more closely aligned with substantive legal subjects, such as contract, tort, public law, criminal law or the law of property.

Having established the ground rules of the task, it is then important to deploy a consistent approach to tackling the advice that you would give the party (or parties) you have been asked to advise. The predominant approach used is one that is termed IRAC. This means that you identify the Issues, you state the Relevant legal rule, you Apply the legal rule, then you articulate a Conclusion.

Identifying the issues is key to ensuring that you fully answer the question set. There will likely be several legal issues (that may or may not be linked) within one set of facts. The more problem questions you complete, the more you will instinctively be able to identify the relevant issues. Problem questions are constructs of fiction and so have been created by an academic to allow you to demonstrate your understanding of the law. This may seem an obvious point, but it is one that should be carefully considered. It means that the narrative is deliberate and the choice of words has meaning. There may be the occasional sentence there just to paint a more colourful 'story', but the vast majority of words are there because they reveal something. Reading with purpose is, in this regard, important. The words will have been chosen because they generate a specific legal issue. A first reading of the text should reveal certain *fact patterns* that suggest a particular legal issue. Be very conscious by asking yourself, for each sentence within the problem, 'why has the author chosen these particular facts? What is it that the author wishes me to take from this fact pattern?'. Keep note of the issue and move to the next set of fact patterns. That separate list of issues will form the structure of your answer to the problem. The more familiar you are with an area of law, the more likely it is you will be able to tell from the fact patterns the issues it is intended that you identify.

Having identified the issue(s), you then need to consider the relevant law or legal rule. The word *relevant* here is important as problem questions are not invitations to give general expositions of the law; they are intended to elicit concise articulation of the relevant legal principles or rules. Depending on the area of law and the issue at hand, it may be that the legal rule finds expression in Act of Parliament or through the common law and decided cases. You should attempt to articulate the law in as concise and straightforward a way as possible. It is important that every proposition of law or articulation of a legal test is supported by authority (a statute or a case). This authority should be the leading or originating authority for the legal rule you are stating. If there is later authority that supports your argument or reinforces the point, you should also state this. If statutes have been interpreted in particular ways by the courts, then you should cite first the Act of Parliament and then give a clear indication of the interpretation given in the case law.

By grounding your answer in a clear and concise articulation of the law, you avoid a common mistake of answering without a clear understanding of the law. The law here acts as a framework and mitigates against the risk of you answering instinctively and without due regard to the legal principles.

Some areas of law are fact-sensitive, and others are driven much more by broad legal principle. Be clear in your mind whether the *facts* of the case you are using for authority are important due to their similarity or their difference to the *facts* of the problem question. Later cases that deal with the same legal principle but address a different set of material facts can be helpful to support your articulation of the law and to demonstrate your wider and further reading. At the level of stating the relevant legal rule/principle, it is much less likely that academic commentary will be helpful. Here you are establishing what is understood and accepted to be the law. That an erstwhile academic believes that the law should be different is not helpful to a client seeking advice on what the state of the present law is. It would be only on the rarest occasions that a problem question would be asking you to argue that the law is wrongly decided and that you should be advocating for a change. Academic commentary can be helpful where the law is uncertain or difficult to apply, and their exposition helps articulate or reinforce that uncertainty or difficulty of application.

Having established the relevant legal rules, with support from authorities, it important to *apply* those rules to the facts of the problem question. It is here that you are demonstrating your problem-solving skills. You are showing not only your understanding of the rule but also how you can use it for practical purposes. Application will depend on how closely the fact pattern meets the legal rule you have described. If a legal test has multiple factors or strands, then you should address each and express your confidence, based on the facts, that the test has been met. More often than not, there is enough information in the problem question for you to be able to take a balanced or weighted view. If the evidence that a test has been met is overwhelming, then you should say so with certainty or a strong indication that this is the case. However, uncertainty can be caused by a number of things. For example, there may be facts *missing* that do not allow you to come to a firm view, and you should be clear if this is the case.

Alternatively, it may be that there is some uncertainty or conflict between the authorities as to how the law may be applied. It is here that academic commentary, exploring the unresolved uncertainty, could be relevant and hold authority for your analysis. If you cannot be sure, after reviewing the fact pattern, that a legal test has been satisfied either fully or partially, then you can make this clear. Equally, if the fact pattern of the problem question differs significantly to that within the authorities, it may be that you can suggest that the case law should not be applied in the same manner.

A common pitfall for those new to application of rules to scenarios is to start, at this stage, hypothesising on alternative facts. Deal with the facts that you have been given, not those that you wish you had. There is no need to create alternative realities where the parties are a different age or behaved differently or had other different characteristics.

Having applied the legal test to the facts, it is necessary to form some conclusions. These conclusions will take numerous forms and follow a logical sequence. First of all, you will need to articulate whether your application means that the conditions of the legal rule have been met. This type of conclusion is particularly important if a legal test is made up of several factors or stages, as you will need to decide whether cumulatively the test has been met. Following on from this, you need to trace back to the original legal issue that was identified. The application of the legal test to the facts will help you come to this conclusion, but it is important that you frame this in terms of the initial legal issue. A legal test being met, partially met or not met will have a consequence for the rights, obligations or liabilities of one or more of the parties. Ensuring that your application leads to a meaningful conclusion of the legal issue will ensure a full and complete answer.

TAKING THINGS FURTHER

The website that accompanies this textbook contains an example hypothetical problem question in a substantive area of law. The website contains step-by-step instructions on how to consider and tackle such a problem question with an annotated answer.

THE BROADER SKILLS DEVELOPED BY LEGAL STUDY

Law is a human construct, and a major function of law is the management of human relationships. It is no surprise, therefore, that there are a range of soft people-focussed skills that benefit those who undertake legal study. Not all these skills are tested or developed (or at least not formally) explicitly through legal study. Some are developed just by the nature of study and of being around others and of participating in timetabled activities, such as seminars and lectures. Others feature more explicitly as part of formal learning opportunities, such as assessment.

These broader skills include teamworking – both leading and being a part of a team – and as well as networking falls into this category. Equally important in this area are skills of oral communication, developed through presenting ideas or through advocacy or practical-type assessments.

TAKING THINGS FURTHER

Given the focus of this textbook on the legal system of England and Wales, there is not sufficient space to consider these broader legal skills in detail. The website that accompanies this textbook contains further information about these skills and provides signposts to other valuable resources for their development.

THE WEBSITE

The website that accompanies this textbook contains many useful resources that you can use to consolidate and further your knowledge of the law, to hone your skills of critical analysis and to test your knowledge. This includes a set of multiple-choice questions (MCQs) that can be used to test your knowledge and understanding of the material.

INDEX

ABTA: role of 398
academic writings: influence of 37
Act of Parliament: coming into force 96–98; commencement 96–97
Administrative Appeals Chamber 364
Administrative Court 359–361; judicial review 359–361; supervisory jurisdiction 359
administrative justice 353–370; elements of 355
administrative law 354–356
agent for change: law as 8
appointment of judges 200–206; context 200; justices of the Supreme Court 202; Lord Chancellor, and 204–205; misconduct 207–212; qualification requirements 202; recommendation process 204; recorders 197; selection process 204
approaching legal study 4–5; comparative and pluralistic approach 17–18
arbitration 382–400; advantages 399–400; commercial 393–394; common examples 393; common forms 393; disadvantages 399–400; faith-based 394–398; family law 398; litigation, and 383–384; powers and duties of arbitrators and tribunal 392–393
Arbitration Act 1996 383–393; general provisions 387–388; party choice 387–388; powers of court 389–392; rationale 384–387; structure 386
barristers: complaints against 442; current route to qualification 439–441; pupillage 440; qualification 440; range of work 431–433; regulation 422–430

Benson Review 419
between equal equities the first in order of time shall prevail 35
bias: jury 342–343
Bichard Inquiry 78
Bills 66–72; amendments 95; classification 66–72; committee stage 92–94; drafting 87; first reading 89; nature of 66; origin classification 68; preservation 102–103; public reading 90; public reading stage pilot 90; report stage 94; second reading 91; third reading 94
books of authority 36–38
BPTC 439–440
branches of the state 48
breach of contract: civil justice, and 279
Briggs Report 277–278
bringing rights home 74
British Overseas Territories 19; byelaws 129–131; breach of 131; examples of powers conferred through 130–132; standard form 131

case management 287
categorising law of England and Wales 39–44
Central London County Court: mediation 414
Chancery Division 233
charging the accused 311–312
civil justice 273–298; allocation 288–290; Briggs Report 277; case management 287; costs penalties 293; damages 293; developments 274–278; enforcement 298; equitable remedy 293; fast track 290; from dispute to trial 279–281; history 274–278; interim relief 293; issue 287; Jackson Report 277; multi-track 290; offer to settle 288; overriding objective 282; Part 36 offers 288; paying for legal services 279–281; post-Lord Woolf 277; pre-action steps 282–286; pre-Woolf 275–279; remedies 292–293; responding to particulars 287–288; small claims track 289; starting proceedings 286; terminology 274–275; tracks 286–290; trial 290–292; Woolf Report 277
civil law 16–17
civil matters: jury, and 333–335
Civil Procedure Rules (CPR) 281–290; overriding objective 282
civil service 55
civil trial 292
CJEU: precedent 263
codes of conduct 131
codes of practice 131
Commencement Order 121
commercial arbitration 393–394
Commercial Court 233
Committee of the Whole House 94–95
common law 31–32; civil law, and 41; equity, and 40; statute, and 40
common law systems 16
Commonwealth 19
complaints: legal professionals (*see* legal professionals)
constable: meaning 302
constitutional law 42–45
constitutional or ordinary law 40
coroner's courts: jury, and 335–336
costs 293
costs lawyer 423

County Court 231–233; appellate jurisdiction 236; High Court, and 233–235
Court of Appeal (Civil Division): precedent 261
Court of Appeal (Criminal Division): precedent 262
Court of Appeal 236; civil jurisdiction 236; jurisdiction 241
Court of Justice of the European Union 243, 263
court structure 225–247; critical approach 244; tracks system 235; tribunals, and 361–366; visiting courts 227–228
Criminal Cases Review Commission (CCRC) 242
criminal court process 312–320
criminal court system 238–242; adversarial and inquisitorial differences 248; magistrates 238–240
criminal justice 299–321; summary 312–314
criminal law: civil law, and 40
critical legal studies 13–14
Crown Court 240, 328–330; appellate jurisdiction 240; closing speeches 319; defence case 318; order of speeches and evidence 317; prosecution case 317; sentencing 320; summing up 319; trial on indictment 316; trial process 317–321; verdict 319
Crown Dependencies 19
Crown in Parliament 52
custom and practice 32–34

damages 293
Dangerous Dogs Act 1991 85
delegated legislation 29, 109–141, secondary legislation; committees of Parliament, and 137, 141; effectiveness of system of scrutiny 142; judicial review 143–148; procedural *ultra vires* 144; substantive *ultra vires* 144
Delegated Legislation Committees 138
Departmental Select Committees 144–145
detecting crime 302–308
detention: police station, at 309–311
devolution: statutory instruments, and 125
dispute resolution 373–415; appropriate forum for discussion 381; burden of proof 407; Commercial Court 412; compulsion 405–411; costs 381, 407; encouragement from within formal legal system 411–414; government encouragement 412–414; *Halsey*, and 406–408; hybrid forums 380; multi-levelled cyclical dispute resolution 380; party control of process 379; principles 374–382; rationale 379; small claims track 411; types 376; use within formal legal system 402; Woolf reforms 404–405
disputes: resolving 11

either way offences 313
employment tribunals 366

equitable remedy 293
equity 34–36; maxims 35
equity acts in personam 35
European Court of Human Rights: precedent 264–266
European Courts: precedent 263
executive 52–55
executive agencies 54

faith-based arbitrations 394–398
family cases: mediation 402
Family Division 233
family law arbitrations 393
fast track 290
framework of senior and inferior courts 226–230

General Regulatory Chamber 363
golden rule 168
Government Bills 68–72; success rate 69
Government Departments 53
Green Papers 86

he who comes to equity must come with clean hands 35
Heads of Division 197
Health, Education and Social Care Chamber 364
Henry VIII clauses 118–119
hierarchy of norms and sources 42–44
High Court 233–235; County Court, and 231–235; precedent 262
House of Commons 49; legislative procedure: committee stage 89–94; first reading 89; Programme Motion 91; Programme Order 91; public reading 90; report stage 94; second reading 91; third reading 94
House of Lords 94; legislative procedure 94; reform 51–52
House of Lords Secondary Legislation Scrutiny Committee 139–141
Hunting Act 2004: progress of 100
Hybrid Bills 67

Immigration and Asylum Chamber 364, 365
indictable offences 315–317
individual freedoms: protection of 10
inferior courts 228; precedent 263
inferior judges 197–198
inquiries 367–370
Inquiries Act 2005: structure of 77
institutions of law-making 48–55
institutions of state: regulating powers of 8–9
institutions of the legal system 47–60

international law 38; obligations 83
internet: jury, and 349–350

Jackson Report 280
Joint Committee on Statutory Instruments (JCSI) 137
judges: leaders of inquiry, as 59
Judicial Appointments Commission 202–206; membership 203
judicial branch 55
judicial office holders 196–199
judicial review: Administrative Court, and 359–361; delegated legislation 142–148; rise of 146–147
judiciary 191–222; appointment (*see* appointment of judges); beyond the courts 193; categorisation of complaints 207; complaints 207; discipline 207; diversity 218–221; gender split 221; immunity 218; independence 213; legal system, and 191–196; misconduct 207; neutrality 213–215; plagiarism, and 211–212; poor judgement 210–211; power of judicial personality 198–199; public perception 209–213; removal 207; retirement 213; role 191–196; sanctions for conduct 208; tasks 194–195; training 208
jurisprudence in action 14
jury 323–351; bench trials in criminal matters 330–333; challenge for cause 342; challenges 341–344; challenging array 342; civil matters 333–335; confidentiality of deliberation 346–348; conscience 345; coroners' courts 335; criminal trials 328–330; different legal cultures, and 326–327; disqualification 338; eligibility 336; equity 345; from summons to serving 341; function 327–330; grounds for excusal or deferral 340; human rights, and 327; importance of 324; ineligibility 338; internet, and 349–350; juror behaviour 348–350; majority decisions 344; origin 325; other jurisdictions, and 326–327; qualification 337; rationale 325–327; selection 336–340; separation of powers, and 325; serious or complex fraud cases 330–331; serious risk of tampering 331–332; summoning 336; stand by 343; tampering 331; underpinning principles 344–350; vetting 343
jus cogens 38–39
Justices of the Supreme Court 198

King's Bench Divisions 228, 233
King's Speech 87

Lands Chamber 365
Law Commission 81–83; 13th programme of reform 81; function 81
law reform: investigating 81
Law Reports 252
law: colliding functions 11; discipline, as 11–12; functions of 4–11; meaning 1, 3–4; rules, as 3–4
law-making, influences on 72–84
legal advice: costs 279–281
legal aid 281; reform 281
legal certainty 248–249
Legal Ombudsman 443
legal positivism 12–13
legal professionals 417–447; complaints 441–444; education 433–440; future of 446; historical context 418–422; regulation 422–430; work of 430–433
legal realism 13
Legal Services Act 2007 423
Legal Services Board 424
legal services: paying for 279
legal skills 449–477; artificial intelligence 463–467; critical thinking 453–458; legal terminology 460; reading 467–471; research 461; referencing 462; study environment 449; study habits 449; note-taking 450
legal systems 14–21; British Overseas Territories 19; classification 14–21; classification of United Kingdom 18–21; Commonwealth 19; Crown dependencies 19; England and Wales 19–21; Northern Ireland 19; Scotland 19
legal theory 11–14
legislation 29–32; delegated 29; primary 30, 65–109; secondary 30
legislative landscape 42, 104–106
legislative process 86, 88–98; post-legislative review 98; special procedures 98–104
legislature 48–52
literal rule 167–168
Local Bills 66
Lord and Lady Justices of Appeal 197
Lord Chancellor: judicial appointments, and 204–205
Lord Chief Justice 197

magistrates: summary offences before 313
magistrates courts 230–231; civil cases 231; criminal jurisdiction 230–231
manifesto pledges 72–75; political force 74–75
mediation 400–404; advantages 403; court-based schemes 402–404; disadvantages 403; examples 402–404; family cases 402; principles 400–402; small claims track 411; unreasonable behaviour 409–410

mischief rule 169
Monarch 52

natural law theory 12
natural rights 12
non-departmental public bodies 54
Northern Ireland 19

obiter dicta 255
Officers of Parliament 50
Ombudsman 366–367
Orders in Council 122–123
origin of Bill classification 68–72

PACE Codes 304–306
paralegals 428
Parliament Acts 99–102; Jackson case 102
parliamentary sovereignty 64
passage through Parliament 88–104
PCSOs 303
police 302–311; complaints 304; detecting crime 302–311; investigation powers 302–311; keeping order 302–311; organisation 302–311
police station 304–307; detention 308–311; questioning 308; taking samples 309
pre-action protocols 282–286
precedent 247–271; binding element 253; CJEU 263; Court of Appeal (Civil Division) 261; Court of Appeal (Criminal Division) 262; discerning value of judgments 253; distinguishing 266; European Court of Human Rights 264–266; European Courts 263; hierarchy 257–260; High Court 262; inferior courts 263; legal certainty 248; mechanisms for avoiding 266–268; non-binding 268–270; overruling 268; *per incuriam* 268; practical considerations 250–253; rationale 248; reporting of cases 250–253; reversing 267; senior courts 261; Supreme Court 257–261
pre-legislative process 86
pressure groups 83; successful campaigns 84
primary legislation 29, 63–107; relationship with secondary legislation 110
Prime Minister: choosing 53
Private Bills 66
Private Members' Bills 70–72; ballot 71; success 71; ten-minute rule 71
Privy Council 237, 241
procedural or substantive law 41
Programme Motion 91
Programme Order 91
Property Chamber 364
prorogation of parliament 9, 20–21
Public Bill Committee 92–93
Public Bills 66
public inquiries 78–79; recent 81
public order, preservation of 5–7
public pressure 84–86
puisne judges 197
pupillage 440
purposive rule 170

ratio decidendi 254; identifying 255
regulations 123
regulators, professional 425
regulatory reform orders 126
relationships: regulating 10
religious systems 17
remedial order 124–126
Royal Assent 96–97
Royal Commissions 75
rules 3–4

samples: taking at police station 309
Scotland 19
search of premises 310
secondary legislation 29, 109–149; delegated legislation; courts, and 142–148; Courts and Legal Services Act 1990 111–112; detail vs principle 115; emergencies 116; expansion of state 115; expertise, need for 115; growth of 113–114; implementation of EU law 116; judicial review 142; nature of 110–114; need for 114–118; Parliamentary scrutiny 136–141; politicising Civil Contingencies Act 2004 120–121; process for adopting 132–136; speed of response 116; types 119–126; updating of rules 115
Senedd Cymru 30
senior courts 229; precedent 261–263
sentencing: Crown Court 320
separation of powers 57–60; institutions and public law 56; managing overlaps between branches of state 60; models 57; within legal system of England and Wales 57
serious or complex fraud cases: jury, and 330–331
Social Entitlement Chamber 363
solicitor: complaints against 458–459, 460; current route to qualification 441; qualification 436; regulation 422–428; reserved activities 426–428; routes to qualification 436
sources of law 27–45; statement of compatibility 89
statutory instruments 120–128; affirmative resolution procedure 134; devolution, and 126; negative resolution procedure 133; passage of 132–136

statutory interpretation 151–188; aids 179–186; always speaking, statutes 172; approaches to parliamentary drafting 156; dangers of 163–166; difficulties of turning policy into law 157–159; golden rule 168; Hansard 184–186; Human Rights Act 1998 174; importance 152; influences of law-making 163; Interpretation Act 1978 173; judicial interpretative toolkit 154; legal meaning of words 161–163; literal rule 167; mischief rule 169; multiple or uncertain meanings of words 155; natural meaning of words 167; need for 155–163; new situations 159; *pari materia* 183; poor drafting 157; presumptions 174–177; principles 166, 170; responding to technological change 160; rules 166; rules of language 177–179; students, importance for 153
summary offences 312
summary trial process 313; allocation procedure 314
Supreme Court 236, 242; precedent, and 257–261

Tax and Chancery Chamber 365
Tax Chamber 364
tertiary legislation 131
Thoburn case 105
treaties 38
tribunal 361–380; courts, and 358; First Tier 363–364; reformed framework 361; Upper Tribunal 364

UK government 53
ultra vires 144; procedural 144; substantive 144

values of society: reflecting and influencing 7
verdict: Crown Court 319; jury 344
visiting courts 227

War Pensions and Armed Forces Compensation Chamber 364
White Papers 86
Woolf Report 277
writing 470–477